Background Readings
for Instructors Using

THE
BEDFORD
HANDBOOK
FOR
WRITERS

Background Readings
for Instructors Using

THE
BEDFORD
HANDBOOK
FOR
WRITERS

Fourth Edition

Glenn B. Blalock

University of North Carolina
at Chapel Hill

BEDFORD BOOKS *of* ST. MARTIN'S PRESS | BOSTON

Acknowledgments

Gloria Anzaldúa, "How to Tame a Wild Tongue," from *Borderlands/La Frontera: The New Mestiza* © 1987 by Gloria Anzaldúa. Reprinted by permission of Aunt Lute Books (415) 558-8116.

David Bartholomae, "Inventing the University." From *When a Writer Can't Write: Studies in Writer's Block and Other Composing Problems,* edited by Mike Rose. Reprinted by permission of The Guilford Press. "The Study of Error," *College Composition and Communication,* October 1980. Copyright © 1980 by the National Council of Teachers of English. Reprinted with permission.

Richard Beach, "Demonstrating Techniques for Assessing Writing in the Writing Conference," *College Composition and Communication,* February 1986. Copyright © 1986 by the National Council of Teachers of English. Reprinted with permission.

Wendy Bishop, "Helping Peer Writing Groups Succeed," *Teaching English in the Two-Year College,* May 1988. Copyright © 1988 by the National Council of Teachers of English. Reprinted with permission.

Patricia Bizzell and Bruce Herzberg, "Research as a Social Act," *The Clearing House* 60 (March 1987): 303–306. Reprinted with permission of the Helen Dwight Reid Educational Foundation. Published by Heldref Publications, 1319 Eighteenth St., N.W., Washington, D.C. 20036-1801. Copyright © 1987. "Writing Across the Curriculum: A Bibliographic Essay." This essay first appeared in *The Territory of Language: Linguistics, Stylistics, and the Teaching of Composition* (Carbondale: Southern Illinois University Press, 1986) and is reprinted with the permission of the authors and the copyright holder, Donald A. McQuade.

Acknowledgments and copyrights are continued at the back of the book on pages 493–495, which constitute an extension of the copyright page.

PREFACE

In her preface, Diana Hacker writes that she intends *The Bedford Handbook for Writers* to be useful to a wide range of students. Similarly, I intend *Background Readings for Instructors Using The Bedford Handbook for Writers* to be useful to a wide range of instructors with diverse backgrounds and different levels of experience. My purpose is to challenge new and experienced instructors to consider how and why they do what they do as writing teachers, to suggest helpful, practical solutions to common problems and concerns, and to provide useful and accessible references for further reading and study. I like to think that these readings will engage instructors in an ongoing professional dialogue about teaching writing.

I selected the readings in this collection from among the extensive annotated bibliographical references included throughout the *Instructor's Annotated Edition of The Bedford Handbook for Writers*. I chose them for their potential to complement, supplement, or enhance the teaching done in courses using *The Bedford Handbook for Writers* and for their potential to stimulate further reading. These selections are representative of the rich body of research that makes up contemporary composition studies and that informs Diana Hacker's textbook.

The organization of *Background Readings* follows exactly that of *The Bedford Handbook for Writers,* with at least one article for each of the twelve parts of the handbook. Just as you may skip around in the handbook throughout the semester, so too you may skip around in this book of readings. No matter where you are in Diana Hacker's text or how you incorporate the text into your course plans, there is something in this collection to complement your teaching.

My intrusions in this text are few. Each part has a brief introduction that explores the possible relationships between the part, the readings, and the ways of teaching them. The selection headnotes attempt only to introduce the author, to give a sense of the selection's original context, and to offer a short synopsis or overview of the reading. I choose not to interpret, prescribe methods, or advocate theories; instead, I attempt to provide a forum for composition scholars to share their insights with composition instructors.

The second edition of *Background Readings* has several new features:

- More than half of the articles are new to this edition and reflect the important ongoing work being done in composition studies. Further, this collection includes fewer excerpts, offering readers fuller discussions of important concerns.
- The section on teaching ESL students has been expanded to reflect current understandings of how to teach writing more effectively in our multicultural society.

- To match the handbook's new coverage of document design, I have included articles that will help teachers understand more fully the implications of this increasingly important aspect of composing.
- A new appendix of articles on writing across the curriculum offers a thorough introduction to WAC, with practical suggestions for establishing and maintaining different WAC initiatives. An extensive, up-to-date bibliography can help instructors continue to pursue questions and concerns related to WAC.
- Finally, a bibliography for further reading at the end of this book points instructors to a range of articles and books on topics discussed in *Background Readings*. For convenient reference, the organization of this bibliography mirrors that of the readings.

Acknowledgments

Working on the second edition of *Background Readings* has given me a new appreciation of the collaborative nature of composing, and I want to acknowledge the numerous people who have contributed in various ways to this book. Of course, without Diana Hacker's *Bedford Handbook for Writers* this collection would not have a reason to be; her comments at various stages ensured that *Background Readings* would be a worthy accompaniment to the handbook.

I would like to thank several reviewers for taking the time to respond in thoughtful detail to the first edition of this collection. Their comments challenged me to reconceive this book and to clarify and defend more carefully the choices I made as I considered possible revisions. I extend my gratitude to Wendy Bishop, Florida State University; Patricia Bizzell, College of the Holy Cross; Jane Dugan, Cleveland State University; Richard Fabrizio, Pace University; Kathryn Flannery, Indiana University at Bloomington; Rebecca Moore Howard, Colgate University; Kate Mangelsdorf, University of Texas at El Paso; and Thomas Recchio, University of Connecticut, Storrs.

At the University of North Carolina at Chapel Hill, Erika Lindemann established and maintains the environment that encourages and values this kind of work; her confidence in my abilities enabled me to accept this project. Robert Bain and Jim Williams have also supported my work in important ways. Sarah Marino and Harry Crockett contributed significantly to my thinking on this project from the beginning, provoking me regularly to consider alternatives that I would have overlooked.

Working with Bedford Books continues to be a wonderful experience, and several individuals deserve special mention for their work on this edition. Joan Feinberg initially conceived of this project and trusted me to attempt it; I have tried to repay that trust throughout this project. Managing Editor Elizabeth Schaaf paid close attention at crucial stages. Copyeditor Barbara Flanagan fine-tuned my prose with her usual care and skill. Ann Sweeney ably guided the manuscript through production, providing helpful insights along the way. Andrea Goldman researched and assembled the biographical information; I appreciate her significant contributions. Kim Chabot provided valuable editorial assistance. For me, the most important member of the Bedford team has been Beth Castrodale, the developmental editor for this project. Beth worked closely with me from the beginning, guiding me through the complex process of revision and skillfully managing the often confusing exchanges of manuscripts and ideas. I have benefited especially from her intellectual engagement with the project and from her willingness to listen, to read, and to respond honestly to my ideas. She has made this seem easy.

Glenn B. Blalock
University of North Carolina, Chapel Hill

Contents

COMPOSING AND REVISING

The first part of *The Bedford Handbook for Writers* introduces students to the composing process and guides them through it. The articles included in the first part of *Background Readings* complement that coverage by recognizing that writing is fundamentally a social activity and that composing is a complex process. Our understanding of the writing situation and the writing process governs the ways we teach students about planning, drafting, and revising and informs our methods of responding to and assessing student writing. The articles in Part One raise a number of important questions that instructors must consider as they develop their course plans and class activities:

- How can instructors help students assess the writing situation?
- What assumptions are instructors making when they teach the writing process in a certain way?
- How many different ways can writers think of audience? What alternatives should students consider as they attempt to analyze their audience?
- How can instructors help students develop more effective strategies for exploring and developing a topic? How can instructors help students consider alternative plans for their writing?
- Is revision the same for everyone? How can instructors help students get more effective feedback on writings-in-progress?
- What effect does word processing have on composing and revision strategies? How can students use word processing more effectively?
- What do instructors do — and what should they consider doing — as they respond to student writing? How can instructors help students become more effective self-evaluators?
- What do instructors do when they assess writing? What alternatives do they have for assessing student writing?

THE WRITING SITUATION

DISCOURSE COMMUNITY: WHERE WRITERS, READERS, AND TEXTS COME TOGETHER

Bennett A. Rafoth

[From The Social Construction of Written Communication. *Ed. Bennett A. Rafoth and Donald L. Rubin. Norwood, NJ: Ablex, 1988. 131–46.]*

Bennett Rafoth directs the writing center at Indiana University of Pennsylvania and teaches courses in applied linguistics, composition theory and research, and research methods. In addition to coediting The Social Construction of Written Communication, *Rafoth has published articles in* Research and the Teaching of English, Written Communication, *and* Writing Program Administration.

The idea for this article came out of Rafoth's study of two related concepts that had not been discussed together before: the notion of "speech communities," studied by sociolinguists, and the notion of "audience," studied by rhetoricians. Rafoth acknowledges that composition scholars have recently offered several ways to think about audience, but he contends that their studies do not define audience in ways that account for the complex interactions among writers, readers, and texts. He asks students and teachers to "subsume the notion of audience within . . . [the notion of] discourse community." By doing this, he argues, we can describe and explain more effectively "the forces that bind and separate writers, readers, and texts." Rafoth's discussion of the discourse community enhances the discussion of the writing situation in The Bedford Handbook.

Introduction

Research in rhetoric and composition has yielded many different perspectives on audience, or what may be called the reader-writer relationship. For centuries, Aristotle's discussion of persuasion and the demographic characteristics of a given listening audience guided most approaches to audience. With the New Rhetoric of the 20th century, however, views about the nature of persuasion *vis-à-vis* those who would be persuaded began to change, and classical notions about audience grew more complex as the study of rhetoric began to draw heavily upon social and psychological research. . . . When attention turned to writing as distinct from speech, some theorists argued that the writer's audience was, after all, "a fiction." Now in recent years, the notion of audience seems to grow even more diffuse as researchers from various disciplines probe the interdependence of writers, readers, and texts.

In composition research, the goal of most perspectives on audience is to show how a particular view of audience helps to describe and explain a variety of composing process phenomena and a variety of features in written products. If there is anything that these perspectives share, it is that they address, to one degree or another, some aspect of writers/speakers, readers/listeners, and the discourse between them by means of the term "audience." It would thus seem that audience has a conceptual status more or less independent of the various perspectives that inform it. Capturing the essence of this conceptual status has proven difficult, however. Whether audience is given a concrete or abstract representation, identifying the center of gravity around which its various perspectives might revolve has been troublesome.

Recently, for example, Ede and Lunsford (1984) have suggested a kind of dual approach to audience that enables focus on the reader, on one hand, and focus on the writer, on the other. And Kroll (1984), in a synthesis of current perspectives on audience, offers a conceptual framework based on three different perspectives: rhetorical, informational, and social. Both of these articles help to show the viability of competing perspectives;

they also illustrate the way in which notions of audience tend to be split from the outset — in two directions by Ede and Lunsford and in three by Kroll. The point *from* which such splits occur is hard to pinpoint. Yet until we can identify a pivotal center from which different perspectives of audience emanate, audience will remain an ambiguous concept. This ambiguity is problematic because it indicates there may be a more fundamental concept for capturing the range of linguistic and rhetorical phenomena for which we typically invoke the notion of *audience*.

In this chapter, I will suggest that *discourse community* may be conceptually more useful than audience for capturing the language phenomena that relate writers, readers, and texts. Whereas the audience metaphor tends naturally to represent readers or listeners as primary, and to admit writers and texts only as derivatives, discourse community admits writers, readers, and texts all together. Instead of forcing the question "Who is the audience for this writer or this text?" (Park, 1982, 1986), discourse community directs attention to the contexts that give rise to a text, including the range of conventions that govern different kinds of writing. . . . To explore the advantages of discourse community over audience, it is helpful to look at a few fields which have already begun to use a similar concept to help overcome problems like those posed by audience in composition studies. I will proceed, therefore, by first turning to the fields of rhetoric, literary criticism, and linguistics in order to show how these fields have attempted to achieve, via notions of *field* or *community*, some degree of explanatory control over a variety of context-sensitive language phenomena. I will then return to composition theory to suggest why a notion such as *discourse community* is a better alternative to *audience*.

Argument Field, Interpretive Community, Speech Community

In such fields as rhetoric, literary criticism, and linguistics, writing theorists can find theoretical problems that impinge on their own, especially questions of how to explain a seemingly endless variety of language phenomena with reference to a few basic concepts. In contemporary rhetoric, argument theorist David Zarefsky (1982) investigates how we can best explain how arguments originate, how they compare and contrast, and how they can be judged valid. In literary criticism, critic Stanley Fish (1980) inquires about the proper role of literary criticism in the face of two seemingly opposing facts: (1) Readers can and do interpret texts in very different ways, and (2) texts are stable. And in linguistics a number of scholars, beginning with ethnographer Dell Hymes (1972), question how language variations reflect social categories, and how these social categories define and constrain interpersonal interaction in communicative situations (Romaine, 1982; Saville-Troike, 1982). In all three cases, and in composition studies as well, theorists pursue the same general goal: to understand the relationships between writers/speakers, readers/listeners, and the discourse between them.

Argument field. How do arguments originate? How may they be compared? What standard may be used to judge their validity? Answers to fundamental questions about the origin, comparison, and validity of arguments have proved difficult to ascertain because of the many sociocontextual variables that influence argument. The doctrine of "separate but equal," for example, was in its time founded on arguments that would be dismissed in most present-day U.S. courts (but likely accepted in a different arena, such as South Africa). Most arguments are not simply a matter of logic, but neither are they ruled by chaos. What counts as a good argument is always determined in light of some cultural context. Public debate on a national issue such as abortion is affected by individual beliefs, which are in turn shaped by media coverage and opinion polls. As one theorist notes, "Deliberative rhetoric is a form of argumentation through which citizens test and create social knowledge in order to uncover, assess, and resolve shared problems" (Goodnight, 1982, p. 214). To understand fully any particular argument about shared problems, it is necessary to look beyond claims and warrants; the student of argumentation must instead look to who is involved in the argument, what standards of deliberation these participants adhere to, and what values they hold dear. Thus there are differences in the standards for arguments among friends versus those for academic arguments versus those for legal debate, for example (Goodnight, 1982; Willard, 1981, 1983).

In searching for underlying principles of argument, rhetorical theorists in recent years have found it useful to speak of *argument fields* as a way of marking the frame of reference for examining arguments. By identifying the field in which a particular argument takes place, one may better understand how that argument came about, how it differs from related arguments, and how it may be evaluated. For example, in the legal profession lawyers often develop arguments based on judicial precedent and then compare the case at hand with previous judgments; judges then evaluate these precedent arguments to arrive at a decision. Lawyers and judges function together in the courtroom by presuming certain norms for arguing. Similarly, in addressing juries or explaining the proceedings and outcomes of adjudication to the press, lawyers and judges work hard at getting relative outsiders socialized into the field. A critic's understanding of this kind of deliberation must begin with the legal profession and its standards for argument (Zarefsky, 1982). Similarly, one who wishes to engage lawyers in debate on a legal point must also be familiar with these standards when following or criticizing them. In short, effective discourse in law depends largely on one's familiarity with the argument field of law.

Shared standards and community norms are thus essential to what makes up a field of argument. According to Willard (1981), fields are social comparison processes in which individuals "check their thinking against the views of others. As we study [fields], we are studying how [people] build order as a social enterprise" (p. 28). With the notion of argument field, theorists have tried to look beyond logic, which can be psychologically impotent when opposed by tradition, popular authorities, or short-term interests. Theorists have also tried to look beyond audience, recognizing that audiences can sometimes have little importance to the origin, differences, and evaluation of arguments. In terms of evaluation, for example, a good argument is not necessarily one an audience will accept; the Surgeon General offers excellent arguments for quitting smoking, but many smokers reject them.

Interestingly, Zarefsky's questions about the origin, comparison, and validity of arguments reflect broad concerns in composition research: Where do writers' ideas come from? How does one essay compare with another? How can essays be properly evaluated? Each of these questions has been addressed through some notion or other of audience. Thus some researchers have investigated the origin of writers' ideas and found that talking with readers is a productive source . . . (Flower, 1981; Murray, 1979; Rubin, 1983). . . . Other studies have compared written products and found that essays may be sorted according to their intended audience (Britton et al., 1975; Faigley & Hansen, 1985; Grobe, 1981; Rafoth, 1984, 1985; Rubin & Piché, 1979). . . . And finally, there are studies that have evaluated essays according to how well they meet the needs of an audience (Lloyd-Jones, 1977; Odell, 1981).

Interpretive community. Literary texts are permanent and often remote in time and space from their readers. This, according to Fish (1980), has made it relatively easy for critics to cast themselves as model readers, lending an authority to their interpretations that is not always deserved. It is a trap that Fish says he fell into as a critical theorist. He explains that he was struck by the problem that the concept of audience poses for literary interpretation: Divergent interpretations of a text result from the fact that there are as many audiences as there are readers, and audiences are continually created anew. As a way out of this critical quagmire, Fish at first suggested two levels of critical interpretation: one, the shared reading, based on the linguistic competence or shared system of rules that holds between readers; and two, the emotional reaction to the first level. This second level was considered subjective and idiosyncratic, unlike the primary, objective level. Accordingly, the proper role of literary criticism was to suppress the subjective in favor of the objective. This meant that it was necessary to posit an ideal reader who was consummately well informed and with whom only deficient readers would disagree: "Agreement was secured by making disagreement aberrant" (pp. 14–15).

Ideal readers, however, are no more plausible than homogeneous, ideal speakers. In later rejecting his original formulation, Fish (1980) proposed the notion of *interpretive community,* which he explained in such a way as to preserve both subjectivity and objectivity:

> An interpretive community is not objective because as a bundle of interests, of particular purposes and goals, its perspective is interested rather than neutral; but by the same reasoning, the meanings and texts produced by an interpretive community are not subjective because they do not proceed from an isolated individual but from a public and conventional point of view. (p. 14)

Fish went on to conclude that what is seen as real and normative is a function of a particular interpretive community, and that there is no such thing as a natural or correct reading, only "ways of reading that are extensions of community perspectives" (pp. 15–16). The business of criticism was therefore to determine how readings proceed from a number of possible perspectives:

> This determination will not be made once and for all by a neutral mechanism of adjudication, but will be made and remade again whenever the interests and tacitly understood goals of one interpretive community replace or dislodge the interests and goals of another. The business of criticism, in other words, was not to decide between interpretations by subjecting them to the test of disinterested evidence but to establish by political and persuasive means . . . the set of interpretive assumptions from the vantage of which the evidence (and the facts and the intentions and everything else) will hereafter be specifiable. (p. 16)

With the concept of interpretive community, Fish thus attempted to offer literary criticism a means for grounding in social context the variety and similarity of interpretations. In so doing, he tried to overcome the problem of granting absolute authority to certain ways of reading, while at the same time avoiding a nontheory in which anything goes. Like the idea of a discourse community, Fish's interpretive community is based on prevailing norms about how any given writers, readers, and texts should be related.

The significance of interpretive community may be seen in a recent analysis of how students learn to write in the social sciences. Faigley and Hansen (1985) followed one student through two courses, one on writing in the social sciences taught by an English professor, and one on crime taught by a sociology professor. On the very same essay, the student received a B– from the English professor and an A from the sociology professor. In contrasting the two instructors' comments, Faigley and Hansen observed the English professor's almost exclusive attention to matters of style, expression, and sentence structure, as opposed to the sociology professor's concern for the breadth and depth of information. The two researchers also noted the apparent difficulty that the English professor had in following his own grading criteria: " 'I will ask questions such as, "Would a professional in your field consider this worthwhile reading?" ' "

Speech community. The concept of speech community in linguistics may be traced back as early as 1933, when Leonard Bloomfield sought to show that similarities in speech patterns among particular groups were due to the frequency of interaction among their members (and not due to environmental factors such as climate and topography, as conventional wisdom in the 19th century held). Since then, the speaker's definition of the situation, particularly how that speaker identifies with others, has been shown to provide a more satisfactory explanation of language subgroups than frequency of contact. Today definitions of speech community tend to emphasize the role of speakers' shared rules and norms, following Hymes (1972): "A speech community is defined as a community sharing rules for the conduct and interpretation of speech, and rules for the interpretation of at least one linguistic variety" (p. 54). Since Bloomfield, however, the notion of speech community has served the same fundamental purpose: to relate social interaction to linguistic variation and change (Hymes, 1972). Thus Labov (1970) argued that pronunciation variation on Martha's Vineyard has social significance because speakers who use the centralized variants of two diphthongs mark solidarity with their community, thereby strongly identifying themselves with the local people and life on the island.

Sociolinguists and ethnographers have used speech community as a theoretical construct to describe and explain the persistence of both widespread variety and (relative) uniformity in language use among different groups of people: Why many native Southerners in the United States continue to speak "Southern," why many Black American speakers frequently alternate between Black dialect and Standard American English, and so on. The idea of speech community helps researchers identify boundaries that reflect certain sociolinguistic parameters which speakers themselves recognize. Researchers then use these speech community boundaries in explaining how language differences relate to social separation, unity, and stratification. Within some Armenian communities in the United States, for example, Armenian is the language of choice between Armenians. Because they also live and function in the larger American community, they also use English to participate in the Standard American English speech community, while Armenian continues to serve as a means of maintaining a separate identity in that community (Saville-Troike, 1982).

Nystrand (1982) notes that writers, like speakers, are also influenced by the "speech" community of their readers. He points out that the writer's audience is different from the writer's speech community because writers can affect their audience on a particular occasion through particular texts. The writer's speech community, by contrast, is a much more stable entity and is rarely so affected by particular occasions and texts; instead, the community affects the writer by tacitly imposing conformity to its ways of writing. . . .

Community vs. Audience in Writing

Taken together, the concepts of argument field in rhetoric, interpretive community in criticism, and speech community in linguistics offer important insights for composition theory generally and for the problem of audience specifically. First, all three concepts attempt to derive their descriptive and predictive power from a pluralistic view of what is normal and expected. Different communities of arguers, readers, or speakers will have different yet valid expectations for carrying on arguments, formulating correct readings of a text, or speaking appropriately. In a similar vein, various groups of writers and readers have different, yet valid, expectations for what written discourse should be like.

Second, all three concepts show the need for interweaving communicators, messages, and pertinent contexts into a single fabric: Argument theory, long dominated by formal approaches focusing on the logical structure of messages, has found it necessary to give wider acceptance to the roles of participants and particular topical domains. Literary criticism has recognized the limitations of granting interpretive authority to certain privileged readers and so acknowledges the various perspectives of different readership communities. And linguistics, with deep roots in the acontextual study of phonology, morphology, and syntax of "ideal speakers," has nonetheless asserted a position for sociolinguistics and contextual studies of language in use. In other words, whereas argument theory may be said to have been once largely concerned with idealized messages or texts, literary criticism with ideal readers, and linguistics with ideal speakers, all three fields have more recently found reason to subordinate these initial formulations to the larger framework of community.

Focus on discourse community differs from approaches to audience in composition, where perspectives that emphasize either writers, texts, or readers emerge not from a single, underlying framework but stand more or less independent of, and sometimes in opposition to, each other. The result is a diversity of perspectives that have only a vague and ill-defined notion of audience as their point in common.

Kroll's (1984) framework illustrates this diversity by showing three current perspectives on audience which, despite their relative strengths, are each limited in the particular aspect of audience they address. This same diversity reveals itself more subtly (and less acutely) in Ede and Lunsford's (1984) notion of dual emphases, toward audience-addressed and audience-invoked. Ede and Lunsford recognize implicitly, however, that the underlying ecology of their two alternatives is "the complex series of obligations, resources, needs, and constraints embodied in the writer's concept of audience" (p. 165). They also note that a sense of audience is guided by a sense of purpose and "by the peculiarities of a specific rhetorical situation . . ." (p. 166). Here we see a theory of audience which, though still split, begins to face head-on the conceptual problem of the *nature* of audience. The dual emphasis on audience-addressed and audience-invoked reflects, like other perspectives, a concern for two important ways one's sense of audience can be manifested, while the recognition of "obligations, resources, needs, and constraints" hints at the more fundamental questions that audience theory must address.

How then can the notion of community help define and unify audience in composition studies? Before addressing this question directly, it is necessary to bring into better focus some of the more important issues that have been addressed under the banner of audience. This will then lead to why audience per se is a conceptually inadequate term for addressing these problems, and how a better concept can emerge from the notion of community.

The Writer as Agent and Object of Influence

Good writers are often said to possess a keen sense of audience. Exactly what constitutes a sense of audience has been difficult to pinpoint, however. In various notions of audience, composition theorists have seen the universe of discourse as shaping different kinds of relationships between participants. On the one hand, audience has been used to suggest that the writer is an *agent* of influence on readers. By this account, writers are the primary actors in discursive events. This may be seen in what Ede and Lunsford call the "audience-addressed" view or in what Kroll (1984) calls the "rhetorical" perspective, where the writer is viewed as adopting communication strategies that will most effectively take advantage of the audience's predispositions, and hence be most convincing. . . . In addition, the writer as agent of influence also coincides with Ong's (1975) notion of "fictionalized" audience, or what Ede and Lunsford label "audience-invoked." This view points to the absence of any known, specific body of readers in many writing situations and emphasizes the great freedom writers have in conceptualizing their own audience — to invoke, create, or fictionalize a potential audience. Despite the contrasts that have been drawn between "audience-addressed" and "audience-invoked" (Ede & Lunsford, 1984; see also Long, 1980), both show the power the writer has in effecting change in readers, whether it be a tangible audience the writer knows and exploits or a remote audience who "play[s] the role in which the author has cast him . . ." (Ong, 1975, p. 12).

On the other hand, audience suggests that the writer is at the same time an *object* of outside influences. This account emphasizes the constraints an audience exerts on the writer. It may be seen in what Nystrand (1982) calls the "linguistics of writing," which is the "examination of the effects of readers, as speech community of the writer, upon writers and the texts they compose" (p. 2). It may also be seen in what Kroll (1984) labels the "informational perspective" of audience, which draws upon cognitive processing theories about readers' short- and long-term memory limitations and emphasizes how best to "get information into the reader's head" (p. 176). The linguistic and rhetorical devices that enable readers' "uptake" of information therefore become norms constraining writers' encoding of information. The notion of writer as object is likewise present in the rhetorical perspective, because in adapting to an audience, the author accepts certain constraints, as in the 1960s when white Americans dropped "Negro" from their vocabularies and replaced it with "Black."

To one degree or another these views reflect the familiar struggle between individual and society in which every person is both separate from the group and capable of individual action and at the same time a part of the group and subject to group influences. . . . It is an opposition which seems to be rooted in the very nature of language and to permeate all types of communication. Thus Edward Sapir (1933) wrote that language is perhaps the greatest force of socialization that exists, and then later in the same essay, "In spite of the fact that language acts as a socializing and uniformizing force, it is at the same time the most potent single known factor for the growth of individuality" (p. 19). Many ordinary acts of politeness, for example, are a means for dealing with this opposition between individual and society by making one's needs or opinions known without appearing to impose on others (Brown & Levinson, 1978). Writers are both agents of influence when effecting change in their readers, and at the same time the object of influence when conforming to established constraints.

An adequate theory of audience thus needs to balance several concerns: writers, who influence and are influenced by, readers; readers, who influence and are influenced by, writers; and texts, which can over time come to embody the norms for writers writing and readers reading. Most theories of audience, however, have found it difficult to balance simultaneously these concerns (but see Bruffee, 1984; Walzer, 1985). The notion *audience* has itself been an obstacle to achieving this balance, denoting as it does the literal interpretation of *audience as readers* and thereby evoking a static Aristotelian notion of writers acting to influence identifiable yet passive readers (Rubin, 1984).

In seeking an alternative to audience we therefore look to a concept that would represent writers, readers, and texts as dynamically interactive, and thus help to (1) describe the interrelationships between discoursers and their texts, and (2) explain the constraints under which these relationships function. Such a concept may lie in the notion of *discourse community.*

Norms in a Discourse Community

The writer who can successfully engage readers is also one who knows and can manipulate the norms for written discourse, norms that are held consensually between readers and writers and embodied in texts. As both agent and object of influence, the writer functions together with readers in a community of particular norms. These reflect standard assumptions about how readers, writers, and texts can be related to each other, and as such help to impose order on the limitless variety of alternatives in the universe of discourse. Community norms and expectations are embodied not only in writers who address and invoke audiences, nor only in the audiences themselves, but in the particular *community* of writers and readers who engage themselves through the medium of text, all together (writers, readers, texts) making up a discourse community. Thus texts, which are often the only visible manifestation of a community (such as readers of Nancy Drew mysteries, for example, or subscribers to *The New Yorker* magazine), also embody community norms. Community norms are like the guidelines readers and writers use to navigate a text, much as roadways are the means by which motorists get from here to there.

Indulge, for a moment, an extension of this analogy. A road is normative in the sense that it is the commonly accepted means for getting from one point to another. Some roads are more normative than others: highways are efficient, but backroads can lead to the same destination. Roadways are not absolute norms but changing ones: New roads are created and old ones abandoned or widened as needs change. Some travelers stray, by accident or design, from the road entirely and find themselves quite alone. The point is obvious: Writers and readers use the norms of their discourse community to construct and construe a text, usually taking the familiar route over the offbeat, and often capable of effecting gradual change on accepted ways.

What are the norms for writers, readers, and texts? Essentially, they are the familiar and expected ways of reading and writing discourse, as embodied in the way most writers write, most readers read, and most texts appear in any given discourse community. Norms are thus probabilistic rather than absolute, and always linked to a particular community, such as evolutionary biologists or computer hackers. These ways of reading and writing discourse are not merely mechanisms for facilitating information processing, like indenting paragraphs or maintaining cohesive ties. Rather, they are ways of reading and writing that influence content as well as form (see Rubin, 1984), reflecting the unique ways a community creates and organizes its knowledge (Bizzell, 1986). For example, in scientific discourse certain topics, such as ESP or divination, are not to be taken seriously by members of the scientific community or those who read scientific writing. In the discourse of tabloids found at the checkout lanes of supermarkets, on the other hand, such topics are stock in trade. Similarly, in the discourse of high-school theme papers, summary conclusions are often considered desirable, while in the discourse of college students' essays, conclusions that merely summarize are considered naive.

Norms and expectations that obtain in different kinds of reader-writer-text relationships pertain to five general areas, resembling several of Dell Hymes's (1972) categories for the description of communicative events: *Purpose, Participants, Genre, Setting,* and *Code.* Each of these may be associated with a set of norms. A persuasive *purpose* is attended by such norms as frequent use of "should," for example, and claims supported by facts, the restatement of key arguments, and documentation — all features which tend to distinguish deliberately persuasive aims from expressive ones, for instance. *Participants* include those writers and readers who share a text, such as reporter, editor, and newspaper reader. Norms for particular *genres* are the conventions which by and large constitute the genre, such as length (for short stories and sonnets), opening lines ("Once upon a time" for bedtime stories), and formats (hypothesis, procedures, results for lab reports). *Setting* includes the norms that come into play by virtue of physical and institutional circumstances surrounding writer, reader, and text: whether a text is composed in class or out of class, whether it is a first or final draft, whether the reader has read it once or more than once, and whether it appears alone or with related texts. And *code* refers to norms concerning the writer's native language(s), grammatical and stylistic conventions (including the "right" of a writer to violate conventions as well as the reader's tolerance for such violations), structuring of given-new information, and whether the text is in Braille or visual print. By determining the operative norms in these areas for writers, readers, and texts, one may begin to form the outline of a particular discourse community.

Conclusion

If we can subsume the notion of audience within something like *discourse community,* considerable leverage is gained over the many phenomena for which "audience" is only marginally helpful. This is because the conceptual metaphor of audience inevitably orients our thinking toward readers and questions about their possible responses to texts, stereotypes about their likely attitudes and beliefs, and musings about whether they really exist at all — all important questions, but only features of some larger picture which concepts of audience never quite seem to capture. The notion of discourse community at least holds within its literal level the idea of writers and readers (community) and text (discourse). The notion of community, from Latin *communitae* ("held in common"), includes the dimension of shared knowledge and norms, which describe what writers and readers bring to a text and carry from it. The notion of discourse, from Late Latin *discursus* ("conversation") and Latin ("a running back and forth"), refers to the dynamic nature of negotiated meaning.

Theories of audience have often been criticized for privileging the role of readers while failing to appreciate the writer's powers of imagination and reflection. As Elbow (1987) has stated, "What most readers value in really excellent writing is not prose that is right for readers but prose that is right for thinking, right for language, or right for the subject being written about" (p. 54). In other words, claims Elbow, writers are sometimes at their best when ignoring audience. The concept of discourse community is not incompatible with this argument because individual interests do not necessarily conflict with community interests; the two are often complementary. Whole communities have been redefined or redirected by the private initiatives of individuals such as William Shakespeare, Charles Darwin, or Noam Chomsky. Creativity in thought and expression is highly regarded (normative, in a sense) in many communities. Writing teachers, in fact, have a responsibility to establish creativity and reflective thought as characteristic of the community of writers.

The concept of discourse community does have limitations, which it shares with argument field, interpretive community, and speech community. Some proponents of argument fields have been criticized for excessive relativism in virtually ignoring the propositional content of arguments (Wenzel, 1982) or for failing to emphasize the role of purpose in argument (Rowland, 1982). The notion of interpretive community has been called "elusive" and leading to "an explosion of communities with no important gain" in the ability to predict a community's stands on specific issues (Beaugrande, 1984, p. 551; see also Goodheart, 1983; Stiebel, 1984). And the notion of speech community, at least as employed by Labov (1966, 1972), has been challenged for its failure to accommodate the linguistic change that occurs when members of a community do not share identical constraints on how a variable rule gets applied (Romaine, 1982).

To one degree or another, the many criticisms of the three concepts point to the problem of relativism: Fields and communities have fuzzy boundaries that allow for a good deal of overlap, making the application of such concepts difficult. The same may certainly be said of discourse communities. Human beings, such as they are, have multiple allegiances that overlap and conflict, and human discourse reflects this overlap and conflict all too well. For all these problems, and they are significant, I believe the notion of community is better suited to exploring the relationship between writers, readers, and texts than is audience. Indeed, in argument theory, literary criticism, and linguistics, we see it is not sufficient to understand spoken and written discourse as a straightforward matter of senders and receivers. Rather, the communities in which writers/speakers and readers/listeners align themselves, together with the discourse norms by which these communities have been symbolized, give a theoretically more powerful concept by which we can describe and explain the forces that bind and separate writers, readers, and texts.

References

Beaugrande, R., de. (1984). Writer, reader, critic: Comparing critical theories as discourse. *College English, 46,* 533–559.

Bizzell, P. (1986). What happens when basic writers come to college? *College Composition and Communication, 37,* 294–301.

Bloomfield, L. (1933). *Language.* New York: Holt, Rinehart, & Winston.

Britton, J. L., Burgess, T., Martin, N., McLeod, A., & Rosen, H. (1975). *The development of writing abilities (11–18).* London: Macmillan Education.

Brown, P., & Levinson, S. (1978). Universals in language usage. In E. N. Goody (Ed.), *Questions and politeness: Strategies in social interaction* (pp. 56–289). Cambridge, England: Cambridge University Press.

Bruffee, K. A. (1984). Collaborative learning and the "conversation of mankind." *College English, 46,* 635–652.

Ede, L., & Lunsford, A. (1984). Audience addressed/audience invoked: The role of audience in composition theory and pedagogy. *College Composition and Communication, 35,* 115–171.

Elbow, P. (1987). Closing my eyes as I speak: An argument for ignoring audience. *College English, 49,* 50–69.

Faigley, L., & Hansen, K. (1985). Learning to write in the social sciences. *College Composition and Communication, 36,* 140–149.

Fish, S. (1980). *Is there a text in this class? The authority of interpretive communities.* Cambridge, MA: Harvard University Press.

Flower, L. (1981). *Problem-solving strategies for writers.* New York: Harcourt Brace Jovanovich.

Goodheart, E. (1983). The text and the interpretive community. *Daedalus, 112,* 215–231.

Goodnight, G. T. (1982). The personal, technical, and public spheres of argument: A speculative inquiry into the art of public deliberation. *Journal of the American Forensic Association, 18,* 215–227.

Grobe, C. (1981). Syntactic maturity, mechanics, and vocabulary as predictors of quality ratings. *Research in the Teaching of English, 15,* 75–85.

Hymes, D. (1972). Models of the interaction of language and social life. In J. J. Gumperz & D. Hymes (Eds.), *Directions in sociolinguistics* (pp. 35–71). New York: Holt, Rinehart, & Winston.

Kroll, B. M. (1984). Writing for readers: Three perspectives on audience. *College Composition and Communication, 35,* 172–185.

Labov, W. (1966). *The social stratification of English in New York City.* Washington, DC: Center for Applied Linguistics.

Labov, W. (1970). The study of language in its social context. *Studium Generale, 23,* 66–84.

Labov, W. (1972). *Sociolinguistic patterns.* Philadelphia: University of Pennsylvania Press.

Lloyd-Jones, R. (1977). Primary trait scoring of writing. In C. R. Cooper & L. Odell (Eds.), *Evaluating writing: Describing, measuring, judging.* Urbana, IL: National Council of Teachers of English.

Long, R. C. (1980). Writer-audience relationships: Analysis or invention? *College Composition and Communication, 31*, 221–226.

Murray, D. (1979). The listening eye: Reflections on the writing conference. *College English, 41*, 13–18.

Nystrand, M. (1982). Rhetoric's "audience" and linguistics' "speech community": Implications for understanding writing, reading, and text. In M. Nystrand (Ed.), *What writers know* (pp. 1–28). New York: Academic Press.

Odell, L. (1981). Defining and assessing competence in writing. In C R. Cooper (Ed.), *The nature and measurement of competency in English* (pp. 95–138). Urbana, IL: National Council of Teachers of English.

Ong, W. J. (1975). The writer's audience is always a fiction. *Publications of the Modern Language Association, 90*, 9–21.

Park, D. (1982). The meanings of "audience." *College English, 44*, 247–257.

Park, D. (1986). Analyzing audiences. *College Composition and Communication, 37*, 478–488.

Rafoth, B. A. (1984). Audience awareness and adaptation in the persuasive writing of proficient and nonproficient college freshmen (Doctoral dissertation, University of Georgia, 1984). *Dissertation Abstracts International, 45*, 2788A.

Rafoth, B. A. (1985). Audience adaptation in the essays of proficient and nonproficient freshman writers. *Research in the Teaching of English, 19*, 237–253.

Romaine, S. (1982). What is a speech community? In S. Romaine (Ed.), *Sociolinguistic variation in speech communities* (pp. 13–24). London: Edward Arnold.

Rowland, R. C. (1982). The influence of purpose on fields of argument. *Journal of the American Forensic Association, 18*, 229–245.

Rubin, D. L. (1983). *Oral communication instruction to improve writing skills among four populations of basic writers.* Athens, GA: University of Georgia, Department of Language Education.

Rubin, D. L. (1984). Social cognition and written communication. *Written Communication, 1*, 211–245.

Rubin, D. L., & Piché, G. (1979). Development in syntactic and strategic aspects of audience adaptation skills in written persuasive communication. *Research in the Teaching of English, 13*, 293–316.

Sapir, E. (1949). Language. In D. G. Mandelbaum (Ed.), *Edward Sapir: Culture, language and personality* (pp. 1–44). Berkeley, CA: University of California Press. (Originally published 1933, in E. R. A. Seligman & A. Johnson [Eds.], *Encyclopedia of the social sciences* [Vol. 9, pp. 155–168]. New York: Macmillan)

Saville-Troike, M. (1982). *The ethnography of communication.* Oxford: Basil Blackwell.

Stiebel, A. (1984). But is it life? Some thoughts on modern critical theory. *Modern Language Studies, 14*, 3–12.

Walzer, A. E. (1985). Articles from the "California Divorce Project": A case study of the concept of audience. *College Composition and Communication, 36*, 150–159.

Wenzel, J. W. (1982). On fields of argument as propositional systems. *Journal of the American Forensic Association, 18*, 205–213.

Willard, C. A. (1981). Field theory: A Cartesian meditation. In G. Ziegelmueller & J. Rhodes (Eds.), *Dimensions of argument: Proceedings of the second summer conference on argumentation* (pp. 21–42a). Annandale, VA: Speech Communication Association.

Willard, C. A. (1983). *Argumentation and the social grounds of knowledge.* University, AL: University of Alabama Press.

Zarefsky, D. (1982). Persistent questions in the theory of argument fields. *Journal of the American Forensic Association, 18*, 192–203.

INVENTING THE UNIVERSITY

David Bartholomae

[From When a Writer Can't Write: Studies in Writer's Block and Other Composing Problems. *Ed. Mike Rose. New York: Guilford, 1985. 134–65.]*

David Bartholomae, professor of English and former director of composition at the University of Pittsburgh, has been a leading scholar in composition studies for more than a decade. He coedited, with Anthony Petrosky, Facts, Artifacts, and Counterfacts *(1986) and* Ways of Reading *(3rd ed., 1993). Bartholomae has published numerous articles in leading journals and in several important collections. He has also chaired the Conference on College Composition and Communication and the second Modern Language Association conference on literacy. His article "The Study of Error" (1980), which is excerpted in Part Five of this book, won the Richard Braddock Award from CCCC in 1981.*

In this now classic and often reprinted essay, Bartholomae discusses academic writing situations. He argues that the writing that students do in colleges and universities takes place in a complex context of already ongoing disciplinary discourses. Bartholomae shows that assessing an academic writing situation is more complex than determining purpose and analyzing audience. Instead, students have to learn the languages of the academy, and those languages are embedded in and are the products of a complex academic culture governed in part by disciplinary and institutional conventions. Illustrating his discussion with several student essays, Bartholomae examines ways in which students attempt to join various academic discourse communities. In the process of his analyses, Bartholomae offers several solid suggestions for how teachers can more effectively engage students in purposeful writing projects, initiating them, in a sense, to the business of the academy.

> Education may well be, as of right, the instrument whereby every individual, in a society like our own, can gain access to any kind of discourse. But we well know that in its distribution, in what it permits and in what it prevents, it follows the well-trodden battle-lines of social conflict. Every educational system is a political means of maintaining or of modifying the appropriation of discourse, with the knowledge and the powers it carries with it.
>
> —Foucault, "The Discourse on Language"

Every time a student sits down to write for us, he has to invent the university for the occasion — invent the university, that is, or a branch of it, like History or Anthropology or Economics or English. He has to learn to speak our language, to speak as we do, to try on the peculiar ways of knowing, selecting, evaluating, reporting, concluding, and arguing that define the discourse of our community. Or perhaps I should say the *various* discourses of our community, since it is in the nature of a liberal arts education that a student, after the first year or two, must learn to try on a variety of voices and interpretive schemes — to write, for example, as a literary critic one day and an experimental psychologist the next, to work within fields where the rules governing the presentation of examples or the development of an argument are both distinct and, even to a professional, mysterious.

The students have to appropriate (or be appropriated by) a specialized discourse, and they have to do this as though they were easily and comfortably one with their audience, as though they were members of the academy, or historians or anthropologists or economists; they have to invent the university by assembling and mimicking its language, finding some compromise between idiosyncrasy, a personal history, and the requirements of convention, the history of a discipline. They must learn to speak our language. Or they must dare to speak it, or to carry off the bluff, since speaking and writing will most certainly be required long before the skill is "learned." And this, understandably, causes problems.

Let me look quickly at an example. Here is an essay written by a college freshman, a basic writer:

> In the past time I thought that an incident was creative was when I had to make a clay model of the earth, but not of the classical or your everyday model of the earth which consists of the two cores, the mantle and the crust. I thought of these things in a dimension of which it would be unique, but easy to comprehend. Of course, your materials to work with were basic and limited at the same time, but thought help to put this limit into a right attitude or frame of mind to work with the clay.
>
> In the beginning of the clay model, I had to research and learn the different dimensions of the earth (in magnitude, quantity, state of matter, etc.). After this, I learned how to put this into the clay and come up with something different than any other person in my class at the time. In my opinion color coordination and shape was the key to my creativity of the clay model of the earth.
>
> Creativity is the venture of the mind at work with the mechanics relay to the limbs from the cranium, which stores and triggers this action. It can be a burst of energy released at a precise time a thought is being transmitted. This can cause a frenzy of the human body, but it depends of the characteristics of the individual and how they can relay the message clearly enough through mechanics of the body to us as an observer. Then we must determine if it is creative or a learned process varied by the individuals thought process. Creativity is indeed a tool which has to exist, or our world will not succeed into the future and progress like it should.

I am continually impressed by the patience and good will of our students. This student was writing a placement essay during freshman orientation. (The problem set to him was "Describe a time when you did something you felt to be creative. Then, on the basis of the incident you have described, go on to draw some general conclusions about 'creativity.'") He knew that university faculty would be reading and evaluating his essay, and so he wrote for them.

In some ways it is a remarkable performance. He is trying on the discourse even though he doesn't have the knowledge that makes the discourse more than a routine, a set of conventional rituals and gestures. And he does this, I think, even though he *knows* he doesn't have the knowledge that makes the discourse more than a routine. He defines himself as a researcher, working systematically, and not as a kid in a high school class: "I thought of these things in a dimension of . . ."; "had to research and learn the different dimensions of the earth (in magnitude, quantity, state of matter, etc.)." He moves quickly into a specialized language (his approximation of our jargon) and draws both a general, textbook-like conclusion ("Creativity is the venture of the mind at work . . .") and a resounding peroration ("Creativity is indeed a tool which has to exist, or our world will not succeed into the future and progress like it should"). The writer has even, with that "indeed" and with the qualifications and the parenthetical expressions of the opening paragraphs, picked up the rhythm of our prose. And through it all he speaks with an impressive air of authority.

There is an elaborate but, I will argue, a necessary and enabling fiction at work here as the student dramatizes his experience in a "setting" — the setting required by the discourse — where he can speak to us as a companion, a fellow researcher. As I read the essay, there is only one moment when the fiction is broken, when we are addressed differently. The student says, "Of course, your materials to work with were basic and limited at the same time, but thought help to put this limit into a right attitude or frame of mind to work with the clay." At this point, I think, we become students and he the teacher, giving us a lesson (as in, "You take your pencil in your right hand and put your paper in front of you"). This is, however, one of the most characteristic slips of basic writers. It is very hard for them to take on the role — the voice, the person — of an authority whose authority is rooted in scholarship, analysis, or research. They slip, then, into the more immediately available and realizable voice of authority, the voice of a teacher giving a lesson or the voice of a parent lecturing at the dinner table. They offer advice or homilies rather than "academic" conclusions. There is a similar break in the final paragraph, where the conclusion that pushes for a definition ("Creativity is the venture of the mind at work with the mechanics relay to the limbs from the cranium . . .") is replaced by a conclusion which speaks in the voice of an Elder ("Creativity is indeed a tool which has to exist, or our world will not succeed into the future and progress like it should").

It is not uncommon, then, to find such breaks in the concluding sections of essays written by basic writers. Here is the concluding section of an essay written by a student about his work as a mechanic. He had been asked to generalize about "work" after reviewing an on-the-job experience or incident that "stuck in his mind" as somehow significant: "How could two repairmen miss a leak? Lack of pride? No incentive? Lazy? I don't know." At this point the writer is in a perfect position to speculate, to move from the problem to an analysis of the problem. Here is how the paragraph continues, however (and notice the change in pronoun reference):

> From this point on, I take my time, do it right, and don't let customers get under your skin. If they have a complaint, tell them to call your boss and he'll be more than glad to handle it. Most important, worry about yourself, and keep a clear eye on everyone, for there's always someone trying to take advantage of you, anytime and anyplace.

We get neither a technical discussion nor an "academic" discussion but a Lesson on Life.[1] This is the language he uses to address the general question "How could two repairmen miss a leak?" The other brand of conclusion, the more academic one, would have required him to speak of his experience in our terms; it would, that is, have required a special vocabulary, a special system of presentation, and an interpretive scheme (or a set of commonplaces) he could use to identify and talk about the mystery of human error. The writer certainly had access to the range of acceptable commonplaces for such an explanation: "lack of pride," "no incentive," "lazy." Each would dictate its own set of phrases, examples, and conclusions, and we, his teachers, would know how to write out each argument, just as we would know how to write out more specialized arguments of our own. A "commonplace," then, is a culturally or institutionally authorized concept or statement that carries with it its own necessary elaboration. We all use commonplaces to orient ourselves in the world; they provide a point of reference and a set of "prearticulated" explanations that are readily available to organize and interpret experience. The phrase "lack of pride" carries with it its own account for the repairman's error just as, at another point in time, a reference to "original sin" would provide an explanation, or just as, in a certain university classroom, a reference to "alienation" would enable a writer to continue and complete the discussion. While there is a way in which these terms are interchangeable, they are not all permissible. A student in a composition class would most likely be turned away from a discussion of original sin. Commonplaces are the "controlling ideas" of our composition textbooks, textbooks that not only insist upon a set form for expository writing but a set view of public life.[2]

When the student above says, "I don't know," he is not saying, then, that he has nothing to say. He is saying that he is not in a position to carry on this discussion. And so we are addressed as apprentices rather than as teachers or scholars. To speak to us as a person of status or privilege, the writer can either speak to us in our terms — in the privileged language of university discourse — or, in default (or in defiance), he can speak to us as though we were children, offering us the wisdom of experience.

I think it is possible to say that the language of the "Clay Model" paper has come through the writer and not from the writer. The writer has located himself (he has located the self that is represented by the *I* on the page) in a context that is, finally, beyond him, not his own and not available to his immediate procedures for inventing and arranging text. I would not, that is, call this essay an example of "writer-based" prose. I would not say that it is egocentric or that it represents the "interior monologue of a writer thinking and talking to himself" (Flower 63). It is, rather, the record of a writer who has lost himself in the discourse of his readers. There is a context beyond the reader that is not the world but a way of talking about the world, a way of talking that determines the use of examples, the possible conclusions, the acceptable commonplaces, and the key words of an essay on the construction of a clay model of the earth. This writer has entered the discourse without successfully approximating it.

Linda Flower has argued that the difficulty inexperienced writers have with writing can be understood as a difficulty in negotiating the transition between writer-based and reader-based prose. Expert writers, in other words, can better imagine how a reader will respond to a text and can transform or restructure what they have to say around a goal shared with a reader. Teaching students to revise for readers, then, will better prepare them to write initially with a reader in mind. The success of this pedagogy depends upon the degree to which a writer can imagine and conform to a reader's goals. The difficulty of this act of imagination, and the burden of such conformity, are so much at the heart of the problem that a teacher must pause and take stock before offering revision as a solution. Students like the student who wrote the "Clay Model" paper are not so much trapped in a private language as they are shut out from one of the privileged languages of public life, a language they are aware of but cannot control.

Our students, I've said, have to appropriate (or be appropriated by) a specialized discourse, and they have to do this as though they were easily or comfortably one with their audience. If you look at the situation this way, suddenly the problem of audience awareness becomes enormously complicated. One of the common assumptions of both composition research and composition teaching is that at some "stage" in the process of composing an essay a writer's ideas or his motives must be tailored to the needs and expectations of his audience. A writer has to "build bridges" between his point of view and his readers'. He has to anticipate and acknowledge his readers' assumptions and biases. He must begin with "common points of departure" before introducing new or controversial arguments. There is a version of the pastoral at work here. It is assumed that a person of low status (like a shepherd) can speak to a person of power (like a courtier), but only (at least so far as the language is concerned) if he is not a shepherd at all, but actually a member of the court out in the field in disguise.

Writers who can successfully manipulate an audience (or, to use a less pointed language, writers who can accommodate their motives to their readers' expectations) are writers who can both imagine and write from a position of privilege. They must, that is, see themselves within a privileged discourse, one that already includes and excludes groups of readers. They must be either equal to or more powerful than those they would address. The writing, then, must somehow transform the political and social relationships between basic writing students and their teachers.

If my students are going to write for me by knowing who I am — and if this means more than knowing my prejudices, psyching me out — it means knowing what I know; it means having the knowledge of a professor of English. They have, then, to know what I know and how I know what I know (the interpretive schemes that define the way I would work out the problems I set for them); they have to learn to write what I would write, or to offer up some approximation of that discourse. The problem of audience awareness, then, is a problem of power and finesse. It cannot be addressed, as it is in most classroom exercises, by giving students privilege and denying the situation of the classroom, by having students write to an outsider, someone excluded from their privileged circle: "Write about 'To His Coy Mistress,' not for your teacher, but for the students in your class"; "Describe Pittsburgh to someone who has never been there"; "Explain to a high school senior how best to prepare for college"; "Describe baseball to a Martian."

Exercises such as these allow students to imagine the needs and goals of a reader and they bring those needs and goals forward as a dominant constraint in the construction of an essay. And they argue, implicitly, what is generally true about writing — that it is an act of aggression disguised as an act of charity. What they fail to address is the central problem of academic writing, where students must assume the right of speaking to someone who knows Pittsburgh or "To His Coy Mistress" better than they do, a reader for whom the general commonplaces and the readily available utterances about a subject are inadequate. It should be clear that when I say that I know Pittsburgh better than my basic writing students I am talking about a way of knowing that is also a way of writing. There may be much that they know that I don't know, but in the setting of the university classroom I have a way of talking about the town that is "better" (and for arbitrary reasons) than theirs.

I think that all writers, in order to write, must imagine for themselves the privilege of being "insiders" — that is, of being both inside an established and powerful discourse, and of being granted a special right to speak. And I think that right to speak is seldom conferred upon us — upon any of us, teachers or students — by virtue of the fact that we have invented or discovered an original idea. Leading students to believe that they are responsible for something new or original, unless they understand what those words mean with regard to writing, is a dangerous and counterproductive practice. We do have the right to expect students to be active and engaged, but that is more a matter of being continually and stylistically working against the inevitable presence of conventional language; it is not a matter of inventing a language that is new.

When students are writing for a teacher, writing becomes more problematic than it is for the students who are describing baseball to a Martian. The students, in effect, have to assume privilege without having any. And since students assume privilege by locating themselves within the discourse of a particular community — within a set of specifically acceptable gestures and commonplaces — learning, at least as it is defined in the liberal arts curriculum, becomes more a matter of imitation or parody than a matter of invention and discovery.

What our beginning students need to learn is to extend themselves into the commonplaces, set phrases, rituals, gestures, habits of mind, tricks of persuasion, obligatory conclusions, and necessary connections that determine the "what might be said" and constitute knowledge within the various branches of our academic community. The course of instruction that would make this possible would be based on a sequence of illustrated assignments and would allow for successive approximations of academic or "disciplinary" discourse. Students will not take on our peculiar ways of reading, writing, speaking, and thinking all at once. Nor will the command of a subject like sociology, at least as that command is represented by the successful completion of a multiple choice exam, enable students to write sociology. Our colleges and universities, by and large, have failed to involve basic writing students in scholarly projects, projects that would allow them to act as though they were colleagues in an academic enterprise. Much of the written work students do is test-taking, report or summary, work that places them outside the working discourse of the academic community, where they are expected to admire and report on what we do, rather than inside that discourse, where they can do its work and participate in a common enterprise.[3] This is a failure of teachers and curriculum designers who, even if they speak of writing as a mode of learning, all too often represent writing as a "tool" to be used by a (hopefully) educated mind.

Pat Bizzell is one of the most important scholars writing now on basic writers and on the special requirements of academic discourse.[4] In a recent essay, "Cognition, Convention, and Certainty: What We Need to Know about Writing," she argues that the problems of basic writers might be

> better understood in terms of their unfamiliarity with the academic discourse community, combined, perhaps, with such limited experience outside their native discourse communities that they are unaware that there is such a thing as a discourse community with conventions to be mastered. What is underdeveloped is their knowledge both of the ways experience is constituted and interpreted in the academic discourse community and of the fact that all discourse communities constitute and interpret experience. (230)

One response to the problems of basic writers, then, would be to determine just what the community's conventions are, so that those conventions can be written out, "demystified," and taught in our classrooms. Teachers, as a result, could be more precise and helpful when they ask students to "think," "argue," "describe," or "define." Another response would be to examine the essays written by basic writers — their approximations of academic discourse — to determine more clearly where the problems lie. If we look at their writing, and if we look at it in the context of other student writing, we can better see the points of discord when students try to write their way into the university.

The purpose of the remainder of this paper will be to examine some of the most striking and characteristic problems as they are presented in the expository essays of basic writers. I will be concerned, then, with university discourse in its most generalized form — that is, as represented by introductory courses — and not with the special conventions required by advanced work in the various disciplines. And I will be concerned with the difficult, and often violent, accommodations that occur when students locate themselves in a discourse that is not "naturally" or immediately theirs.

I have reviewed five hundred essays written in response to the "creativity" question used during one of our placement exams. (The essay cited at the opening of this paper was one of that group.) Some of the essays were written by basic writers (or, more properly, those essays led readers to identify the writers as "basic writers"); some were written by students who "passed" (who were granted immediate access to the community of writers at the university). As I read these essays, I was looking to determine the stylistic resources that enabled writers to locate themselves within an "academic" discourse. My bias as a reader should be clear by now. I was not looking to see how the writer might represent the skills demanded by a neutral language (a language whose key features were paragraphs, topic sentences, transitions, and the like — features of a clear and orderly mind). I was looking to see what happened when a writer entered into a language to locate himself (a textual self) and his subject, and I was looking to see how once entered, that language made or unmade a writer.

Here is one essay. Its writer was classified as a basic writer. Since the essay is relatively free of sentence level errors, that decision must have been rooted in some perceived failure of the discourse itself.

> I am very interested in music, and I try to be creative in my interpretation of music. While in high school, I was a member of a jazz ensemble. The members of the ensemble were given chances to improvise and be creative in various songs. I feel that this was a great experience for me, as well as the other members. I was proud to know that I could use my imagination and feelings to create music other than what was written.
>
> Creativity to me, means being free to express yourself in a way that is unique to you, not having to conform to certain rules and guidelines. Music is only one of the many areas in which people are given opportunities to show their creativity. Sculpting, carving, building, art, and acting are just a few more areas where people can show their creativity.
>
> Through my music I conveyed feelings and thoughts which were important to me. Music was my means of showing creativity. In whatever form creativity takes, whether it be music, art, or science, it is an important aspect of our lives because it enables us to be individuals.

Notice, in this essay, the key gesture, one that appears in all but a few of the essays I read. The student defines as his own that which is a commonplace. "Creativity, to *me,* means being free to express yourself in a way that is unique to you, not having to conform to certain rules and guidelines." This act of appropriation constitutes his authority; it constitutes his authority as a writer and not just as a musician (that is, as someone with a story to tell). There were many essays in the set that told only a story, where the writer's established presence was as a musician or a skier or someone who painted designs on a van, but not as a person removed from that experience interpreting it, treating it as a metaphor for something else (creativity). Unless those stories were long, detailed, and very well told (unless the writer was doing more than saying, "I am a skier or a musician or a van-painter"), those writers were all given low ratings.

Notice also that the writer of the jazz paper locates himself and his experience in relation to the commonplace (creativity is unique expression; it is not having to conform to rules or guidelines) regardless of whether it is true or not. Anyone who improvises "knows" that improvisation follows rules and guidelines. It is the power of the commonplace (its truth as a recognizable, and, the writer believes, as a final statement) that justifies the example and completes the essay. The example, in other words, has value because it stands within the field of the commonplace. It is not the occasion for what one might call an "objective" analysis or a "close" reading. It could also be said that the essay stops with the articulation of the commonplace. The following sections speak only to the power of that statement. The reference to "sculpting, carving, building, art, and acting" attest to the universal of the commonplace (and it attests to the writer's nervousness with the status he has appropriated for himself — he is saying, "Now, I'm not the only one here who's done something unique"). The commonplace stands by itself. For this writer, it does not need to be elaborated. By virtue of having written it, he has completed the essay and established the contract by which we may be spoken to as equals: "In whatever form creativity takes, whether it be music, art, or science, it is an important aspect of *our lives* because it enables *us* to be individuals." (For me to break that contract, to argue that *my* life is not represented in that essay, is one way for me to begin as a teacher with that student in that essay.)

I said that the writer of the jazz paper offered up a commonplace regardless of whether it was "true" or not, and this, I said, was an example of the power of a commonplace to determine the meaning of an example. A commonplace determines a system of interpretation that can be used to "place" an example within a standard system of belief. You can see a similar process at work in this essay.

> During the football season, the team was supposed to wear the same type of cleats and the same type socks, I figured that I would change this a little by wearing my white shoes instead of black and to cover up the team socks with a pair of my own white ones. I thought that this looked better than what we were wearing, and I told a few of the other people on the team to change too. They agreed that it did look better and they changed there combination to go along with mine. After the game people came up to us and said that it looked very good the way we wore our socks, and they wanted to know why we changed from the rest of the team.
>
> I feel that creativity comes from when a person lets his imagination come up with ideas and he is not afraid to express them. Once you create something to

do it will be original and unique because it came about from your own imagination and if any one else tries to copy it, it won't be the same because you thought
of it first from your own ideas.

This is not an elegant paper, but it seems seamless, tidy. If the paper
on the clay model of the earth showed an ill-fit between the writer and his
project, here the discourse seems natural, smooth. You could reproduce
this paper and hand it out to a class, and it would take a lot of prompting
before the students sense something fishy and one of the more aggressive
ones might say, "Sure he came up with the idea of wearing white shoes and
white socks. Him and Billy White-shoes Johnson. Come on. He copied the
very thing he said was his own idea, 'original and unique.'"

The "I" of this text, the "I" who "figured," "thought," and "felt" is located
in a conventional rhetoric of the self that turns imagination into origination
(I made it), that argues an ethic of production (I made it and it is mine),
and that argues a tight scheme of intention (I made it because I decided
to make it). The rhetoric seems invisible because it is so common. This "I"
(the maker) is also located in a version of history that dominates classroom
accounts of history. It is an example of the "Great Man" theory, where
history is rolling along — the English novel is dominated by a central,
intrusive narrative presence; America is in the throes of a great depression;
during football season the team was supposed to wear the same kind of
cleats and socks — until a figure appears, one who can shape history —
Henry James, FDR, the writer of the football paper — and everything is
changed. In the argument of the football paper, "I figured," "I thought," "I
told," "they agreed," and, as a consequence, "I feel that creativity *comes
from* when a person lets his imagination come up with ideas and he is not
afraid to express them." The story of appropriation becomes a narrative of
courage and conquest. The writer was able to write that story when he was
able to imagine himself in that discourse. Getting him out of it will be a
difficult matter indeed.

There are ways, I think, that a writer can shape history in the very act
of writing it. Some students are able to enter into a discourse, but, by
stylistic maneuvers, to take possession of it at the same time. They don't
originate a discourse, but they locate themselves within it aggressively,
self-consciously.

Here is one particularly successful essay. Notice the specialized vocabulary, but also the way in which the text continually refers to its own
language and to the language of others.

Throughout my life, I have been interested and intrigued by music. My mother
has often told me of the times, before I went to school, when I would "conduct"
the orchestra on her records. I continued to listen to music and eventually started
to play the guitar and the clarinet. Finally, at about the age of twelve, I started
to sit down and to try to write songs. Even though my instrumental skills were
far from my own high standards, I would spend much of my spare time during
the day with a guitar around my neck, trying to produce a piece of music.

Each of these sessions, as I remember them, had a rather set format. I would
sit in my bedroom, strumming different combinations of the five or six chords I
could play, until I heard a series which sounded particularly good to me. After
this, I set the music to a suitable rhythm, (usually dependent on my mood at the
time), and ran through the tune until I could play it fairly easily. Only after this
section was complete did I go on to writing lyrics, which generally followed along
the lines of the current popular songs on the radio.

At the time of the writing, I felt that my songs were, in themselves, an original creation of my own; that is, I, alone, made them. However, I now see that, in this sense of the word, I was not creative. The songs themselves seem to be an oversimplified form of the music I listened to at the time.

In a more fitting sense, however, I *was* being creative. Since I did not purposely copy my favorite songs, I was, effectively, originating my songs from my own "process of creativity." To achieve my goal, I needed what a composer would call "inspiration" for my piece. In this case the inspiration was the current hit on the radio. Perhaps with my present point of view, I feel that I used too much "inspiration" in my songs, but, at that time, I did not.

Creativity, therefore, is a process which, in my case, involved a certain series of "small creations" if you like. As well, it is something, the appreciation of which varies with one's point of view, that point of view being set by the person's experience, tastes, and his own personal view of creativity. The less experienced tend to allow for less originality, while the more experienced demand real originality to classify something a "creation." Either way, a term as abstract as this is perfectly correct, and open to interpretation.

This writer is consistent and dramatically conscious of herself forming something to say out of what has been said *and* out of what she has been saying in the act of writing this paper. "Creativity" begins, in this paper, as "original creation." What she thought was "creativity," however, she now calls "imitation" and, as she says, "in this sense of the word" she was not "creative." In another sense, however, she says that she *was* creative since she didn't purposefully copy the songs but used them as "inspiration."

The writing in this piece (that is, the work of the writer within the essay) goes on in spite of, or against, the language that keeps pressing to give another name to her experience as a song writer and to bring the discussion to closure. (Think of the quick closure of the football shoes paper in comparison.) Its style is difficult, highly qualified. It relies on quotation marks and parody to set off the language and attitudes that belong to the discourse (or the discourses) it would reject, that it would not take as its own proper location.[5]

In the papers I've examined in this essay, the writers have shown a varied awareness of the codes — or the competing codes — that operate within a discourse. To speak with authority student writers have not only to speak in another's voice but through another's "code"; and they not only have to do this, they have to speak in the voice and through the codes of those of us with power and wisdom; and they not only have to do this, they have to do it before they know what they are doing, before they have a project to participate in and before, at least in terms of our disciplines, they have anything to say. Our students may be able to enter into a conventional discourse and speak, not as themselves, but through the voice of the community. The university, however, is the place where "common" wisdom is only of negative value; it is something to work against. The movement toward a more specialized discourse begins (or perhaps, best begins) when a student can both define a position of privilege, a position that sets him against a "common" discourse, and when he can work self-consciously, critically, against not only the "common" code but his own.

The stages of development that I've suggested are not necessarily marked by corresponding levels in the type or frequency of error, at least not by the type or frequency of sentence level errors. I am arguing, then, that a basic writer is not necessarily a writer who makes a lot of mistakes. In fact, one of the problems with curricula designed to aid basic writers is that they too often begin with the assumption that the key distinguishing feature of a basic writer is the presence of sentence level error. Students are placed in courses because their placement essays show a high frequency of such errors and those courses are designed with the goal of making those errors go away. This approach to the problems of the basic writer ignores the degree to which error is not a constant feature but a marker in the development of a writer. Students who can write reasonably correct narratives may fall to pieces when faced with more unfamiliar assignments. More importantly, however, such courses fail to serve the rest of the curriculum. On every campus there is a significant number of college freshmen who require a course to introduce them to the kinds of writing that are required for a university education. Some of these students can write correct sentences and some cannot, but as a group they lack the facility other freshmen possess when they are faced with an academic writing task.

The "White Shoes" essay, for example, shows fewer sentence level errors than the "Clay Model" paper. This may well be due to the fact, however, that the writer of that paper stayed well within the safety of familiar territory. He kept himself out of trouble by doing what he could easily do. The tortuous syntax of the more advanced papers on my list is a syntax that represents a writer's struggle with a difficult and unfamiliar language, and it is a syntax that can quickly lead an inexperienced writer into trouble. The syntax and punctuation of the "Composing Songs" essay, for example, shows the effort that is required when a writer works against the pressure of conventional discourse. If the prose is inelegant (although I'll confess I admire those dense sentences), it is still correct. This writer has a command of the linguistic and stylistic resources (the highly embedded sentences, the use of parentheses and quotation marks) required to complete the act of writing. It is easy to imagine the possible pitfalls for a writer working without this facility.

There was no camera trained on the "Clay Model" writer while he was writing, and I have no protocol of what was going through his mind, but it is possible to speculate that the syntactic difficulties of sentences like the following are the result of an attempt to use an unusual vocabulary and to extend his sentences beyond the boundaries that would be "normal" in his speech or writing:

> In past time I thought that an incident was creative was when I had to make a clay model of the earth, but not of the classic or your everyday model of the earth which consists of the two cores, the mantle and the crust. I thought of these things in a dimension of which it would be unique, but easy to comprehend.

There is reason to believe, that is, that the problem is with this kind of sentence, in this context. If the problem of the last sentence is a problem of holding together these units — "I thought," "dimension," "unique," and "easy to comprehend" — then the linguistic problem is not a simple matter of sentence construction.

I am arguing, then, that such sentences fall apart not because the writer lacks the necessary syntax to glue the pieces together but because he lacks the full statement within which these key words are already operating. While writing, and in the thrust of his need to complete the sentence, he has the key words but not the utterance. (And to recover the utterance, I suspect, he will need to do more than revise the sentence.) The invisible conventions, the prepared phrases remain too distant for the statement to be completed. The writer must get inside of a discourse he can only partially imagine. The act of constructing a sentence, then, becomes something like an act of transcription, where the voice on the tape unexpectedly fades away and become inaudible.

Mina Shaughnessy speaks of the advanced writer as a writer with a more facile but still incomplete possession of this prior discourse. In the case of the advanced writer, the evidence of a problem is the presence of dissonant, redundant, or precise language, as in a sentence such as this: "No education can be *total*, it must be *continuous*." Such a student, Shaughnessy says, could be said to hear the "melody of formal English" while still unable to make precise or exact distinctions. And, she says, the prepackaging feature of language, the possibility of taking over phrases and whole sentences without much thought about them, threatens the writer now as before. The writer, as we have said, inherits the language out of which he must fabricate his own messages. He is therefore in a constant tangle with the language, obliged to recognize its public, communal nature and yet driven to invent out of this language his own statements (19).

For the unskilled writer, the problem is different in degree and not in kind. The inexperienced writer is left with a more fragmentary record of the comings and goings of academic discourse. Or, as I said above, he often has the key words without the complete statements within which they are already operating.

It may very well be that some students will need to learn to crudely mimic the "distinctive register" of academic discourse before they are prepared to actually and legitimately do the work of the discourse, and before they are sophisticated enough with the refinements of tone and texture to do it with grace or elegance. To say this, however, is to say that our students must be our students. Their initial progress will be marked by their abilities to take on the role of privilege, by their abilities to establish authority. From this point of view, the student who wrote about constructing the clay model of the earth is better prepared for his education than the student who wrote about playing football in white shoes, even though the "White Shoes" paper was relatively error-free and the "Clay Model" paper was not. It will be hard to pry the writer of the "White Shoes" paper loose from the tidy, pat discourse that allows him to dispose of the question of creativity in such a quick and efficient manner. He will have to be convinced that it is better to write sentences he might not so easily control, and he will have to be convinced that it is better to write muddier and more confusing prose (in order that it may sound like ours), and this will be harder than convincing the "Clay Model" writer to continue what he has begun.[6]

Notes

[1] David Olson has made a similar observation about school-related problems of language learning in younger children. Here is his conclusion: "Depending upon whether children assumed language was primarily suitable for making assertions and conjectures or primarily for making direct or indirect commands, they will either find school texts easy or difficult" (107).

[2] For Aristotle there were both general and specific commonplaces. A speaker, says Aristotle, has a "stock of arguments to which he may turn for a particular need."

If he knows the *topic* (regions, places, lines of argument) — and a skilled speaker will know them — he will know where to find what he wants for a special case. The general topics, or *common*places, are regions containing arguments that are common to all branches of knowledge. . . . But there are also special topics (regions, places, *loci*) in which one looks for arguments appertaining to particular branches of knowledge, special sciences, such as ethics or politics. (154–55)

And, he says "The topics or places, then, may be indifferently thought of as in the science that is concerned, or in the mind of the speaker." But the question of location is "indifferent" *only* if the mind of the speaker is in line with set opinion, general assumption. For the speaker (or writer) who is not situated so comfortably in the privileged public realm, this is indeed not an indifferent matter at all. If he does not have the commonplace at hand, he will not, in Aristotle's terms, know where to go at all.

[3] See especially Bartholomae and Rose for articles on curricula designed to move students into university discourse. The movement to extend writing "across the curriculum" is evidence of a general concern for locating students within the work of the university: see especially Bizzell or Maimon et al. For longer works directed specifically at basic writing, see Ponsot and Deen, and Shaughnessy. For a book describing a course for more advanced students, see Coles.

[4] See especially Bizzell, and Bizzell and Herzberg. My debt to Bizzell's work should be evident everywhere in this essay.

[5] In support of my argument that this is the kind of writing that does the work of the academy, let me offer the following excerpt from a recent essay by Wayne Booth ("The Company We Keep: Self-Making in Imaginative Art, Old and New"):

I can remember making up songs of my own, no doubt borrowed from favorites like "Hello, Central, Give Me Heaven," "You Can't Holler Down My Rain Barrel," and one about the ancient story of a sweet little "babe in the woods" who lay down and died, with her brother.

I asked my mother, in a burst of creative egotism, why nobody ever learned to sing my songs, since after all I was more than willing to learn *theirs*. I can't remember her answer, and I can barely remember snatches of two of "my" songs. But I can remember dozens of theirs, and when I sing them, even now, I sometimes feel again the emotions, and see the images, that they aroused then. Thus who I am now — the very shape of my soul — was to a surprising degree molded by the works of "art" that came my way.

I set "art" in quotation marks, because much that I experienced in those early books and songs would not be classed as art according to most definitions. But for the purposes of appraising the effects of "art" on "life" or "culture," and especially for the purposes of thinking about the effects of the "media," we surely must include every kind of artificial experience that we provide for one another.
. . .
In this sense of the word, all of us are from the earliest years fed a steady diet of art. . . . (58–59)

While there are similarities in the paraphrasable content of Booth's arguments and my student's, what I am interested in is each writer's method. Both appropriate terms from a common discourse (about *art* and *inspiration*) in order to push against an established way of talking (about tradition and the individual). This effort of opposition clears a space for each writer's argument and enables the writers to establish their own "sense" of the key words in the discourse.

[6] Preparation of this manuscript was supported by the Learning Research and Development Center of the University of Pittsburgh, which is supported in part by the National Institute of Education. I am grateful also to Mike Rose, who pushed and pulled at this paper at a time when it needed it.

Works Cited

Aristotle. *The Rhetoric of Aristotle.* Trans. L. Cooper, Englewood Cliffs: Prentice, 1932.

Bartholomae, D. "Writing Assignments: Where Writing Begins." *Forum.* Ed. P. Stock. Montclair: Boynton/Cook, 1983. 300–312.

Bizzell, P. "The ethos of academic discourse." *College Composition and Communication* 29 (1978): 351–55.

———. "Cognition, Convention, and Certainty: What We Need to Know about Writing." *Pre/text* 3 (1982): 213–44.

———. "College Composition: Initiation into the Academic Discourse Community." *Curriculum Inquiry* 12 (1982): 191–207.

Bizzell, P., and B. Herzberg. "'Inherent' Ideology, 'Universal' History, 'Empirical' Evidence, and 'Context-Free' Writing: Some Problems with E. D. Hirsch's *The Philosophy of Composition.*" *Modern Language Notes* 95 (1980): 1181–1202.

Coles, W. E., Jr. *The Plural I.* New York: Holt, 1978.

Flower, Linda S. "Revising Writer-Based Prose." *Journal of Basic Writing* 3 (1981): 62–74.

Maimon, E. P., G. L. Belcher, G. W. Hearn, B. F. Nodine, and F. X. O'Connor. *Writing in the Arts and Sciences.* Cambridge: Winthrop, 1981.

Olson, D. R. "Writing: The Divorce of the Author from the Text." *Exploring Speaking-Writing Relationships: Connections and Contrasts.* Ed. B. M. Kroll and R. J. Vann. Urbana: National Council of Teachers of English, 1981.

Ponsot, M., and R. Deen. *Beat Not the Poor Desk.* Montclair: Boynton/Cook, 1982.

Rose, M. "Remedial Writing Courses: A Critique and a Proposal." *College English* 45 (1983): 109–28.

Shaughnessy, Mina. *Errors and Expectations.* New York: Oxford UP, 1977.

ANALYZING AUDIENCES

Douglas B. Park

[College Composition and Communication *37 (1986): 478–88.*]

Douglas Park is professor of English at Western Washington University, where he served as department chair for ten years. He has published articles on composition and rhetoric in several journals; "Analyzing Audiences" continues an article published in College English *in 1982.*

Park recognizes that few teachers agree on how best to teach audience analysis. He offers options for expanded discussions of audience, and he emphasizes that audience analyses will be most successful if students recognize how their writing will function in a reasonable social context. As a result, Park affirms the pragmatic, functional approach to audience analysis that The Bedford Handbook *promotes.*

What do we expect analysis of audience to do for writers? What form should analysis of audience take; or, more precisely, what makes certain kinds of analysis more or less appropriate in given situations?

The centrality of audience in the rhetorical tradition and the detail with which current writing texts provide advice on analyzing an audience might suggest that the answers to such questions are well established. But they clearly are not. Side by side with the growing awareness in recent discussions that audience is a rich and complex concept exists a growing dissatisfaction with traditional audience analysis — those familiar questions about an audience's age, sex, education, and social background that form the core of most proposed heuristics. (See, for instance, Barry Kroll, "Writing for Readers: Three Perspectives on Audience," *CCC*, 35 [May 1984], 172–75; Russell Long, "Writer–Audience Relationships," *CCC*, 31 [May 1980], 221–26; Arthur Walzer, "Articles from the 'California Divorce Project': A Case Study of the Concept of Audience," *CCC*, 36 [May 1985], 155–58.)

The general import of the explicit criticism is that traditional audience analysis is too limited a tool: It works only for persuasive discourse; it seems inapplicable to discourse situations with general audiences about whom specific questions cannot be arrived at. But underneath these criticisms lies a greater uncertainty about the whole subject, characterized on the one hand by a sense that traditional analysis somehow fails altogether to provide what we now expect from audience analysis and on the other by the lack of any other widely shared way of thinking about the subject.

To address this uncertainty, we need to return to first principles and examine just what it is that we do expect audience analysis to accomplish and just how the assumptions behind traditional analysis relate to those expectations. This examination will show why traditional analysis, for all the apparent sanction of tradition, has so little practical rhetorical value for us. More important, it will provide a backdrop for a broader and, I hope, more useful view of what can go into analyzing audiences.

In a broad sense, the purpose of audience analysis is obvious enough: to aid the writer or speaker in understanding a social situation. The advice to "know your audience" carries much of the social meaning of "know" as in knowing who another person is or what that person is like. The advice to "consider your audience" suggests a deliberate weighing of the characteristics of the audience with a view to an appropriate shaping of the discourse. If we look at a set of hypothetical discourses chosen to illustrate a range of different audiences, we can describe more precisely these undifferentiated purposes for analysis. Consider

a legal argument on behalf of an accused embezzler;

a local businessman's letter to City Council protesting a zoning decision;

a grant proposal to develop computer instruction;

a memo from a provost to his university faculty arguing for annual evaluations;

a panel presentation on invention at CCCC;

an article on food in the Pacific Northwest contemplated by a freelance journalist;

an essay on rock and roll contemplated by an English 101 student.

In all but the last two cases, the most obvious specific purpose for analysis will be to understand where a given audience stands in relation to the particular aim and issues at hand. The goal is the immediately strategic one of adapting argument to audience: What are the criteria on which the grant review board makes its decisions? Why are most of the faculty so hostile to annual evaluations? What are the current issues in the discipline's discussions of invention?

In the last two cases above, however, the writers are not yet ready for this sort of strategic analysis. The freelance writer must first choose an audience — a journal such as *Sunset Magazine* — in order to be able to think about rhetorical strategy. The student, in a yet more difficult position, must somehow imagine or invent an audience in a situation where no audience naturally exists. Here the primary purpose of audience analysis becomes not the usual one of providing information about an existing audience but rather a means of actually helping students to discover an audience. And this raises the questions of just how they are to do that. What must they think about to imagine their papers as having or being capable of having an audience?

The special context of the classroom creates a peculiar purpose for audience analysis, one for which it was never intended. It does, however, usefully focus the essential question of what we mean by "having an audience." What is an audience, anyway? — as our baffled students often seem to ask. And this is just a generalized form of a need that all writers experience to understand the identity of the audience that they know they have: What does it mean to be in the situation of addressing a CCCC audience or a grant review board or a City Council? Questions of this sort are, I think, another important part of the meaning of "know your audience." They point to a purpose for analysis which lies underneath the more obvious strategic purpose of determining the audience's responses to particular issues.

Both these purposes for analysis — the fundamental identifying and defining of an audience and the strategic analysis of particular attitudes — involve describing situations, because audience is an inherently situational concept (Lisa Ede, "On Audience and Composition," *CCC*, 30 [October 1979], 294ff.). The notion of accommodating discourse to an audience is one of participating in a dynamic social relationship. And "audience" itself refers to the idea of a collective entity that can exist only in relation to a discourse; it means a group of people engaged in a rhetorical situation. Therefore if we are to identify an audience and say anything useful about it, we will have to speak in terms of the situation that brings it into being and gives it identity.

From this perspective, it becomes easy to see why traditional audience analysis so often seems unsatisfactory. What it does is to take literally the idea of "knowing" an audience as examining a group already assembled and describing any or all of the characteristics that those assembled may happen to have. In so doing it directly addresses neither the situation that has brought the audience into being as an audience nor the particular states of mind that the audience may possess in relation to the issues at hand. It tries rather to describe general traits from which rhetorically useful inferences may be drawn.

> [The elderly] are positive about nothing; in all things they err by an extreme moderation. . . . The rich are insolent and superior. . . . Now the hearer is always receptive when a speech is adapted to his own character and reflects it. (*The Rhetoric of Aristotle*, trans. Lane Cooper [Englewood Cliffs, N.J., Prentice-Hall, 1932], pp. 134–38)

> Different habits . . . and different occupations in life . . . make one incline more to one passion, another to another. . . . With men of genius the most successful topic will be fame; with men of industry, riches; with men of fortune, pleasure. (George Campbell, *The Philosophy of Rhetoric*, 2 vols. [Edinburgh, 1776], 1, 241–42)

> It is . . . to begin by recording certain information about an audience and then, on the basis of experience and research, to infer about the audience such matters as knowledge, temperament, attitudes, habits of thought, language preferences or other matters that will enter into their responses to communication. (Theodore Clevenger, Jr., *Audience Analysis* [Indianapolis, Ind.: Bobbs-Merrill, 1966], p. 43)

Clearly, both Campbell and Aristotle envision the possibility of topoi appropriate for various ages and conditions of men. If an assembled audience in a particular situation can be seen to have a salient trait or quality — what classical rhetoric calls the "character" of the audience — then various lines of argument will fit that character more or less effectively. Perhaps most of the City Council are like our letter-writer businessman "men of industry," practical men who will respond best to arguments from "riches." As a general idea — which is how audience analysis usually appears in classical rhetoric (e.g., Quintilian, *Institutio Oratoria*, III, viii, 38) — the notion seems plausible. Certainly in situations involving small, immediate audiences, most of us have had the experience of sensing the overall personality of an audience, or of dominant members in it, and the need to adjust to those qualities in a general and impressionistic way. But inflated to a social-science method of the sort that the modern description suggests, traditional analysis almost completely loses touch with rhetorical usefulness. Aside from the fact that large generalizations about the psychology of age or sex are suspect in any particular application, the accumulation of demographic facts about an audience has no clear goal or limit (Clevenger, pp. 45ff.). All it can do is amass information unlikely to add up to any sort of "character." "The characters of men," admits George Campbell, beating a retreat from the subject, "may be infinitely diversified" (243). One of our industrious business executives may also be a man of genius and education who might therefore be motivated by arguments from fame. Another is perhaps rich and therefore "insolent." Two might be in their 30's, one in his 50's, two in their 60's. Two might have high-school educations, and so on ad infinitum, the writer having no clear way to determine the relevance or weight of any of this information to the task at hand.

Of course the general assumption informing traditional audience analysis as we find it in modern speech communication texts is that it aims at the social traits held in common that shape the responses of the audience as a whole. (See, for instance, Paul Holtzman's *The Psychology of Speakers' Audiences* [Glenview, Ill.: Scott Foresman, 1970], pp. 73–79.) So we can observe that a CCCC audience will share many social traits: most will have advanced degrees in English; most will be between 25 and 65; probably at least half will be women; most will be politically liberal. Certainly all will have modest incomes. But although such facts might well interest a social scientist, they are merely symptoms of the situation that actually gives the audience its identity. If we were to send a speaker to the podium, shanghaied, blindfolded, armed only with the subject and the result of a demographic analysis, our victim would angrily or plaintively want to know, "But who is my audience?" The answer of course is "conferees attending a CCCC panel," a simple identification that compresses for someone in the know a wealth of necessary knowledge about the identity of the audience as an entity assembled for a collective purpose.

Bizarre as the case of the blindfolded speaker may be, it describes exactly the mistaken way in which traditional analysis is used to help students discover audiences by amassing detailed information about people, real or imaginary. "They [students] must construct in imagination an audience that is as nearly a replica as is possible of those many readers who actually exist in the world of reality and who are reading the writer's words" (Fred R. Pfister and Joanne F. Petrick, "A Heuristic Model for Creating a Writer's Audience," *CCC*, 30 [May 1980], 213). Following this principle, discussions commonly suggest as audiences groups with analyzable traits. "Thus a reader might be delineated as being a university administrator, over 40, male, white, etc., or a group of readers might be defined as businessmen in a small [midwestern] community" (Winifred B. Horner, "Speech-Act and Text-Act Theory: 'Theme-ing' in Freshman Composition," *CCC*, 30 [May 1979], 168). But obviously the problem that students face is not one of just visualizing hypothetical real people; it is one of grasping a situation in which real readers could constitute an "audience." In what conceivable situations, for instance, could our student writing about rock and roll be addressing a group of midwestern businessmen?

How then do we go about describing the situations that bring audiences into being and give them their identities? Or to put the question in a more basic way, how is it that discourses of any sort can have audiences? If we look at the most concrete possible image of an audience assembled to hear a speech and ask how they come to be there, the immediate answer will be that a particular occasion has brought them together. This, indeed, is the most common way we tend to think about and characterize audiences, as a particular group assembled to hear a particular speech. But a moment's reflection shows that while an audience assembles only for a particular discourse, the discourse alone cannot bring the audience into being. Lawyers do not defend their clients on street corners; passers-by do not wander into Holiday Inns to hear lectures on teaching composition; freelance journalists do not mimeograph their articles and leave them in mailboxes — unless they have become really desperate.

In brief, an audience can assemble on a particular occasion only because a social setting already exists in which a certain kind of discourse performs a recognized function. Note that the ancient classification of judicial, deliberative, and epideictic discourse follows this principle and amounts, as Chaim Perelman points out, to the identification of three basic audiences (*The New Rhetoric: A Treatise on Argumentation,* trans. John Wilkinson and Purcell Weaver [Notre Dame, Ind.: University of Notre Dame Press, 1969], p. 21). To define other audiences we need simply to amplify the principle to its broadest extent, as follows.

An audience can exist when there is (1) an established social institution or social relationship, a judicial system, a legislative process, an institutional hierarchy, a charitable foundation, a social compact of any sort, a club, a nation, even a friendship between two people; (2) and an evolved and understood function that discourse performs within and for that social relationship. Speech-act theory — and sociolinguistics in general — has taught us to see all discourse as representing action performed within and conditioned by a social situation. We can name these actions in very general terms — making statements, contracts, promises, implications, requests. But it is also important to see that all discourse, especially of the more public or formalized kind, functions in and can be described as part of a social transaction that has defined roles for both writers and readers. If I write a grant proposal, I am making a request, but I am also participating in a highly conventionalized activity evolved to enable the distribution of resources, the manipulation of tax laws, the satisfaction of political and public relations imperatives. I write as the representative of one institution.

My audience exists in terms of and reads as representatives of the granting agency.

(3) Finally, for an audience to "assemble," there must be a physical setting. For written discourse, the exact analog to the place of assembly is the means of publication or distribution. Much has been made of the distance between writers and readers as opposed to the closeness of speakers and audience. Walter Ong argues that the readers of written discourse do not form an audience, a "collectivity," as do the listeners to a speech ("The Writer's Audience Is Always a Fiction," *PMLA*, 90 [January 1975], 11). In some senses this must of course be true, but because a written discourse always exists within some larger social setting and reaches its dispersed readers through a given physical means of distribution for an accepted social function, readers of prose are very much part of a collectivity. When I read a memo from the Provost in my office mail or a copy of *Sunset Magazine* in the public mail, I understand that I am participating in a social activity together with others. The major difference between speech and writing in their roles in social settings is that writing has been able to develop a wider range of functions. In the instance of popular journalism, the means of publication has been able to become a social institution in its own right. The reader of a newspaper or a magazine participates in a social relationship that has been largely created by the development of newspapers and magazines themselves.

All these intertwined elements of the social context for discourse define the terms in which the identity of an audience is best understood. This is why when we respond most directly and effectively to the question, "Who is the audience," we always respond in terms of the social institution and function that the discourse serves — a court, members of City Council, a grant review board, the college faculty, CCCC conferees, readers of *Sunset Magazine.* Unspoken but always present in any such simple identification of an audience is the whole complex of the social situation that has brought that audience into being. This unspoken presence is so compressed into the identification that it is easy to take for granted. But a writer who understands the identity of the audience grasps a wealth of tacit and explicit knowledge about the form of the discourse and the way the subject can be treated.

This knowledge informs the obvious rhetorical choices about appropriate formats, matters of tone, diction, stance toward the reader, kinds of allowable openings, structure, evidence, and argument. It also includes more subtle, crucial presuppositions about such things as how much the purpose of the discourse or the writer's own authority can be presumed or needs to be explained and justified. In many cases where the setting is subject specific — e.g., periodical journalism or scholarship — knowledge of the audience's identity also includes a great deal that the audience can be taken to know about the subject at hand. Awareness of the audience's identity provides, in short, all the sense of situation that makes it possible for a writer or speaker to proceed with a sense of being engaged in purposeful communication.

The identity of the audience, as I have described it above, constitutes, therefore, the necessary foundation for audience analysis. It constitutes as well the setting that shapes further considerations of strategy about the specific subject. For example, the lawyer pleading the case before the court will be concerned with the attitudes of the jurors toward the client and the issues of the case. But strategies to play on those attitudes will have to acknowledge the decorum of the courtroom and the jurors' own awareness of their special role as jurors. As Chaim Perelman points out, "It is quite common for members of an audience to adopt attitudes connected with the role they play in certain social institutions" (p. 21). In the case of the audience for the CCCC presentation, almost everything that one can say about their attitudes toward the subject at hand will, as Arthur Walzer suggests, have to be defined in terms of that particular "rhetorical or interpretive community" and in terms of the role that academic audiences are expected to play (p. 157).

To summarize the above discussion, I would suggest that what a writer needs to understand about an audience, what we mean by "knowing" an audience, can be adequately described by two interrelated levels of questions:

I. What is the identity of the audience?
   A. What is the institution or social relationship of writer(s) and audience that the discourse serves (or creates)?
   B. How does the discourse function in that relationship?
   C. What is the physical setting or means of distribution that brings the discourse to the audience and what are the conventions and formats associated with it?
II. How does the audience view the specific subject matter and how may it view the intentions of the discourse?
   A. What is known or can be projected about specific attitudes and knowledge in the audience that affect what the discourse will have to do in order to accomplish its purpose?
   B. To what extent are the audience's attitudes toward subject and purpose affected by or describable by reference to its collective identity as audience?

Although this outline has the appearance of a heuristic, I propose it more as a general framework for thinking about what writers may actually do when they attend to audience. How much, and at what points in the process of composing, such attention may profitably take the form of deliberate analysis of the audience are questions that I hope the above framework may help others to explore further. In particular, I think this framework helps to open a more adequate view of how different kinds of writing situations may require very different kinds of attention to audience. The elements of the audience that I have described above seem in different situations to take on different forms, to claim varying degrees of precedence and to interact in different ways.

For instance, our businessman writing to City Council probably knows the members of the Council well and has several social relationships to them — friend, enemy, fellow member of the Chamber of Commerce, and so on — any of which might be involved explicitly or implicitly in the letter. He has, therefore, a number of ways to conceive of and address his audience. But his attention seems most likely to be concentrated on their individual attitudes and predispositions toward the zoning issues. In the case of the grant proposal, by contrast, the writer's conception of the audience will be necessarily defined by their role as agents of the institution and by the conventions of grant proposals. The means of distribution for the discourse maintains distance, even anonymity, between the writer and the audience. Here, everything that can be said about the audience's attitudes will concern the kinds of argument that this particular granting agency is most responsive to. Yet again, in other kinds of institutional prose, like the provost's memo to the faculty, a piece of discourse may serve more than one function and audience — e.g., the President as well as the faculty. Much of the initial attention to audience will have to fall on actually identifying and defining these multiple audiences and then on juggling issues in recognition of all of them, while perhaps explicitly addressing only one audience. (See C. H. Knoblauch, "Intentionality in the Writing Process: A Case Study," *CCC*, 31 [May 1980], 153–59. See also Mathes and Stevenson, *Designing Technical Reports* [Indianapolis, Ind.: Bobbs-Merrill, 1976], pp. 9–23.)

In spite of the differences in the attention to audience in the above examples, all are alike in that they aim toward the second level of the audience's specific attitudes and knowledge, and the appropriate strategies to accommodate them. This is so because the general function of the writings is transactional, by which I mean that they work to produce specific actions or responses from an audience who, as members of the institution involved, have an active part to play.

The kinds of attention a writer pays to audience seem likely to alter significantly, in ways that we do not understand at all well, when the function of discourse moves away from the transactional, as it does in the typical periodical essay and in much of what we call discourse written for a general audience. The audience for such discourse is not part of an institution — members of a jury, faculty at University X — within which the discourse performs some function. The audience comes rather to the discourse to participate in the social relationship — a sort of one-sided conversation — that is offered there. Here, understanding the identity of the audience means understanding what readers expect, the nature of the "conversation," the conventions which govern that kind of prose. In particular, it usually means understanding the setting of publication, e.g. *Sunset Magazine*, that ties those conventions to a specific format or to a set of assumed interests and attitudes in readers.

In such discourse, second-level analysis of the audience in relation to the specific subject and purpose often seems almost irrelevant, or so different from the analysis in transactional discourse that we need to find other ways of talking about it. The traditional model sees the writer as assessing and accommodating specific attitudes. The discourse is an instrument of negotiation. But here the writer is in the position of offering readers a social relationship — for entertainment, for intellectual stimulation, for general information — which they may or may not choose to enter.

One familiar way to talk about this very different relationship between discourse and audience is to draw on Walter Ong's idea of the audience as a fiction evoked by the text, a series of roles that the text offers to readers, or a series of presuppositions it makes about readers that the readers can accept or not ("The Writer's Audience Is Always a Fiction," *PMLA*, 90 [January 1975], 9–21; see also Douglas Park, "The Meanings of 'Audience,'" *College English*, 44 [March 1982], 247–57). Accordingly, Russell Long suggests that young writers should not try to analyze their audiences but to ask rather "Who do I want my audience to be?" (Writer–Audience Relationships: Analysis or Invention?" *CCC*, 31 [May 1980], 225).

Although this idea has force, it has remained too undeveloped. Further, it seems clear that all discourse must in some fashion attend to the constraints imposed by the requirements of real audiences. (See Lisa Ede and Andrea Lunsford, "Audience Addressed/Audience Invoked: The Role of Audience in Composition Theory and Pedagogy," *CCC*, 35 [May 1984], 155–71.) Writers, that is to say, can set out to engage readers in conversation only by some appropriate estimate of what they are actually likely to find intelligible, credible, or interesting. In practice, the setting for publication usually yields such information. But it seems probable that what writers work with here is not precise formulations of particular attitudes or states of knowledge but rather an awareness of a range of possible viewpoints. Robert Roth, for example, describes successful student revisions that evolve by appealing to a variety of possible responses from readers, by casting a wider rather than a narrower net ("The Evolving Audience: Alternatives to Audience Accommodation," *CCC*, 38 [February 1987], 47–55). The general aim of such attention to audience might perhaps be described not as fitting discourse to audience but as making it possible for a variety of readers to become an audience.

This survey is too brief to give more than an idea of the range of considerations that can go into audience analysis. But it will do to indicate how the framework I have laid out might be used, and to indicate as well some areas that need more investigation. For teachers of writing, I hope this discussion demonstrates that analysis of audience cannot profitably be seen as a set of all-purpose questions to be tacked on to an assignment to help students invent or identify an audience. To identify an audience means identifying a situation. So the primary issue that our current concern with audience analysis poses for teachers of writing is not how we can help students analyze their audiences but, first, how and to what extent we can help them define situations for their writing. And to this question there are no simple answers.

The most obvious way to define a situation for writing is to pose hypothetical cases — Imagine you are a resident assistant writing a report for the Dean of Students; write an article for *Sports Illustrated* — or to use the composition class for "real" writing such as a letter to the hometown paper. In fact the only way to have an audience analyzable in the detail we usually envision when we speak of audience analysis is to have a situation for writing that includes a concrete setting for "publication." For such assignments, I hope this discussion will facilitate more useful analyses of audience than those evoked by traditional advice.

Most teachers, however, will resist turning their composition courses entirely over to the writing of letters for various occasions. They feel, with good reason, that too much emphasis upon specific and often imaginary situations can lead to crude pretense and mechanical emphasis on format that robs student writing of all genuineness. They want students' writing to be in some elusive but important sense real and self-generated. Unfortunately, this ideal is difficult to reconcile with the obvious need many students have for a clearer sense of audience. Well-meaning advice like, "Be your own audience," while it seems to get at a truth, can leave many students with no way to understand their writing as being for anyone or any purpose at all.

The student who escapes this limbo — perhaps our hypothetical student writing about rock and roll — will do so partly by using various conventions of written prose to evoke the shadow of a situation, by writing like a freelance journalist or a musicologist, or an encyclopedist, or a columnist, or some creative pastiche of these. The very use of a certain recognizable "register" (M. A. K. Halliday and R. Hasan, *Language as Social Semiotic* [London: Longmans, 1976], pp. 65–73) — a way of addressing the readers, of opening the subject, of organizing material, and so on — even though it is accompanied by no identifiable setting for publication, will evoke a sense of the paper's possessing an audience. If the student's paper is sufficiently like other discourse that exists in real settings for publication, then it too will be felt to some extent to have an audience. But such a sense of audience will, I would suggest, always be informed by a grasp of the social function of the prose — that is to say how it works as public discourse, what general kind of thing it offers to readers.

If we are to help students who do not have this grasp on audience, we need to learn more about it ourselves. We need, first of all, to give more attention to defining the social functions of various kinds of public discourse. It is easy enough to see that different composition courses and different teachers have preferences — too often barely conscious or impressionistically defined — for different kinds of audiences. Students in one course may be expected to write like popular journalists about their personal knowledge, in another like apprentice philosophers, in another like informal essayists in the grand tradition. The current trend to center composition courses on the varieties of academic discourse seems especially constructive because it is accompanied by an attempt to understand and make more explicit the nature of such discourse (Walzer, p. 157).

Second, we need to learn more about how different kinds of discourse written for public or "general" audiences actually work rhetorically. Recognizing that the model of audience accommodation which works for transactional prose does not apply well to all discourse situations is a starting point. Doing more to describe the conventions of such prose would also be useful, as for instance in George Dillon's *Constructing Texts* (Bloomington, Ind.: Indiana University Press, 1981). His description of how students fail to understand some of the basic conventions of expository prose gets at a fundamental part of what we mean by a sense of audience. Although it is difficult to say how far such material should be taught directly, my own experience is that students are more receptive to descriptions and discussions of writing conventions as matters of social form and function than they are to descriptions of absolute criteria for good writing.

Finally, we need to keep in mind that the culture of the classroom can be a pervasive influence on a student's ability to understand an audience. In "Collaborative Learning and the 'Conversation of Mankind'" (*College English,* 46 [November 1984], 635–52), Kenneth Bruffee provides a fine account of the way that students can learn through social interaction to internalize and then re-externalize the kind of "conversation" that defines "a community of knowledgeable peers" (p. 642). At this point the discussion may appear to have moved far from analysis of audience, but at its most basic the issue of audience in writing instruction is one of social development and maturation — of student writers learning to see themselves as social beings in a social situation. Only in such a context can the art of rhetoric and of audience analysis have any real meaning or force in our teaching of writing.

THE WRITING PROCESS

COMPETING THEORIES OF PROCESS: A CRITIQUE AND A PROPOSAL

Lester Faigley

[College English *48 (1986): 527–42.*]

Lester Faigley is professor of English and director of the Division of Rhetoric and Composition at the University of Texas, Austin. He has published numerous journal articles, including "Analyzing Revision" (College Composition and Communication, 1981) with Stephen Witte and "Learning to Write in the Social Sciences" (College Composition and Communication, 1985) with Kristine Hansen. His book Fragments of Rationality: Postmodernity and the Subject of Composition *was published in 1992.*

Through his wide reading about the writing process, Faigley came to see the variety of notions that have been advanced about the process. "Competing Theories of Process" is an effort to sort out those notions and to examine their intellectual backgrounds. Faigley offers an overview of the three prevailing views of composing — the expressive, the cognitive, and the social — and examines the assumptions that each view makes about writers, writing, and the composing process. The article reminds instructors that the choices they make in their course plans and daily classroom practices are informed by an implicit or explicit theory of composing. Faigley's argument is particularly valuable for its suggestive synthesis of the three competing theoretical views. His discussion of writing processes complements The Bedford Handbook's *flexible approach to process.*

The recognition of the study of writing as an important area of research within English in North America has also led to a questioning of its theoretical underpinnings. While the teaching of writing has achieved programmatic or departmental status at many colleges and universities, voices from outside and from within the ranks question whether a discipline devoted to the study of writing exists or if those who teach writing simply assume it exists because they share common problems and interests. The convenient landmark for disciplinary historians is the Richard Braddock, Richard Lloyd-Jones, and Lowell Schoer review of the field in 1963, a survey that found a legion of pedagogical studies of writing, most lacking any broad theoretical notion of writing abilities or even awareness of similar existing studies. Contemporary reviewers of writing research point out how much happened in the years that followed, but no development has been more influential than the emphasis on writing as a process. For the last few years, Richard Young's and Maxine Hairston's accounts of the process movement as a Kuhnian paradigm shift have served as justifications for disciplinary status. Even though the claim of a paradigm shift is now viewed by some as an overstatement, it is evident that many writing teachers in grade schools, high schools, and colleges have internalized process assumptions. In the most optimistic visions, writing teachers K–13 march happily under the process banner. Slogans such as "revising is good for you" are repeated in nearly every college writing textbook as well as in many secondary and elementary classrooms. Paradigm, pre-paradigm, or no paradigm, nearly everyone seems to agree that writing as a process is good and "current-traditional rhetoric" is bad. It would seem, therefore, that any disciplinary claims must be based on some shared definition of process.

The problem, of course, is that conceptions of writing as a process vary from theorist to theorist. Commentators on the process movement (e.g., Berlin, *Writing Instruction*) now assume at least two major perspectives on composing, an *expressive view* including the work of "authentic voice" proponents such as William Coles, Peter Elbow, Ken Macrorie, and Donald Stewart, and a *cognitive view* including the research of those who analyze composing processes such as Linda Flower, Barry Kroll, and Andrea Lunsford. More recently, a third perspective on composing has emerged, one that contends processes of writing are social in character instead of originating within individual writers. Statements on composing from the third perspective, which I call the *social view,* have come from Patricia Bizzell, Kenneth Bruffee, Marilyn Cooper, Shirley Brice Heath, James Reither, and authors of several essays collected in *Writing in Nonacademic Settings* edited by Lee Odell and Dixie Goswami.

Before I contrast the assumptions of each of these three views on composing with the goal of identifying a disciplinary basis for the study of writing, I want to raise the underlying assumption that the study and teaching of writing *should* aspire to disciplinary status. In a radical critique of education in America, Stanley Aronowitz and Henry Giroux see the development of writing programs as part of a more general trend toward an atheoretical and skills-oriented curriculum that regards teachers as civil servants who dispense pre-packaged lessons. Here is Aronowitz and Giroux's assessment:

> We wish to suggest that schools, especially the colleges and universities, are now battlegrounds that may help to determine the shape of the future. The proliferation of composition programs at all levels of higher education may signal a new effort to extend the technicization process even further into the humanities. . . . The splitting of composition as a course from the study of literature, [*sic*] is of course a sign of its technicization and should be resisted both because it is an attack against critical thought and because it results in demoralization of teachers and their alienation from work. (52)

While I find their conclusions extreme, their critique provokes us to examine writing in relation to larger social and political issues. Unlike most other Marxist educational theorists, Aronowitz and Giroux do not present a pessimistic determinism nor do they deny human agency. They allow for the possibility that teachers and students can resist domination and think critically, thus leaving open the possibility for a historically aware theory and pedagogy of composing.

I will outline briefly the histories of each of the dominant theoretical views of composing, drawing on an earlier book by Giroux, *Theory and Resistance in Education,* for a critical review of the assumptions of each position.[1] In the concluding section of this essay, however, I reject Aronowitz and Giroux's dour assessment of the study of writing as a discipline. Each of the theoretical positions on composing has given teachers of writing a pedagogy for resisting a narrow definition of writing based largely on "correct" grammar and usage. Finally, I argue that disciplinary claims for writing must be based on a conception of process broader than any of the three views.

The Expressive View

The beginnings of composing research in the mid-1960s hardly marked a revolution against the prevailing line of research; in fact, early studies of composing issues typically were isolated pedagogical experiments similar to those described by Braddock, Lloyd-Jones, and Schoer. One of these experiments was D. Gordon Rohman and Albert Wlecke's study of the effects of "pre-writing" on writing performance, first published in 1964. Rohman and Wlecke maintained that thinking was different from writing and antecedent to writing; therefore, teachers should stimulate students' thinking by having them write journals, construct analogies, and, in the spirit of the sixties, meditate before writing essays. Young cites the Rohman and Wlecke study as one that helped to overturn the current-traditional paradigm. What Young neglects to mention is that Rohman and Wlecke revived certain Romantic notions about composing and were instigators of a "neo-Romantic" view of process. Rohman defines "good writing" as

> that discovered combination of words which allows a person the integrity to dominate his subject with a pattern both fresh and original. "Bad writing," then, is an echo of someone else's combination which we have merely taken over for the occasion of our writing. . . . "Good writing" must be the discovery by a responsible person of his uniqueness within his subject. (107–08)

This definition of "good writing" includes the essential qualities of Romantic expressivism — integrity, spontaneity, and originality — the same qualities M. H. Abram uses to define "expressive" poetry in *The Mirror and the Lamp*.

Each of these expressivist qualities has motivated a series of studies and theoretical statements on composing. We can see the influence of the first notion — integrity — in the transmission of Rohman and Wlecke's definitions of "good" and "bad" writing. In 1969 Donald Stewart argued that the unified aim for writing courses should be writing with integrity. He illustrated his argument with a student paper titled "Money Isn't as Valuable as It Seems" that contained a series of predictable generalities. Stewart criticized the student not for failing to support his generalizations but because he "doesn't believe what he is saying. Worse yet, it is possible that he doesn't even realize he doesn't believe it" (225).[2] The problem with using integrity as a measure of value is obvious in retrospect. Not only is the writer of the paper Stewart reproduces bound by his culture, as Stewart argues, but so too are Stewart's criticisms. Stewart's charges of insincerity are based on the assumption that the student is parroting the antiestablishment idealism of the late sixties. Conversely, career-oriented students of today are so unlikely to write such a paper, that if one started an essay with the same sentences as Stewart's example ("Having money is one of the least important items of life. Money only causes problems and heartaches among one's friends and self."), a teacher likely would assume that the student believed what she was saying, no matter how trite or predictable.

Because the sincerity of a text is finally impossible to assess, a second quality of Romantic expressivism — spontaneity — became important to the process movement primarily through Peter Elbow's *Writing without Teachers*, a book that was written for a broad audience, and that enjoyed great popular success. Elbow adopted Macrorie's method of free writing, but he presented the method as practical advice for writing spontaneously, not as a way of discovering "the truth." Elbow questioned Rohman and Wlecke's separation of thinking from writing, a model he maintained led to frustration. Instead, Elbow urged that we think of writing as an organic, developmental process in which you start writing at the very beginning — before you know your meaning at all — and encourage your words gradually to change and evolve. Only at the end will you know what you want to say or the words you want to say it with. (15)

Elbow chose the metaphor of organic growth to describe the operations of composing, the same metaphor Edward Young used to describe the vegetable concept of genius in 1759 and Coleridge borrowed from German philosophers to describe the workings of the imagination (see Abrams 198–225). Coleridge contrasted two kinds of form — one mechanical, when we impress upon any material a predetermined form, the other organic, when the material shapes itself from within. Coleridge also realized the plant metaphor implied a kind of organic determinism. (Tulip bulbs cannot grow into daffodils.) He avoided this consequence by insisting upon the free will of the artist, that the artist has foresight and the power of choice. In much the same way, Elbow qualifies his organic metaphor:

It is true, of course, that an initial set of words does not, like a young live organism, contain within each cell a *plan* for the final mature stage and all the intervening stages that must be gone through. Perhaps, therefore, the final higher organization in words should only be called a borrowed reflection of a higher organization that is really in me or my mind. (23)

Elbow's point is one of the standards of Romantic theory: that "good" writing does not follow rules but reflects the processes of the creative imagination.

If writing is to unfold with organic spontaneity, then it ought to expose the writer's false starts and confused preliminary explorations of the topic. In other words, the writing should proceed obliquely as a "striving toward" — a mimetic of the writer's actual thought processes — and only hint at the goal of such striving. The resultant piece of writing would then seem fragmentary and unfinished, but would reveal what Coleridge calls a progressive method, a psychological rather than rhetorical organization, unifying its outwardly disparate parts. On the other hand, insofar as a piece of writing — no matter how expressive — is coherent, it must also be mimetic and rhetorical. At times Wordsworth and to a lesser extent Coleridge seem to argue that expressivism precludes all intentionality — as if such meditations as Wordsworth's "Tintern Abbey" and Coleridge's "This Lime-Tree Bower My Prison" weren't carefully *arranged* to seem spontaneous. Peter Elbow's solution to the dilemma of spontaneity comes in *Writing with Power*, where he discusses revision as the shaping of unformed material.

A third quality of Romantic expressivism — originality — could not be adapted directly to current theories of composing because the Romantic notion of originality is linked to the notion of natural genius, the difference between the poet who is born and the poet who is made. The concept of natural genius has been replaced in contemporary expressive theory with an emphasis on the innate potential of the unconscious mind. More limited statements of this position recommend teaching creative writing to stimulate originality.[3] Stronger statements come from those expressive theorists who apply the concept of "self-actualization" from psychoanalysis to writing. Rohman says teachers "must recognize and use, as the psychologists do in therapy, a person's desire to actualize himself" (108). The implication is that personal development aids writing development or that writing development can aid personal development, with the result that better psychologically integrated people become better writers. (Case histories of twentieth-century poets and novelists are seldom introduced in these discussions.) In an essay on meditation and writing James Moffett extends the self-actualization notion introduced by Rohman, saying "good therapy and composition aim at clear thinking, effective relating, and satisfying self-expression" (235).

Giroux, however, would see Moffett's essay as emblematic of what is wrong with the expressive view. Although Giroux grants that expressive theory came as a reaction against, to use his words, the "technicization" of education, he contends the result of the quest for "psychic redemption" and "personal growth" is a turning away from the relation of the individual to the social world, a world where "social practices situated in issues of class, gender, and race shape everyday experience" (219). For Giroux, the expressive view of composing ignores how writing works in the world, hides the social nature of language, and offers a false notion of a "private" self. Before I defend the expressive position against Giroux's attack, I will move on to the cognitive view where Giroux's strongest criticisms center.

The Cognitive View

In addition to promoting expressive assumptions about composing, Rohman and Wlecke helped inspire research that led to the current cognitive view. Several researchers in the late sixties were encouraged by Rohman and Wlecke's mention of *heuristics* and their finding that students who were taught "pre-writing" activities wrote better essays. More important, Rohman and Wlecke's proposal of three linear stages in the writing process stimulated research in response. In 1964 Janet Emig first argued against a linear model of composing, and she redoubled her attack in her 1969 dissertation, later published as an NCTE research monograph. Emig was among the first writing researchers to act on calls for research on cognitive processes issued at the influential 1966 Dartmouth Seminar on English. She observed that high school writers, in contrast to standard textbook advice of the time, did not use outlines to compose and that composing "does not occur as a left-to-right, solid, uninterrupted activity with an even pace" (84). Instead, Emig described composing as "recursive," an adjective from mathematics that refers to a formula generating successive terms. While the term is technically misapplied, since writing processes do not operate this simply, the extent to which it is used by other researchers attests to Emig's influence. Another measure of Emig's influence is that denunciations of Rohman and Wlecke's *Pre-Writing, Writing, Re-writing* model became a trope for introductions of later articles on composing.

In a recent consideration of Emig's monograph, Ralph Voss credits her with developing a "'science consciousness' in composition research" (279). Emig appropriated from psychology more than the case-study approach and think-aloud methodology. Her monograph is a mixture of social science and literary idioms, with one sentence talking about a "sense of closure," the next about "a moment in the process when one feels most godlike" (44). Emig's work was well received because writing researchers wanted to enter the mainstream of educational research. For example, Janice Lauer began a 1970 article directing writing researchers to psychologists' work in problem solving with the following sentence: "Freshman English will never reach the status of a respectable intellectual discipline unless both its theorizers and its practitioners break out of the ghetto" (396). Emig provided not only a new methodology but an agenda for subsequent research, raising issues such as pausing during composing, the role of rereading in revision, and the paucity of substantial revision in student writing. Her monograph led to numerous observational studies of writers' composing behavior during the next decade.[4]

The main ingredient Emig did not give researchers was a cognitive theory of composing. When writing researchers realized Chomsky's theory of transformational grammar could not explain composing abilities, they turned to two other sources of cognitive theory. The first was cognitive-developmental psychology, which James Britton and his colleagues applied to the developing sense of audience among young writers. Britton argued that children as speakers gain a sense of audience because the hearer is a reactive presence, but children as writers have more difficulty because the "other" is not present. Consequently, a child writing must imagine a generalized context for the particular text in all but the most immediate writing situations (such as an informal letter). Britton condemned most school writing assignments for failing to encourage children to imagine real writing situations (see *Development* 63–65). Other researchers probed the notion of developmental stages in writing. Barry Kroll adapted Jean Piaget's concept of *egocentrism* — the inability to take any perspective but one's own — to explain young children's lack of a sense of audience. He hypothesized, like Britton, that children's ability to *decenter* — to imagine another perspective — develops more slowly in writing than in speaking. Andrea Lunsford extended Piaget's stages of cognitive development to college basic writers, arguing that their tendency to lapse into personal narrative in writing situations that call for "abstract" discourse indicates they are arrested in an "egocentric stage."

The second source of cognitive theory came from American cognitive psychology, which has spawned several strands of research on composing. Many college writing teachers were introduced to a cognitive theory of composing through the work of Linda Flower and John R. Hayes. Flower and Hayes' main claims — that composing processes intermingle, that goals direct composing, and that experts compose differently from inexperienced writers — all have become commonplaces of the process movement. Less well understood by writing teachers, however, are the assumptions underlying Flower and Hayes' model, assumptions derived from a cognitive research tradition. Flower and Hayes acknowledge their debt to this tradition, especially to Allen Newell and Herbert A. Simon's *Human Problem Solving,* a classic work that helped define the aims and agenda for a cognitive science research program. Newell and Simon theorize that the key to understanding how people solve problems is in their "programmability"; in other words, how people use "a very simple information processing system" to account for their "problem solving in such tasks as chess, logic, and cryptarithmetic" (870). The idea that thinking and language can be represented by computers underlies much research in cognitive science in several camps, including artificial intelligence, computational linguistics, and cognitive psychology. Newell and Simon's historical overview of this movement credits Norbert Wiener's theory of *cybernetics* as the beginnings of contemporary cognitive science.[5] The basic principle of cybernetics is the *feedback loop,* in which the regulating mechanism receives information from the thing regulated and makes adjustments.

George A. Miller was among the first to introduce cybernetic theory as an alternative to the stimulus-response reflex arc as the basis of mental activity. In *Plans and the Structure of Behavior,* Miller, Eugene Galanter, and Karl Pribram describe human behavior as guided by plans that are constantly being evaluated as they are being carried out in a feedback loop. They theorize that the brain — like a computer — is divided into a *memory* and a *processing unit.* What Miller, Galanter, and Pribram do not attempt to theorize is where plans come from. To fill in this gap, Newell and Simon add to the feedback loop an entity they call the *task environment,* defined in terms of a goal coupled with a specific environment. Newell and Simon claim the resulting loop explains how people think.

If we look at the graphic representation of the Flower and Hayes model in the 1980 and 1981 versions, we can see how closely the overall design follows in the cognitive science tradition. The box labeled *Writing Processes* is analogous to the central processing unit of a computer. In the 1980 version, diagrams representing the subprocesses of composing (*planning, translating,* and *reviewing*) are presented as computer flowcharts. Like Newell and Simon's model of information processing, Flower and Hayes' model makes strong theoretical claims in assuming relatively simple cognitive operations produce enormously complex actions, and like Emig's monograph, the Flower and Hayes model helped promote a "science consciousness" among writing teachers. Even though cognitive researchers have warned that "novice writers cannot be turned into experts simply by tutoring them in the knowledge expert writers have" (Scardamalia 174), many writing teachers believed cognitive research could provide a "deep structure" theory of *the* composing process, which could in turn specify how writing should be taught. Furthermore, the Flower and Hayes model had other attractions. The placement of *translating* after *planning* was compatible with the sequence of invention, arrangement, and style in classical rhetoric. It also suited a popular conception that language comes after ideas are formed, a conception found in everyday metaphors that express ideas as objects placed in containers (e.g., "It's difficult to put my ideas into words").[6]

Giroux's response to the cognitive view of composing can be readily inferred. To begin, Giroux would be highly critical of any attempt to discover universal laws underlying writing. Writing for Giroux, like other acts of literacy, is not universal but social in nature and cannot be removed from culture. He would fault the cognitive view for collapsing cultural issues under the label "audience," which, defined unproblematically, is reduced to the status of a variable in an equation. He further would accuse the cognitive view of neglecting the content of writing and downplaying conflicts inherent in acts of writing. As a consequence, pedagogies assuming a cognitive view tend to overlook differences in language use among students of different social classes, genders, and ethnic backgrounds.

At this point I'll let Giroux's bricks fly against my windows and use an article on revision I wrote with Steve Witte as a case in point. In this study Witte and I attempt to classify revision changes according to the extent they affect the content of the text. We apply a scheme for describing the structure of a text developed by the Dutch text linguist, Teun van Dijk. What seems obviously wrong with this article in hindsight is the degree to which we assign meaning to the text. Now even van Dijk admits there are as many macrostructures for a text as there are readers. Although our conclusions criticize the artificiality of the experiment and recognize that "revision cannot be separated from other aspects of composing," the intent of the study still suffers from what Giroux sees as a fundamental flaw of cognitivist research — the isolation of part from whole.

The Social View

The third perspective on composing I identified at the beginning of this essay — the social view — is less codified and less constituted at present than the expressive and cognitive views because it arises from several disciplinary traditions. Because of this diversity a comprehensive social view cannot be extrapolated from a collection of positions in the same way I have described the expressive and cognitive views of composing. Statements that propose a social view of writing range from those urging more attention to the immediate circumstances of how a text is composed to those denying the existence of an individual author. My effort to outline a social view will be on the basis of one central assumption: human language (including writing) can be understood only from the perspective of a society rather than a single individual. Thus taking a social view requires a great deal more than simply paying more attention to the context surrounding a discourse. It rejects the assumption that writing is the act of a private consciousness and that everything else — readers, subjects, and texts — is "out there" in the world. The focus of a social view of writing, therefore, is not on how the social situation influences the individual, but on how the individual is a constituent of a culture.

I will attempt to identify four lines of research that take a social view of writing, although I recognize that these positions overlap and that each draws on earlier work (e.g., Kenneth Burke). These four lines of research can be characterized by the traditions from which they emerge: poststructuralist theories of language, the sociology of science, ethnography, and Marxism.

In the last few years, writing researchers influenced by poststructuralist theories of language have brought notions of discourse communities to discussions of composing. Patricia Bizzell and David Bartholomae, for example, have found such ideas advantageous in examining the writing of college students. Those who believe that meaning resides in the text accuse any other position of solipsism and relativism, but concepts of discourse communities provide an alternative position, offering solutions to difficult problems in interpretative theory. Reading is neither an experience of extracting a fixed meaning from a text nor is it a matter of making words mean anything you want them to in *Alice in Wonderland* fashion. Ambiguity in texts is not the problem for humans that it is for computers — not so much because we are better at extracting meaning but because language is social practice; because, to paraphrase Bakhtin, words carry with them the places where they have been.

This view of language raises serious problems for cognitive-based research programs investigating adults' composing processes. For instance, Bizzell criticizes the separation of "Planning" and "Translating" in the Flower and Hayes model. Even though Flower and Hayes allow for language to generate language through rereading, Bizzell claims the separation of words from ideas distorts the nature of composing. Bizzell cites Vygotsky, whom many cognitive researchers lump together with Piaget, but whose understanding of language is very different from Piaget's. Vygotsky studied language development as a historical and cultural process, in which a child acquires not only the words of language but the intentions carried by those words and the situations implied by them.

From a social perspective, a major shortcoming in studies that contrast expert and novice writers lies not so much in the artificiality of the experi- .

mental situation, but in the assumption that expertise can be defined outside of a specific community of writers. Since individual expertise varies across communities, there can be no one definition of an expert writer. David Bartholomae explores the implications for the teaching of college writing. He argues that writing in college is difficult for inexperienced writers not because they are forced to make the transition from "writer-based" to "reader-based" prose but because they lack the privileged language of the academic community. Bartholomae's point is similar to Bizzell's: when students write in an academic discipline, they write in reference to texts that define the scholarly activities of interpreting and reporting in that discipline. Bartholomae alludes to Barthes' observation that a text on a particular topic always has "off-stage voices" for what has previously been written about that topic. Thus a social view of writing moves beyond the expressivist contention that the individual discovers the self through language and beyond the cognitivist position that an individual constructs reality through language. In a social view, any effort to write about the self or reality always comes in relation to previous texts.

A substantial body of research examining the social processes of writing in an academic discourse community now exists in the sociology of science. Most of this research has been done in Britain, but Americans Charles Bazerman and Greg Myers have made important contributions. . . . Research in scientific writing displays many of the theoretical and methodological differences mentioned at the beginning of this section, but this literature taken as a whole challenges the assumption that scientific texts contain autonomous presentations of facts; instead, the texts are "active social tools in the complex interactions of a research community" (Bazerman 3). In the more extreme version of this argument, which follows from Rorty and other pragmatists, science itself becomes a collection of literary forms. Writing about the basis of economics, Donald McCloskey calls statistics "figures of speech in numerical dress" (98). He goes on to say that "the scientific paper is, after all, a literary genre, with an actual author, an implied author, an implied reader, a history, and a form" (105). In contrast, current British research understands a dialectical relationship between external reality and the conventions of a community. A good introduction to this field is Nigel Gilbert and Michael Mulkay's 1984 book, *Opening Pandora's Box*.[7]

A third line of research taking a social view of composing develops from the tradition of ethnography. Ethnographic methodology in the 1970s and 1980s has been used to examine the immediate communities in which writers learn to write — the family and the classroom. These researchers have observed that for many children, the ways literacy is used at home and in the world around them matches poorly with the literacy expectations of the school.[8] The most important of these studies to date is Shirley Brice Heath's analysis of working-class and middle-class families in the Carolina Piedmont. Heath found that how children learn to use literacy originates from how families and communities are structured. Another line of research using ethnographic methodology investigates writing in the workplace, interpreting acts of writing and reading within the culture of the workplace (see Odell and Goswami for examples).

Finally, I include Marxist studies of literacy as a fourth social position on composing. The essential tenet of a Marxist position would be that any act of writing or of teaching writing must be understood within a structure of power related to modes of production. A Marxist critique of the other social positions would accuse each of failing to deal with key concepts such as class, power, and ideology.[9] Giroux finds discourse communities are often more concerned with ways of excluding new members than with ways of admitting them. He attacks non-Marxist ethnographies for sacrificing "theoretical depth for methodological refinement" (98). Indeed, much Marxist scholarship consists of faulting other theorists for their lack of political sophistication.

Toward a Synthesis

At the beginning of this essay I quoted Aronowitz and Giroux's conclusion that the spread of writing programs and, by implication, the process movement itself are part of a general movement toward "atheoretical" and "skills-oriented" education in America. Now I would like to evaluate that claim. If process theory and pedagogy have up to now been unproblematically accepted, I see a danger that it could be unproblematically rejected. Process theory and pedagogy have given student writing a value and authority absent in current-traditional approaches. Each view of process has provided teachers with ways of resisting static methods of teaching writing — methods based on notions of abstract form and adherence to the "rules" of Standard English. Expressive theorists validate personal experience in school systems that often deny it. Cognitive theorists see language as a way of negotiating the world, which is the basis of James Berlin's dialogic redefinition of epistemic rhetoric (*Rhetoric and Reality*). And social theorists such as Heath have found that children who are labeled remedial in traditional classrooms can learn literacy skills by studying the occurrences of writing in the familiar world around them (see *Ways with Words,* chapter 9).

But equally instructive is the conclusion of Heath's book, where she describes how the curriculum she helped create was quickly swept away. It illustrates how social and historical forces shape the teaching of writing — relationships that, with few exceptions, are only now beginning to be critically investigated. If the process movement is to continue to influence the teaching of writing and to supply alternatives to current-traditional pedagogy, it must take a broader conception of writing, one that understands writing processes are historically dynamic — not psychic states, cognitive routines, or neutral social relationships. This historical awareness would allow us to reinterpret and integrate each of the theoretical perspectives I have outlined.

The expressive view presents one of two opposing influences in discourse — the unique character of particular acts of writing versus the conventions of language, genre, and social occasion that make that act understandable to others. The expressive view, therefore, leads us to one of the key paradoxes of literacy. When literacy began to be widespread in Northern Europe and its colonies during the eighteenth and nineteenth centuries, it reduced differences between language groups in those countries and brought an emphasis on standard usage. But at the same time linguistic differences were being reduced, individuals became capable of changing the social order by writing for a literate populace (witness the many revolutionary tracts published during the nineteenth century). Furthermore, modern notions of the individual came into being through the widespread publication of the many literary figures and philosophers associated with the Romantic movement and the later development of psychology as a discipline in the nineteenth century. Current technologies for electronic communications bring the potential for gaining access to large bodies of information from the home, yet at the same time these technologies bring increased potential for control through surveillance of communication and restriction of access. People, however, find ways to adapt technologies for their own interests. In organizations where computer technologies have become commonplace, people have taken advantage of opportunities for horizontal communication on topics of their choice through computer "bulletin boards," which function like radio call-in programs. For example, on ARPANET, the Department of Defense's computer network linking research facilities, military contractors, and universities, popular bulletin boards include ones for science fiction, movie reviews, and even a lively debate on arms control. How the possibilities for individual expression will be affected by major technological changes in progress should become one of the most important areas of research for those who study writing.

In a similar way, historical awareness would enhance a cognitive view of composing by demonstrating the historical origins of an individual writer's goals. The cognitive view has brought attention to how writers compose in the workplace. Many writing tasks on the job can be characterized as rhetorical "problems," but the problems themselves are not ones the writers devise. Writing processes take place as part of a structure of power. For instance, Lee Iacocca's autobiography reveals how writing conveys power in large organizations. Iacocca says he communicated good news in writing, but bad news orally. Surely Iacocca's goals and processes in writing are inseparable from what he does and where he works, which in turn must be considered in relation to other large corporations, and which finally should be considered within a history of capitalism.

Some social approaches to the study of discourse entail historical awareness, but a social view is not necessarily historical. The insight that the learning of literacy is a social activity within a specific community will not necessarily lead us to a desirable end. Raymond Williams observes that the term *community* has been used to refer to existing social relationships or possible alternative social relationships, but that it is always used positively, that there is no opposing term. Yet we know from the sad experiences of the twentieth century that consensus often brings oppression. How written texts become instruments of power in a community is evident in the history of colonial empires, where written documents served to implement colonial power. Some of the earliest recorded uses of writing in Mesopotamia and ancient Egypt were for collecting taxes and issuing laws in conquered territories. Written documents made possible the incident George Orwell describes in "The Hanging" — an essay frequently anthologized but rarely analyzed in writing classes for its political significance. Furthermore, in the effort to identify conventions that define communities of writers, commentators on writing processes from a social viewpoint have neglected the issue of what *cannot* be discussed in a particular community, exclusions Foucault has shown to be the exercise of power.

These questions are not mere matters of ivory-tower debate. The preoccupation with an underlying theory of the writing process has led us to neglect finding answers to the most obvious questions in college writing instruction today: why college writing courses are prevalent in the United States and rare in the rest of the world; why the emphasis on teaching writing occurring in the aftermath of the "literacy crisis" of the seventies has not abated; why the majority of college writing courses are taught by graduate students and other persons in nontenurable positions. Answers to such questions will come only when we look beyond who is writing to whom to the texts and social systems that stand in relation to that act of writing. If the teaching of writing is to reach disciplinary status, it will be achieved through recognition that writing processes are, as Stanley Fish says of linguistic knowledge, "contextual rather than abstract, local rather than general, dynamic rather than invariant" (438).

Notes

[1] Giroux directly criticizes "romantic" and "cognitive developmental" traditions of teaching literacy in *Theory and Resistance in Education*. Bruce Herzberg has extended Giroux's critique to particular composition theorists.

[2] Even more strident attacks on clichés and conventional writing assignments came from Ken Macrorie, who damned "themes" as papers "not meant to be read but corrected" (686), and from William Coles, who accused textbook authors of promoting "themewriting" by presenting writing "as a trick that can be played, a device that can be put into operation . . . just as one can be taught or learn to run an adding machine, or pour concrete" (134–42).

[3] For example, Art Young advocates having students write poems, plays, and stories in writing-across-the-curriculum classes. During the 1920s and 1930s, there were numerous appeals to incorporate creative writing into the English curriculum; see, for example, Lou LaBrant.

[4] For a bibliographic review of cognitive studies of composing, see Faigley, Cherry, Jolliffe, and Skinner, chapters 1–5.

[5] Wiener used the term *cybernetics* — derived from the Greek word for the pilot of a ship — as a metaphor for the functioning mind. He claimed as a precedent James Watt's use of the word *governor* to describe the mechanical regulator of a steam engine. Wiener's metaphor explained the mind as a control mechanism such as an automatic pilot of an airplane. For a historical overview of cybernetics and the beginnings of cognitive science, see Bell.

[6] Reddy discusses some of the consequences of the "conduit" metaphor for our understanding of language.

[7] Gilbert and Mulkay provide a bibliography of social studies of scientific discourse on 194–95.

[8] Heath includes an annotated bibliography of school and community ethnographies in the endnotes of *Ways with Words*.

[9] Richard Ohmann's *English in America* remains the seminal Marxist analysis of American writing instruction.

Works Cited

Abrams, M. H. *The Mirror and the Lamp*. New York: Oxford UP, 1953.

Aronowitz, Stanley, and Henry A. Giroux. *Education under Siege*. South Hadley, MA: Bergin, 1985.

Bartholomae, David. "Inventing the University." *When a Writer Can't Write*. Ed. Mike Rose. New York: Guilford, 1985. 134–65.

Bazerman, Charles. "Physicists Reading Physics: Schema-Laden Purposes and Purpose-Laden Schema." *Written Communication* 2 (1985): 3–23.

Bell, Daniel. *The Social Sciences since the Second World War*. New Brunswick, NJ: Transaction, 1982.

Berlin, James. *Rhetoric and Reality: Writing in American Colleges, 1900–1985*. Carbondale: Southern Illinois UP, 1984.

———. *Writing Instruction in Nineteenth-Century American Colleges*. Carbondale: Southern Illinois UP, 1984.

Bizzell, Patricia. "Cognition, Convention, and Certainty: What We Need to Know about Writing." *PRE/TEXT* 3 (1982): 213–43.

Braddock, Richard, Richard Lloyd-Jones, and Lowell Schoer. *Research in Written Composition.* Urbana: NCTE, 1963.

Britton, James, Tony Burgess, Nancy Martin, Alex McLeod, and Harold Rosen. *The Development of Writing Abilities (11–18).* London: Macmillan, 1975.

Bruffee, Kenneth A. "Collaborative Learning and the 'Conversion of Mankind.'" *College English* 46 (1984): 635–52.

Coleridge, Samuel Taylor. "On Method." *The Portable Coleridge.* Ed. I. A. Richards. New York: Viking, 1950. 339–86.

Coles, William, Jr. "Freshman Composition: The Circle of Unbelief." *College English* 31 (1969): 134–42.

Cooper, Marilyn M. "The Ecology of Writing." *College English* 48 (1986): 364–75.

Elbow, Peter. *Writing without Teachers.* New York: Oxford UP, 1973.

———. *Writing with Power.* New York: Oxford UP, 1981.

Emig, Janet. *The Composing Processes of Twelfth Graders,* NCTE Research Report No. 13. Urbana: NCTE, 1971.

———. "The Uses of the Unconscious in Composing." *College Composition and Communication* 16 (1964): 6–11.

Faigley, Lester, Roger D. Cherry, David A. Jolliffe, and Anna M. Skinner. *Assessing Writers' Knowledge and Processes of Composing.* Norwood, NJ: Ablex, 1985.

Faigley, Lester, and Stephen P. Witte. "Analyzing Revision." *College Composition and Communication* 32 (1981): 400–14.

Fish, Stanley. "Consequences." *Critical Inquiry* 11 (1985): 433–58.

Flower, Linda, and John R. Hayes. "A Cognitive Process Theory of Writing." *College Composition and Communication* 31 (1980): 365–87.

Foucault, Michel. *Power/Knowledge: Selected Interviews and Other Writings, 1972–1977.* Ed. Colin Gordon. New York: Pantheon, 1980.

Gilbert, G. Nigel, and Michael Mulkay. *Opening Pandora's Box: A Sociological Analysis of Scientists' Discourse.* Cambridge: Cambridge UP, 1984.

Giroux, Henry A. *Theory and Resistance in Education.* South Hadley, MA: Bergin, 1983.

Hairston, Maxine. "The Winds of Change: Thomas Kuhn and the Revolution in the Teaching of Writing." *College Composition and Communication* 33 (1982): 76–88.

Hayes, John R., and Linda Flower. "Identifying the Organization of Writing Processes." *Cognitive Processes in Writing: An Interdisciplinary Approach.* Ed. Lee Gregg and Erwin Steinberg. Hillsdale, NJ: Erlbaum, 1980. 3–30.

Heath, Shirley Brice. *Ways with Words.* New York: Cambridge UP, 1983.

Herzberg, Bruce. "The Politics of Discourse Communities." Paper presented at the Conference on College Composition and Communication, New Orleans, March 1986.

Iacocca, Lee. *Iacocca: An Autobiography,* New York: Bantam, 1984.

Kroll, Barry M. "Cognitive Egocentrism and the Problem of Audience Awareness in Written Discourse." *Research in the Teaching of English* 12 (1978): 269–81.

LaBrant, Lou. "The Psychological Basis for Creative Writing." *English Journal* 25 (1936): 292–301.

Lauer, Janice. "Heuristics and Composition." *College Composition and Communication* 21 (1970): 396–404.

Lunsford, Andrea. "The Content of Basic Writers' Essays." *College Composition and Communication* 31 (1980): 278–90.

Macrorie, Ken. "To Be Read." *English Journal* 57 (1968): 686–92.

McCloskey, Donald N. "The Literary Character of Economics." *Daedalus* 113.3 (1984): 97–119.

Miller, George A., Eugene Galanter, and Karl Pribram. *Plans and the Structure of Behavior.* New York: Holt, 1962.

Moffett, James. "Writing, Inner Speech, and Meditation." *College English* 44 (1982): 231–44.

Myers, Greg. "Texts as Knowledge Claims: The Social Construction of Two Biologists' Articles." *Social Studies of Science* 15 (1985): 593–630.

———. "Writing Research and the Sociology of Scientific Knowledge: A Review of Three New Books." *College English* 48 (1986): 595–610.

Newell, Alan, and Herbert A. Simon. *Human Problem Solving.* Englewood Cliffs, NJ: Prentice, 1972.

Odell, Lee, and Dixie Goswami, eds. *Writing in Nonacademic Settings.* New York: Guilford, 1985.

Ohmann, Richard. *English in America: A Radical View of the Profession.* New York: Oxford UP, 1976.

Reddy, Michael J. "The Conduit Metaphor." *Metaphor and Thought.* Ed. Andrew Ortony. Cambridge: Cambridge UP, 1979. 284–324.

Reither, James A. "Writing and Knowing: Toward Redefining the Writing Process." *College English* 47 (1985): 620–28.

Rohman, D. Gordon. "Pre-Writing: The Stage of Discovery in the Writing Process." *College Composition and Communication* 16 (1965): 106–12.

Rohman, D. Gordon, and Alfred O. Wlecke. "Pre-Writing: The Construction and Application of Models for Concept Formation in Writing." U.S. Department of Health, Education, and Welfare Cooperative Research Project No. 2174. East Lansing: Michigan State U, 1964.

Scardamalia, Marlene, Carl Bereiter, and Hillel Goelman. "The Role of Production Factors in Writing Ability." *What Writers Know: The Language, Process, and Structure of Written Discourse.* Ed. Martin Nystrand. New York: Academic, 1982. 173–210.

Stewart, Donald. "Prose with Integrity: A Primary Objective." *College Composition and Communication* 20 (1969): 223–27.

Voss, Ralph. "Janet Emig's *The Composing Processes of Twelfth Graders*: A Reassessment." *College Composition and Communication* 34 (1983): 278–83.

Williams, Raymond. *Keywords: A Vocabulary of Culture and Society.* new York: Oxford UP, 1976.

Young, Art. "Considering Values: The Poetic Function of Language." *Language Connections.* Ed. Toby Fulwiler and Art Young. Urbana: NCTE, 1982. 77–97.

Young, Richard. "Paradigms and Problems: Needed Research in Rhetorical Invention." *Research on Composing: Points of Departure.* Ed. Charles R. Cooper and Lee Odell. Urbana: NCTE, 1978. 29–47.

Joseph Alkana, Andrew Cooper, Beth Daniell, Kristine Hansen, Greg Myers, Carolyn Miller, and Walter Reed made helpful comments on earlier drafts of this essay.

PLANNING AND DRAFTING

EXPLORING THE POTENTIAL OF FREEWRITING

Joy Marsella and Thomas L. Hilgers

[From Nothing Begins with N: New Investigations of Freewriting. Ed. Pat Belanoff, Peter Elbow, and Sheryl I. Fontaine. Carbondale: Southern Illinois UP, 1991. 93–110.]

Joy Marsella is professor of English and director of the Hawaii site of the National Writing Project. Thomas Hilgers, professor of English at the University of Hawaii, directs the university's campuswide writing program and has published articles in several journals, including Written Communication *and* Research in the Teaching of English. *In 1992 Marsella and Hilgers published* Making Your Writing Program Work: A Guide to Good Practices.

Those who subscribe to social views of composition tend to devalue freewriting as a serious strategy for discovery and invention, arguing that it is representative of an expressivist or "me-centered" view of writing that has been shown to be naive or inadequate. But Marsella and Hilgers argue that freewriting is more than an expressive discovery strategy, more than a way to get started. They describe a freewriting sequence that can be used as a broad heuristic, "a series of operations" that guide and promote discovery. This essay expands fruitfully on the discussion of freewriting in The Bedford Handbook *and offers practical suggestions for exploring freewriting's potential.*

"Our last master plan emphasized freewriting, but our new one goes beyond it and incorporates newer approaches." This comment, which we overheard at a recent national convention, reminded us that the field of composition, so recently entrenched in the traditional, has now become almost trend-driven, to the point where making changes may be equated with making progress. Some of the repercussions of this situation are well illustrated by the history of "freewriting." The term became important in the composition lexicon with the publication of Ken Macrorie's *Writing to Be Read* in 1968, and Peter Elbow's *Writing without Teachers* in 1973. Classroom use of "freewriting exercises" caught on rather quickly, and by the late 1970s many composition textbooks were recommending freewriting in their chapters on "getting started" or "prewriting." But very few theorists seemed to believe, as Elbow apparently did, that freewriting could be important in the generation of analytic prose. It was fine for personal writing, for overcoming writer's block, for priming the pump. Beyond that, it seemed to hold little promise. By the later 1980s, freewriting was primarily associated with "naturalistic" writing (Hillocks 1986) or a relatively naive ideological "expressionism" (Berlin 1988).

Though theorists relegate it to minor roles, and though the age of collaboration has dawned in the writing classroom, freewriting continues to hold its own among student writers and their teachers. Researchers, however, tend to overlook it, especially now that invention is no longer fashionable as an area of study. This is unfortunate. Until freewriting is subjected to analysis and investigation, composition specialists are unlikely to learn just why so many people find it useful. And people will continue to use the term *freewriting* without definition, much as *writing* was used until recently as the term for everything from penmanship to editing.

This chapter argues for hard-nosed investigation of freewriting in its many uses and particularly as applied to analytic tasks. We build our argument in three steps: after our introductory comments, we summarize a research study that demonstrated that training in the use of a freewriting heuristic can promote positive results more readily than training in techniques that appear to be more analytically based; second, we explain in some detail the freewriting heuristic that was employed in the study; and, finally, we make suggestions to teachers and researchers for further exploration of freewriting's potential.

Our argument rests on the use of freewriting as a broad heuristic, a heuristic that prompts not only ideas but also analysis of those ideas. We hope that our discussion will at least provoke doubts among those who see freewriting as valuable only within a me-centered pedagogy. We also hope that our presentation will provoke researchers to look at the variety of practices now lumped together as *freewriting*, sort them out, and show which practices may be effective under which circumstances.

We are not the first to describe freewriting as a heuristic. A decade ago, James Kinney proposed that freewriting be seen as a heuristic for invention. Heuristics, or "rules of thumb," are often expressed as a series of operations or questions that guide discovery. To many, their use involves a writer in something that freewriting does not: the systematic application of reason to a writer's problems. Kinney argued that freewriting could be viewed as an interplay between intuition and reason.

Young, Becker, and Pike's tagmemic analysis is more frequently cited in discussions of heuristics for invention; however, heuristics based on freewriting may be more widely used, although they may not be so identified. For example, freewriting was often recommended in Elbow's second book, *Writing with Power* (1981), as a part of several procedures that a writer might use to guide the production of analytic writing. Although Elbow himself did not identify these procedures as heuristics, it is appropriate to think of them as such.

At the heart of the procedures we describe here is a three-step sequence that we shall call the *freewriting heuristic*. The sequence is adapted directly from Elbow's *Writing without Teachers.* We used the three-step freewriting heuristic to create one set of classroom practices around which Hilgers designed a study of the effects of teaching college students to use heuristics for composition. That study has been reported in detail elsewhere (Hilgers). We will summarize it here and then elaborate the activities that the freewriting heuristic comprises.

Freewriting and Problem-Solving Heuristics: An Evaluative Study

Hilgers's study involved forty-seven students enrolled in two sections of the introductory course in composition at the University of Hawaii. Several weeks into the term, a randomly chosen half of the students were assigned to special classes in which they would learn to use problem-solving heuristics to deal with audience, purpose, voice, and other components associated with writing as communication. A significant number of studies in applied psychology suggest that there are several steps that can be taught to people who lack the skills associated with effective problem solving. In fact much of the attention focused on cognitive psychology during the last two decades derived from studies of problem-solving processes. The early research of Flower and Hayes (for example, "Problem-solving Strategies and the Writing Process," "Process-based Evaluation of Writing") suggested that such processes were commonly used by experienced writers.

The other half of the students were assigned to special classes involving practice in the use of freewriting, reflection, and writing of a "summing-up" assertion. This sequence, suggested in early writings by Macrorie and Elbow, seems more intuitive than do the rational operations prescribed in problem-solving heuristics. But when the sequence is repeated again and again, it functions nonetheless as a heuristic for the generation of both material and ideas.

To approximate what would be feasible in a one-semester college class, the classes in heuristics were limited to six fifty-minute sessions. Joy Marsella, who was intuitively convinced of the value of freewriting as a heuristic, designed and taught the classes of the freewriting sequence. Tom Hilgers, rationally confident of the effectiveness of problem-solving heuristics, designed and taught classes on problem solving applied to writing. Marsella and Hilgers acted as guest lecturers for the two-week period these special classes were conducted; they were not regularly assigned to teach these sections. Both trainers were well matched in terms of education, experience, student evaluations, peer evaluations, and classroom "enthusiasm." Marsella and Hilgers used the same content for writing exercises during the last three training sessions, but students were encouraged to use the different heuristics to deal with that content.

Though Hilgers expected to be able to show the superiority of the problem-solving heuristics, the research design was of necessity neutral and aimed to pinpoint differences in the writing produced by students in the two groups.

The study called for analysis of three pieces of writing done by all students. The first was a brief "article," written in class, offering freshmen advice on how to deal with registration. The assignment for this piece of writing was presented to the students by their regular instructor and completed before the "experimental" portion of the study began. The second writing assignment was introduced to all students toward the end of the fourth special class; the writing was to be done outside class and collected during the sixth special session. The assignment included a sheet of facts about a hearing aid, facts that the students were to use in writing a "letter" in response to a plea from a distraught high-school coach. The final writing assignment, completed during the sixth special class, gave students forty minutes to write a "speech" with advice for sophomores at the high school from which the writers had graduated. Although not traditional essays, all three of the writings called for students to *analyze* personal experience, situations, and facts and to draw some conclusions based on them.

Compositions by the thirty-seven students who had completed all three of the writing assignments were evaluated by two paid readers, experienced instructors who knew nothing of the design or purpose of the study, or even that the students had been trained in different groups. All three types of composition were ranked with holistic scores between 1 and 7. The "letter" subsequently was also ranked on several scales: (1) attention to needs of the audience; (2) clarity and appropriateness of writer's voice; (3) development of a central idea; (4) appropriateness of ideas and materials; (5) appropriateness of organization; and (6) attention to conventions of grammar and usage. The correlations between scores assigned by the two readers ranged from 0.60 to 0.78. The score assigned to an individual essay was the sum of the two readers' rankings; thus, scores ranged from 0 to 14.

To answer the question Was there a difference in the writing produced by students in the two groups?, scores were run through a multivariate analysis of covariance with scores from the "article" used as the covariate. Subsequent tests showed that there was indeed a significant difference in the "letters" written by students in the two groups ($F = 4.16$, $df = 2$, 36, $p = 0.05$). As is clear from table 5–1, students who were trained to use the freewriting heuristic (Group FW on table 5–1) scored 2 points higher on the average than students trained to use the problem-solving heuristics (Group CAPS). Although the freewriting students scored higher on all of the subscales, the difference was most pronounced in scores assigned for appropriateness of ideas and materials in the letters.

Because the study was conducted in the real world rather than a laboratory, answers to the research questions have to be appended by caveats. First, the groups were not taught by the same person; though the two teachers were equal on several measures of student satisfaction, unknown variables may have come into play; and second, although all student writers used the heuristics they had been taught, many complied less than fully with guidelines. Nearly all students noted that using the heuristics required more time than they were used to giving a writing assignment. Although these are real limitations, a different research design would likely have generated other limitations. If, for example, the study had been conducted under conditions of near-laboratory control, we would have to wonder about the likelihood of its applicability to everyday circumstances.

To our knowledge, this has been the only controlled study of freewriting. The study shows that freewriting, when used according to the sequence of activities explained in the next section, accomplishes more than most commentators seem willing to grant. We think the following sections help explain why this is so.

Defining the Freewriting Heuristic

Let us explore in more detail the series of operations, derived from Elbow's *Writing without Teachers,* that make up the freewriting heuristic as it was used by students in the study.

The first step calls for writers to freewrite, following Elbow's directives:

> Write for ten minutes (later on, perhaps fifteen or twenty). Don't stop for anything. Go quickly without rushing. Never stop to look back to cross something out, to . . . think about what you are doing. If you can't think of a word or a spelling, just use a squiggle. . . . The easiest thing is just to put down whatever is in your mind. If you get stuck it's fine to write "I can't think of what to say. . . ." The only requirement is that you *never* stop. (3)

For purposes of the heuristic, we refer to this procedure as the *freewriting exercise.*

A variant of this basic exercise calls for the writer to begin writing with an object, a concept, a question, or an assertion in mind. Using this focus as a point of departure, the writer writes freely, following her ideas where they take her; whenever she reaches the point where she "can't think of anything to say," she returns to the focus. It is this variant of the exercise, *focused freewriting,* that is at the heart of the heuristic.

Early in *Writing without Teachers,* Elbow gives an example of "how you might go about" a typical writing task "if you adopted the developmental model" of the writing process. The operation described in the example involves, first, performance of the freewriting exercise, or of focused freewriting, according to set guidelines. After the exercise is completed, the operation requires the writer to read and reflect on what he or she has written, seeking to identify its "center of gravity." Finally, the "center" is

Table 5–1. *Mean Scores of Texts Written by Students Trained with Problem-Solving and Freewriting Heuristics*

	Raw Scores				Scores Adjusted on Covariate		F	p
	Group: CAPS (N = 20)		FW (N = 19)		CAPS	FW		
	Mean	SD	Mean	SD				
Article (preintervention)	8.20	2.55	7.31	2.85	—	—	1.05	—
Letter	7.15	2.62	8.89	3.45	7.03	9.02	4.16	.05
Speech	7.80	3.07	8.21	3.02	7.60	8.43	0.77	—
Components of Letter								
1. Audience awareness	8.05	3.14	7.95	3.31	7.96	8.05	0.01	—
2. Clarity of voice	8.10	2.65	7.89	3.43	7.98	8.02	0.00	—
3. Controlling idea	7.60	2.91	8.42	3.25	7.44	8.59	1.44	—
4. Materials appropriateness	6.65	3.18	9.42	2.43	6.61	9.47	9.41	.004
5. Organization	7.35	3.01	8.68	3.06	7.24	8.80	1.97	—
6. Conventions (grammar, etc.)	7.10	2.83	8.95	3.06	6.89	9.16	6.50	.01

*Second ranking.
(Adapted from Hilgers 1980)

formulated into an assertion. The assertion then becomes the starting point for another performance of focused freewriting; the product of that exercise is then read, its new "center of gravity" is identified, and a new assertion is formulated. This procedure of freewriting, reflecting, and asserting is repeated again and again until the emerging assertion becomes settled and the writer is ready to shape the piece of writing for readers. This basic three-step operation — perform the (focused) freewriting exercise; read, reflect, identify; formulate an assertion — is the basic *freewriting heuristic.*

To make clearer how the freewriting heuristic can be used within the larger writing process, we will first describe how we teach student writers to use the heuristic and then provide an example to illustrate the heuristic's use. The procedure we describe later takes about five hours of class time to teach.

Teaching the Freewriting Heuristic

To learn how to use the freewriting heuristic, students must first experience themselves as capable of sustained, uncensored writing. This experience can result from practice with the *freewriting exercise.* Thus, we initiate students into freewriting by providing Elbow's directives for the freewriting exercise and then asking them to write for ten minutes, following the directives. It is important for the teacher to freewrite along with the students: as practice with the heuristic develops, her writing can provide crucial examples. The exercise has to be followed by a discussion of the experience, in that some students, especially those who have assimilated what they were taught in the past about "good writing," are likely to have difficulty with uncensored writing and have to be assured that such writing is not mentally lax.

From experience, we learned that the goal of teaching at this point is to induce students to do three things: to retrieve bits of information and experience stored in their memories, to let those bits interact, and to record some of the interactions. To accomplish this, the teacher may explicitly have to nurture uncensored free association by encouraging students to follow their ideas wherever they lead. If free exploration is really to happen, students must know that their writing at this point is totally private: only they will be reading what they produce in the freewriting exercise. But at this point the teacher can read what he or she produced during the freewriting exercise. Hearing the teacher's authentic freewriting, with its associative, sometimes incoherent patterns, can give reluctant students the "permission" they need to unlock ideas via the freewriting exercise.

We find that most students enjoy doing the basic freewriting exercise, if only because it seems a ready antidote to "writer's block." Therefore, most of them are willing to repeat the exercise several times if repetitions are assigned at this time.

The next step is to teach *focused freewriting.* To the directives for the basic freewriting exercise are added two additional guidelines: begin with a subject in mind, and try to hold that subject in mind; and follow digressions when they occur, returning to your subject as each digression winds down. We have our students practice focused freewriting in class with two kinds of subject. The first is an object, word, or phrase — we have used chopsticks, the word *sand,* and song titles. The second kind of subject is a full-sentence proposition, such as "Flowering trees are more trouble than they're worth."

After students have experienced timed focused freewriting exercises with each type of subject, they are ready to be introduced to the conscious decision-making processes involved in the use of the freewriting heuristic. At this point they should read over what they have produced during one of the focused-freewriting periods. The goal of this reading is to find the central idea or concept (Elbow's "center of gravity") around or toward which the writing seems to be moving. The center each finds may be quite far removed from the initial focus. Frequently this center is most apparent in the writing done during the last few minutes of the freewriting period. Sometimes it is simply one idea or sentence that stands out from all the rest. Sometimes it is elusive (like a split or an implied topic sentence in a paragraph). And sometimes it is simply not there; in such a case perhaps more time must be given to the unlocking of ideas. In any event, what a writer sees as his or her "center" is at this point not "carved in stone." The primary purpose of the center is to spur further discovery. Thus, even an arbitrarily selected idea will do.

Next comes a critical, and sometimes difficult, activity: formulating an assertion about the "center" that each student has found in his or her writing. The assertion should be a full sentence. It should in part sum up what the writer has discovered about his or her center. But it has to do more: it has to push beyond, extend the boundaries of, the writer's thinking, for it has to allow room for further discovery. It should shape the "center" of the focused freewriting into something fresh. Failure to formulate the center-of-gravity assertion properly can cause the writer subsequently to write again what he or she has already said. Once students have formulated their own assertions, some may volunteer theirs as bases for further discussion of what constitutes a useful assertion. And, of course, once again the teacher can share examples from his or her own writing, explaining how the assertion summarizes yet introduces something new to explore. Our examples in the next section show several assertions that prove to be good points of departure.

After each student has formulated an assertion, the teacher can monitor another ten- or fifteen-minute focused freewriting. This time, the focus of the freewriting is the assertion that the writer has created from material in one of the earlier focused freewriting sessions.

Upon completion of this session, students again read what they have written, each searching for a center. It is likely that their centers will have shifted somewhat if they have followed the guidelines for focused freewriting: exploration and discovery should be going on. (This is a good time for the teacher to point out that freewriting sessions subsequent to the initial one are not rewriting sessions; instead, they are continuing searches for ideas, materials, and insights.) Once students have identified their new centers, they should formulate them into new assertion statements.

Although its utility will not yet be clear, the process that the students will have experienced is that of the *freewriting heuristic,* which involves repetitions of the three steps of performing the (focused) freewriting exercise, reading and reflecting to identify a center, and formulating an assertion statement based on the center. It is useful at this time to assign students a sequence of writing involving at least three repetitions of the three-step process, in which each focused freewriting exercise begins with the assertion statement derived from the previous focused freewriting exercise. For this sequence of repetitions, the teacher can suggest a focus for the initial freewriting, can ask students to select their own initial focus, or can ask students to begin with the basic freewriting exercise, from which a focus should emerge.

Subsequent instruction in the use of the freewriting heuristic must demonstrate how repetitions of this three-step process can be used to generate the makings of a full-fledged piece of finished prose. Repetitions of the write-reflect-assert process are in effect initially explorations around an embryonic thesis, then refinement of that thesis, and then a testing of the thesis's validity. Once employment of the freewriting heuristic has generated a clear, defendable central-idea statement, a writer can go back over the pieces of freewriting that led up to the statement and select materials that are relevant to the statement. These materials finally have to be "shaped" into a piece of prose that accomplishes a particular purpose with a specific audience.

An Example of the Freewriting Heuristic in Use

We find it useful to cap our teaching of the freewriting heuristic by walking our students through the process of essay composition using the freewriting heuristic. Where a writer has a topic in mind, or has been assigned a topic, he or she begins to use the freewriting heuristic with the performance of the focused freewriting exercise. Alternatively, the writer without even a topic can begin the process with the basic freewriting exercise. Such a case involves Warren, a student trained in use of the freewriting heuristic who had come to class midway through the semester without a topic for his next essay. We provide examples of what Warren wrote as a concrete illustration of the freewriting heuristic in use and as reference points for other comments we want to make.

This is Warren's first run through the freewriting exercise:

Another freewriting — wonder how many times I'll sit, lay, stand doing this. Kenny's question about this and term papers — good question. Am surprised that I can feel eager about a writing class — was wondering last Fri if I was really up for it. Up for it where does that come from? Sexual meaning, no doubt Doubt doubt is it good not to doubt? If we didn't doubt, could we ever advance as a society? If Adam hadn't doubted, supposedly, there'd be no sin. If Darwin hadn't doubted there'd be no evolution. If there were no evolution there'd be no me or us — at least we wouldn't have evolved to the point I really hate the noise of this building Does anyone think education can happen with trucks and back-up horns — who invented those mournful things anyway — they intrude on my airspace! Why don't they make Walkman back up horns people can hear privately only over earphones. Should I go complain — just saw Catherine scratch with her writing hand complain — I've complained about noise here before and what's happened? Only more noise. Wonder if we could make noise a positive thing "The Hotel that blasts your blues with the noises — morning noon, and specially at night" Wonder if some cultures love noise? It may sound racist, but those suitcase radios seem a lot more popular with some cultures than others. Maybe quiet is the real problem is some groups and for some people. Mom used to have the radio on all the time — that same almost silent music where every song sounds the same — Simon and Garfunkle humming. But it may be that even for an American mom silence, real silence, is bad. Am I lying when I say I hate noise. Maybe even I can't live without it.

After completing this, Warren had another ten minutes to proceed through the next two steps of the heuristic: reflecting on what he had written in order to find its center and formulating a tentative assertion. At the bottom of his page, Warren added

Center of gravity: noise, something about noise — it annoys me but others enjoy it

Assertion: While the noisey are noisily protesting noise as pollution, many silent ones are, consciously or unconsciously, enjoying noise.

Using his assertion as his first sentence, a point of departure, Warren produced this piece of focused freewriting:

While the noisey are noisily protesting noise as pollution, many silent ones are, consciously or unconsciously, enjoying noise. Citezens against Noise are noisey — I remember the time they even disrupted a class in Kuykendall by bring in a noise-meter! And I hate noise hate those big suitcase radios and all who carry them hate especially people who bring radios to the pool the resident manager yelling out the window at that guy "Didn't you read the sign" and he said "It said no *loud* radios" and his was absolutely sahking windows up on the 33rd floor and the man. says "Yours is loud, kid" and the guy looked incredulous. I was glad the manager yelled — even tho I was pissed I didn't want to hassle with anyone carrying a suitcase radio. Wonder if they're a sign of macho? Noise-bearers are macho! Show you're macho by increasing your volume! Certainly they seem to stare defiantly at anyone who would tell them to wear earphones. I talked with one in Waikiki one night and he was sure he was making people happier by sharing his vibes with them! Right?! Mom and her radio In Japan being shocked at that lake resort — Otsu? no it was Lake Biwa — at the melange of broadcast noise every beach stand broadcasting something over horn speakers, each one it's own contribution to a horrid cacophony and yet everyone all over the beach seeming oblivious, playing and splashing and talking and warm-up exercising — see not, speak not, *hear* not? Even I sometimes turn on FM sometimes just because it gets too quiet. The quietest quiet, the exciting silence, made more pungent by the addition of a sound — the silent ironwood grove above Kalaupapa, so totally quiet, till the wind blew through just a single tree — what a magnificent quiet swish of sound! Sometimes after a week of studying for finals, gotta blast out with a night a Bobby McGees. The problem is that silence is selectively golden — I really cherish it most of the time, but even I want to escape it sometimes and other people lots more times? But how give people freedom to indulge or escape when noise is a public commodity? (Noise = sound)

After some thought, Warren wrote:

Center of gravity: Silence is selectively golden. Sometimes sound can add to — everything from image to aesthetic experience

Assertion: Silence and sound are both sometimes golden, and societies must create spaces where their members are free to find their gold-for-the-moment.

After three more sessions of focused freewriting (done out of class), Warren reported that he had a clear enough central idea and enough examples to go on to produce a first draft. Under the title "Sounds and Silences," he provided an analysis, not of noise, but of sounds and silences. This description led to a list of suggestions — some practical, some fanciful — for ways in which a sound-and-silence-conscious society might assure an individual's right to pursue either sounds or silence, whichever might be his or her pleasure. And, according to the rules operating in Warren's class, it was this first draft, and not the freewriting that had led up to it, which he read to his "feedback group" during its weekly meeting.

We provide this partial example from a series of runs through the freewriting heuristic to illustrate how centers of gravity do appear, how this identification is partly a matter of interest and choice, and how they can be woven into an assertion that will guide further exploration. We provide the example for other reasons also. The first is to suggest how use of the freewriting heuristic is likely to change the way in which writers write. On the basis of our teaching experience, we assert that most students, faced with a writing assignment, latch onto their first "idea," develop it as best they can in a "first draft," and then type it up with their minimum of spelling and grammar errors. To use the freewriting heuristic, on the other hand, is to experience writing as a process of invention and shaping, an experience many students will find new and rewarding. Warren's example illustrates how use of the freewriting heuristic fosters exploration, discovery, and, ultimately, the confidence of having a considered position on a topic.

It further suggests some limits of the freewriting heuristic. Use of the heuristic itself is not the generation of progressive drafts. Its use does nothing to guarantee the production of purposeful, audience-aware, convention-observing prose, although it was precisely these components that made the writing of the students in the study described previously effective. Instead, its use helps writers to identify subjects and to discover where they stand on those subjects; it provides writers with written information banks that they can consult in supporting their stands.

In Hilgers's study, the most pronounced difference between the freewriters and the problem solvers was not in presence of writer's "voice," as advocates of freewriting might have predicted. It was, rather, in the inclusion of material that was appropriate for purpose and audience. Freewriters also scored higher on presence of a controlling idea, on organization, and on observance of conventions of grammar (see table 5–10). These are important dimensions of reader-based prose and of analytic writing. It would seem that the use of the freewriting heuristic, which pushes the writer to discover ideas, reflect on those ideas, and transform them through further writing and reflection, can prompt the generation of prose that has many of the hallmarks we associate with transactional writing.

The Hilgers study and our subsequent experience in teaching the freewriting heuristic support the contention that training in freewriting results in an improved written product. But the research we have done and the observations we have made only begin to make a dent in what we need to do and understand about freewriting. In our next section we suggest what teachers and researchers can do to further our understanding of what is known, generically, as freewriting.

Exploring Freewriting's Potential

Let us return to our initial concern that the full potential for freewriting be understood. We have several recommendations for how this may be done.

1. Recognize that freewriting is not a single entity: investigate freewriting phenomena with the aim of describing and differentiating among the activities now called freewriting.

Freewriting is a generic term that is attached to any number of activities, including nonstop writing in which writers follow ideas wherever they lead them; freewriting performed as timed exercise; focused freewriting; and any one of these combined in a series of systematic operations that act as a heuristic.

One common variant is loop writing, described in a major chapter of *Writing with Power*. When writers "loop" write, (1) they perform a series of focused freewritings aimed to give them different perspectives on the analytic writing task they wish to accomplish; (2) they review and reflect on the focused freewritings to glean insights; and (3) they rewrite, using the accumulated information and shaping their ideas for a public audience.

Consider our freewriting heuristic and Elbow's loop. They seem similar. But there is a difference between them. Whereas the freewriting heuristic prompts an evolving analysis through the freewriting-reflecting-asserting sequence, loop writing prompts examination of a topic from various perspectives through focused freewrites and the gleaning of these multiple freewritten texts for the production of a final text. We suspect that the two procedures may produce different types of texts or may be more applicable to some contexts than others.

The need for differentiation is also obvious when we note, in Elbow's same text on loop writing, his description of thirteen different prompts for focused freewritings. For example, he suggests that writers may write dialogues, create scenes or portraits in response to a given subject. We ask, along with Elbow, which circumstances are appropriate for which prompt. At present, we rely on intuition to suggest which prompts may be most effective for given situations. But differences, even subtle differences, may be critical to the effectiveness of one or another variant of freewriting; those differences deserve attention.

Let us continue to describe some of the many activities frequently referred to with the single simple term *freewriting*. Classroom teachers devoted to learning through writing often ask their students at the beginning of a class to do focused freewriting to connect their assigned reading to the topic under discussion for the day. Similarly, write-to-learn journals are often freewritten. In other circumstances, focused freewriting "happens" without the writer's intending to freewrite. Think of accounts of "breakthroughs" in which a scientist who has been pondering a problem for some time suddenly has an insight and, in a fit of nonstop writing, explains fully and precisely the complex elements that interact to constitute the breakthrough. All of use who are experienced writers have had at least one experience of "magic writing," a burst in which we said exactly what we wanted to say in exactly the way we wanted to say it. What we wrote was perfect. It may have been a short or long passage. It may have been part or all of a personal letter, a speech, a case study, a report. Our "magic writing" may have followed a period of some contemplation of the subject or been a flash of insight on a new subject.

The circumstances, purposes, and cues for these different types of "focused freewriters" vary. What is common to all of these variants is method. Freewriting, generically, is a *method,* potentially appropriate for use in any circumstance, to accomplish any end, in any ideology. Practitioners need to develop a freewriting vocabulary that makes distinctions among the kinds of freewriting described; such distinctions may help writers to choose a particular variant of freewriting, according to purpose, audience, degree of knowledge of the topic under consideration, or factors of which we are now unaware. Elbow himself has suggested that the freewriting heuristic that we explain here and that we derived from *Writing without Teachers* may be more appropriate when the purpose and form of the writing are undefined, whereas the heuristics suggested in the "Loop Writing" chapter of *Writing with Power* are useful when responding to assignments in which the purpose and form are prescribed.

It is especially important that we take care in defining our terms and understanding the ramifications of their use now that English faculty are responsible for explaining to their colleagues in other disciplines how writing is an effective tool for learning. Our experience is that workshop presenters who encourage freewriting sometimes mislead or discourage teachers because they have merely presented the guidelines and asked teachers to practice the freewriting exercise without explaining what qualities of writing operate to foster discovery, without explaining how the removal of certain constraints via freewriting further fosters that discovery. By emphasizing the practice part of freewriting, they seem to value fluency more than analysis; as a result, workshop participants are skeptical about freewriting's potential for tasks that require analysis, synthesis, or argumentation.

2. Explore the possibility that there is little that is "free" — and perhaps much that is analytic — in freewriting.

We cannot resist speculating that the word *freewriting* itself probably generates misunderstanding. What, after all, is so free about freewriting? The luxury to follow ideas where they take you. The freedom not to worry, for the moment, about how good the ideas are or whether they make sense. The reprieve from "correctness," from having to follow the conventions of public writing. Not much else. The rest is hard work, as writers know after a session that consists of three repetitions of the freewriting heuristic.

Yes, freewriting is writing after all, and some of the constraints that operate in regular writing operate in freewriting. In the very act of following your ideas there is order and shape. James Britton has written eloquently on how we count on our ability to make associations when we start a conversation with a stranger, not knowing where we will end. We take a thought and go with it, "shaping at the point of utterance." The important word here is *shape:* we don't go helter-skelter but strive to make sense. Britton argues that in writing, as in conversation, the act of starting creates a momentum, and seeing words on the page provides further impetus to flesh out and shape a thought ("Shaping at the Point of Utterance" 62–63). In other words, there is a movement toward sense making even though under the rules of the freewriting exercise writers are given permission not to worry about making sense. Writers are permitted to make leaps normally not allowed. And in those leaps writers somehow make new meaning. In reflecting on their writing, our students often find their leaps create associative patterns. Articulating such patterns through reflection and more writing often is a key to not only thesis but also pattern of development and organization.

How else does freewriting promote shaping, perhaps even the emergence of arguments? Writing is a context for making connections. Examine the writing act itself. Three tenses of experience occur simultaneously as we put pen to paper: at the same moment we must remember what we have just written, write, and think of what we will write. Past, present, and future are encapsulated in the moment.

We are well on our way to establishing that there is less that is free in freewriting than those who charge it with being "soft" might realize. In fact, the compression of the writing activity, the charge to keep writing no matter what, may serve to increase the opportunity for connections while downplaying them. The exercise itself acts as a precipitant, and the simultaneous nature of the qualities of writing provides for heightened meaning making. The method has more rigor than skeptics realize; the skeptics' position has been bolstered because freewriting's very name masks its rigor.

3. Understand that the freewriting exercise as defined by Elbow and described here is only one step in a series of operations that lead to effective writing. Focus attention on what users of the freewriting heuristic do *after* they complete the freewriting exercise.

What happens to a piece of freewriting once it is completed is at least as important as the act of freewriting itself. The heuristic embodies a push-pull dynamic: after ideas are pushed out via the freewriting exercise, they must be pulled at in a period of review and reflection to see what can be made of them. Although writers might normally take hours, even days, to reflect on where they might go after writing a first draft, the freewriting heuristic compresses the activity by insisting that the writer shape an assertion to use as a point of departure for immediate further discovery.

What happens while the writer reflects may be essential to successful use of the freewriting heuristic. The "center of gravity" changes, depending on how the material in the freewriting pushes and how text is pulled. Warren's writing, which we explored earlier, is instructive here. He identified his first center of gravity as being "something about noise — it annoys me but others enjoy it." He then shaped an assertion around how silent people might consciously or unconsciously be enjoying noise. What if he had formed an assertion on how various situations evoke a need for either noise or silence? The way the material is processed during reflection determines the shape the next text takes.

The function of the assertions that are the "focus" of subsequent freewriting sessions also may be critical to the effectiveness of the freewriting heuristic. Back-and-forth movement from opening assertion to emerging text is a form of dialectic. The dialectic may prompt a move away from "expressive" emphasis on the individual writer to an emphasis on language and meaning as the writer wants to convey it to the larger community.

Although not explicitly addressing the demands of audience, the heuristic procedure takes more time, holds off closure, and allows for consideration of new perspectives, perhaps thus accounting for improvement in ideas. In engaging in the natural dialectic that occurs while using the heuristic, writers become clearer on what they're saying. In becoming clear on meaning, they become clear on organization (form follows function, after all), and thus meet some of the demands of public audience while focusing only on themselves as private audience.

4. In the classroom, build upon the strengths of the freewriting heuristic.

The freewriting heuristic works. Exactly why, we're not sure. But it offers several strengths upon which teachers can build. First, freewriting is writing. The medium is the message. The message is transformed over time, but it need not be translated. In this, the freewriting heuristic stands apart from most invention procedures in that it requires writers to solve their basic invention problems by writing. One possible reason that the freewriters in Hilgers's study wrote better prose is that they began writing immediately and produced a larger quantity of writing.

The act of freewriting is also multisensory. The urges to connect and continue are nurtured by writing's enactive nature: the brain, eye, and hands are engaged. This multisensory stimulation makes it possible to go further in shaping than we might if we "freethink" or "freetalk." Powerful as they may be, thinking and talking are still ephemeral and they are not manifested in language on the computer screen. The advantages of simultaneity in the act of freewriting promote freewriters' compliance with the heuristic. What they do when they follow the rules works unconsciously to their advantage.

Finally, the freewriting heuristic has the marks of an effective heuristic. It gets potentially high marks on Janice Lauer's categories for the evaluation of heuristic procedures: generative capacity, flexibility, and transcendency.

Freewriting encourages *generation of ideas* by encouraging free association, a technique that has been successful among users of the "brainstorming" approach to problem solving. For the writer who has trouble getting words on paper, the heuristic is generative because it pushes the writer to begin and continue.

The freewriting heuristic seems to offer writers a *flexible direction.* The basic movement from freewriting to reasoned formulation is repeated again and again, until the writer is satisfied that his or her ideas are effectively uncovered, whether in a single paragraph or a monograph. The freewriter is not bound to a thesis statement that has emerged from prewriting activities. The freewriter is bound instead to be guided by a series of central-idea assertions that are reformulated as discovery-by-writing proceeds. The center of gravity concept seems to be a good image for how the ideas we get as we write keep affecting and altering what we want our thesis to be. It connotes change: as the writer's perspective, position, and writing experience change, so does the center of gravity of the prose being generated.

It is this availability of drafts for review that makes writing a particularly effective tool for discovery. Janet Emig refers to this as writing's epigenetic quality ("Writing as a Mode of Learning" 127). She explains that one reason writing promotes discovery and exploration is that the record of a writer's evolution of thought can be traced through first written notes, through drafts, to written products. The heuristic's procedure fosters discovery by sending the writer back through a progressive series of drafts to review, reshape, and draft again. In other words, the heuristic capitalizes on writing's epigenetic quality.

We can go a bit beyond speculation when we look at freewriting in terms of *transcendency.* In Hilgers's program evaluation, the freewriting heuristic was used in conjunction with the writing of a speech and a business letter. Teachers we have worked with in workshops have found that the freewriting heuristic allows the genres of writing to emerge as ideas begin to shape themselves; its use led participants to produce poems, autobiographical sketches, short fiction, and critical essays. Our experience, then, seems to support the contention that the freewriting heuristic can be used in a wide variety of writing situations; nothing in the formulation of the heuristic suggests any writing exigencies with which it cannot be used.

It might prove useful to add a fourth dimension to Lauer's three: the dimension of *simplicity.* Student writers in Hilgers's study reported a higher degree of compliance with the freewriting heuristic than with the problem-solving heuristic, perhaps as a result of the heuristic's relative simplicity. The most commonly employed writer's heuristic — the who? what? when? where? why? questions of the journalist — is popular because of its relative simplicity. We have heard of instructors who spent much time teaching the relatively complex tagmemic heuristics only to find that students did not consciously employ them in satisfying most writing assignments. It may well be that the likelihood of a student writer's use of any given heuristic is in large part a function of the heuristic's simplicity. As we have shown, it is relatively easy to teach the effective use of the freewriting heuristic in a few hours, to reinforce the initial teaching occasionally over the course of a semester or year, and still have ample time to devote to problems with audience, arrangement, grammar, mechanics, and editing.

Although we are excited about the possibilities of freewriting formulated as a heuristic, we fully realize that a great deal of research must be done before all of its comparative strengths and weaknesses can be listed and understood. In the meantime we suggest that it is a good idea for teachers to devote some of their energy to teaching freewriting as a heuristic. The freewriting exercise has always been recognized as a valuable tool to help writers get started and to fight writer's block; the "freewriting three-step" incorporates that useful tool in a heuristic approach that is somewhat new, somewhat empirically validated, and full of promise for writers struggling to produce original, intelligent, and effective pieces of writing.

Works Cited

Berlin, James. "Rhetoric and Ideology in the Writing Class." *College English* 50 (1988): 477–94.

Britton, James. *Language and Learning.* New York: Penguin, 1970.

Elbow, Peter. *Writing without Teachers.* New York: Oxford UP, 1973.

———. *Writing with Power: Techniques for Mastering the Writing Process.* New York: Oxford UP, 1981.

Emig, Janet. "Writing as a Mode of Learning." *College Composition and Communication* 28 (1977): 122–28. Rpt. in *The Web of Meaning: Essays on Writing, Teaching, Learning, and Thinking.* Ed. Dixie Goswami and Peter Stillman. Upper Montclair, NJ: Boynton/Cook, 1983. 122–131.

Flower, Linda, and John R. Hayes. "Problem-Solving Strategies and the Writing Process." *College English* 39 (1977): 449–61.

———. "Process-Based Evaluation of Writing: Changing the Performance, Not the Product." Paper presented at American Educational Research Assn. meeting, San Francisco, April 1979.

Hilgers, Thomas. "Training Composition Students in the Use of Freewriting and Problem-Solving Heuristics for Rhetorical Invention." *Research in the Teaching of English* 14 (1980): 293–307.

Hillocks, George, Jr. *Research on Written Composition: New Directions for Teaching.* Urbana: Natl. Conference on Research in English and Natl. Inst. of Education, 1986.

Kinney, James. "Why Freewriting Works." Unpublished essay. Virginia Commonwealth University, n.d.

Lauer, Janice. "Toward a Metatheory of Heuristic Procedures." *College Composition and Communication* 30 (1979): 268–69.

Macrorie, Ken, with John Bennett. "An Intense Teacher." *Teaching English: Reflections on the State of the Art.* Ed. Stephen Tchudi. Rochelle Park, NJ: Hayden Book, 1979. 29–38.

Young, R., Alton L. Becker, and Kenneth L. Pike. *Rhetoric: Discovery and Change.* New York: Harcourt, 1970.

RIGID RULES, INFLEXIBLE PLANS, AND THE STIFLING OF LANGUAGE: A COGNITIVIST ANALYSIS OF WRITER'S BLOCK

Mike Rose

[College Composition and Communication 31 (1980): 389–401.]

Associate director of the writing programs at the University of California–Los Angeles, Mike Rose is the author of numerous works on language and literacy. His books include Writer's Block: The Cognitive Dimension *(1984) and* Lives on the Boundary: The Struggles and Achievements of America's Underprepared *(1989). Rose coedited, with Malcolm Kiniry,* Critical Strategies for Academic Thinking and Writing *(2nd edition, 1993). He has won awards from the National Council of Teachers of English, the Conference on College Composition and Communication, and the Modern Language Association.*

In this article investigating causes of writer's block, Rose reports on his study of ten undergraduates, five with writer's block and five without. Rose discovered that rigid rules and inflexible plans were a significant cause of writer's block. He argues that stymied writers do not necessarily need more rules and plans, as much previous research has suggested. Rose contends instead that writers may well need different, more flexible plans and rules. He closes the article with several suggestions for helping students who suffer from writer's block.

Ruth will labor over the first paragraph of an essay for hours. She'll write a sentence, then erase it. Try another, then scratch part of it out. Finally, as the evening winds on toward ten o'clock and Ruth, anxious about tomorrow's deadline, begins to wind into herself, she'll compose that first paragraph only to sit back and level her favorite exasperated interdiction at herself and her page: "No. You can't say that. You'll bore them to death."

Ruth is one of ten UCLA undergraduates with whom I discussed writer's block, that frustrating, self-defeating inability to generate the next line, the right phrase, the sentence that will release the flow of words once again. These ten people represented a fair cross-section of the UCLA student community; lower-middle-class to upper-middle-class backgrounds and high schools, third-world and Caucasian origins, biology to fine arts majors, C+ to A– grade point averages, enthusiastic to blasé attitudes toward school. They were set off from the community by the twin facts that all ten could write competently, and all were currently enrolled in at least one course that required a significant amount of writing. They were set off among themselves by the fact that five of them wrote with relative to enviable ease while the other five experienced moderate to nearly immobilizing writer's block. This blocking usually resulted in rushed, often late papers and resultant grades that did not truly reflect these students' writing ability. And then, of course, there were other less measurable but probably more serious results: a growing distrust of their abilities and an aversion toward the composing process itself.

What separated the five students who blocked from those who didn't? It wasn't skill; that was held fairly constant. The answer could have rested in the emotional realm — anxiety, fear of evaluation, insecurity, etc. Or perhaps blocking in some way resulted from variation in cognitive style. Perhaps, too, blocking originated in and typified a melding of emotion and cognition not unlike the relationship posited by Shapiro between neurotic feeling and neurotic thinking.[1] Each of these was possible. Extended clinical interviews and testing could have teased out the answer. But there was one answer that surfaced readily in brief explorations of these students' writing processes. It was not profoundly emotional, nor was it embedded in that still unclear construct of cognitive style. It was constant, surprising, almost amusing if its results weren't so troublesome, and, in the final analysis, obvious: the five students who experienced blocking were all operating either with writing rules or with planning strategies that impeded rather than enhanced the composing process. The five students who were not hampered by writer's block also utilized rules, but they were less rigid ones, and thus more appropriate to a complex process like writing. Also, the plans these non-blockers brought to the writing process were more functional, more flexible, more open to information from the outside.

These observations are the result of one to three interviews with each student. I used recent notes, drafts, and finished compositions to direct and hone my questions. This procedure is admittedly non-experimental, certainly more clinical than scientific; still, it did lead to several inferences that lay the foundation for future, more rigorous investigation: (a) composing is a highly complex problem-solving process[2] and (b) certain disruptions of that process can be explained with cognitive psychology's problem-solving framework. Such investigation might include a study using "stimulated recall" techniques to validate or disconfirm these hunches. In such a study, blockers and non-blockers would write essays. Their activity would be videotaped and, immediately after writing, they would be shown their respective tapes and questioned about the rules, plans, and beliefs operating in their writing behavior. This procedure would bring us close to the composing process (the writers' recall is stimulated by their viewing the tape), yet would not interfere with actual composing.

In the next section I will introduce several key concepts in the problem-solving literature. In section three I will let the students speak for themselves. Fourth, I will offer a cognitivist analysis of blockers' and non-blockers' grace or torpor. I will close with a brief note on treatment.

Selected Concepts in Problem Solving: Rules and Plans

As diverse as theories of problem solving are, they share certain basic assumptions and characteristics. Each posits an *introductory period* during which a problem is presented, and all theorists, from Behaviorist to Gestalt to Information Processing, admit that certain aspects, stimuli, or "functions" of the problem must become or be made salient and attended to in certain ways if successful problem-solving processes are to be engaged. Theorists also believe that some conflict, some stress, some gap in information in these perceived "aspects" seems to trigger problem-solving behavior. Next comes a *processing period,* and for all the variance of opinion about this critical stage, theorists recognize the necessity of its existence — recognize that man, at the least, somehow "weighs" possible solutions as they are stumbled upon and, at the most, goes through an elaborate and sophisticated information-processing routine to achieve problem solution. Furthermore, theorists believe — to varying degrees — that past learning and the particular "set," direction, or orientation that the problem solver takes in dealing with past experience and present stimuli have critical bearing on the efficacy of solution. Finally, all theorists admit to a *solution period,* an end-state of the process where "stress" and "search" terminate, an answer is attained, and a sense of completion or "closure" is experienced.

Theses are the gross similarities, and the framework they offer will be useful in understanding the problem-solving behavior of the students discussed in this paper. But since this paper is primarily concerned with the second stage of problem-solving operations, it would be most useful to focus this introduction on two critical constructs in the processing period: rules and plans.

Rules

Robert M. Gagné defines "rule" as "an inferred capability that enables the individual to respond to a class of stimulus situations with a class of performances."[3] Rules can be learned directly[4] or by inference through experience.[5] But, in either case, most problem-solving theorists would affirm Gagné's dictum that "rules are probably the major organizing factor, and quite possibly the primary one, in intellectual functioning."[6] As Gagné implies, we wouldn't be able to function without rules; they guide response to the myriad stimuli that confront us daily, and might even be the central element in complex problem-solving behavior.

Dunker, Polya, and Miller, Galanter, and Pribram offer a very useful distinction between two general kinds of rules: algorithms and heuristics.[7] Algorithms are precise rules that will always result in a specific answer if applied to an appropriate problem. Most mathematical rules, for example, are algorithms. Functions are constant (e.g., pi), procedures are routine (squaring the radius), and outcomes are completely predictable. However, few day-to-day situations are mathematically circumscribed enough to warrant the application of algorithms. Most often we function with the aid of fairly general heuristics or "rules of thumb," guidelines that allow varying degrees of flexibility when approaching problems. Rather than operating with algorithmic precision and certainty, we search, critically, through alternatives, using our heuristic as a divining rod — "if a math problem stumps you, try working backwards to solution"; "if the car won't start, check x, y, or z," and so forth. Heuristics won't allow the precision or the certitude afforded by algorithmic operations; heuristics can even be so "loose" as to be vague. But in a world where tasks and problems are rarely mathematically precise, heuristic rules become the most appropriate, the most functional rules available to us: "a heuristic does not guarantee the optimal solution or, indeed, any solution at all; rather, heuristics offer solutions that are good enough most of the time."[8]

Plans

People don't proceed through problem situations, in or out of a laboratory, without some set of internalized instructions to the self, some program, some course of action that, even roughly, takes goals and possible paths to that goal into consideration. Miller, Galanter, and Pribram have referred to this course of action as a plan: "A plan is any hierarchical process in the organism that can control the order in which a sequence of operations is to be performed" (p. 16). They name the fundamental plan in human problem-solving behavior the TOTE, with the initial T representing a *test* that matches a possible solution against the perceived end-goal of problem completion. O represents the clearance to *operate* if the comparison between solution and goal indicates that the solution is a sensible one. The second T represents a further, post-operation, *test* or comparison of solution with goal, and if the two mesh and problem solution is at hand the person *exits* (E) from problem-solving behavior. If the second test presents further discordance between solution and goal, a further solution is attempted in TOTE-fashion. Such plans can be both long-term and global and, as problem solving is underway, short-term and immediate.[9] Though the mechanicality of this information-processing model renders it simplistic and, possibly, unreal, the central notion of a plan and an operating procedure is an important one in problem-solving theory; it at least attempts to metaphorically explain what earlier cognitive psychologists could not — the mental procedures (see pp. 390–91) underlying problem-solving behavior.

Before concluding this section, a distinction between heuristic rules and plans should be attempted; it is a distinction often blurred in the literature, blurred because, after all, we are very much in the area of gestating theory and preliminary models. Heuristic rules seem to function with the flexibility of plans. Is, for example, "If the car won't start, try x, y, or z" a heuristic or a plan? It could be either, though two qualifications will mark it as heuristic rather than plan. (A) Plans subsume and sequence heuristic and algorithmic rules. Rules are usually "smaller," more discrete cognitive capabilities; plans can become quite large and complex, composed of a series of ordered algorithms, heuristics, and further planning "sub-routines." (B) Plans, as was mentioned earlier, include criteria to determine successful goal-attainment and, as well, include "feedback" processes — ways to incorporate and use information gained from "tests" of potential solutions against desired goals.

One other distinction should be made: that is, between "set" and plan. Set, also called "determining tendency" or "readiness,"[10] refers to the fact that people often approach problems with habitual ways of reacting, a predisposition, a tendency to perceive or function in one way rather than another. Set, which can be established through instructions or, consciously or unconsciously, through experience, can assist performance if it is appropriate to a specific problem,[11] but much of the literature on set has shown its rigidifying, dysfunctional effects.[12] Set differs from plan in that set represents a limiting and narrowing of response alternatives with no inherent process to shift alternatives. It is a kind of cognitive habit that can limit perception, not a course of action with multiple paths that directs and sequences response possibilities.

The constructs of rules and plans advance the understanding of problem solving beyond that possible with earlier, less developed formulations. Still, critical problems remain. Though mathematical and computer models move one toward more complex (and thus more real) problems than the earlier research, they are still too neat, too rigidly sequenced to approximate the stunning complexity of day-to-day (not to mention highly creative) problem-solving behavior. Also, information-processing models of problem-solving are built on logic theorems, chess strategies, and simple planning tasks. Even Gagné seems to feel more comfortable with illustrations from mathematics and science rather than with social science and humanities problems. So although these complex models and constructs tell us a good deal about problem-solving behavior, they are still laboratory simulations, still invoked from the outside rather than self-generated, and still founded on the mathematico-logical.

Two Carnegie-Mellon researchers, however, have recently extended the above into a truly real, amorphous, unmathematical problem-solving process — writing. Relying on protocol analysis (thinking aloud while solving problems), Linda Flower and John Hayes have attempted to tease out the role of heuristic rules and plans in writing behavior.[13] Their research pushes problem-solving investigations to the real and complex and pushes, from the other end, the often mysterious process of writing toward the explainable. The latter is important, for at least since Plotinus many have viewed the composing process as unexplainable, inspired, infused with the transcendent. But Flower and Hayes are beginning, anyway, to show how writing generates from a problem-solving process with rich heuristic rules and plans of its own. They show, as well, how many writing problems arise from a paucity of heuristics and suggest an intervention that provides such rules.

This paper, too, treats writing as a problem-solving process, focusing, however, on what happens when the process dead-ends in writer's block. It will further suggest that, as opposed to Flower and Hayes' students who need more rules and plans, blockers may well be stymied by possessing rigid or inappropriate rules, or inflexible or confused plans. Ironically enough, these are occasionally instilled by the composition teacher or gleaned from the writing textbook.

"Always Grab Your Audience" — The Blockers

In high school, *Ruth* was told and told again that a good essay always grabs a reader's attention immediately. Until you can make your essay do that, her teachers and textbooks putatively declaimed, there is no need to go on. For Ruth, this means that beginning bland and seeing what emerges as one generates prose is unacceptable. The beginning is everything. And what exactly is the audience seeking that reads this beginning? The rule, or Ruth's use of it, doesn't provide for such investigation. She has an edict with no determiners. Ruth operates with another rule that restricts her productions as well: if sentences aren't grammatically "correct," they aren't useful. This keeps Ruth from toying with ideas on paper, from the kind of linguistic play that often frees up the flow of prose. These two rules converge in a way that pretty effectively restricts Ruth's composing process.

The first two papers I received from *Laurel* were weeks overdue. Sections of them were well written; there were even moments of stylistic flair. But the papers were late and, overall, the prose seemed rushed. Furthermore, one paper included a paragraph on an issue that was never mentioned in the topic paragraph. This was the kind of mistake that someone with Laurel's apparent ability doesn't make. I asked her about this irrelevant passage. She knew very well that it didn't fit, but believed she had to include it to round out the paper. "You must always make three or more points in an essay. If the essay has less, then it's not strong." Laurel had been taught this rule in high school and in her first college English class; no wonder, then, that she accepted its validity.

As opposed to Laurel, *Martha* possesses a whole arsenal of plans and rules with which to approach a humanities writing assignment, and, considering her background in biology, I wonder how many of them were formed out of the assumptions and procedures endemic to the physical sciences.[14] Martha will not put pen to first draft until she has spent up to two days generating an outline of remarkable complexity. I saw one of these outlines and it looked more like a diagram of protein synthesis or DNA structure than the time-worn pattern offered in composition textbooks. I must admit I was intrigued by the aura of process (vs. the static appearance of essay outlines) such diagrams offer, but for Martha these "outlines" only led to self-defeat: the outline would become so complex that all of its elements could never be included in a short essay. In other words, her plan locked her into the first stage of the composing process. Martha would struggle with the conversion of her outline into prose only to scrap the whole venture when deadlines passed and a paper had to be rushed together.

Martha's "rage for order" extends beyond the outlining process. She also believes that elements of a story or poem must evince a fairly linear structure and thematic clarity, or — perhaps bringing us closer to the issue — that analysis of a story or poem must provide the linearity or clarity that seems to be absent in the text. Martha, therefore, will bend the logic of her analysis to reason ambiguity out of existence. When I asked her about a strained paragraph in her paper on Camus' "The Guest," she said, "I didn't want to admit that it [the story's conclusion] was just hanging. I tried to force it into meaning."

Martha uses another rule, one that is not only problematical in itself, but one that often clashes directly with the elaborate plan and obsessive rule above. She believes that humanities papers must scintillate with insight, must present an array of images, ideas, ironies gleaned from the literature under examination. A problem arises, of course, when Martha tries to incorporate her myriad "neat little things," often inherently unrelated, into a tightly structured, carefully sequenced essay. Plans and rules that govern the construction of impressionistic, associational prose would be appropriate to Martha's desire, but her composing process is heavily constrained by the non-impressionistic and non-associational. Put another way, the plans and rules that govern her exploration of text are not at all synchronous with the plans and rules she uses to discuss her exploration. It is interesting to note here, however, that as recently as three years ago Martha was absorbed in creative writing and was publishing poetry in high school magazines. Given what we know about the complex associational, often non-neatly-sequential nature of the poet's creative process, we can infer that Martha was either free of the plans and rules discussed earlier or they were not as intense. One wonders, as well, if the exposure to three years of university physical science either established or intensified Martha's concern with structure. Whatever the case, she now is hamstring by conflicting rules when composing papers for the humanities.

Mike's difficulties, too, are rooted in a distortion of the problem-solving process. When the time of the week for the assignment of writing topics draws near, Mike begins to prepare material, strategies, and plans that he believes will be appropriate. If the assignment matches his expectations, he has done a good job of analyzing the professor's intentions. If the assignment *doesn't* match his expectations, however, he cannot easily shift approaches. He feels trapped inside his original plans, cannot generate alternatives, and blocks. As the deadline draws near, he will write something, forcing the assignment to fit his conceptual procrustien bed. Since Mike is a smart man, he will offer a good deal of information, but only some of it ends up being appropriate to the assignment. This entire situation is made all the worse when the time between assignment of topic and generation of product is attenuated further, as in an essay examination. Mike believes (correctly) that one must have a plan, a strategy of some sort in order to solve a problem. He further believes, however, that such a plan, once formulated, becomes an exact structural and substantive blueprint that cannot be violated. The plan offers no alternatives, no "sub-routines." So, whereas Ruth's, Laurel's, and some of Martha's difficulties seem to be rule-specific ("always catch your audience," "write grammatically"), Mike's troubles are more global. He may have strategies that are appropriate for various writing situations (e.g., "for this kind of political science assignment write a compare/contrast essay"), but his entire approach to formulating plans and carrying them through to problem solution is too mechanical. It is probable that Mike's behavior is governed by an explicitly learned or inferred rule: "Always try to 'psych out' a professor." But in this case this rule initiates a problem-solving procedure that is clearly dysfunctional.

While Ruth and Laurel use rules that impede their writing process and Mike utilizes a problem-solving procedure that hamstrings him, *Sylvia* has trouble deciding which of the many rules she possesses to use. Her problem can be characterized as cognitive perplexity: some of her rules are inappropriate, others are functional; some mesh nicely with her own definitions of good writing, others don't. She has multiple rules to invoke, multiple paths to follow, and that very complexity of choice virtually paralyzes her. More so than with the previous four students, there is probably a strong emotional dimension to Sylvia's blocking, but the cognitive difficulties are clear and perhaps modifiable.

Sylvia, somewhat like Ruth and Laurel, puts tremendous weight on the crafting of her first paragraph. If it is good, she believes the rest of the essay will be good. Therefore, she will spend up to five hours on the initial paragraph: "I won't go on until I get that first paragraph down." Clearly, this rule — or the strength of it — blocks Sylvia's production. This is one problem. Another is that Sylvia has other equally potent rules that she sees as separate, uncomplementary injunctions: one achieves "flow" in one's writing through the use of adequate transitions; one achieves substance to one's writing through the use of evidence. Sylvia perceives both rules to be "true," but several times followed one to the exclusion of the other. Furthermore, as I talked to Sylvia, many other rules, guidelines, definitions were offered, but none with conviction. While she *is* committed to one rule about initial paragraphs, and that rule is dysfunctional, she seems very uncertain about the weight and hierarchy of the remaining rules in her cognitive repertoire.

"If It Won't Fit My Work, I'll Change It" — The Non-blockers

Dale, Ellen, Debbie, Susan, and Miles all write with the aid of rules. But their rules differ from blockers' rules in significant ways. If similar in content, they are expressed less absolutely — e.g., "*Try* to keep audience in mind. " If dissimilar, they are still expressed less absolutely, more heuristically — e.g., "I can use as many ideas in my thesis paragraph as I need and then develop paragraphs for each idea." Our non-blockers do express some rules with firm assurance, but these tend to be simple injunctions that free up rather than restrict the composing process, e.g., "When stuck, write!" or "I'll write what I can." And finally, at least three of the students openly shun the very textbook rules that some blockers adhere to: e.g., "Rules like 'write only what you know about' just aren't true. I ignore those." These three, in effect, have formulated a further rule that expresses something like: "If a rule conflicts with what is sensible or with experience, reject it."

On the broader level of plans and strategies, these five students also differ from at least three of the five blockers in that they all possess problem-solving plans that are quite functional. Interestingly, on first exploration these plans seem to be too broad or fluid to be useful and, in some cases, can barely be expressed with any precision. Ellen, for example, admits that she has a general "outline in [her] head about how a topic paragraph should look" but could not describe much about its structure. Susan also has a general plan to follow, but, if stymied, will quickly attempt to conceptualize the assignment in different ways: "If my original idea won't work, then I need to proceed differently." Whether or not these plans operate in TOTE-fashion, I can't say. But they do operate with the operate-test fluidity of TOTEs.

True, our non-blockers have their religiously adhered-to rules: e.g., "When stuck, write," and plans, "I couldn't imagine writing without this pattern," but as noted above, these are few and functional. Otherwise, these non-blockers operate with fluid, easily modified, even easily discarded rules and plans (Ellen: "I can throw things out") that are sometimes expressed with a vagueness that could almost be interpreted as ignorance. There lies the irony. Students that offer the least precise rules and plans have the least trouble composing. Perhaps this very lack of precision characterizes the functional composing plan. But perhaps this lack of precision simply masks habitually enacted alternatives and sub-routines. This is clearly an area that needs the illumination of further research.

And then there is feedback. At least three of the five non-blockers are an Information-Processor's dream. They get to know their audience, ask professors and T.A.s specific questions about assignments, bring half-finished products in for evaluation, etc. Like Ruth, they realize the importance of audience, but unlike her, they have specific strategies for obtaining and utilizing feedback. And this penchant for testing writing plans against the needs of the audience can lead to modification of rules and plans. Listen to Debbie:

> In high school I was given a formula that stated that you must write a thesis paragraph with *only* three points in it, and then develop each of those points. When I hit college I was given longer assignments. That stuck me for a bit, but then I realized that I could use as many ideas in my thesis paragraph as I needed and then develop paragraphs for each one. I asked someone about this and then tried it. I didn't get any negative feedback, so I figured it was o.k.

Debbie's statement brings one last difference between our blockers and non-blockers into focus; it has been implied above, but needs specific formulation: the goals these people have, and the plans they generate to attain these goals, are quite mutable. Part of the mutability comes from the fluid way the goals and plans are conceived, and part of it arises from the effective impact of feedback on these goals and plans.

Analyzing Writer's Block

Algorithms Rather Than Heuristics

In most cases, the rules our blockers use are not "wrong" or "incorrect" — it is good practice, for example, to "grab your audience with a catchy opening" or "craft a solid first paragraph before going on." The problem is that these rules seem to be followed as though they were algorithms, absolute dicta, rather than the loose heuristics that they were intended to be. Either through instruction, or the power of the textbook, or the predilections of some of our blockers for absolutes, or all three, these useful rules of thumb have been transformed into near-algorithmic urgencies. The result, to paraphrase Karl Dunker, is that these rules do not allow a flexible penetration into the nature of the problem. It is this transformation of heuristic into algorithm that contributes to the writer's block of Ruth and Laurel.

Questionable Heuristics Made Algorithmic

Whereas "grab your audience" could be a useful heuristic, "always make three or more points in an essay" is a pretty questionable one. Any such rule, though probably taught to aid the writer who needs structure, ultimately transforms a highly fluid process like writing into a mechanical lockstep. As heuristics, such rules can be troublesome. As algorithms, they are simply incorrect.

Set

As with any problem-solving task, students approach writing assignments with a variety of orientations or sets. Some are functional, others are not. Martha and Jane (see footnote 14), coming out of the life sciences and social sciences respectively, bring certain methodological orientations with them — certain sets or "directions" that make composing for the humanities a difficult, sometimes confusing, task. In fact, this orientation may cause them to misperceive the task. Martha has formulated a planning strategy from her predisposition to see processes in terms of linear, interrelated steps in a system. Jane doesn't realize that she can revise the statement that "committed" her to the direction her essay has taken. Both of these students are stymied because of formative experiences associated with their majors — experiences, perhaps, that nicely reinforce our very strong tendency to organize experiences temporally.

The Plan That Is Not A Plan

If fluidity and multi-directionality are central to the nature of plans, then the plans that Mike formulates are not true plans at all but, rather, inflexible and static cognitive blueprints.[15] Put another way, Mike's "plans" represent a restricted "closed system" (vs. "open system") kind of thinking, where closed system thinking is defined as focusing on "a limited number of units or items, or members, and those properties of the members which are to be used are known to begin with and do not change as the thinking proceeds," and open system thinking is characterized by an "adventurous exploration of multiple alternatives with strategies that allow redirection once 'dead ends' are encountered."[16] Composing calls for open, even adventurous thinking, not for constrained, no-exit cognition.

Feedback

The above difficulties are made all the more problematic by the fact that they seem resistant to or isolated from corrective feedback. One of the most striking things about Dale, Debbie, and Miles is the ease with which they seek out, interpret, and apply feedback on their rules, plans, and productions. They "operate" and then they "test," and the testing is not only against some internalized goal, but against the requirements of external audience as well.

Too Many Rules — "Conceptual Conflict"

According to D. E. Berlyne, one of the primary forces that motivate problem-solving behavior is a curiosity that arises from conceptual conflict — the convergence of incompatible beliefs or ideas. In *Structure and Direction in Thinking,*[17] Berlyne presents six major types of conceptual conflict, the second of which he terms "perplexity":

> This kind of conflict occurs when there are factors inclining the subject toward each of a set of mutually exclusive beliefs. (p. 257)

If one substitutes "rules" for "beliefs" in the above definition, perplexity becomes a useful notion here. Because perplexity is unpleasant, people are motivated to reduce it by problem-solving behavior that can result in "disequalization":

> Degree of conflict will be reduced if either the number of competing . . . [rules] or their nearness to equality of strength is reduced. (p. 259)

But "disequalization" is not automatic. As I have suggested, Martha and Sylvia hold to rules that conflict, but their perplexity does *not* lead to curiosity and resultant problem-solving behavior. Their perplexity, contra Berlyne, leads to immobilization. Thus "disequalization" will have to be effected from without. The importance of each of. particularly, Sylvia's rules needs an evaluation that will aid her in rejecting some rules and balancing and sequencing others.

A Note on Treatment

Rather than get embroiled in a blocker's misery, the teacher or tutor might interview the student in order to build a writing history and profile: How much and what kind of writing was done in high school? What is the student's major? What kind of writing does it require? How does the student compose? Are there rough drafts or outlines available? By what rules does the student operate? How would he or she define "good" writing? etc. This sort of interview reveals an incredible amount of information about individual composing processes. Furthermore, it often reveals the rigid rule or the inflexible plan that may lie at the base of the student's writing problem. That was precisely what happened with the five blockers. And with Ruth, Laurel, and Martha (and Jane) what was revealed made virtually immediate remedy possible. Dysfunctional rules are easily replaced with or counter-balanced by functional ones if there is no emotional reason to hold onto that which simply doesn't work. Furthermore, students can be trained to select, to "know which rules are appropriate for which problems."[18] Mike's difficulties, perhaps because plans are more complex and pervasive than rules, took longer to correct. But inflexible plans, too, can be remedied by pointing out their dysfunctional qualities and by assisting the student in developing appropriate and flexible alternatives. Operating this way, I was successful with Mike. Sylvia's story, however, did not end as smoothly. Though I had three forty-five minute contacts with her, I was not able to appreciably alter her behavior. Berlyne's theory bore results with Martha but not with Sylvia. Her rules were in conflict, and perhaps that conflict was not exclusively cognitive. Her case keeps analyses like these honest; it reminds us that the cognitive often melds with, and can be overpowered by, the affective. So while Ruth, Laurel, Martha, and Mike could profit from tutorials that explore the rules and plans in their writing behavior, students like Sylvia may need more extended, more affectively oriented counseling sessions that blend the instructional with the psychodynamic.

Notes

[1] David Shapiro, *Neurotic Styles* (New York: Basic Books, 1965).

[2] Barbara Hayes-Ruth, a Rand cognitive psychologist, and I are currently developing an information-processing model of the composing process. A good deal of work has already been done by Linda Flower and John Hayes (see p. 70 of this article). I . . . recommend . . . their "Writing as Problem Solving" (paper presented at American Educational Research Association, April 1979).

[3] *The Conditions of Learning* (New York: Holt, Rinehart and Winston, 1970), p. 193.

[4] E. James Archer, "The Psychological Nature of Concepts," in H. J. Klausmeier and C. W. Harris, eds., *Analysis of Concept Learning* (New York: Academic Press, 1966), pp. 37–44; David P. Ausubel, *The Psychology of Meaningful Verbal Behavior* (New York: Grune and Stratton, 1963); Robert M. Gagné, "Problem Solving," in Arthur W. Melton, ed., *Categories of Human Learning* (New York: Academic Press, 1964), pp. 293–317; George A. Miller, *Language and Communication* (New York: McGraw-Hill, 1951).

[5] George Katona, *Organizing and Memorizing* (New York: Columbia Univ. Press, 1940); Roger N. Shepard, Carl I. Hovland, and Herbert M. Jenkins, "Learning and Memorization of Classifications," *Psychological Monographs*, 75, No. 13 (1961) (entire No. 517); Robert S. Woodworth, *Dynamics of Behavior* (New York: Henry Holt, 1958), chs. 10–12.

[6] *The Conditions of Learning*, pp. 190–91.

[7] Karl Dunker, "On Problem Solving," *Psychological Monographs*, 58, No. 5 (1945) (entire No. 270); George A. Polya, *How to Solve It* (Princeton: Princeton Univ. Press, 1945); George A. Miller, Eugene Galanter, and Karl H. Pribram, *Plans and the Structure of Behavior* (New York: Henry Holt, 1960).

[8] Lyle E. Bourne, Jr., Bruce R. Ekstrand, and Roger L. Dominowski, *The Psychology of Thinking* (Englewood Cliffs, N.J.: Prentice-Hall, 1971).

[9] John R. Hayes, "Problem Topology and the Solution Process," in Carl P. Duncan, ed., *Thinking: Current Experimental Studies* (Philadelphia: Lippincott, 1967), pp. 167–81.

[10] Hulda J. Rees and Harold E. Israel, "An Investigation of the Establishment and Operation of Mental Sets," *Psychological Monographs*, 46 (1925) (entire No. 210).

[11] Ibid.; Melvin H. Marx, Wilton W. Murphy, and Aaron J. Brownstein, "Recognition of Complex Visual Stimuli as a Function of Training with Abstracted Patterns," *Journal of Experimental Psychology*, 62 (1961), 456–60.

[12] James L. Adams, *Conceptual Blockbusting* (San Francisco: W. H. Freeman, 1974); Edward DeBono, *New Think* (New York: Basic Books, 1958); Ronald H. Forgus, *Perception* (New York: McGraw-Hill, 1966), ch. 13; Abraham Luchins and Edith Hirsch Luchins, *Rigidity of Behavior* (Eugene: Univ. of Oregon Books, 1959); N. R. F. Maier, "Reasoning in Humans. I. On Direction," *Journal of Comparative Psychology*, 10 (1920), 115–43.

[13] "Plans and the Cognitive Process of Writing," paper presented at the National Institute of Education Writing Conference, June 1977; "Problem Solving Strategies and the Writing Process," *College English*, 39 (1977), 449–61. See also footnote 2.

[14] Jane, a student not discussed in this paper, was surprised to find out that a topic paragraph can be rewritten after a paper's conclusion to make that paragraph reflect what the essay truly contains. She had gotten so indoctrinated with Psychology's (her major) insistence that a hypothesis be formulated and then left untouched before an experiment begins that she thought revision of one's "major premise" was somehow illegal. She had formed a rule out of her exposure to social science methodology, and the rule was totally inappropriate for most writing situations.

[15] Cf. "A plan is flexible if the order of execution of its parts can be easily interchanged without affecting the feasibility of the plan . . . the flexible planner might tend to think of lists of things she had to do; the inflexible planner would have his time planned like a sequence of cause-effect relations. The former could rearrange his lists to suit his opportunities, but the latter would be unable to strike while the iron was hot and would generally require considerable 'lead-time' before he could incorporate any alternative sub-plans" (Miller, Galanter, and Pribram, p. 120).

[16] Frederic Bartlett, *Thinking* (New York: Basic Books, 1958), pp. 74–76.

[17] *Structure and Direction in Thinking* (New York: John Wiley, 1965), p. 255.

[18] Flower and Hayes, "Plans and the Cognitive Process of Writing," p. 26.

ON IMPOSED VERSUS IMITATIVE FORM

Richard Fulkerson

[Journal of Teaching Writing 7.2 (1988): 143–55.]

Richard Fulkerson teaches at East Texas State University, where he is director of graduate studies and coordinator of composition. His articles have appeared in such journals as College Composition and Communication, Rhetoric Review, Informal Logic, *and* Quarterly Journal of Speech.

Many students, Fulkerson argues, use an "imitative" strategy of writing, organizing papers by "repeating the shape of the materials discussed." These students must be encouraged, however, to take authority in their writing and impose a form that suits the points they wish to make — not merely an imitative form. Fulkerson provides examples of the ways in which students use imitative forms and suggests ways of helping them consider alternatives. By helping students explore alternatives for structuring their writing, instructors also help them understand that writing is a rhetorical act and that composing is a process of choosing and testing options.

In "Confessions of a Former Sailor," a wonderful essay about her own writing process, Professor Sue Lorch tells a traumatic tale from her undergraduate experience in advanced composition. The story is revealing, I think, about some important principles of one of the least understood and least discussed features of writing, the arrangement of a discourse. Lorch's first assignment was to visit the art department and write a descriptive paper about a painting of cows in a field. Lorch, who had always been a "good writer," sailed up, applied the description formula she had been taught, going left to right and top to bottom, and produced a description so thorough it even numbered the spots on the cows. Having never received less than a B on a piece of writing in sixteen years of schooling, she was naturally shocked when her work received an F, an F for being boring.

Since her teacher required that Lorch rewrite the paper, shock became despair. How could she make a description of a boring painting anything but boring? "I tried to imagine what would interest [the professor] — an effective use of colons perhaps, more adjectives, maybe an allusion to a classical myth. What was the name of that cow Jove courted in the form of a bull?" (168).

Finally, she gave up and returned to reexamine the now hated painting. The moment was a revelation. She suddenly saw that one cow had a different look on its face, a look that undercut the surface impression of bucolic bliss. By focusing on that cow and that insight, Lorch rewrote and achieved the painful breakthrough that transformed her writing process for all time. Instead of sailing smoothly down the page, her "progress is now that of a '39 Ford negotiating hard terrain, a Ford operated by a slightly dim twelve-year-old child lacking entirely any experience with stick shift" (170). She does not describe the structure of the revised piece, but she does indicate that it had to be completely redesigned: "My all-purpose sea chart for getting through a description — begin at the upper left of whatever and move clockwise until you come round again to the starting point — was not going to get me where I needed to be" (170). A new form was required.

Structurally Lorch's original paper mirrored the shape of the topic she was writing about. Whatever appeared at the top left of the picture would be discussed first, whatever was in the middle next, etc. In other words, the form of the painting controlled the form of the discourse. That is what I will call "natural" or "imitative" order in discourse. On the other hand, when Lorch rewrote the paper to focus on the importance of that one cow and its odd look, she had to restructure the paper on her own. Whatever form she used, she had to create. This is "imposed" form, form not found in the topic, but chosen by the writer.

Not all topics manifest an inherent shape. Those that do involve either chronology or spatiality. Time and space, the two dimensions of the Newtonian universe, seem also to be the two dimensions of natural form in discourse.

Imposed form in contrast *restructures* the topical material in some significant way. Now imposed form itself has at least two variants. It includes the standard forms we sometimes teach — such as the alternating comparison-contrast structure — the forms of development that Frank D'Angelo presents as conceptual paradigms for various types of writing, what Coleridge called mechanical form. But imposed form also includes the organic form favored by the British Romantics, and by such essayists as Didion, Baldwin, Carlyle, and Emerson.

Having postulated the existence of two broad categories of form, I now offer the Theorem of Student Selected Structure: Whenever possible, students tend to arrange papers by repeating the shape of the materials discussed. In other words, students choose imitative rather than imposed form.

Let me illustrate the Theorem with a personal anecdote. It's the story of one of those times in teaching when what seems like a really good idea at the moment turns into a disaster whose only virtue is that you learn not to do that again. At my university's annual spring symposium in honor of alumnus Sam Rayburn, David Schoenbrun was the featured speaker. All classes were canceled, and we were to "encourage" students to attend.

Now what better way to encourage attendance than to make the speech the subject of a writing assignment? I did not want to ask for anything complex from first-semester freshmen, so I asked them to attend the lecture, then write an account of it as a news story — no critical analysis of the positions taken, just summation of what was said with some attention to what was most important. I explained the 5 W's briefly, devoted at least thirty seconds to inverted pyramidal form, and encouraged them to take notes or even record the session.

When I read the papers, I was aghast. The major problem was structure. As the ritual on such occasions goes, the program had not begun with Schoenbrun but with our student body president, who introduced a regional newscaster, who in turn introduced Schoenbrun. And a good many of my students' papers followed that same order, beginning with the student, then the Dallas newscaster, then Schoenbrun. Of course the papers also mirrored the order of his speech, which had the effect of leaving the most interesting material near the end. My students had enacted what some literary critic once called the fallacy of imitative form.

I was expecting the mechanical imposed form of the journalist's inverted pyramid, but I got imitative chronology. They had written the minutes of the assembly, not news accounts of it.

The students certainly were not at fault — except perhaps in the general sense that they are not very familiar with what a news article sounds like. They had done what students seem to do naturally: they had built their papers in the shape of the material being discussed. But *I* was at fault for providing such an opportunity.

When asked to write a paper based on personal experiences, students also "naturally" seize on chronological order. I often assign students an essay evaluating a teacher they have had, addressed to an appropriate audience, such as the school board or future teachers of that discipline. Unless I take pains to explain the logic of evaluation, they tend to shape the papers by chronicling their experiences with that teacher, beginning with the first day in the classroom, or sometimes even before, with the rumors they had heard. They tend to be quite detailed about the first week or two, and then collapse the rest of the year into a paragraph or so.

Students are in fact ingenious about finding a natural structure, even where one would think it impossible. Last term I spent four weeks teaching research papers. We examined sample papers by other students, stressed use of multiple types of sources, and emphasized locating cognitive dissonance among the sources in order to focus a paper and contribute to the ongoing dialogue on the topic. So I was perplexed at a paper I received with five main points about the effects of teacher personality on elementary students. It had one for each of the five articles the student had located. That particular sort of natural order had seemed so unlikely that I had never warned against it. Later it occurred to me that I had seen exactly the same thing happen in doctoral dissertations in the obligatory review of the literature, which is frequently treated chronologically and exhaustingly. That same term I read such a section that was seventeen paragraphs long.

I know its length because it summarized seventeen prior studies, one study per paragraph, in the order of publication.

Why do students tend to seize on natural orders? First, a powerful economy may be at work: natural form is already there, but imposing some alternate form takes extra energy and control of text. Throwing out the form already present and hunting for another seems wasteful.

Second, our textbooks *teach* such orders. When students need to describe a place, person, or object (including Lorch's painting), the books direct them to follow the innate structure of the scene by moving left to right, or top to bottom, etc., although in my experience most published description does not follow such a structure. (Have you ever hunted for such a passage to supplement your textbook?)

Third, the structure our students are most familiar with from media of *all* types may well be chronology. From movies and TV shows, to the literary works we teach, to the U.S. history they study, the majority of the extended discourse they receive is chronologically oriented. Undoubtedly, of course, the urge to hear and tell stories is deeply embedded in the human psyche. Such structure is thus *natural* in the deepest sense of the word.

My second theorem, therefore, is certain to be more controversial: "Natural order is usually ineffective." For mnemonic purposes, we can call it the INS theorem, with INS standing for the "ineffectiveness of natural structure." I base my INS theorem largely on the experience of having read so many ineffective natural-order papers, such as those news stories on David Schoenbrun, papers which could have been presented to a reader clearly and effectively if the same material had merely been reshaped.

I have neither the space nor the inclination to document these theorems directly by comparing alternate versions of student papers. Instead I count on readers having had pedagogical experiences similar to mine that illustrate both points.

I see two explanations for why natural order is less effective than imposed order.

(1) I take it as a given that writing is a purposeful activity. It is also non-algorithmic, meaning no set sequence of steps will guarantee a solution. Consequently, writers are inherently in the business of making choices to achieve their purposes. Certainly not a revolutionary idea.

Writers choose what to include and what to omit; they make stylistic choices, and grammatical choices — and structural choices. The grounds for all these choices ought to be, in the largest sense, rhetorical. That is, the choices should be based on the question "Which of my various options at this point will best help me achieve my purpose for my readers?" Students who follow natural form forfeit the right to make such purposive structural choices. They let the shape of perceived reality deprive them of their privilege to control movement to achieve a goal. They trade freedom for security.[1]

Jack Selzer says this extreme rhetorical view privileges audience-based choices inappropriately. I maintain, however, that whether one is writing science, persuasion, information, evaluation, or a note to the paperboy, audience-based choices *should* be privileged. We write to audiences in order to communicate to them, in order to affect them in some way. Any choice we make that interferes with the audience's reception of that message — whether the choice is in spelling, vocabulary, title, readability level, or structure — is a defective choice, one that *should* have been made otherwise. (See Martin Nystrand's discussion of the principle of "reciprocity" that should operate in discourse.)

I do not wish to oversimplify this matter. Peter Elbow has made a powerful "argument for ignoring audience" in which he asserts — correctly, I think — that "we often do not really develop a strong, authentic voice in our writing till we find important occasions for *ignoring* audience" (55) in order to concentrate on what we need to say. He concludes, however, that "we must nevertheless *revise* with conscious awareness of audience in order to figure out which pieces of writer-based prose are good as they are — and how to discard or revise the rest" (55).

That is my point as well: not that at all moments during writing a student should be conscious of audience, but that *finally* all decisions need to rest on audience — even the decision to retain some natural order discourse.

(2) The second reason for the ineffectiveness of natural order grows from the presumption that discourse is unified, elaborated predication. That is, discourse asserts a claim about a subject (a rheme about a theme, to use the jargon). Natural order focuses on the subject (such as Lorch's painting of the cows), rather than on the claim. Natural order takes whatever noun referent is being discussed — whether it be "pornography," or "my summer vacation," or "the Elizabethan world picture" — locates its spatial or chronological parts and builds the discourse around them, using some variation of a list construction. Natural order thus de-emphasizes the predication and foregrounds the subject.

But the *point* of writing is what the writer predicates.

One useful corollary of the INS theorem applies to writing about writing: in writing about another text, following the structure of that text rarely works. This holds whether one reviews a new textbook, refutes a previous article, or interprets a poem.

My own struggles with textbook reviewing remind me of this point constantly. Inevitably I draft a review that is mainly a summary of the book, with evaluative remarks tied on, clanking like tin cans behind the newlyweds' car. And I defend the structure to myself on the grounds that one major purpose of the review is to tell other teachers what the book includes so they can judge whether it interests them. I maintain that charade through perhaps two drafts before acknowledging that reading even my own summary is boring, that the structure seems childish, mechanical (in the pejorative sense), and lacking in insight. At that point I know I must reconstruct the review, basing it not on the book's structure, but on my own evaluative insights, with supporting detail included but subordinated. In short, I must act on my INS theorem.

Another common example: When students are asked to interpret a poem, they automatically adopt a structure both spatial and chronological: namely, first stanza, second stanza, etc. If asked to analyze a character in a work of fiction, they will typically follow the character through the narrative. If asked to discuss several characters, they will discuss one, then another *seriatim,* often in separate paragraphs.

How often have we asked for more interpretation and less summary from our students? I submit that the problem is frequently not so much quantitative as structural. Following the shape of the work tends to produce summary and bury interpretation.

So far, this has all been personal speculation and pontification. But a fair amount of careful research supports the view that imitative order is generally less effective than imposed order.

The evidence comes from three different sorts of research: cognitive psychology, discourse analysis, and reading research.

Frankly, much of what I have been saying could have been entitled "Footnote to Linda Flower." In her classic "Writer-Based Prose: A Cognitive Basis for Problems in Writing," she asserts that "in its *structure* writer-based prose reflects the associative, narrative path of the writer's own confrontation with her subject" (269). Flower illustrates by comparing two versions of a report, written by students analyzing problems faced by the Oskalossa Brewing Company. When the group first drafted its report, it repeated the order of its own investigation, thus including a great deal of background material about the company that would be unnecessary, in fact counter productive, for the intended audience of company executives.

As Flower points out, such a structure has "an inner logic of its own . . . either a narrative framework or a survey form" (276), what I have been calling chronology or spatiality. But as she further points out, "a narrative obscures the more important logical and hierarchical relations between ideas" (276). This describes much of what our students write when asked to deal with a work of literature, as well as what often happens when they write about their own experiences. Now an argument can be made for the dramatic values of taking a reader through an experience with you — if indeed the experience itself happened to be well structured. Ken Macrorie and others have asserted a natural human "bias toward narrative" (see Dillon 65). But if one wants to make a more complex point about that experience, such as in my earlier example of evaluating a teacher, telling the story in its own order often isn't enough. Even the strict single experience narrative is often improved by using some version of flashback rather than following the natural order of the materials. Narration need not equal chronology.

Suzanne Jacobs used Flower's concept of writer-based prose in a case study of Rudy and his weekly in-class essays in advanced physiology. His teacher regularly gave the class an opening sentence designed to make them focus the ideas in that week's lectures, such as "Muscle cells are cells specialized for contraction" (35). Rudy knew a lot about muscle cells, and his essay retold that information in the order he had learned it — with no attention to the predicate, "specialized for contraction." Jacobs refers in a telling phrase to "the difficulty of fighting against the structure of remembered information" (38). Rudy imitated the order in which the teacher had presented the material. That order had worked for her purposes. But it would not work for his. He produced what we disdainfully call regurgitation. It is information-full, but not well formed.

In an article less well known than Flower's but equally brilliant, entitled "Perceiving Structure in Professional Prose," Gregory Colomb and Joseph Williams categorized the structures of prose in the professions: "There are, we believe, roughly three kinds of large-scale order. The first originates in experience, the second in historical convention, the third in something we will very crudely characterize as logic" (121).

The authors name the type "originating in experience" "iconic order." It is what I have been calling natural or imitative form. The other two types represent varieties of imposed form, a mechanical one imposed by generic conventions, such as the form of a grant application, and an organic one created to help realize the discourse as an argument.

Based on their studies of business prose, Colomb and Williams conclude bluntly, "iconic order characterizes the worst professional prose: the order of information follows the associations of the writer, or the sequence of inquiry the writer engaged in, or the structure of the object under discussion" (122). The INS theorem again.

In a very different sort of study, Richard Haswell examined impromptu essays by 160 writers representing different age groups, ranging from 18-year-old new freshmen in college to working adults age 30 and over already judged by their job supervisors to be competent writers. He discovered fourteen different macro structures and was able to classify them into simple patterns such as partition, seriation, and consequence, or chained patterns made up by joining simple patterns. The important finding for my point is that the simple or unchained patterns could be further divided into symmetrical patterns and asymmetrical patterns. In symmetrical patterns, the parts are "categories of a common class, as in chronology where the parts are all units of time" (404). In asymmetrical patterns such as "consequence" and "problem/solution," different parts are not subdivisions of one class. The five symmetrical patterns he found correspond to what I have been calling "natural" order. Nearly one-fourth of the 128 impromptu essays used "partition" (a natural pattern), but only one of the 32 essays by effective adult writers did (409).

The findings are complex, but in general the mature and effective writers tended to use the more complex asymmetrical and chained patterns, the ones I have been lumping as "imposed" structures. "Asymmetrical construction," Haswell says, "lends itself to the adventurous kind of writing that competent adults favor" (413).

In an earlier related study Aviva Freedman and Ian Pringle compared the abstraction levels of essays written by high school seniors and third-year college students in the same academic subjects. In doing so they created a four part schema in which the two lower parts, the ones showing less use of intellectual abstracting (report and commentary), are written in natural order, while the two higher forms reflect imposed orders. College writers were found to use the forms involving higher level abstraction much more frequently than did the high school students. Thus the use of imposed form was found to correlate with developmental level, a conclusion that seems consistent with Haswell's.

Finally, probably the most elaborate explanation of why imposed structure (what Colomb and Williams call "principled order" and Flower calls "reader-based prose") is generally superior comes from the work of reading researcher Bonnie J. F. Meyer. She categorizes prose structures into five main groups: description, collection (which includes time-order), antecedent/consequent, comparison, and response (which includes such structures as question and answer, and problem-solution) ("Prose Analysis: Purposes, Procedures, and Problems" 11). Her first two structures, description and collection, are simple symmetrical patterns; the other three are asymmetrical. Meyer has done extensive research on how much information readers can recall when texts containing identical information are structured along different lines. (See Meyer and Freedle, "Effects of Discourse Type on Recall.") "Some of our ongoing studies suggest that the descriptive plan is the least effective when people read or listen to text for the purpose of remembering it" ("Reading Research and the Composition Teacher: The Importance of Plans" 41). Meyer's work again suggests the superiority of imposed forms.

In 1980 a national survey of leaders in composition revealed that the inability to organize papers effectively was considered the second most important weakness in student writing, with nearly 70 percent of the 219 respondents identifying it as a "major problem" (Bossone and Larson 12).

If we agree that this is a widespread problem, and we accept the principle that imposed forms are generally superior to imitative forms, what then do we do to help students structure their prose more effectively? On this issue, existing scholarship is much less helpful. Meyer suggests that we ought to teach students conscious use of effective schemata. So does Richard Coe, but he cautions "not by pontificating about form; rather by creating processes that allow them to experience both the constraining and generative powers of forms" ("An Apology for Form" 21). Just what he means by that isn't clear, since in his own pedagogy he begins with description and narration, which he agrees lend themselves to imitative form. He does, at least, have students try out alternate structural versions of the same paper so that they can discover for themselves the effects of alternate patterns (*Form and Substance* 238–41).

It is difficult to teach form directly without returning to the empty formalism for which current-traditional, or product, pedagogies have been widely criticized. Direct teaching of form almost inevitably divorces form from purpose by asking students to locate material suitable for pouring into the mold we have designed rather than imposing whatever form will achieve their purpose.

Instead, I suggest we begin simply by giving students the advice of Leonard Podis that "every paper ought to have a consciously crafted scheme of arrangement" (197) and thus stressing the superiority of imposed form. Then we can follow the lead of a number of teachers who include some discussion of the relevant structural issues when making specific assignments. Jean Jensen, for example, describes an interview assignment for high school students that includes the following directive: "If possible, try to organize by idea rather than by time" (40). Simply telling students not to use the most obvious form might lead them to discover workable alternatives, but probably showing them model interview essays, one organized by time and one done in some other way, would further sensitize them to the general preferability of imposed form. Similarly, Judith and Geoffrey Summerfield discuss at length a personal narrative paper they assign in which students are to "break the hold on chronology" (111) and avoid the natural "bed-to-bed" structure (111). Their chapter includes two versions of a student's autobiographical paper, done six weeks apart. The revision dramatically alters the initial "bed-to-bed" chronological structure (113–21).

Of course, I am assuring that we will teach composition as an extended process — allowing both time for considering alternative structures and opportunities for revisions in which different structures, not just improved surface features, can be tried. And I am assuming that we teach composition from a rhetorical rather than a formalist axiology. In a course based on rhetorical considerations, explicit discussions of natural versus imposed orders would not be out of order.

I already teach writing as a rhetorical process. Maybe in the future I will remember my own advice and spend time discussing preferable structures every time I make a writing assignment. Then, if I am lucky, I won't have to spend my weekends reading papers beginning, "At 9:00 this morning, student body president Martin Solis welcomed a large crowd to the University Auditorium and introduced Gloria Campos, news anchor for WFAA-TV, Dallas. Ms. Campos, in turn, introduced David Schoenbrun. Mr. Schoenbrun opened his speech by saying. . . ."

Note

[1] Obviously in some cases natural order is also the superior rhetorical order — such as in giving directions for carrying out a linear process. I am not opposing *all* natural order, just natural order used without consideration of potentially superior rhetorical alternatives.

Works Cited

Bossone, Richard, and Richard Larson. *Needed Research in the Teaching of Writing.* New York: Center for Advanced Study in Education, The Graduate School and University Center of the City University of New York, 1980.

Coe, Richard. "An Apology for Form; or, Who Took the Form Out of the Process?" *College English* 49 (Jan. 1987): 13–28.

———. *Form and Substance: An Advanced Rhetoric.* New York: John Wiley, 1981.

Colomb, Gregory G., and Joseph M. Williams. "Perceiving Structure in Professional Prose: A Multiply Determined Experience." *Writing in Nonacademic Settings.* Ed. Lee Odell and Dixie Goswami. New York: Guilford, 1985. 87–128.

D'Angelo, Frank. *Process and Thought in Composition.* 2nd ed. Cambridge, Mass.: Winthrop, 1980.

Dillon, George. *Constructing Texts: Elements of a Theory of Composition and Style.* Bloomington: Indiana UP, 1981.

Elbow, Peter. "Closing My Eyes as I Speak: An Argument for Ignoring Audience." *College English* 49 (Jan. 1987): 50–69.

Flower, Linda. "Writer-Based Prose: A Cognitive Basis for Problems in Writing." *College English* 41 (Sept. 1979): 19–37. Rpt. Gary Tate and E. P. J. Corbett, eds. *A Writing Teacher's Sourcebook.* New York: Oxford UP, 1981. 268–92.

Freedman, Aviva, and Ian Pringle. "Writing in the College Years." *College Composition and Communication* 31 (1980): 311–24.

Haswell, Richard. "The Organization of Impromptu Essays." *College Composition and Communication* 37 (Dec. 1986): 402–15.

Jacobs, Susanne. "Composing the In-Class Essay: A Case Study of Rudy." *College English* 46 (January 1984): 34–46.

Jensen, Jean. "The Evolution of a Writing Program." *Teaching Writing: Essays from the Bay Area Writing Project.* Ed. Gerald Camp. Montclair, NJ: Boynton/Cook, 1982. 24–43.

Lorch, Sue. "Confessions of a Former Sailor." *Writers on Writing.* Ed. Tom Waldrep. New York: Random House, 1985. 165–71.

Meyer, Bonnie J. F. "Prose Analysis: Purposes, Procedures, and Problems." *Understanding Expository Text: Theoretical and Practical Handbook for Analyzing Explanatory Text.* Hillsdale, NJ: Lawrence Erlbaum, 1985. 11–64.

————. "Reading Research and the Composition Teacher: The Importance of Plans." *College Composition and Communication* 37 (Feb. 1982): 37–49.

Meyer, Bonnie J. F., and Roy O. Freedle. "Effects of Discourse Type on Recall." *American Educational Research Journal* 21 (Spring 1984): 121–43.

Nystrand, Martin. *The Structure of Written Communication: Studies in Reciprocity between Writers and Readers.* Orlando, FL: Academic Press, Harcourt Brace Jovanovich, 1986.

Podis, Leonard. "Teaching Arrangement: Defining a More Practical Approach." *College Composition and Communication* 31 (May 1980): 197–204.

Selzer, Jack. "A Catalog of Arrangement Considerations and Choices for Writers." Paper presented at CCCC, 1987.

Summerfield, Judith, and Geoffrey Summerfield. *Texts and Contexts: A Contribution to the Theory and Practice of Teaching Composition.* New York: Random House, 1986.

REVISING

REVISION STRATEGIES OF STUDENT WRITERS AND EXPERIENCED ADULT WRITERS

Nancy Sommers

[College Composition and Communication 31 (1980): 378–88.]

Nancy Sommers is associate director of the Expository Writing Program at Harvard University. One of the most respected scholars in the field of composition studies, Sommers is widely known for her work on the revision process and on responding to student writing. She received the Promising Researcher Award from NCTE in 1979 and the Richard Braddock Award from CCCC in 1983.

This study was among the first to investigate with any methodological rigor the revision process of specific writers, and Sommers's findings caused writing teachers to reconsider how they present revision to their students. The Bedford Handbook's extensive section on revision recognizes implicitly the results of Sommers's research, emphasizing the creative, cyclical, recursive nature of revision.

Although various aspects of the writing process have been studied extensively of late, research on revision has been notably absent. The reason for this, I suspect, is that current models of the writing process have directed attention away from revision. With few exceptions, these models are linear; they separate the writing process into discrete stages. Two representative models are Gordon Rohman's suggestion that the composing process moves from prewriting to writing to rewriting and James Britton's model of the writing process as a series of stages described in metaphors of linear growth, conception — incubation — production.[1] What is striking about these theories of writing is that they model themselves on speech: Rohman defines the writer in a way that cannot distinguish him from a speaker ("A writer is a man who . . . puts [his] experience into words in his own mind" — p. 15); and Britton bases his theory of writing on what he calls (following Jakobson) the "expressiveness" of speech.[2] Moreover, Britton's study itself follows the "linear model" of the relation of thought and language in speech proposed by Vygotsky, a relationship embodied in the linear movement "from the motive which engenders a thought to the shaping of the thought, *first* in inner speech, *then* in meanings of words, and *finally* in words" (quoted in Britton, p. 40). What this movement fails to take into account in its linear structure — "first . . . then . . . finally" — is the recursive shaping of thought by language; what it fails to take into account is *revision*. In these linear conceptions of the writing process revision is understood as a separate stage at the end of the process — a stage that comes after the completion of a first or second draft and one that is temporally distinct from the prewriting and writing stages of the process.[3]

The linear model bases itself on speech in two specific ways. First of all, it is based on traditional rhetorical models, models that were created to serve the spoken art of oratory. In whatever ways the parts of classical rhetoric are described, they offer "stages" of composition that are repeated in contemporary models of the writing process. Edward Corbett, for instance, describes the "five parts of a discourse" — *inventio, dispositio, elocutio, memoria, pronuntiatio* — and, disregarding the last two parts since "after rhetoric came to be concerned mainly with written discourse, there was no further need to deal with them,"[4] he produces a model very close to Britton's conception [*inventio*], incubation [*dispositio*], production [*elocutio*]. Other rhetorics also follow this procedure, and they do so not simply because of historical accident. Rather, the process represented in the linear model is based on the irreversibility of speech. Speech, Roland Barthes says, "is irreversible":

> A word cannot be retracted, except precisely by saying that one retracts it. To cross out here is to add: If I want to erase what I have just said, I cannot do it without showing the eraser itself (I must say: "*or rather . . .*" "*I expressed myself badly . . .*"); paradoxically, it is ephemeral speech which is indelible, not monumental writing. All that one can do in the case of a spoken utterance is to tack on another utterance.[5]

What is impossible in speech is *revision*: Like the example Barthes gives, revision in speech is an afterthought. In the same way, each stage of the linear model must be exclusive (distinct from the other stages) or else it becomes trivial and counterproductive to refer to these junctures as "stages."

By staging revision after enunciation, the linear models reduce revision in writing, as in speech, to no more than an afterthought. In this way such models make the study of revision impossible. Revision, in Rohman's model, is simply the repetition of writing; or to pursue Britton's organic metaphor, revision is simply the further growth of what is already there, the "preconceived" product. The absence of research on revision, then, is a function of a theory of writing which makes revision both superfluous and redundant, a theory which does not distinguish between writing and speech.

What the linear models do produce is a parody of writing. Isolating revision and then disregarding it plays havoc with the experiences composition teachers have of the actual writing and rewriting of experienced writers. Why should the linear model be preferred? Why should revision be forgotten, superfluous? Why do teachers offer the linear model and students accept it? One reason, Barthes suggests, is that "there is a fundamental tie between teaching and speech," while "writing begins at the point where speech becomes *impossible.*"[6] The spoken word cannot be revised. The possibility of revision distinguishes the written text from speech. In fact, according to Barthes, this is the essential difference between writing and speaking. When we must revise, when the very idea is subject to recursive shaping by language, then speech becomes inadequate. This is a matter to which I will return, but first we should examine, theoretically, a detailed exploration of what student writers as distinguished from experienced adult writers *do* when they write and rewrite their work. Dissatisfied with both the linear model of writing and the lack of attention to the process of revision, I conducted a series of studies over the past three years which examined the revision processes of student writers and experienced writers to see what role revision played in their writing processes. In the course of my work the revision process was redefined as *a sequence of changes in a composition — changes which are initiated by cues and occur continually throughout the writing of a work.*

Methodology

I used a case study approach. The student writers were twenty freshmen at Boston University and the University of Oklahoma with SAT verbal scores ranging from 450 to 600 in their first semester of composition. The twenty experienced adult writers from Boston and Oklahoma City included journalists, editors, and academics. To refer to the two groups, I use the terms *student writers* and *experienced writers* because the principal difference between these two groups is the amount of experience they had in writing.

Each writer wrote three essays, expressive, explanatory, and persuasive, and rewrote each essay twice, producing nine written products in draft and final form. Each writer was interviewed three times after the final revision of each essay. And each writer suggested revisions for a composition written by an anonymous author. Thus extensive written and spoken documents were obtained from each writer.

The essays were analyzed by counting and categorizing the changes made. Four revision operations were identified: deletion, substitution, addition, and reordering. And four levels of changes were identified: word, phrase, sentence, theme (the extended statement of one idea). A coding system was developed for identifying the frequency of revision by level and operation. In addition, transcripts of the interviews in which the writers interpreted their revisions were used to develop what was called a *scale of concerns* for each writer. This scale enabled me to codify what were the writer's primary concerns, secondary concerns, tertiary concerns, and whether the writers used the same scale of concerns when revising the second or third drafts as they used in revising the first draft.

Revision Strategies of Student Writers

Most of the students I studied did not use the term *revision* or *rewriting*. In fact, they did not seem comfortable using the word *revision* and explained that revision was not a word they used, but the word their teachers used. Instead, most of the students had developed various functional terms to describe the type of changes they made. The following are samples of these definitions:

Scratch Out and Do Over Again: "I say scratch out and do over, and that means what it says. Scratching out and cutting out. I read what I have written and I cross out a word and put another word in; a more decent word or a better word. Then if there is somewhere to use a sentence that I have crossed out, I will put it there."

Reviewing: "Reviewing means just using better words and eliminating words that are not needed. I go over and change words around."

Reviewing: "I just review every word and make sure that everything is worded right. I see if I am rambling; I see if I can put a better word in or leave one out. Usually when I read what I have written, I say to myself, 'that word is so bland or so trite,' and then I go and get my thesaurus."

Redoing: "Redoing means cleaning up the paper and crossing out. It is looking at something and saying, no that has to go, or no, that is not right."

Marking Out: "I don't use the word *rewriting* because I only write one draft and the changes that I made are made on top of the draft. The changes that I made are usually just marking out words and putting different ones in."

Slashing and Throwing Out: "I throw things out and say they are not good. I like to write like Fitzgerald did by inspiration, and if I feel inspired then I don't need to slash and throw much out."

The predominant concern in these definitions is vocabulary. The students understand the revision process as a rewording activity. They do so because they perceive words as the unit of written discourse. That is, they concentrate on particular words apart from their role in the text. Thus one student quoted above thinks in terms of dictionaries, and, following the eighteenth-century theory of words parodied in *Gulliver's Travels,* he imagines a load of things carried about to be exchanged. Lexical changes are the major revision activities of the students because economy is their goal. They are governed, like the linear model itself, by the Law of Occam's razor that prohibits logically needless repetition: redundancy and superfluity. Nothing governs speech more than such superfluities; speech constantly repeats itself precisely because spoken words, as Barthes writes, are expendable in the cause of communication. The aim of revision according to the students' own description is therefore to clean up speech; the redundancy of speech is unnecessary in writing, their logic suggests, because writing, unlike speech, can be reread. Thus one student said, "Redoing means cleaning up the paper and crossing out." The remarkable contradiction of cleaning by marking might, indeed, stand for student revision as I have encountered it.

The students place a symbolic importance on their selection and rejection of words as the determiners of success or failure for their compositions. When revising, they primarily ask themselves: Can I find a better word or phrase? A more impressive, not so clichéd, or less humdrum word? Am I repeating the same word or phrase too often? They approach the revision process with what could be labeled as a "thesaurus philosophy of writing"; the students consider the thesaurus a harvest of lexical substitutions and believe that most problems in their essays can be solved by rewording. What is revealed in the students' use of the thesaurus is a governing attitude toward their writing: that the meaning to be communicated is already there, already finished, already produced, ready to be communicated, and all that is necessary is a better word "rightly worded." One student defined revision as "redoing"; "redoing" meant "just using better words and eliminating words that are not needed." For the students, writing is translating: the thought to the page, the language of speech to the more formal language of prose, the word to its synonym. Whatever is translated, an original text already exists for students, one which need not be discovered or acted upon, but simply communicated.[7]

The students list repetition as one of the elements they most worry about. This cue signals to them that they need to eliminate the repetition either by substituting or deleting words or phrases. Repetition occurs, in large part, because student writing imitates — transcribes — speech; attention to repetitious words is a manner of cleaning speech. Without a sense of the developmental possibilities of revision (and writing in general) students seek, on the authority of many textbooks, simply to clean up their language and prepare to type. What is curious, however, is that students are aware of lexical repetition, but not conceptual repetition. They only notice the repetition if they can "hear" it; they do not diagnose lexical repetition as symptomatic of problems on a deeper level. By rewording their sentences to avoid the lexical repetition, the students solve the immediate problem but blind themselves to problems on a textual level; although they are using different words, they are sometimes merely restating the same idea with different words. Such blindness, as I discovered with student writers, is the inability to "see" revision as a process: the inability to "review" their work again, as it were, with different eyes, and to start over.

The revision strategies described above are consistent with the students' understanding of the revision process as requiring lexical changes but not semantic changes. For the students, the extent to which they revise is a function of their level of inspiration. In fact, they use the word *inspiration* to describe the ease or difficulty with which their essay is written, and the extent to which the essay needs to be revised. If students feel inspired, if the writing comes easily, and if they don't get stuck on individual words or phrases, then they say that they cannot see any reason to revise. Because students do not see revision as an activity in which they modify and develop perspectives and ideas, they feel that if they know what they want to say, then there is little reason for making revisions.

The only modification of ideas in the students' essays occurred when they tried out two or three introductory paragraphs. This results, in part, because the students have been taught in another version of the linear model of composing to use a thesis statement as a controlling device in their introductory paragraphs. Since they write their introductions and their thesis statements even before they have really discovered what they want to say, their early close attention to the thesis statement, and more generally the linear model, function to restrict and circumscribe not only the development of their ideas, but also their ability to change the direction of these ideas.

Too often as composition teachers we conclude that students do not willingly revise. The evidence from my research suggests that it is not that students are unwilling to revise, but rather that they do what they have been taught to do in a consistently narrow and predictable way. On every occasion when I asked students why they hadn't made any more changes, they essentially replied, "I knew something larger was wrong, but I didn't think it would help to move words around." The students have strategies for handling words and phrases and their strategies helped them on a word or sentence level. What they lack, however, is a set of strategies to help them identify the "something larger" that they sensed was wrong and work from there. The students do not have strategies for handling the whole essay. They lack procedures or heuristics to help them reorder lines of reasoning or ask questions about their purposes and readers. The students view their compositions in a linear way as a series of parts. Even such potentially useful concepts as "unity" or "form" are reduced to the rule that a composition, if it is to have form, must have an introduction, a body, and a conclusion, or the sum total of the necessary parts.

The students decide to stop revising when they decide that they have not violated any of the rules for revising. These rules, such as "Never begin a sentence with a conjunction" or "Never end a sentence with a preposition," are lexically cued and rigidly applied. In general, students will subordinate the demands of the specific problems of their text to the demands of the rules. Changes are made in compliance with abstract rules about the product, rules that quite often do not apply to the specific problems in the text. These revision strategies are teacher-based, directed toward a teacher-reader who expects compliance with rules — with preexisting "conceptions" — and who will only examine parts of the composition (writing comments about those parts in the margins of their essays) and will cite any violations of rules in those parts. At best the students see their writing altogether passively through the eyes of former teachers or their surrogates, the textbooks, and are bound to the rules which they have been taught.

Revision Strategies of Experienced Writers

One aim of my research has been to contrast how student writers define revision with how a group of experienced writers define their revision processes. Here is a sampling of the definitions from the experienced writers:

Rewriting: "It is a matter of looking at the kernel of what I have written, the content, and then thinking about it, responding to it, making decisions, and actually restructuring it."

Rewriting: "I rewrite as I write. It is hard to tell what is a first draft because it is not determined by time. In one draft, I might cross out three pages, write two, cross out a fourth, rewrite it, and call it a draft. I am constantly writing and rewriting. I can only conceptualize so much in my first draft — only so much information can be held in my head at one time; my rewriting efforts are a reflection of how much information I can encompass at one time. There are levels and agenda which I have to attend to in each draft."

Rewriting: "Rewriting means on one level, finding the argument, and on another level, language changes to make the argument more effective. Most of the time I feel as if I can go on rewriting forever. There is always one part of a piece that I could keep working on. It is always difficult to know at what point to abandon a piece of writing. I like this idea that a piece of writing is never finished, just abandoned."

Rewriting: "My first draft is usually very scattered. In rewriting, I find the line of argument. After the argument is resolved, I am much more interested in word choice and phrasing."

Revising: "My cardinal rule in revising is never to fall in love with what I have written in a first or second draft. An idea, sentence, or even a phrase that looks catchy, I don't trust. Part of this idea is to wait a while. I am much more in love with something after I have written it than I am a day or two later. It is much easier to change anything with time."

Revising: "It means taking apart what I have written and putting it back together again. I ask major theoretical questions of my ideas, respond to those questions, and think of proportion and structure, and try to find a controlling metaphor. I find out which ideas can be developed and which should be dropped. I am constantly chiseling and changing as I revise."

The experienced writers describe their primary objective when revising as finding the form or shape of their argument. Although the metaphors vary, the experienced writers often use structural expressions such as "finding a framework," "a pattern," or "a design" for their argument. When questioned about this emphasis, the experienced writers responded that since their first drafts are usually scattered attempts to define their territory, their objective in the second draft is to begin observing general patterns of development and deciding what should be included and what excluded. One writer explained, "I have learned from experience that I need to keep writing a first draft until I figure out what I want to say. Then in a second draft, I begin to see the structure of an argument and how all the various subarguments which are buried beneath the surface of all those sentences are related." What is described here is a process in which the writer is both agent and vehicle. "Writing," says Barthes, unlike speech, "develops like a seed, not a line,"[8] and like a seed it confuses beginning and end, conception and production. Thus, the experienced writers say their drafts are "not determined by time," that rewriting is a "constant process," that they feel as if they "can go on forever." Revising confuses the beginning and end, the agent and vehicle; it confuses, *in order to find*, the line of argument.

After a concern for form, the experienced writers have a second objective: a concern for their readership. In this way, "production" precedes "conception." The experienced writers imagine a reader (reading their product) whose existence and whose expectations influence their revision process. They have abstracted the standards of a reader and this reader seems to be partially a reflection of themselves and functions as a critical and productive collaborator — a collaborator who has yet to love their work. The anticipation of a reader's judgment causes a feeling of dissonance when the writer recognizes incongruities between intention and execution, and requires these writers to make revision on all levels. Such a reader gives them just what the students lacked: new eyes to "re-view" their work. The experienced writers believe that they have learned the causes and conditions, the product, which will influence their reader, and their revision strategies are geared toward creating these causes and conditions. They demonstrate a complex understanding of which examples, sentences, or phrases should be included or excluded. For example, one experienced writer decided to delete public examples and add private examples when writing about the energy crisis because "private examples would be less controversial and thus more persuasive." Another writer revised his transitional sentences because "some kinds of transitions are more easily recognized as transitions than others." These examples represent the type of strategic attempts these experienced writers use to manipulate the conventions of discourse in order to communicate to their reader.

But these revision strategies are a process of more than communication; they are part of the process of *discovering meaning* altogether. Here we can see the importance of dissonance; at the heart of revision is the process by which writers recognize and resolve the dissonance they sense in their writing. Ferdinande de Saussure has argued that meaning is differential or "diacritical," based on differences between terms rather than "essential" or inherent qualities of terms. "Phonemes," he said, "are characterized not, as one might think, by their own positive quality but simply by the fact that they are distinct."[9] In fact, Saussure bases his entire *Course in General Linguistics* on these differences, and such differences are dissonant; like musical dissonances which gain their significance from their relationship to the "key" of the composition which itself is determined by the whole language, specific language (parole) gains its meaning from the system of language (langue) of which it is a manifestation and part. The musical composition — a "composition" of parts — creates its "key" as in an overall structure which determines the value (meaning) of its parts. The analogy with music is readily seen in the compositions of experienced writers: Both sorts of composition are based precisely on those structures experienced writers seek in their writing. It is this complicated relationship between the parts and the whole in the work of experienced writers which destroys the linear model; writing cannot develop "like a line" because each addition or deletion is a reordering of the whole. Explicating Saussure, Jonathan Culler asserts that "meaning depends on difference of meaning."[10] But student writers constantly struggle to bring their essays into congruence with a predefined meaning. The experienced writers do the opposite: They seek to discover (to create) meaning in the engagement with their writing, in revision. They seek to emphasize and exploit the lack of clarity, the differences of meaning, the dissonance, that writing as opposed to speech allows in the possibility of revision. Writing has spatial and temporal features not apparent in speech — words are recorded in space and fixed in time — which is why writing is susceptible to reordering and later addition. Such features make possible the dissonance that both provokes revision and promises, from itself, new meaning.

For the experienced writers the heaviest concentration of changes is on the sentence level, and the changes are predominantly by addition and deletion. But, unlike the students, experienced writers make changes on all levels and use all revision operations. Moreover, the operations the students fail to use — reordering and addition — seem to require a theory of the revision process as a totality — a theory which, in fact, encompasses the *whole* of the composition. Unlike the students, the experienced writers possess a nonlinear theory in which a sense of the whole writing both precedes and grows out of an examination of the parts. As we saw, one writer said he needed "a first draft to figure out what to say," and "a second draft to see the structure of an argument buried beneath the surface." Such a "theory" is both theoretical and strategical; once again, strategy and theory are conflated in ways that are literally impossible for the linear model. Writing appears to be more like a seed than a line.

Two elements of the experienced writers' theory of the revision process are the adoption of a holistic perspective and the perception that revision is a recursive process. The writers ask: What does my essay as a *whole* need for form, balance, rhythm, or communication? Details are added, dropped, substituted, or reordered according to their sense of what the essay needs for emphasis and proportion. This sense, however, is constantly in flux as ideas are developed and modified; it is constantly "reviewed" in relation to the parts. As their ideas change, revision becomes an attempt to make their writing consonant with that changing vision.

The experienced writers see their revision process as a recursive process — a process with significant recurring activities — with different levels of attention and different agenda for each cycle. During the first revision cycle their attention is primarily directed toward narrowing the topic and delimiting their ideas. At this point, they are not as concerned as they are later about vocabulary and style. The experienced writers explained that they get closer to their meaning by not limiting themselves too early to lexical concerns. As one writer commented to explain her revision process, a comment inspired by the summer 1977 New York power failure: "I feel like Con Edison cutting off certain states to keep the generators going. In first and second drafts, I try to cut off as much as I can of my editing generator, and in a third draft, I try to cut off some of my idea generators, so I can make sure that I will actually finish the essay." Although the experienced writers describe their revision process as a series of different levels or cycles, it is inaccurate to assume that they have only one objective for each cycle and that each cycle can be defined by a different objective. The same objectives and subprocesses are present in each cycle, but in different proportions. Even though these experienced writers place the predominant weight upon finding the form of their argument during the first cycle, other concerns exist as well. Conversely, during the later cycles, when the experienced writers' primary attention is focused upon stylistic concerns, they are still attuned, although in a reduced way, to the form of the argument. Since writers are limited in what they can attend to during each cycle (understandings are temporal), revision strategies help balance competing demands on attention. Thus, writers can concentrate on more than one objective at a time by developing strategies to sort out and organize their different concerns in successive cycles of revision.

It is a sense of writing as discovery — a repeated process of beginning over again, starting out new — that the students failed to have. I have used the notion of dissonance because such dissonance, the incongruities between intention and execution, governs both writing and meaning. Students do not see the incongruities. They need to rely on their own internalized sense of good writing and to see their writing with their "own" eyes. Seeing in revision — seeing beyond hearing — is at the root of the word *revision* and the process itself; current dicta on revising blind our students to what is actually involved in revision. In fact, they blind them to what constitutes good writing altogether. Good writing disturbs: It creates dissonance. Students need to seek the dissonance of discovery, utilizing in their writing, as the experienced writers do, the very difference between writing and speech — the possibility of revision.

Notes

¹ D. Gordon Rohman and Albert O. Wlecke, "Pre-writing: The Construction and Application of Models for Concept Formation in Writing." Cooperative Research Project No. 2174, U.S. Office of Education, Department of Health, Education, and Welfare; James Britton, Anthony Burgess, Nancy Martin, Alex McLeod, Harold Rosen, *The Development of Writing Abilities (11–18)* (London: Macmillan Education, 1975).

² Britton is following Roman Jakobson, "Linguistics and Poetics," in T. A. Sebeok, *Style in Language* (Cambridge, Mass: MIT Press, 1960).

³ For an extended discussion of this issue see Nancy Sommers, "The Need for Theory in Composition Research," *College Composition and Communication,* 30 (February 1979), 46–49.

[4] *Classical Rhetoric for the Modern Student* (New York: Oxford University Press, 1965), p. 27.

[5] Roland Barthes, "Writers, Intellectuals, Teachers," in *Image-Music-Text*, trans. Stephen Heath (New York: Hill and Wang, 1977), pp. 190–191.

[6] "Writers, Intellectuals, Teachers," p. 190.

[7] Nancy Sommers and Ronald Schleifer, "Means and Ends: Some Assumptions of Student Writers," *Composition and Teaching*, II (in press).

[8] *Writing Degree Zero* in *Writing Degree Zero and Elements of Semiology*, trans. Annette Lavers and Colin Smith (New York: Hill and Wang, 1968), p. 20.

[9] *Course in General Linguistics*, trans. Wade Baskin (New York: McGraw-Hill 1966), p. 119.

[10] Jonathan Culler, *Saussure* (Penguin Modern Masters Series; London: Penguin Books, 1976), p. 70.

Acknowledgment: The author wishes to express her gratitude to Professor William Smith, University of Pittsburgh, for his vital assistance with the research reported in this article and to Patrick Hays, her husband, for extensive discussions and critical editorial help.

COMPOSING BEHAVIORS OF ONE- AND MULTI-DRAFT WRITERS

Muriel Harris

[College English 51 (1989): 174–91.]

Muriel Harris, professor of English and director of the writing lab at Purdue University, is author of Teaching One-to-One: The Writing Conference *(1986) and the* Prentice Hall Reference Guide to Grammar and Usage *(2nd edition, 1994). In addition to editing* Writing Lab Newsletter, *Harris has published articles in* College English, College Composition and Communication, Written Communication, *and* Writing Center Journal.

Harris suggests that we think of revising behaviors (and thus of revision strategies) as ranging on a continuum from writers who produce only one draft to writers who produce multiple drafts. According to Harris, one writer may exhibit several different revision behaviors, in some instances producing only one draft or doing little revision and in other instances producing multiple drafts and doing extensive revision. The variety of composing and revising behaviors, she contends, is not necessarily attributable to experience or abilities. Harris's approach to understanding revision offers instructors a powerful and flexible explanation of revising, one that accounts more fully for the variety of writing tasks that students encounter and provides them with a variety of effective composing strategies for accomplishing those tasks.

A belief shared by teachers of writing, one that we fervently try to inculcate in our students, is that revision can improve writing. This notion, that revision generally results in better text, often pairs up with another assumption, that revision occurs as we work through separate drafts. Thus, "hand in your working drafts tomorrow and the final ones next Friday" is a common assignment, as is the following bit of textbook advice: "When the draft is completed, a good critical reading should help the writer re-envision the essay and could very well lead to substantial rewriting" (Axelrod and Cooper 10). This textbook advice, hardly atypical, is based on the rationale that gaining distance from a piece of discourse helps the writer to judge it more critically. As evidence for this assumption, Richard Beach's 1976 study of the self-evaluation strategies of revisers and non-revisers demonstrated that extensive revisers were more capable of detaching themselves and gaining aesthetic distance from their writing than were non-revisers. Nancy Sommers' later theoretical work on revision also sensitized us to students' need to re-see their texts rather than to view revision as an editing process at the limited level of word changes.

A logical conclusion, then, is to train student writers to re-see and then re-draft a piece of discourse. There are other compelling reasons for helping students view first or working drafts as fluid and not yet molded into final form. The opportunities for outside intervention, through teacher critiques and suggestions or peer evaluation sessions, can be valuable. And it is equally important to help students move beyond their limited approaches and limiting tendency to settle for whatever rolls out on paper the first time around. The novice view of a first draft as written-in-stone (or fast-drying cement) can preclude engaging more fully with the ideas being expressed. On the other hand, we have to acknowledge that there are advantages in being able, where it is appropriate, to master the art of one-draft writing. When students write essay exams or placement essays and when they go on to on-the-job writing where time doesn't permit multiple drafts, they need to produce first drafts which are also coherent, finished final drafts. Yet, even acknowledging that need, we still seem justified in advocating that our students master the art of redrafting to shape a text into a more effective form.

The notion that reworking a text through multiple drafts and/or visible changes is generally a beneficial process is also an underlying assumption in some lines of research. This had been particularly evident in studies of computer-aided revision, where counts were taken of changes in macro-structure and microstructure with and without word processing. If more changes were made on a word processor than were written by hand, the conclusion was that word processors are an aid to revision. Such research is based on the premise that revision equals visible changes in a text and that these changes will improve the text.

Given this widely entrenched notion of redrafting as being advantageous, it would be comforting to turn to research results for clearcut evidence that reworking of text produces better writing. But studies of revision do not provide the conclusive picture that we need in order to assert that we should continue coaxing our students into writing multiple drafts. Lillian Bridwell's 1980 survey of revision studies led her to conclude that "questions about the relationship between revision and qualitative improvement remain largely unanswered" (199), and her own study demonstrated that the most extensively revised papers "received a range of quality ratings from the top to the bottom of the scale" (216). In another review of research on revision, Stephen Witte cites studies which similarly suggest that the amount of redrafting (which Witte calls "retranscription") often bears little relation to the overall quality of completed texts ("Revising" 256). Similarly, Linda Flower and John Hayes et al., citing studies which also dispute the notion that more re-drafting should mean better papers, conclude that the amount of change is not a key variable in revision and that revision as an obligatory stage required by teachers doesn't necessarily produce better writing. (For a teacher's affirmation of the same phenomenon, see Henley.)

Constricting revision to retranscription (i.e., to altering what has been written) also denies the reality of pre-text, a composing phenomenon studied by Stephen Witte in "Pre-Text and Composing." Witte defines a writer's pre-text as "the mental construction of 'text' prior to transcription" (397). Pre-text thus "refers to a writer's linguistic representation of intended meaning, a 'trial locution' that is produced in the mind, stored in the writer's memory, and sometimes manipulated mentally prior to being transcribed as written text" (397). Pre-texts are distinguished from abstract plans in that pre-texts approximate written prose. As the outcome of planning, pre-text can also be the basis for further planning. In his study Witte found great diversity in how writers construct and use pre-text. Some writers construct little or no pre-text; others rely heavily on extensive pre-texts; others create short pre-texts; and still others move back and forth between extensive and short pre-texts. The point here is that Witte has shown us that revision can and does occur in pre-texts, before visible marks are made on paper. In an earlier paper, "Revising, Composing Theory, and Research Design," Witte suggests that the pre-text writers construct before making marks on paper is probably a function of the quality, kind, and extent of planning that occurs before transcribing on paper. The danger here is that we might conclude that the development from novice to expert writer entails learning to make greater use of pre-text prior to transcribing. After all, in Linda Flower's memorable phrase, pre-text is "the last cheap gas before transcribing text" (see Witte, "Pre-Text" 422). But Witte notes that his data do not support a "vote for pre-text" ("Pre-Text" 401). For the students in Witte's study, more extensive use of pre-text doesn't automatically lead to better written text. Thus it appears so far that the quality of revision can neither be measured by the pound nor tracked through discreet stages.

But a discussion of whether more or fewer drafts is an indication of more mature writing is itself not adequate. As Maxine Hairston reminds us in "Different Products, Different Processes," we must also consider the writing task that is involved in any particular case of generating discourse. In her taxonomy of writing categories, categories that depict a variety of revision behaviors that are true to the experience of many of us, Hairston divides writing into three classes: first, routine maintenance writing which is simple communication about uncomplicated matters; second, extended, relatively complex writing that requires the writer's attention but is self-limiting in that the writer already knows most of what she is going to write and may be writing under time constraints; and third, extended reflective writing in which the form and content emerge as the writing proceeds. Even with this oversimplified, brief summary of Hairston's classes of writing, we recognize that the matter of when and if re-drafting takes place can differ according to the demands of different tasks and situations as well as the different skills levels of writers.

Many — or perhaps even most — of us may nod in agreement as we recognize in Hairston's classes of writing a description of the different types of writing we do. But given the range of individual differences that exist among writers, we still cannot conclude that the nature of effective revision is always tied to the writing task, because such a conclusion would not account for what we know also exists — some expert writers who, despite the writing task, work at either end of the spectrum as confirmed, consistent one-drafters or as perpetual multi-drafters. That writers exhibit a diversity of revising habits has been noted by Lester Faigley and Stephen Witte in "Analyzing Revision." When testing the taxonomy of revision changes they had created, Faigley and Witte found that expert writers exhibited "extreme diversity" in the ways they revised:

> One expert writer in the present study made almost no revisions; another started with an almost stream-of-consciousness text that she then converted to an organized essay in the second draft; another limited his major revisions to a single long insert; and another revised mostly by pruning. (410)

Similarly, when summarizing interviews with well-known authors such as those in the *Writers at Work: The Paris Review Interviews* series, Lillian Bridwell notes that these discussions reveal a wide range of revision strategies among these writers, from rapid producers of text who do little revising as they proceed to writers who move along by revising every sentence (198).

More extensive insights into a variety of composing styles are offered in Tom Waldrep's collection of essays by successful scholars working in composition, *Writers on Writing*. Here too as writers describe their composing processes, we see a variety of approaches, including some writers who plan extensively before their pens hit paper (or before the cursor blips on their screens). Their planning is so complete that their texts generally emerge in a single draft with minor, if any, editing as they write. Self-descriptions of some experienced writers in the field of composition give us vivid accounts of how these one-drafters work. For example, Patricia Y. Murray notes that prior to typing, she sees words, phrases, sentences, and paragraphs taking shape in her head. Her composing, she concludes, has been done before her fingers touch the typewriter. though as she also notes, she revises and edits as she types (234). William Lutz offers a similar account:

> Before I write, I write in my mind. The more difficult and complex the writing, the more time I need to think before I write. Ideas incubate in my mind. While I talk, drive, swim, and exercise I am thinking, planning, writing. I think about the introduction, what examples to use, how to develop the main idea, what kind of conclusion to use. I write, revise, rewrite, agonize, despair, give up, only to start all over again, and all of this before I ever begin to put words on paper. . . . Writing is not a process of discovery for me. . . . The writing process takes place in my mind. Once that process is compiete the product emerges. Often I can write pages without pause and with very little, if any, revision or even minor changes. (186–87)

Even with such descriptions from experienced writers, we are hesitant either to discard the notion that writing *is* a process of discovery for many of us or to typecast writers who make many visible changes on the page and/or work through multiple drafts as inadequate writers. After all, many of us, probably the majority, fall somewhere along the continuum from one- to multi-drafters. We may find ourselves as both one- and multi-drafters with the classes of writing that Hairston describes, or we may generally identify ourselves as doing both but also functioning more often as a one- or multi-drafter. Just as we have seen that at one end of the spectrum there are some confirmed one-drafters, so too must we recognize that at the other end of that spectrum there are some confirmed multi-drafters, expert writers for whom extensive revising occurs when writing (so that a piece of discourse may go through several or more drafts or be reworked heavily as the original draft evolves). David Bartholomae, a self-described multi-drafter, states that he never outlines but works instead with two pads of paper, one to write on and one for making plans, storing sentences, and taking notes. He views his first drafts as disorganized and has to revise extensively, with the result that the revisions bear little resemblance to the first drafts (22–26). Similarly, Lynn Z. Bloom notes that she cannot predict at the outset a great deal of what she is going to say. Only by writing does she learn how her content will develop or how she will handle the structure, organization, and style of her paragraphs, sentences, and whole essay (33).

Thus, if we wish to draw a more inclusive picture of composing behaviors for revision, we have to put together a description that accounts for differences in levels of ability and experience (from novice to expert), for differences in writing tasks, and also for differences in the as yet largely unexplored area of composing process differences among writers. My interest here is in the composing processes of different writers, more particularly, the reality of those writers at either end of that long spectrum, the one-drafters at one end and the multi-drafters at the other. By one-draft writers I mean those writers who construct their plans and the pre-texts that carry out those plans as well as do all or most of the revising of those plans and pre-texts mentally, before transcribing. They do little or no retranscribing. True one-drafters have not arrived at this developmentally or as a result of training in writing, and they should not be confused with other writers who — driven by deadlines, lack of motivation, insufficient experience with writing, or anxieties about "getting it right the first time" — do little or no scratching out of what they have written. Multi-drafters, on the other hand, need to interact with their transcriptions in order to revise. Independent of how much planning they do or pre-text they compose, they continue to revise after they have transcribed words onto paper. Again, true multi-drafters have not reached this stage developmentally or as a result of any intervention by teachers. This is not to say that we can classify writers into two categories, one- and multi-drafters, because all the evidence we have and, more importantly, our own experience tells us that most writers are not one or the other but exist somewhere between these two ends of the continuum.

However, one- and multi-drafters do exist, and we do need to learn more about them to gain a clearer picture not only of what is involved in different revising processes but also to provide a basis for considering the pedagogical implications of dealing with individual differences. There is a strong argument for looking instead at the middle range of writers who do some writing in single drafts and others in multiple drafts or with a lot of retranscribing as they proceed, for it is very probable that the largest number of writers cluster there. But those of us who teach in the individualized setting of conferences or writing lab tutorials know that we can never overlook or put aside the concerns of every unique individual with whom we work. Perhaps we are overly intrigued with individual differences, partly because we see that some students can be ill-served in the group setting of the classrooms and partly because looking at individual differences gives us such enlightening glimpses into the complex reality of composing processes. Clinicians in other fields would argue that looking at the extremes offers a clearer view of what may be involved in the behaviors of the majority. But those who do research in writing also acknowledge that we need to understand dimensions of variation among writers, particularly those patterned differences or "alternate paths to expert performance" that have clear implications for instruction (Freedman et al. 19). In this case, whatever we learn about patterns of behavior among one- and multi-drafters has direct implications for instruction as we need to know the various trade-offs involved in any classroom instruction which would encourage more single or multiple drafting. And, as we will see when looking at what is involved in being able to revise before drafting or in being able to return and re-draft what has been transcribed, there are trade-offs indeed. Whatever arguments are offered, we must also acknowledge that no picture of revision is complete until it includes all that is known and observed about a variety of revision behaviors among writers.

But what do we know about one- and multi-drafters other than anecdotal accounts that confirm their existence? Much evidence is waiting to be gathered from the storehouse of various published interviews in which well-known writers have been asked to describe their writing. And Ann Ruggles Gere's study of the revising behaviors of a blind student gives us a description of a student writer who does not redraft but writes "first draft/final draft" papers, finished products produced in one sitting for her courses as a master's degree candidate. The student describes periods of thinking about a topic before writing. While she doesn't know exactly what she will say until actually writing it, she typically knows what will be contained in the first paragraph as she types the title. Her attention is not focused on words as she concentrates instead on images and larger contexts. A similar description of a one-drafter is found in Joy Reid's "The Radical Outliner and the Radical Brainstormer." Comparing her husband and herself, both composition teachers, Reid notes the differences between herself, an outliner (and a one-drafter), and her husband, a brainstormer (and a multi-drafter), differences which parallel those of the writers in *Writers on Writing* that I have described.

The descriptions of all of the one- and multi-draft writers mentioned so far offer a fairly consistent picture, but these descriptions do little more than reaffirm their existence. In an effort to learn more, I sought out some one- and multi-drafters in order to observe them composing and to explore what might be involved. Since my intent was not to determine the percentage of one- and multi-drafters among any population of writers (though that would be an interesting topic indeed, as I suspect there are more than we may initially guess — or at least more who hover close to either end of the continuum), I sought out experienced writers who identify themselves as very definitely one- or multi-drafters. The subjects I selected for observation were graduate students who teach composition or communications courses, my rationale being that these people can more easily categorize and articulate their own writing habits. From among the group of subjects who described themselves as very definitely either one- or multi-drafters, I selected those who showed evidence of being experienced, competent writers. Of the eight selected subjects (four one-drafters and four multi-drafters), all were at least several years into their graduate studies in English or communications and were either near completion or had recently completed advanced degrees. All had received high scores in standardized tests for verbal skills such as the SAT or GRE exams; all had grade point averages ranging from B+ to A in their graduate courses; and all wrote frequently in a variety of tasks, including academic papers for courses and journal publications, conference papers, the usual business writing of practicing academics (e.g., letters of recommendation for students, memos, instructional materials for classes, etc.), and personal writing such as letters to family and friends. They clearly earned their description as experienced writers. Experienced writers were used because I also wished to exclude those novices who may, through development of their writing skills, change their composing behaviors, and also those novices whose composing habits are the result of other factors such as disinterest (e.g., the one-drafter who habitually begins the paper at 3 a.m. the night before it's due) or anxiety (e.g., the multi-drafter who fears she is never "right" and keeps working and reworking her text).

The experienced writers whom I observed all confirmed that their composing behaviors have not changed over time. That is, they all stated that their writing habits have not altered as they became experienced writers and/or as they moved through writing courses. However, their descriptions of themselves as one- or multi-drafters were not as completely accurate as might be expected. Self-reporting, even among teachers of writing, is not a totally reliable measure. As I observed and talked with the eight writers, I found three very definite one-drafters, Ted, Nina, and Amy; one writer, Jackie, who tends to be a one-drafter but does some revising after writing; two very definite multi-drafters, Bill and Pam; and two writers, Karen and Cindy, who described themselves as multi-drafters and who tend to revise extensively but who can also produce first draft/final draft writing under some conditions. To gather data on their composing behaviors, I interviewed each person for an hour, asking questions about the types of writing they do, the activities they engage in before writing, the details of what happens as they write, their revision behaviors, the manner in which sentences are composed, and their attitudes and past history of writing. Each person was also asked to spend an hour writing in response to an assignment. The specific assignment was a request from an academic advisor asking for the writers' descriptions of the skills needed to succeed in their field of study. As they wrote, all eight writers were asked to give thinking-aloud protocols and were videotaped for future study. Brief interviews after writing focused on eliciting information about how accurately the writing session reflected their general writing habits and behaviors. Each type of information collected is, at best, incomplete because accounts of one's own composing processes may not be entirely accurate, because thinking-aloud protocols while writing are only partial accounts of what is being thought about, and because one-hour writing tasks preclude observing some of the kinds of activities that writers report. But even with these limitations I observed patterns of composing behaviors that should differentiate one-draft writers from multi-draft writers.

Preference for Beginning with a Developed Focus vs. Preference for Beginning at an Exploratory Stage

Among the consistent behaviors that one-drafters report is the point at which they can and will start writing. All of the four one-drafters expressed a strong need to clarify their thinking prior to beginning to transcribe. They are either not ready to write or cannot write until they have a focus and organization in mind. They may, as I observed Jackie and Ted doing, make some brief planning notes on paper or, as Amy and Nina did, sit for awhile and mentally plan, but all expressed a clearly articulated need to know beforehand the direction the piece of writing would take. For Nina's longer papers, she described a planning schedule in which the focus comes first, even before collecting notes. Ted too described the first stage of a piece of writing as being a time of mentally narrowing a topic. During incubation times before writing, two of these writers described some global recasting of a paper in their minds while the other two expressed a need to talk it out, either to themselves or friends. There is little resorting of written notes and little use of written outlines, except for some short lists, described by Ted as "memory jogs" to use while he writes. Amy explained that she sometimes felt that in high school or as an undergraduate she should have written outlines to please her teachers, but she never did get around to it because outlines served no useful purpose for her. Consistent throughout these accounts and in my observation of their writing was these writers' need to know where they are headed beforehand and a feeling that they are not ready to write — or cannot write — until they are at that stage. When asked if they ever engaged in freewriting, two one-drafters said they could not, unless forced to, plunge in and write without a focus and a mental plan. Ted, in particular, noted that the notion of exploration during writing would make him so uncomfortable that he would probably block and be unable to write.

In contrast to the one-drafters' preference for knowing their direction before writing, the two consistent multi-drafters, Pam and Bill, explained that they resist knowing, resist any attempt at clarification prior to writing. Their preference is for open-ended exploration as they write. They may have been reading and thinking extensively beforehand, but the topic has not taken shape when they decide that it is time to begin writing. Bill reported that he purposely starts with a broad topic while Pam said that she looks for something "broad or ambiguous" or "something small that can grow and grow." As Bill explained, he doesn't like writing about what he already knows as that would be boring. Pam too expressed her resistance to knowing her topic and direction beforehand in terms of how boring it would be. Generally, Bill will do about four or five drafts as he works through the early parts of a paper, perhaps two to four pages, before he knows what he will write about. He and Pam allow for — and indeed expect — that their topic will change as they write. Pam explained: "I work by allowing the direction of the work to change if it needs to. . . . I have to allow things to go where they need to go." When I observed them writing, Pam spent considerable time planning and creating pre-texts before short bursts of transcribing while Bill wrote several different versions of an introduction and, with some cutting and pasting, was about ready to define his focus at the end of the hour. He reported that he depends heavily on seeing what he has written in order to find his focus, choose his content, and organize. Pam also noted that she needs to see chunks of what she has transcribed to see where the piece of discourse is taking her.

The other two writers who characterized themselves as multi-drafters, Karen and Cindy, both described a general tendency to plunge in before the topic is clear. Karen said that she can't visualize her arguments until she writes them out and generally writes and rewrites as she proceeds, but for writing tasks that she described as "formulaic" in that they are familiar because she has written similar pieces of discourse, she can write quickly and finish quickly — as she did with the writing task for this study. Since she had previously written the same kind of letter assigned in this study, she did not engage in the multi-drafting that would be more characteristic, she says, of her general composing behaviors. Cindy, the other self-described multi-drafter, almost completed the task in a single draft, though as she explained with short pieces, she can revert to her "journalistic mode" of writing, having been a working journalist for a number of years. For longer papers, such as those required in graduate courses, her descriptions sound much like those of Bill, Pam, and Karen. All of these writers, though, share the unifying characteristic of beginning to write before the task is well defined in their minds, unlike the one-drafters who do not write at that stage.

Preference for Limiting Options vs. Preference for Open-ended Exploring

Another consistent and clearly related difference between one- and multi-drafters is the difference in the quantity of options they will generate, from words and sentences to whole sections of a paper, and the way in which they will evaluate those options. As they wrote, all four of the one-drafters limited their options by generating several choices and then making a decision fairly quickly. There were numerous occasions in the think-aloud protocols of three of the four one-drafters in which they would stop, try another word, question a phrase, raise the possibility of another idea to include, and then make a quick decision. When Ted re-read one of his paragraphs, he saw a different direction that he might have taken that would perhaps be better, but he accepted what he had. ("That'll do here, OK . . . OK" he said to himself and moved on.) Nina, another one-drafter, generated no alternate options aloud as she wrote.

As is evident in this description of one-drafters, they exhibited none of the agonizing over possibilities that other writers experience, and they appear to be able to accept their choices quickly and move on. While observers may question whether limiting options in this manner cuts off further discovery and possibly better solutions or whether the internal debate goes on prior to transcribing, one-drafters are obviously efficient writers. They generate fewer choices, reach decisions more quickly, and do most or all of the decision-making before transcribing on paper. Thus, three of the four one-drafters finished the paper in the time allotted, and the fourth writer was almost finished. They can pace themselves fairly accurately too, giving me their estimates of how long it takes them to write papers of particular lengths. All four one-drafters describe themselves as incurable procrastinators who begin even long papers the night before they are due, allowing themselves about the right number of hours in which to transcribe their mental constructs onto paper. Nina explained that she makes choices quickly because she is always writing at the last minute under pressure and doesn't have time to consider more options. Another one-drafter offered a vivid description of the tension and stress that can be involved in these last minute, all-night sessions.

While they worry about whether they will finish on time, these one-drafters generally do. Contributing to their efficiency are two time-saving procedures involved as they get words on paper. Because most decisions are made before they commit words to paper, they do little or no scratching out and re-writing; and they do a minimum of re-reading both as they proceed and also when they are finished. The few changes I observed being made were either single words or a few short phrases, unlike the multi-drafters who rejected or scratched out whole sentences and paragraphs. As Nina wrote, she never re-read her developing text, though she reported that she does a little re-reading when she is finished with longer papers. The tinkering with words that she might do then, she says, is counterproductive because she rarely feels that she is improving the text with these changes. (Nina and the other one-drafters would probably be quite successful at the kind of "invisible writing" that has been investigated, that is, writing done under conditions in which writers cannot see what they are writing or scan as they progress. See Blau.)

In contrast to the one-drafters' limited options, quick decisions, few changes on paper and little or no re-reading, the multi-drafters were frequently observed generating and exploring many options, spending a long time in making their choices, and making frequent and large-scale changes on paper. Bill said that he produces large quantities of text because he needs to see it in order to see if he wants to retain it, unlike the one-drafters who exhibit little or no need to examine their developing text. Moreover, as Bill noted, the text he generates is also on occasion a heuristic for more text. As he writes, Bill engages in numerous revising tactics. He writes a sentence, stops to examine it by switching it around, going back to add clauses, or combining it with other text on the same page or a different sheet of paper. For the assigned writing task, he began with one sheet of paper, moved to another, tore off some of it and discarded it, and added part back to a previous sheet. At home when writing a longer paper, he will similarly engage in extensive cutting and pasting. In a somewhat different manner, Pam did not generate as many options on paper for this study. Instead, her protocol recorded various alternative plans and pre-texts that she would stop to explore verbally for five or ten minutes before transcribing anything. What she did write, though, was often heavily edited so that at the end of the hour, she, like Bill, had only progressed somewhat through an introductory paragraph of several sentences. Thus, while Bill had produced large amounts of text on paper that were later rejected after having been written, Pam spent more of her time generating and rejecting plans and pre-texts than crossing out transcriptions.

Writing is a more time-consuming task for these multi-drafters because they expect to produce many options and a large amount of text that will be discarded. Both Bill and Pam described general writing procedures in which they begin by freewriting, and, as they proceed, distilling from earlier drafts what will be used in later drafts. Both proceed incrementally, that is, by starting in and then starting again before finishing a whole draft. Both writers are used to rereading frequently, partly to locate what Pam called "key elements" that will be retained for later drafts and partly, as Bill explained, because the act of generating more options and exploring them causes him to lose track of where he is.

Because both Bill and Pam seem to be comfortable when working within an as-yet only partially focused text, it would be interesting to explore what has been termed their "tolerance for ambiguity," a trait defined as a person's ability to function calmly in a situation in which interpretation of all stimuli is not completely clear. (See Budner, and Frenkel-Brunswick.) People who have little or no tolerance for ambiguity perceive ambiguous situations as sources of psychological discomfort, and they may try to reach conclusions quickly rather than to take the time to consider all of the essential elements of an unclear situation. People with more tolerance for ambiguity enjoy being in ambiguous situations and tend to seek them out. The relevance here, of course, is the question of whether one-drafters will not begin until they have structured the task and will also move quickly to conclusions in part, at least, because of having some degree of intolerance for ambiguity. This might be a fruitful area for further research.

For those interested in the mental processes which accompany behaviors, another dimension to explore is the Myers-Briggs Type Indicator (MBTI), a measure of expressed preferences (i.e., not performance tasks) in four bipolar dimensions of personality. The work of George H. Jensen and John K. DiTiberio has indicated some relationships between the personality types identified by the MBTI and writing processes. Of particular interest here is that Bill, who had independently taken the MBTI for other reasons, reported that he scored highly in the dimensions of "extraversion" and "perceiving." Extraverts, say Jensen and DiTiberio, "often leap into tasks with little planning, then rely on trial and error to complete the task" (288), and they "often find freewriting a good method for developing ideas, for they think better when writing quickly, impulsively, and uncritically" (289). Perceivers, another type described by Jensen and DiTiberio, appear to share tendencies similar to those with a tolerance for ambiguity, for perceivers "are willing to leave the outer world unstructured. . . . Quickly made decisions narrow their field of vision" (295). Perceiving types tend to select broad topics for writing, like a wide range of alternatives, and always want to read one more book on the subject. Their revisions thus often need to be refocused (296). The similarities here to Bill's writing behaviors show us that while the MBTI is somewhat circular in that the scoring is a reflection of people's self-description, it can confirm (and perhaps clarify) the relationship of writing behaviors to more general human behaviors.

The Preference for Closure vs. Resistance to Closure

From these descriptions of one- and multi-drafters it is readily apparent that they differ in their need for closure. The one-drafters move quickly to decisions while composing, and they report that once they are done with a paper, they prefer not to look back at it, either immediately to re-read it or at some future time, to think about revising it. Ted explained that he generally is willing to do one rereading at the time of completing a paper and sometimes to make a few wording changes, but that is all. He shrugged off the possibility of doing even a second re-reading of any of his writing once it is done because he says he can't stand to look at it again. All of the one-drafters reported that they hardly, if ever, rewrite a paper. This distaste for returning to a completed text can be the source of problems for these one-drafters. Forced by a teacher in a graduate course who wanted first drafts one week and revisions the next week, Nina explained that she deliberately resorted to "writing a bad paper" for the first submission in order to submit her "real" draft as the "revised" paper. Writing a series of drafts is clearly harder for one-drafters such as Nina than we have yet acknowledged.

These one-drafters are as reluctant to start as they are impatient to finish. Although they tend to delay the drafting process, this does not apply to their preparation, which often starts well in advance and is the "interesting" or "enjoyable" part for them. With writing that produces few surprises or discoveries for any of them because the generative process precedes transcription, drafting on paper is more "tedious" (a word they frequently used during their interviews) than for other writers. Said Ted, "Writing is something I have to do, not something I want to do." Even Jackie, who allows for some revising while drafting in order to develop the details of her plan, reported that she has a hard time going back to revise a paper once it is completed. She, like the others, reported a sense of feeling the paper is over and done with. "Done, dead and done, done, finished, done," concluded another of these one-drafters.

On the other hand, the multi-drafters observed in this study explained that they are never done with a paper. They can easily and willingly go back to it or to keep writing indefinitely. Asked when they know they are finished, Bill and Pam explained that they never feel they are "done" with a piece of discourse, merely that they have to stop in order to meet a deadline. As Pam said, she never gets to a last draft and doesn't care about producing "neat packages." Understandably, she has trouble with conclusions and with "wrapping up" at the end of a piece of discourse. Asked how pervasive her redrafting is for all of her writing, Pam commented that she writes informal letters to parents and friends every day and is getting to the point that she doesn't rewrite these letters as much. Bill too noted that he fights against products and hates to finish. As a result, both Bill and Pam often fail to meet their deadlines. Cindy, bored by her "journalistic one-draft writing," expressed a strong desire to return to some of her previously completed papers in order to rewrite them.

Writer-Based vs. Reader-Based Early Drafts

One way of distinguishing the early drafts produced by the multi-drafters for this study from the drafts produced by the one-drafters is to draw upon Linda Flower's distinction between Writer-Based and Reader-Based prose. Writer-Based prose, explains Flower, is "verbal expression written by a writer to himself and for himself. It is the working of his own verbal thought. In its *structure*, Writer-Based prose reflects the associative, narrative path of the writer's own confrontation with her subject" (19–20). Reader-Based prose, on the other hand, is "a deliberate attempt to communicate something to a reader. To do that it creates a shared language and shared context between writer and reader. It also offers the reader an issue-oriented rhetorical structure rather than a replay of the writer's discovery process" (20). Although Flower acknowledges that Writer-Based prose is a "problem" that composition courses are designed to correct, she also affirms its usefulness as a search tool, a strategy for handling the difficulty of attending to multiple complex tasks simultaneously. Writer-Based prose needs to be revised into Reader-Based prose, but it can be effective as a "medium for thinking." And for the multi-drafters observed in this study, characterizing the initial drafts of two of the multi-drafters as Writer-Based helps to see how their early drafts differ from those of the one-drafters.

One feature of Writer-Based prose, as offered by Flower, is that it reflects the writer's method of searching by means of surveying what she knows, often in a narrative manner. Information tends to be structured as a narrative of the discovery process or as a survey of the data in the writer's mind. Reader-Based prose, on the other hand, restructures the information so that it is accessible to the reader. Both the protocols and the written drafts produced by the two confirmed multi-drafters, Bill and Pam, reveal this Writer-Based orientation as their initial way into writing. Bill very clearly began with a memory search through his own experience, made some brief notes. and then wrote a narrative as his first sentence in response to the request that he describe to an academic counselor the skills needed for his field: "I went through what must have been a million different majors before I wound up in English and it was actually my first choice." Pam spent the hour exploring the appropriateness of the term "skills."

In distinct contrast, all four of the one-drafters began by constructing a conceptual framework for the response they would write, most typically by defining a few categories or headings which would be the focus or main point of the paper. With a few words in mind that indicated his major points, Ted then moved on to ask himself who would be reading his response, what the context would be, and what format the writing would use. He moved quickly from a search for a point to considerations of how his audience would use his information. Similarly, Amy rather promptly chose a few terms, decided to herself that "that'll be the focus," and then said, "OK, I'm trying to get into a role here. I'm responding to someone who... This is not something they are going to give out to people. But they're going to read it and compile responses, put something together for themselves." She then began writing her draft and completed it within the hour. Asked what constraints and concerns she is most aware of when actually writing, Amy said that she is generally concerned with clarity for the reader. The point of contrast here is that the search process was both different in kind and longer for the multi-drafters. Initially, their time was spent discovering what they think about the subject, whereas the one-drafters chose a framework within a few minutes and moved on to orient their writing to their readers. Because the transformation or reworking of text comes later for the multi-drafters, rewriting is a necessary component of their writing. The standard bit of advice, about writing the introductory paragraph later, would be a necessary step for them but would not be a productive or appropriate strategy for one-drafters to try. For the one-drafters, the introductory paragraph is the appropriate starting point. In fact, given what they said about the necessity of knowing their focus beforehand, the introductory paragraph is not merely appropriate but necessary.

Because the early stages of a piece of writing are, for multi-drafters, so intricately bound up with mental searching, surveying, and discovering, the writing that is produced is not oriented to the reader. For their early drafts, Bill and Pam both acknowledged that their writing is not yet understandable to others. When Pam commented that in her early drafts, "the reader can't yet see where I'm going," she sighed over the difficulties this had caused in trying to work with her Master's thesis committee. If some writers' early drafts are so personal and so unlikely to be accessible to readers, it is worth speculating about how effective peer editing sessions could be for such multi-drafters who appear in classrooms with "rough drafts" as instructed.

Conclusions

One way to summarize the characteristics of one- and multi-drafters is to consider what they gain by being one-drafters and at what cost they gain these advantages. Clearly, one-drafters are efficient writers. This efficiency is achieved by mentally revising beforehand, by generating options verbally rather than on paper, by generating only a limited number of options before settling on one and getting on with the task, and by doing little or no re-reading. They are able to pace themselves and can probably perform comfortably in situations such as the workplace or in in-class writing where it is advantageous to produce first-draft, final-draft pieces of discourse. Their drafts are readily accessible to readers, and they can expend effort early on in polishing the text for greater clarity. But at what cost? One-drafters are obviously in danger of cutting themselves off from further exploration, from a richer field of discovery than is possible during the time in which they generate options. When they exhibit a willingness to settle on one of their options, they may thereby have eliminated the possibility of searching for a better one. In their impatience to move on, they may even settle on options they know could be improved on. Their impulse to write dwindles as these writers experience little or none of the excitement of discovery or exploration during writing. The interesting portion of a writing task, the struggle with text and sense of exploration, is largely completed when they begin to commit themselves to paper (or computer screen). Because they are less likely to enjoy writing, the task of starting is more likely to be put off to the last minute and to become a stressful situation, thus reinforcing their inclination not to re-read and their desire to be done and to put the paper behind them forever once they have finished. And it appears that it is as hard for true one-drafters to suspend the need for closure as it is for multi-drafters to reach quick decisions and push themselves rapidly toward closure.

Multi-drafters appear to be the flip side of the same coin. Their relative inefficiency causes them to miss deadlines, to create Writer-Based first drafts, to produce large quantities of text that is discarded, and to get lost in their own writing. They need to re-read and re-draft, and they probably appear at first glance to be poorer writers than one-drafters. But they are more likely to be writers who will plunge in eagerly, will write and re-write, and will use writing to explore widely and richly. They also are more likely to affirm the value of writing as a heuristic, the merits of freewriting, and the need for cutting and pasting of text. They may, if statistics are gathered, be the writers who benefit most from collaborative discussions such as those in writing labs with tutors. Their drafts are truly amenable to change and available for re-working.

Implications

Acknowledging the reality of one- and multi-drafting involves enlarging both our perspectives on revision and our instructional practices with students. In terms of what the reality of one-drafting and multi-drafting tells us about revision, it is apparent that we need to account for this diversity of revision behaviors as we construct a more detailed picture of revision. As Stephen Witte notes, "revising research that limits itself to examining changes in written text or drafts espouses a reductionist view of revising as a stage in a linear sequence of stages" ("Revising" 266). Revision can and does occur when writers set goals, create plans, and compose pre-text, as well as when they transcribe and re-draft after transcription. Revision can be triggered by cognitive activity alone and/or by interaction with text; and attitudes, preferences, and cognitive make-up play a role in when and how much a writer revises — or is willing to revise — a text.

Yet, while recognizing the many dimensions to be explored in understanding revision, we can also use this diversity as a source for helping students with different types of problems and concerns. For students who are one-drafters or have tendencies toward single drafting, we need to provide help in several areas. They'll have to learn to do more reviewing of written text both as they write and afterwards, in order to evaluate and revise. They will also need to be aware that they should have strategies that provide for more exploration and invention than they may presently allow themselves. While acknowledging their distaste for returning to a draft to open it up again, we also need to help them see how and when this can be productive. Moreover, we can provide assistance in helping one-drafters and other writers who cluster near that end of the spectrum recognize that sometimes they have a preference for choosing an option even after they recognize that it may not be the best one. When Tim, one of the one-drafters I observed, noted at one point in his protocol that he should take a different direction for one of his paragraphs but won't, he shows similarities to another writer, David, observed by Witte ("Pre-Text and Composing" 406), who is reluctant to spend more than fifteen seconds reworking a sentence in pre-text, even though he demonstrates the ability to evoke criteria that could lead to better formulations if he chose to stop and revise mentally (David typically does little revision of written text). This impatience, this need to keep moving along, that does not always allow for the production of good text, can obviously work against producing good text, and it is unlikely that such writers will either recognize or conquer the problem on their own. They may have snared themselves in their own vicious circles if their tendency to procrastinate puts them in a deadline crunch, which, in turn, does not afford them the luxury of time to consider new options. Such behaviors can become a composing habit so entrenched that it is no longer noticed.

As we work with one-drafters, we will also have to learn ourselves how to distinguish them from writers who see themselves as one-drafters because they are not inclined, for one reason or another, to expend more energy on drafting. Inertia, lack of motivation, lack of information about what multiple drafts can do, higher priorities for other tasks, and so on are not characteristic of true one-drafters, and we must be able to identify the writer who might take refuge behind a label of "one-drafter" from the writer who exhibits some or many of the characteristics of one-draft composing and who wants to become a better writer. For example, in our writing lab I have worked with students who think they are one-drafters because of assorted fears, anxieties, and misinformation. "But I have to get it right the first time," "My teachers never liked to see scratching out on the paper, even when we wrote in class," or "I hate making choices, so I go with what I have" are not the comments of true one-drafters.

With multiple-drafters we have other work to do. To become more efficient writers, they will need to become more proficient planners and creators of pre-text, though given their heavy dependence on seeing what they have written, they will probably still rely a great deal on reading and working with their transcribed text. They will also need to become more proficient at times at focusing on a topic quickly, recognizing the difficulties involved in agonizing endlessly over possibilities. In the words of a reviewer of this paper, they will have to learn when and how "to get on with it."

Besides assisting with these strategies, we can help students become more aware of their composing behaviors. We can assist multi-drafters in recognizing that they are not slow or inept writers but writers who may linger too long over making choices. For writers who have difficulty returning to a completed text in order to revise, we can relate the problem to the larger picture, an impatience with returning to any completed task. Granted, this is not a giant leap forward, but too many students are willing to throw in the towel with writing skills in particular without recognizing the link to their more general orientations to life. Similarly, the impatient writer who, like Ted, proclaims to have a virulent case of the "I-hate-to-write" syndrome may be a competent one-drafter (or have a preference for fewer drafts) who needs to see that it is the transcribing stage of writing that is the source of the impatience, procrastination, and irritation. On the other hand, writers more inclined to be multi-drafters need to recognize that their frustration, self-criticism, and/or low grades may be due to having readers intervene at too early a stage in the drafting. What I am suggesting here is that some writers unknowingly get themselves caught in linguistic traps. They think they are making generalizations about the whole act of "writing," that blanket term for all the processes involved, when they may well be voicing problems or attitudes about one or another of the processes. What is needed here is some assistance in helping students define their problems more precisely. To do this, classroom teachers can open conferences like a writing lab tutorial, by asking questions about the student's writing processes and difficulties.

In addition to individualizing our work with students, we can also look at our own teaching practices. When we offer classroom strategies and heuristics, we need to remind our students that it is likely that some will be very inappropriate for different students. Being unable to freewrite is not necessarily a sign of an inept writer. One writer's written text may be just as effective a heuristic for that writer as the planning sheets are for another writer. Beyond these strategies and acknowledgments, we have to examine how we talk about or teach composing processes. There is a very real danger in imposing a single, "ideal" composing style on students, as Jack Selzer found teachers attempting to do in his survey of the literature. Similarly, as Susan McLeod notes, teachers tend to teach their own composing behaviors in the classroom and are thus in danger either of imposing their redrafting approaches on students whose preference for revising prior to transcribing serves them well or of touting their one- or few-draft strategies to students who fare better when interacting with their transcribed text. Imposing personal preferences, observes McLeod, would put us in the peculiar position of trying to fix something that isn't broken. And there's enough of that going around as it is.

Works Cited

Axelrod, Rise B., and Charles R. Cooper. *The St. Martin's Guide to Writing*. New York: St. Martin's, 1985.

Bartholomae, David. "Against the Grain." Waldrep I:19–29.

Beach, Richard. "Self-Evaluation Strategies of Extensive Revisers and Nonrevisers." *College Composition and Communication* 27 (1976): 160–64.

Blau, Sheridan. "Invisible Writing: Investigating Cognitive Processes in Composition." *College Composition and Communication* 34 (1983): 297–312.

Bloom, Lynn Z. "How I Write." Waldrep I:31-37.

Bridwell, Lillian S. "Revising Strategies in Twelfth Grade Students' Transactional Writing." *Research in the Teaching of English* 14 (1980): 197–222.

Budner, S. "Intolerance of Ambiguity as a Personality Variable." *Journal of Personality* 30 (1962): 29–50.

Faigley, Lester, and Stephen Witte. "Analyzing Revision." *College Composition and Communication* 32 (1981): 400–14.

Flower, Linda. "Writer-Based Prose: A Cognitive Basis for Problems in Writing." *College English* 41 (1979): 19–37.

Flower, Linda, John R. Hayes, Linda Carey, Karen Shriver, and James Stratman. "Detection, Diagnosis, and the Strategies of Revision." *College Composition and Communication* 37 (1986): 16–55.

Freedman, Sarah Warshauer, Anne Haas Dyson, Linda Flower, and Wallace Chafe. *Research in Writing: Past, Present, and Future*. Technical Report No. 1. Center for the Study of Writing. Berkeley: University of California, 1987.

Frenkel-Brunswick, Else. "Intolerance of Ambiguity as an Emotional and Perceptual Personality Variable." *Journal of Personality* 18 (1949): 108–43.

Gere, Ann Ruggles. "Insights from the Blind: Composing without Revising." *Revising: New Essays for Teachers of Writing.* Ed. Ronald Sudol. Urbana, IL: ERIC/NCTE, 1982. 52–70.

Hairston, Maxine. "Different Products, Different Processes: A Theory about Writing." *College Composition and Communication* 37 (1986): 442–52.

Henley, Joan. "A Revisionist View of Revision." *Washington English Journal* 8.2 (1986): 5–7.

Jensen, George, and John DiTiberio. "Personality and Individual Writing Processes." *College Composition and Communication* 35 (1984): 285–300.

Lutz, William. "How I Write." Waldrep I:183–88.

McLeod, Susan. "The New Orthodoxy: Rethinking the Process Approach." *Freshman English News* 14.3 (1986): 16-21.

Murray, Patricia Y. "Doing Writing." Waldrep I:225–39.

Reid, Joy. "The Radical Outliner and the Radical Brainstormer: A Perspective on Composing Processes." *TESOL Quarterly* 18 (1985): 529–34.

Selzer, Jack. "Exploring Options in Composing." *College Composition and Communication* 35 (1984): 276–84.

Sommers, Nancy. "Revision Strategies of Student Writers and Experienced Adult Writers." *College Composition and Communication* 31 (1980): 378–88.

Waldrep, Tom, ed. *Writers on Writing. Vol. 1.* New York: Random House, 1985. 2 vols.

Witte, Stephen P. "Pre-Text and Composing." *College Composition and Communication* 38 (1987): 397–425.

———. "Revising, Composing Theory, and Research Design." *The Acquisition of Written Language: Response and Revision.* Ed. Sarah Warshauer Freedman. Norwood, NJ: Ablex, 1985. 250–84.

HELPING PEER WRITING GROUPS SUCCEED

Wendy Bishop

[Teaching English in the Two-Year College *15 (1988): 120-25.]*

Wendy Bishop, associate professor of English at Florida State University, is the author of several books, including Something Old, Something New: College Writing Teachers and Classroom Change *(1990),* Working Words: The Process of Creative Writing *(1992), and* The Subject Is Writing: Essays by Teachers and Students *(1993). Currently, she is at work on a new book,* Colors of a Different Horse: Rethinking Creative Writing, Theory, and Pedagogy.

More and more teachers are establishing writing workshops in their classrooms. In these settings, students work in small groups, collaborating on assignments, sharing works-in-progress, and offering feedback on one another's writing. But establishing and maintaining effective peer writing groups requires serious planning, training, and monitoring on the part of the teacher. Bishop explores causes for successes and failures of peer writing groups and offers practical advice for instructors. Her discussion complements the guidelines for peer reviewers in The Bedford Handbook.

An idealized but obtainable writing classroom is one in which students join together in collaborative work and develop their writing abilities in a non-threatening environment. This article explores that concept by reviewing research and by offering a plan for preparing and training students.

Research on Peer Writing Groups

The value of using peer writing groups as a teaching method has at times been overrated and has sometimes been oversimplified. In general, collaborative peer writing groups do benefit the student. The claims for the efficacy of the method are many and various.[1] Beaven, discussing peer evaluation, claims that the collaborative method allows students to develop audience awareness, to check their perceptions of reality, to strengthen their interpersonal skill, and to take risks; the entire process results in improvement in writing and students' ability to revise. Hawkins agrees that students strengthen their interpersonal skills and risk-taking or creative abilities.

Bruffee ("Brooklyn Plan") found that peer tutors and tutees at work in a collaborative environment deal with higher order concerns such as paper focus and development. Researchers like Danis ("Peer Response Groups"), who found that 75 percent of the students in her study correctly identified both major and minor writing problems, and Gere, who felt that student responses did deal with meaning, seem to support Bruffee's contention that students in peer groups do more than simply act as proofreaders of each other's work. Recent research by Gere and Abbott has reaffirmed the power of peer writing groups to stay focused on discussions about writing. Their research also shows that group discussions where teachers are present are significantly different from those where teachers are absent.

Because collaborative learning can be time consuming (Beaven; Abercrombie) for those writing about this method, it is agreed that some training of group members is necessary with emphasis on student-centered discussion rather than teacher/lecture dominated classrooms.

Danis ("Weaving the Web of Meaning") found that students are not always sure of their group role, aren't able to stand back from their own writing, don't know what they want to know, and have a reluctance to offer critical comments. Flynn stated that students lacked critical ability and attributed this to students' tendencies to supply missing information in a paper in order to make sense out of what they were reading. The fact that students need to develop a critical vocabulary with which to discuss their works is supported in Bruffee's articles ('Writing and Reading," "Collaborative Learning"). Clearly, there is a need to introduce writing students to the vocabulary and terminology of the composition community.

When peer groups are fully developed, the method is exciting and rewarding for both student and teacher, but when peer group interactions are underdeveloped or break down, the method is discouraging and group work all too often feels like a matter of luck.

The teacher needs a way to begin to sort out group interaction patterns. George distinguishes among task-oriented, leaderless, and dysfunctional groups. Teachers need to be aware of the attributes of successful groups and learn what can be done to move groups from failure to success, for doing so will enable composition teachers to feel more comfortable using peer writing groups.

Following is a list of causes for group failure or success with the names of researchers or writers who touch on these concerns when discussing peer writing groups.

Causes for Peer Writing Group Failure

- Too much or too little leadership (Hawkins; Elbow; George)
- Poor attendance or participation or preparation of some students, leading to resentment between members (Hawkins; Flynn)
- Unclear group goals; group doesn't value work or works too quickly (Johnson & Johnson *Learning*; Hawkins; George)
- Group doesn't feel confident of group members' expertise or members are afraid to offer criticism (Lagana; Danis; Flynn)
- Group doesn't understand new role of instructor (Ziv)
- Group never develops adequate vocabulary for discussing writing (Danis; Bruffee "Writing and Reading," "Collaborative Learning")
- Group fails to record suggestions or to make changes based on members' suggestions (Ziv; George)

Causes for Peer Writing Group Success

- Group successfully involves all members (Johnson & Johnson *Learning*; Hawkins; Elbow)
- Group works to clarify goals and assignments (Johnson & Johnson; Elbow; Danis)
- Group develops a common vocabulary for discussing writing (Beaven; Bruffee "Writing and Reading," "Collaborative Learning"; Danis)
- Group learns to identify major writing problems such as organization, tone, and focus, as well as minor writing problems such as spelling errors, and so on (Bruffee "Brooklyn Plan"; Danis; Gere; Gere and Abbott)
- Group learns to value group work and to see instructor as a resource which the group can call on freely (Rogers; Danis; Flynn)

Preparing for Peer Writing Groups

Most writers are in agreement: students and teachers need preparation and training for successful peer group work.

Students can work together to discuss readings, to complete exercises, to explore writing invention strategies, and to help members with forming very early drafts.

Teachers who want to use peer writing groups in their classroom should plan ahead and read widely in this area. A teacher should ask several questions:

- Do I understand the theory behind peer writing groups?
- Do I have a clear use for this method in my classroom?
- What are my goals for students when using this method?

The well prepared teacher will acquaint students with concepts of collaborative learning through prepared handouts, class discussion, and continual monitoring of group work. Students need to develop a group identity. To function well, group members must be present, which requires a class attendance policy. I use groups 50 to 75 percent of my available class periods. This percentage allows my students to develop a group identity yet regroup into a class on a regular basis in order to maintain a class identity also.

Classroom communities are formed by the school registrar, academic departments, and the enrolling student. Teachers may divide a class into sets of four to five students, or students may start working collaboratively in pairs and then pairs may be joined. First week diagnostic writings may be used to organize groups with a balance of strong and weak writers. Students may rate themselves on matters such as ability to lead, to help, to take risks, and so on, and groups may be balanced with a member strong in each area. In addition, I group by gender and age.

Groups work best when they are balanced, focused, and comfortable. I let groups work together for at least four sessions, and I rarely leave a group together for an entire semester.

Sometimes a teacher needs to intervene and change group membership (placing an overly dominant member in another, more challenging group, and so on), but often it is wiser to let the group itself solve group problems. Ideally, groups staying together over a long period develop a strong group identity and sense of shared community. Equally, groups that change membership, partially or wholly, are often revitalized and ready to undertake new course challenges with greater enthusiasm.

Choosing a group name can help members identify with their new community. Ordering and clarifying group members' roles, such as monitor and historian and general member, also assures that group work will be carried on in an orderly manner. Group projects should be clearly articulated in handout form or as directions on the chalkboard, and group work should be real work, contributing to each member's writing development.

Reporting on what the group accomplished each session, in the form of historian's notes in a group folder, provides useful artifacts for group self-evaluation and teacher evaluation of the group session.

Training Peer Writing Groups

Peer writing groups need training in two areas: group roles and writing critiquing. A monitor acts as the group caretaker, making sure each member gets time to respond to writing and time to have writing discussed. The historian records group discussions, insuring continuity from session to session. When groups are first formed, handouts to elected members, as well as a handout detailing the responsibilities of a member in general — attendance, support, sharing, and so on — can speed the training in this area.

Teaching each other to talk about writing can be initiated by the teacher, reinforced by the class text, and nurtured by whole class discussion, but it will be brought to fruition in the group itself as members learn to improve their writing. The teacher may begin by teaching the class necessary terminology (concerning writing process and writing analysis) and by training writers and readers to work together through such activities as role playing and reviewing sample essays. Groups can work to answer set questions or can learn to develop their own critical concerns for papers. If composition terms such as prewriting, drafting, revising, focus, organization, and tone are introduced in class discussion, show up on group handouts, are reinforced in peer writing group discussions and recorded in group minutes, such terms will soon become part of the peer group's working vocabulary.

Monitoring Peer Writing Groups

Sometimes the best thing teachers can do is to listen and watch the groups quietly and unobtrusively; sometimes teachers must participate in groups to insure that each group is working efficiently. Teachers should keep records of the groups (a personal journal is a good place to start); teachers can monitor groups by sight (regularly noting what is happening in each by direct observation); by sound (listening to tape recordings of groups at a later date); by direct contact (visits to and participation in groups); and by reviewing group or individual artifacts (learning logs, group weekly reports, group self-evaluations, and questionnaires).

Evaluating Peer Writing Groups

Teachers can determine if students are attaining the goals set for group work. Group folders when examined tell a story of good attendance, completed work, and enlarged understanding. Self-evaluation, on the part of students and teacher, can chronicle success with the method and pinpoint areas for future work and improvement. And most important, gains in individual student writing can be assessed.[2]

Measurements of student growth in collaborative learning techniques and writing in general can be accomplished with pre and post testing in the following areas:

- pre and post written descriptions of what students feel can be accomplished in writing groups
- pre and post written descriptions of student's writing process
- pre and post writing apprehension tests
- pre and post essay samples

Teachers who hope to use peer writing groups should prepare for success. Teachers must become researchers in the classroom. They must plan for the class, train group members, monitor and evaluate them, and, the next semester, begin the process over, refining and developing talents as a group facilitator based on personal observations. These teachers will be willing to experiment, to redefine group failures as steps in a larger process that leads to success, and to have realistic expectations for this holistic teaching method. Before long, those expectations will be met and hopefully surpassed.

Notes

[1] For an in-depth review of research on peer writing groups, see Bishop.

[2] For detailed discussions of methods for evaluating peer writing groups, see Cooper; McAndrew; and Weiner.

Works Cited

Abercrombie, Minnie Louie Johnson. *Aims and Techniques of Group Teaching.* 3rd ed. London: Soc. for Research into Higher Educ. Ltd., 1974.

Beaven, Mary H. "Individualized Goal Setting, Self-Evaluation, and Peer Evaluation." *Evaluating Writing: Describing, Measuring, Judging.* Ed. Charles R. Cooper and Lee Odell. Urbana: NCTE, 1977. 135–56.

Bishop, Wendy. "Research, Theory, and Pedagogy of Writing Peer Groups: An Annotated Bibliography." 1987. Forthcoming in ERIC.

Bruffee, Kenneth A. "The Brooklyn Plan: Attaining Intellectual Growth through Peer Group Tutoring." *Liberal Education* 64 (1978): 447–69.

_____. "Writing and Reading as Collaborative or Social Acts." *The Writer's Mind: Writing as a Mode of Thinking.* Ed. Janet L. Hays and others. Urbana: NCTE, 1983.

_____. "Collaborative Learning and the Conversation of Mankind." *College English* 46 (1984): 635–52.

Cooper, Charles. "Measuring Growth in Writing." *English Journal* 64 (1975): 111–20.

Danis, Francine. "Peer-Response Groups in a College Writing Workshop: Students' Suggestions for Revising Compositions." *DAI* 41 (1980): 5008A–5009A.

_____. "Weaving the Web of Meaning: Interactions Patterns in Peer-Response Groups." Paper presented at CCCC, San Francisco, March 1982. ERIC ED 214 202.

Elbow, Peter. *Writing with Power.* New York: Oxford UP, 1981.

Flynn, Elizabeth A. "Freedom, Restraint and Peer Group Interaction." Paper presented at CCCC, San Francisco, March 1982. ERIC ED 216 365.

George, Diana. "Writing with Peer Groups in Composition." *College Composition and Communication* 35 (1984): 320–36.

Gere, Anne Ruggles. "Students' Oral Response to Written Composition." Seattle: Washington, 1982. ERIC ED 229 781.

Gere, Anne Ruggles, and Robert D. Abbott. "Talking about Writing: The Language of Writing Groups." *Research in the Teaching of English* 19 (1985): 362–81.

Hawkins, Thom. *Group Inquiry Techniques in Teaching Writing.* Urbana: NCTE, 1976.

Johnson, David W., and Roger T. Johnson. *Learning Together and Alone: Cooperation, Competition, and Individualization.* Englewood Cliffs: Prentice, 1975.

_____. "Cooperative Small-Group Learning." *Curriculum Report* 14 (1984): 1–6. ERIC ED 249 625.

Lagana, Jean Remaly. "The Development, Implementation, and Evaluation of a Model for Teaching Composition Which Utilizes Individualized Learning and Peer Grouping." *DAI* 33 (1973): 4063A.

McAndrew, Donald A. "Measuring Holistic and Syntactic Quality in a Semester Writing Course." *The English Record* 29 (1978): 16–17.

Rogers, Carl R. *On Becoming a Person.* Boston: Houghton, 1961.

Weiner, Harvey S. "Collaborative Learning in the Classroom: A Guide to Evaluation." *College English* 48 (1986): 52–61.

Ziv, Nina D. "Peer Groups in the Composition Classroom: A Case Study." Paper presented at CCCC, Detroit, March 1983. ERIC ED 229 799.

WORD PROCESSING

THE ACCUMULATIVE RHETORIC OF WORD PROCESSING
Ronald A. Sudol

[College English 53 (1991): 920–33.]

Ronald A. Sudol is professor of rhetoric at Oakland University. His articles have appeared in such publications as College English, College Composition and Communication, Quarterly Journal of Speech, *and* The Writing Instructor.

In this article, Sudol examines the effects of word processing on student writing and concludes that the technology itself does not promote more effec-

tive revisions; rather, it offers an efficient means for writers who choose to revise. Sudol argues that students use and appreciate word processing because it allows them to easily generate and accumulate text. However, such generation and accumulation are not necessarily desirable. Sudol describes three harmful effects of word processing for inexperienced writers and suggests ways of countering those effects. Sudol describes how word processing can help in the "gestation" phase of writing, and instructors can find even more suggestions in The Bedford Handbook's *discussion of "Composing and Revising on a Word Processor."*

Writers disciplined by the arduous steps of mechanical composing are quick to affirm the liberating effects of word processing. For James Fallows, the ease of word processing is "satisfying to the soul." In this electronic prelapsarian state "each maimed and misconceived passage can be made to vanish instantly, by the word or by the paragraph, leaving a pristine green field on which to make the next attempt" (84). Just like that. Addressing novice writers, William Zinsser promises "you will really enjoy writing on a word processor when you see your sentences growing in strength, literally before your eyes, as you get rid of the fat. . . . With its help I cut hundreds of unnecessary words and didn't replace them" (100). These testimonials are typical responses of experienced writers set free from the material limits of composing with an outmoded technology. However, there is nothing in the new technology itself that helps them detect maimed and misconceived passages or distinguish between fat and fiber. Nor does digital writing provide the gumption to cut or the skill to rewrite. But it does provide an efficient means for executing decisions experienced writers have already formed mentally.

Students in college composition courses do not as easily recognize the maimed, misconceived, and corpulent. And even when they do, they lack these writers' ruthless integrity and determination to cut and start over. That kind of enthusiasm comes from having developed habits of composing in an environment of mechanical inscription. Thus, professional writers and composition instructors who learned writing with pencils and typewriters keenly admire the word processor's capacity for clean, revisionary cutting and replacing. Many of today's students composing with word processors, however, have bypassed the rigors of mechanical inscription and have missed opportunities to internalize some of the specific habits of composing that physical limits impose on an emerging text. So it is not surprising that students experience word processing primarily for its capacity to generate and accumulate. They struggle mainly to create text, not revise it. The technology encourages adding, not cutting. Even before the advent of the new technology, we emphasized invention and process in recognition of their need to accumulate the material substance of writing.

These differences in the way practiced and novice writers experience word processing should guide how we go about integrating word processing in composition classes. Researchers have conducted study after study comparing the written products of students composing with and without computers (Hawisher). The word processing groups in these studies generally reveal less than impressive revising skill or motivation — a finding that should not be surprising when we recognize the extent to which our notions of revising have been shaped by the experience of writers seasoned by the rigors of mechanical print. In the absence of the kind of well-honed judgment and practiced skill cultivated by such experience, student writers enjoy little more revising advantage from word processing than they do from an eraser. For them, ease and volume of production are the principal advantages of writing with a word processor — its basic feature, the one that most directly shapes meaning and its communication. I propose here to explore this accumulative rhetoric of word processing as it is experienced by student writers — what it is, how it may affect language and thought, what use can be made of it in teaching.

The Perils of Accumulation

The ease of production made possible by word processing really opens the spigot for any loquacious individual with a message to convey or some other urge to communicate. Several years ago in a "Dear Abby" column, "Nervous in Delaware" described a sister-in-law whose newsy Christmas letters to relatives, friends, old schoolmates, and casual acquaintances included gossip about the entire extended family — legal problems, children gone astray, separations, affairs, divorces, jilted lovers, the works. To make matters worse, the sister-in-law had received a word processor from her husband for Christmas, and "Nervous in Delaware" was afraid the letters would now be even longer. "How can we stop her'?" she asked Abby, anticipating a voluminous, uncensored, and embarrassing Christmas message. Like other educational Christmas gifts, the new word processor is a toy before it becomes a tool.

This story of the verbal excess feared by Abby's correspondent reveals one apparent effect on language and thought of the new technology in an early stage of its evolution, before it becomes a tool of genuine communication. The ease of production leads to voluminous output, everything in the writer's mind gushing without the monitoring and regulation that a slower, more laborious writing process imposes. Given the constraints of time they feel in their lives, students using word processors quickly come to appreciate their efficiencies of production — of creating and adding. Professional writers, in contrast, appreciate the efficiency of revision — of cutting and polishing. Indeed, our taste for clarity and brevity in prose presupposes the writer's ability and willingness to engage in the slow revision of what is unclear and verbose. The image of revision as polishing reinforces the idea that improvement comes only with hard effort applied to recalcitrant material. In physical terms, polishing means removing by force whatever is not shiny and smooth.

When word processing seems to make the material less recalcitrant, distinctive stylistic effects begin to appear — the absence of polished brevity, for example, that Russell Baker pokes fun at in one of his columns. The joke in the column is that Baker switches from mechanical writing to word processing halfway through his essay. He begins in the plain style fostered by the quill pen technology of his colonial forebears.

> For a long time after going into the writing business, I wrote. It was hard to do. That was before the word processor was invented. Whenever writers got together, it was whine, whine, whine. How hard writing was. How they wished they had gone into dry cleaning, stonecutting, anything less toilsome than writing.

He eventually overcomes his timidity about new technology, abandons the quaintness of ordinary writing, and switches to processing words:

It is so easy, not to mention so much fun — listen, folks, I have just switched right here at the start of this very paragraph you are reading — right there I switched from the old typewriter (talk about goose-quill pen days!) to my word processor, which is clicking away so quietly and causing me so little effort that I don't think I'll ever want to stop this sentence because — well, why should you want to stop a sentence when you're really well launched into the thing — the sentence, I mean — and it's so easy just to keep her rolling right along and never stop since, anyhow, once you stop, you are going to have to start another sentence, right? — which means coming up with another idea. (vi: 14)

The giddy and loose processed language sounds like inner speech even though we perceive it in written form. This semi-orality accounts, in part, for the apparent ease of production. The writer feels unimpeded by the rhetorical constraints of either writing or speaking. Baker's persona, for example, becomes oblivious to such constraints as audience and message, preferring not to have to think of a new idea in order to justify a new sentence. The sister-in-law of "Nervous in Delaware" will publish a written document produced with the ease and volume of an oral message but without the face-to-face inducement to tact that normally attends oral discourse. In his book *Electric Language: A Philosophical Study of Word Processing*, Michael Heim considers the effects of this semi-orality on what he calls the "formulation" of writing:

> [W]ord processing reclaims something of the direct flow of oral discourse. But, as a consequence, a certain step is bypassed in composition. Though the step of considering audience belongs more properly to rhetoric and communication, it might be added to the general erosion of the gestation period of formulation, the long inner ferment a writer must endure when working with physically resistant materials. While there is in word processing a closer approximation to oral-aural language, paradoxically, a certain "forgetting the situation" occurs in which any writing, as written and not spoken, takes place. (209)

The freedom and immediacy of this kind of writing can lead to what users of computerized telecommunications call "flaming" — "the tendency to write messages on the computer so directly that the usual norms of civility and politeness fall away." Some researchers have found that electronic mail promotes a confrontational style because, although moving with the speed of an oral telephone message, it is received and read as a written document at a later time without the small talk that would normally accompany conversation (Heim 209).

Few students aspire to the status of fussy professional writers like Baker and Zinsser, but a good many of them will become professionals whose work requires them to write. Gerald Grow has noted some effects of word processing on this breed of competent writers. There is, for example, the editing trap in which writers exhaust themselves by tinkering with microscopic editorial changes but neglect global revisions of thought and content. Other professionals who write may embrace the opportunities for collaborative writing facilitated by computers, but their aim is inclusive rather than interactive. Word processed collaboration can be additive rather than dialogic, and the prose that emerges may be schizophrenic. Other writers may rely on boilerplate passages easily transported from other documents. Accumulating language becomes more important (perhaps because easier to do) than placing it in context. Indeed, the small screen confounds context by preventing some writers from grasping a sense of the whole. For others the finished appearance of printouts prevents them from distinguishing between clean copy and completed copy. For professionals who write, then, word processing may invite production more enticingly than communication. The speed of this production is achieved by short-circuiting steps in a slower process. One might as well try to speed up the wine-making process: to do so will require losses and trade-offs. Through the rapid digital processing of words we lose some of the barriers and hazards that encouraged economy of style, clear thinking, and focused presentation.

The thrilling anguish of wholesale rewriting is part of the writer's lore. Our intuition that multiple drafts improve the quality of a document is so powerful we have incorporated multiple drafting into our pedagogy, sometimes even building it into the syllabus. Get something down first — fix it later. In contrast, the physical circumstances of, say, a blind writer writing at a conventional keyboard will compel her to get it right the first time — revising before composing in order to avoid the inconvenience of finding someone to read preliminary drafts out loud (Gere). But most of us compose with the assumption that it is all quite temporary. A polite way of criticizing a piece of writing is to say it is fine as a first draft.

These assumptions about a progressively fixable text when carried over to the environment of infinite revision in word processing can lead to highly unstable communication — language unanchored by fixed principles, undirected by firm purpose, and possibly empty of meaning. To illustrate this point Heim quotes former Secretary of the Treasury Donald T. Regan testifying before Congress on tax reform proposals: "It's in the word processor. It can be changed" (212). This flexibility may be admirable from a practical and political standpoint, but from a philosophical and pedagogical standpoint it raises doubts about the stability of meanings and principles to which mechanical inscription has accustomed us. Such notions as "it is written" and "get it in writing" seem undermined. The easy interchange of words, facts, and ideas so smoothly assisted by word processing reinforces the notion that language is merely a code for transmitting information from sender to receiver.

In summary, then, the accumulative power of word processing brings with it three potentially harmful effects for inexperienced writers: (1) *overproduction*, the tendency to include voluminous data indiscriminately as well as emotions and reactions unregulated by rhetorical and interpersonal constraints; (2) *a flabby and verbose style* resulting from the semi-orality of video text where writing seems to be a transcription of speech; and (3) *a diminution of meaning and a trivialization of content*, where meanings destabilized by easy changes become subject to sudden reversal by whatever wind is blowing. Underlying all of these effects is the way the technology encourages us to postpone hard decisions. We add rather than decide. With all the messiness, limitation, slowness, and multiple drafting of mechanical inscription, when we used pencils and typewriters we tried to get it right, if not the first time then at least the second or third. A reluctance to have to make changes may have made writers more thoughtful when they committed words to paper, though other writers trying to do the same thing would think themselves into writer's block.

Indeed, the premier advantage of the accumulative power of word processing for students, it seems, is the way in which it helps unblock the flow of language not only at the point of production but also through the sense of context and collaboration encouraged by the public character of its video display. Moreover, the protean quality of electronic display relieves much anxiety about error, and the clean appearance of printed products fosters a sense of pride and accomplishment. For these benefits the new technology has provided the material means for bringing the process movement in the teaching of writing to its conclusion. That is, the notion of "process" is so intrinsically linked with the technology itself, now that writing with word processors is becoming normative, we may no longer need to organize composition classes by an explicit process model. It remains to be seen, then, what might be done about the perils of accumulation, of processing gone amok.

Compensatory Disciplines

In *Electric Language* Heim bases his critique of word processing on the various ways western philosophy has responded to transformations in communications technology. From orality to manuscripts to print to electronics each transformation has altered the way we manipulate symbols, thus determining our construction of meaning. The mechanical and linear modes of inscription characteristic of the Platonic tradition fostered contemplation, the stability of written forms. and the solitude of the culture of books. Word processing, on the other hand, fosters information exchange, the instability of the direct flow of oral discourse, and the culture of information management. Writing becomes digitized, fragmented, abstract, and writer-based. The psychic drama of the writer struggling with the resistant materials of writing, and forming language and thought as a result, succumbs to the easy flow and strict rationality of digital writing.

Heim's argument is complex but convincing, not only for its richly textured reading of the relevant texts (especially Plato, Heidegger, and Ong) but also for how it helps account for the different ways experienced and novice writers employ the revising capability of word processing. Experienced writers have been able to import the struggle of formulation, through which they have practiced and learned composing in the past, into the environment of digital writing. For other writers, compensatory disciplines are indicated. I want to suggest here some compensatory disciplines worth considering as part of a program integrating word processing into the writing class. They are presented in two groups, one as part of the gestation or formulation of meaning in writing, the other as part of the explicit teaching of style. In each case, the compensatory disciplines take advantage of the accumulative power of word processing by encouraging extensive writing practice in highly structured forms but taking place in the background of specific writing assignments. In general, the suggestions are adaptations of some quite venerable, if old-fashioned, notions about the teaching of writing.

Gestation

In a passage quoted earlier Heim observes how word processing has precipitated "the general erosion of the gestation period of formulation, the long inner ferment a writer must endure when working with physically resistant materials" (209). It is surprising how rarely one sees the word "gestation" used in connection with the writing process, for it seems superior to its more popular alternatives. "Invention" and "discovery," for example, rather dauntingly suggest writers need to have episodes of insight. Because of their emphasis on problem-solving, "brainstorming" and "heuristics" may be limiting for some writers. "Freewriting" and "prewriting" sound vague, and "nutshelling" and "clustering" sound silly. But as a metaphorical concept, "gestation" carries with it a number of useful entailments. Unlike any of the alternatives, it situates formulation firmly in time. It is organic, requires nurturing, and proceeds inexorably according to some incipient design. Its outcome is not so much a solution to a problem or a bit of information as something formed.

Whatever name we apply to this kind of preliminary activity, over the last twenty years the scope of writing instruction has expanded to include attention to it: the writer's own background and development, the rhetorical situation or social context of a given assignment, predictions about how a message will be received by particular audiences under particular circumstances, the accumulation and forming of the language through which meaning will be made and conveyed. Applied to student writing this expansion has tended to divide writing into separate components or stages — preliminary work followed by composing followed by revising, editing, and publishing. Although teachers and theorists emphasize the importance of writers moving recursively among these stages — and for experienced writers word processing greatly facilitates recursiveness — students often bypass the critical struggles of composing/revising in the middle of the process and submit edited prewriting instead of fully composed pieces. The knowledge that publishing is just a few keystrokes away provides a powerful inducement to jump ahead.

Various forms of invention (or whatever) have evolved in the era of manuscript and print technology to help writers gather and focus information and ideas outside the confines of sentences and paragraphs targeted toward an audience. But the protean environment of word processing may offer the user of such techniques excessive freedom, to the extent that the preliminary activity takes on a life of its own. In applying Peter Elbow's concept of "writing with power," for example, students are called upon to write freely and then subject what they have written to rigorous criticism, a dynamic and often effective way of getting something written. Inexperienced writers are more productive on the creative and expressive side of the formula but come up short on the critical and analytical side. Writing with electric power accentuates this tendency by encouraging transcription rather than formulation, getting down inner speech rather than making meaning. It is true, of course. that the initial transcription can subsequently be shaped and formulated, but this sequencing separates content from form and reinforces the notion that form can be merely applied to content.

"Forming" and "making meaning" in the pedagogies described and advocated by Ann Berthoff (in *Forming/Thinking/Writing,* for example) show promise of being worthy compensatory disciplines for digital writing because they resist the easy separation of form and content. By imposing various dialectical tensions on the flow of inner speech, teachers can help student writers formulate rather than merely transcribe the flow. Placed within such boundaries, the accumulative rhetoric of word processing can be turned to advantage by allowing focused writing practice to occur extensively and repetitively, entailing what Berthoff calls "consciousness of consciousness." The teacher, "by means of a careful sequence of lessons or assignments, can assure that the students are conscious of their minds in action, can develop their language by means of exercising deliberate choice"

("Is Teaching Still Possible?" 747). The accumulative rhetoric of word processing makes it easier to bring criticism to the front end of the composing process. With mechanical inscription teachers had good reason to delay criticism because they did not want to short circuit the flow. But the flow in word processing is more resilient and stands a better chance of surviving the stress of early critical attention.

Another way to nurture formulation early in the process is to distinguish between files and documents by treating files as writer-based accumulations and documents as reader-based drafts. Separate files, or individual components of a single file, may be used for accumulating focused writing about different aspects of the rhetorical situation — audience, purpose, persona, context, design, and the broad outlines of the message. Such files are expressive in mode but analytical in purpose. They create a context within which the document itself will be drafted, and they also serve as a point of reference for the critical and constructive intervention of peers or instructor. Indeed, the effect is to introduce criticism even before the writer starts drafting in a document file. Formulation precedes drafting, much as it does when experienced writers mull over these elements of a writing situation in their minds before they actually start writing. When they do start writing, they discover that bits and pieces have already been formed. Electric files make a visible, recoverable record of these insights of short-term memory.

"Formulation" implies structure, outlining, and planning. Implicit in the process view of composition is that the formal structure of a piece of writing emerges from the very act of composing. This is in contrast to the more classical conception of pre-existing ideal structures to facilitate discovery. As teachers we may acknowledge the heuristic value of outlines but avoid prescribing them to students. We promote a more romantic psychology that form follows function because we don't want students to be stuck with a structure that, after the effort of composing, turns out to be inappropriate. Of course, being stuck with an inappropriate structure is a legacy of mechanical inscription. The flexibility of word processing, however, makes it relatively easy to rearrange the parts of something written under a false outline. The spaceless environment of word processing removes much of the physical limitation of outlines. The writer can anticipate and enter proposed headings, for example, without having to anticipate the length of text belonging there.

So as a compensatory discipline it may be useful to move a notch or two toward more exact planning, toward recognizing that the effort of finding a form or making a design has value as part of the gestation of a piece of writing. This is not to endorse computerized outliners, however. As application programs designed for experienced writers already fully in touch with the material content of their subjects, these serve little instructional purpose for students, whose academic writings usually commit them to the tentativeness of learning and discovering.

The point of compensatory disciplines is to help students internalize the gestation process, to discover how they can bring their own intellects and personalities to bear on the making of meaning. Rather than using the accumulative power of word processing to produce more papers or longer ones, students should do more pedagogically directed writing in the process of formulation — by confronting dialectical tensions and working within modest structural and rhetorical constraints.

Style

Perhaps because it has been unfairly associated with the derelict pedagogies overthrown by the process movement, the direct teaching of style in composition classes has languished. The prevailing assumption seems to be that there is not a strong enough connection between teaching style as a subject and students' own writings to justify the time spent on such work. Furthermore, what we define as style can go to extremes, too easily drifting into effete literary analysis or lapsing into the particulars of usage and mechanics. The latter is especially susceptible to the utilitarian aims of modern communications in the form of electronic style checkers, which reduce style to a set of publishing conventions.

Indeed, by threatening to displace the teaching of style altogether, the advent of style checkers promises to reopen the debate over whether and how style should be taught. At their worst the narrow prescriptions, arch commentaries, and smarmy personalities of style checkers make easy targets for ridicule, but they can also be valuable adjuncts to a word processing program, especially for experienced writers. The stylistic conventions they check for are the same ones endorsed by textbooks and applied by editors, so there is little point in quibbling about their content. The quibble is with how student writers should use them. Applied post hoc to student writing, style check programs help erode the process of formulation by encouraging students to submit prewriting to the checker's cleansing authority. A quick write followed by a quick fix. Such a procedure downgrades style to the level of spelling where checking programs quite appropriately enforce standard conventions. Intervention late in the process carries no liabilities where spelling is concerned. A misspelled word corrected only moments before publication will have had no adverse effect on the work in progress. But matters of style — verbalization, predication, nominalization, agency, diction, syntactic structure, and the like — are so bound to meanings and messages that the writer who delays critical attention to them until the last moment fails to allow for the interplay of language and thought along the way and misses opportunities for fresh insights and perspectives.

A typical style checker is programmed to pounce on uses of the passive voice (as, for example, it would on this very sentence). A student who considers her writing finished except for style checking might eliminate a passive construction identified by the checker. (These programs assume the user is capable of executing appropriate changes or overriding the checker's admonitions. For my sentence I would override on the grounds that the active agent "programmers" is immaterial, and the sentence has all the action it needs in the infinitive "to pounce.") As is often the case in matters of style, however, this student's potential change from passive to active involves more than the verb. The writer needs to figure out who is doing what to whom, the kind of fundamental question that, while better asked late than never, could more usefully have been asked closer to the point of formulation. The whole sentence may have to be rearranged. Some of it may disappear altogether. At this late stage the student is looking for correction, not formulation. But making a correction in one sentence sends ripples to others nearby. Turning the sentence around in order to get the active agent up front may break the original connections between sentences and interrupt the sequence of nouns and predicates in the paragraph. So fixing one problem creates a mess somewhere else, and the checker will not help clean it up. It has lunged onward in search of the next solecism.

The objection to style checkers, then, is not what they prescribe nor how experienced writers use them but how these programs separate form and content for student writers by treating all levels of stylistic lapses in the same way — as correctable errors having little effect on the shaping of discourse. The solution is certainly not to avoid using these programs. In applying accepted standards they perform adequately and can be expected to improve in the future. Furthermore, they can initiate reformulation of a text — if only belatedly — and they have some instructional value if students apply the checkers' queries and messages to their next writing task. But to compensate for the easy accumulation of unformulated writing in the first place, students should possess the skill and judgment to connect language and thought at the point of composing. The best way to acquire such skill and judgment is by cultivating a lifelong habit of extensive and attentive reading. Within the limits of a ten- or fifteen-week semester, however, the next best thing is to provide for direct instruction. extensive practice, and immediate application. In the environment of high-tech writing this may seem a retrograde pedagogy, but the accumulative power of the technology itself makes it necessary and effective.

As a canon of rhetoric, style cycles in and out of favor according to the philosophical climate of the times. It is out of favor when prevailing attitudes place nature over nurture, or, in linguistic terms, acquiring language over learning it. Ian Pringle succinctly summarizes prevailing opinion in a commentary on one of the few books that attempts to teach style explicitly, Joseph Williams' *Style: Ten Lessons in Clarity and Grace:*

> If students are to produce literate writing, they will do so primarily on the basis of what they have acquired, and what they acquire will come to them not through the explicit study of style (or for that matter grammar), but from "comprehensible input," from reading good, relevant models, not because they are prescribed, but because they are interesting, intellectually engaging, exciting, new. (94)

And if our intuitions as teachers fail to convince us this is true, Pringle adds, "I know of no empirical studies which demonstrate that teaching about style at this level of explicitness can improve style" (95). As such, the criticism is fair. Williams is frankly prescriptive and treats style from the point of view of intended readers trying to make sense of fully formed messages that have been unclearly or pretentiously expressed. He advocates a particular style to improve the quality of written expression in government and the professions. His lessons may or may not improve style, but within the framework of the accumulative tendency of digital writing the question may not be whether teaching style improves style but whether it improves writing.

Although Williams' approach is to repair what is already written, one finds on nearly every page of his first eight lessons ways to improve writing at the point of formulation. Stylistic guidelines introduce tensions as valuable there as at the point of editing and clarifying for an audience. When Fallows uses the words "maimed" and "misconceived" to describe what goes wrong with sentences, he reveals the two levels at which style influences writing. A sentence may be maimed stylistically, but when we apply stylistic guidelines to fix it we discover it is misconceived as well, or even as a consequence.

Two representative sources provide a sound pedagogical basis for bringing the explicit teaching of style into the world of electric writing: Winston Weathers' "Teaching Style: A Possible Anatomy" and Frank J. D'Angelo's "Imitation and Style," both reprinted in the second edition of Tate and Corbett's *The Writing Teacher's Sourcebook*. Weathers identifies three obligatory tasks for the instructor: making style "significant and relevant," revealing it as "measurable and viable," and making it "believable and real." He recommends a variety of exercises designed to compel students to write according to specific directions or following prescribed models in order to discover the principles of style underlying all writing. He argues that such work constitutes the kind of practice needed to perfect any skill. D'Angelo argues on behalf of the paradox that students become more original by engaging in imitation, which, by expanding the student's repertoire of alternative modes of expression, acquires generative power. Following Francis Christensen's generative rhetoric of the sentence, D'Angelo analyzes some samples to illustrate the mutual influence of syntactic structure and rhetorical aims that can be learned or acquired — through imitation.

The debate about whether the kind of work advocated by Weathers, D'Angelo, and others constitutes empty learning or useful acquisition of language skills will certainly continue, but the advent of word processing should to some extent mollify the critics of explicit teaching of style. One objection is that stylistic exercises are busywork — mechanical, fatiguing, cumbersome, time consuming, and unengaging. In the context of the accumulative power of word processing, however, such exercises can be accomplished quickly and easily. As files rather than documents, directed writing practice can also be done extensively and intensively. If students can use text files to work out such metacognitive concerns as audience and purpose, why not practice alternative modes of expression there as well? Is imitating various argumentative styles in a text file any less valuable than rehearsing a line of argument there? Given the right teaching and learning environment, practicing stylistic principles can be as engaging as writing essays, perhaps more so since it is easier. In the huge volume of writing the text files of a word processing system can accommodate, there ought to be ample room for writing practice in forms other than the drafts of compositions. To do original composing to the extent possible in word processing would tax any writer.

The classroom technology that allows overhead projection of the computer's video display also makes it easier to engage students in the application and effect of stylistic principles. Rather than referring to static textbook examples, instructors can display composing in progress by entering text with a voice-over disclosure of what a writer thinks about while composing, think-aloud protocols for instructional rather than research purposes. In the context of a representative writing situation the instructor can illustrate in real-time projection the alternative ways a writer might solve the problems of forming sentences, clarifying ideas, finding words — producing and inviting further alternatives and commentary on the effects of various stylistic choices and their relationship to all the other choices a writer makes. Since students face similar problems when they write, they should find this kind of classroom use of word processing relevant and instructive.

Another criticism of direct teaching of style is that students do not easily transfer whatever they may learn about style to their own writing. Certainly there will always be a gap between learning and acquisition of this sort, but word processing can narrow the gap in a couple of ways. First, with word processing a student can be immersed in intensive writing practice. This active experience compensates to some degree for lack of extensive reading in the past, providing a sense of the forms and rhythms of the language and helping students more easily recognize and repair maimed or misconceived passages. Second, once they have been trained to do so, students can use the pliability of electric text to multiply options within the borders of a text-in-progress, a technique Zinsser recommends in his early word processing guidebook (101). The physical limits of print technology have bestowed negative conceptions of revising by emphasizing the detection of error and its deletion and replacement. An alternative principle of addition in word processing is more positive. Here the writer suspends judgment and uses the computer's short-term memory to produce multiple options. With options made visible, the writer is able to judge comparatively (Sudol 334–35). Directed practice in style — variations of syntactic structure, for example — combined with the capacity to open a text and multiply options at the very point of composing or revising should hasten students along the path from learning to acquiring.

Discussion of the explicit teaching of style and the additive principle of word processed composing leads inevitably to Christensen's generative rhetoric of the sentence and, by extension, sentence combining, for these are the only contemporary alternatives to classical precepts of imitation. Although both modern methods are based on solid research and good thinking, they have suffered in application and testing. The classroom materials derived from this research have been either cumbersome or misused, and testing of them has been narrowly behaviorist in its focus on discrete treatments. Attempting to quantify syntactic fluency, syntactic maturity, and t-units has accentuated the vaguest and least valuable aspects of these materials, and the whole Christensen/sentence combining enterprise is in decline. And this is unfortunate because many of us find so much merit in the possibility of "buckling down to the hard work of making a difference in the student's understanding and manipulation of language" as Christensen puts it. We would avoid the composition course where "we do not really teach our captive charges to write better — we merely *expect* them to" (25). The Christensen and sentence combining methods provide specific ways for us to do more than expect good writing as long as producing good writing — and not some particular change in writing style — remains our principal aim.

Advocating Christensen or sentence combining in the context of computer applications to writing implies that I am promoting computer programs to teach these methods. Quite the contrary. Any computer program, no matter how friendly and interactive, that attempts to give instruction on levels of generality, the cumulative sentence, and kernel combining would merely replicate in an even more superficial way the kinds of exercises aimed at changing style, the kinds of materials we have already had. In order to plumb the rich depths of contemporary rhetorics of the sentence, students need to discover alternative ways of thinking about how sentences get put together.

Exercises in the mechanics of doing so play a role, to be sure, but reflexive thinking can best be cultivated by analyzing and imitating samples, judging multiple alternatives in context, and applying generative principles in text files as part of the background of making meaning through writing.

Such work parallels the process of formulation, where students tease meaning out of dialectical tensions and philosophical questioning. What teachers need to do is design and sequence writing tasks that take advantage of the vast capacity for accumulation in word processing, but also to keep the accumulation in the background, in the files as part of the gestation of documents. This point brings me to a brink where I should go no further, for I have made bedfellows of Ann Berthoff and sentence combining. But such is the power of the new technology.

Works Cited

Baker, Russell. "The Processing Process." *New York Times* 10 Feb. 1985. Rpt. in *Textfiles: A Rhetoric for Word Processing.* Ronald A. Sudol. San Diego: Harcourt, 1987. 2–3.

Berthoff, Ann E. *Forming/Thinking/Writing: The Composing Imagination.* Rochelle Park, NJ: Hayden, 1978.

———. "Is Teaching Still Possible? Writing, Meaning, and Higher Order Reasoning." *College English* 46 (1984): 743–55.

Christensen, Francis, and Bonniejean Christensen. *Notes toward a New Rhetoric: 9 Essays for Teachers.* 2nd ed. New York: Harper, 1978.

D'Angelo, Frank J. "Imitation and Style." *College Composition and Communication* 24 (1973): 283–90.

Elbow, Peter. *Writing with Power.* New York: Oxford UP, 1981.

Fallows, James. "Toys: Living with a Computer." *Atlantic* July 1982: 84–91.

Gere, Anne Ruggles. "Insights from the Blind: Composing without Revising." *Revising: New Essays for Teachers of Writing.* Ed. Ronald A. Sudol. Urbana: NCTE, 1982. 52–70.

Grow, Gerald. "Lessons from the Computer Writing Problems of Professionals." *College Composition and Communication* 39 (1988): 217–20.

Hawisher, Gail E. "Research and Recommendations for Computers." *Critical Perspectives on Computers and Composition Instruction.* Ed. Gail E. Hawisher and Cynthia Selfe. New York: Teachers College, 1989. 44–69.

Heim, Michael. *Electric Language: A Philosophical Study of Word Processing.* New Haven: Yale UP, 1987.

Pringle, Ian. "Why Teach Style? A Review Essay." *College Composition and Communication* 34 (1983): 91–98.

Sudol, Ronald A. "Applied Word Processing: Notes on Authority, Responsibility, and Revision in a Workshop Model." *College Composition and Communication* 36 (1985): 331–35.

Tate, Gary, and Edward P. J. Corbett. eds. *The Writing Teacher's Sourcebook.* 2nd ed. New York: Oxford UP, 1988.

Weathers, Winston. "Teaching Style: A Possible Anatomy." *College Composition and Communication* 21 (1970): 144–49.

Williams, Joseph M. *Style: Ten Lessons in Clarity and Grace.* Glenview, IL.: Scott, 1985.

Zinsser, William. *Writing with a Word Processor.* New York: Harper, 1983.

THE STYLE-CHECKER AS TONIC, NOT TRANQUILIZER

Louie Crew

[Journal of Advanced Composition 8 (1988): 66–70.]

Louie Crew, associate professor in the Department of Academic Founda-tions at Rutgers University in Newark, has written several books on religion and on gay studies and is the author of a style checker called Styled *(1986).*

The idea for this article came to Crew while he was working on a com-puter-assisted analysis of style in Dickens's language of protest. To demon-strate the usefulness of style checkers, Crew takes two prose passages by leading composition scholars, runs them through Grammatik, *and revises them in light of the computer's advice. The revisions are tighter and much easier to read.*

D. N. Dobrin argues that style-checkers, like Valium, distract writers from "thoughts [that] make sense or are worth saying" (30). I argue that checkers quicken writers precisely when they already have an idea worth saying, worth saying well.

When you have annotated a hundred student papers and pick up a journal like *CCC* to recharge your professional battery, which version would you prefer?

Version 1
Finally, a cognitive process model of the sort presented here is both a theory and a distillation of data. It represents in our case the range of processes observed in detailed data on fourteen writers, whose behavior, we should add, invalidated a number of other "reasonable" models we constructed along the way. Because such a model is data-based rather than speculative, it reflects behavior of indi-vidual writers rather than of the world as a whole. However, this means that it can offer us a concrete working hypothesis which can be tested against new evidence.

Version 2
We observed fourteen writers and theorized about their cognitive processes. Their behavior invalidated several "reasonable" models we constructed along the way. We derived our final model from data, not from our speculation. Our model reflects how these fourteen write, not how others do. Now we can test a concrete hypothesis against new evidence.

GRAMMATIK, a computer program, helped me revise the original, writ-ten by Linda Flower, John R. Hayes, Linda Carey, Karen Shriver, and James Stratman (21). GRAMMATIK checked three forms of the verb *to be.* As Joseph M. Williams counsels, I replaced *to be* with strong verbs; and I compressed.

If you prefer the original, stop now. I have nothing more to say to you.

I contend that those who prefer the original value jargon more than clarity. I acknowledge that the original "sounds" more academic. These overtones help to explain why *academic* functions as a pejorative in the lexicon of many intelligent citizens.

The clearest prose often requires prodigious amounts of time. After GRAMMATIK focused my strategies, I spent twenty minutes on this one paragraph. At that rate, I would require 100 minutes per printed page. I would need sixty-one hours and forty minutes to revise their entire thirty-seven-page article. I think their research deserves that much extra effort.

I did not expect the computer to think for me. GRAMMATIK flagged *to be* only because I told it to. The 987 items in its master list do not include forms of *to be;* my own drafting file does. My file also flags nominalizations, which I negotiate more cautiously. Nominalizations often contain action which I can put back into verbs.

GRAMMATIK allows writers to harness it for their own strategies. In files for special occasions, users specify what and how GRAMMATIK should annotate. GRAMMATIK can both describe and prescribe. For example, another of my files prompts GRAMMATIK to identify a few problems specific to my Chinese students of English; users can expand it. I have created still other files: one to monitor emphatic forms to gauge possible stridency; two more to monitor first- and second-person pronouns; another to count conjunctives, subordinators, and transitionals.

I would never load all these files at one time. I use my drafting file mainly for a preliminary draft. I use the modified master file in the final stages, usually after I have checked spelling. Some files best analyze completed texts, not drafts.

Ron Bauer observes in his manual for GRAMMATIK that "if GRAMMATIK II has a flaw, it's versatility." Ironically, the versatility that I most respect cost GRAMMATIK points when *PC Magazine* reviewed it:

> It is loaded with options that make your document analysis reflect the writing you do. Unfortunately, many users are not in a position to handle the responsibility this imposes — partly because entering phrases is so difficult and partly because they buy a program to follow its rules, not write their own. (Raskin 192)

Some teachers buy new software also to "follow its rules, not write their own." Some prefer a pacifier to a prod. Many have no precise goals for their syntax, and some who do know the kind of syntax they want still refuse to learn all but the simplest computer terminology required to make a program serve them.

A colleague once complained that she finds GRAMMATIK "too mechanical," yet she admitted she does not know how to edit out those features that annoy her or how to add others. She could learn these skills quickly enough from GRAMMATIK's manual but has chosen not to. She has learned neither to use the windows of her word processor nor how to add her students' names to her spelling checker. The few hours it took me to explore GRAMMATIK's options have paid off plentifully. GRAMMATIK has helped me with most of my essays published during the past four years.

I control GRAMMATIK; it does not control me. Before the second version supplied one, I wrote my own program to prepare my own dictionaries for GRAMMATIK. Because I do not write to avoid potholes, I welcome GRAMMATIK as a way to negotiate potholes purposefully after my ideas have momentum.

I do not ask GRAMMATIK to advise me every time I use *principle* or *principal,* but I do need it to prompt me for *discrete* and *discreet.* A reviewer found that I misspelled one of these in a book, and I shall not burn again for the same offense. I also ask GRAMMATIK to flag -*ize* words as well as my pet Latin — for example, *e.g., viz., et al.* I do not let it compare my prose to that of Hemingway, "The Gettysburg Address," or an insurance policy, although GRAMMATIK will do so. I leave glib gimmicks to readers of *PC Magazine,* to whom Raskin appeals.

I delete few of these functions, however. Occasionally, GRAMMATIK shocks me with evidence that I said something I thought I *never* say. Although I rarely wash out my mouth with soap, I carefully launder my manuscript.

All writers need mechanical help; that's why they buy a faster printer, a more versatile word processor, a larger thesaurus or spelling checker, a ram disk for more speed. I welcome help with the mechanical matters. Several phrases make us wordy; certain phrases mark us as pretentious. At times, I even ask GRAMMATIK to scold me with advice I deplore, as when it tells me I've begun a sentence with a coordinate conjunction or I've split an infinitive. Sometimes I ignore the prompt; sometimes I heed it, especially when I know an editor holds those prejudices, and I don't want to miss the publication's readers.

Stephen Reid and Gilbert Findlay warn against style-checkers:

> In order to meet the second condition, that the analysis should lead to direct improvements in a revision, even the measurements which do correlate with essay quality need to be used with some caution. Research which studies the relationship of revised essays to holistic scores should provide more accurate guidance in this area, but our initial findings suggest some starting points. Reducing the percentage of abstract words and spelling errors can be accomplished directly and with measurable effect on essay quality; however, students should not expect that direct changes in word length, sentence length, or readability will improve an essay. The correlation of average word length to quality, for instance, cannot be directly addressed in revision. Substitution of lexical units for the mere sake of length would change the data and practice in writing which increase active vocabulary; a student could meaningfully raise his or her average word length from the low mean (4.3) to the high limit of 5.0. The fact that these measurements can be improved only indirectly suggests the overall importance of scribal fluency. Since sentence length, word length, and readability are all measurements of scribal fluency, the results of this study seem to suggest that more classroom time should be spent on improving scribal behavior than on practicing those discrete grammatical and stylistic elements which do not correlate significantly with essay quality. (22–23)

Abandon style; it does not earn good grades. How's that for nurture?

Reid and Findlay retreat as they prescribe. I used my drafting file to revise their prose:

> A student who expects to improve prose must apply our analysis cautiously. Even when our counts correlate with good grades, further research needs to define precisely how the correlation occurs. For example, we found that grades go up when students spell correctly and use few abstract words; but one cannot exchange a word for another as mechanically as one can alter spelling. Perhaps students should read more if they expect to use words effectively. Then possibly they can raise average word length from the low mean (4.3) to the high limit of 5.0. Sentence length, word length, and readability measure scribal fluency. Classes need to improve these rather than practice with those discrete grammatical and stylistic elements which do not correlate significantly with grades.

Stripped of academese, Reid and Findlay sound silly. They conclude only that students should read more, and only to win higher grades. For their own prose style, Reid and Findlay either did not consult, did not understand, or did not agree with their own style-checker: Writer's Workbench.

Recently, I sent one of my own programs to several who have published about computers and composition. Some reported to me that I had sent them a bugged copy. When the program requested a carriage return, it did so with the symbol "<>," as do dozens of computer programs and manuals. These respondents, however, entered the "less-than" and "greater-than" keys, and the program bombed. I improved the program when I expunged this jargon, but I also realized new vulnerabilities for those who depend on software chosen by persons who demand absolute simplicity.

The computer is a Rolls Royce for which much software provides only a hand crank. I, too, welcome easier starts, but I prefer to crank by hand rather than to use the Rolls for its ash trays. I also suspect that only when writers and teachers learn to program will we get truly sophisticated software for writers.

My dean at the University of Wisconsin once asked me, "Oh, word processing — you can teach that in about three hours, can't you?" Yes, with the same rewards as when you spend your first three hours with Shakespeare at a production of *Hamlet.* It profits little to know how to move a block of text if you have no good strategy for the move.

Works Cited

Bauer, Ron. *GRAMMATIK II: The Writing Analyst.* Manual for GRAMMATIK II. N.p.: Reference Software, 1986.

Dobrin, D. N. "Style Analyzers Once More." *Computers and Composition* 3.3 (1986): 22–32.

Flower, Linda, et al. "Detection, Diagnosis, and the Strategies of Revision." *College Composition and Communication* 37 (1986): 16–55.

Raskin, Robin. "The Quest for Style." *PC Magazine* May 1986: 187–91.

Reid, Stephen, and Gilbert Findlay. "Writer's Workbench Analysis of Holistically Scored Essays." *Computers and Composition* 3.2 (1986): 6–32.

Williams, Joseph M. *Style: Ten Lessons in Clarity and Grace.* 2nd ed. Scott, 1985.

RESPONDING TO STUDENT WRITING

RESPONDING TO STUDENT WRITING

Nancy Sommers

[College Composition and Communication 33 (1982): 148–56.]

(For biographical information, see page 86.)

This article reports on research Sommers conducted to examine how instructors' responses to student writing actually contributed to subsequent revisions. Her findings, supported with specific examples and extensive observations, revealed discouraging tendencies in teacher responses, and her advice can help teachers avoid these problems. Teachers can apply Sommers's advice to avoid the tendency to attach responses that are too general by following The Bedford Handbook*'s guidelines for peer reviewers (pp. 42–43), which offer a ready-made list of features to consider while responding to student writing, encouraging text-specific comments that reinforce particular revision strategies.*

More than any other enterprise in the teaching of writing, responding to and commenting on student writing consumes the largest proportion of our time. Most teachers estimate that it takes them at least 20 to 40 minutes to comment on an individual student paper, and those 20 to 40 minutes times 20 students per class, times 8 papers. more or less, during the course of a semester add up to an enormous amount of time. With so much time and energy directed to a single activity, it is important for us to understand the nature of the enterprise. For it seems, paradoxically enough, that although commenting on student writing is the most widely used method for responding to student writing, it is the least understood. We do not know in any definitive way what constitutes thoughtful commentary or what effect, if any, our comments have on helping our students become more effective writers.

Theoretically, at least, we know that we comment on our students' writing for the same reasons professional editors comment on the work of professional writers or for the same reasons we ask our colleagues to read and respond to our own writing. As writers we need and want thoughtful commentary to show us when we have communicated our ideas and when not, raising questions from a reader's point of view that may not have occurred to us as writers. We want to know if our writing has communicated our intended meaning and, if not, what questions or discrepancies our reader sees that we, as writers, are blind to.

In commenting on our students' writing, however. we have an additional pedagogical purpose. As teachers, we know that most students find it difficult to imagine a reader's response in advance, and to use such responses as a guide in composing. Thus, we comment on student writing to dramatize the presence of a reader, to help our students to become that questioning reader themselves, because, ultimately, we believe that becoming such a reader will help them to evaluate what they have written and develop control over their writing.[1]

Even more specifically, however. we comment on student writing because we believe that it is necessary for us to offer assistance to student writers when they are in the process of composing a text, rather than after the text has been completed. Comments create the motive for doing something different in the next draft; thoughtful comments create the motive for revising. Without comments from their teachers or from their peers, student writers will revise in a consistently narrow and predictable way. Without comments from readers, students assume that their writing has communicated their meaning and perceive no need for revising the substance of their text.[2]

Yet as much as we as informed professionals believe in the soundness of this approach to responding to student writing, we also realize that we don't know how our theory squares with teachers' actual practice — do teachers comment and students revise as the theory predicts they should?

For the past year my colleagues, Lil Brannon, Cyril Knoblach, and I have been researching this problem, attempting to discover not only what messages teachers give their students through their comments, but also what determines which of these comments the students choose to use or to ignore when revising. Our research has been entirely focused on comments teachers write to motivate revisions. We have studied the commenting styles of thirty-five teachers at New York University and the University of Oklahoma, studying the comments these teachers wrote on first and second drafts, and interviewing a representative number of these teachers and their students. All teachers also commented on the same set of three student essays. As an additional reference point one of the student essays was typed into the computer that had been programmed with the "Writer's Workbench," a package of twenty-three programs developed by Bell Laboratories to help computers and writers work together to improve a text rapidly. Within a few minutes, the computer delivered editorial comments on the student's text, identifying all spelling and punctuation errors, isolating problems with wordy or misused phrases, and suggesting alternatives, offering a stylistic analysis of sentence types, sentence beginnings, and sentence lengths, and finally, giving our freshman essay a Kincaid readability score of eighth-grade which, as the computer program informed us, "is a low score for this type of document." The sharp contrast between the teachers' comments and those of the computer highlighted how arbitrary and idiosyncratic most of our teachers' comments are. Besides, the calm, reasonable language of the computer provided quite a contrast to the hostility and mean-spiritedness of most of the teachers' comments.

The first finding from our research on styles of commenting is that *teachers' comments can take students' attention away from their own purposes in writing a particular text and focus that attention on the teachers' purpose in commenting*. The teacher appropriates the text from the student by confusing the student's purpose in writing the text with her own purpose in commenting. Students make the changes the teacher wants rather than those that the student perceives are necessary, since the teachers' concerns imposed on the text create the reasons for the subsequent changes. We have all heard our perplexed students say to us when confused by our comments: "I don't understand how you want me to change this" or "Tell me what you want me to do." In the beginning of the process there was the writer, her words, and her desire to communicate her ideas. But after the comments of the teacher are imposed on the first or second draft, the student's attention dramatically shifts from "This is what I want to say," to "This is what *you* the teacher are asking me to do."

This appropriation of the text by the teacher happens particularly when teachers identify errors in usage, diction, and style in a first draft and ask students to correct these errors when they revise; such comments give the student an impression of the importance of these errors that is all out of proportion to how they should view these errors at this point in the process. The comments create the concern that these "accidents of discourse" need to be attended to before the meaning of the text is attended to.

It would not be so bad if students were only commanded to correct errors, but, more often than not, students are given contradictory messages; they are commanded to edit a sentence to avoid an error or to condense a sentence to achieve greater brevity of style, and then told in the margins that the particular paragraph needs to be more specific or to be

developed more. An example of this problem can be seen in the following
student paragraph:

> *wordy- be precise*   *which Sunday?*   *Comma needed*
>
> Every year on 'one Sunday in the middle of January tens of millions of people
>
> *word choice*
>
> cancel all events, plans or work to watch the Super Bowl. This audience in-
>
> *Be specific -*
> *wordy*   *what reasons?*
>
> cludes little boys and girls, old people, and housewives and men. Many reasons
>
> *and why*
>
> have been given to explain why the Super Bowl has become so popular that
>
> *what spots?*
>
> *awkward*
>
> commercial spots cost up to $100,000.00. One explanation is that people like
>
> *another what?*   *spelling*
>
> to take sides and root for a team. Another is that some people like the pagentry
>
> and excitement of the event. These reasons alone, however, do not explain a
>
> *too*
> *colloquial*
>
> happening as big as the Super Bowl.

(margin left, bottom-to-top): you need to do more research.

(margin right, bottom-to-top): This paragraph needs to be expanded in order to be more interesting to the reader.

In commenting on this draft, the teacher has shown the student how to
edit the sentences, but then commands the student to expand the paragraph in order to make it more interesting to a reader. The interlinear
comments and the marginal comments represent two separate tasks for
this student; the interlinear comments encourage the student to see the
text as a fixed piece, frozen in time, that just needs some editing. The
marginal comments, however, suggest that the meaning of the text is not
fixed, but rather that the student still needs to develop the meaning by
doing some more research. Students are commanded to edit and develop
at the same time; the remarkable contradiction of developing a paragraph
after editing the sentences in it represents the confusion we encountered
in our teachers' commenting styles. These different signals given to students, to edit and develop, to condense and elaborate, represent also the
failure of teachers' comments to direct genuine revision of a text as a
whole.

Moreover, the comments are worded in such a way that it is difficult for
students to know what is the most important problem in the text and what
problems are of lesser importance. No scale of concerns is offered to a
student with the result that a comment about spelling or a comment about
an awkward sentence is given weight equal to a comment about organization or logic. The comment that seemed to represent this problem best was
one teacher's command to his student: "Check your commas and semicolons and think more about what you are thinking about." The language of
the comments makes it difficult for a student to sort out and decide what
is most important and what is least important.

When the teacher appropriates the text for the student in this way,
students are encouraged to see their writing as a series of parts — words,

sentences, paragraphs — and not as a whole discourse. The comments encourage students to believe that their first drafts are finished drafts, not invention drafts, and that all they need to do is patch and polish their writing. That is, teachers' comments do not provide their students with an inherent reason for revising the structure and meaning of their texts, since the comments suggest to students that the meaning of their text is already there, finished, produced, and all that is necessary is a better word or phrase. The processes of revising, editing, and proofreading are collapsed and reduced to a single trivial activity, and the students' misunderstanding of the revision process as a rewording activity is reinforced by their teachers' comments.

It is possible, and it quite often happens, that students follow every comment and fix their texts appropriately as requested. but their texts are not improved substantially, or, even worse, their revised drafts are inferior to their previous drafts. Since the teachers' comments take the students' attention away from their own original purposes, students concentrate more, as I have noted, on what the teachers commanded them to do than on what they are trying to say. Sometimes students do not understand the purpose behind their teachers' comments and take these comments very literally. At other times students understand the comments, but the teacher has misread the text and the comments, unfortunately, are not applicable. For instance, we repeatedly saw comments in which teachers commanded students to reduce and condense what was written, when in fact what the text really needed at this stage was to be expanded in conception and scope.

The process of revising always involves a risk. But, too often revision becomes a balancing act for students in which they make the changes that are requested but do not take the risk of changing anything that was not commented on, even if the students sense that other changes are needed. A more effective text does not often evolve from such changes alone, yet the student does not want to take the chance of reducing a finished, albeit inadequate, paragraph to chaos — to fragments — in order to rebuild it, if such changes have not been requested by the teacher.

The second finding from our study is that *most teachers' comments are not text-specific and could be interchanged, rubber-stamped, from text to text*. The comments are not anchored in the particulars of the students' texts, but rather are a series of vague directives that are not text-specific. Students are commanded to "think more about [their] audience, avoid colloquial language, avoid the passive, avoid prepositions at the end of sentences or conjunctions at the beginning of sentences, be clear, be specific, be precise, but above all, think more about what [they] are thinking about." The comments on the following student paragraph illustrate this problem:

Begin by telling your reader what you are going to write about

↓ In the sixties it was drugs, in the seventies it was rock and roll. Now in the

avoid "one of the"

eighties, <u>one of the</u> most controversial subjects is nuclear power. The United

elaborate

States is <u>in great need of its own</u> source of power. Because of environmental-

think more →

ists, coal is not an acceptable source of energy. Solar and wind power have not

be specific   avoid "it seems"

yet received the technology necessary to use them. It seems that nuclear power

about your reader

is the only feasible means right now for obtaining self-sufficient power. How-

ever, too large a percentage of the population are against nuclear power claim-

be precise

ing it is unsafe. With as many problems as the United States is having con-

Thesis sentence needed.

cerning energy, it seems a shame that the public is so quick to "can" a very

feasible means of power. Nuclear energy should not be given up on, but rather,

more nuclear plants should be built.

One could easily remove all the comments from this paragraph and rubber-stamp them on another student text, and they would make as much or as little sense on the second text as they do here.

We have observed an overwhelming similarity in the generalities and abstract commands given to students. There seems to be among teachers an accepted, albeit unwritten canon for commenting on student texts. This uniform code of commands, requests, and pleadings demonstrates that the teacher holds a license for vagueness while the student is commanded to be specific. The students we interviewed admitted to having a great difficulty with these vague directives. The students stated that when a teacher writes in the margins or as an end comment, "choose precise language," or "think more about your audience," revising becomes a guessing game. In effect, the teacher is saying to the student, "Somewhere in this paper is imprecise language or lack of awareness of an audience and you must find it." The problem presented by these vague commands is compounded for the students when they are not offered any strategies for carrying out these commands. Students are told that they have done something wrong and that there is something in their text that needs to be fixed before the text is acceptable. But to tell students that they have done something wrong is not to tell them what to do about it. In order to offer a useful revision strategy to a student, the teacher must anchor that strategy in the specifics of the student's text. For instance, to tell our student, the author of the above paragraph, "to be specific," or "to elaborate," does not show our student what questions the reader has about the meaning of the text, or what breaks in logic exist, that could be resolved if the writer supplied information; nor is the student shown how to achieve the desired specificity.

Instead of offering strategies, the teachers offer what is interpreted by students as rules for composing; the comments suggest to students that writing is just a matter of following the rules. Indeed, the teachers seem to impose a series of abstract rules about written products even when some of them are not appropriate for the specific text the student is creating.[3] For instance, the student author of our sample paragraph presented above is commanded to follow the conventional rules for writing a five paragraph essay — to begin the introductory paragraph by telling his reader what he is going to say and to end the paragraph with a thesis sentence. Somehow these abstract rules about what five-paragraph products should look like do not seem applicable to the problems this student must confront when revising, nor are the rules specific strategies he could use when revising. There are many inchoate ideas ready to be exploited in this paragraph, but the rules do not help the student to take stock of his (or her) ideas and use the opportunity he has, during revision, to develop those ideas.

The problem here is a confusion of process and product; what one has to say about the process is different from what one has to say about the product. Teachers who use this method of commenting are formulating their comments as if these drafts were finished drafts and were not going to be revised. Their commenting vocabularies have not been adapted to revision and they comment on first drafts as if they were justifying a grade or as if the first draft were the final draft.

Our summary finding, therefore, from this research on styles of commenting is that the news from the classroom is not good. For the most part, teachers do not respond to student writing with the kind of thoughtful commentary which will help students to engage with the issues they are writing about or which will help them think about their purposes and goals in writing a specific text. In defense of our teachers, however, they told us that responding to student writing was rarely stressed in their teacher-training or in writing workshops; they had been trained in various prewriting techniques, in constructing assignments, and in evaluating papers for grades, but rarely in the process of reading a student text for meaning or in offering commentary to motivate revision. The problem is that most of us as teachers of writing have been trained to read and interpret literary texts for meaning, but, unfortunately, we have not been trained to act upon the same set of assumptions in reading student texts as we follow in reading literary texts.[4] Thus, we read student texts with biases about what the writer should have said or about what he or she should have written, and our biases determine how we will comprehend the text. We read with our preconceptions and preoccupations, expecting to find errors, and the result is that we find errors and misread our students' texts.[5] We find what we look for; instead of reading and responding to the meaning of a text, we correct our students' writing. We need to reverse this approach. Instead of finding errors or showing students how to patch up parts of their texts, we need to sabotage our students' conviction that the drafts they have written are complete and coherent. Our comments need to offer students revision tasks of a different order of complexity and sophistication from the ones that they themselves identify, by forcing students back into the chaos, back to the point where they are shaping and restructuring their meaning.[6]

For if the content of a text is lacking in substance and meaning, if the order of the parts must be rearranged significantly in the next draft, if paragraphs must be restructured for logic and clarity, then many sentences are likely to be changed or deleted anyway. There seems to be no point in having students correct usage errors or condense sentences that are likely to disappear before the next draft is completed. In fact, to identify such problems in a text at this early first draft stage, when such problems are likely to abound, can give a student a disproportionate sense of their importance at this stage in the writing process.[7] In responding to our students' writing, we should be guided by the recognition that it is not spelling or usage problems that we as writers first worry about when drafting and revising of our texts.

We need to develop an appropriate level of response for commenting on a first draft, and to differentiate that from the level suitable to a second or third draft. Our comments need to be suited to the draft we are reading. In a first or second draft, we need to respond as any reader would, registering questions, reflecting befuddlement, and noting places where we are puzzled about the meaning of the text. Comments should point to breaks in logic, disruptions in meaning, or missing information. Our goal in commenting on early drafts should be to engage students with the issues they are considering and help them clarify their purposes and reasons in writing their specific text.

For instance, the major rhetorical problem of the essay written by the student who wrote the first paragraph (the paragraph on nuclear power) quoted above was that the student had two principal arguments running through his text, each of which brought the other into question. On the one hand, he argued that we must use nuclear power, unpleasant as it is, because we have nothing else to use; though nuclear energy is a problematic source of energy, it is the best of a bad lot. On the other hand, he also argued that nuclear energy is really quite safe and therefore should be our primary resource. Comments on this student's first draft need to point out this break in logic and show the student that if we accept his first argument, then his second argument sounds fishy. But if we accept his second argument, his first argument sounds contradictory. The teacher's comments need to engage this student writer with this basic rhetorical and conceptual problem in his first draft rather than impose a series of abstract commands and rules upon his text.

Written comments need to be viewed not as an end in themselves — a way for teachers to satisfy themselves that they have done their jobs — but rather as a means for helping students to become more effective writers. As a means for helping students, they have limitations; they are, in fact, disembodied remarks — one absent writer responding to another absent writer. The key to successful commenting is to have what is said in the comments and what is done in the classroom mutually reinforce and enrich each other. Commenting on papers assists the writing course in achieving its purpose; classroom activities and the comments we write to our students need to be connected. Written comments need to be an extension of the teacher's voice — an extension of the teacher as reader. Exercises in such activities as revising a whole text or individual paragraphs together in class, noting how the sense of the whole dictates the smaller changes, looking at options, evaluating actual choices, and then discussing the effect of these changes on revised drafts — such exercises need to be designed to take students through the cycles of revising and to help them overcome their anxiety about revising: that anxiety we all feel at reducing what looks like a finished draft into fragments and chaos.

The challenge we face as teachers is to develop comments which will provide an inherent reason for students to revise; it is a sense of revision as discovery, as a repeated process of beginning again, as starting out new, that our students have not learned. We need to show our students how to seek, in the possibility of revision, the dissonances of discovery — to show them through our comments why new choices would positively change their texts, and thus to show them the potential for development implicit in their own writing.

Notes

[1] C. H. Knoblach and Lil Brannon, "Teacher Commentary on Student Writing: The State of the Art," *Freshman English News*, 10 (Fall 1981), 1–3.

[2] For an extended discussion of revision strategies of student writers see Nancy Sommers, "Revision Strategies of Student Writers and Experienced Adult Writers," *College Composition and Communication*, 31 (December 1980), 378–388.

[3] Nancy Sommers and Ronald Schleifer, "Means and Ends: Some Assumptions of Student Writers," *Composition and Teaching*, 2 (December 1980), 69–76.

[4] Janet Emig and Robert P. Parker, Jr., "Responding to Student Writing: Building a Theory of the Evaluating Process," unpublished paper, Rutgers University.

[5] For an extended discussion of this problem see Joseph Williams, "The Phenomenology of Error," *College Composition and Communication*, 32 (May 1981), 152–168.

[6] Ann Berthoff, *The Making of Meaning* (Montclair, N.J.: Boynton/Cook Publishers, 1981).

[7] W. U. McDonald, "The Revising Process and the Marking of Student Papers," *College Composition and Communication*, 24 (May 1978), 167–170.

MONITORING STUDENT WRITING: HOW NOT TO AVOID THE DRAFT

Margie Krest

[Journal of Teaching Writing *7.1 (1988): 27–39.]*

Margie Krest is an associate at the Center for Research in Rhetoric at the University of Colorado at Denver. She has published articles in English Journal *and the* Journal of Teaching Writing.

In the years since Nancy Sommers's groundbreaking article "Responding to Student Writing" (reprinted on p. 132), instructors have come to understand that student writing improves when students receive meaningful feedback on works-in-progress. Krest describes her strategies for providing this feedback at various stages of the drafting and revising process. She also describes several roles that teachers can adopt when they offer feedback to students. Using drafts from three students, Krest illustrates how her approach can help students make effective revisions.

Monitoring student writing is a challenge because it involves a number of teaching skills, all aimed at effectively guiding students from a first to a final draft. Monitoring is different from evaluating because it does not involve assigning the student a grade or making a final assessment; rather, it helps students direct their attention to aspects of their drafts that they might change to improve their writing. This article is designed to help teachers monitor student writing. In section one, I discuss the rationale for monitoring; in section two, I demonstrate the monitoring procedure on three papers from an English 101 class at the University of Colorado–

Denver; in section three, I summarize the major considerations to remember when monitoring writing.

Rationale

When we monitor students' writing with the primary purposes of helping them improve their writing skills and helping them maintain or attain a positive attitude about writing, we must consider a number of important points. The way we phrase our responses to students is just as important as what we actually tell them. And, of course, neither of these can be done in a vacuum. First, we must consider the point in the semester at which a paper is written: what we expect on the first paper should be much less than what we expect on the fifth paper. Second, we must consider the stage of drafting the student is in: what we respond to in a first draft will be different from what we respond to on a third draft. As a general rule, teachers should hold students responsible for implementing skills only after those skills are introduced and discussed in class.

Focus, Development, Organization

Recognizing what to monitor on a student's paper can be simplified when we keep a few major concerns in mind. Instead of approaching a paper looking for problems, we should approach a paper considering how and why communication either failed or succeeded (Lindemann). The question is how to determine what leads to a failure in writing. Certainly sentence structure and mechanics can hinder writing. However, if a student's focus, development and/or organization are not apparent, correcting sentence structure or mechanics will not clarify an idea. Thus, it makes sense to direct our own attention to the paper's focus, development and organization, especially on initial drafts (McDonald; Sommers). Reigstad and McAndrew suggest that teachers divide their own thinking into High Order Concerns (HOCs) and Low Order Concerns (LOCs). HOCs include focus, organization, development and voice. Analyzing these areas only on all initial drafts will first tell us how well the students communicated their ideas, and second, direct the students' attention to these, *as their own* areas of concern on all early drafts.

Style

Determining the point at which we should monitor sentence structure, mechanics, spelling and usage is not difficult when we remember to focus on these only after students have a handle on their HOCs. To simplify monitoring, I make a separate category for sentence structure (variety, subordination, phrasing) calling them "Middle Order Concerns" (MOCs). Once students have focused, organized and developed their content, concentrating on MOCs serves to direct the students' attention to *how* to express ideas (McDonald). When a teacher points out *why* a sentence is awkward and suggests one or two ways to clarify it, students can then work on their own to revise particular sentences. What's more, after students spend class time discussing sentence variety, subordination and coordination and practice using these during class sessions, most students simply need to have their lack of variety or subordination pointed out to them in order to improve their sentences.

Mechanics, Spelling, Usage

As a rule, I rarely spend time responding to individual LOCs such as spelling and mechanics on specific papers when I monitor except when a student asks me to check for a particular pattern of errors (see below). This is not to suggest that LOCs are not important; however, it does say that my emphasis is first on content, then on style, and then on mechanics and spelling (Bridges). Mechanics and spelling are areas for which students can take more responsibility (Hirsch, cited in Lees) once they understand their own pattern of errors (Bridges; Kroll & Schafer; Lindemann: Shaughnessy). That is, instead of students seeing themselves as never knowing how to use a comma, they can begin to see that they omit commas after introductory clauses or use a comma before every coordinating conjunction. Most LOCs, such as mechanics, spelling and usage, can and should be worked on in editing groups in class sessions before the final paper is due but after the student has revised for content and style. Working in mini-groups on a common problem or "error pattern" is effective because group members can work together to isolate and correct a particular error.

Roles

Finally, when we read a student's paper and begin to formulate in our own minds what we want to discuss with the student, it is most important to determine how we will phrase our responses to the student so that we facilitate positive attitudes about writing (Johnston). From the first class session we need to strive to get to know our students and learn to be sensitive to their feelings about who they are as writers.

As we get to know students and develop our own sensitivities to them, we should also be able to assume various roles as teacher (Britton; Calabrese). When I monitor students' writing I assume one of four roles — the partner or trusted adult, the coach. the diagnostician, or the critic:

- As a partner or trusted adult, I give my honest reactions regarding a paper. For example, I might express my own confusion about a certain passage that I do not understand because of a lack of detail or sentence structure; or, I might express my feeling of sadness after reading a certain passage.
- As a coach, I work to direct a student's energies in a certain direction to help him or her accomplish a goal. For me, coaching means asking the writer specific questions. For instance, I might ask a series of questions throughout the paper, all for the purpose of helping the writer answer those questions to find a focus.
- As a diagnostician my role is to analyze or identify what is being said or how something is being said in the paper. For example, I might simply point out that in a particular paragraph, each sentence begins with the subject/verb pattern. I do not praise or criticize this — I simply diagnose or identify it.
- Finally, as a critic, I direct my comments to those areas of the paper that are either "not working" or simply wrong, and *tell* the writer such very openly and directly — much more directly than as a diagnostician. As a critic, a teacher should be sure to explain why something is wrong and refrain from making negative value judgments about the person.

The teacher needs to assume different roles for different students on different papers, during various drafts at various times throughout the semester. In other words, one student may need a partner on a first draft but a critic on a third draft. And another may need a coach on a first draft and a diagnostician on a second. The point is that we need to be *flexible* in our role when monitoring student writing, and this flexibility in our role should coincide with the actual comments that we make. Overall, the role we assume must be determined by (A) the personality of the student and (B) the academic needs of the student because our role as monitor is not only to help students improve their writing but also help them maintain or attain a positive attitude toward writing.

Application

Kay

The following is a copy of Kay's first draft. The assignment, given during the third week of the semester, was to write a one to two page character sketch in which she was to describe a person in terms of a specific quality, trait or characteristic. We spent the class period in which the assignment was given on pre-writing activities specifically relating to the assignment: brainstorming, mapping and free writing about a person. We then discussed how to limit oneself to a single aspect of a person's personality. At this point in the semester, I knew little about Kay or her background in writing. (All student papers in this article are reproduced exactly as written.)

> Up in the morning here we go again, into the shower or maybe not into the shower. washing one face awake. Drawers full of blue shorts, white socks and blue T-shirts. Jocks everwhere thrown all over the place, colors and styles of who only knows what kind. Grabbing one of any kind into the shorts and on goes the T-shit, socks and tennis shoes.
>
> Just a repeat going through the motions, on with the hat and out of the house. Vitamins breakfact some nutrion of that kind. Arriving day to day all jokes aside, Back and forth up and down the floor we go, white lines. red lines up and down I go. Wet like a pig the sweat just pours down his forehead, neck and slowly down the spin.
>
> All the yelling screamin spearing, on this may go however we only know to what extent it really goes, on our mission is to score. As it all ends I must keep in mind in another days time the motion will return

My first response to Kay's paper was in the form of a simple question in our workshop group in class. I asked her what she wanted to get across to us, her audience. Her reply was that she wanted to describe her messy husband in the morning. I then commented that what confused me was the use of different pronouns such as I, one, we, his. I suggested that she focus just on him — what *he* did or thought or where *he* went. Then, I added one additional comment — that it would be nice for me as a reader to have more information that "showed" he was messy.

Obviously, there are many stylistic and mechanical problems in Kay's paper. However, it was important for her to understand that her content was of primary importance in communication. So, she needed to know why her *content* failed to communicate her idea. Because I was merely a member of her workshop group, I responded to her primarily as a partner and a trusted adult, giving my honest responses to her essay.

Kay's second draft contained approximately nine to eleven additional sentences that showed his messiness; she used one "I" pronoun and "he" or "his" in all other places. After reading her second draft, I told her that I was beginning to see how messy he was and that she *had* focused the paper on him. My only suggestion for change was that she might arrange all the information in the order that it happened.

During the remainder of our conference, I talked to Kay about herself. My goal was to understand Kay as a person and learn why she was in school. I wanted to find out why she wrote as she did and the amount of motivation she had to improve her writing. I hoped that in knowing her motivation I would also find out her reaction to criticisms or suggestions so that I could *phrase* my responses accordingly.

Kay was just starting college, 13 years after finishing high school. She always did "awful" in high school but was now training to be an airline stewardess and felt the need to better her education. Kay hated to read. Even at the age of 30, she disliked reading newspapers or magazines. Her only contact with written English was in the form of instructions or mail.

Kay's writing suffered from a lack of exposure to written communication. However, although her skills were very weak, her motivation was very high. Also, she liked the idea of revising her papers and was eager to do so. Kay was not overly sensitive about her writing so I could easily assume the role of a diagnostician and/or critic.

We discussed this third draft several days later.

> Throwing the covers back off the bed, he begins slowly to stroll. Up in the morning, made it once again into the shower or . . . maybe not into the shower he goes. Rubbing his eyes to see clear the view headed straight for the bathroom door. Feeling the running water looking into the fogged mirrors just can't seem to focus a view. Stepped into the shower splashing water all over his body and fact beginning to surface a view. Out of the shower onto the bare floor his feet are stuck to the towel that was left on the floor.
>
> On with the robe and down the stairs he goes, leaving tracks of water dripping from his body onto the floor. Opens the door picking up the newspaper sits at the dining room table, off comes the rubberband and onto the floor. Papers sorted thrown here and thrown there, goes to the kitchen and fixes a bowl of cheerios, dripping milk from the bowl to his mouth realizing the time and away their he goes.
>
> Into the drawers begins the search for daily wear, underwear that are throun hear and there grabbing a pair and on they go. Pulling another drawer open to find a T-shirt, wrinkled and studded no one else would dare, put it on to wear. Sorting through the socks mixed and some matched some long and some short who will ever know. Ties and belts accessories who know where they are, in a pocket or on some slack Lord only knows. Grab a shirt half way hanging on a hook and a pair of slack that are from before. Oh what about his hair a couple of stroked of the comb and out of the door he goes.

Within three drafts, Kay had basically attained a focus (her husband in the morning), given details to support her focus and succeeded at a sense of organization (the order in which he did things in the morning). Kay had made progress with HOCs within three drafts. It became apparent that the next major failure in her communications was due to her lack of proper sentence structure (MOCs). However, marking R.O., Frag. or Awk. beside every sentence would not help Kay in any way. She simply did not understand the function of subjects and verbs in sentences, so the editorial markings would make no sense. First, Kay needed to hear how a correctly written sentence *sounded* when read aloud. She then needed to understand the function of the subject and verb in a sentence so that she could be sure to include them in every sentence she wrote.

I first took a paragraph or two and simply put in subjects and verbs, retaining as much of her own wording as possible. For example:

> He put on the robe and went down the stairs leaving tracks of water dripping from his body onto the floor. He opened the door, picked up the newspaper, and sat at the dining room table. He took off the rubberband and threw it onto the floor. Papers were thrown here and there. He went to the kitchen and fixed a bowl of cheerios. As he read one section of the news and ate his cheerios, milk dripped from his mouth to the bowl. Realizing the time, he went upstairs.

I asked Kay to read this aloud a number of times. We worked on another of her paragraphs, concentrating solely on identifying subjects and verbs in each sentence. I then assigned her exercises in a simple grammar book on sentence fragments and run-ons. We also did some group work in class on how to identify a subject and verb in a sentence and correct run-ons and fragments.

These are the only areas we worked on in this paper. Over a period of two weeks Kay made noticeable progress on the paper and the fact that she still wished to continue writing, knowing that she had numerous hurdles to overcome, encouraged both of us.

Steve

The following is a copy of Steve's third draft. It was the seventh week of the semester, and class discussions had included essay structure, paragraph structure, use of details, methods of organization, and identification and correction of run-ons and fragments. In this assignment he was to write an essay in which he described a person's influence upon him.

> One day while walking through the green and flowered gardens of Kensington park I encountered a man that forever changed my dull view towards music. The man was Bill Wyman the bassest for the Rolling Stones, a legend in the rock music world.
>
> Having met such a renowned person without having heard his work, I decided to listen to some of his bands particular type of music. I went to the largest record store in the city where I found an enormous selection of Rolling Stones albums. I listened to several of their albums and ended up buying my first real rock and roll album. This new album began opening up many new relationships and ideas.
>
> One of the relationships that sprang from my new awakening to rock music was, that I met more musicaly inclined people. They were always interested in playing and listening to different music. An other relationship was that I began participating in a band where I could learn more about musiciams and their instruments. Through these people and the band, I learned how to play the bass guitar as well as recognize different styles and tastes in music. My new friends tastes in music were varied which gave me thoughts of the type of music that excited me. These thoughts led me to choose jazz as the music that I enjoyed listening to. My interest in jazz began with the blues and blossomed into a more progressive instrument style.
>
> Occasionly I hear different types of jazz that brings back memories of how I had become acquainted with this type of music. Only by having met Bill Wyman would I have eventualy had the influences I did and discovered the music I really liked.

Because it was the seventh week of the semester, I had had some time to get to know Steve. He was 27 years old, had spent four years in the

Navy, had worked full time and had just decided to return to school. He had spent much of the semester developing the essay structure and developing details. Steve was a humorous person but extremely sensitive about his writing ability. When given abrupt or negative comments such as "This sentence doesn't make sense" or "I don't understand this at all," his reaction was severe: his facial muscles tightened and he became very discouraged. Consequently, I learned that *how* I phrased my comments to Steve was extremely important. Generally, in order to avoid his interpreting my written responses negatively, I tried to talk so that my tone of voice might convey encouragement or humor. I found that assuming the role of partner or coach relaxed Steve the most while at the same time elicited positive responses.

I began by commenting on the flow of the first sentence and the obvious improvement he had made on paragraphing, noting the different idea each paragraph conveyed. Even though this was his third draft, focus, organization and details in the third paragraph still needed revising so it was on this paragraph that I focused my attention.

I summarized his third paragraph by saying, "This is what I hear you saying in this paragraph. Tell me if I'm correct. Because of Bill, you started listening to music, meeting people interested in music, and really got into jazz." He was excited that I had understood his idea, and the positive feedback encouraged him. My next comment would be an important one for Steve because he would need to understand that the way in which he conveyed these ideas was not clear and detailed. However, knowing Steve, I also knew that I would not need to be blunt because when I simply questioned a statement or suggested another way of saying something, Steve would immediately assume that he didn't get his point across. I started by asking him if "that I met . . . people" and "participating in a band" were "relationships." As he quickly understood that he needed to rephrase his ideas, I voiced my interest in knowing what he meant by such phrases as "musically inclined people" and "different music" and "tastes in music" and a more "progressive instrument style." He began to understand that this paper could use a lot of revision. However, most important for Steve was the fact that he was not devastated or overwhelmed by comments which would discourage him from writing, and he actually became excited at the prospect of revising his content, which he went on to do.

Matt

Approximately eleven weeks into the semester, Matt submitted this paper as his "almost final" draft. In this essay he was to describe and give his own reactions to a situation that he saw but was not involved in. When the paper was submitted, the class had just completed two class sessions on sentence variety (in length and opening) and subordination and coordination of ideas.

They faced each other. Joe was really mad. He kept yelling and pushing Rob around. Rob repeated, "If you push me again, I'm gonna kill you." Joe did not head this warning. Another shove and Robs head hit the locker. I guess that's when he lost it.

In raged, Rob jumped at Joe, fist flying. I was wondering what provoked this incident. A right hook landed on Joes brow. It looked quite painful. Rob paused and waited for Joes return blow. I don't know why he waited except that they were best friends. Joe, being stunned did not return a punch. I thought it was over, but Rob seemed to desire a punch in the head just to make it even. Again Rob swung and another blow struck and split Joe's lip. Why won't Joe fight back I wondered. By now Joe was being held up by the lockers. I was really mad at both guys. They are best friends. Why are they fighting I though.

I know Rob often jokes around too much. Maybe Joe got fed up with his pranks; however, Rob gave Joe fair warning. Why did Joe want to fight so bad and why isn't he fighting now that he has the chance. Rob continued to pummel Joe's face.

Bleeding from about the eyes and lip, Joe slid to the floor. Some guys pulled Rob off the beaten pile of flesh. Rob quickly ran off somewhere. I asked around and found my hypothesis to be correct. Rob and Joe were having punch wars and Rob hit Joe too hard when Joe didn't expect it. Joe blew up and forced this whole thing. A bunch of questions came to mind. Will they still be friends? Will they see the dean and get suspended? Why didn't some one stop the fight? Why didn't I?

As it turned out the dean did not suspend them because they were best friends and both said they were very sorry. I don't think that really mattered. Sorrow did not help the situation. I wondered how their parents felt. Parents can't win in this situation. The victors parents must be angry at their sons violent agression. And the losers parents must be disappointed in their sons performance. It just proves that fighting serves no purpose for anyone involved.

Matt was 19 years old and interested in writing but overconfident about his writing abilities. In class he quickly responded to discussions on mechanics, grammar and content and could verbalize rules for mechanics and grammar and identify possible problems in essays. However, he did not apply the rules and his insight to his own work. In many ways, it seemed that his overconfidence was his greatest hindrance because he never felt that he was the type of person who needed to revise. Also, Matt often chose not to work on his papers unless someone was very firm with him, pointing out errors directly. "Suggestions" to Matt were merely another way of saying something that he perceived as already well said. Often, encouragement resulted in his working less on his papers because hearing the encouragement, he seemed to consider the weaknesses unimportant.

There are many types of errors on his paper, even though this is his "almost final" draft. His focus and development obviously need to be revised. So, I started by *telling* him that there were three major weaknesses in his content that he needed to work on. One, there were numerous "telling" statements such as "It looked quite painful" rather than "showing" statements; two, there was a paragraphing problem in the fourth paragraph; and three, there was a shift in focus in the last paragraph. Matt understood why these areas were weak and said that he just hadn't taken the time to change them and went on to explain how he would revise them. If when I pointed out to him the weaknesses in his focus and development he could not have told me how and why he would change these, it would have been premature to discuss his style.

However, for Matt, a discussion of style motivated him to place more demands on himself, demands which he knew how to make but too often chose not to. I first asked him to analyze the pattern and length of each sentence in the first two paragraphs, commenting that they did not show application of the skills we had worked on in class. I then had him count the number of coordinating and subordinating ideas. Within a couple of minutes, Matt saw that his first two paragraphs contained many short, choppy sentences and did not give his reader insight into what ideas should be stressed. When I asked him how he might change the situation, he readily rattled off three or four different techniques for sentence opening and sentence combining and illustrated how he would combine his first three sentences. He then took the paper home and revised it. Matt had the skills for being a good writer, but he needed a critic to "encourage" him to use his skills.

Students use and learn from our comments when we monitor their writing rather than simply evaluate their final papers. When students have the opportunity immediately to incorporate ideas and changes into a paper, they understand the value of a particular comment. One student noted this idea quite succinctly in a journal entry: "The more important fact to notice here is that the conference is held *before* the paper is graded. This allows the teacher and student to thoroughly discuss and revise the paper. I believe that everyone should have the right to perfect something to make it the best it can be."

So, as we work to apply the theory behind monitoring writing and help students "make it the best it can be," we must remember four key points: (1) When we respond to student writing, our first concerns must relate to focus, development, organization and voice. (2) Only after students have a handle on these in any given paper should we direct their attention to style. (3) When further revision in these areas is no longer necessary, and students are contemplating their final drafts, we can work with them to help them identify their pattern of errors regarding mechanics and spelling. (4) At each point in our monitoring we must strive to be sensitive to our students as writers so that our comments foster positive attitudes about writing.

Successful monitoring, then, is really a matter of organizing our own expectations for papers and developing our own skills as communicators. As we develop in these areas, our students' writing will develop as well.

Works Cited

Bridges, Charles. "The Basics and the New Teacher," in *Training the New Teacher of College Composition*. Ed. Charles Bridges. Urbana, Ill.: NCTE, 1986.

Britton, James, et al. *The Development of Writing Abilities (11–18)*. London: Macmillan Education LTD, 1975.

Calabrese, Marylyn E. "I Don't Grade Papers Anymore." *English Journal*, 71, 1 (1982): 28–31.

Hirsch, E. D., Jr. *The Philosophy of Composition*. Chicago: University of Chicago Press, 1977.

Johnston, Brian. "Non-Judgmental Response to Students' Writing." *English Journal*, 71, 4 (1982): 50–53.

Kroll, Barry M., and John C. Schafer. "Error-Analysis and the Teaching of Composition." *College Composition and Communication*, 29 (1978): 242–248.

Lees, Elaine O. "Evaluating Student Writing." *College Composition and Communication*, 30 (1979): 370–374.

Lindemann, Erika. *A Rhetoric for Writing Teachers*. New York: Oxford University Press, 1982.

McDonald, W. U., Jr. "The Revising Process and the Marking of Student Papers." *College Composition and Communication*, 24 (1978): 167–170.

Reigstad, Thomas J., and Donald A. McAndrew. *Training Tutors for Writing Conferences*. Urbana, Ill: NCTE, 1984.

Shaughnessy, Mina P. *Errors and Expectations.* New York: Oxford University Press, 1977.

Sommers, Nancy. "Responding to Student Writing." *College Composition and Communication,* 33 (1982): 148–156.

DEMONSTRATING TECHNIQUES FOR ASSESSING WRITING IN THE WRITING CONFERENCE

Richard Beach

[College Composition and Communication 37 (1986): 56–65.]

Richard Beach is a professor of English education at the University of Minnesota, Twin Cities, campus. His recent books include Teaching Literature in the Secondary School *(1991) and* A Teacher's Introduction to Reader-Response Theories *(1993). Beach's articles have appeared in* Linguistics and Education, College Composition and Communication, *and* Research in the Teaching of English.

As more classrooms provide environments in which students share and respond to one another's works-in-progress, instructors continue to seek ways to increase and improve on the feedback that writers give each other. Beach argues that students will not necessarily learn to evaluate writing on their own just from reading instructors' responses to their writing. Rather, instructors need to model for students the various strategies for reading and assessing; in essence, students must be taught how to assess.

In a conference, I ask a student to tell me how she feels about her draft. "Oh, I feel pretty good about it," is her response; "maybe it needs a few more details." Having read the draft, I know that it's riddled with more serious problems than lack of details.

How can this student be taught to critically assess her writing? As experienced teachers know, simply telling the students what their problems are and what to do about those problems doesn't help them learn to become their own best readers. It teaches them only how to follow instructions.

Moreover, in giving students "reader-based feedback" — how I respond as a reader — which presumably implies to students that certain problems exist, I must assume that they are capable of defining the implied problem, which is often not the case.

The majority of students who have difficulty assessing their own writing need some instruction in how to assess. Teachers typically demonstrate techniques for assessing writing by discussing rhetorical or logical problems in published and/or students' texts. Unfortunately, students often have difficulty applying this instruction to assessment of problems in their own texts. For these students, a teacher may then need to augment classroom instruction in assessing techniques by demonstrating these techniques in writing conferences — showing them how to assess their own unique problems — and then having them practice this assessing in the conference.

This more individualized approach to teaching assessing in conferences involves the following steps:

1. determining a student's own particular difficulty by analyzing his or her use of certain assessing techniques;
2. demonstrating the stages of assessing: describing, judging, and selecting appropriate revisions;
3. describing the different components of the rhetorical context — purpose, rhetorical strategies, organization, and audience, showing students how each component implies criteria for judging drafts and selecting appropriate revisions;
4. having students practice the technique that was just demonstrated.

Techniques of Assessing

In order to discuss ways of demonstrating different assessing techniques, I propose a model of assessing. As illustrated in the following chart, assessing involves three basic stages: describing, judging, and selecting/testing out revisions. I will briefly define each of these stages and then, for the remainder of this paper, discuss how I demonstrate these techniques in a conference.

As depicted in this chart, each of the first two stages implies a subsequent stage. By *describing* their goals, strategies, or audience, writers have

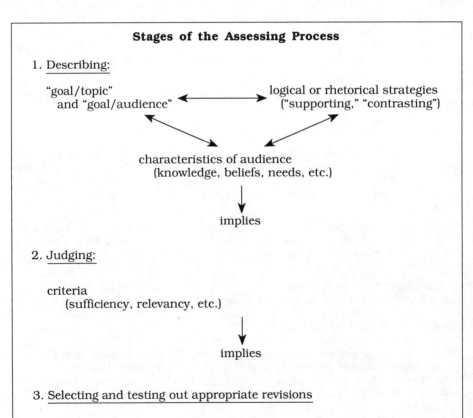

Stages of the Assessing Process

1. Describing:

   "goal/topic" and "goal/audience"   ⟷   logical or rhetorical strategies ("supporting," "contrasting")

   characteristics of audience
   (knowledge, beliefs, needs, etc.)

   ↓

   implies

2. Judging:

   criteria
   (sufficiency, relevancy, etc.)

   ↓

   implies

3. Selecting and testing out appropriate revisions

some basis for making judgments about their drafts. For example, a writer describes his strategy — that in the beginning of his story, he is "setting the scene in order to show what a small-town world is like." He describes his audience — noting that the audience probably knows little about that particular setting. Now he can infer appropriate criteria for judging his setting — whether he has included enough information to convey the sense of a "small-town world" to his reader. This judgment, in turn, helps him in the final stage, *selecting appropriate revisions* — in this case, adding more information about the setting.

In demonstrating assessing techniques, I am therefore showing students more than how to use a specific technique. I am also showing them that describing audience implies criteria for judging or that defining a problem implies criteria for selecting revisions. These demonstrations help students appreciate the value of describing and judging in helping them make revisions.

One benefit of a conference is that it provides a forum for students to practice their assessing with a teacher. The teacher can then note instances in which a student is having difficulty and, instead of simply telling the student how to improve her assessing, demonstrate how to assess. The student then has a concrete guide for trying out a certain assessing technique.

Determining Difficulties in Assessing

In order to know which technique to demonstrate, I try to pinpoint a student's difficulty in using particular technique. I therefore have students begin the conference by giving me their reactions to and sense of the difficulties with their draft, listening carefully for difficulties in describing, judging, or selecting revisions. However, given the brevity of many conferences, I often can't diagnose students' difficulties by relying solely on their comments in the conference. I therefore use guided assessing forms, which students complete prior to the conference.

The questions on these forms are based on the three assessing stages, as listed below:

The Guided Assessing Form

Describing

1. What are you trying to say or show in this section?
2. What are you trying to do in this section?
3. What are some specific characteristics of your audience?
4. What are you trying to get your audience to do or think?

Judging

5. What are some problems you perceive in achieving 1, 2, and 4?

Selecting appropriate revisions

6. What are some changes you can make to deal with these problems?

In using the forms, students divide their draft into sections, answering the questions on the form for each section. The students don't necessarily need to begin with the "describing" questions; they may begin by noting problems and then working back to the describing stage.

By reading over the form in the beginning of the conference and by listening to their reactions to the draft, I try to determine a student's particular difficulty in assessing her draft. If, for example, for each of three sections in her draft a student has difficulty describing what she is "trying to say or show," I might conclude that she has difficulty defining her intentions. The fact that she's also had difficulty answering my questions about goals further suggests that inferring intentions is a problem for her.

I then demonstrate how I would identify intentions. Rather than using my own writing, which the student isn't familiar with, I use the student's writing. I adopt the student's role or persona, demonstrating how I, from her perspective, would infer intentions. I stress to the student that while I am showing her how *I* would infer intentions, I am not implying that my approach is the "one correct way." I also *avoid* telling the students what they ought to be saying, for example, by telling them what I think they are "really trying to say." Rather, I am showing students how to do something rather than telling them what to say.

After I demonstrate a certain technique, I then ask the student to make her own inferences. If she continues to have difficulty, I demonstrate that technique further.

All of this requires careful attention to clues suggesting difficulties, as well as a conceptual framework for sorting out and isolating certain strategies. Based on my own experience and research on assessing, I will now discuss how I demonstrate each of the stages of the assessing process — describing, judging, and selecting revisions.

The Describing Stage

The describing stage consists of describing goals for content (What am I trying to say?), audience (What do I want my audience to do or think?), logical or rhetorical strategies (What am I trying to do: supporting, contrasting, shifting to a different point?), and audience characteristics (knowledge, traits, needs, etc.). Writers obviously use goals as criteria for judging whether their text says or does what they want it to say or do. Once they identify their goals, they can detect dissonance between their goals and their text, dissonance that leads to judgments about problems in achieving their goals.

This is not to imply that writers must always articulate their goals in order to assess their writing. Writers often have only a "felt sense" of their intentions without ever articulating them, but they know how to use their unarticulated intentions to determine that something is amiss and to decide what to do about their problems.

In a conference, it is often useful to have students articulate their goals because those goals are necessary for judging, for determining the extent to which those goals have or have not been fulfilled. If students are to be able to make these judgments, they may need help articulating goals.

Difficulties in describing goal/topics and goal/audience. In my research on use of the guided assessing forms, I asked students to describe what they were trying to say or show ("goal/topic") or what they wanted their audience to do or think ("goal/audience") in each of several sections of their draft.[1] Many students in these studies have difficulty stating what it is that they are trying to say or show. They often simply restate their text *verbatim* rather than stating their intended topic or idea. For example, in writing an analysis of citizen participation in the government of her hometown, a student described her draft section as saying that "a lot of citizens in the town don't vote and there often aren't enough candidates to run for local offices," almost a verbatim restatement of what she was saying in the draft. She did not go beyond that restatement to recognize a point of that section, her "goal/topic" — that citizens aren't involved in town government. She also had difficulty identifying her "goal/audience," what she wanted her audience to do or think having read her essay. Because she had difficulty identifying these goals, she had difficulty judging her draft.

To some degree, identifying these goals is difficult, particularly if students don't perceive the purpose for defining goals — to further assess their draft. I therefore try to show students that clearly defining goals helps them in judging their draft.

In demonstrating definitions of goal/topic, I demonstrate the difference between simply restating the content of a section of their draft and recognizing the goal or purpose of that section. In working with the student writing about her local government, I first take her restatement of the text, "that citizens don't vote and there aren't enough candidates" and, playing the role of the "dumb reader," to use Walker Gibson's term, ask the question, "what's the point?" I then infer a goal statement — that the citizens aren't involved — and show her that, in contrast to her restatement, I can use this goal statement to pinpoint disparities between goal and text.

Another problem with students' identifications of goal/topic is that they are often so global that they are not very useful for perceiving disparities between goals and text.[2] For example, in writing an autobiographical narrative about a series of shoplifting incidents, a student states that he was "trying to show what I was like when I was a teenager." This description is too global for assessing what it is he wants to show about this past self. The student needs to identify what the incidents show about his past self.

Having diagnosed the student's goals as too global, I then propose, using his other comments in the conference, a more precise goal statement: "in portraying my shoplifting, I'm trying to show that I was so lonely that I would do anything to be popular with my peers." I then use this inferred goal to review the shoplifting episodes, judging whether or not the descriptions of the student's behavior in each episode convey his need for friendship. Again, I am demonstrating the value of goal statements, particularly precise goal statements.

Difficulties in describing rhetorical or logical strategies. In describing rhetorical or logical strategies, writers are defining what they are doing in their texts — supporting, defining, stating, requesting, contrasting, describing, evaluating, specifying, etc. In naming these strategies, writers go beyond simply summarizing what they are trying to say, to identifying what they are trying to do, conceiving of their text from a functional or pragmatic perspective.

Each of these strategies implies certain criteria for assessing the success or failure of that strategy. By describing these strategies, writers evoke the particular criteria necessary for judging the use of that strategy. Writers then narrow down the criteria in light of their particular goals and the characteristics of their audience. For example, the strategy, *supporting,* implies the criteria, *sufficiency, relevancy,* or *specificity of support:* do I have enough support? is my support relevant to my thesis? is my support specific enough? Given an audience which the writer assumes knows little about the topic, the writer is particularly concerned about the sufficiency of information — is there enough supportive information for that audience to understand a point? Or, in requesting, as suggested by speech-act theorists, I am concerned about my power, right, or ability to make a request; my reader's ability to fulfill my request; and my reader's perception of my sincerity in making a request. Given a reader who may doubt my right to make a request, I'm particularly concerned that my request implies that I have the right to make such a request.

For example, the administration at my university has decided to reduce my program, but without giving any clear rationale for the proposed reduction. In writing to the administration requesting some clarification of their rationale, I somewhat cynically anticipate their response — that I have no right to make such a request. In my request, I argue that I have the right to ask for clarification because further reductions would jeopardize my program and my job. I therefore clearly define my affiliation with the program in order to imply my right to make such a request.

Describing strategies and inferring implied criteria is a complicated process that requires a pragmatic perspective on writing — conceiving of writing as doing things rather than simply conveying information. It also requires tacit knowledge of the conditions governing the use of these strategies. It is therefore not surprising that, as our analysis of the assessing forms indicated, many students had difficulty describing their strategies and inferring implied criteria.[3] When asked to describe their strategies, students often had difficulty going beyond describing what they were trying to "say" to inferring what it is they were trying to "do." They frequently restated content — "I am writing about my high school and college courses," rather than inferring strategy — "I am contrasting my high school and college courses." These students, with only a restatement of content, then had difficulty making judgments about their text. Those students who identified a strategy were more likely to make a judgment because they had some basis for making it — for example, whether or not they were able to successfully contrast high school and college courses.

In demonstrating the difference between a summary of content and a description of strategy I again demonstrate how descriptions of strategies can be used to imply criteria. For example, having inferred that the student is contrasting high school and college classes, I then note that "contrasting" implies, among other criteria, the importance of information relevant to the contrast and the validity of the contrast — whether or not the information constitutes valid evidence for a contrast.

Difficulties in describing characteristics of audience. Making inferences about characteristics of audience is also a complex process. There is much debate regarding the conflicting evidence about how much writers actually think about their audience.[4]

I would argue that, rather than conceiving of audience as a unified global construct, writers infer or create specific prototypical characteristics such as what and how much members of an audience know about a topic, what they believe about a topic, and their needs, status, power, attitudes, or expectations. For example, in writing a set of directions for windsurfing, a writer may conceive of her audience as "someone who knows little about windsurfing." Or, in arguing the case for nationalizing the steel industry, a writer conceives of his audience as "someone who is opposed to my belief about nationalization." These conceptions are prototypical because writers often never know, even with familiar audiences, exactly what their audience knows, believes, needs, etc. They must therefore rely on prototypical constructs derived from approximations of their audience.

Writers also derive these characteristics from their defined goals and strategies. In giving a set of directions for windsurfing, a writer knows that she needs to consider what her audience may or may not know about windsurfing, because that characteristic is particularly useful for judging the relevancy and sufficiency of information in her directions. Writers therefore infer these prototypical constructs because, as with decisions about goals and strategies, the constructs imply relevant criteria for judging their writing.

Inferring these characteristics of audience also allows writers to adopt a reader's schema, as they must in order to distance themselves from their text. Having created the construct, "someone who is opposed to nationalizing the steel industry," they can then assess the text from that perspective.

When, in our research, Sarah Eaton and I asked students to infer characteristics of their audience on their assessing form, most of the students made few if any references to specific audience characteristics.[5] Most of their inferences consisted of anticipated emotional responses such as "my reader should like this beginning" or "my audience will be bothered by this section," inferences reflecting an egocentric orientation. They were more concerned with how their audience would react to their writing than with how to adapt their text to their audience.

When I sense that students are having difficulty inferring characteristics of audience, I demonstrate how I infer these characteristics from my description of strategies or goals. For example, in writing her paper about the lack of citizen participation in affairs of her hometown, the student previously cited began her paper by describing the town's government, noting that she's trying to "provide background information in order to set the scene." However, she has difficulty judging her use of this defined strategy — setting the scene — because she has difficulty inferring audience.

Using her description of her "backgrounding" strategy, I note that in giving background information, I need to determine how much her audience may know about her hometown. Once I've isolated the appropriate attribute — knowledge — I create the construct, "someone who knows little about the town." I then use that construct to judge her descriptions of the town.

The Judging Stage

Sensing dissonance. Having described these components of the rhetorical context, writers then judge their text. In judging, a writer needs to sense dissonance between goals and the text, dissonance that serves as an incentive to revise.

However, many students in our research had difficulty sensing dissonance because they had difficulty adopting a reader's perspective. In order to demonstrate ways of sensing dissonance, I go back and describe goals, strategies, characteristics of audience, and intended effects. As instructor, I then review the text from the perspective of a member of an audience with one of these characteristics, for example, "someone who knows little about book publishing." I, as instructor, then cite instances in which I, as a reader, didn't have enough background information to understand the draft. Given my goal, as the writer, of informing my reader about book publishing, I know that, from the reader's perspective, something is amiss.

Applying criteria. Once writers sense the dissonance, they need to specify the reason for the problem, why something is amiss.

Students often have difficulty specifying reasons for their problems. They may say that "this is awkward" or "this doesn't flow"; but these judgments often don't point towards any predicted solutions, because they are too vague. In contrast, judgments such as, "I don't have enough examples to support my thesis," imply some specific directions: add more examples.

One reason students aren't able to specify their reasons is that they simply don't know or don't know how to apply criteria such as sufficiency, relevancy, validity, clarity, appropriateness, or coherence. For example, a student thinks that there is a problem with her extended illustration of an ineffective teaching technique, but she can't define the reason for the problem. I then show her how to define a reason for her problem. Having defined her strategy, *giving examples,* I infer implied criteria — relevancy, sufficiency, or clarity of the information in terms of illustrating the point. I then ask the question — given the goals and characteristics of audience, is this a problem of relevancy, sufficiency, or clarity? I then note that, from my perspective as reader, the illustration is too long. This suggests that sufficiency of information serves as a useful criterion for selecting and testing out appropriate revisions. One can hope that the student will then recognize the value of specifying criteria in order to make revisions.

Selecting and Testing Out Appropriate Revisions

Once writers have defined their problem, they select and test out those revisions that will best solve the problem. A writer may select a certain revision strategy — adding, deleting, modifying, rewording, etc. — and/or formulate the content involved in using that revision strategy ("I will add more information about the appearance of the house").

Difficulties in selecting revisions. Just as writers' descriptions imply judgments, their judgments imply appropriate revisions. If their information is irrelevant, then they need to delete that information or make it more relevant. However, when students in our study were asked to answer the question on the form, "What are you going to do about your problem?" many had difficulty identifying possible revisions because they hadn't clearly defined their problem or the reasons for their problem.[6]

In these instances, I go back to the judging stage and demonstrate how specifying problems and reasons for problems implies revisions.

Difficulties in testing out optional revisions. Once students select a revision, they often assume that that revision will do the job, failing to consider why or how that revision works according to their goals, strategies, and characteristics of audience. For example, in writing about police corruption, a student notes that he wants to add some more examples of police corruption, but he doesn't know why he's adding the examples. I then show him how to review his revisions in terms of his goals, strategies, or audience characteristics. The student then realizes that the additional examples help bolster his charge — his central point — that the police corruption exists in all areas of society. Having reaffirmed his goal, he can test out whether each additional example supports his contention that "corruption is everywhere."

In showing students how to justify their revisions by considering their goals, strategies, or audience characteristics, I am illustrating that in assessing, it is essential to constantly cycle back to conceptions of the rhetorical context in order to reaffirm, clarify, or modify those conceptions in light of their advancing comprehension of that context as they write.

Diagnosing Students' Response to Modeling: Comprehending and Applying

These, then, are some of the techniques of assessing that I demonstrate in the conference. In most cases, I demonstrate no more than one or two of these techniques in any one conference. Otherwise, I end up dominating the conference rather than having the students practice their own assessing. After I complete my demonstration, I ask the students whether or not they understood the technique I was demonstrating. If a student didn't understand the technique, I repeat the demonstration until I am confident that the student not only understood the technique but also could actually employ that technique.

In subsequent conferences, I often find that my demonstrations have benefitted students in that they are able to use these techniques on their own, either in the conferences or on the guided assessing forms. In an attempt to determine the influence of the demonstrations, I conducted a study of one teacher's use of demonstrations with a group of eight college freshman students enrolled in a remedial composition course.[7] I analyzed (1) the transcripts of conferences and the students' assessing forms for evidence of students' use of assessing techniques, and (2) the students' revisions from the beginning to the end of the course. Over time, most of the students demonstrated marked changes, particularly in their ability to describe goals and strategies and to use those descriptions to judge their drafts and make revisions that improved their writing.

If learning to assess drafts is central to learning to revise and improve writing quality, then demonstrating these assessing techniques assumes a central role in composition instruction.

Notes

[1] Richard Beach and Sarah Eaton, "Factors Influencing Self-assessing and Revising of College Freshmen," in Richard Beach and Lillian Bridwell, ed., *New Directions in Composition Research* (New York: Guilford Press, 1984), pp. 149–70.

[2] Beach and Eaton, ibid.

[3] Beach and Eaton, "Factors."

[4] Donald Rubin, Gene Piché, Michael Michlin, and Fern Johnson, "Social-Cognitive Ability as a Predictor of the Quality of Fourth-Graders' Written Narratives," in Richard Beach and Lillian Bridwell, *New Directions;* Brant Burleson and Katherine Rowan, "Are Social-Cognitive Ability and Narrative Writing Skill Related?" *Written Communication* 2 (January 1985), 25–43.

[5] Beach and Eaton, "Factors."

[6] Beach and Eaton, "Factors."

[7] Richard Beach, "The Self-assessing Strategies of Remedial College Students," paper presented at the annual meeting of the American Educational Research Association," New York, 1977.

ASSESSING STUDENT WRITING

From *PREPARING TO TEACH WRITING*
James D. Williams

[From Preparing to Teach Writing. *Belmont, CA: Wadsworth, 1989. 256-61.]*

James D. Williams is an associate professor of English and director of the undergraduate writing program at the University of North Carolina at Chapel Hill. He has published numerous journal articles and, in addition to authoring Preparing to Teach Writing, *he is coauthor (with Grace Capizzi Snipper) of* Literacy and Bilingualism *(1990) and (with David Huntley and Christine Hanks)* The Interdisciplinary Reader *(1991).*

In this excerpt, Williams questions the notion that grades can reflect writing ability; rather, grades "appear to reflect a degree of success on a particular task." In determining what to measure when assessing writing, Williams says, instructors need to consider validity — *"the match between what's being taught and what's being evaluated. . . . Quite simply, we need to be certain that we are truly measuring what we believe we are teaching."*

Validity: What Are We Measuring?

Most researchers who study evaluation have found widespread confusion over what writing teachers are assessing when they give students grades on their papers. Are they measuring "writing ability," or are they measuring students' performance on a given task at a particular time? Many people, both in and out of education, assume that the grade is a measure of writing ability. In fact, you may share this assumption and may never have questioned it. But careful consideration suggests that this assumption may be wrong, or at least simplistic.

We begin to see the difficulties in this assumption when we note the patterns of students' writing growth. Any given class will have good, average, and poor writers. At the end of the term, all the students will show growth, all will have improved their language skills to some degree. But generally the patterns remain the same: Those who were good writers at the beginning of the term may at the end be excellent writers, those who were average writers may now be good writers, and those who were poor writers may now be average writers. In terms of overall writing ability, it's unusual when students skip ability levels. We just don't often find students who start a term as poor writers and end it as excellent writers, perhaps because growth in writing is such a slow, incremental process.

Nevertheless, we often find students of all ability levels whose performance may differ from assignment to assignment or from task to task. Students who have been writing C– papers for weeks will get excited about an idea or a project, will work away at it for days, and will produce B work or better. But then the next assignment finds them really struggling to put together something meaningful. By the same token, students who generally are very good writers will occasionally stumble, producing a paper that *is* barely passing. In both cases, it is hard to say that the grades on these uncommon papers truly reflect overall writing ability. But they do appear to reflect a degree of success on a particular task.

It may be, of course, that when we add up all of a student's grades at the end of the term we have some indication of overall writing ability, so perhaps we're measuring ability after all. We should note, however, that ability is a comparative concept, which means that in each case we have to match it against something else. University writing teachers experience the reality of ability's comparative nature every fall, when tens of thousands of freshmen enter college having received nothing but A's on all their high school essays. These students are also crushed by the tens of thousands when they can't earn anything higher than a C in freshman composition.

This experience suggests that the terms "good," "average," and "poor" writers are constrained by context. We can apply them with a degree of accuracy only when the group we base our comparisons on is fairly limited and well defined. But if this is the case, then even cumulative or averaged grades may not be true indications of writing ability, at least not in any absolute sense.

What we're left with is the idea that the grades we put on papers are related to performance on a specific task at a given time, not to the broader concept of ability. Indeed, it looks more and more as though writing ability itself is coming to be viewed as the application of quite specific rhetorical skills to equally specific rhetorical situations. In other words, one doesn't simply learn how to write, but rather learns how to write very particular texts for particular audiences (Bizzell, 1987; Faigley et al., 1985).

This isn't to suggest, however, that we *cannot* measure writing ability. But any straightforward effort to do so in a composition class is likely to have undesirable pedagogical consequences.

We know that we can usually determine what a teacher is evaluating by looking at the way he or she teaches, because what one intends to measure will affect methodology (see Faigley et al., 1985; Greenberg, Wiener, & Donovan, 1986). For example, teachers who want to evaluate how successfully students use writing in a social context, how they respond to specific writing situations, and how they revise are likely to use a method that stresses making students feel good about themselves as writers, providing realistic writing situations, and offering ample opportunities for revision. They will probably search for relevant, interesting topics, and they will probably make much use of workshops and conferences, where instruction is as individualized as possible. Grades in this case will reflect a complex array of abilities, such as cooperation with others during group activities, not just writing ability.

Evaluation can also serve a pedagogical function, as when poor writers occasionally receive an average grade on a paper that is barely passing in order for the teacher to build their self-confidence and sense of accomplishment. Evaluation in this case is not a measure of writing ability at all but is, if anything, a pedagogical tool used to manipulate student behavior and attitudes.

If one were concerned strictly with measuring writing ability, there would be no need to consider the relevance of writing assignments, and certainly one wouldn't use grades to manipulate behavior. The chief interest would be in making certain that the assignments were *valid tests* of writing ability. Each assignment would be structured so that the good writers would consistently receive high grades on their responses and the poor writers would consistently receive low grades. The issue would be how accurately the task and the subsequent assessment measure students' abilities.

In trying to determine what we teachers are measuring when we assess writing, we're really dealing with a question of *validity*, or the match between what's being taught and what's being evaluated. It's our responsibility as instructors to give more attention to validity in writing assessment, because it is crucial to just about everything that takes place in a writing class. Quite simply, we need to be certain that we are truly measuring what we believe we are teaching (White, 1986).

If, for example, revision is an important part of our instruction on every project, we need some way to account for this skill when we evaluate students' work. Some teachers therefore assign grades or scores to rough drafts, as well as to participation in work groups. This approach has at least two drawbacks, however. First, it reflects an attempt to grade process, even though composing processes appear to differ from person to person and from task to task. There really is no such thing as *the* composing process, and evaluation is only valid when we measure similar student behavior against a preestablished standard. Second, this approach defeats the purpose of formative evaluations by adding a summative component that too easily results in a shift in focus from, for example, having a rough draft to having a good rough draft. Such a shift is significant and counterproductive because it reinforces the erroneous perception students have that the only difference between a first draft and a final draft is neatness.

It seems that a more effective means of evaluating something like revision skill would involve having students submit their rough drafts along with final drafts to allow for comparisons between the revisions and the finished product. By comparing the initial drafts and then matching them against the final draft, one can more clearly evaluate how successfully any given student is grasping the skill being taught. The grade on the final draft, the summative evaluation, would therefore reflect the quality of the finished paper as well as revision skill, because realistically the two are inseparable. In other words, one grade would indicate an overall assessment.

. . . Assessment validity can be affected by the way one structures assignments. If teachers give students poorly planned tasks that allow them to choose from a list of topics that call for different kinds of writing, teachers have no principled way to evaluate responses. If one student writes a narrative report and another an argument in response to the same assignment, which may ask for description, our criteria for what constitutes a successful response will vary from essay to essay, seriously compromising evaluation validity. Often students who attempt the more difficult task, the argument, will receive a lower grade on the assignment than they would have received had they performed the easier task and written a narrative report. Under these circumstances, teachers have almost no way of knowing *what* they are measuring.

Reliability

The second problem we face in evaluation is uniformity of assessment, or what is called *reliability*. Suppose, for example, you wrote a paper in one of your English classes that your professor thought was very good. In fact, suppose she thought it was so good she passed it around among her colleagues and asked them to tell her how they liked it — in other words, she asked them to assess it. If her colleagues' assessments are *reliable,* they should all see it as a very good paper. Thus we see that reliability simply describes the degree of consistency from one evaluation to another. But it need not be limited to different evaluators of the same paper: If your professor came across the paper a year or two later, she would still think it was well written, if she is a reliable evaluator.

In our own classrooms, we will want our evaluation of students' writing to be as reliable as possible for several reasons. Students need to know that assessment is consistent and objective, not capricious and subjective. Just as important, we will want reliable evaluations throughout our schools to avoid situations in which a student receives D's on written tasks in one class and A's in another. Unfortunately, reliability doesn't usually occur spontaneously. Unless teachers in a school work together to make their assessments reliable, some students will indeed get high grades on papers in one class and low grades in another, even though their writing remains pretty much the same from teacher to teacher. The problem is that different teachers will look for different things in a well written assignment — hence the inconsistency in evaluation. In such circumstances, students are forced to conclude, quite correctly, that writing assessment is largely subjective, which has the effect of motivating them to write to please the teacher.

Writing for that audience of one, of course, is just another arhetorical exercise that fails to improve discourse skills. A key, then, to better writing performance may well lie in making our assessment more reliable. The only way to accomplish this task, however, *is* to reach an agreement on what constitutes good writing and what doesn't. As difficult as such agreement may initially appear, it isn't very hard at all. Later in the chapter we'll explore how it's done.

References

Bizzell, P. (1987). What can we know, what must we do, what may we hope: Writing assessment. *College English,* 49, 575–584.

Faigley, L., Cherry, R., Joliffe, D., & Skinner, A (1985). *Assessing writers' knowledge and processes of composing.* Norwood, NJ: Ablex.

Greenburg, K., Wiener, H., & Donovan, T. (Eds.) (1986). *Writing assessment: Issues and strategies.* New York: Longman.

White, E. (1986). *Teaching and assessing writing.* San Francisco: Jossey-Bass.

RANKING, EVALUATING, AND LIKING:
SORTING OUT THREE FORMS OF JUDGMENT

Peter Elbow

[College English 55 (1993): 187–206.]

Professor of English at the University of Massachusetts–Amherst and author of the classic Writing without Teachers *(1973), Peter Elbow coedited (with Pat Belanoff and Sheryl Fontaine)* Nothing Begins with N: New Investigations of Freewriting *(1990) and authored* "What Is English?, *published by the Modern Language Association in 1990.* "The Challenge for Sentence Combining" *is one of twenty-three articles collected in* Sentence Combining: A Rhetorical Perspective *(1985), edited by Don Daiker, Andrew Kerek, and Max Morenberg. Elbow won CCCC's prestigious Richard Braddock Award in 1986.*

Eventually, students submit their writing for a grade, no matter how much their instructors promote multiple, significant revisions. At that point instructors assess student writing — not to help guide revisions, but to decide how effectively students have achieved their goals or met assignment criteria. Elbow reflects on several alternatives available for assessing student writing, alternatives he characterizes as ranking, evaluating, and liking. He discusses the problems with ranking and the benefits of evaluating, suggesting that teachers do portfolio assessments where possible. He explores, too, the limitations of evaluation and the benefits of evaluation-free zones. Finally, Elbow discusses how simply liking students' writing — enjoying and taking a sincere interest in their work — can help motivate students and foster more effective criticism. Elbow offers several suggestions for teachers who want to explore alternative assessment strategies.

This essay is my attempt to sort out different acts we call assessment — some different ways in which we express or frame our judgments of value. I have been working on this tangle not just because it is interesting and important in itself but because assessment tends so much to drive and control *teaching.* Much of what we do in the classroom is determined by the assessment structures we work under.

Assessment is a large and technical area and I'm not a professional. But my main premise or subtext in this essay is that we nonprofessionals can and should work on it because professionals have not reached definitive conclusions about the problem of how to assess writing (or anything else, I'd say). Also, decisions about assessment are often made by people even less professional than we, namely legislators. Pat Belanoff and I realized that the field of assessment was open when we saw the harmful effects of a writing proficiency exam at Stony Brook and worked out a collaborative portfolio assessment system in its place (Belanoff and Elbow; Elbow and Belanoff). Professionals keep changing their minds about large-scale testing and assessment. And as for classroom grading, psychometricians provide little support or defense of it.

The Problems with Ranking and the Benefits of Evaluating

By ranking I mean the act of summing up one's judgment of a performance or person into a single, holistic number or score. We rank every time we give a grade or holistic score. Ranking implies a single scale or continuum or dimension along which all performances are hung.

By evaluating I mean the act of expressing one's judgment of a performance or person by pointing out the strengths and weaknesses of different features or dimensions. We evaluate every time we write a comment on a paper or have a conversation about its value. Evaluation implies the recognition of different criteria or dimensions — and by implication different contexts and audiences for the same performance. Evaluation requires going *beyond* a first response that may be nothing but a kind of ranking ("I like it" or "This is better than that"), and instead looking carefully enough at the performance or person to make distinctions between parts or features or criteria.

It's obvious, thus, that I am troubled by ranking. But I will resist any temptation to argue that we can get rid of all ranking — or even should. Instead I will try to show how we can have *less* ranking and *more* evaluation in its place.

I see three distinct problems with ranking: it is inaccurate or unreliable; it gives no substantive feedback; and it is harmful to the atmosphere for teaching and learning.

(1) First the unreliability. To rank reliably means to give a *fair* number, to find the single quantitative score that readers will agree on. But readers don't agree.

This is not news — this unavailability of agreement. We have long seen it on many fronts. For example, research in evaluation has shown many times that if we give a paper to a set of readers, those readers tend to give it the full range of grades (Diederich). I've recently come across new research to this effect — new to me because it was published in 1912. The investigators carefully showed how high school English teachers gave different grades to the same paper. In response to criticism that this was a local problem in English, they went on the next year to discover an even greater variation among grades given by high school geometry teachers and history teachers to papers in their subjects. (See the summary of Daniel Starch and Edward Elliott's 1913 *School Review* articles in Kirschenbaum, Simon, and Napier 258–59.)

We know the same thing from literary criticism and theory. If the best critics can't agree about what a text means, how can we be surprised that they disagree even more about the quality or value of texts? And we know that nothing in literary or philosophical theory gives us any agreed-upon rules for settling such disputes.

Students have shown us the same inconsistency with their own controlled experiments of handing the same paper to different teachers and getting different grades. This helps explain why we hate it so when students ask us their favorite question, "What do you want for an A?": it rubs our noses in the unreliability of our grades.

Of course champions of holistic scoring argue that they *can* get agreement among readers — and they often do (White). But they get that agreement by "training" the readers before and during the scoring sessions. What "training" means is getting those scorers to stop reading the way they normally read — getting them to stop using the conflicting criteria and standards they normally use outside the scoring sessions. (In an impressive and powerful book, Barbara Herrnstein Smith argues that whenever we have widespread inter-reader reliability, we have reason to suspect that difference has been suppressed and homogeneity imposed — almost always at the expense of certain groups.) In short, the reliability in holistic scoring is not a measure of how texts are valued by real readers in natural settings, but only of how they are valued in artificial settings with imposed agreements.

Defenders of holistic scoring might reply (as one anonymous reviewer did), that holistic scores are not perfect or absolutely objective readings but just "judgments that most readers will agree are the appropriate ones given the purpose of the assessment and the system of communication." But I have been in and even conducted enough holistic scoring sessions to know that even that degree of agreement doesn't occur unless "purpose" and "appropriateness" are defined to mean acceptance of the single set of standards imposed on that session. We know too much about the differences among readers and the highly variable nature of the reading process. Supposing we get readings only from academics, or only from people in English, or only from respected critics, or only from respected writing programs, or only from feminists, or only from sound readers of my tribe (white, male, middle-class, full professors between the ages of fifty and sixty). We *still* don't get agreement. We can sometimes get agreement among readers from some subset, a particular community that has developed a strong set of common values, perhaps *one* English department or *one* writing program. But what is the value of such a rare agreement? It tells us nothing about how readers from other English departments or writing programs will judge — much less how readers from other domains will judge.

(From the opposite ideological direction, some skeptics might object to my skeptical train of thought: "So what else is new?" they might reply. "Of *course* my grades are biased, 'interested' or 'situated' — always partial to my interests or the values of my community or culture. There's no other possibility." But how can people consent to give grades if they feel that way? A single teacher's grade for a student is liable to have substantial consequences — for example on eligibility for a scholarship or a job or entrance into professional school. In grading, surely we must not take anything less than genuine fairness as our goal.)

It won't be long before we see these issues argued in a court of law, when a student who has been disqualified from playing on a team or rejected from a professional school sues, charging that the basis for his plight — teacher grades — is not reliable. I wonder if lawyers will be able to make our grades stick.

(2) Ranking or grading is woefully uncommunicative. Grades and holistic scores are nothing but points on a continuum from "yea" to "boo" — with no information or clues about the criteria behind these noises. They are 100 percent evaluation and 0 percent description or information. They quantify the degree of approval or disapproval in readers but tell nothing

at all about what the readers actually approve or disapprove of. They say nothing that couldn't be said with gold stars or black marks or smiley-faces. Of course our first reactions are often nothing but global holistic feelings of approval or disapproval, but we need a system for communicating our judgments that nudges us to move beyond these holistic feelings and to articulate the basis of our feeling — a process that often leads us to change our feeling. (Holistic scoring sessions sometimes use rubrics that explain the criteria — though these are rarely passed along to students — and even in these situations, the rubrics fail to fit many papers.) As C. S. Lewis says, "People are obviously far more anxious to express their approval and disapproval of things than to describe them" (7).

(3) Ranking leads students to get so hung up on these oversimple quantitative verdicts that they care more about scores than about learning — more about the grade we put on the paper than about the comment we have written on it. Have you noticed how grading often forces us to write comments to justify our grades? — and how these are often *not* the comment we would make if we were just trying to help the student write better? ("Just try writing several favorable comments on a paper and then giving it a grade of D" [Diederich 21].)

Grades and holistic scores give too much encouragement to those students who score high — making them too apt to think they are already fine — and too little encouragement to those students who do badly. Unsuccessful students often come to doubt their intelligence. But oddly enough, many "A" students also end up doubting their true ability and feeling like frauds — because they have sold out on their own judgment and simply given teachers whatever yields an A. They have too often been rewarded for what they don't really believe in. (Notice that there's more cheating by students who get high grades than by those who get low ones. There would be less incentive to cheat if there were no ranking.)

We might be tempted to put up with the inaccuracy or unfairness of grades if they gave good diagnostic feedback or helped the learning climate; or we might put up with the damage they do to the learning climate if they gave a fair or reliable measure of how skilled or knowledgeable students are. But since they fail dismally on both counts, we are faced with the striking question of why grading has persisted so long.

There must be many reasons. It is obviously easier and quicker to express a global feeling with a single number than to figure out what the strengths and weaknesses are and what one's criteria are. (Though I'm heartened to discover, as I pursue this issue, how troubled teachers are by grading and how difficult they find it.) But perhaps more important, we see around us a deep *hunger to rank* — to create pecking orders: to see who we can look down on and who we must look up to, or in the military metaphor, who we can kick and who we must salute. Psychologists tell us that this taste for pecking orders or ranking is associated with the authoritarian personality. We see this hunger graphically in the case of IQ scores. It is plain that IQ scoring does not represent a commitment to looking carefully at people's intelligence; when we do that, we see different and frequently uncorrelated *kinds* or *dimensions* of intelligence (Gardner). The persistent use of IQ scores represents the hunger to have a number so that everyone can have a rank. ("Ten!" mutter the guys when they see a pretty woman.)

Because ranking or grading has caused so much discomfort to so many students and teachers, I think we see a lot of confusion about the process.

It is hard to think clearly about something that has given so many of us such anxiety and distress. The most notable confusion I notice is the tendency to think that if we renounce ranking or grading, we are renouncing the very possibility of judgment and discrimination — that we are embracing the idea that there is no way to distinguish or talk about the difference between what works well and what works badly.

So the most important point, then, is that *I am not arguing against judgment or evaluation.* I'm just arguing against that crude, oversimple way of *representing* judgment — distorting it, really — into a single number, which means ranking people and performances along a single continuum.

In fact I am arguing *for evaluation.* Evaluation means looking hard and thoughtfully at a piece of writing in order to make distinctions as to the quality of different features or dimensions. For example, the process of evaluation permits us to make the following kinds of statements about a piece of writing:

- The thinking and ideas seem interesting and creative.
- The overall structure or sequence seems confusing.
- The writing is perfectly clear at the level of individual sentences and even paragraphs.
- There is an odd, angry tone of voice that seems unrelated or inappropriate to what the writer is saying.
- Yet this same voice is strong and memorable and makes one listen even if one is irritated.
- There are a fair number of mistakes in grammar or spelling: more than "a sprinkling" but less than "riddled with."

To rank, on the other hand, is to be forced to translate those discriminations into a single number. What grade or holistic score do these judgments add up to? It's likely, by the way, that more readers would agree with those separate, "analytic" statements than would agree on a holistic score.

I've conducted many assessment sessions where we were not trying to impose a set of standards but rather to find out how experienced teachers read and evaluate, and I've had many opportunities to see that good readers give grades or scores right down through the range of possibilities. Of course good readers sometimes agree — especially on papers that are strikingly good or bad or conventional, but I think I see difference more frequently than agreement when readers really speak up.

The process of evaluation, because it invites us to articulate our criteria and to make distinctions among parts or features or dimensions of a performance, thereby invites us further to acknowledge the main fact about evaluation: that different readers have different priorities, values, and standards.

The conclusion I am drawing, then, in this first train of thought is that we should do less ranking and more evaluation. Instead of using grades or holistic scores — single number verdicts that try to sum up complex performances along only one scale — we should give some kind of written or spoken evaluation that discriminates among criteria and dimensions of the writing — and if possible that takes account of the complex context for writing: who the writer is, what the writer's audience and goals are, who we are as readers and how we read, and how we might differ in our reading from other readers the writer might be addressing.

But how can we put this principle into practice? The pressure for ranking seems implacable. Evaluation takes more time, effort, and money. It seems as though we couldn't get along without scores on writing exams. Most teachers are obliged to give grades at the end of each course. And many students — given that they have become conditioned or even addicted to ranking over the years and must continue to inhabit a ranking culture in most of their courses — will object if we don't put grades on papers. Some students, in the absence of that crude gold star or black mark, may not try hard enough (though how hard is "enough" — and is it really our job to stimulate motivation artificially with grades — and is grading the best source of motivation?).

It is important to note that there are certain schools and colleges that do *not* use single-number grades or scores, and they function successfully. I taught for nine years at Evergreen State College, which uses only written evaluations. This system works fine, even down to getting students accepted into high quality graduate and professional schools.

Nevertheless we have an intractable dilemma: that grading is unfair and counterproductive but that students and institutions tend to want grades. In the face of this dilemma there is a need for creativity and pragmatism. Here are some ways in which I and others use *less ranking* and *more evaluation* in teaching — and they suggest some adjustments in how we score large-scale assessments. What follows is an assortment of experimental compromises—sometimes crude, seldom ideal or utopian — but they help.

(a) Portfolios. Just because conventional institutions oblige us to turn in a single quantitative course grade at the end of every marking period, it doesn't follow that we need to grade individual papers. Course grades are more trustworthy and less damaging because they are based on so many performances over so many weeks. By avoiding frequent ranking or grading, we make it *somewhat* less likely for students to become addicted to oversimple numerical rankings — to think that evaluation always translates into a simple number — in short, to mistake ranking for evaluation. (I'm not trying to defend conventional course grades since they are still uncommunicative and they still feed the hunger for ranking.) Portfolios permit me to refrain from grading individual papers and limit myself to writerly evaluative comments — and help students see this as a positive rather than a negative thing, a chance to be graded on a body of their best work that can be judged more fairly. Portfolios have many other advantages as well. They are particularly valuable as occasions for asking students to write extensive and thoughtful explorations of their own strengths and weaknesses.

A midsemester portfolio is usually an informal affair, but it is a good occasion for giving anxious students a ballpark estimate of how well they are doing in the course so far. I find it helpful to tell students that I'm perfectly willing to tell them my best estimate of their course grade — but only if they come to me in conference and only during the second half of the semester. This serves somewhat to quiet their anxiety while they go through seven weeks of drying out from grades. By midsemester, most of them have come to enjoy not getting those numbers and thus being able to think better about more writerly comments from me and their classmates.

Portfolios are now used extensively and productively in larger assessments, and there is constant experimentation with new applications (Belanoff and Dickson; *Portfolio Assessment Newsletter; Portfolio News*).

(b) Another useful option is to make a strategic retreat from a wholly negative position. That is, I sometimes do a *bit* of ranking even on individual papers, using two "bottom-line" grades: H and U for "Honors" and "Unsatisfactory." I tell students that these translate to about A or A– and D or F. This practice may seem theoretically inconsistent with all the arguments I've just made, but (at the moment, anyway) I justify it for the following reasons.

First, I sympathize with a *part* of the students' anxiety about not getting grades: their fear that they might be failing and not know about it — or doing an excellent job and not get any recognition. Second, I'm not giving *many* grades; only a small proportion of papers get these H's or U's. The system creates a "non-bottom-line" or "non-quantified" atmosphere. Third, these holistic judgments about best and worst do not seem as arbitrary and questionable as most grades. There is usually a *bit* more agreement among readers about the best and worst papers. What seems most dubious is the process of trying to rank that whole middle range of papers — papers that have a mixture of better and worse qualities so that the numerical grade depends enormously on a reader's priorities or mood or temperament. My willingness to give these few grades goes a long way toward helping my students forgo most bottom-line grading.

I'm not trying to pretend that these minimal "grades" are truly reliable. But they represent a very small amount of ranking. Yes, someone could insist that I'm really ranking every single paper (and indeed if it seemed politically necessary, I could put an OK or S [for satisfactory] on all those middle range papers and brag, "Yes, I grade everything"). But the fact is that I am doing *much less sorting* since I don't have to sort them into five or even twelve piles. Thus there is a huge reduction in the total amount of unreliability I produce.

(It might seem that if I use only these few minimal grades I have no good way for figuring out a final grade for the course — since that requires a more fine-grained set of ranks. But I don't find that to be the case. For I also give these same minimal grades to the many other important parts of my course such as attendance, meeting deadlines, peer responding, and journal writing. If I want a mathematically computed grade on a scale of six or A through E, I can easily compute it when I have such a large number of grades to work from — even though they are only along a three-point scale.)

This same practice of crude or minimal ranking is a big help on larger assessments outside classrooms, and needs to be applied to the process of assessment in general. There are two important principles to emphasize. On the one hand we must be prudent or accommodating enough to admit that despite all the arguments against ranking, there *are* situations when we need that bottom-line verdict along one scale: which student has not done satisfactory work and should be denied credit for the course? which student gets the scholarship? which candidate to hire or fire? We often operate with scarce resources. But on the other hand we must be bold enough to insist that we do far more ranking than is really needed. We can get along not only with fewer occasions for assessment but also with fewer

Strong	OK	Weak	
			CONTENT, INSIGHTS, THINKING, GRAPPLING WITH TOPIC
			GENUINE REVISION, SUBSTANTIVE CHANGES, NOT JUST EDITING
			ORGANIZATION, STRUCTURE, GUIDING THE READER
			LANGUAGE: SYNTAX, SENTENCES, WORDING, VOICE
			MECHANICS: SPELLING, GRAMMER, PUNCTUATION, PROOFREADING
			OVERALL [Note: this is not a sum of the other scores.]

Figure 1.

gradations in scoring. If we decide what the *real* bottom-line is on a given occasion — perhaps just "failing" or perhaps "honors" too — then the reading of papers or portfolios is enormously quick and cheap. It leaves time and money for evaluation — perhaps for analytic scoring or some comment.

At Stony Brook we worked out a portfolio system where multiple readers had only to make a binary decision: acceptable or not. Then individual teachers could decide the actual course grade and give comments for their own students — so long as those students passed in the eyes of an independent rater (Elbow and Belanoff; Belanoff and Elbow). The best way to begin to wean our society from its addiction to ranking may be to permit a tiny bit of it (which also means less unreliability) — rather than trying to go "cold turkey."

(c) Sometimes I use an analytic grid for evaluating and commenting on student papers. An example is given in Figure 1.

I often vary the criteria in my grid (e.g. "connecting with readers" or "investment") depending on the assignment or the point in the semester.

Grids are a way I can satisfy the students' hunger for ranking but still not give in to conventional grades on individual papers. Sometimes I provide nothing but a grid (especially on final drafts), and this is a very quick way to provide a response. Or on midprocess drafts I sometimes use a grid in addition to a comment: a more readerly comment that often doesn't so much tell them what's wrong or right or how to improve things but rather tries to give them an account of what is *happening to me* as I read their words. I think this kind of comment is really the most useful thing of all for students, but it frustrates some students for a while. The grid can help these students feel less anxious and thus pay better attention to my comment.

I find grids extremely helpful at the end of the semester for telling students their strengths and weaknesses in the course — or what they've done well and not so well. Besides categories like the ones above, I use categories like these: "skill in giving feedback to others," "ability to meet deadlines," "effort," and "improvement." This practice makes my final grade much more communicative.

(d) I also help make up for the absence of ranking — gold stars and black marks — by having students share their writing with each other a great deal both orally and through frequent publication in class magazines. Also, where possible, I try to get students to give or send writing to audiences outside the class. At the University of Massachusetts at Amherst, freshmen pay a ten dollar lab fee for the writing course, and every teacher publishes four or five class magazines of final drafts a semester. The effects are striking. Sharing, peer feedback, and publication give the best reward and motivation for writing, namely, getting your words out to many readers.

(e) I sometimes use a kind of modified *contract grading.* That is, at the start of the course I pass out a long list of all the things that I most want students to do — the concrete activities that I think most lead to learning — and I promise students that if they do them *all* they are guaranteed a certain final grade. Currently, I say it's a B — it could be lower or higher. My list includes these items: not missing more than a week's worth of classes; not having more than one late major assignment; *substantive* revising on all major revisions; good copy editing on all final revisions; good effort on peer feedback work; keeping up the journal; and substantial effort and investment on each draft.

I like the way this system changes the "bottom-line" for a course: the intersection where my authority crosses their self-interest. I can tell them, "You have to work very hard in this course, but you can stop worrying about grades." The crux is no longer that commodity I've always hated and never trusted: a numerical ranking of the quality of their writing along a single continuum. Instead the crux becomes what I care about most: the *concrete behaviors* that I most want students to engage in because they produce more learning and help me teach better. Admittedly, effort and investment are not concrete observable behaviors, but they are no harder to judge than overall quality of writing. And since I care about effort and investment, I don't mind the few arguments I get into about them; they seem fruitful. ("Let's try and figure out why it looked to me as though you didn't put any effort in here.") In contrast, I hate discussions about grades on a paper and find such arguments fruitless. Besides, I'm not making fine distinctions about effort and investment — just letting a bell go off when they fall palpably low.

It's crucial to note that I am *not* fighting evaluation with this system. I am just fighting ranking or grading. I still write evaluative comments and often use an evaluative grid to tell my students what I see as strengths and weaknesses in their papers. My goal is not to get rid of evaluation but in fact to emphasize it, enhance it. I'm trying to get students to listen *better* to my evaluations — by uncoupling them from a grade. In effect, I'm doing this because I'm so fed up with students *following* or *obeying* my evaluations too blindly — making whatever changes my comments suggest but doing it for the sake of a grade; not really taking the time to make up their own minds about whether they think my judgments or suggestions really make sense to them. The worst part of grades is that they make students obey us without carefully thinking about the merits of what we say. I love the situation this system so often puts students in: I make a criticism or suggestion about their paper, but it doesn't matter to their grade whether they go along with me or not (so long as they genuinely revise in some fashion). They have to think; to decide.

Admittedly this system is crude and impure. Some of the really skilled students who are used to getting A's and desperate to get one in this course remain unhelpfully hung up about getting those H's on their papers. But a good number of these students discover that they can't get them, and they soon settle down to accepting a B and having less anxiety and more of a learning voyage.

The Limitations of Evaluation and the Benefits of Evaluation-free Zones

Everything I've said so far has been in praise of evaluation as a substitute for ranking. But I need to turn a corner here and speak about the *limits* or *problems* of evaluation. Evaluating may be better than ranking, but it still carries some of the same problems. That is, even though I've praised evaluation for inviting us to acknowledge that readers and contexts are different, nevertheless the very word *evaluation* tends to imply fairness or reliability or getting beyond personal or subjective preferences. Also, of course, evaluation takes a lot more time and work. To rank you just have to put down a number; holistic scoring of exams is cheaper than analytic scoring.

Most important of all, evaluation harms the climate for learning and teaching — or rather *too much* evaluation has this effect. That is, if we evaluate *everything* students write, they tend to remain tangled up in the assumption that their whole job in school is to give teachers "what they want." Constant evaluation makes students worry more about psyching out the teacher than about what they are really learning. Students fall into a kind of defensive or on-guard stance toward the teacher: a desire to hide what they don't understand and try to impress. This stance gets in the way of learning. (Think of the patient trying to hide symptoms from the doctor.) Most of all, constant evaluation by someone in authority makes students reluctant to take the risks that are needed for good learning — to try out hunches and trust their own judgment. Face it: if our goal is to get students to exercise their own judgment, that means exercising an immature and undeveloped judgment and making choices that are obviously wrong to us.

We see around us a widespread hunger to be evaluated that is often just as strong as the hunger to rank. Countless conditions make many of us walk around in the world wanting to ask others (especially those in authority), "How am I doing, did I do OK?" I don't think the hunger to be evaluated is as harmful as the hunger to rank, but it can get in the way of learning. For I find that the greatest and most powerful breakthroughs in learning occur when I can get myself and others to *put aside* this nagging, self-doubting question ("How am I doing? How am I doing?") — and instead to take some chances, trust our instincts or hungers. When everything is evaluated, everything counts. Often the most powerful arena for deep learning is a kind of "time out" zone from the pressures of normal evaluated reality: make-believe, play, dreams — in effect, the Shakespearian forest.

In my attempts to get away from too much evaluation (not from all evaluation, just from too much of it), I have drifted into a set of teaching practices which now feel to me like the *best* part of my teaching. I realize now what I've been unconsciously doing for a number of years: creating "evaluation-free zones."

(a) The paradigm evaluation-free zone is the ten minute, nonstop freewrite. When I get students to freewrite, I am using my authority to create unusual conditions in order to contradict or interrupt our pervasive habit of always evaluating our writing. What is essential here are the two central features of freewriting: that it be private (thus I don't collect it or have students share it with anyone else); and that it be nonstop (thus there isn't time for planning, and control is usually diminished). Students quickly catch on and enter into the spirit. At the end of the course, they often tell me that freewriting is the most useful thing I've taught them (see Belanoff, Elbow, and Fontaine).

(b) A larger evaluation-free zone is the single unevaluated assignment — what people sometimes call the "quickwrite" or sketch. This is a piece of writing that I ask students to do — either in class or for homework — without any or much revising. It is meant to be low stakes writing. There is a bit of pressure, nevertheless, since I usually ask them to share it with others and *I* usually collect it and read it. But I don't write any comments at all — except perhaps to put straight lines along some passages I like or to write a phrase of appreciation at the end. And I ask students to refrain from giving evaluative feedback to each other — and instead just to say "thank you" or mention a couple of phrases or ideas that stick in mind. (However, this writing-without-feedback can be a good occasion for students to discuss the *topic* they have written about — and thus serve as an excellent kick-off for discussions of what I am teaching.)

(c) These experiments have led me to my next and largest evaluation-free zone — what I sometimes call a "jump start" for my whole course. For the last few semesters I've been devoting the first three weeks *entirely* to the two evaluation-free activities I've just described: freewriting (and also more leisurely private writing in a journal) and quickwrites or sketches. Since the stakes are low and I'm not asking for much revising, I ask for *much more* writing homework per week than usual. And every day we write in class: various exercises or games. The emphasis is on getting rolling, getting fluent, taking risks. And every day all students read out loud something they've written — sometimes a short passage even to the whole class. So despite the absence of feedback, it is a very audience-filled and sociable three weeks.

At first I only dared do this for two weeks, but when I discovered how fast the writing improves, how good it is for building community, and what a pleasure this period is for me, I went to three weeks. I'm curious to try an experiment with teaching a whole course this way. I wonder, that is, whether all that evaluation we work so hard to give really does any more good than the constant writing and sharing (Zak).

I need to pause here to address an obvious rejoinder: "But withholding evaluation is not normal!" Indeed, it is *not* normal — certainly not normal in school. We normally tend to emphasize evaluations — even bottom-line ranking kinds of evaluations. But I resist the argument that if it's not normal we shouldn't do it.

The best argument for evaluation-free zones is from experience. If you try them, I suspect you'll discover that they are satisfying and bring out good writing. Students have a better time writing these unevaluated pieces; they enjoy hearing and appreciating these pieces when they don't have to evaluate. And *I* have a much better time when I engage in this astonishing activity: reading student work when I don't have to evaluate and respond. And yet the writing improves. I see students investing and risking more, writing more fluently, and using livelier, more interesting voices. This writing gives me and them a higher standard of clarity and voice for when we move on to more careful and revised writing tasks that involve more intellectual pushing — tasks that sometimes make their writing go tangled or sodden.

The Benefits and Feasibility of Liking

Liking and disliking seem like unpromising topics in an exploration of assessment. They seem to represent the worst kind of subjectivity, the merest accident of personal taste. But I've recently come to think that the phenomenon of liking is perhaps the most important evaluative response for writers and teachers to think about. In effect, I'm turning another corner in my argument. In the first section I argued against ranking — with evaluating being the solution. Next I argued not *against* evaluating — but for no-evaluation zones in *addition* to evaluating. Now I will argue neither against evaluating nor against no-evaluation zones, but for something very different in addition, or perhaps underneath, as a foundation: liking.

Let me start with the germ story. I was in a workshop and we were going around the circle with everyone telling a piece of good news about their writing in the last six months. It got to Wendy Bishop, a good poet (who has also written two good books about the teaching of writing), and she said, "In the last six months, I've learned to *like* everything I write." Our jaws dropped; we were startled — in a way scandalized. But I've been chewing on her words ever since, and they have led me into a retelling of the story of how people learn to write better.

The old story goes like this: We write something. We read it over and we say, "This is terrible. I *hate* it. I've got to work on it and improve it." And we do, and it gets better, and this happens again and again, and before long we have become a wonderful writer. But that's not really what happens. Yes, we vow to work on it — but we don't. And next time we have the impulse to write, we're just a *bit* less likely to start.

What really happens when people learn to write better is more like this: We write something. We read it over and we say, "This is terrible. . . . But I *like* it. Damn it, I'm going to get it good enough so that others will like it too." And this time we don't just put it in a drawer, we actually work hard on it. And we try it out on other people too — not just to get feedback and advice but, perhaps more important, to find someone else who will like it.

Notice the two stories here — two hypotheses. (a) "First you improve the faults and then you like it." (b) "First you like it and then you improve faults." The second story may sound odd when stated so baldly, but really it's common sense. Only if we like something will we get involved enough to work and struggle with it. Only if we like what we write will we write again and again by choice — which is the only way we get better.

This hypothesis sheds light on the process of how people get to be published writers. Conventional wisdom assumes a Darwinian model: poor writers are unread; then they get better; as a result, they get a wider audience; finally they turn into Norman Mailer. But now I'd say the process is more complicated. People who get better and get published really tend to be driven by how much *they* care about their writing. Yes, they have a small audience at first — after all, they're not very good. But they try reader after reader until finally they can find people who like and appreciate their writing. I certainly did this. If someone doesn't like her writing enough to be pushy and hungry about finding a few people who also like it, she probably won't get better.

It may sound so far as though all the effort and drive comes from the lonely driven writer — and sometimes it does (Norman Mailer is no joke). But, often enough, readers play the crucially active role in this story of how writers get better. That is, the way writers *learn* to like their writing is by the grace of having a reader or two who likes it — even though it's not good. Having at least a few appreciative readers is probably indispensable to getting better.

When I apply this story to our situation as teachers I come up with this interesting hypothesis: *good writing teachers like student writing* (and like students). I think I see this borne out — and it is really nothing but common sense. Teachers who hate student writing and hate students are grouchy all the time. How could we stand our work and do a decent job if we hated their writing? Good teachers see what is only *potentially* good, they get a kick out of mere possibility — and they encourage it. When I manage to do this, I teach well.

Thus, I've begun to notice a turning point in my courses — two or three weeks into the semester: "Am I going to like these folks or is this going to be a battle, a struggle?" When I like them everything seems to go better — and it seems to me they learn more by the end. When I don't and we stay tangled up in struggle, we all suffer — and they seem to learn less.

So what am I saying? That we should like bad writing? How can we see all the weaknesses and criticize student writing if we just like it? But here's the interesting point: if I *like* someone's writing it's *easier* to criticize it.

I first noticed this when I was trying to gather essays for the book on freewriting that Pat Belanoff and Sheryl Fontaine and I edited. I would read an essay someone had written, I would want it for the book, but I had some serious criticism. I'd get excited and write, "I really like this, and I hope we can use it in our book, but you've got to get rid of this and change that, and I got really mad at this other thing." I usually find it hard to criticize, but I began to notice that I was a much more critical and pushy reader when I liked something. It's even fun to criticize in those conditions.

It's the same with student writing. If I like a piece, I don't have to pussyfoot around with my criticism. It's when I don't like their writing that I find myself tiptoeing: trying to soften my criticism, trying to find something nice to say — and usually sounding fake, often unclear. I see the same thing with my own writing. If I like it, I can criticize it better. I have faith that there'll still be something good left, even if I train my full critical guns on it.

In short — and to highlight how this section relates to the other two sections of this essay — liking is not the same as ranking or evaluating. Naturally, people get them mixed up: when they like something, they assume it's good; when they hate it, they assume it's bad. But it's helpful to uncouple the two domains and realize that it makes perfectly good sense to say, "This is terrible, but I like it." Or, "This is good, but I hate it." In short, I am not arguing here *against* criticizing or evaluating. I'm merely arguing *for* liking.

Let me sum up my clump of hypotheses so far:

- It's not improvement that leads to liking, but rather liking that leads to improvement.

- It's the mark of good writers to like their writing.
- Liking is not the same as evaluating. We can often criticize something better when we like it.
- We learn to like our writing when we have a respected reader who likes it.
- Therefore, it's the mark of good teachers to like students and their writing.

If this set of hypotheses is true, what practical consequences follow from it? How can we be better at liking? It feels as though we have no choice — as though liking and not-liking just happen to us. I don't really understand this business. I'd love to hear discussion about the mystery of liking — the phenomenology of liking. I sense it's some kind of putting oneself out — or holding oneself open — but I can't see it clearly. I have a hunch, however, that we're not so helpless about liking as we tend to feel.

For in fact I can suggest some practical concrete activities that I have found fairly reliable at increasing the chances of liking student writing:

(a) I ask for lots of private writing and merely shared writing, that is, writing that I don't read at all, and writing that I read but don't comment on. This makes me more cheerful because it's so much easier. Students get *better* without me. Having to evaluate writing — especially bad writing — makes me more likely to hate it. This throws light on grading: it's hard to like something if we know we have to give it a D.

(b) I have students share lots of writing with each other — and after a while respond to each other. It's easier to like their writing when I don't feel myself as the only reader and judge. And so it helps to build community in general: it takes pressure off me. Thus I try to use peer groups not only for feedback, but for other activities too, such as collaborative writing, brainstorming, putting class magazines together, and working out other decisions.

(c) I increase the chances of my liking their writing when I get better at finding what *is* good — or *potentially* good — and learn to praise it. This is a skill. It requires a good eye, a good nose. We tend — especially in the academic world — to assume that a good eye or fine discrimination means *criticizing*. Academics are sometimes proud of their tendency to be bothered by what is bad. Thus I find I am sometimes looked down on as dumb and undiscriminating: "He likes bad writing. He must have no taste, no discrimination." But I've finally become angry rather than defensive. It's an act of discrimination to see what's good in bad writing. Maybe, in fact, this is the secret of the mystery of liking: to be able to see potential goodness underneath badness.

Put it this way. We tend to stereotype liking as a "soft" and sentimental activity. Mr. Rogers is our model. Fine. There's nothing wrong with softness and sentiment — and I love Mr. Rogers. But liking can also be hard-assed. Let me suggest an alternative to Mr. Rogers: B. F. Skinner. Skinner taught pigeons to play ping-pong. How did he do it? Not by moaning, "Pigeon standards are falling. The pigeons they send us these days are no good. When I was a pigeon . . ." He did it by a careful, disciplined method that involved close analytic observation. He put pigeons on a ping-pong table with a ball, and every time a pigeon turned his head 30 degrees toward the ball, he gave a reward (see my "Danger of Softness").

What would this approach require in the teaching of writing? It's very simple . . . but not easy. Imagine that we want to teach students an ability they badly lack, for example how to organize their writing or how to make their sentences clearer. Skinner's insight is that we get nowhere in this task by just telling them how much they lack this skill: "It's disorganized. Organize it!" "It's unclear. Make it clear!"

No, what we must learn to do is to read closely and carefully enough to show the student little bits of *proto*-organization or *sort of* clarity in what they've already written. We don't have to pretend the writing is wonderful. We could even say, "This is a terrible paper and the worst part about it is the lack of organization. But I will teach you how to organize. Look here at this little organizational move you made in this sentence. Read it out loud and try to feel how it pulls together this stuff here and distinguishes it from that stuff there. Try to remember what it felt like writing that sentence — creating that piece of organization. Do it some more." Notice how much more helpful it is if we can say, "Do *more* of what you've done here," than if we say, "Do something *different* from anything you've done in the whole paper."

When academics criticize behaviorism as crude it often means that they aren't willing to do the close careful reading of student writing that is required. They'd rather give a cursory reading and turn up their nose and give a low grade and complain about falling standards. No one has undermined behaviorism's main principle of learning: that reward produces learning more effectively than punishment.

(d) I improve my chances of liking student writing when I take steps to get to know them a bit as people. I do this partly through the assignments I give. That is, I always ask them to write a letter or two to me and to each other (for example about their history with writing). I base at least a couple of assignments on their own experiences, memories, or histories. And I make sure some of the assignments are free choice pieces — which also helps me know them.

In addition, I make sure to have at least three conferences with each student each semester — the first one very early. I often call off some classes in order to keep conferences from being too onerous (insisting nevertheless that students meet with their partner or small group when class is called off). Some teachers have mini-conferences with students during class — while students are engaged in writing or peer group meetings. I've found that when I deal only with my classes as a whole — as a large group — I sometimes experience them as a herd or lump — as stereotyped "adolescents"; I fail to experience them as individuals. For me, personally, this is disastrous since it often leads me to experience them as that scary tribe that I felt rejected by when *I* was an eighteen-year-old — and thus, at times, as "the enemy." But when I sit down with them face to face, they are not so stereotyped or alien or threatening — they are just eighteen-year-olds.

Getting a glimpse of them as individual people is particularly helpful in cases where their writing is not just bad, but somehow offensive — perhaps violent or cruelly racist or homophobic or sexist — or frighteningly vacuous. When I know them just a bit I can often see behind their awful attitude to the person and the life situation that spawned it, and not hate their writing so much. When I know students I can see that they are smart behind that dumb behavior; they are doing the best they can behind that bad behavior. Conditions are keeping them from acting decently; something is holding them back.

(e) It's odd, but the more I let myself show, the easier it is to like them and their writing. I need to share some of my own writing — show some of my own feelings. I need to write the letter to them that they write to me — about my past experiences and what I want and don't want to happen.

(f) It helps to work on my own writing — and work on learning to *like* it. Teachers who are most critical and sour about student writing are often having trouble with their own writing. They are bitter or unforgiving or hurting toward their own work. (I think I've noticed that failed PhDs are often the most severe and difficult with students.) When we are stuck or sour in our own writing, what helps us most is to find spaces free from evaluation such as those provided by freewriting and journal writing. Also, activities like reading out loud and finding a supportive reader or two. I would insist, then, that if only for the sake of our teaching, we need to learn to be charitable and to like our own writing.

A final word. I fear that this sermon about liking might seem an invitation to guilt. There is enough pressure on us as teachers that we don't need someone coming along and calling us inadequate if we don't *like* our students and their writing. That is, even though I think I am right to make this foray into the realm of feeling, I also acknowledge that it is dangerous — and paradoxical. It strikes me that we also need to have permission to hate the dirty bastards and their stupid writing.

After all, the conditions under which they go to school bring out some awful behavior on their part, and the conditions under which we teach sometimes make it difficult for us to like them and their writing. Writing wasn't meant to be read in stacks of twenty-five, fifty, or seventy-five. And we are handicapped as teachers when students are in our classes against their will. (Thus high school teachers have the worst problem here, since their students tend to be the most sour and resentful about school.)

Indeed, one of the best aids to liking students and their writing is to be somewhat charitable toward ourselves about the opposite feelings that we inevitably have. I used to think it was terrible for teachers to tell those sarcastic stories and hostile jokes about their students: "teacher room talk." But now I've come to think that people who spend their lives teaching *need* an arena to let off this unhappy steam. And certainly it's better to vent this sarcasm and hostility with our buddies than on the students themselves. The question, then, becomes this: do we help this behavior function as a venting so that we can move past it and not be trapped in our inevitable resentment of students? Or do we tell these stories and jokes as a way of staying stuck in the hurt, hostile, or bitter feelings — year after year — as so many sad teachers do?

In short I'm not trying to invite guilt, I'm trying to invite hope. I'm trying to suggest that if we do a sophisticated analysis of the difference between liking and evaluating, we will see that it's possible (if not always easy) to like students and their writing — without having to give up our intelligence, sophistication, or judgment.

Let me sum up the points I'm trying to make about ranking, evaluating, and liking:

- Let's do as little ranking and grading as we can. They are never fair and they undermine learning and teaching.
- Let's use evaluation instead — a more careful, more discriminating, fairer mode of assessment.
- But because evaluating is harder than ranking, and because too much evaluating also undermines learning, let's establish small but important evaluation-free zones.
- And underneath it all — suffusing the whole evaluative enterprise — let's learn to be better likers: liking our own and our students' writing, and realizing that liking need not get in the way of clear-eyed evaluation.

Works Cited

Belanoff, Pat, and Peter Elbow. "Using Portfolios to Increase Collaboration and Community in a Writing Program." *WPA: Journal of Writing Program Administration* 9.3 (Spring 1986): 27–40. (Also in *Portfolios: Process and Product*. Ed. Pat Belanoff and Marcia Dickson. Portsmouth, NH: Boynton/Cook-Heinemann, 1991.)

Belanoff, Pat, Peter Elbow, and Sheryl Fontaine, eds. *Nothing Begins with N: New Investigations of Freewriting*. Carbondale: Southern Illinois UP, 1991.

Bishop, Wendy. *Something Old, Something New: College Writing Teachers and Classroom Change*. Carbondale: Southern Illinois UP, 1990.

———. *Released into Language: Options for Teaching Creative Writing*. Urbana: NCTE, 1990.

Diederich, Paul. *Measuring Growth in English*. Urbana: NCTE, 1974.

Elbow, Peter. "The Danger of Softness." *What Is English?* New York: MLA, 1990. 197–210.

Elbow, Peter, and Pat Belanoff. "State University of New York: Portfolio-Based Evaluation Program." *New Methods in College Writing Programs: Theory into Practice*. Ed. Paul Connolly and Teresa Vilardi. New York: MLA, 1986. 95–105. (Also in *Portfolios: Process and Product*. Ed. Pat Belanoff and Marcia Dickson. Portsmouth, NH: Boynton/Cook-Heinemann, 1991.)

Gardner, Howard. *Frames of Mind: The Theory of Multiple Intelligences*. New York: Basic, 1983.

Kirschenbaum, Howard, Sidney Simon, and Rodney Napier. *Wad-Ja-Get? The Grading Game in American Education*. New York: Hart, 1971.

Lewis, C. S. *Studies in Words*. 2nd ed. London: Cambridge UP, 1967.

Portfolio Assessment Newsletter. Five Centerpointe Drive, Suite 100, Lake Oswego, Oregon 97035.

Portfolio News. c/o San Dieguito Union High School District, 710 Encinitas Boulevard, Encinitas, CA 92024.

Smith, Barbara Herrnstein. *Contingencies of Value: Alternative Perspectives for Critical Theory*. Cambridge: Harvard UP, 1988.

White, Edward M. *Teaching and Assessing Writing*. San Francisco: Jossey-Bass, 1985.

Zak, Frances. "Exclusively Positive Responses to Student Writing." *Journal of Basic Writing* 9.2 (1990): 40–53.

PART TWO

PARAGRAPHS

Part II of *The Bedford Handbook*, "Constructing Paragraphs," reminds students regularly that paragraphs contribute to the overall effectiveness of a piece of writing. And although it presents patterns of paragraph development, coverage of topic sentences and discussions of coherence, the handbook emphasizes flexibility and an approach to paragraphing that stresses writing's communicative function. The following selections address one of the central questions that teachers grapple with as they decide how to teach students about paragraphs and paragraphing:

* What are some of the alternatives to teaching rigid patterns and prescriptive rules about development and coherence?

From PARAGRAPHING FOR THE READER

Rick Eden and Ruth Mitchell

[College Composition and Communication 37 (1986): 416–30.]

Rick Eden is a writer/analyst at the RAND Corporation. He has published articles and reviews in several journals, and he has taught a wide variety of composition and rhetoric courses. Ruth Mitchell is author of First Steps *(1990) and* Testing for Learning *(1991).*

The following excerpt is the introduction and first part of Eden and Mitchell's article "Paragraphing for the Reader," in which they react to the prevalent method of teaching paragraphing found in many textbooks. Arguing that teaching students formulas for constructing paragraphs is ineffective, they demonstrate convincingly that we should teach writers to make paragraphing decisions in light of "purpose, audience, and rhetorical stance," always attending to readers' expectations.

The teaching of paragraphs needs a revolution. Classroom instruction offers patterns and precepts which cannot be applied to the ordinary process of writing and which, moreover, are unsupported by current research. Researchers in English like Braddock, Meade and Ellis, and Knoblauch report findings which directly contradict the textbooks' platitudes:[1] Paragraphs in admired professional writing do not necessarily contain topic sentences, they rarely follow prescribed patterns, and they seem essentially accidental, invented as the writer composes.

We have found that textbooks do not heed these warnings. Students perceive a strange disjunction between the paragraphs they read and those they are asked to write in class. Too often the latter are miniature five-element themes — introductory and concluding sentences, with three intervening sentences connected by "therefore" and "in addition."

We believe that paragraphing is best presented to student writers as an important signaling system, based on signals of two sorts, visual and substantive. To readers, the strip of indented white space separating paragraphs indicates both connection and discontinuity. It heightens their attention. To the writer, marking paragraphs offers opportunity for manipulating the reader's focus. Strategically paragraphed prose not only streamlines a message but also molds and shapes it to achieve the writer's purpose.

We shall argue for a reader-oriented theory of the paragraph.[2] In order to paragraph effectively, a writer needs to know, not the five, ten, fifteen, or twenty most common paragraph patterns that current theories enumerate, but how indentions affect the reader's perception of prose discourse. Knowing how readers perceive prose, the writer can arrange his text to mesh with their perception.

Our argument proposes (and, we hope, proves) two main theses:

1. Paragraphs depend for their effectiveness on the exploitation of psycholinguistic features — that is, of the reader's conventional expectations and perceptual patterns. For example, readers treat the first sentence of a paragraph as the orienting statement necessary for them to understand the rest, regardless of whether the writer so intended. Thus a paragraph does not "need" a topic sentence: Every paragraph has one, willy-nilly. The question for the writer is not "Where shall I put my topic sentence?" but "Do I want this initial statement to direct the reader's understanding of the paragraph?" A good deal of our argument will explicate and extend these psycholinguistic features and their consequences.
2. Paragraphing is not part of the composing but of the editing process. To think about paragraphs too early may invoke the blocking mechanisms that Mike Rose has described in "Rigid Rules, Inflexible Plans, and the Stifling of Language: A Cognitivist Analysis of Writer's Block" (*College Composition and Communication*, 41 [December 1980], 389–400) [p. 66 in this book]. Current paragraph theory has assumed that paragraphing is part of the process of generating, whereas it properly belongs with revision. It refines and shapes material already on the page.

Our argument is divided into four parts. In the first we explain the reader's expectations of paragraphs and point out research which has clarified these expectations. Part Two demonstrates the strengths and weaknesses of the most popular current model of paragraph structure, the scheme devised by Francis Christensen to explain paragraph structure according to levels of generality. In Part Three an extended example demonstrates the power of rhetorical paragraphing. In Part Four we lay out pedagogical implications of our reader-oriented theory.[3]

1

Paragraphing for the reader means meeting the reader's expectations. These expectations are unconscious and remain so unless repeatedly disappointed. Some are rooted in cognition itself, in the reader's patterns of perception and comprehension. Others are rooted in rhetorical convention, in current practices of formatting prose.

What are these expectations?

1. Readers expect to see paragraphs when they read a piece of extended prose. They expect to see regularly spaced indentions. This is only an expectation about the appearance of the page. How frequently readers expect the indentions to appear — i.e., how long they expect the average paragraph to run — will vary according to several factors, including the size and genre of the text as a whole. Readers conventionally expect a book on philosophy to have many very long paragraphs, some filling entire pages. They do not expect the same from a modern narrow-column newspaper. Reading typescript, they need relief upon encountering pages unbroken by indentions — too many such pages make a coffee break irresistible.

   This initial, visual expectation — that prose will be indented at regular intervals — is conventional, and it changes as continually as other social conventions. In the nineteenth century, for instance, readers expected newspapers virtually to eschew indentions. The other expectations, which follow, are derived from human cognitive processes and are thus universal.

2. Readers expect paragraphs to be unified simply because they perceive them as units. Readers expect the paragraph's formal unity to signal substantive unity and they infer one from the other as they half-find and half-fashion significance in the text.

3. Readers expect the initial sentences of a paragraph to orient them, to identify the context in which succeeding sentences are to be understood. Readers accept the initial sentences as instructions for integrating what they are about to read with what they have just read.

   These instructions do little good if readers receive them only as they finish reading a paragraph: To work effectively the instructions must appear initially. People understand material most readily when it is presented to them in a top-down fashion, with details and reasons preceded by orienting statements.[4]

4. Readers expect to find at each paragraph's peripheral points something which merits special attention, because readers naturally attend to endpoints. As they read a paragraph, their attention is greatest as they begin and end. This is simply a fact about perception — a principle of peripherality.[5] We shall show that it has implications for the rhetorical organization of paragraphs.

5. Readers expect paragraphs to be coherent, both internally and externally. The demand for external coherence is implied by the expectation for unity. To distinguish external from internal coherence, we will term the latter "cohesiveness." The reader expects each paragraph to cohere internally as well as externally, to contain a sensible sequence of thought within itself as well as to continue one begun in previous paragraphs.

Current rhetorics teach various strategies, such as repeating words and structures and supplying transitional words and phrases, to help the writer make the text cohere for the reader, and it is important that writers learn them. However, important as these strategies are in practice, in theory they have nothing to do with paragraphing. Readers expect paragraphs to be cohesive only because they expect all prose, all discourse, to be so. Rhetorics would have to teach these strategies even if we did not conventionally organize prose into paragraphs.

The same is true of the many plans of development — compare/contrast, topic/comment, question/answer, and so on — that rhetorics teach as ways to organize paragraphs internally. These patterns also have nothing inherent to do with the practice of indention. They are characterized in some texts as "types" of paragraphs simply because paragraphs provide conveniently sized forums in which to discuss, illustrate, and practice them. Francis Christensen made this point twenty years ago, but no one seems much to have heeded him:

> These methods [of paragraph development] are real, but they are simply methods of development — period. They are no more relevant to the paragraph than, on the short side, to the sentence or, on the long side, to a run of several paragraphs or to a paper as long as this or a chapter. They are the topoi of classical rhetoric. They are the channels our minds naturally run in whether we are writing a sentence or a paragraph or planning a paper. [*Notes toward a New Rhetoric*, 2nd ed. [New York: Harper & Row, 1978], p. 77)

Not many researchers have investigated how paragraphing influences the reader's interpretation of the text, but during the 1960s Koen, Becker, and Young performed a series of experiments which support our characterization of the reader's expectations.[6] They established that paragraphs are both visual and structural units. A writer sets up a paragraph by framing it with white space. He unifies its structure with three kinds of internal markers, representing the three systems which interact to produce cohesion. The lexical system depends on reiterated nouns and pronouns producing a chain of references over several sentences. These are the lexical markers. The grammatical system is signaled by inflections, the grammatical markers. The rhetorical system consists of expository patterns or modes of development — topic and illustration, for example. Its markers consist of so-called "collocational sets," that is, words whose meanings cluster round a general topic. Formal markers — such as conjunctions and transitional words and phrases — permitted subjects in Koen, Becker, and Young's experiments to recognize the systems even in nonsense passages. When prose is well paragraphed, these markers permit readers to predict paragraph boundaries in unindented passages.

The experimenters established an important principle: reparagraphing — i.e., moving indention points — is not only typographical but also substantive. Because the visual breaks direct the reader's attention, changing them changes the reader's interpretation of the text. They thus showed that paragraphs have a psychological as well as a physical reality. Their results pointed toward a reader-oriented theory of the paragraph.

More recent research, conducted by David Kieras, a psychologist at the University of Arizona, also supports our reader-oriented approach. His work corroborates our characterization of the reader's expectations for initial, orienting material. Kieras has found that "information appearing first in the passage has more influence on the reader's perception of the main idea compared to the very same information appearing later in the passage" ("How Readers Abstract Main Ideas from Technical Prose: Some Implications for Document Design," paper presented at a Document Design Center Colloquium, American Institute for Research, Washington, D.C., 17 November 1980, p. 6). These results led him to endorse the initial placement of orienting sentences: "the topic sentence of a passage really should be first, because that is where a reader expects to find the important information" (p. 7). A paragraph which violates this expectation may remain comprehensible, of course, especially if the content is familiar to the reader, but it takes longer to read and demands more work of the reader, who must revise his notion of the paragraph's main point as he proceeds.

Paragraphing is as complex as the reader's pattern of comprehension and expectation. A writer who understands these complexities commands a powerful and flexible rhetorical resource. With paragraphs, writers can shape their text so as to influence its reading. Indeed, paragraphing offers the prose writer the poet's privileges. Prose writers cannot govern the placement of sentences — where they begin and end depends on layout design, choice of typeface, size of page, and so on. But they can choose where the white indentions will indicate paragraphs. That choice offers them opportunity and responsibility, the opportunity to manipulate the reader's attention and the responsibility to do so effectively. To paragraph well, writers must exploit and reinforce the visual impact of indentions. They must provide the unity and cohesion that the paragraph's visual form promises.

Current text-oriented writing theory and pedagogy misrepresent paragraphing by oversimplifying it. Text-centered approaches abbreviate the writing process; they treat the text rather than the reader as its endpoint. This over-simplification creates unnecessary complications in the form of poorly motivated prescriptions (e.g., for unity) and fossilized taxonomies.

The inadequacy of these taxonomies is evident to anyone who has tried to learn or teach them. They are not and cannot possibly become exhaustive. They can't list every type of paragraph, every strategy for paragraphing. Thus, they don't give the student the flexibility he will need to handle unanticipated rhetorical demands. Nor can the taxonomies help us to evaluate paragraphs: It's impossible to know whether a paragraph which doesn't fall under one of the types is a poor paragraph or a new species.

Formal definitions of the paragraph also vitiate much research and pedagogy. Too many researchers and rhetoricians take the paragraph to be a conveniently sized, self-contained piece of prose — a sort of latter-day *chreia*. Roger C. Schank, for instance, in a paper entitled "Understanding Paragraphs" (Technical Report, Instituto per gli studi semantici e cognitivi, Castagnola, Switzerland, 1974), investigates the structures of inferences in what he calls paragraphs but what are in fact "short stories." Sharing Schank's misconception of the paragraph as a self-contained rhetorical form, composition instructors often ask students to "write a paragraph" when they mean a short story, summary, or writing sample.

Inflexible formal definitions also lie behind the frequent proscription against the one-sentence paragraph. Although student writers are commonly denied this tool by edict, any attentive reading of effective prose will demonstrate its usefulness and its frequent occurrence. A one-sentence paragraph packs a double punch: It has the normal emphasis of a sentence as well as the visual emphasis of a paragraph.

By taking into account the reader's needs, we can clear up the current muddle of principles and patterns in our theories and our texts. We can't make paragraphing appear simple, because it isn't, but we can make its complexities appear sensible and well motivated. . . .

Notes

The authors wish to thank the following colleagues who generously gave their time to criticize earlier versions of this paper: Molly Faulkner, Connie Greaser, Carol Hartzog, Richard Lanham, Alan Purves, Mike Rose, Mary Vaiana, and Joseph Williams.

[1] Richard Braddock, "The Frequency and Placement of Topic Sentences in Expository Prose," *Research in the Teaching of English*, 8 (Winter 1974), 287–302. Richard A. Meade and W. Greiger Ellis, "Paragraph Development in the Modern Age of Rhetoric," *English Journal*, 59 (February 1970), 219–26; C. H. Knoblauch, "Some Formal and Nonformal Properties of Paragraphs and Paragraph Sequences," a paper delivered in session B-12, "Revisiting the Rhetoric of the Paragraph," Conference on College Composition and Communication, Dallas, Texas, March 1981.

[2] Ruth Mitchell and Mary Vaiana Taylor laid out a reader-oriented model for composition in their article "The Integrative Perspective: An Audience-Response Model for Writing," *College English*, 41 (November 1979), 247–70. The present essay offers an extension and specific application of their model.

[3] There is a considerable history to the paragraph, documented in James R. Bennett, Betty Brigham, Shirley Carson, John Fleischauer, Turner Kobler, Foster Park, and Allan Thies, "The Paragraph: An Annotated Bibliography," *Style*, 9 (Spring 1977), 107–18. Paul C. Rodgers claimed that Alexander Bain first systematically formulated paragraph theory ("Alexander Bain and the Rise of the Organic Paragraph," *Quarterly Journal of Speech*, 51 [December 1965], 399–403). His view was modified by Ned A. Shearer ("Alexander Bain and the Genesis of Paragraph Theory," *Quarterly Journal of Speech*, 58 [December 1972], 408–17). Shearer claimed that Bain had unacknowledged predecessors and furthermore derived his paragraph theory from the unity of the sentence: a paragraph was a larger sentence, a sentence a smaller paragraph.

[4] Top-down processing means proceeding from an orienting statement to details. It applies to all units of prose larger than the sentence. A top-down arrangement presents the reader with a thesis statement which allows him to understand why he is being told what follows. But composing processes . . . often proceed bottom-up — they don't begin with an orienting statement but end with one. The consequences of top-down processing for paragraph comprehension have been investigated by Perry Thorndyke in "Cognitive Structures in Comprehension and Memory of Narrative Discourse," *Cognitive Psychology*, 9 (January 1977), 77–110, and by Bonnie Meyer in *The Organization of Prose and Its Effects on Memory* (Amsterdam: North-Holland, 1975). Perhaps the most striking example of dependence on top-down processing is supplied by J. D. Bransford and M. K. Johnson, "Considerations of Some Problems of Comprehension," in W. G. Chase, ed., *Visual Information Processing* (New York: Academic Press, 1973). They found that experimental subjects could not understand or remember the following passage, which does not identify its orienting topic:

> The procedure is actually quite simple. First you arrange things into different groups depending on their makeup. Of course, one pile may be sufficient, depending on how much there is to do. If you have to go somewhere else due to lack of facilities, that is the next step, otherwise, you are pretty well set. It is important not to overdo any particular endeavor. That is, it is better to do too few things at once than too many. . . .

Readers must be told first that the passage describes washing clothes. Without that information, they cannot make sense of it.

[5] The principle of peripherality is well established in cognitive psychology. For a discussion of the literature see J. A. McGeoch and A. L. Irion, *The Psychology of Human Learning* (New York: Longmans Green, 1952).

[6] Frank Koen, Alton Becker, and Richard Young, "The Psychological Reality of the Paragraph, Part I," *Studies in Language and Language Behavior,* 4 (February 1967), University of Michigan; rpt. in *Technical Communication: Selected Publications by the Faculty,* Department of the Humanities, College of Engineering, University of Michigan, 1977. This article is not listed in the *Style* bibliography of the paragraph cited in note 3.

AN APPETITE FOR COHERENCE: AROUSING AND FULFILLING DESIRES

Kristie S. Fleckenstein

[College Composition and Communication *43 (1992): 81–87.]*

Kristie S. Fleckenstein is an independent research scholar in Overland Park, Kansas; her research interests include imagery and effect in reading and writing. Her articles have appeared in such publications as the Journal of Advanced Composition, English Journal, Teaching English in the Two-Year College, *and* College Composition and Communication.

Fleckenstein suggests that coherence is so difficult to teach, in part, because it is as much a "reader-based phenomenon as it is a writer-based creation." She describes a sequence of classroom activities that help students see their writing from a reader's perspective. Fleckenstein also includes examples from her students' work to illustrate how her suggestions help students become more effective at perceiving coherence (or incoherence) in their own writing. She suggests activities for individuals, peer groups, and the whole class.

The American Dream is to lose weight quickly and to keep it off without going hungry. But that's all it is: a dream. Wouldn't it be great if you could lose weight by swallowing a pill? The truth is no diet aid or diet pill will take excess weight off unless a person takes in less calories than he/she burns. Some pill packets even suggest a 1,200-calorie-a-day diet program for weight loss. How effective and safe are these diet products, though? Every year seems to bring a new drug for weight loss, and every year Americans seem to spend millions of dollars on diet aids that are ineffective and may even be dangerous.

Wouldn't it be great if you could lose weight by swallowing a pill? The American dream is to lose weight quickly and to keep it off without going hungry. Some pill packets even suggest a 1,200-calorie-a-day diet program for weight loss. But that's all it is: a dream. The truth is no diet aid or diet pill will take excess weight off unless a person takes in fewer calories than he/she burns. Yet every year seems to bring a new drug for weight loss, and every year Americans seem to spend millions of dollars on diet aids that are ineffective and may even be dangerous.

These two introductory paragraphs, so similar but so different, demonstrate the "before" and "after" texts created by Shelly, a struggling writer in an introductory college composition course. Beyond one or two minor stylistic changes and the omission of a single sentence, the two paragraphs are identical, save in the arrangement of the sentences. And that revision in order is the difference between a coherent introductory paragraph and an incoherent introductory paragraph.

Helping students create coherent texts is one of the most difficult jobs that composition teachers have. Part of that difficulty lies in the fact that coherence is as much a reader-based phenomenon as it is a writer-based creation. As Robert de Beaugrande and Wolfgang Dressler point out in *Introduction to Text Linguistics*, writers may provide the linguistic cues, but it is the readers who fill the gaps between ideas by building relationships that bridge ideas, and who thereby create their sense of order (Longman, 1981). Form is not a product, but a process, Kenneth Burke says, "an arousing and fulfillment of desires," "the creation of an appetite in the mind of the auditor, and the adequate satisfying of that appetite" (qtd. in Sonja Foss, Karen Foss, and Robert Trapp, *Contemporary Perspectives on Rhetoric*, Waveland, 1985, 162).

No wonder it is difficult for inexpert — and expert — writers to create coherent texts, both locally, at the sentence and paragraph levels, and globally, at the full-text level. To judge the success or failure of a particular passage requires the writer to step out of his or her shoes as a writer and examine the passage as a reader. Writers need to perceive the desires or expectations their texts arouse in their projected readers and then check to see if those desires are satisfied. Such a difficult role reversal is not easy to achieve, especially for students previously taught that form, for instance the five-paragraph form, is imposed on content or for those students taught to write without a consideration of their readers.

A method that helps writers shift perspectives involves getting them outside their texts. The technique requires students to examine what they do as readers to create coherent meaning, apply those discoveries to an incoherent text, then examine their own in-progress essays for problems with coherence.

The first part of this classroom strategy demonstrates that coherence is not "in the text," but something that readers create with the aid of cues provided by the writer. Begin this process by offering students the following brief passage, instructing them to read it, noting any words or sentences they don't understand, and then, if possible, to summarize it:

> Sally first tried setting loose a team of gophers. The plan backfired when a dog chased them away. She then entertained a group of teenagers and was delighted when they brought their motorcycles. Unfortunately, she failed to find a Peeping Tom listed in the Yellow Pages. Furthermore, her stereo system was not loud enough. The crab grass might have worked, but she didn't have a fan that was sufficiently powerful. The obscene phone calls gave her hope until the number was changed. She thought about calling a door-to-door salesman but decided to hang up a clothesline instead. It was the installation of blinking neon lights across the street that did the trick. She eventually framed the ad from the classified section.

Most students are unable to create a coherent meaning out of this passage, although they understand all the words and most of the sentences. They merely can't weave the disparate ideas into any understandable pattern. So the next step is to discuss the reasons for their difficulty. For instance, three sentences that commonly confuse my students are (1) "The crab grass might have worked, but she didn't have a fan that was sufficiently powerful"; (2) "She thought about calling a door-to-door salesman but decided to hang up a clothesline instead"; and (3) "She eventually framed the ad from the classified section." During full-class discussions, my students complain that they can't connect crab grass to fans in the first sample sentence. They point to a similar problem between door-to-door salesman and clothesline. Finally, in the last sample sentence, students say that they don't know what ad Sally refers to.

Following a discussion of reading frustrations, provide students with the following sentence: "Sally disliked her neighbors and wanted them to leave the area." Students discover that this sentence provides them a context to draw from. Now, they can use their background knowledge about human motivation, neighborhood irritations, and offensive strategies to build relationships within and between sentences. Thus, they are able to relate crab grass and fan by filling the gaps with the cause-effect knowledge (1) that crab grass is the bane of the suburbanite's lawn and (2) that the fan was meant to infest the neighbor's lawn with crab grass. Door-to-door salesmen and clotheslines are connected in an additive relationship as ploys designed to irritate the neighbors, and the ad, associated with Sally's implied goal of driving her neighbors out, is the real estate ad announcing the sale of the neighbor's home.

These observations serve as a basis for the discovery that coherent meaning results from the relationships we as readers build between ideas. — If we can't build relationships by bridging the gaps between ideas — ideas such as crab grass and fans — we create no coherent sense of the text.

The orienting statement about Sally's sentiments can also be used to demonstrate that readers approach a text with an array of expectations already cued (including the expectation that the text confronting us is coherent). Then, as we read, we are guided by those expectations, or appetites, and sample the text to satisfy or revise those appetites. By discussing the expectations the first sentence elicits, students discover how those expectations become predictions, hypotheses, and guesses which they validate or revise as they read.

The next step of this strategy is to move students from a contemplation of themselves as readers to practical work as peer editors. Sharing and revising an incoherent text helps effect this shift from reader to writer. Using an overhead projector, project an incoherent paragraph, but separate each sentence with three to four lines of space. With a sheet of paper, cover everything except the first sentence. Ask students to write down (a) what they think the idea of the sentence is, (b) what they think will come next, and (c) what they think the entire essay will concern. Uncover the second sentence and ask the students to decide if this sentence is consistent with their expectations. Discuss differences in opinion, but without attempting to arrive at any premature closure. Then, with the first two sentences as a basis, ask students to again write down what they think the essay will be about and what will come next. Continue predicting and discussing those predictions throughout the paragraph. As the last step in the exercise, have the students pool their observations and decide, as a class, how best to revise the paragraph so that it achieves a greater sense of coherence. Ask students to make specific suggestions for revisions: what to rearrange, add, or delete.

Following this whole-class work, divide the students into small groups, pass out copies of a second paragraph, and ask each group to read, analyze, and suggest changes for that paragraph, just as they had done for the first one. Finally, ask students to take the first one or two paragraphs of their current essays-in-progress and "stretch them out" — separate each sentence by three or four lines of space — and bring them to share with their peer partners for an analysis of paragraph coherence.

   During the third stage of this experience with coherence, students apply to *each other's papers* the techniques they applied previously as a group. The sample below illustrates a typical interchange between writer and peer partner. I have selected this particular interaction for a variety of reasons. First, both the writer, Trish, and the peer editor, Terry, were average writers from a developmental college writing class. Second, this sample reflects Trish's work with her first complete, formal draft of her first essay. Finally, I chose this sample because Terry did not follow the precise instructions provided in class; however, he still produced valuable reactions and advice for Trish. For instance, students were asked to (a) jot down the focus of the sentence under analysis, (b) jot down what they expect next, and (c) jot down what they expect from the entire essay. Terry frequently failed to include his expectations and the focus; instead, he explained why the sentence under examination did or did not meet his expectations, and he provided on-the-spot advice. Terry's success as a peer editor illustrates that the effectiveness of the strategy is not a product of its exact application.

1. In high school I had been in the printing class for about 3 and 1/2 years.
   a. The sentence is about printing class.
   b. Your essay's about printing class.

2. When we started out, there were 6 or 7 black students in a class that was predominately white and hispanic.
   a. It's about the kids in the class.
   b. The sentence doesn't correspond with the previous sentence. I am a bit confused.
   c. The paper is still about printing class.

3. As the years progressed and I was in my junior year there was one black student left: me.
   a. This should have been your second sentence because it corresponds with the first sentence.
   b. The problems she had in her class because she was the only black person.
   c. The essay's going to be about the problem that she had for being black.

4. I had become extremely talented with lithographic photography, which is making negatives of line copy (words), halftone pictures (regular pictures into dot form), and the PMT process (taking drawn art and making it usable for printing).
   a. This sentence doesn't fit because you started talking about being the only black and then you start explaining what you did in the class. The reader is like, the only black and so what?
   b. Being the only black gave these advantages of learning how to work the many different equipments.
   c. Learning how to work the equipment in the printing class.

5. Due to the fact I was working with light sensitive film a lot, I was in the darkroom, which is away from the rest of the class, and where I am hardly seen.

   a. This sentence doesn't fit. What does light sensitive film have to do with equipment or being the only black? About now I am confused.

   b. The sentence is about her class work.

   c. I'm not sure what the paper will be about. Discrimination in the printing class? her work?

6. This made the class look as if it was all white and hispanic, and gave the impression to the customers as well.

   a. This sort of follows because she's still talking about working out of sight, but what customers is she talking about?

   b. The customers gave all the credit to the white students.

   c. The discrimination from the printing class.

7. When I was seen in the class room, which was rare, and a customer would walk in, they would be shocked to see me.

   a. This sentence fits and your essay is starting to make sense. I think it is about being discriminated by your printing class.

8. It was then I realized the subtle prejudice of my printshop teacher, Mr. H—.

   a. I finally got the connection in your last sentence and the topic of the essay is clearer.

Suggestions for Revision I finally figured out your topic, but I still can't make all the sentences fit. Maybe you should explain about your print class and the customers. Why were you in the same class for 3 years? Maybe take out the sentence on what you did in class. I don't know how to fit it in. Can you combine the ideas in the first three sentences? Or start out with your first sentence, add a couple of sentences about the class, then explain that by your junior year you were the only black? Then say you were out of sight a lot?

Trish revised her first paragraph into the following:

In high school I had been in a printing class for about 3 and 1/2 years. The class was a production class, which meant that students could take it for a number of years and that we learned about printing by doing jobs for customers. When I started out as a freshman, there were about 6 or 7 other black students in a predominately white and hispanic class, but by my junior year I was the only black student left. Also, because I was working with light sensitive film much of the time, I was in the darkroom, away from the class and hardly seen. Customers had the impression that the class was all white and hispanic. When customers saw me in the class room, which was rare, they would be shocked. It was then that I realized the subtle prejudice of my printshop teacher, Mr. H—.

With Terry's help, Trish was able to revise her first paragraph into a much tighter introduction, one that consistently cued her topic for the entire paper and one that maintained greater unity between ideas.

Beyond the value of this technique as a revision tool, it also helps students achieve more writing control. For instance, one pedagogical goal in any writing class is to wean our students from dependence on our judgment and to foster reliance on their own judgment. This strategy for creating coherence facilitates that movement, in that it provides what Carl Bereiter and Marlene Scardamalia call executive controls: a method of determining when the composing process derails and a procedure for correcting the derailment (*The Psychology of Written Composition*, Erlbaum, 1987). This strategy does that; it can be effectively wielded by writers without access to peer partners or with less-than-satisfactory peer partners, as the following example demonstrates. The three sample paragraphs below are from the first, second, and final drafts of a paper by a writer in a developmental freshman composition class. Tina, whose peer partner frustrated her with an inconsistent performance, applied the strategy herself, as she worked through several versions of her introduction.

> *Draft I:* Remember if you don't follow your dreams, you'll never know what's on the other side of the rainbow; you'll never know what you can find at the top of the mountain; you'll never know your journey's best. By being a pushover, you let people dictate what you can and cannot do. Letting people run over you, or pushing your thoughts aside and not caring how you feel, you'll never know what you're capable of in terms of success but the failures you possess will always carry with you. Of course the failure is being afraid to speak and tell somebody or anybody how you truly feel. By bottling up your personal frustrations that you have problems saying aloud, your insides are going to explode. That explosion can be dangerous or even fatal that you get to the point of going out and killing that person who pushes you around or develop a high blood pressure which will eventually result in a heart attack. On the other hand, you can let your frustrations out and let that weak point of your character work to your advantage. Believe me, the second choice is safer and more productive.

> *Draft II:* For all of you pushovers out there, never let anyone tell you what to do or what's impossible for you. Remember, if you don't follow your dreams, you'll never know what's on the other side of the rainbow or what's at the top of the mountain. So always speak up for what you believe in, because if you don't do it for yourself, no one will. If you continue to be a pushover, a sucker for the rest of your life, you'll be a rug for the rest of your life. People will continue to step all over you. Believe me. I know. I was once a pushover myself. A pushover. An opponent who is easy to defeat or a victim who is capable of no effective resistance. Do not and I repeat do not subject yourself to that despicable low-life group called: the suckers.

> *Draft III:* Pushover. An opponent who is easy to defeat or a victim who is capable of no effective resistance. Do not, and I repeat, do not subject yourself to that despicable, low-life group called the suckers. If you continue to be a sucker for the rest of your life, you'll be a rug for the rest of your life. People will continue to step all over you. Believe what I am saying. I was once a pushover myself.

Although Tina's introduction still has problems, it does reflect a tighter focus and greater coherence than do her previous two efforts.

This way to help students perceive incoherence in their writing also possesses peripheral benefits. First, it emphasizes the importance of reading in writing. To be good writers, students must also be good readers. The focus of discussions can switch easily from the students' writing process to an examination of specific cues that can help readers create the relationships the writers seemingly have in mind. Second, the strategy also offers a productive way to introduce transitions and cohesive ties as linguistic cues that signal to readers an underlying relationship. This method centers students' attention on the underlying relationship of the transitional word cues, not on the word itself. Finally, students can examine the texts of professional writers, tracing shifts and noting how these writers ensure smooth bridges between ideas, gaining a greater sense of the rhetorical conventions that govern discourse. Again, this fosters the students' growth as readers, as well as writers.

Shelly's, Trish's, and Tina's revisions are hardly problem free, but each demonstrates the increasingly effective coherence this strategy promotes. Perhaps the most rewarding outgrowth of this technique is watching students gain confidence in their own ability to create meaningful texts and to create meaning from texts without a teacher's continued intercession.

EFFECTIVE SENTENCES AND WORD CHOICE

Parts III and IV of *The Bedford Handbook*, "Crafting Sentences" and "Choosing Words," offer students easy-to-understand advice about how to solve sentence-level problems, supplemented with examples that model revision possibilities. In these discussions, the handbook emphasizes the rhetorical impact of sentence structure and word choice.

The articles that follow raise several critical questions for teachers to consider as they decide how to teach students about sentences and word choice:

- How can sentence-combining strategies improve students' writing abilities, and how can writing teachers incorporate sentence combining in their instruction?
- How can instructors help students become more sensitive to obscure language such as jargon or doublespeak?
- What can instructors do to make students conscious of sexist or discriminatory language, and how can they help students avoid using it?

From *PREPARING TO TEACH WRITING*

James D. Williams

[From *Preparing to Teach Writing.* Belmont, CA: Wadsworth, 1989. 124–30.]

(For biographical information, see page 158.)

This excerpt concludes "Stylistics," chapter five of Williams's book. In it, Williams reviews interest and research in the study of style and the relation of stylistics to the teaching of writing. He opens the chapter with a historical review of the relation of style and composition and then discusses the "sociology of stylistics," charting how the increased interest in teaching style matches the increase of nontraditional students in composition classrooms. In the excerpt, Williams reviews the development of the sentence-combining movement and its claims about improvements in writing style. He questions those claims, emphasizing instead, as does The Bedford Handbook, *developing writing skills by focusing on rhetorical concerns during all stages of the composition process.*

Style and Sentence Combining

Kellogg Hunt (1965) was one of the first researchers to use the transformational-generative framework to examine the relationship between stylistic maturity and cognitive maturity. He studied maturation by comparing student writing at three grade levels to the writing of "superior" adults who published regularly in magazines and journals. Before Hunt's work, stylistic maturity had been measured in terms of sentence length. He immediately found that sentence length was a poor standard for defining a mature style and that a much better indicator was clause length, or what he called a "minimal-terminal unit," or simply *T-unit,* the shortest grammatical construction that can be punctuated as a sentence.

Underlying Hunt's research is a hypothesized linear relationship between age and style (which has prompted Witte and Cherry [1986] to ask whether we should predict such a thing as "syntactic senility"). Within limits, such a relationship does exist. The older and more experienced writers in Hunt's study produced sentences with longer T-units which prompted him to link *syntactic maturity* with *developmental maturity.*

Sentences (1)–(3), which follow, illustrate this finding. A third-grade student, for example, would use two sentences to express two propositions, as in (1) and (2), producing two short T-units, whereas the adult would embed one proposition in the other in a single sentence, creating a single T-unit, as in (3):

1. The woman had red hair.
2. The woman laughed.
3. The woman who laughed had red hair.

Based on what you now know about competence and performance, you can perhaps see that Hunt's study suggests a goal of composition instruction would be to raise students' linguistic competence to the level of performance. In other words, we know that third graders, for instance, can understand sentences with embedded subordinate clauses, like (3), even though they themselves don't produce such sentences as often as adults. Hunt's study suggested that at least one factor involved in moving from competence to performance in writing was to get students to produce longer T-units by embedding dependent clauses. That is, instruction could increase the *rate* of syntactic maturation.

Mellon (1969), drawing extensively on Hunt's findings, recognized these embeddings as having a transformational basis, and he hypothesized that teaching students how to perform grammatical transformations would have a significant effect on T-unit length. He gave a group of seventh-grade students intensive training in applying transformations over a period of nine weeks and then presented them with sentences like (1) and (2) above, with a relative-clause marker indicating the appropriate transformation. Pretest-posttest analysis of T-units indicated a significant increase in length, from 9.98 to 11.25 words. Unfortunately, although the subjects managed to produce longer T-units, trained readers did not judge their writing to be particularly better overall.

Despite these problematic results, the theory underlying the technique of combining short sentences into longer ones seemed flawless. Then O'Hare (1973) saw a difficulty in Mellon's methodology. He reasoned that subjects did not need any formal instruction in grammar to perform transformations, because such transformations were already part of their linguistic competence: That is, students did not need to know the formal aspects of, say, the relative-clause transformation in order to form a sentence with a relative clause.

Using 95 percent of the sentences from Mellon's study, O'Hare simply had students manipulate them to form the combinations, which they were able to do quite easily. His results showed an increase in T-unit length 5 times greater than what Mellon reported, and 23 times greater than the "normal" increase reported by Hunt. Moreover, trained readers rated the quality of the subjects' posttreatment writing as better than the writing of the control group.

One result of these studies, particularly O'Hare's, has come to be known as the "sentence-combining movement." Another was dozens of sentence-combining textbooks and the subsequent development of sentence-combining methodology as a major feature of composition pedagogy.

We should note at this point that many teachers were asking students to combine sentences long before the studies summarized here were published. The technique was not really "new." We must also recognize, however, that the work by Hunt, Mellon, and O'Hare achieved nationwide attention. In this regard it is significantly different from earlier combining experiences. . . .

Francis Christensen (1967) took a somewhat different approach to syntactic maturity. After studying the work of professional writers, he determined that they used short base (or independent) clauses to which they attached modifying phrases that add detail and depth. The following student sentences illustrate this technique. The underlined portion of the sentences is the base clause:

22. <u>I danced with excitement,</u> winding myself around my nana's legs, balling my hands in her apron, tugging at her dress, stepping on her toes, until finally she gave me a swat across the bottom and told me to go play.
23. <u>I dragged a chair to the counter and climbed up,</u> grasping the counter edge with my hands, stretching my body, pulling up with my arms until my head was above the tiles.

Unlike other sentence-combining techniques, this one emphasizes having students start out with short base clauses, then asking them to supply modifying detail on the basis of close observation. Modifying constructions are usually added to the end of the base clauses, producing what Christensen refers to as a "cumulative sentence." These sentences, found with great frequency in narration and description, have an ebb-and-flow movement from the general to the specific, what Christensen calls changes in "levels of generality." His approach focuses on helping students shift from one level of generality to another.

Both methodologies were instantly popular, in part because sentence combining fit neatly into the already established focus on style in student writing. In addition, it was noted that many students find an element of fun in figuring out different ways to join sentences together. The task has a puzzlelike fascination. Even more important, teachers began to see that sentence combining seemed to improve writing performance. Students who practiced it gained greater control over their sentences and were able to develop more variety in sentence types.

These classroom observations have been supported by many studies showing that students who engage in regular sentence-combining exercises increase the length of their T-units and improve overall composition quality (see Combs, 1977; Daiker, Kerek, and Morenberg, 1978; Howie, 1979; Pedersen, 1978). For example, after reviewing the major investigations related to sentence combining, Kerek, Daiker, and Morenberg (1980) state that sentence combining "has been proven again and again to be an effective means of fostering growth in syntactic maturity" (p. 1067).

One of the major attractions of sentence combining is that it can be used effectively by students at all grade and ability levels (O'Hare, 1973; Sullivan, 1978; Waterfall, 1978). If anything, in fact, poor writers seem to benefit most from this technique.

Part of the explanation appears to be that sentence combining offers an algorithmic approach to teaching writing that many teachers and most students are very comfortable with, owing to composition instruction's lack of content. The perception is that if writing is a skill, it should be reducible to a series of steps that can be articulated by teachers and followed by students. And certainly sentence combining satisfies these desires, because students are given a series of short sentences and asked to combine them into longer ones. Occasional difficulties arise with older students who have generally been told to perform just the opposite task, taking long sentences and reducing them to short ones, but these are certainly not insurmountable.

As positive as this review of sentence combining sounds, however, several questions are associated with the technique. Various studies have suggested that over time, the gains in sentence length and writing quality attributed to sentence combining disappear (Callaghan, 1978; Green, 1973; Sullivan, 1978). Kerek, Daiker, and Morenberg (1980), for example, in the same study that comments on the positive effects of the technique, found that two years after instruction, no measurable differences were perceived between the writing of students who had practiced sentence combining and of students who had not. The control group had completely caught up with the treatment group, which over the two-year period had made no further gains. If the results are transient or mitigated by time, teachers must carefully evaluate the energy and effort involved in using the technique.

In addition, it should be noted that rhetorical mode may affect measures of syntactic maturity. Studies by Perron (1977) and Crowhurst and Piche (1979) suggest that narration and description result in the shortest T-units, whereas analysis and argumentation result in the longest. Furthermore, having students write regularly in the argumentative mode seems to produce gains in T-unit length and writing quality equal to those related to sentence-combining exercises.

Ample data indicate the reality of what we might think of as a "complexity continuum" for rhetorical modes (see Britton et al., 1975; Williams, 1983). At least in regard to classroom compositions, analysis and argumentation are cognitively more demanding than description, so the frequently noted correlation between complexity of thought and syntactic maturity would serve to explain the effect of mode on performance (see Williams, 1983, 1987). (This isn't to suggest, of course, that we don't find complex constructions in description; we do. But generally these constructions consist of short T-units with attached modifying phrases [see Christensen, 1967]).

Along these lines, Kinneavy (1979) and Witte (1980) argue that the gains in T-unit length and writing quality attributed to sentence combining may actually be the result of teaching rhetorical principles like analysis and synthesis inductively, principles that are inherent in the process of combining. If this is the case, teaching these principles directly, no doubt through the associated rhetorical modes, would probably be more efficient. In other words, it may well be that teachers can have a significant effect on syntactic maturity and writing performance simply by focusing more attention on more demanding writing tasks, such as analysis and argument.

This suggestion is an important one, because it raises a serious question not only for sentence combining but for any approach to writing instruction that emphasizes style. The issue is this: Will students benefit more from working on isolated sentences or on whole essays?

Over the last few years, as composition pedagogy and theory have increasingly adopted a position that advocates an emphasis on the process of writing rather than the finished product, many teachers have come down solidly on the side of the whole essay. Writing, like reading, has come to be viewed as primarily a top-down process rather than bottom-up. In this view, to focus on style is to deal with the surface features of discourse, with matters of form. As we have already seen in our discussion of the phonics approach to reading, an emphasis on surface features tends to lead to error correction that slights the rhetorical, functional nature of discourse. Content, meaning, and purpose too often get ignored in such a learning environment, and an emphasis on style in general and sentence combining in particular may not be conducive to successful writing instruction over the long term.

But in spite of these significant theoretical difficulties, style remains a powerful force in most writing classes and in many of the discussions about teaching writing. Proponents of sentence combining, for example, have frequently skirted the theoretical problem by falling back on the flawed work of those writers who claim that mastery of surface features and the conventions of written discourse are linked to cognitive development.

On this basis, sentence combining is seen as a comprehensive model for constructing texts, its advocates maintaining that increasing "syntactic fluency" affects global discourse skills. Christensen (1967), for example, claims that work on sentences will provide a discovery procedure that will enable students to find things to say about a topic. To date, however, there is no solid evidence to support the idea that teaching students to write better sentences will lead to their writing a better essay. . . .

References

Britton, J., Burgess, T., Martin, N., McLeod, A., and Rosen, H. (1975). *The Development of Writing Abilities (11–18)*. London: Macmillan Education Ltd.

Callaghan, T. (1978). The effects of sentence-combining exercises on the syntactic maturity, quality of writing, reading ability, and attitudes of ninth-grade students. *Dissertation Abstracts International, 39*, 637-A.

Christensen, F. (1967). *Notes toward a New Rhetoric: Six Essays for Teachers*. New York: Harper & Row.

Combs, W. (1977). Sentence-combining practice: Do gains in judgments of writing "quality" persist? *Journal of Education Research, 70*, 318–321.

Crowhurst, J., and Piche, G. (1979). Audience and mode of discourse effects on syntactic complexity in writing at two grade levels. *Research in the Teaching of English, 13*, 101–109.

Daiker, D., Kerek, A., and Morenberg, M. (1978). Sentence-combining and syntactic maturity in freshman English. *College Composition and Communication,* 29, 36–41.

Green, E. (1973). An experimental study of sentence-combining to improve written syntactic fluency in fifth-grade children. *Dissertation Abstracts International,* 33, 4057-A.

Howie, S. (1979). A study: The effects of sentence combining practice on the writing ability and reading level of ninth-grade students. *Dissertation Abstracts International,* 40, 1980-A.

Hunt, K. (1965). *Grammatical Structures Written at Three Grade Levels.* NCTE Research Report Number 3. Champaign, Ill.: National Council of Teachers of English.

Kerek, A., Daiker, D., and Morenberg, M. (1980). Sentence combining and college composition. *Perceptual and Motor Skills,* 51, 1059–1157.

Kinneavy, J. (1979). Sentence combining in a comprehensive language framework. In D. Daiker, A. Kerek, and M. Morenberg (Eds.), *Sentence combining and the teaching of writing.* Conway, Ark.: University of Akron and University of Central Arkansas.

Mellon, J. (1969). *Transformational Sentence-Combining: A Method for Enhancing the Development of Syntactic Fluency in English Composition.* NCTE Research Report Number 10. Champaign, Ill.: National Council of Teachers of English.

O'Hare, F. (1973). *Sentence Combining: Improving Student Writing without Formal Grammar Instruction.* NCTE Committee on Research Report Series, Number 15. Urbana, Ill.: National Council of Teachers of English.

Pedersen, E. (1978). Improving syntactic and semantic fluency in writing of language arts students through extended practice in sentence-combining. *Dissertation Abstracts International,* 38, 5892-A.

Perron, J. (1977). *The Impact of Mode on Written Syntactic Complexity.* Athens: University of Georgia Studies in Language Education Series.

Sullivan, M. (1978). The effects of sentence-combining exercises on syntactic maturity, quality of writing, reading ability, and attitudes of students in grade eleven. *Dissertation Abstracts International,* 39, 1197-A.

Waterfall, C. (1978). An experimental study of sentence-combining as a means of increasing syntactic maturity and writing quality in the compositions of college-age students enrolled in remedial English classes. *Dissertation Abstracts International,* 38, 7131-A.

Williams, J. D. (1983). Covert language behavior during writing. *Research in the Teaching of English,* 17, 301–312.

Williams, J. D. (1987). Covert linguistic behavior during writing tasks: Psychophysiological differences between above-average and below-average writers. *Written Communication,* 4, 310–328.

Witte, S. (1980). Toward a model for research in written composition. *Research in the Teaching of English,* 14, 73–81.

Witte, S., and Cherry, R. (1986). Writing processes and written products in composition research. In C. Cooper and S. Greenbaum (Eds.), *Studying Writing: Linguistic Approaches.* Beverly Hills, Calif.: Sage.

THE CHALLENGE FOR SENTENCE COMBINING

Peter Elbow

[From Sentence Combining: A Rhetorical Perspective. *Ed. Don Daiker, Andrew Kerek, and Max Morenberg. Carbondale: Southern Illinois UP, 1985. 232–45.]*

(For biographical information, see page 162.)

Elbow's essay resulted from observations he made at a conference on sentence combining, where he was invited to give a talk. Elbow argues that, though sentence combining is one possible strategy for revising or restructuring ineffective sentences, other strategies are equally effective, including "decombining" and leaving syntax alone. The Bedford Handbook never presents sentence combining as an exercise in itself, but recommends sentence combining as one alternative among many and emphasizes that sentence revision must serve the larger rhetorical concerns of the writing. Peter Elbow affirms that approach, and as he challenges teachers to reconsider the "institution" of sentence combining, he offers, as usual, practical uses and alternatives.

Writing Courses with Writing at the Center

My premise is that a writing course is seriously flawed if it doesn't devote most of its time to writing itself (from finding a topic to revising), to talking about what happens as we write, to giving one's writing to readers, and to getting these readers to talk to us about what happens as they read. When we don't center our courses on this full writing process, we leave students unaided, writing as it were in the dark, and as a result they tend to learn only the sordid gutter or cloakroom story about what people actually do when they write — learning for instance:

- that no self-respecting person ever allows herself to derive pleasure from it;
- that the best you can do is put it off until it can no longer be escaped;
- that it's all a matter of duty and giving satisfaction to the other party — in this case the teacher — and never getting any satisfaction back;
- that it helps to feign enthusiasm even if you don't feel it; but in the end feigning only makes you hate it worse;
- that the only satisfaction comes from an extrinsic reward or payoff, a grade, which has no real connection with writing; though one can get some pleasure in keeping complete control oneself while subtly manipulating the receiver so he feels he's in control;
- that composition is something you do in school or college but it has nothing to do with what real writers do;
- that writing equals grammar and grammar is boring;
- that one is entirely helpless about whether one's writing goes well or badly; some people have the knack and others don't, and there's no way to change it;
- that there's no use fighting this mystery because, almost invariably, the harder you try, the worse it comes out.

I think sentence combining is vulnerable to attack for being so arhetorical — so distant from the essential process of writing. In sentence combining the student is not engaged in figuring out what she wants to say or saying what is on her mind. And because it provides prepackaged words and ready-made thoughts, sentence combining reinforces the pushbutton, fast-food expectations in our culture. As a result the student is not saying anything to anyone: The results of her work are more often "answers" given to a teacher for correction — not "writing" given to readers for reactions.[1]

But I am not, as a matter of fact, trying to attack. I've just stated my misgivings in their most extreme form. In what follows I will, in effect, back off and try to find common ground between sentence combining and my own concerns. I will try to be a constructive if critical ally to the institution of sentence combining. (It does seem to be an institution and perhaps that tempts attack.) I am trying to write a challenge *for* sentence combining, not a challenge *to* sentence combining.[2]

Sentence Combining as Exercises

A first step in backing off. Who could reasonably demand that *nothing* go on in writing courses except real writing? Exercises can help. I try to play the viola and I find exercises useful and even satisfying. I long ago discovered that I am not even tempted to spend *all* my time playing music. Thus, some of my misgivings ought to be translated into a simple plea that sentence combining as it is commonly practiced take up no more than a small part of any writing course. Sentence combining must clearly announce itself and be felt by students as *ancillary* to the writing process — a genuine handmaiden, never the focus of the writing course.

This is a plea for humility. It's a vote in favor of those small and flexible sentence-combining texts — better yet, reproducible exercise sheets — which lend themselves to ancillary use, rather than those texts which try to determine the shape and style of a course. I take it that if a teacher or student conceives of a writing course as a sentence-combining course, that signals a problem: Adjunct exercises are being implied as a paradigm for the writing process. But I hasten to add that such a plea for humility is also an invitation to ambition: If sentence combining can be genuinely ancillary, then it might fit *any* teacher, not just "sentence combiners."

But which exercises shall we use in our writing courses? Writing is long and our courses are short. It's my prejudice that closed exercises where there's always a right or best answer are not what we want in our limited time. They reinforce our students' worst assumption, namely that writing is a matter of finding the right answer of pleasing the teacher. Open exercises face students with an *array* of acceptable or even good answers — as writing does.

One of the main reasons people have trouble with writing is that they feel helpless and not in control. Open sentence-combining exercises would increase their sense that they can find options and choose freely among them — and reduce their sense that there is some hidden magic involved in producing effective syntax. "I can make changes; my syntax is not cast in concrete: It's a matter of manipulating well." There is a deep human desire for control that is stymied for most people when they try to write. But it can be tapped in the teaching of writing, and surely these exercises are one way to tap it.

When students must choose among acceptable options on the basis of trade-offs between competing advantages and disadvantages, they will almost inevitably make intuitive judgments *by ear.* Nothing could be more helpful and appropriate. We might be tempted to try to prevent this intuitive strategy — perhaps by constructing rules of thumb about certain constructions being better in certain conditions. But the study of language shows that people are in trouble if they have to operate by conscious rules. The ear, in the last analysis, is the most trustworthy and powerful organ for learning syntax; and fortunately it is the easiest to teach — as long as we give some time to it. We may complain that students have undeveloped ears, but time devoted to developing their ears is far more efficient than time devoted to teaching syntactic rules.

In the interests of this ear training (and for other advantages too) I would commend two practices which I gather are used by only a few sentence-combining teachers: oral exercises and the use of groups.

Unless students actually *speak* the syntax in question, they will often bypass the use of their ears. We must get students to check their syntactic hypotheses against their actual sensations in their throats and ears. Besides, oral work is quicker, giving students a chance to try out more hypotheses in less time and with less drudgery; it gives more sense of play; it emphasizes the ability to make changes in midspeech and thus acknowledges that we tend to generate sentences as we go along rather than planning them in advance. One of the goals of sentence combining is fluency or automaticity, but I fear a hidden message in it that sentences ought to be planned in advance. In short, oral sentence combining would help convey that necessary sense that writing can scarcely be rich and strong unless it grows out of the matrix of living speech.

Small peer groups are the natural context for spoken sentence-combining exercises. Groups are also ideal places for reading out loud answers to written sentence-combining exercises: The precious thing is to discover the actual effects of different constructions upon listeners and readers. We can sometimes even ask groups to agree on a construction, thereby compelling students to articulate why they prefer a given version. (And of course asking groups to agree on something is a good community-building activity to improve the spirit in a class.)

But no matter how clever and fruitful sentence-combining exercises are, I suspect we will end up having to take a defensive stance against them because they *are* exercises and not written.

For it's in the nature of exercises, because they are exercises, to begin to take up too much time and attention in the minds of students and teachers alike. The better and more fruitful the exercises, the worse the danger. We see it in the case of grammar and spelling. Exercises are inevitably clearer, simpler, and more coherent than writing. We can feel more in control of exercises than of writing. Indeed, we can *teach* exercises and make steady discernible progress — whereas teaching writing itself seems impossible because progress is seldom steady or, in the short run, even discernible. (As a person begins to use a higher level skill, her actual performance often deteriorates, that is, a student's writing often gets worse when she tries a harder task or tries to use a higher level skill. The classic statement of this principle is in Jerome S. Bruner's *Studies in Cognitive Growth.*[3] It is hard to see progress when writing gets worse.) As a result, teachers are almost inevitably tempted to slide imperceptibly over into teaching the exercise rather than teaching writing, because we yearn to see progress.

Perhaps some will argue that there's nothing wrong with such a slide — that is with a frank emphasis on the teaching of exercises. Music teachers often claim, "Of course I teach scales. Scales are teachable. Teaching scales helps my students play better. I don't teach musicality or musicianship because they are not teachable." Playing scales does help people play better, but there's a crucial difference between scales and sentence-combining exercises. Scales consist of performances that actually occur in the playing of almost any music. Sentence combining, on the other hand — building complex sentences from kernels — does not seem to be an activity people ever actually engage in while writing.

I've been told that string students at the Curtis Institute spend their entire first year doing nothing but left-hand finger exercises: no use of the right hand or the bow. A bit extreme; no doubt effective; but they can get away with it because they have such a good reputation and students come eagerly to get what they have to offer. If they had to teach everyone to play the violin and most of their students were there under compulsion, they would undermine their chance of success by asking for too much undiluted exercise. They would have to "sink" to exploiting more of the self-reinforcing power of music itself. Similarly, if I am teaching an advanced-writing course which students take by choice, I can build my course around exercises. But if I am teaching a required course — if the students are thus already half-disposed to fight me, yet what I need most for good writing is their genuine involvement or investment in their own words — I must be careful not to overshadow writing itself. I must exploit the only intrinsic reinforcement we have available in writing: the basic human process of making meaning and the basic social process of communicating.

Sentence Combining as Writing

But in fact it wouldn't take much to transform sentence combining from a mere exercise into writing itself. For of course there is a central part of the writing process where writers do exactly what sentence combining asks, namely to take a set of already written sentences and transform or manipulate them in order to improve them. Thus sentence combining *is* revising, you may say, and I was wrong to call it mere exercise.

Yet the essential fact that revising — and the essential difficulty — derives from the fact that it is one's own writing one is trying to improve. It is one's own syntax that somehow makes rewriting hard.

It happens to me, it happens to other writers, and I know it happens to students at all levels: I sit before a passage from my draft. I know it's not right, but as I try and try and try to improve it, I cannot. I turn the sentence or the passage this way and that, but nothing seems progress. Nothing comes that is not odd or silly or a deviation from what I want to say. After a while all meaning drains from the language, and I begin to feel that perhaps I had nothing at all to say in the first place. Finally my head begins to swim.

The point is that when I have generated my own syntax — particularly when the syntax embodies a train of thought I've had to struggle for — somehow my own language is inescapable. I've spent all my syntactic capital getting the thought into words at all. I've used up all my cognitive and linguistic strength cutting *one* opening through into this piece of meaning. There's no more strength left for making other openings. When I go back through the opening, I'm back into the outer darkness of brute nonmeaning.

The only way into the meaning again is through that one opening. And so at this point the revising process bogs down into a desultory wandering back and forth through that one opening: saying it in the form one has said it, letting go of that version and not coming up with anything better, then saying it again the first way in hopes it will seem better this time but of course it's still not right, then letting go again in hopes one will find another version, another door, but still no luck. Is this not the central cognitive/psychological event that makes revising difficult? It centers around the numbing, medusaficatory effect of one's own struggled-for syntax.

But one could take something very like sentence combining — perhaps it should be called sentence transforming — and *make* it part of the actual process of revising. As follows. The student writes a draft. She finds passages which are problematic: not quite clear, something a bit off in the emphasis, muddy, tinny, thin, whatever. No need to diagnose the problem; one simply finds it by ear and intuition.[4]

Having found a problem passage, the students *decombine* it down into kernels. Sentence combiners will have to provide us with some exercises to teach decombining, but I would ask for something brief and less than perfect. No need for textbooks. After all, the sentences needn't be pulverized into pure Chomskyan kernels — merely broken down into mostly simple sentences.

Occasionally in the middle of decombining there will be a click, and the sentence or passage will right itself. Usually, of course, recombining will be needed. As in open sentence-combining exercises, the student will try different constructions to find the best option. But for this recombining process we will specifically refrain from implying to students that their T-units or clauses ought to end up longer than they started. More often than not the average clause length will end up shorter — especially since most of these problem passages are tangles of some sort.[5]

It is crucial to add the social dimension here: other students in groups as readers and as fellow writers. Readers are crucial not only for helping identify problem passages but also for hearing or reading various rewritings and describing how they affect real readers. The writer herself must do the actual decombining and recombining, but other students, as fellow writers, might also join in on their own — simply for the sake of showing the writer more alternatives. (This might be particularly useful for weak writers who have trouble with the process: There might be a group effort on one passage.)

But my plea would be that the same principle should hold here as in all feedback groups: Readers are in charge of telling their responses (to original drafts and to possible revisions), and sometimes they even suggest alternatives of their own; but the writer is always in charge of deciding what changes to make — if any. Perhaps the main way to help students act like writers is by treating them like writers, that is, by insisting that they are in charge of their own texts.

Peer readers would thus fulfill the natural functions of audience. The process would reinforce the notion that writing is not a matter of finding correct answers but writing sentences that do to readers what you want to do. This would help emphasize that you can't decide what is a good or a poor sentence apart from who it is aimed at and where it comes in a whole piece. There's no such thing as a "good sentence" abstractly considered.

This activity of sentence transforming or manipulating — this de- and recombining activity — appeals to me because it is at once both an exercise and "the real thing." These are real papers for real readers. And the process should gradually strengthen students' ability to revise *without* full decombining. That is, the exercise should gradually put itself out of business, yet always be available when a passage is particularly tangled. The power of an exercise comes from allowing you to choose a *small behavior* that is too difficult when it is part of a larger complex sequence of behaviors in "the real thing" — and work on it in isolation in a structured way and thereby master it.[6]

The difficulty of the real performance stems not only from how *many* behaviors are involved but also from the fact that these behaviors often *interfere* with each other. That is, revising a tangled passage requires the contrary acts of breaking down and recombining syntax. Skilled revisers make this complex performance in one step, but we could all occasionally benefit by separating these opposite syntactic processes.

Notice how sentence combining-as-revising brings *thought* more to the fore. Breaking a problem passage into small bits allows thought to remake or readjust itself by prying open the fist of our original syntax which had locked us into a particular shade of meaning or train of emphasis. Indeed, de- and recombining is a formula for figuring out what you think. You cannot break down your prose into simple sentences without asking yourself "What am I really asserting?" Sentence combiners and their adversaries may debate about whether syntax drives thought or thought drives syntax, but I suspect we should work on writing from both ends. Sentence combining-as-revising is a way to work on syntax, but it's also syntax-work that peels syntax away to permit thought-work.[7]

Manipulating Your Syntax but Leaving It Alone, Too

Sophisticated defenders of sentence combining have dissociated themselves from the notorious implication that better writing equals writing with more complex syntax: that in measuring T-unit lengths or clause lengths we get a measure of syntactic maturity and thereby (sometimes stated, sometimes merely implied) a measure also of good writing. But there is no way to untangle this dangerous implication from sentence combining as it presently exists. The exercises are nothing but constant practice in turning simple sentences into complex embedded ones. Many exercises ask students to change perfectly good sentences into worse ones. Defenders may argue that this is just practice in manipulation, but when it all goes in one direction, what message does this send to students — especially in a culture which tends to mistake fancy syntax for good writing? (And it is not just the culture, it's also our profession. We all know the recent research by Joseph M. Williams and Rosemary L. Hake that shows writing teachers themselves preferring the very complications of syntax they say they specifically disapprove of — such as passives and heavy nominalizations.)[8] William L. Smith and Warren E. Combs set out to measure whether the mere fact of asking students to do sentence-combining exercises seemed in itself to communicate the message, "write more complex syntax." The answer was a resounding yes.[9]

When we remove the dangerous message, a lovely healthy message emerges — a message that was buried there all the time — namely, that good writing involves the ability to manipulate syntax or transform sentences.

Surely this is the right message to send. And notice the shift from product to process: from "good writing is a product characterized by more complexity" to "good writing is a process characterized by manipulating your syntax."

And yet, lovely and wholesome as that message is, I am not willing to leave things here. That is, till this point in my paper I've been accepting the premise in sentence combining that the ability consciously to manipulate and transform one's syntax is central to good writing. Now I must step back and take a larger perspective and insist that the premise can only be affirmed if we also affirm its opposite, which is equally true and important, namely that *good writing as a process is also characterized by the ability to leave your syntax alone.*

How can I defend such an odd assertion? First, what do I mean by the phrase "leave your syntax alone?" Marlene Scardamalia and Carl Bereiter remark in passing upon the "natural tendency to let syntax be determined by the order in which words come to mind."[10] My argument for this last section is that though of course we must teach students how to manipulate their syntax, we must also — perverse as it may sound — show them how to let syntax be determined by the order in which words come to mind.

What does this mean in practice? Obviously it means freewriting or nonstop, uncensored writing. It also means using fast uncensored writing when you are exploring a topic or generating raw first draft writing. It may seem perverse to defend lack of care or neglect in syntax, but it simply turns out to be helpful to leave your syntax alone when exploring and generating thought. It makes writing easier, you get more written more quickly, and it is reinforcing since you discover ideas you didn't know you had. As an exercise it is far less onerous than sentence combining. (Notice, by the way, how freewriting and sentence combining-as-revising complement each other as activities which are at once exercises yet also real writing.)

This is reason enough for telling students to leave their syntax alone as they explore their thoughts and write first drafts. And, interestingly enough, the process needs to be taught. That is, even though we should present freewriting in the most nonjudgmental light as an activity you cannot fail at if you just keep writing at all, nevertheless people don't get the full benefit till they really do learn to put down words in the actual order they come to mind. Some students and teachers conclude that freewriting is no help because they haven't learned how to do this. After all, for students, writing always implies writing for a teacher's scrutiny, and thus always implies constant vigilance against just putting down what comes to mind. Thus, even when they learn to keep their pencil moving in a freewriting exercise, they may not learn how to follow where their minds are trying to go and how to allow themselves really to write down words in the order they come to mind.

But the fact that writing is easier to engage in when you leave syntax alone is a process-oriented reason for doing it. I would like to give some product-oriented reasons that might be more controversial but more interesting to an audience interested in sentence combining.

First, quickly. When students put words down in the order they come to mind (as in freewriting) they are often led to syntax that is *more complex* than they use in papers they hand in for credit. Tangled or vexed syntax sometimes, yes, but nevertheless strikingly more complex and interesting. (Indeed, freewriting can lead to some T-units with no termination in sight.) One of the main reasons students hand in papers with awful dick-and-jane syntax is to avoid errors in grammar and punctuation: They play it safe. After all, they usually pay a bigger price for mistakes in mechanics than for overly simple syntax.

Second, quicker still. There is good ear training in putting words down in the order they come to mind. They come by ear rather than by calculation. I wonder if experiments might not show that practice in freewriting — genuinely safe feedback taught by a teacher who understands its use — might not produce greater increases in T-unit length than an equal amount of sentence combining.

Third. When students put down words in the order they come to mind their syntax is usually clearer than what they achieve in their more careful writing. I realize this is hard for many teachers to believe. We see so much *unclear* writing which is also careless writing. How can we not infer that what the writing needs is more care? And of course it does — to be genuinely good. But let us remember nevertheless something obvious but profound which linguists have taught us: Words never come to mind in sequences that are unintelligible or even ungrammatical. That is, when the human mind generates words in a truly uninterrupted and natural fashion, they always follow the natural grammar of the speaker's language. ("Grammar," of course, as the linguist understands the term, not the schoolmarm.)

Of course I'm not saying that a transcription of the natural and uninterrupted language generated in the head of a college freshman would be good writing. But it *would* be syntactically intelligible and indeed usually clear and lively at every moment — which we cannot say of the papers the freshman tends to hand in.

What is the moral? Not that the students should transcribe or freewrite all their thoughts — what a job — but that every one of our students at every moment is *capable* of generating a perfectly intelligible, lively sentence. This is part of what is called linguistic "competence." Of course student "performance" frequently falls short. But the way to bring performance closer to competence, in this instance at least, is not by making more transformations in syntax but by leaving syntax more alone — that is, by learning to do a better job of writing down words in the order in which they come to mind. It is a skill that can be taught: the skill of tapping into that stream of syntax that is always intelligible and usually lively.

Once I really began to believe that this syntax is always there for students, I began to see student writing in a very different light. Now whenever I see a passage of tangled or unclear student writing I can almost *feel* behind it one of the following events:

• The student made a change in the syntax that came to mind — probably because of some doubt or hesitation or a sense that something was wrong the first time and a change was needed (see the NAEP tests that show how common it is for students to make their writing worse when they revise);

• or the student wrote part of a sentence or clause and then paused to think and then, when she came back to continue, she wasn't on the same syntactic track she had been on;

- or the student referred to material she had in mind that she neglected to tell the reader and therefore she produced unclear *meaning or reference* (but not unclear syntax);
- or, in the case of freewriting, the writer abandoned one thought before finishing it and started another — perhaps even in the middle.

In short, either the student didn't put the words down in the order they really came to mind or else — and this may be a more frequent problem — she never got herself into a condition where words really *were* coming to mind in what could be called a genuine order, that is, she was putting down words of a sentence about *King Lear* in the order that the words of that sentence happened to come to mind, but that sentence was interrupted three or four times by a completely *different* (and more felt and lively) internal discourse about, say, how baffled or unsatisfied she is with her sentence about *King Lear*. All of this is a topic for fruitful research.

Many teachers cannot believe that syntax which is truly left alone is always intelligible because they have never seen syntax truly left alone. You will never see it unless you help your students produce it — that is, unless you ensure that students do lots of freewriting in class and help them learn to do it well. And one of the main ways to help them is by never collecting it and assuring students that you will not collect it. Then, gradually, after plenty of time for trust to build up along with a large reservoir of freewritings, you can request (not require) that students hand you some pieces of their choice. Gradually you will see enough to trust that you are not just seeing atypically "good syntax." And you will see "terrible" passages mixed in with what the student wanted to show you that was "good." Those terrible pieces will be terrible in every imaginable way except for being syntactically unclear. (Or where they are syntactically unclear, you'll sense that you are not reading words put down in the order they came to mind.)

Despite the many faults that often result when students put down words in the order they come to mind, it is an important and empowering revelation to realize that students are *always capable* of clear syntax. Teachers sometimes think certain students are incapable of it; they fear brain damage or "low levels of cognitive development" on some Piagetian or Perrian scale. And many *students* fear they are incapable of writing clear language. All parties need to know the truth.[11]

Let me restate in practical terms my third argument for leaving syntax alone. To put down words in the order they come to mind provides a resting point midway in the fearfully huge gulf that separates the chaos in our heads from the coherence, organization, good thinking, and correctness needed in a good piece of writing. It's too large a gulf for most of us to leap all at once. Putting down words as they come shows us that the chaos in our heads is basically not syntactic chaos, and that therefore we can produce a fluent text that conveys clearly what we have in mind. We need to know we can do that much at least (for what it's worth) — and do it without much effort.

My fourth and final argument for learning to leave syntax alone centers on voice: a spoken sound in the text and a sense that the sound somehow fits or matches the writer. Frost wrote, "All that can save [sentences] is the speaking tone of voice somehow entangled in the words and fastened to the page for the ear of the imagination" (from the introduction, Robert Frost,

A Way Out [New York: Harbor Press, 1929]). This quality of the writer's *presence* in the words somehow makes readers more likely to keep on reading and paying attention. Voice is also helpful to writers because when they start using voice, their writing tends to improve in other ways too. I find that leaving syntax alone usually increases voice in one's writing.

At this point I must come out of the closet with something that has been making me uncomfortable among sentence combiners. I often find myself preferring the uncombined sentences to the combined ones. A couple of unremarkable examples:

I put my foot down. The car surged forward.
                        vs.
Because I put my foot down, the car surged forward.
Having put my foot down, the car surged forward.
After I put my foot down, the car surged forward.

Being smart is one thing. Making others feel dumb is something else.
                        vs.
Although being smart is one thing, making others feel dumb is something else.

I prefer the unembedded sentences because I feel *something going on* in them — whereas in the embedded sentences I feel *something having gone on,* something already completed. The simple sentences seem to express or embody an ongoing mental event — as though the writer's mind is in action — and this seems to put the reader's mind more into action. Sentence combining seems to be practice in packaging past or completed mental events because it is practice in embedding and because it always provides the student with someone else's completed thoughts.

I think this "going on" quality is one of the things that gives voice to prose, gives life to syntax. It's also reinforcing to the writer. It's why students like to do freewriting or rough exploratory writing (when they learn how): Holding the pen, they feel something alive in their hands.

This is tricky business. Am I saying that "something going on" is good enough? No. If that's all we have, we have nothing but freewriting and that's not usually good writing. For writing to be good we also need something *already having gone on.* That is, we must revise our prose and polish it till it is the way we want it, and that means the final syntax will also represent something having gone on, something completed.

Can we have it both ways? Yes. For writing takes place in time and therefore good prose usually represents *both* something going on and something having gone on. That is, when writing goes well, there is usually something going on during the act of writing: a process of ongoing, live engagement in the thinking. Yet it is rare that the writing so produced doesn't also need some revising — and thus also embody completed and fully examined mental events. But if we know how to revise well, we can preserve the quality of present "going on" mental life *within* what is also completed and pondered. If prose embodies *only* the completed mental events, precious life and voice is usually missing.

My point echoes what Francis Christensen said about the "cumulative sentence": It "doesn't represent the idea as conceived, pondered over, reshaped, packaged, and delivered cold. It is dynamic rather than static, representing the mind thinking."[12]

I suspect that leaving syntax alone or putting down words in the order they come to mind leads to simple sentences and cumulative sentences more often than to embedded ones. But I want to back off here again. I don't really think voice or life is a matter of certain syntactic forms being better — of cumulative or simple sentences always being more alive than embedded ones. In making the following hypothesis perhaps I'm being both literal-minded and mystical at the same time, but I suspect it's a matter of whether something in fact *was going on* — whether thinking *was* in action while the sentence was being written. Was the sentence impelled by live thought? Was the writer, at the moment of writing, actually engaged in her topic? Is the sentence an embodiment and expression of presently ongoing mental life? If so, it is likely to have that "going on" quality and the voice that often goes with it. But when a writer is engaged in this way, she will not necessarily restrict herself to simple or cumulative sentences. She will no doubt produce some deeply and complexly embedded sentences. Surely we see them all around us in good prose that is alive. Thus in the case of my sample sentences above, the simple sentences may have seemed to have more "going on" in them than the embedded ones partly because we were comparing them in isolation without context. If a writer is really engaged in thought, of course she might write, "Having put my foot down, the car surged forward," and end up imparting enormous voice and life to that embedding.

But sentence combining as a model for *generating* worries me nevertheless. It gives the wrong model for generating by implying that when we produce a sentence we are making a package for an already completed mental act. For revising, however, sentence combining is not such a dangerous model. Revising is necessarily (if not entirely) a process of transforming sentences so that they successfully package completed mental events — adjusting them to make them clear and to make them say what we have *already* decided we mean. (Good revising also, however, should try to preserve the life entangled in the mess of the rough draft, and even — if the writer is skilled — to inject some new life that wasn't there before.)

Conclusion

I'm worried that I end up sounding merely naive and sentimental. Yes, I'm making a naive claim — that "warbling one's woodnotes wild" or leaving one's syntax alone creates syntactic value and voice. But that claim is only half of a larger position that I think is complex, paradoxical, and sophisticated. It's not a matter of either/or — of choosing between learning to transform one's syntax or to leave it alone — or even stressing one process over the other. I'm arguing for the necessity of both, however confusing that may be to teachers and students. But once we consider writing under the aspect of time — which of course is inevitable when we look at writing as process — we must heed opposites and they need not conflict with each other. (Hegel was interested in history, the realm where contraries can reinforce rather than undermine each other.) We can put words down in the order they come to mind and also manipulate and transform our syntax if we engage first in the one activity and then the other. Interestingly, we cannot do it the other way around: Time's arrow points only one way. Therefore we need to teach both leaving syntax alone and manipulating syntax. And we need to know how to live with opposites.[13]

Notes

[1] Some teachers maintain that basic writers need sentence combining to provide the semantic content because they are not fluent in producing written text. But, in fact, basic writers are good at generating their own words and ideas on paper when released from their preoccupation with mistakes. They, most of all, need to generate their own writing.

[2] I am grateful to Bill Strong for showing me a draft of his paper for this conference and thereby giving me some reassurance that my misgivings are not farfetched even to sentence combiners.

[3] Jerome S. Bruner, *Studies in Cognitive Growth* (New York: Wiley, 1966).

[4] Objection: "But the trouble with students is precisely that they *don't* seem to notice problems in their drafts." Of course this is true to a degree. This is part of why they are unskilled writers, and my proposal will help. But students are not, in fact, as bad at sensing problems as they appear to be. It's because they feel so helpless about fixing problems — or lazy about it — that they find it so easy not to notice them. Why notice problems if you can't do anything about them? If we improve their skill at making improvements, we'll see them notice more problems.

[5] I had the sensation of figuring out this use of sentence combining myself, but I discover that the idea was in fact planted in a conversation a number of years ago with Professor Susan Hubbuch, an insightful and effective teacher who has used the approach at Lewis and Clark College.

[6] This process is illustrated by the simple but effective musical exercise for fast, difficult passages. One practices them in a dotted rhythm so exaggerated that one relaxes on every other note while playing the alternate ones as fast as possible. The dottedness is then reversed: this time one relaxes on the notes previously played fast. This is a perfect example of making an exercise out of the real thing in order to conquer it.

[7] Two thoughts about revising: (1) When I reflect on the fact that my misgivings about sentence combining dissipate when it is made part of revising, I see a pattern. It seems to happen that most pieces of problematic advice about writing turn into good advice when restricted to revising rather than applied to the whole writing process. For example: "Get your meaning clear in mind before proceeding further"; "Make an outline"; "Think about your audience." (2) We might call revising that part of the writing process which most needs disciplined exercise and instruction: Revising requires the most cognitive skill and disciplined practice, it doesn't come naturally (like generating), and it tends to hurt. No doubt these are some of the reasons why writing instruction has tended to center on revision and ignore invention or generation. Yet I'm scared to focus instruction and exercise on revising. In many ways generating is *more* important: not only must generating come first since there's no revising till you have material to work on; in addition, all other instruction in writing tends to backfire if generating is not healthy. And it turns out that students do need instruction in how to generate productively and well.

[8] Joseph M. Williams and Rosemary L. Hake, "Style and Its Consequences: Do as I Do, Not as I Say," *CE*, 43 (1981), 433–51.

[9] William L. Smith and Warren E. Combs, "The Effects of Overt and Covert Cues on Written Syntax," *RTE*, 14 (1980), 19–38.

[10] Marlene Scardamalia and Carl Bereiter, "Written Composition" (Ontario Institute for Studies in Education, 1983, circulated manuscript), 33–34.

[11] I am frightened at the many teachers and researchers who make inferences about students' cognitive and linguistic development on the basis of syntax intended for teachers. These texts may present a valid picture of syntactic *decisions* students end up making under pressure — that is, while worrying about what the teacher or the exam is looking for ("Let's see — that word I started to write must be wrong —

I better find a different one — or change the punctuation at least"). But surely they are not a valid picture of how the student's mind actually generates syntax. Therefore, we must reject any inferences from syntax about the students' mental development.

[12] Francis Christensen and Bonniejean Christensen, *Notes Toward a New Rhetoric,* 2nd ed. (New York: Harper & Row, 1978). The quotation is from "A Generative Rhetoric of the Sentence," in *A Writing Teacher's Sourcebook,* ed. Gary Tate and Edward P. J. Corbett (New York: Oxford University Press, 1981), p. 356.

[13] I am grateful for helpful feedback on drafts of this paper from Pat Belanoff, Paul Connolly, Helen Cooper, Adrienne Munich, and David Laurence.

ANOTHER CASE IN POINT:
THE JARGONAUTS AND THE NOT-SO-GOLDEN FLEECE
Dwight Bolinger

[From Language, the Loaded Weapon: The Use and Abuse of Language Today. *New York: Longman, 1980. 125–37.]*

Dwight Bolinger is emeritus professor of Romance languages and literatures at Harvard University, where he taught from 1963 to 1973. He has written several books on linguistics; the third edition of his popular introductory text, Aspects of Language, *was published in 1981. In addition, he has published articles in a wide array of professional journals.*

The selection that follows is chapter 11 of Bolinger's Language, the Loaded Weapon: The Use and Abuse of Language Today *(1980). In his book, Bolinger explores and explains language as a means by which we construct realities, focusing primarily on the intentional and unintentional misuses of that power. This chapter on "jargon — gobbledegook — doubletalk — doublespeak" explores causes and effects of obscure language, offering explanations, suggestions, and ample material for teachers to consider.*

When the U.S. Department of State appointed a Consumer Affairs Coordinator to look after the Department's interests in what has come to be called consumerism, it fell to the Deputy Secretary for Management, Lawrence Eagleburger, to draw up a description for the job. Here, in part, is what he wrote:

> The purpose of the Department's plan is two-fold, to confirm and reinforce the Department's sensitivity to consumer rights and interests as they impact upon the Department and to take those steps necessary and feasible to promote and channel these rights and interests with respect to the maintenance and expansion of an international dialogue and awareness.

The Coordinator's duties were to "review existing mechanisms of consumer input, thruput and output, and seek ways of improving these linkages via the consumer communication channel."[1] For this achievement in prose, Mr. Eagleburger was presented with the annual Doublespeak Award from the National Council of Teachers of English, through its Committee on Public Doublespeak.

That there should be such a committee — formed in 1971 — is one of many signs of growing irritation and alarm at the spread of obscure language. Next to "Why can't Johnny read (or write)?," the most-debated question of language today is "Why can't officials use plain language?" Not that officials are the only offenders, but their pronouncements affect the general public and the general public feels it has a RIGHT to understand what is going on.

Jargon — gobbledegook — doubletalk — doublespeak. Johnny's encounters with English are part of the problem. Writing is such an alien activity that he overreaches himself. Stepping into a written paragraph for him is like stepping into a Paris salon — to play safe he dons the most formal style he can lay hands on, and since he has little acquaintance with formal styles, he combines purple tails with a frilled shirt and forgets that he is still wearing his work trousers. As more and more Johnnies spread by capillary action through the professions, the level of prose sinks with a dead weight.

By sheer numbers, Johnny's ineptitudes are transformed. The more Johnnies there are in contact with one another and performing the same activities, the more their altered language becomes a badge of their class. Jargon takes on the functions of a SOCIOLECT. The same can be said of jargon as of another sociolect, the slang of marijuana-users: that it becomes "one of the most important active media for transmitting certain kinds of social awareness through the culture"[2] — a Solidarity of Bureaucrats, whose bureaucratese is their password. Like other forms of secret language — the slang of the "now" generation, the argot of pickpockets, the Latinisms of medicine — it identifies its users to one another and shields them from intrusion. Combating it calls for something more than instruction in English. The antijargoneer encounters the same obstacles as the campaigner against environmental pollution: Success is not a question of eliminating a few supposed errors but of changing a way of life.

Except that all play their part in group reinforcement, there would seem to be little in common between jargon and other secret languages. Yet there are so many of them that it is easy to find unofficial styles that share the sources of jargon as well as some of its purposes. Take the language-for-sociability that the anthropologist Bronislaw Malinowski called "phatic communion." Its main purpose is not to exchange information but to warm the conversants to each other and keep the talk going. Ostensibly conversation has to be about something, so phatic talk — when it gets beyond the standard greetings and leavetakings — makes a stab at being informative; but content is outweighed by sound and stroking. In California, phatic communion luxuriates in a rank growth of "psychobabble," as R. D. Rosen calls it. . . . The topics follow the latest psychic fad, disdaining precision, affecting modish variation of the same trite ideas, a music to accompany the clink of cocktail glasses:

> At a dinner party, a new acquaintance tells me about her intimate life. Although she is still "processing" her ex-husband . . . , she just spent a weekend with another man from whom she gets "a lot of ego reinforcement. My therapist keeps telling me to go where the energies are," she says, "so that's what I'm doing, because that's what went wrong last time. I didn't just kick back and go with the energies."[3]

The mark of pseudoscience is on this passage, and reading another, from McFadden's book *The Serial*, one understands why. It lists the character Rita's curriculum of psycho-courses; Rita had "been through"

> Gurdjieff, Silva Mind Control, actualism, analytical tracking, parapsychology, Human Life Styling, postural integration, the Fischer–Hoffman Process, hatha and raja yoga, integral massage, orgonomy, palmistry,

and she was commuting twice a week for "polarity balancing manipulation."[4]

For jargon, science is both source and motive. The social sciences imitate the hard sciences, the pseudo-sciences imitate the social sciences, and mod speaker takes his cues from all three. Why does an ordinarily plain-spoken person advise keeping detergent away from indoor plants because *it causes an adverse reaction* instead of *it is bad for them?* The metaphors of scientism tempt us with a sham authority; they keep the ordinary from sounding commonplace. English is particularly susceptible because of its openness to borrowings from everywhere, and scientists are notorious for their snatches of Latin and Greek, and for applying rules of affixiation that result in verbal monstrosities. Their nomenclatures are intended to be internally consistent — *deoxyribonuclease* is made to have each of its elements, *de + oxy + rib + nucle + ase,* relate the compound to some trait in the whole family of organic compounds, but this goes counter to the essential contrastiveness of words; in natural language it is more practical to keep things apart than to show their interrelationships, and when such terms are taken into everyday speech they trade the reality of scientific precision for its pretense. The charlatan passes for a scientist by sounding like one, and writing and conversation swell with the concepts, metaphors, and polysyllables of our white-coated oracles. In some professions — notably those dealing with public safety, such as fire and police — the affectation becomes comical: *At least seventy-five people evacuated safely from the premises*, goes a radio report,[5] to let us know they all got away.

The full riches of jargon are best savored in the softest of the soft sciences, sociology and its branches. An anonymous wag a few years ago circulated a "Folklore Article Reconstitution Kit" consisting of four sections which, when compiled phrase by phrase in 1–2–3–4 order, would yield sentences suitable for a folklore article. Readers can try their hand:

Section 1

1. Obviously,
2. On the other hand,
3. From the intercultural standpoint,
4. Similarly,
5. As Lévi-Strauss contends,
6. In this regard,
7. Based on my own fieldwork in Guatemala,
8. For example,
9. Thus, within given parameters,
10. In respect to essential departmental goals,

Section 2

1. a large proportion of intercultural communicative coordination
2. a constant flow of field-collected input ordinates

3. the characterization of critically co-optive criteria
4. initiation of basic charismatic subculture development
5. our fully integrated field program
6. any exponential Folklife coefficient
7. further and associated contradictory elements
8. the incorporation of agonistic cultural constraints
9. my proposed independent structuralistic concept
10. a primary interrelationship between systems and/or subsystems logistics

Section 3

1. must utilize and be functionally interwoven with
2. maximizes the probability of project success while minimizing cross-cultural shock elements in
3. adds explicit performance contours to
4. necessitates that coagulative measures be applied to
5. requires considerable further performance analysis and computer studies to arrive at
6. is holistically compounded, in the context of
7. presents a valuable challenge showing the necessity for
8. recognizes the importance of other disciplines, while taking into account
9. effects a significant implementation of
10. adds overwhelming Folkloristic significance to

Section 4

1. Propp's basic formulation
2. the anticipated epistemological repercussions
3. improved subcultural compatibility-testing
4. all deeper structuralistic conceptualization
5. any communicatively programmed computer techniques
6. the profound meaning of *The Raw and the Cooked*
7. our hedonic Folklife perspectives over a given time-period
8. any normative concept of the linguistic/holistic continuum
9. the total configurational rationale
10. Krappe's Last Tape

Not to be outdone, the Open University's magazine *Sesame* published the following reduced-complexity homeomorphic co-varying exercises in sociological conceptualization:

The Instant Sociological Jargon Matrix

0	relative	0	charismatic
1	peripheral	1	hierarchical
2	traditional	2	bureaucratic
3	internalized	3	conceptual
4	functional	4	homeostatic
5	normative	5	pre-industrial
6	symbolic	6	deviant
7	multi-variate	7	anomic
8	reciprocal	8	empirical
9	affective	9	psychometric

0	model
1	regression
2	alienation
3	paradigm
4	reification
5	hypothesis
6	commitment
7	expectations
8	syndrome
9	deprivation[6]

Jargon spares no institution, not even the sacred ones, where, we are told, the minister of the Gospel lives in a *pastorium, interacts* with and gets *input and feedback* from his *prayer-cell circle of the Committed* in a *Christian Life Center, raps* with *teens* in special *after-glow* services, *opts for alternatives* to *implement, restructure, finalize,* and *firm up a meaningful Operation Involvement Outreach Explosion* to *bridge* the *Generation Credibility Gap* of the *unchurched* through a *Koinonia, Agape Multine dia Thrust.*[7]

The organ supplies strains of rock music in the background.

Most jargon is not quite so condensed — it takes rhapsodic compilations like these to make good reading. The antijargoneer is not above exaggerating a bit to make his point. Here is a "translation" of the beginning of the Twenty-third Psalm from the gospel according to Alan Simpson, former President of Vassar College:

> The Lord is my external-internal integrative mechanism.
> I shall not be deprived of gratifications for my viscerogenic hungers
>   or my need-dispositions.
> He motivates me to orient myself towards a nonsocial object with
>   affective significance.
> He positions me in a nondecisional situation.
> He maximizes my adjustment.[8]

But the real thing is almost a match for the caricature. Here is a true-to-life sentence from an article on linguistics:

> In traditional linguistics it has been assumed that the analysis of sentences can be performed upon examples isolated from the process of interaction within which they naturally emerge.

Deflated, this means "Traditional linguists thought that sentences could be analyzed out of context." Appropriately, the next sentence from the same passage reads *Indeed this has been stated as an explicit tenant by Chomsky.*[9] Malapropisms — like *tenant* for *tenet,* where the writer could just as well have said *principle* — are a regular adornment of jargon. The writer or speaker strains for the more erudite and exotic synonym, but has no sure idea of what he is looking for. An official of a chemical company boasts that *During our 33-year history, only one employee died of chemical exposure and his death was largely due to panic on his behalf* — jargon in the phrase *chemical exposure* as well as in the malapropism *behalf* for *part.*[10] A caller on a radio talk show says *It become inherent on us* — stumbling on the way from the simple *It is our duty* to the elegant *It is incumbent on us.*[11] Another true-to-life passage:

> Over the past ten years the school has evolved a child-centred individual-learning situation with a degree of integrated day organisation and close co-operation between each year's mixed-ability classes. Basic-work morning programmes are carefully structured but allow for integration. . . .[12]

The spelling tells us that jargon is firmly established on both sides of the Atlantic, with roots deep in the educational establishment — as yet another true-to-life passage extravagantly proves:

> Our school's Cross-Graded, Multi-Ethnic, Individualized Learning Program is designed to enhance the concept of an Open-Ended Learning Program with emphasis on a continuum of multi-ethnic academically enriched learning, using the identified intellectually gifted child as the agent or director of his own learning. Major emphasis is on a cross-graded, multi-ethnic learning with the main objective being to learn respect for the uniqueness of a person.

This was in a letter received by a Houston, Texas, father inviting him to a meeting about a new high school program.[13]

Like any other style, jargon is complex and hard to define. Pure jargon would have to be a condensation of only those ingredients shared by no other style, and obviously such an extreme would be annihilated by its own destiny, a sort of verbal black hole. But take certain qualities and pack them close together, and you get a pretty solid approximation of the undenatured thing:

First, basic words — pseudoscientific, much of it layered with Greek and Latin prefixes and suffixes, most of it a substitution of the unusual for the usual. Not that unusualness is bad if the ideas are unusual: The rarity of the words hardly counts against a sentence like *The piebald mare trampled the yarrow underfoot.*[14] But *The identical theory offers a basis for development of X* is authentic jargon: for *identical*, read *same*; for *offers a basis*, read *from*; for *development*, read *develop* — which translates to *From the same theory we develop X.* Jargon even invades the prepositions: *before* becomes *prior to*, *after* becomes *following* or *subsequent to*, *from* in a causative sense becomes *due to (She broke down due to overwork)*, *in* becomes *as far as (It is striking as far as appearance).* The unusual soon becomes usual — statistically — as the jargon word catches on and becomes a vogue word. *Government programs impact on people's needs. Things are prioritized and reprioritized. Bureaucrats coordinate, facilitate and disseminate, especially on the interface.*[15] The lexicon of jargon quickly degenerates into a catalog of clichés.

After basic words come the compounds. Here thrive the hyphenations that make it appear as if every passing encounter between two ideas deserved a permanent record in the dictionary. On a Greyhound bus appears the sign *The coach is restroom equipped for your convenience* — to have a restroom becomes a new verb, *to restroom-equip.* The city jail in Madison, Wisconsin, is called a *total-incarceration facility. Correctional facility* has become a kind of standard euphemism for *jail* or *prison.*

Third, the syntax of phrases. Richard Nixon's lieutenant Gordon Liddy, outlining *Operation Diamond*, aimed at preventing demonstrations at political conventions, explained a bit of strategy:

We will have a second operational arm that could be of even greater preventive use. These teams are experienced in surgical relocation activities. In a word, General, they can kidnap a hostile leader with maximum secrecy and minimal use of force.[16]

The simple noun *kidnapping* grows to a noun modified by a noun modified by an adjective. A radio station announces a new venture in religion: *Program emphasis will be on Christian living.*[17] We have a new technical entity, *program emphasis*, to replace the humdrum activity of emphasizing something in a program. An ad for a magazine inquires, *How can you tell if you are heart-attack prone?*[18] Piling up plethoric adjectives gives a similar effect: *ambient noncombatant personnel* for *refugees*[19] and *waterborne logistic craft* for *sampans*,[20] both from the rich harvest of jargon from Vietnam. A common practice in these phrases is to attach heavyweight modifiers to lightweight nouns. The noun *facility* covers virtually anything intended for general use and having an established location, from an insane asylum to a lavatory: *sanitary facility, health facility* (hospital), *parking facility* (public garage), *recycling facility* (junkyard), besides Madison's *incarceration facil-*

ity. A traffic-spotter helicopter, reporting light rain, observes *a lot of windshield wiper activity*. We hear *firefighting operation* for *firefighting*, *supervisory personnel* for *supervisors*, *age level* for *age*. Among the most frequent empty nouns are *phase, process, condition, nature phenomenon*. In advertising the favorite is *system:* a motel calls its beds *sleep systems*, and a water bed is a *flotation system;* a vacuum cleaner is a *sanitation system*. But the general favorite for a number of years has been *situation* — empty enough to cover any situation. When the telephone lines were jammed during a heavy storm in the winter of 1977–78, a patron called the company to complain, and the operator explained, *Yes, we know, everyone's having the same trouble — we're in a slow-talk situation.*[21] A radio report says that *the weather does not permit a helicopter to maintain a landing situation.*[22] Two people in a fight are in a *conflict situation*. The result of no rain for six months is a *drought situation*. The nice thing about *situation* is that you can add it to any self-sufficient action noun: *crime situation, inflation situation, strike situation, attack situation, retreat situation*.

Verb phrases are like noun phrases except that the lightweight is an empty verb instead of an empty noun. A passage quoted earlier had *perform an analysis* in place of *analyze. To be in receipt of* substitutes for simple *receive, to have need of* for simple *need*. In some cases there is a true contrast; for instance, *They had an argument* pictures the argument as finished, *They argued* suggests that there is more to this story. But this does not explain why the San Francisco police chief who wanted to get rid of prostitutes referred to *having an absence* of them.[23]

Many phrases are hard to classify, but all are the same in substituting the roundabout for the direct: *other considerations to the contrary notwithstanding* for *in spite of other considerations, over and above* for *more than* or *beyond, from this it follows that* for *so* or *therefore, it is a function of* for *it depends on*. In the larger unit of the sentence the combined resources are infinite: In the Nixon era, *The input process is going on* stood for *The president is listening*.

As for the syntax of jargon, it predictably circumnavigates. There are passives in abundance (*It is thought that* for *I think that*), double negative (*a not unintentional remark* for *an insult*), inversions and extractions (*It is security that people want* or *What people want is security* for *People want security*), repetitions of words that could be dropped or replaced with pronouns (*They accepted the document and said document was affirmed*), continual admonitions to the hearer or reader that the speaker or writer means what he is saying (*it should be understood that, it is noteworthy that, it is necessary to be aware of the fact that, bear in mind that, it cannot be stressed too strongly that*), transitions pointing to what is obvious on inspection (*to begin, we next turn to, in conclusion*), phrases with which the author pats himself on the back (*interestingly enough, the important fact is, we have made it clear that*). And so on. For every way of driving straight to a goal, jargon discovers a dozen ways of beating around the bush — for whatever reason: self-importance, obfuscation, ineptitude. Expanded constructions have their place, but not whole colonies of them.

The most consistent feature of jargon is SEMANTIC. It is elevated, ameliorative, euphemistic in the most general sense. It tries to improve appearances, both in what the message is about and in the message itself. The listener is reassured that reality is at worst not threatening and at best attractive, and that the message and its giver have authority. The first purpose is served by avoiding the unpleasant, and the second by sounding weighty. The ideal piece of jargon does both at once. There are not supposed to be secrets from the American people — so *secret* is removed from the secret file and replaced with *classified,* which makes things seem less conspiratorial and at the same time creates visions of busy, efficient people classifying documents in a scientific way. The Department of Physical Education of the California State University at San Jose covers its sweat and dons academic respectability as the *Department of Human Performance* (*physical education* was already the jargon of another era, when *physical exercise* was seeking status in institutions of higher *education*). The *Bay Area* (San Francisco) *Air Pollution Control District* went itself one better in 1978 as the *Bay Area Air Quality Management District.*[24] For many years now we have dialed *Directory Assistance* when all we want is *Information.* Vietnam was a verbal as well as a military minefield, a place where

> troops were advisors, where men were not murdered but wasted, and where the CIA shunned assassination in favor of termination with prejudice. . . . "You always write it's bombing, bombing, bombing," Col. David H. E. Opfer, air attaché at the U.S. Embassy in Phnom Penh, complained to reporters. "It's not bombing. It's air support."[25]

Business uses glossy jargon for advertising, but evasive jargon for self-protection. When the Ford Motor Company recalled their Torinos and Rancheros,

> They sent out a letter: ". . . Continued driving with a failed bearing could result in disengagement of the axle shaft and adversely affect vehicle control."[26]

Adversely affect vehicle control is a pseudoscientist lecturing a moronic public, and *continued driving* puts the responsibility on YOU. George Herman, on the Washington Staff of CBS News, tells of a business executive who erected a verbal screen at a Senate hearing by promising the optimum maximization of the potentialities or the maximum optimization of the potentialities, he wasn't sure which.

> I tried to figure out what it meant either way. Optimum maximization, I figure, is the best possible way of making something big, whereas maximum optimization is the biggest possible way of making something the best. Neither way does it make much sense. I listened some more and eventually I realized that it wasn't supposed to make much sense — it was part of a new language of antisemantics, a strange hybrid tongue designed to keep your meaning so unclear that if anyone tries to quarrel with you, you can hastily beat a retreat by saying that wasn't what you meant at all.[27]

Herman errs only in thinking the language to be new. It is more rampant now, but it is as old as speech, renewing only its manifestations.

There is always some obstacle to penetrating the essential meaning of a piece of jargon. As with the last example, likely as not when we have got to the center of it we find the room empty. This happens most often in advertising, as in the pure illogic of *Not everybody likes Kava but Kava likes everybody,* or *People eat more McDonalds than anybody.* Or the nonsense may be added on. Intonation can be used for this: An advertisement for Chevette cars went *A choice of TWO engines instead of no choice at ALL!*[28] The least possible choice is a choice from two, but *least* is made to sound like *most.* As these examples show, the conjuring of something out of nothing can be done with plain words as well as with woolly abstractions: The gobbledegook is in the logic rather than in the terms. Whether this should be called jargon is a matter of definition. It lacks the ingredient of impressiveness. The brand of soup that carries on its label the wording *Full strength: no water needs to be added* is merely aiming to deceive, with its substitution of *full strength* for *already diluted.*

Who the first jargoneer was, nobody knows. He — or as likely she — probably antedated articulate speech, and substituted fancy gestures for plain ones. No one has compiled a history of jargon, but recorded objections to it go back a long way. Over two hundred years ago the Secretary to the Commissioner of Excise admonished an official of the town of Pontefract to stop his "schoolboy way of writing," with "affected phrases and incongruous words, such as *illegal procedure, harmony, etc.*"[29] A century ago, the director of the U.S. Geological Survey, Dr. George Otis Smith,

> chided a colleague for writing "The argillaceous character of the formation is very prominent in some localities, although it is usually subsidiary to the arenaceous phase." What he meant was: "At some places the formation included considerable clay, but generally it is made up chiefly of sand."[30]

Jargon at its worst is partly a product of unfinished education, and if we have more of it today, one reason is that we have more half-educated people in a position to afflict the public with their words — and, as often as not, a wish to hide something.

Reaction was inevitable, and it has taken two forms: an effort to reeducate, and an attack on deliberate unclarity. Industry and government are concerned about the bad impression their employees make on the public and the trouble they have understanding one another. President Carter made it official by demanding that federal regulations be written in plain English, and a number of agencies looked for ways to reform themselves or called in outside help. The Federal Trade Commission hired Rudolph Flesch, author of *Why Johnny Can't Read,* as consultant, the Department of Housing and Urban Development began taking advice from the former head of the English Department at Goucher College, Ruth Limmer, and the Department of Health, Education, and Welfare launched an "Operation Common Sense" directed by a lawyer and a writer, Inez Smith Reid, in a five-year plan to reedit six thousand pages of regulations. Its office of Civil Rights employed a former reporter and editor, Norma Mohr, to help "push back the tide of turgid prose." Here is a sample of an old regulation on hearing aids, and its new rendition by Flesch:

> No seller shall represent that it or any of its employees, agents, sales persons and/or representatives is a physician or an audiologist, unless such is the fact.
>
> Don't say or hint that you or anyone in your firm is a doctor of medicine or an audiologist if it isn't so.[31]

Some local governments too began taking stock of their language. The Planning Division of San Mateo County, California, hired a specialist in plain writing whose blue pencil "regularly changes *utilize* to *use, inaugurate* to *start,* and *at this point in time* to *now.*"[32] In Milwaukee a consulting firm was set up by a journalism graduate, Caroline Poh, to serve business clients in rewriting such products as advertisements, articles for trade magazines, and executives' speeches.[33]

Conspicuous by their absence among these experts are the professional linguists. It cannot be just because linguists are among the worst offenders themselves — as claimed by David Ferris of Exeter University, who devised a scale to measure jargon and put theoretical linguists at the top.[34] It is partly because linguists have not come forward with advice, and partly because shamanism is still the rule in treating the ills of language — glottotherapy, if you please.

When jargon is deliberate, education in direct, unambiguous speech and writing is of little use. If the deliberate jargoneer is a diplomat, he needs his indirections for the sparring matches he has to play with others of his kind. Here, perhaps, jargon has its place, in encounters where suspicion is high and talk has to be kept going without presuming on a frankness that might cause offense. But deliberate jargoneering "to advance the career of the speaker (or the issue, cause or product he is agent for) by a kind of verbal sleight of hand," as L. E. Sissman describes it,[35] calls for countermeasures. There is one response that offers at least psychological relief: A public that feels put upon but helpless to do anything about it strikes back with gallows humor. Professor Don Nilson of Arizona State University collects antijargon graffiti:

> When in doubt, do as the President does — take a guess.
>
> Studies at the University of Michigan have proved that the average blond has an IQ equalling that of a medium-sized radish.
>
> There is a relationship between stable government and horse sense.
>
> Bureaucrats never change the course of the ship of state; they simply adjust the compass.[36]

But sarcasm is too often an admission of defeat, and besides, not every public servant deserves to be publicly ridiculed. The logical target of the antijargoneer is specific jargon and its motives. Frankness and honesty are more apt to come in our one-way language-consuming world when we demand them frankly and honestly. And if the deliberate jargoneer cannot be educated, his victims can, to recognize what is being done to them. When Edwin Newman says of jargon that "it serves as a fence that keeps others outside and respectful, or leads them to ignore what is going on because it is too much trouble to find out,"[37] he exposes the attitude that makes this kind of deception possible. We are surrounded by the products of scientific magicians whose methods and formulas we do not understand and are afraid to question lest we expose our ignorance. Confident that if the scientific is accepted as unintelligible the unintelligible will be accepted as scientific, the pseudoscientists parade their pseudoformulas, persuading us to buy their products on the basis of misleading claims, or to accept a course of action that we would never endorse if it were clearly labeled. Jargoneering deception depends on ignorance; seen through, it collapses. We are the students in a class where the professor talks over our heads. We have paid our fees, and have a right to stop his lecture every time he gets ahead of us.

But to catch jargon aimed at us we must understand our own all too easy retreat into it. Words pass for solutions because we permit language to become automatic. This too we inherit from science — applied science, that is, which is forever on the lookout for tricks that will save people from having to do for themselves — in transportation, food preparation, computing, pest control, child rearing — even to brushing teeth and opening a tin can. We have convenience foods and we want a convenience language, one with a formula for every emergency. For all things there have to be specialists, and specialists are those who have mastered the incantations of their science. If formulas have that power, how is the ordinary word to stand up against them?

The answer is to renew our own faith in ordinary language as the most powerful instrument we have. It produced all those special languages in the first place and can recall them when they prove defective. Formulas are good for putting ideas into a small space and testing them for consistency, but the formula that defies translation into intelligible prose is probably a fraud. The test of survival is to face the world of problems unarmed except with a functioning brain and the birthright of a common language. It is the unrestricted code, the organizer of our universe, not to be shamed by false notions of refinement nor cowed by the condescensions of those for whom promises are commitments and driving the blacks out of the slums is urban renewal in the inner city.

Having battered jargon for all these pages, is there any good we can say of it? Perhaps that along with slang it is part of the exuberance of language always striving to keep one jump ahead of reality. If the expressions are there, even though vague and often deceptive at first, some of them may serve as half-finished material for ideas that are steadily refined. As we saw in an earlier chapter [of Bolinger's book *Language, the Loaded Weapon: The Use and Abuse of Language Today*], things are not only assigned their words, but reach out to things. The process of adjustment is never-ending — and what other word can we use here than *process?* In its day, *complex* was a jargoneering loan from psychology. *To contact* was jargon fifty years ago, but now we find it a useful abstraction a level higher than *to call, write,* or *see,* all unnecessarily specific; and it is certainly less clumsy than *get in touch with.* Today's *lifestyle* instead of *way of living* dramatizes what a whole generation insists on as its right, a new conceptual entity. Though terribly overused, *viable* in its proper sphere has no substitute. Jargon is an ABUSE of terms whose main fault is that some of them tempt us to abuse them. Otherwise they have a certain right to protest their innocence, for their other faults are no worse than those of hundreds of terms that pass our lips daily, unnoticed because we are used to them. A new word, or an old one that rockets to popularity, like *meaningful,* flags us down because we expected something else. With our attention riveted on it, there is no way for it to hide the semantic vagueness that afflicts all abstractions. Yet *meaningful* comes as a potentially useful antonym of a term that no one would think of as jargon. When Britt Ekland declares, *My love affairs have always been meaningful,*[38] she is saying that they were not *frivolous. Serious* will not quite serve. Old vices are accepted, new ones viewed with horror — the familiar jargon is the alcohol of our verbal drug culture, the unfamiliar jargon is its marijuana.

For all that one would like to throttle them, it would be neither good nor possible to ABOLISH the special ways of talking and writing that serve little purpose except to set groups apart from one another. But it is essential to learn when not to be fooled by them. It makes no sense for a society to spend millions on bilingual programs to break down the barriers between languages, and do nothing about the rank growth of sociolects that raise new ones. Or do nothing about the oppressive side of the standard itself, which in some of its forms — and to some degree in the scheme as a whole — is designed as a barrier of social class. The standard, too, is a sociolect.

220   *Effective Sentences and Word Choice*

Notes

¹ *Public Doublespeak Newsletter* 3 (1977) 3.5.

² Geoffrey Nunberg, "Slang, Usage-conditions, and l'Arbitraire du Signe," in Donka Farkas, Wesley M. Jacobson, and Karol W. Todrys (eds.), *Parasession on the Lexicon.* Chicago: Chicago Linguistic Society, 1978, 301–11, p. 305.

³ "California Spinach Talk," San Francisco, California, *Chronicle,* Sunday Punch section, 4 December 1977, p. 2.

⁴ Cited by Mary Ann Seawell, "Satirist Skewers 'Self-indulgent' Marin Lifestyle," Palo Alto, California, *Times,* 10 October 1977, p. 13.

⁵ San Francisco radio KCBS, 2 July 1978, 7:25 am.

⁶ Kindly supplied by Geoffrey Leech.

⁷ D. G. Kehl, "Religious Doublespeak and the Idols of the Marketplace," *Public Doublespeak Newsletter* 3 (1977) 4.1–2.

⁸ Alan Simpson, "Liberal Education in a University," *Washington University Magazine,* February 1961, 14–18, p. 17.

⁹ From a paper by Charles Goodwin titled "The Interactive Construction of the Sentence within the Turn at Talk in Natural Conversation," at the annual meeting of the American Anthropological Association, 1975, MS p. 33.

¹⁰ San Francisco *Examiner and Chronicle,* 25 January 1976, p. A12.

¹¹ San Francisco radio KGO, 21 July 1974.

¹² Cited by David C. Ferris, "Scoring Jargon," *Verbatim* 4 (1977) 2.3–4.

¹³ *Reader's Digest,* September 1977, p. 95.

¹⁴ Ferris, op. cit.

¹⁵ Donald Zochert, "Don't Freak Out — *Some* Slang Is Here to Stay," Chicago *Daily News,* 17 September 1977, p. 1.

¹⁶ John Dean, *Blind Ambition.* New York: Simon and Schuster, 1976, p. 81.

¹⁷ San Francisco radio KGO, 13 June 1976, 7:40 am.

¹⁸ San Francisco radio KCBS, 27 June 1978, for *Better Homes and Gardens.*

¹⁹ *Newsweek,* 15 April 1974, p. 7.

²⁰ Henry Steele Commager, "The Defeat of America," *New York Review of Books,* 5 October 1972, p. 10.

²¹ Example from D. R. Ladd, private communication.

²² San Francisco radio KCBS, 6 September 1978, 10:04 pm.

²³ Radio report, 27 June 1978.

²⁴ Palo Alto, California, *Times,* 27 September 1978, p. 1.

²⁵ Israel Shenker, "Zieglerrata," *The New Republic,* 12 April 1974, pp. 21–23, cited *Public Doublespeak Newsletter* 1 (1974) 3.7–8.

²⁶ Cited ibid., p. 7.

²⁷ Cited by Robert Kirk Mueller, *Buzzwords: A Guide to the Language of Leadership.* New York: Van Nostrand Reinhold Co., 1974, p. 21.

²⁸ Example from D. R. Ladd, private communication.

²⁹ Cited by Ernest Gowers, *Plain Words: Their ABC.* New York: Knopf, 1962, pp. 46–47.

³⁰ Morrie Landsberg, "Speak Not in Doublespeak," Sacramento, California, *Bee,* 30 October 1975, p. B4.

³¹ Robert Reinhold, "A Federal Crackdown: Gobbledegook Has to Go!," San Francisco *Examiner and Chronicle,* This World section, 1 January 1978, p. 26.

³² Carrie Peyton, "Man Changes Gobbledegook into English," Palo Alto, California, *Times,* 25 November 1977, p. 7.

³³ AP dispatch, Palo Alto, California, *Times,* 18 April 1978, p. 33.

³⁴ Op. cit., p. 4.

³⁵ "Plastic English," *Atlantic Monthly,* October 1972, p. 32.

³⁶ "Graffiti vs. Doublespeak: The Anti-Establishment 'Strikes Back,'" *English Journal,* February 1978, pp. 20–25.

[37] *A Civil Tongue.* Indianapolis and New York: Bobbs-Merrill, 1976, p. 146.
[38] *National Enquirer,* 11 July 1978, p. 18.

From *THE HANDBOOK OF NONSEXIST WRITING*

Casey Miller and Kate Swift

[From The Handbook of Nonsexist Writing. *2nd ed. New York: Harper,
1988. 1–9]*

*Freelance writers and editors Casey Miller and Kate Swift have published
as partners since 1970. Over the years, their work on sexism and language
has been published widely, and* The Handbook of Nonsexist Writing *has
been the standard recommended text on the topic since its first appearance
in 1980.*

*In the following selection, the introduction to their book, Miller and Swift
argue forcefully for continued efforts to change sexist language. The balance
of the book exposes the widespread sexism in language, provides historical
analyses of sexist usage, and offers practical suggestions for avoiding sexist
language. The* Bedford Handbook's *expanded discussion of sexist language,
including the helpful chart on page 200, testifies to the continued concern
about sexism and language.*

Introduction: Change and Resistance to Change

When the first edition of *The Handbook of Nonsexist Writing* appeared in
1980, efforts to eliminate linguistic sexism had already gained support
from a wide assortment of national and local organizations, both public
and private. Guidelines for nonsexist usage had been issued by most major
textbook publishers, and professional and academic groups ranging from
the Society of Automotive Engineers to the American Psychological Association were developing their own guidelines, as were such diverse public
institutions as the City of Honolulu and the University of New Hampshire.
Churches and synagogues were struggling with the problems of perception
raised by traditional male-oriented language; librarians were rethinking the
wording of catalog entries; and groups as varied as philanthropic founda-
tions, political councils, and consumer cooperatives were recasting their
charters, bylaws, application forms, and other materials in gender-neutral
terms. Advertising copy had begun to acknowledge that bankers, insurance
agents, scientists, consumers at every level, farmers, and athletes are female as well as male.

By the mideighties the movement toward nonsexist usage had gained so
much momentum that researchers who studied its impact by analyzing
three recently published American dictionaries of new words were prepared
to state, in the cautious phraseology of scholarship, that their results
showed "a trend toward nonsexism" in written language. The data, they
said, "provided a judgment of the efficacy of feminists' efforts toward nonsexist vocabulary," and they ventured the opinion that the "importance and
justice of the subject have been recognized."

During the same period, a marked increase occurred in academic research into language use and its relation to women, and the number of books and articles on the subject addressed to the general public continues to grow. So extensive is this outpouring, in fact, that a newsletter established in 1976 to report on activities in the field grew in only ten years from a 4-page pamphlet to a 64-page periodical called *Women and Language.* Not all this interest has been on the side of linguistic reform, of course; opposition to the concept of nonsexist language continues and in some quarters has stiffened. But during the past ten years, some of the most influential opponents of linguistic change have been persuaded that the problem is not going to disappear as obligingly as ground fog on an autumn morning.

The increased use of nonsexist language by those in major channels of communication provides a graphic demonstration of the mysterious ways in which reality affects language and is, in turn, affected by it. For as women become more prominent in fields from which they were once excluded, their presence triggers questions of linguistic equity that, once having been asked and answered, bring new visibility to women. How does one refer to a woman who is a member of Congress, or address a woman who sits on her country's highest court or is its chief of state? What does one call a woman who flies in space? Superficial as such questions may seem, their existence brings into focus a new awareness of women's potential. When *Time* magazine named Corazon Aquino its "Woman of the Year," it paid tribute to her extraordinary achievements and, at least by implication, made two other statements: (1) the year's most newsworthy person need not be a man, and (2) some of the connotations once assumed to be communicated only by the word *man* are now attaching themselves to the word *woman.* Still to come, however, is widespread acceptance of a gender-inclusive term that, in such a context, would concentrate attention on the person's newsworthiness rather than on the irrelevant factor of gender.

Notable among recent acknowledgments of the need for more even-handed usage was the change of policy adopted by the *New York Times* regarding titles of courtesy. First the *Times* stopped prefixing women's names with honorifics in both headlines and sports stories — thereby including women under the same rubric it had followed for years with respect to men. Then the newspaper dropped its ban on the courtesy title *Ms.* because, as an Editor's Note explained, "The *Times* now believes that 'Ms.' has become part of the language." Since the *Times* moves to a majestic beat, it is not about to rush headlong into the unqualified adoption of a nonsexist lexicon, but the recognition of *Ms.* wasn't its first move in that direction, and each day brings new evidence that it was not intended to be its last.

As individuals and the media gradually work out the logic involved in each new linguistic quandary, the presence of women in government and business and in the arts and professions becomes more and more apparent. Which is not to say that as women gain positive linguistic visibility they magically gain recognition and respect. But something "magical" does happen whenever people — singly or as a class — begin to sense their potential as fully integrated members of society, and it is this "magic" that using nonsexist language helps to bring about.

One subtle, and therefore particularly harmful, linguistic practice that has not changed much in the last few years is the use of common-gender terms as though they automatically refer only to males. When a member of Congress says on a televised news program, "Any politician would have trouble running against a woman," or a newspaper reports that a man "went berserk . . . and murdered his neighbor's wife," the effect is to make women irrelevant. Politicians become, once again, an all-male breed, and a woman, denied even the identity of "neighbor," is relegated instead to that of "neighbor's wife."

The reason the practice of assigning masculine gender to neutral terms is so enshrined in English is that every language reflects the prejudices of the society in which it evolved, and English evolved through most of its history in a male-centered, patriarchal society. We shouldn't be surprised, therefore, that its vocabulary and grammar reflect attitudes that exclude or demean women. But we are surprised, for until recently few people thought much about what English — or any other language for that matter — was saying on a subliminal level. Now that we have begun to look, some startling things have become obvious. What standard English usage says about males, for example, is that they are the species. What it says about females is that they are a subspecies. From these two assertions flow a thousand other enhancing and degrading messages, all encoded in the language we in the English-speaking countries begin to learn almost as soon as we are born.

Many people would like to do something about these inherited linguistic biases, but getting rid of them involves more than exposing them and suggesting alternatives. It requires change, and linguistic change is no easier to accept than any other kind. It may even be harder.

At a deep level, changes in a language are threatening because they signal widespread changes in social mores. At a level closer to the surface they are exasperating. We learn certain rules of grammar and usage in school, and when they are challenged it is as though we are also being challenged. Our native language is like a second skin, so much a part of us we resist the idea that it is constantly changing, constantly being renewed, though we know intellectually that the English we speak today and the English of Shakespeare's time are very different, we tend to think of them as the same — static rather than dynamic. Emotionally, we want to agree with the syndicated columnist who wrote that "grammar is as fixed in its way as geometry."

One of the obstacles to accepting any kind of linguistic change — whether it concerns something as superficial as the pronunciation of *tomato* or as fundamental as sexual bias — is this desire to keep language "pure." In order to see change as natural and inevitable rather than as an affront, we need perspective, and to gain perspective it helps to take a look at some of the changes that have already taken place in English.

To start with, if it were true that "grammar is as fixed in its way as geometry," we would still, in the twentieth century, be speaking Old English, the earliest version of the tongue we know today: Our vocabulary would be almost totally different; we would still be altering a word's form to change the meaning of a sentence instead of shifting words about — as in "Dog bites man," "Man bites dog" — to do the same thing; and we would still have "grammatical" rather than "natural" gender. The last change is important because the gender assigned to nouns and pronouns in Old English, as in most modern European languages, often had no relationship to sex or its absence. The word for "chair," for example, was masculine; the word for "table" was feminine; and the word of "ship" was neuter. In modern English we match gender with sex. That is, we reserve feminine and masculine gender for human beings and other sex-differentiated animals or, in flights of fancy, for nonliving things (like ships) onto which we project human associations. At least theoretically all other English nouns and pronouns are neuter or, in the case of agent-nouns like *teacher* and *president,* gender-neutral.

Greatly as these grammatical simplifications invigorated English, some of its special richness comes from the flexibility of its vocabulary. The English lexicon is a kind of uninhibited conglomeration put together over the centuries from related Indo-European languages and, though far less frequently, from languages as unrelated to English as Chinese, Nahuatl, and Yoruba.

Yet despite the hospitality of English to outside as well as internal influences, many people, including many language experts, become upset when confronted with new words or grammatical modifications they happen not to like. H. W. Fowler, whose widely used *Dictionary of Modern English Usage* was first published in 1926, deplored such "improperly formed" words as *amoral, bureaucrat, speedometer, pacifist,* and *coastal,* terms so commonly used today we take them for granted. His scorn for *electrocute* (formed by analogy to *execute*) pushed him beyond compassion or reason. The word, he wrote, "jars the unhappy latinist's nerves much more cruelly than the operation denoted jars those of its victims" (an emotional excess Sir Ernest Gowers, editor of the current edition of Fowler, mercifully deleted).

Lexicographers are less judgmental. In compiling dictionaries, they try to include as many commonly used words as space allows, whether the words are "properly formed" or not. Dictionaries, however, cannot help but lag behind actual usage, so they are not always reliable indicators of new or altered meanings. The 1986 edition of Webster's Ninth New Collegiate Dictionary defines *youth* as (among other things) "a young person; esp: a young male between adolescence and maturity." Essentially the same definition appears in several other current dictionaries, and some people continue to use the word in that limited sense. When film director Martha Coolidge approached a Hollywood producer about making a "low-budget youth picture," he is reported to have said, "No gays or women; it's a male subject." Actually the accepted meaning of *youth* is shifting faster than the producer realized or dictionaries can keep up with. Under the headline "Stolen Horse Is Found by Relentless Searcher," a news story in the *New York Times* referred to the horse's owner, a sixteen-year-old girl, as a youth: "After Rocky was stolen . . . the youth called every stable and horse handler she could find" and "the youth's parents brought a trailer . . . for the trip home." Though the term may once have been anomalous when used of a young woman, today it is a recognized common-gender noun, and the next round of dictionaries will no doubt add their authority to the change.

Changes in usage often occur slowly and imperceptibly, but some take place seemingly overnight. Such was the case in the 1960s when *black* replaced *Negro.* How the change occurred and something of the power of the words was described by Shirley Chisholm:

> A few short years ago, if you called most Negroes "blacks," it was tantamount to calling us niggers. But now black is beautiful, and black is proud. There are relatively few people, white or black, who do not recognize what has happened.

Black people have freed themselves from the dead weight of albatross blackness that once hung around their necks. They have done it by picking it up in their arms and holding it out with pride for all the world to see. . . . [A]nd they have found that the skin that was once seen as symbolizing their chains is in reality their badge of honor.

Although a few people are still reluctant to accept this use of *black*, the balance has clearly shifted in its favor, and the familiar alternatives *Negro, colored,* and *Afro-American* are heard less often.

Ironically, those who deal with words professionally or avocationally can be the most resistant to linguistic changes. Like Fowler, they may know so much about etymology that any deviation from the classical pattern of word formation grates on their ears. Or having accepted certain rules of grammar as correct, they may find it impossible to acknowledge that those particular rules could ever be superseded.

What many people find hardest to accept is that a word which used to mean one thing now means another, and that continuing to use it in its former sense — no matter how impeccable its etymological credentials — can only invite misunderstanding. When the shift in meaning happened centuries ago, no problem lingers. One may be fully aware that *girl* once meant "a young person of either sex" (as it did in Chaucer's time) and yet not feel compelled to refer to a sexually mixed group of children as girls. When the change happens in one's lifetime, recognition and acceptance may be harder.

The word *intriguing* is such a case. Once understood to mean "conniving" or "deceitful" (as a verb, *intrigue* comes through the French *intriguer*, "to puzzle," from the Latin *intricare*, "to entangle"), *intriguing* now means "engaging the interest to a marked degree," as Webster's Third New International Dictionary noted over three decades ago. People still make statements like "They are an intriguing pair" with the intention of issuing a warning, but chances are the meaning conveyed is "They are a fascinating pair," because that is how a new generation of writers and speakers understands and uses the word. In one sense precision has been lost; in another it has only shifted.

The transformation of *man* over the past thousand years may be the most troublesome and significant change ever to overtake an English word. Once a synonym for "human being," *man* has gradually narrowed in meaning to become a synonym for "adult male human being" only. Put simply in the words of a popular dictionary for children, "A boy grows up to be a man. Father and Uncle George are both men." These are the meanings of *man* and *men* native speakers of English internalize because they are the meanings that from infancy on we hear applied to everyday speech. Though we may later acquire the information that *man* has another, "generic" meaning, we do not accept it with the same certainty that we accept the children's dictionary definition and its counterparts: A girl does not grow up to be a man. Mother and Aunt Teresa are not men; they are women.

To go on using in its former sense a word whose meaning has changed is counterproductive. The point is not that we should *recognize semantic change, but that in order to be precise, in order to be understood, we* must. The difference is a fundamental one in any discussion of linguistic bias, for some writers think their freedom of expression and artistic integrity are being compromised when they are asked to avoid certain words or grammatical forms. Is it ever justifiable, for example, for publishers to expect their authors to stop using the words *forefathers, man,* and *he* as though they were sex-inclusive? Is this not unwarranted interference with an author's style? Even censorship?

No, it is not. The public counts on those who disseminate factual information — especially publishers of textbooks and other forms of nonfiction, and those who work in the mass media — to be certain that what they tell us is as accurate as research and the conscientious use of language can make it. Only recently have we become aware that conventional English usage, including the generic use of masculine-gender words, often obscures the actions, the contributions, and sometimes the very presence of women. Turning our backs on that insight is an option, of course, but it is an option like teaching children that the world is flat. In this respect, continuing to use English in ways that have become misleading is no different from misusing data, whether the misuse is inadvertent or planned.

The need today, as always, is to be in command of language, not used by it, and so the challenge is to find clear, convincing, graceful ways to say accurately what we want to say. . . .

PART FIVE

GRAMMATICAL SENTENCES

Part V of *The Bedford Handbook,* "Editing for Grammar," helps students apply rules for grammar and usage as they revise. The handbook keeps these rules in perspective, presenting them in an accessible format that helps students, whatever their backgrounds, to make their writing more effective.

Since Mina Shaughnessy's seminal work on "basic writing" introduced composition specialists to error analysis (*Errors and Expectations,* 1977), instructors have become more attuned to the problems that many students have with sentence grammar and standard usage. We now understand that many students experience conflicts and struggles with issues of grammar and usage that are more fundamental than problems with correctness. Their personal and cultural identities are related inextricably to their use of language.

The following selections present a dialogue about grammar, usage, and error, offering instructors an expanded perspective from which they can consider questions fundamental to the relation of grammar and composition.

- What is error analysis? How can it help students recognize and solve problems with grammar and usage? How can we make error analysis productive for students?
- What are the relations between language and identity? How can we help students learn to use standard edited English without asking them to abandon cultural values? How can we help students understand the implications of choosing or resisting to conform?

From THE STUDY OF ERROR

David Bartholomae

[College Composition and Communication 31 (1980): 253–69.]

(For biographical information, see page 13.)

Bartholomae wrote this article in response to instructors who felt that students' errors were signs that they couldn't write. He opens his article by surveying then current (1980) attitudes about "basic writing," the various pedagogies that instructors have adopted when confronted with "basic writers," and the results of their attempts. He argues for further research into "basic writing" and the concurrent perceptions of errors apparently inherent to basic writers. Aligning his argument with Mina Shaughnessy's groundbreaking work in Errors and Expectations, *Bartholomae proposes error analysis as a method to better understand how writers develop and learn. The excerpt that follows begins at that point, with Bartholomae explaining error analysis and demonstrating its effectiveness with a study of one of his students' assignments in progress.*

Error analysis begins with a theory of writing, a theory of language production and language development, that allows us to see errors as evidence of choice or strategy among a range of possible choices or strategies. They provide evidence of an individual style of using the language and making it work; they are not a simple record of what a writer failed to do because of incompetence or indifference. Errors, then, are stylistic features, information about *this* writer and *this* language; they are not necessarily "noise" in the system, accidents of composing, or malfunctions in the language process. Consequently, we cannot identify errors without identifying them in context, and the context is not the text, but the activity of composing that presented the erroneous form as a possible solution to the problem of making a meaningful statement. Shaughnessy's taxonomy of error, for example, identifies errors according to their source, not their type. A single type of error could be attributed to a variety of causes. Donald Freeman's research, for example, has shown that "subject-verb agreement . . . is a host of errors, not one." One of his students analyzed a "large sample of real world sentences and concluded that there are at least eight different kinds, most of which have very little to do with one another."[1]

Error analysis allows us to place error in the context of composing and to interpret and classify systematic errors. The key concept is the concept of an "interlanguage" or an "intermediate system," an idiosyncratic grammar and rhetoric that is a writer's approximation of the standard idiom. Errors, while they can be given more precise classification, fall into three main categories: errors that are evidence of an intermediate system; errors that could truly be said to be accidents, or slips of the pen as a writer's mind rushes ahead faster than his hand; and, finally, errors of language transfer, or, more commonly, dialect interference, where in the attempt to produce the target language, the writer intrudes forms from the "first" or "native" language rather than inventing some intermediate form. For writers, this intrusion most often comes from a spoken dialect. The error analyst is primarily concerned, however, with errors that are evidence of some intermediate system. This kind of error occurs because the writer *is* an active, competent language user who uses his knowledge that language is rule-governed, and who uses his ability to predict and form analogies, to construct hypotheses that can make an irregular or unfamiliar language more manageable. The problem comes when the rule is incorrect or, more properly, when it is idiosyncratic, belonging only to the language of this writer. There is evidence of an idiosyncratic system, for example, when a student adds inflectional endings to infinitives, as in this sentence, "There was plenty the boy had to *learned* about birds." It also seems to be evident in a sentence like this: "This assignment calls on *choosing* one of my papers and making a last draft out of it." These errors can be further subdivided into those that are in flux and mark a fully transitional stage, and those that, for one reason or another, become frozen and recur across time.

Kroll and Schafer, in a recent *CCC* article, argue that the value of error analysis for the composition teacher is the perspective it offers on the learner, since it allows us to see errors "as clues to inner processes, as windows into the mind."[2] If we investigate the pattern of error in the performance of an individual writer, we can better understand the nature of those errors and the way they "fit" in an individual writer's program for writing. As a consequence, rather than impose an inappropriate or even misleading syllabus on a learner, we can plan instruction to assist a writer's internal syllabus. If, for example, a writer puts standard inflections on irregular verbs or on verbs that are used in verbals (as in "I used to runned"), drill on verb endings will only reinforce the rule that, because the writer is overgeneralizing, is the source of the error in the first place. By charting and analyzing a writer's errors, we can begin in our instruction with what a writer *does* rather than with what he fails to do. It makes no sense, for example, to impose lessons on the sentence on a student whose problems with syntax can be understood in more precise terms. It makes no sense to teach spelling to an individual who has trouble principally with words that contain vowel clusters. Error analysis, then, is a method of diagnosis.

Error analysis can assist instruction at another level. By having students share in the process of investigating and interpreting the patterns of error in their writing, we can help them begin to see those errors as evidence of hypotheses or strategies they have formed and, as a consequence, put them in a position to change, experiment, imagine other strategies. Studying their own writing puts students in a position to see themselves as language users, rather than as victims of a language that uses them.

This, then, is the perspective and the technique of error analysis. To interpret a student paper without this frame of reference is to misread, as for example when a teacher sees an incorrect verb form and concludes that the student doesn't understand the rules for indicating tense or number. I want, now, to examine error analysis as a procedure for the study of errors in written composition. It presents two problems. The first can be traced to the fact that error analysis was developed for studying errors in spoken performance.[3] It can be transferred to writing only to the degree that writing is like speech, and there are significant points of difference. It is generally acknowledged, for example, that written discourse is not just speech written down on paper. Adult written discourse has a grammar and rhetoric that is different from speech. And clearly the activity of producing language is different for a writer than it is for a speaker.

The "second language" a basic writer must learn to master is formal, written discourse, a discourse whose lexicon, grammar, and rhetoric are learned not through speaking and listening but through reading and writing. The process of acquisition is visual not aural. Furthermore, basic writers do not necessarily produce writing by translating speech into print (the way children learning to write would); that is, they must draw on a memory for graphemes rather than phonemes. This is a different order of memory and production from that used in speech and gives rise to errors unique to writing.

Writing also, however, presents "interference" of a type never found in speech. Errors in writing may be caused by interference from the act of writing itself, from the difficulty of moving a pen across the page quickly enough to keep up with the words in the writer's mind, or from the difficulty of recalling and producing the conventions that are necessary for producing print rather than speech, conventions of spelling, orthography, punctuation, capitalization, and so on. This is not, however, just a way of saying that writers make spelling errors and speakers do not. As Shaughnessy pointed out, errors of syntax can be traced to the gyrations of a writer trying to avoid a word that her sentence has led her to, but that she knows she cannot spell.

The second problem in applying error analysis to the composition classroom arises from special properties in the taxonomy of errors we chart in student writing. Listing varieties of errors is not like listing varieties of rocks or butterflies. What a reader finds depends to a large degree on her assumptions about the writer's intention. Any systematic attempt to chart a learner's errors is clouded by the difficulty of assigning intention through textual analysis. The analyst begins, then, by interpreting a text, not by describing features on a page. And interpretation is less than a precise science.

Let me turn to an example. This is part of a paper that a student, John, wrote in response to an assignment that asked him to go back to some papers he had written on significant moments in his life in order to write a paper that considered the general question of the way people change:

> This assignment call on chosing one of my incident making a last draft out of it. I found this very differcult because I like them all but you said I had to pick one so the Second incident was decide. Because this one had the most important insight to my life that I indeed learn from. This insight explain why adulthood mean that much as it dose to me because I think it alway influence me to change and my outlook on certain thing like my point-of-view I have one day and it might change the next week on the same issue. So in these frew words I going to write about the incident now. My exprience took place in my high school and the reason was out side of school but I will show you the connection. The situation took place cause of the type of school I went too. Let me tell you about the sitution first of all what happen was that I got suspense from school. For thing that I fell was out of my control sometime, but it taught me alot about respondability of a growing man. The school suspense me for being late ten time. I had accummate ten dementic and had to bring my mother to school to talk to a conselor and Prinpicable of the school what when on at the meet took me out mentally period.

One could imagine a variety of responses to this. The first would be to form the wholesale conclusion that John can't write and to send him off to a workbook. Once he had learned how to write correct sentences, then he could go on to the business of actually writing. Let me call this the "old style" response to error. A second response, which I'll call the "investigative approach," would be to chart the patterns of error in this particular text. Of the approximately 40 errors in the first 200 words, the majority fall under four fairly specific categories: verb endings, noun plurals, syntax, and spelling. The value to pedagogy is obvious. One is no longer teaching a student to "write" but to deal with a limited number of very specific kinds of errors, each of which would suggest its own appropriate response. Furthermore, it is possible to refine the categories and to speculate on and organize them according to cause. The verb errors almost all involve "s" or "ed" endings, which could indicate dialect interference or a failure to learn the rules for indicating tense and number. It is possible to be even more

precise. The passage contains 41 verbs; only 17 of them are used incorrectly. With the exception of four spelling errors, the errors are all errors
of inflection and, furthermore, these errors come only with regular verbs.
There are no errors with irregular verbs. This would suggest, then, that
when John draws on memory for a verb form, he gets it right; but when
John applies a rule to determine the ending, he gets it wrong.

The errors of syntax could be divided into those that might be called
punctuation errors (or errors that indicate a difficulty perceiving the boundaries of the sentence), such as

> Let me tell you about the situation first of all that happen was that I got suspense
> from school. For thing that I fell was out of my control sometime, but it taught
> me alot about respondability of a growing man.

and errors of syntax that would fall under Shaughnessy's category of consolidation errors,

> This insight explain why adulthood mean that much as it dose to me because I
> think it alway influence me to change and my outlook on certain thing like my
> point-of-view I have one day and it might change the next week on the same
> issue.

One would also want to note the difference between consistent errors, the
substitution of "situation" for "situation" or "suspense" for "suspended," and
unstable ones, as, for example, when John writes "cause" in one place and
"because" in another. In one case John could be said to have fixed on a
rule; in the other he is searching for one. One would also want to distinguish between what might seem to be "accidental" errors, like substituting
"frew" for "few" or "when" for "went," errors that might best be addressed
by teaching a student to edit, and those whose causes are deeper and
require time and experience, or some specific instructional strategy.

I'm not sure, however, that this analysis provides an accurate representation of John's writing. Consider what happens when John reads this
paper out loud. I've been taping students reading their own papers, and
I've developed a system of notation, like that used in miscue analysis,[4] that
will allow me to record the points of variation between the writing that is
on the page and the writing that is spoken, or, to use the terminology of
miscue analysis, between the expected response (ER) and the observed
response (OR). What I've found is that students will often, or in predictable
instances, substitute correct forms for the incorrect forms on the page,
even though they are generally unaware that such a substitution was
made. This observation suggests the limits of conventional error analysis
for the study of error in written composition.

I asked John to read his paper out loud, and to stop and correct or note
any mistakes he found. Let me try to reproduce the transcript of that
reading. I will italicize any substitution or correction and offer some comments in parentheses. The reader might first go back and review the original. Here is what John read:

> This assignment calls on *choosing* one of my incident making a last draft out of
> it. I found this very difficult because I like them all but you said I *had* to pick
> one so the Second incident was decide*d on.* Because (John goes back and rereads,
> connecting up the subordinate clause.) So the second incident was decided on
> because this one had the most important insight to my life that I indeed learn*ed*
> from. This insight explains why adulthood *meant* that much as it dose to me

because I think it always influences me to change and my outlook on certain things like my point-of-view I have one day and it might change the next week on the same issue. (John goes back and rereads, beginning with "like my point-of view," and he is puzzled but he makes no additional changes.) So in these *few* words *I'm* going to write about the incident now. My experience took place *be*-cause of the type of school I went to (John had written "too.") Let me tell you about the situation (John comes to a full stop.) first of all what happen*ed* was that I got *suspended* from school (no full stop) for things that I *felt* was out of my control sometime, but it taught me a lot about *responsibility* of a growing man. The school *suspended* me for being late ten times. I had *accumulated* (for "accumate") ten *demerits* (for "dementic") and had to bring my mother to school to talk to a counselor and *the Principal* of the school (full stop) what *went* on at the meet*ing* took me out mentally (full stop) period (with brio).

I have chosen an extreme case to make my point, but what one sees here is the writer correcting almost every error as he reads the paper, even though he is not able to recognize that there *are* errors or that he has corrected them. The only errors John spotted (where he stopped, noted an error and corrected it) were the misspellings of "situation" and "Principal," and the substitution of "chosing" for "choosing." Even when he was asked to reread sentences to see if he could notice any difference between what he was saying and the words on the page, he could not. He could not, for example, see the error in "frew" or "dementic" or any of the other verb errors, and yet he spoke the correct form of every verb (with the exception of "was" after he had changed "thing" to "things" in "for things that I *felt* was out of my control") and he corrected every plural. His phrasing as he read produced correct syntax, except in the case of the consolidation error, which he puzzled over but did not correct. It's important to note, however, that John did not read the confused syntax as if no confusion were there. He sensed the difference between the phrasing called for by the meaning of the sentence and that which existed on the page. He did not read as though meaning didn't matter or as though the "meaning" coded on the page was complete. His problem cannot be simply a syntax problem, since the jumble is bound up with his struggle to articulate this particular meaning. And it is not simply a "thinking" problem — John doesn't write this way because he thinks this way — since he perceives that the statement as it is written is other than that which he intended.

When I asked John why the paper (which went on for two more pages) was written all as one paragraph, he replied, "It was all one idea. I didn't want to have to start all over again. I had a good idea and I didn't want to give it up." John doesn't need to be "taught" the paragraph, at least not as the paragraph is traditionally taught. His prose is orderly and proceeds through blocks of discourse. He tells the story of his experience at the school and concludes that through his experience he realized that he must accept responsibility for his tardiness, even though the tardiness was not his fault but the fault of the Philadelphia subway system. He concludes that with this realization he learned "the responsibility of a growing man." Furthermore John knows that the print code carries certain conventions for ordering and presenting discourse. His translation of the notion that "a paragraph develops a single idea" is peculiar but not illogical.

It could also be argued that John does not need to be "taught" to pro-duce correct verb forms, or, again, at least not as such things are conven-tionally taught. Fifteen weeks of drill on verb endings might raise his test scores, but they would not change the way he writes. He *knows* how to produce correct endings. He demonstrated that when he read, since he was reading in terms of his grammatical competence. His problem is a problem of performance, or fluency, not of competence. There is certainly no evidence that the verb errors are due to interference from his spoken language. And if the errors could be traced to some intermediate system, the system exists only in John's performance as a writer. It does not operate when he reads or, for that matter, when he speaks, if his oral reconstruction of his own text can be taken as a record of John "speaking" the idiom of academic discourse.[5]

John's case also highlights the tremendous difficulty such a student has with editing, where a failure to correct a paper is not evidence of laziness or inattention or a failure to know correct forms, but evidence of the tremendous difficulty such a student has objectifying language and seeing it as black and white marks on the page, where things can be wrong even though the meaning seems right.[6] One of the hardest errors for John to spot, after all my coaching, was the substitution of "frew" for "few," certainly not an error that calls into question John's competence as a writer. I can call this a "performance" error, but that term doesn't suggest the constraints on performance in writing. This is an important area for further study. Surely one constraint is the difficulty of moving the hand fast enough to translate meaning into print. The burden imposed on their patience and short-term memory by the slow, awkward handwriting of many inexperienced writers is a very real one. But I think the constraints extend beyond the difficulty of forming words quickly with pen or pencil.

One of the most interesting results of the comparison of the spoken and written versions of John's text is his inability to *see* the difference between "frew" and "few" or "dementic" and "demerit." What this suggests is that John reads and writes from the "top down" rather than the "bottom up," to use a distinction made by cognitive psychologists in their study of reading.[7] John is not operating through the lower level process of translating orthographic information into sounds and sounds into meaning when he reads. And conversely, he is not working from meaning to sound to word when he is writing. He is, rather, retrieving lexical items directly, through a "higher level" process that bypasses the "lower level" operation of phonetic translation. When I put *frew* and *few* on the blackboard, John read them both as "few." The lexical item "few" is represented for John by either orthographic array. He is not, then, reading or writing phonetically, which is a sign, from one perspective, of a high level of fluency, since the activity is automatic and not mediated by the more primitive operation of translating speech into print or print into speech. When John was writing, he did not produce "frew" or "dementic" by searching for sound/letter/letter correspondences. He drew directly upon his memory for the look and shape of those words; he was working from the top down rather than the bottom up. He went to stored print forms and did not take the slower route of translating speech into writing.

John, then, has reached a stage of fluency in writing where he directly and consistently retrieves print forms, like "dementic," that are meaningful to him, even though they are idiosyncratic. I'm not sure what all the implications of this might be, but we surely must see John's problem in a new light, since his problem can, in a sense, be attributed to his skill. To ask John to slow down his writing and sound out words would be disastrous.

Perhaps the most we can do is to teach John the slowed down form of reading he will need in order to edit.

John's paper also calls into question our ability to identify accidental errors. I suspect that when John substitutes a word like "when" for "went," this is an accidental error, a slip of the pen. Since John spoke "went" when he read, I cannot conclude that he substituted "when" for "went" because he pronounces both as "wen." This, then, is not an error of dialect interference but an accidental error, the same order of error as the omission of "the" before "Principal." Both were errors John corrected while reading (even though he didn't identify them as errors).

What is surprising is that, with all the difficulty John had identifying errors, he immediately saw that he had written "chosing" rather than "choosing." While textual analysis would have led to the conclusion that he was applying a tense rule to a participial construction, or overgeneralizing from a known rule, the ease with which it was identified would lead one to conclude that it was, in fact, a mistake, and not evidence of an approximative system. What would have been diagnosed as a deep error now appears to be only an accidental error, a "mistake" (or perhaps a spelling error).

In summary, this analysis of John's reading produces a healthy respect for the tremendous complexity of transcription, for the process of recording meaning in print as opposed to the process of generating meaning. It also points out the difficulty of charting a learner's "interlanguage" or "intermediate system," since we are working not only with a writer moving between a first and a second language, but a writer whose performance is subject to the interference of transcription, of producing meaning through the print code. We need, in general, to refine our understanding of performance-based errors, and we need to refine our teaching to take into account the high percentage of error in written composition that is rooted in the difficulty of performance rather than in problems of general linguistic competence.

Let me pause for a moment to put what I've said in the context of work in error analysis. Such analysis is textual analysis. It requires the reader to make assumptions about intention on the basis of information in the text. The writer's errors provide the most important information since they provide insight into the idiosyncratic systems the writer has developed. The regular but unconventional features in the writing will reveal the rules and strategies operating for the basic writer.

The basic procedure for such analysis could be outlined this way. First the reader must identify the idiosyncratic construction; he must determine what is an error. This is often difficult, as in the case of fragments, which are conventionally used for effect. Here is an example of a sentence whose syntax could clearly be said to be idiosyncratic.

> In high school you learn alot for example Kindergarten which I took in high school.[8]

The reader, then, must reconstruct that sentence based upon the most reasonable interpretation of the intention in the original, and this must be done *before* the error can be classified, since it will be classified according to its cause.[9] Here is Shaughnessy's reconstruction of the example given above: "In high school you learn a lot. For example, I took up the study of

Kindergarten in high school." For any idiosyncratic sentence, however, there are often a variety of possible reconstructions, depending on the reader's sense of the larger meaning of which this individual sentence is only a part, but also depending upon the reader's ability to predict how this writer puts sentences together, that is, on an understanding of this individual style. The text is being interpreted, not described. I've had graduate students who have reconstructed the following sentence, for example, in a variety of ways:

> Why do we have womens liberation and their fighting for Equal Rights ect. to be recognized not as a lady but as an Individual.

It could be read, "Why do we have women's liberation and why are they fighting for Equal Rights? In order that women may be recognized not as ladies but as individuals." And, "Why do we have women's liberation and their fight for equal rights, to be recognized not as a lady but as an individual?" There is an extensive literature on the question of interpretation and intention in prose, too extensive for the easy assumption that all a reader has to do is identify what the writer would have written if he wanted to "get it right the first time." The great genius of Shaughnessy's study, in fact, is the remarkable wisdom and sympathy of her interpretations of student texts.

Error analysis, then, involves more than just making lists of the errors in a student essay and looking for patterns to emerge. It begins with the double perspective of text and reconstructed text and seeks to explain the difference between the two on the basis of whatever can be inferred about the meaning of the text and the process of creating it. The reader/researcher brings to bear his general knowledge of how basic writers write, but also whatever is known about the linguistic and rhetorical constraints that govern an individual act of writing. In Shaughnessy's analysis of the "kindergarten" sentence, this discussion is contained in the section on"consolidation errors" in the chapter on "Syntax."[10] The key point, however, is that any such analysis must draw upon extra-textual information as well as close, stylistic analysis.

This paper has illustrated two methods for gathering information about how a text was created. A teacher can interview the student and ask him to explain his error. John wrote this sentence in another paper for my course:

> I would to write about my experience helping 1600 childrens have a happy christmas.

The missing word (I would *like* to write about . . .) he supplied when reading the sentence aloud. It is an accidental error and can be addressed by teaching editing. It is the same kind of error as his earlier substitution of "when" for "went." John used the phrase, "1600 childrens," throughout his paper, however. The conventional interpretation would have it that this is evidence of dialect interference. And yet, when John read the paper out loud, he consistently read "1600 children," even though he said he did not see any difference between the word he spoke and the word that was on the page. When I asked him to explain why he put an "s" on the end of "children," he replied, "Because there were 1600 of them." John had a rule for forming plurals that he used when he wrote but not when he spoke. Writing, as we rightly recognized, has its own peculiar rules and constraints. It is different from speech. The error is not due to interference from his spoken language but to his conception of the "code" of written discourse.

The other method for gathering information is having students read aloud their own writing, and having them provide an oral reconstruction of their written text. What I've presented in my analysis of John's essay is a method for recording the discrepancies between the written and spoken versions of a single text. The record of a writer reading provides a version of the "intended" text that can supplement the teacher's or researcher's own reconstruction and aid in the interpretation of errors, whether they be accidental, interlingual, or due to dialect interference. I had to read John's paper very differently once I had heard him read it.

More importantly, however, this method of analysis can provide access to an additional type of error. This is the error that can be attributed to the physical and conceptual demands of writing rather than speaking; it can be traced to the requirements of manipulating a pen and the requirements of manipulating the print code.[11]

In general, when writers read, and read in order to spot and correct errors, their responses will fall among the following categories:

1. overt corrections — errors a reader sees, acknowledges, and corrects;
2. spoken corrections — errors the writer does not acknowledge but corrects in reading;
3. no recognition — errors that are read as written;
4. overcorrection — correct forms made incorrect, or incorrect forms substituted for incorrect forms;
5. acknowledged error — errors a reader senses but cannot correct;
6. reader miscue — a conventional miscue, not linked to error in the text;
7. nonsense — In this case, the reader reads a nonsentence or a nonsense sentence as though it were correct and meaningful. No error or confusion is acknowledged. This applies to errors of syntax only.

Corrections, whether acknowledged or unacknowledged, would indicate performance-based errors. The other responses (with the exception of "reader miscues") would indicate deeper errors, errors that, when charted, would provide evidence of some idiosyncratic grammar or rhetoric.

John "miscues" by completing or correcting the text that he has written. When reading researchers have readers read out loud, they have them read someone else's writing, of course, and they are primarily concerned with the "quality" of the miscues.[12] All fluent readers will miscue; that is, they will not repeat verbatim the words on the page. Since fluent readers are reading for meaning, they are actively predicting what will come and processing large chunks of graphic information at a time. They do not read individual words, and they miscue because they speak what they expect to see rather than what is actually on the page. One indication of a reader's proficiency, then, is that the miscues don't destroy the "sense" of the passage. Poor readers will produce miscues that jumble the meaning of a passage, as in

Text: Her wings were folded quietly at her sides.
Reader: Her wings were floated quickly at her sides.

or they will correct miscues that do not affect meaning in any significant way.[13]

The situation is different when a reader reads his own text, since this reader already knows what the passage means and attention is drawn, then, to the representation of that meaning. Reading also frees a writer from the constraints of transcription, which for many basic writers is an awkward, laborious process, putting excessive demands on both patience and short-term memory. John, like any reader, read what he expected to see, but with a low percentage of meaning-related miscues, since the meaning, for him, was set, and with a big percentage of code-related miscues, where a correct form was substituted for an incorrect form.

The value of studying students' oral reconstruction of their written texts is threefold. The first is as a diagnostic tool. I've illustrated in my analysis of John's paper how such a diagnosis might take place.

It is also a means of instruction. By having John read aloud and, at the same time, look for discrepancies between what he spoke and what was on the page, I was teaching him a form of reading. The most dramatic change in John's performance over the term was in the number of errors he could spot and correct while rereading. This far exceeded the number of errors he was able to eliminate from his first drafts. I could teach John an editing procedure better than I could teach him to be correct at the point of transcription.

The third consequence of this form of analysis, or of conventional error analysis, has yet to be demonstrated, but the suggestions for research are clear. It seems evident that we can chart stages of growth in individual basic writers. The pressing question is whether we can chart a sequence of "natural" development for the class of writers we call basic writers. If all nonfluent adult writers proceed through a "natural" learning sequence, and if we can identify that sequence through some large, longitudinal study, then we will begin to understand what a basic writing course or text or syllabus might look like. There are studies of adult second language learners that suggest that there is a general, natural sequence of acquisition for adults learning a second language, one that is determined by the psychology of language production and language acquisition.[14] Before we can adapt these methods to a study of basic writers, however, we need to better understand the additional constraints of learning to transcribe and manipulate the "code" of written discourse. John's case illustrates where we might begin and what we must know.[15]

Notes

[1] Donald C. Freeman, "Linguistics and Error Analysis: On Agency," in Donald McQuade, ed., *Linguistics, Stylistics and the Teaching of Composition* (Akron, Ohio: L. & S Books, 1979), pp. 143–44.

[2] Kroll and Schafer, "Error Analysis and the Teaching of Composition."

[3] In the late sixties and early seventies, linguists began to study second language acquisition by systematically studying the actual performance of individual learners. What they studied, however, was the language a learner would speak. In the literature of error analysis, the reception and production of language is generally defined as the learner's ability to hear, learn, imitate, and independently produce *sounds*. Errors, then, are phonological substitutions, alterations, additions, and subtractions. Similarly, errors diagnosed as rooted in the mode of production (rather than, for example, in an idiosyncratic grammar or interference from the first language) are errors caused by the difficulty a learner has hearing or making foreign sounds. When we are studying written composition, we are studying a different mode of

production, where a learner must see, remember, and produce marks on a page. There may be some similarity between the grammar-based errors in the two modes, speech and writing (it would be interesting to know to what degree this is true), but there should be marked differences in the nature and frequency of performance-based errors.

⁴ See Y. M. Goodman and C. L. Burke, *Reading Miscue Inventory: Procedure for Diagnosis and Evaluation* (New York: Macmillan, 1972).

⁵ Bruder and Hayden noticed a similar phenomenon. They assigned a group of students exercises in writing formal and informal dialogues. One student's informal dialogue contained the following:

What going on?
It been a long time . . .
I about through . . .
I be glad . . .

When the student read the dialogue aloud, however, these were spoken as

What's going on?
It's been a long time . . .
I'm about through . . .
I'll be glad . . .

See Mary Newton Bruder and Luddy Hayden, "Teaching Composition: A Report on a Bidialectal Approach," *Language Learning*, 23 (June 1973), 1–15.

⁶ See Patricia Laurence, "Error's Endless Train: Why Students Don't Perceive Errors," *Journal of Basic Writing*, I (Spring 1975), 23–43, for a different explanation of this phenomenon.

⁷ See, for example, J. R. Frederiksen, "Component Skills in Reading" in R. R. Snow, P. A. Federico, and W. E. Montague, eds., *Aptitude, Learning, and Instruction* (Hillsdale, N.J.: Erlbaum, 1979); D. E. Rumelhart, "Toward an Interactive Model of Reading," in S. Dornic, ed., *Attention and Performance VI* (Hillsdale, N.J.: Erlbaum, 1977); and Joseph H. Denks and Gregory O. Hill, "Interactive Models of Lexical Assessment during Oral Reading," paper presented at Conference on Interactive Processes in Reading, Learning Research and Development Center, University of Pittsburgh, September 1979.

Patrick Hartwell argued that "apparent dialect interference in writing reveals partial or imperfect mastery of a neural coding system that underlies both reading and writing" in a paper, "'Dialect Interference' in Writing: A Critical View," presented at CCCC, April 1979. This paper is available through ERIC. He predicts, in this paper, that "basic writing students, when asked to read their writing in a formal situation, . . . will make fewer errors in their reading than in their writing." I read Professor Hartwell's paper after this essay was completed, so I was unable to acknowledge his study as completely as I would have desired.

⁸ This example is taken from Shaughnessy, *Errors and Expectations*, p. 52.

⁹ Corder refers to "reconstructed sentences" in "Idiosyncratic Dialects and Error Analysis."

¹⁰ Shaughnessy, *Errors and Expectations*, pp. 51–72.

¹¹ For a discussion of the role of the "print code" in writer's errors, see Patrick Hartwell, "'Dialect Interference' in Writing: A Critical View."

¹² See Kenneth S. Goodman, "Miscues: Windows on the Reading Process," in Kenneth S. Goodman, ed., *Miscue Analysis: Applications to Reading Instruction* (Urbana, Ill.: ERIC, 1977), pp. 3–14.

¹³ This example was taken from Yetta M. Goodman, "Miscue Analysis for In-Service Reading Teachers," in K. S. Goodman, ed., *Miscue Analysis*, p. 55.

[14] Nathalie Bailey, Carolyn Madden, and Stephen D. Krashen, "Is There a 'Natural Sequence' in Adult Second Language Learning?" *Language Learning,* 24 (June 1974), 235–243.

[15] This paper was originally presented at CCCC, April 1979. The research for this study was funded by a research grant from the National Council of Teachers of English.

CONFLICT AND STRUGGLE:
THE ENEMIES OR PRECONDITIONS OF BASIC WRITING?

Min-Zhan Lu

[College English 54 (1992): 887–913.]

Min-Zhan Lu, assistant professor of English at Drake University, has published articles in such journals as College English, Journal of Basic Writing, *and* Journal of Education. *She is currently at work with Bruce Horner on a book,* Representing the "Other": Basic Writers and the Teaching of Basic Writing.

In this and other recent essays, Lu challenges prevailing views of basic writing. Up to now, many composition theorists have seen the "conflict and struggle" that basic writers experience while learning conventions of standard English as negative — something to be overcome. Lu contests this assumption, arguing that teachers should consider the productive, creative, and positive potential of conflict. "We need to find ways of foregrounding conflict and struggle," Lu asserts, "not only in the generation of meaning and authority, but also in the teaching of conventions of 'correctness' in syntax, spelling, and punctuation, traditionally considered the primary focus of Basic Writing instruction."

Harlem taught me that light skin Black people was better look, the best to suceed, the best off fanicially etc this whole that I trying to say, that I was brainwashed and people aliked.

I couldn't understand why people (Black and white) couldn't get alone. So as time went along I began learned more about myself and the establishment.

— Sample student paper, Shaughnessy, *Errors and Expectations* 278

. . . Szasz was throwing her. She couldn't get through the twelve-and-a-half pages of introduction....

One powerful reason Lucia had decided to major in psychology was that she wanted to help people like her brother, who had a psychotic break in his teens and had been in and out of hospitals since. She had lived with mental illness, had seen that look in her brother's eyes.... The assertion that there was no such thing as mental illness, that it was a myth, seemed incomprehensible to her. She had trouble even entertaining it as a hypothesis.... Szasz's bold claim was a bone sticking in her assumptive craw.

— Mike Rose, *Lives on the Boundary* 183–84

In perceiving conflicting information and points of view, she is subjected to a swamping of her psychological borders.

— Gloria Anzaldúa, *Borderlands/La Frontera: The New Mestiza* 79

In the Preface to *Borderlands,* Gloria Anzaldúa uses her own struggle "living on borders and in margins" to discuss the trials and triumphs in the lives of "border residents." The image of "border residents" captures the conflict and struggle of students like those appearing in the epigraphs. In perceiving conflicting information and points of view, a writer like Anzaldúa is "subjected to a swamping of her psychological borders" (79). But attempts to cope with conflicts also bring "compensation," "joys," and "exhilaration" (Anzaldúa, Preface). The border resident develops a tolerance for contradiction and ambivalence, learning to sustain contradiction and turn ambivalence into a new consciousness — "a *third* element which is *greater* than the sum of its *severed parts*": "a mestiza consciousness" (79–80; emphasis mine). Experience taught Anzaldúa that this developing consciousness is a source of intense pain. For development involves struggle which is "inner" and is played out in the outer terrains (87). But this new consciousness draws energy from the "continual creative motion that keeps breaking down the unitary aspect of each new paradigm" (80). It enables a border resident to act on rather than merely react to the conditions of her or his life, turning awareness of the situation into "inner changes" which in turn bring about "changes in society" (87).

Education as Repositioning

Anzaldúa's account gathers some of the issues on which a whole range of recent composition research focuses, research on how readers and writers necessarily struggle with conflicting information and points of view as they reposition themselves in the process of reading and writing. This research recognizes that reading and writing take place at sites of political as well as linguistic conflict. It acknowledges that such a process of conflict and struggle is a source of pain but constructive as well: a new consciousness emerges from the creative motion of breaking down the rigid boundaries of social and linguistic paradigms.

Compositionists are becoming increasingly aware of the need to tell and listen to stories of life in the borderlands. The CCCC Best Book Award given Mike Rose's *Lives on the Boundary* and the Braddock Award given to Glynda Hull and Mike Rose for their research on students like Lucia attest to this increasing awareness. *College Composition and Communication* recently devoted a whole issue (February 1992) to essays which use images of "boundary," "margin," or "voice" to re-view the experience of reading and writing and teaching reading and writing within the academy (see also Lu, "From Silence to Words"; Bartholomae, "Writing on the Margins"; and Mellix). These publications and their reception indicate that the field is taking seriously two notions of writing underlying these narratives: the sense that the writer writes at a site of conflict rather than "comfortably inside or powerlessly outside the academy" (Lu, "Writing as Repositioning" 20) and a definition of "innovative writing" as cutting across rather than confining itself within boundaries of race, class, gender, and disciplinary differences.

In articulating the issues explored by these narratives from the borderlands, compositionists have found two assumptions underlying various feminist, marxist, and poststructuralist theories of language useful: first, that learning a new discourse has an effect on the re-forming of individual consciousness; and second, that individual consciousness is necessarily heterogeneous, contradictory, and in process (Bizzell; Flynn; Harris; Lunsford, Moglen, and Slevin; Trimbur). The need to reposition oneself and the positive use of conflict and struggle are also explored in a range of research devoted to the learning difficulties of Basic Writers (Bartholomae, "Inventing"; Fox; Horner; Hull and Rose; Lu, "Redefining"; Ritchie; Spellmeyer; Stanley). Nevertheless, such research has had limited influence on Basic Writing instruction, which continues to emphasize skills (Gould and Heyda) and to view conflict as the enemy (Schilb, Brown). I believe that this view of conflict can be traced in the work of three pioneers in Basic Writing: Kenneth Bruffee, Thomas Farrell, and Mina Shaughnessy. In what follows, I examine why this view of conflict had rhetorical power in the historical context in which these pioneers worked and in relation to two popular views of education: education as acculturation and education as accommodation. I also explore how and why this view persists among Basic Writing teachers in the 1990s.

Although Bruffee, Farrell, and Shaughnessy hold different views on the goal of education, they all treat the students' fear of acculturation and the accompanying sense of contradiction and ambiguity as a *deficit*. Even though stories of the borderlands like Anzaldúa's suggest that teachers can and should draw upon students' perception of conflict as a constructive resource, these three pioneers of Basic Writing view evidence of conflict and struggle as something to be dissolved and so propose "cures" aimed at *releasing* students from their fear of acculturation. Bruffee and Farrell present students' acculturation as inevitable and beneficial. Shaughnessy promises them that learning academic discourse will not result in acculturation. Teachers influenced by the work of these pioneers tend to view all signs of conflict and struggle as the *enemy* of Basic Writing instruction. In perpetuating this view, these teachers also tend to adopt two assumptions about language: 1) an "essentialist" view of language holding that the essence of meaning precedes and is independent of language (see Lu, "Redefining" 26); 2) a view of "discourse communities" as "discursive utopias," in each of which a single, unified, and stable voice directly and completely determines the writings of all community members (Harris 12).

In the 1970s, the era of open admissions at CUNY, heated debate over the "educability" of Basic Writers gave these views of language and of conflict exceptional rhetorical power. The new field of Basic Writing was struggling to establish the legitimacy of its knowledge and expertise, and it was doing so in the context of arguments made by a group of writers — including Lionel Trilling, Irving Howe, and W. E. B. DuBois — who could be viewed as exemplary because of their ethnic or racial backgrounds, their academic success, and the popular view that all Basic Writers entering CUNY through the open admissions movement were "minority" students. The writings of Bruffee, Farrell, and Trilling concur that the goal of education is to acculturate students to the kind of academic "community" they posit. Shaughnessy, on the other hand, attempts to eliminate students' conflicting feelings towards academic discourse by reassuring them that her teaching will only "accommodate" but not weaken their existing relationship with their home cultures. Shaughnessy's approach is aligned with the arguments of Irving Howe and W. E. B. DuBois, who urge teachers to honor students' resistance to deracination. Acculturation and accommodation were the dominant models of open admissions education for teachers who recognized teaching academic discourse as a way of empowering students, and in both models conflict and struggle were seen as the enemies of Basic Writing instruction.

This belief persists in several recent works by a new generation of compositionists and "minority" writers. I will read these writings from the point of view of the border resident and through a view of education as a process of repositioning. In doing so, I will also map out some directions for further demystifying conflict and struggle in Basic Writing instruction and for seeing them as the preconditions of all discursive acts.

Education as Acculturation

In *Errors and Expectations,* Mina Shaughnessy offers us one way of imagining the social and historical contexts of her work: she calls herself a trailblazer trying to survive in a "pedagogical West" (4). This metaphor captures the peripheral position of Basic Writing in English. To other members of the profession, Shaughnessy notes, Basic Writing is not one of their "'real' subjects"; nor are books on Basic Writing "important enough" either to be reviewed or to argue about ("English Professor's Malady" 92). Kenneth Bruffee also testifies to feeling peripheral. Recalling the "collaborative learning" which took place among the directors of CUNY writing programs — a group which included Bruffee himself, Donald McQuade, Mina Shaughnessy, and Harvey Wiener — he points out that the group was brought together not only by their "difficult new task" but also by their sense of having more in common with one another than with many of their "colleagues on [their] own campuses" ("On Not Listening" 4–5).

These frontier images speak powerfully of a sense of being *in* but not *of* the English profession. The questionable academic status of not only their students (seen as "ill-prepared") but also themselves (Basic Writing was mostly assigned to beginning teachers, graduate students, women, minorities, and the underemployed but tenured members of other departments) would pressure teachers like Shaughnessy and Bruffee to find legitimacy for their subject. At the same time, they had to do so by persuading both college administrators who felt "hesitation and discomfort" towards open admissions policies and "senior and tenured professorial staff" who either resisted or did not share their commitment (Lyons 175). Directly or indirectly, these pioneers had to respond to, argue with, and persuade the "gatekeepers" and "converters" Shaughnessy describes in "Diving In." It is in the context of such challenges that we must understand the key terms the pioneers use and the questions they consider — and overlook — in establishing the problematics of Basic Writing.

One of the most vehement gatekeepers at CUNY during the initial period of open admissions was Geoffrey Wagner (Professor of English at City College). In *The End of Education,* Wagner posits a kind of "university" in which everyone supposedly pursues learning for its own sake, free of all "worldly" — social, economic, and political — interests. To Wagner, open admissions students are the inhabitants of the "world" outside the sort of scholarly "community" which he claims existed at Oxford and City College. They are dunces (43), misfits (129), hostile mental children (247), and the most sluggish of animals (163). He describes a group of Panamanian "girls" taking a Basic Writing course as "abusive, stupid, and hostile" (128). Another student is described as sitting "in a half-lotus pose in back of class with a transistor strapped to his Afro, and nodding off every two minutes" (134). Wagner calls the Basic Writing program at City a form of political psychotherapy (145), a welfare agency, and an entertainment center (173). And he calls Shaughnessy "the Circe of CCNY's remedial English program"

(129). To Wagner, Basic Writers would cause "the end of education" because they have intellects comparable to those of beasts, the retarded, the psychotic, or children, and because they are consumed by non-"academic" — i.e., racial, economic, and political — interests and are indifferent to "learning."

Unlike the "gatekeepers," Louis Heller (Classics Professor, City College) represents educators who seemed willing to shoulder the burden of converting the heathens but disapproved of the ways in which CUNY was handling the conversion. Nonetheless, in *The Death of the American University* Heller approaches the "problems" of open admissions students in ways similar to Wagner's. He contrasts the attitudes of open admissions students and of old Jewish City College students like himself:

> In those days ["decades ago"] there was genuine hunger, and deprivation, and discrimination too, but when a child received failing marks no militant parent group assailed the teacher. Instead parent and child agonized over the subject, placing the responsibility squarely on the child who was given to know that *he* had to measure up to par, not that he was the victim of society, a wicked school system, teachers who didn't understand him, or any of the other pseudosociological nonsense now handed out. (138)

According to Heller, the parents of open admissions students are too "militant." As a result, the students' minds are stuffed with "pseudosociological nonsense" about their victimization by the educational system. The "problem" of open admissions students, Heller suggests, is their militant attitude, which keeps them from trying to "agonize over the subject" and "measure up to par."

Wagner predicts the "end of education" because of the *"arrival* in urban academe of *large,* indeed *overwhelming, numbers* of *hostile* mental children" (247; emphasis mine). As the titles of Heller's chapters suggest, Heller too believes that a "Death of the American University" would inevitably result from the "Administrative Failure of Nerve" or "Capitulation Under Force" to "Violence on Campus" which he claims to have taken place at City College. The images of education's end or death suggest that both Wagner and Heller assume that the goal of education is the acculturation of students into an "educated community." They question the "educability" of open admissions students because they *fear* that these students would not only be hostile to the education they promote but also take it over — that is, change it. The apocalyptic tone of their book titles suggests their fear that the students' "hostile" or "militant" feelings towards the existing educational system would weaken the ability of the "American University" to realize its primary goal — to acculturate. Their writings show that their view of the "problems" of open admissions students and their view of the goal of education sustain one another.

This view of education as a process of acculturation is shared by Lionel Trilling, another authority often cited as an exemplary minority student (see, for example, Howe, "Living" 108). In a paper titled "The Uncertain Future of the Humanistic Educational Ideal" delivered in 1974, Trilling claims that the view of higher education "as the process of initiation into membership" in a "new, larger, and more complex community" is "surely" not a "mistaken conception" (*The Last Decade* 170). The word "initiation," Trilling points out, designates the "ritually prescribed stages by which a person is brought into a community" (170–71). "Initiation" requires "sub-

244 Grammatical Sentences

mission," demanding that one "shape" and "limit" oneself to "*a self, a life*" and "preclude any other kind of selfhood remaining available" to one (171, 175; emphasis mine). Trilling doubts that contemporary American culture will find "congenial" the kind of "initiation" required by the "humanistic educational ideal" (171). For contemporary "American culture" too often encourages one to resist any doctrine that does not sustain "a multiplicity of options" (175). And Trilling admits to feeling "saddened" by the unlikelihood that "an ideal of education closely and positively related to the humanistic educational traditions of the past" will be called into being in contemporary America (161).

The trials of "initiation" are the subject of Trilling's short story "Notes on a Departure." The main character, a young college professor about to leave a university town, is portrayed as being forced to wrestle with an apparition which he sometimes refers to as the "angel of Jewish solitude" and, by the end of the story, as "a red-haired comedian" whose "face remained blank and idiot" (*Of This Time* 53, 55). The apparition hounds the professor, often reminding him of the question "'What for?' Jews did not do such things" (54). Towards the end of the story, the professor succeeds in freeing himself from the apparition. Arriving at a state of "readiness," he realizes that he would soon have to "find his *own* weapon, his *own* adversary, his *own* things to do" — findings in which "this red-haired figure . . . would have *no* part" (55; emphasis mine).

This story suggests — particularly in view of Trilling's concern for the "uncertain future" of the "humanistic educational ideal" in the 1970s — that contemporary Americans, especially those from minority cultural groups, face a dilemma: the need to combat voices which remind them of the "multiplicity of options." The professor needs to "wrestle with" two options of "selfhood." First, he must free himself from the authority of the "angel"/ "comedian." Then, as the title "Notes on a Departure" emphasizes, he must free himself from the "town." Trilling's representation of the professor's need to "depart" from the voice of his "race" and of the "town" indirectly converges with the belief held by Wagner and Heller that the attitudes "parents" and "society" transmit to open admissions students would pull them away from the "university" and hinder their full initiation — acculturation — into the "educated" community.

Read in the 1990s, these intersecting approaches to the "problems" of "minority" students might seem less imposing, since except perhaps for Trilling, the academic prestige of these writers has largely receded. Yet we should not underestimate the authority these writers had within the academy. As both the publisher and the author of *The End of Education* (1976) remind us within the first few pages of the book, Wagner is not only a graduate of Oxford but a full professor at City College and author of a total of twenty-nine books of poetry, fiction, literary criticism, and sociology. Heller's *The Death of the American University* (1973) indicates that he has ten years' work at the doctoral or postdoctoral level in three fields, a long list of publications, and years of experience as both a full professor of classics and an administrator at City College (12). Furthermore, their fear of militancy accorded with prevalent reactions to the often violent conflict in American cities and college campuses during the 1960s and 70s. It was in the context of such powerful discourse that composition teachers argued for not only the "educability" of open admissions students but also the ability of the "pioneer" educators to "educate" them. Bruffee's and Farrell's eventual success in establishing the legitimacy of their knowledge and expertise as Basic Writing teachers, I believe, comes in part from a conjuncture in the arguments of the two Basic Writing pioneers and those of Wagner, Heller, and Trilling.

For example, Thomas Farrell presents the primary goal of Basic Writing instruction as acculturation — a move from "orality" to "literacy." He treats open admissions students as existing in a "residual orality": "literate patterns of thought have not been interiorized, have not displaced oral patterns, in them" ("Open Admissions" 248). Referring to Piaget, Ong, and Bernstein, he offers environmental rather than biological reasons for Basic Writers' "orality" — their membership in "communities" where "orality" is the dominant mode of communication. To Farrell, the emigration from "orality" to "literacy" is unequivocally beneficial for everyone, since it mirrors the progression of history. At the same time, Farrell recognizes that such a move will inevitably be accompanied by "anxiety": "The *psychic strain* entailed in moving from a highly oral frame of mind to a more literate frame of mind is *too great* to allow rapid movement" (252; emphasis mine). Accordingly, he promotes teaching strategies aimed at "reducing anxiety" and establishing "a supportive environment." For example, he urges teachers to use the kind of "collaborative learning" Bruffee proposes so that they can use "oral discourse to improve written discourse" ("Open Admissions" 252–53; "Literacy" 456–57). He reminds teachers that "highly oral students" won't engage in the "literate" modes of reasoning "unless they are shown how and reminded to do so often," and even then will do so only "gradually" ("Literacy" 456).

Kenneth Bruffee also defines the goal of Basic Writing in terms of the students' acculturation into a new "community." According to Bruffee, Basic Writers have already been acculturated within "local communities" which have prepared them for only "the narrowest and most limited" political and economic relations ("On Not Listening" 7). The purpose of education is to "reacculturate" the students — to help them "gain membership in another such community" by learning its "language, mores, and values" (8). However, Bruffee believes that the "trials of changing allegiance from one cultural community to another" demand that teachers use "collaborative learning" in small peer groups. This method will "create a *temporary transition* or 'support' group that [one] can join *on the way*" (8; emphasis mine). This "transition group," he maintains, will offer Basic Writers an arena for sharing their "trials," such as the "uncertain, nebulous, and protean thinking that occurs in the process of change" and the "painful process" of gaining new awareness ("On Not Listening" 11; "Collaborative Learning" 640).

Two points bind Bruffee's argument to Farrell's and enhance the rhetorical power of their arguments for the Wagners, Hellers, and Trillings. First, both arguments assume that the goal of education is acculturation into a "literate" community. The image of students who are "changing allegiance from one cultural community to another" (Bruffee), like the image of students "moving" from "orality" to "literacy" (Farrell), posits that "discourse communities" are discrete and autonomous entities rather than interactive cultural forces. When discussing the differences between "orality" and "literacy," Farrell tends to treat these "discourses" as creating coherent but distinct modes of thinking: "speaking" vs. "reading," "clichés" vs. "explained and supported generalizations," "additive" vs. "inductive or deductive" reasoning. Bruffee likewise sets *"coherent* but *entirely* local communities" against a community which is "broader, highly diverse, *integrated*" ("On Not Listening" 7; emphasis mine). Both Farrell and Bruffee use existing analyses of" discourse communities" to set up a seemingly non-political hierarchy between academic and non-academic "communities." They then use the hierarchy to justify implicitly the students' need to be acculturated by the more advanced or broader "community." Thus, they can be construed as promising "effective" ways of appeasing the kind of "hostility" or "militancy" feared in open admissions students. The appeal of this line of thinking is that it protects the autonomy of the "literate community" while also professing a solution to the "threat" the open admissions students seem to pose to the university. Farrell and Bruffee provide methods aimed at keeping students like Anzaldua, Lucia, and the writer of Shaughnessy's sample paper from moving the points of view and discursive forms they have developed in their home "communities" into the "literate community" and also at persuading such students to willingly "move" into that "literate community."

Second, both Bruffee and Farrell explicitly look for teaching methods aimed at reducing the feelings of "anxiety" or "psychic strain" accompanying the process of acculturation. They thus present these feelings as signs of the students' still being "on the way" from one community to another, i.e., as signs of their failure to complete their acculturation or education. They suggest that the students are experiencing these trials only because they are still in "transition," bearing ties to both the old and new communities but not fully "departed" from one nor comfortably "inside" the other. They also suggest that these experiences, like the transition or support groups, are "temporary" (Bruffee, "On Not Listening" 8). In short, they sustain the impression that these experiences ought to and will disappear once the students get comfortably settled in the new community and sever or diminish their ties with the old. Any sign of heterogeneity, uncertainty, or instability is viewed as problematic; hence conflict and struggle are the enemies of Basic Writing instruction.

This linkage between students' painful conflicts and the teacher's effort to assuage them had rhetorical power in America during the 1970s because it could be perceived as accepting rather than challenging the gatekeepers' and converters' arguments that the pull of non-"academic" forces — "society" (Wagner), "militant parents" (Heller), and minority "race" or "American culture" at large (Trilling) — would render the open admissions students less "educable" and so create a "problem" in their education. It feeds the fear that the pulls of conflicting "options," "selfhoods," or "lives" promoted by antagonistic "communities" would threaten the university's ability to acculturate the Basic Writers. At the same time, this linkage also offers a "support system" aimed at releasing the gatekeepers and converters from their fear. For example, the teaching strategies Farrell promotes, which explicitly aim to support students through their "psychic strain," are also aimed at gradually easing them into "interiorizing" modes of thinking privileged by the "literate community," such as "inductive or deductive" reasoning or "detached, analytic forms of thinking" ("Literacy" 455, 456). Such strategies thus provide a support system for not only the students but also the kind of discursive utopia posited by Trilling's description of the "humanistic educational ideal," Heller's "American University," and Wagner's "education." Directly and indirectly, the pedagogies aimed at "moving" students from one culture to another support and are supported by gatekeepers' and converters' positions towards open admissions students.

The pedagogies of Bruffee and Farrell recognize the "psychic strain" or the "trials" experienced by those reading and writing at sites of contradiction, experiences which are depicted by writers like Trilling ("Notes on a Departure"), Anzaldúa, and Rose and witnessed by teachers in their encounters with students like Lucia and the writer of Shaughnessy's sample paper. Yet, for two reasons, the approaches of Bruffee and Farrell are unlikely to help such students cope with the conflicts "swamping" their "psychological borders." First, these approaches suggest that the students' primary task is to change allegiance, to "learn" and "master" the "language, mores, and values" of the academic community presented in the classroom by passively internalizing them and actively rejecting all points of view or information which run counter to them (Bruffee, "On Not Listening" 8). For the author of Shaughnessy's sample student paper, this could mean learning to identify completely with the point of view of authorities like the Heller of *The Death of the American University* and thus rejecting "militant" thoughts about the "establishment" in order to "agonize over the subject." For Lucia, this could mean learning to identify with the Trilling of "Notes on a Departure," viewing her ability to forget the look in her brother's eyes as a precondition of becoming a psychologist like Szasz. Yet students like Lucia might resist what the classroom seems to indicate they must do in order to achieve academic "success." As Rose reminds us, one of the reasons Lucia decided to major in psychology was to help people like her brother. Students like these are likely to get very little help or guidance from teachers like Bruffee or Farrell.

Secondly, though Bruffee and Farrell suggest that the need to cope with conflicts is a temporary experience for students unfamiliar with and lacking mastery of dominant academic values and forms, Rose's account of his own education indicates that similar experiences of "confusion, anger, and fear" are not at all temporary (Rose 235–36). During Rose's high school years, his teacher Jack MacFarland had successfully helped him cope with his "sense of linguistic exclusion" complicated by "various cultural differences" by engaging him in a sustained examination of "points of conflict and points of possible convergence" between home and academic canons (193). Nevertheless, during Rose's first year at Loyola and then during his graduate school days, he continued to experience similar feelings when encountering texts and settings which reminded him of the conflict between home and school. If students like Rose, Lucia, or the writer of Shaughnessy's sample paper learn to view experiences of conflict — exclusion, confusion, uncertainty, psychic pain or strain — as "temporary," they are also likely to view the recurrence of those experiences as a reason to discontinue their education. Rather than viewing their developing ability to sustain contradictions as heralding the sort of "new mestiza consciousness" Anzaldúa calls for (80), they may take it as signaling their failure to "enter" the academy, since they have been led to view the academy as a place free of contradictions.

Education as Accommodation

Whereas the gatekeepers and converters want students to be either barred from or acculturated into academic culture, Irving Howe (Distinguished Professor of English, Graduate Center of CUNY and Hunter College), another City graduate often cited by the public media as an authority on the education of open admissions students (see Fiske), takes a somewhat different approach. He believes that "the host culture, resting as it does on

the English language and the literary traditions associated with it, has
. . . every reason to be *sympathetic* to the *problems* of those who, from
choice or necessity, may *live with* the *tension of biculturalism*" ("Living" 110;
emphasis mine).

The best way to understand what Howe might mean by this statement
and why he promotes such a position is to put it in the context of two types
of educational stories Howe writes. The first type appears in his *World of
Our Fathers,* in which he recounts the "cultural bleaching" required of
Jewish immigrants attending classes at the Educational Alliance in New
York City around the turn of this century. As Eugene Lyons, one immigrant
whom Howe quotes, puts it, "We were 'Americanized' about as gently as
horses are broken in." Students who went through this "crude" process,
Lyons admits, often came to view their home traditions as "alien" and to
"unconsciously resent and despise those traditions" (234). Howe points out
that education in this type of "Americanization" exacted a price, leaving the
students with a "nagging problem in self-perception, a crisis of identity"
(642). Read in the context of Howe's statement on the open admissions
students cited above, this type of story points to the kind of "problems"
facing students who have to live with the tension between the "minority
subcultures" in which they grow up and a "dominant" "Western" "host
culture" with which they are trying to establish deep contact through education ("Living" 110). It also points to the limitations of an educational
system which is not sympathetic to their problems.

The "Americanization" required of students like Eugene Lyons, Howe
points out, often led Jewish students to seek either "a full return to religious faith or a complete abandonment of Jewish identification" (642). But
Howe rejects both such choices. He offers instead an alternative story —
the struggle of writers like himself to live with rather than escape from "the
tension of biculturalism." In *A Margin of Hope,* he recounts his long journey
in search of a way to "achieve some equilibrium with that earlier self which
had started with childhood Yiddish, my language of naming, and then
turned away in adolescent shame" (269). In "Strangers," Howe praises Jewish
writers like Saul Bellow and the contributors to *Partisan Review* for their
attitudes towards their "partial deracination" (*Selected Writings* 335). He
argues that these writers demonstrated that being a "loose-fish" (with "roots
loosened in Jewish soil but still not torn out, roots lowered into American
soil but still not fixed") is "a badge" to be carried "with pride" (335). Doing
so can open up a whole "range of possibilities" (335), such as the "forced
yoking of opposites: gutter vividness and university refinement, street energy and high-culture rhetoric" Howe sees these writers achieving (338).
This suggests what Howe might mean by "*living with* the tension of
biculturalism." The story he tells of the struggle of these Jewish writers
also proves that several claims made in the academy of the earlier 1970s,
as Howe points out, are "true and urgent": 1) students who grow up in
"subcultures" can feel "pain and dislocation" when trying to "connect with
the larger, cosmopolitan culture"; 2) for these students, "there must always
be some sense of 'difference,' even alienation"; 3) this sense of difference
can "yield moral correction and emotional enrichment" ("Living" 110). The
story of these writers also suggests that when dealing with students from
"subcultures," the dominant culture and its educational system need, as
Howe argues, to be more "sympathetic to" the pain and alienation indicated
by the first two claims, and at the same time should value more highly the

"infusion of vitality and diversity from subcultures" that the third claim suggests these students can bring (110).

Howe believes that the need for reform became especially urgent in the context of the open admissions movement, when a large number of "later immigrants, newer Americans" from racial as well as ethnic "subcultures" arrived at CUNY ("A Foot"). He also believes that, although the dominant culture needs to be more "responsive" and "sympathetic" towards this body of students, it would be "a dreadful form of intellectual condescension — and social cheating" for members of the "host culture" to dissuade students from establishing a "deep connection" with it. The only possible and defensible "educational ideal" is one which brings together commitments to "the widespread diffusion of learning" and to the "preservation of the highest standards of learning" ("Living" 109).

However, as Howe himself seems aware throughout his essay, he is more convinced of the need to live up to this ideal than certain about how to implement it in the day-to-day life of teaching, especially with "the presence of large numbers of ill-prepared students in our classroom" ("Living" 110, 112). For example, the values of "traditionalism" mean that teachers like Howe should try to "preserve" the "English language and the literary traditions" associated with "the dominant culture we call Western" (109, 110). Yet, when Howe tries to teach *Clarissa* to his students, he finds out that he has to help students to "transpose" and "translate" Clarissa's belief in the sanctity of her virginity into their "terms." And he recognizes that the process of transposing would "necessarily distort and weaken" the original belief (112). This makes him realize that there is "reason to take seriously the claim" that "a qualitative transformation of Western culture threatens the survival of literature as we have known it" (112).

Although Howe promotes the images of "loose-fish" and "partial deracination" when discussing the work of Jewish writers, in his discussion of the education of "ill-prepared" students, he considers the possibility of change from only one end of the "tension of bi-culturalism" — that of "Western culture." His essay overlooks the possibility that the process of establishing a deep connection with "Western culture," such as teaching students to "transpose" their "subcultural" beliefs into the terms of "Western culture," might also "distort and weaken" — *transform* — the positions students take towards these beliefs, especially if these beliefs conflict with those privileged in "Western culture." In fact, teachers interested in actively honoring the students' decisions and needs to "live with the tension of bi-culturalism" must take this possibility seriously (see Lu, "Redefining" 33).

In helping students to establish deep connections with "Western culture," teachers who overlook the possibility of students' changing their identification with "subcultural" views are likely to turn education into an accommodation — or mere tolerance — of the students' choice or need to live with conflicts. This accommodation could hardly help students explore, formulate, reflect on, and enact strategies for coping actively with conflicts as the residents of borderlands do: developing a "tolerance for" and an ability to "sustain" contradictions and ambiguity (Anzaldúa 79). Even if teachers explicitly promote the image of "partial deracination," they are likely to be more successful in helping students unconsciously "lower" and "fix" their roots into "Western culture" than in also helping them keep their roots from being completely "torn out" of "subcultures."

Two recurring words in Howe's essay, "preserve" and "survival," suggest a further problematic, for they represent the students as "preservers" of conflicting but unitary paradigms — a canonical "literary tradition" and "subcultures" with "attractive elements that merit study and preservation" ("Living" 110). This view of their role might encourage students to envision themselves as living at a focal point where "severed or separated pieces merely come together" (Anzaldúa 79). Such perceptions might also lead students to focus their energy on "accommodating" their thoughts and actions to rigid boundaries rather than on actively engaging themselves in what to Anzaldúa is the resource of life in the borderlands: a "continual creative motion" which breaks entrenched habits and patterns of behavior (Anzaldúa 79). The residents of the borderlands act on rather than react to the "borders" cutting across society and their psyches, "borders" which become visible as they encounter conflicting ideas and actions. In perceiving these "borders," the mestizas refuse to let these seemingly rigid boundaries confine and compartmentalize their thoughts and actions. Rather, they use these "borders" to identify the unitary aspects of "official" paradigms which "set" and "separate" cultures and which they can then work to break down. That is, for the mestizas, "borders" serve to delineate aspects of their psyches and the world requiring change. Words such as "preserve" and "survival," in focusing the students' attention on accommodation rather than change, could not help students become active residents of the borderlands.

The problematics surfacing from Howe's writings — the kind of "claims" about students from "subcultures" that he considers "true and urgent," the kind of "problems" he associates with students living with the tension of conflicting cultural forces, and the questions he raises as well as those he overlooks when discussing his "educational ideal" — map the general conceptual framework of a group of educators to whose writings I now turn. The writings of Leonard Kriegel, another member of the CUNY English faculty, seem to address precisely the question of how a teacher might implement in the day-to-day teaching of "remedial" students at City College the educational ideal posited by Howe.

In *Working Through: A Teacher's Journey in the Urban University*, Kriegel bases his authority on his personal experience as first a City undergraduate and then a City professor before and during the open admissions movement. Kriegel describes himself as a "working-class Jewish youth" — part of a generation not only eager to "get past [its] backgrounds, to deodorize all smells out of existence, especially the smells of immigrant kitchens and beer-sloppy tables," but also anxious to emulate the "aggressive intellectualism" of City students (32, 123). Kriegel maintains that in his days as a student, there existed a mutual trust between teachers and students: "My teachers could assume a certain intelligence on my part; I, in turn, could assume a certain good will on theirs" (29).

When he was assigned to teach in the SEEK program, Kriegel's first impression was that such a mutual trust was no longer possible. For example, when he asked students to describe Canova's *Perseus Holding the Head of Medusa*, a student opened his paper, "When I see this statue it is of the white man and he is holding the head of the Negro" (176). Such papers led Kriegel to conclude that these students had not only "elementary" problems with writing but also a "racial consciousness [which] seemed to obscure everything else" (176). Yet working among the SEEK students gradually convinced Kriegel that the kind of mutual trust he had previously enjoyed with his teachers and students was not only possible but necessary. He discovered that his black and Puerto Rican students "weren't very different from their white peers": they did not lack opinions and they did want in to the American establishment (175, 178). They can and do trust the "good will" of the teacher who can honestly admit that he is a product of academic culture and believes in it, who rids himself of the "inevitable white guilt" and the fear of being accused of "cultural colonialism," and who permits the students to define their needs in relation to the culture rather than rejecting it for them (180). Kriegel thus urges teachers to "leave students alone" to make their own choices (182).

Kriegel's approach to his journey falls within the framework Howe establishes. The university ought to be "*responsive* to the needs and points of view of students who are of *two minds* about what Western culture offers them" ("Playing It Black" 11; emphasis mine). Yet, when summarizing the lessons he learned through SEEK, Kriegel implies that being "responsive" does not require anything of the teacher other than "*permit[ting]* the student *freedom of choice,* to let him take what he felt he needed and let go of what was not important to him" (*Working Through* 207; emphasis mine). Kriegel ultimately finds himself "mak[ing] decisions based on old values" and "placing greater and greater reliance on the traditional cultural orientation to which [he] had been exposed as an undergraduate" (201–2). The question he does not consider throughout his book is the extent to which his reliance on "old values" and "traditional cultural orientation" might affect his promise to accommodate the students' freedom of choice, especially if they are of "two minds" about what Western culture offers them. That is, he never considers whether his teaching practice might implicitly disable his students' ability to exercise the "freedom" he explicitly "permits" them.

Kriegel's story suggests that business in the classroom could go on as usual so long as teachers openly promise students their "freedom of choice." His story implies that the kind of teaching traditionally used to disseminate the conventions of the "English language or literary tradition" is politically and culturally neutral. It takes a two-pronged approach to educational reform: 1) explicitly stating the teacher's willingness to accommodate — i.e., understand, sympathize with, accept, and respect — the students' choice or need to resist total acculturation; 2) implicitly dismissing the ways in which particular teaching practices "choose" for students — i.e., set pressures on the ways in which students formulate, modify, or even dismiss — their position towards conflicting cultures (for comparable positions by other City faculty, see Volpe and Quinn). This approach has rhetorical currency because it both aspires to and promises to deliver the kind of education envisioned by another group of minority writers with established authority in 1970s America, a group which included black intellectuals W. E. B. DuBois and James Baldwin. Using personal and communal accounts, these writers also argue for educational systems which acknowledge students' resistance to cultural deracination. Yet, because their arguments for such an educational reform are seldom directly linked to discussion of specific pedagogical issues, teachers who share Kriegel's position could read DuBois and Baldwin as authorizing accommodation.

For example, in *The Education of Black People,* DuBois critiques the underlying principle of earlier educational models for black students, such as the "Hampton Idea" or the Fisk program, which do not help students deal with what he elsewhere calls their double-consciousness (12, 51). Instead, such models pressure students to "escape their cultural heritage and the body of experience which they themselves have built-up." As a result, these students may "meet *peculiar frustration* and in the end be unable to achieve success in the new environment or fit into the old" (144; emphasis mine).

DuBois's portrayal of the "peculiar frustration" of black students, like Howe's account of the "problems" of Jewish students, speaks powerfully of the need to consider seriously Howe's list of the "claims" made during the open admissions movement ("Living" 110). It also supports Howe's argument that the dominant culture needs to be more "sympathetic" to the "problems" of students from black and other ethnic cultures. DuBois's writings offer teachers a set of powerful narratives to counter the belief that students' interests in racial politics will impede their learning. In fact, DuBois's life suggests that being knowledgeable of and concerned with racial politics is a precondition to one's eventual ability to "force" oneself "in" and to "share" the world with "the owners" *(Education 77).*

At the same time, DuBois's autobiography can also be read as supporting the idea that once the teacher accepts the students' need to be interested in racial politics and becomes "sympathetic to" — acknowledges — their "peculiar frustration," business in the writing classroom can go on as usual. For example, when recalling his arrival at Harvard "in the midst of a violent controversy about poor English among students," DuBois describes his experiences in a compulsory Freshman English class as follows:

> I was at the point in my intellectual development when the content rather than the form of my writing was to me of prime importance. Words and ideas surged in my mind and spilled out with disregard of exact accuracy in grammar, taste in word or restrain in style. I knew the Negro problem and this was more important to me than literary form. I knew grammar fairly well, and I had a pretty wide vocabulary; but I was bitter, angry and intemperate in my first thesis. . . . Senator Morgan of Alabama had just published a scathing attack on "niggers" in a leading magazine, when my first Harvard thesis was due. I let go at him with no holds barred. My long and blazing effort came back marked "E" — not passed. *(Autobiography* 144*)*

Consequently, DuBois "went to work at" his English and raised the grade to a "C." Then, he "*elected* the best course on the campus for English composition," one which was taught by Barrett Wendell, "then the great pundit of Harvard English" (144–45; emphasis mine).

DuBois depicts his teacher as "fair" in judging his writing "technically" but as having neither any idea of nor any interest in the ways in which racism "scratch[ed] [DuBois] on the raw flesh" (144). DuBois presents his own interest in the "Negro problem" as a positive force, enabling him to produce "solid content" and "worthy" thoughts. At the same time, he also presents his racial/political interest as making him "bitter, angry, and intemperate." The politics of style would suggest that his "disregard of exact accuracy in grammar, taste in word or restraint in style" when writing the thesis might have stemmed not only from his failure to recognize the importance of *form* but also from the particular constraints this "literary form" placed on his effort to "spill out" bitter and angry *contents* against the establishment. Regard for "*accuracy* in grammar, *taste* in word or *re-*

straint in style" would have constrained his effort to "let go at [Senator Morgan] with no holds barred" (emphasis mine). But statements such as "style is *subordinate* to content" but "*carries* a message further" suggest that DuBois accepts wholeheartedly the view that the production of "something to say" takes place before and independent of the effort to "say it well" (144; emphasis mine). Nor does DuBois fault his teachers for failing to help him recognize and then practice ways of dealing with the politics of a "style" which privileges "restraint." Rather, his account suggests only that writing teachers need to become more understanding of the students' racial/political interests and their tendency to view "the Negro problem" as more important than "literary form." Thus, his account allows teachers to read it as endorsing the idea that once the teachers learn to show more interest in what the students "have to say" about racism, they can continue to teach "literary form" in the way DuBois's composition teachers did.

Neither do the writings of James Baldwin, whom Shaughnessy cites as the kind of "mature and gifted writer" her Basic Writers could aspire to become (*Errors* 197), provide much direct opposition to this two-pronged approach to reform. In "A Talk to Teachers" (originally published in the *Saturday Review,* 21 December 1963), Baldwin argues that "any Negro who is born in this country and undergoes the American educational system runs the risk of becoming schizophrenic" (*Price* 326; see also *Conversations* 183), thus providing powerful support for Howe's call for sympathy from the dominant culture. Baldwin does offer some very sharp and explicit critiques of the view of literary style as politically innocent. In "If Black English Isn't a Language, Then Tell Me, What Is?" Baldwin points out that "the rules of the language are dictated by what the language must convey" (*Price* 651). He later explains that standard English "was not designed to carry those spirits and patterns" he has observed in his relatives and among the people from the streets and churches of Harlem, so he "had to find a way to bend it (English]" when writing about them in his first book (*Conversations* 162). These descriptions suggest that Baldwin is aware of the ways in which the style of one particular discourse mediates one's effort to generate content or a point of view alien to that discourse. Yet, since he is referring to his writing experience *after* he has become what Shaughnessy calls a "mature and gifted writer" rather than to experience as a student in a writing classroom, he does not directly challenge the problematics surfacing in discussions of educational reform aimed at accommodation without change.

The seeming resemblances between minority educators and Basic Writers — their "subculture" backgrounds, the "psychic woe" they experience as a result of the dissonance within or among cultures, their "ambivalence" towards cultural bleaching, and their interest in racial/class politics — make these educators powerful allies for composition teachers like Shaughnessy who are not only committed to the educational rights and capacity of Basic Writers but also determined to grant students the freedom of choosing their alignments among conflicting cultures. We should not underestimate the support these narratives could provide for the field of Basic Writing as it struggled in the 1970s to establish legitimacy for its knowledge and expertise. I call attention to this support because of the intersection I see between Shaughnessy's approach to the function of conflict and struggle in Basic Writing instruction and the problematics I have sketched out in discussing the writings of Howe, Kriegel, DuBois, and Baldwin.

Like Howe and DuBois, Shaughnessy tends to approach the problems of Basic Writers in terms of their ambivalence toward academic culture:

> College both beckons and threatens them, offering to teach them useful ways of thinking and talking about the world, promising even to improve the quality of their lives, but threatening at the same time to take from them their distinctive ways of interpreting the world, to assimilate them into the culture of academia without acknowledging their experience as outsiders. (*Errors* 292)

Again and again, Shaughnessy reminds us of her students' fear that mastery of a new discourse could wipe out, cancel, or take from them the points of view resulting from "their experience as outsiders." This fear, she argues, causes her students to mistrust and psychologically resist learning to write. And she reasons that "if students understand why they are being asked to learn something and if the reasons given *do not conflict* with deeper needs for self-respect and loyalty to their group (whether that be an economic, racial, or ethnic group), they *are disposed* to learn it" (*Errors* 125; emphasis mine).

Shaughnessy proposes some teaching methods towards that end. For example, when discussing her students' difficulty developing an "academic vocabulary," she suggests that students might resist associating a new meaning with a familiar word because accepting that association might seem like consenting to a "linguistic betrayal that threatens to wipe out not just a word but the reality that the word refers to" (*Errors* 212). She then goes on to suggest that "if we consider the formal (rather than the contextual) ways in which words can be made to shift meaning we are closer to the kind of practical information about words BW students need" (212). Shaughnessy's rationale seems to be that the "formal" approach (in this case teaching students to pay attention to prefixes and suffixes) is more "practical" because it will help students master the academic meaning of a word *without* reminding them that doing so might "wipe out" the familiar "reality" — the world, people, and meanings — previously associated with that word.

However, as I have argued elsewhere, the "formal" approach can be taken as "practical" only if teachers view the students' awareness of the conflict between the home meaning and the school meaning of a word as something to be "dissolved" at all costs because it will make them less "disposed to learn" academic discourse, as Shaughnessy seems to believe (Lu, "Redefining" 35). However, the experiences of Anzaldúa and Rose suggest that the best way to help students cope with the "pain," "strain," "guilt," "fear," or "confusions" resulting from this type of conflict is not to find ways of "releasing" the students from these experiences or to avoid situations which might activate them. Rather, the "contextual" approach would have been more "practical," since it could help students deal self-consciously with the threat of "betrayal," especially if they fear and want to resist it. The "formal approach" recommended by Shaughnessy, however, is likely to be only a more "practical" way of preserving "academic vocabulary" and of speeding the students' internalization of it. As Rose's experiences working with students like Lucia indicate, it is exactly because teachers like him took the "contextual" approach — "encouraging her to talk through opinions of her own that ran counter to these discussions" (Rose 184–85) — that Lucia was able to get beyond the first twelve pages of Szasz's text and learn the "academic" meaning of "mental illness" posited by Szasz, a meaning which literally threatens to wipe out the "reality" of her brother's illness and her feelings about it.

Shaughnessy's tendency to overlook the political dimensions of the linguistic choices students make when reading and writing also points to the ways in which her "essentialist" view of language and her view of conflict and struggle as the enemies of Basic Writing instruction feed on one another (Lu, "Redefining" 26, 28–29). The supposed separation between language, thinking, and living reduces language into discrete and autonomous linguistic varieties or sets of conventions, rules, standards, and codes rather than treating language as a site of cultural conflict and struggle. From the former perspective, it is possible to believe, as Shaughnessy seems to suggest when opting for the "formal" approach to teaching vocabulary, that learning the rules of a new "language variety" — "the language of public transactions" — will give the student the "ultimate freedom of deciding how and when and where he will use which language" (*Errors* 11, 125). And it makes it possible for teachers like Shaughnessy to separate a "freedom" of choice in "linguistic variety" from one's social being — one's need to deliberate over and decide how to reposition oneself in relationship to conflicting cultures and powers. Thus, it might lead teachers to overlook the ways in which one's "freedom" of cultural alignment might impinge on one's freedom in choosing "linguistic variety."

Shaughnessy's approach to Basic Writing instruction has rhetorical power because of its seeming alignment with positions taken by "minority" writers. Her portrayal of the "ambivalent feelings" of Basic Writers matches the experiences of "wrestling" (Trilling) and "partial deracination" (Howe), "the distinctive frustration" (DuBois), and "schizophrenia" (Baldwin) portrayed in the writings of the more established members of the academy. All thus lend validity to each other's understanding of the "problems" of students from minority cultures and to their critiques of educational systems which mandate total acculturation. Shaughnessy's methods of teaching demonstrate acceptance of and compassion towards students' experience of the kind of "dislocation," "alienation," or "difference" which minority writers like Howe, DuBois, and Baldwin argue will always accompany those trying by choice or need to "live with" the tensions of conflicting cultures. Her methods of teaching also demonstrate an effort to accommodate these feelings and points of view. That is, because of her essentialist assumption that words can express but will not change the essence of one's thoughts, her pedagogy promises to help students master academic discourse without forcing them to reposition themselves — i.e., to re-form their relation — towards conflicting cultural beliefs. In that sense, her teaching promises to accommodate the students' need to establish deep contact with a "wider," more "public" culture by "releasing" them from their fear that learning academic discourse will cancel out points of view meaningful to their non-"academic" activities. At the same time, it also promises to accommodate their existing ambivalence towards and differences from academic culture by assuming that "expressing" this ambivalence and these differences in academic "forms" will not change the "essence" of these points of view. The lessons she learns from her journey in the "pedagogical West" thus converge with those of Kriegel, who dedicates his book to "Mina Shaughnessy, who knows that nothing is learned simply." That is, when discussing her teaching methods, she too tends to overlook the ways in which her methods of teaching "linguistic codes" might weaken her concern to permit the students freedom of choice in their points of view. Ultimately, as I have argued, the teaching of both Shaughnessy and Kriegel might prove to be more successful in preserving the traditions of "English language and literature" than in helping students reach a self-conscious choice on their position towards conflicting cultural values and forces.

Contesting the Residual Power of Viewing Conflict and Struggle as the Enemies of Basic Writing Instruction: Present and Future

The view that all signs of conflict and struggle are the enemies of Basic Writing instruction emerged partly from a set of specific historical conditions surrounding the open admissions movement. Open admissions at CUNY was itself an attempt to deal with immediate, intense, sometimes violent social, political, and racial confrontations. Such a context seemed to provide a logic for shifting students' attention *away* from conflict and struggle and *towards* calm. However, the academic status which pioneers like Bruffee, Farrell, and Shaughnessy have achieved and the practical, effective *cures* their pedagogies seem to offer have combined to perpetuate the rhetorical power of such a view for Basic Writing instruction through the 1970s to the present. The consensus among the gatekeepers, converters, and accommodationists furnishes some Basic Writing teachers with a complacent sense that they already know all about the "problems" Basic Writers have with conflict and struggle. This complacency makes teachers hesitant to consider the possible uses of conflict and struggle, even when these possibilities are indicated by later developments in language theories and substantiated both by accounts of alternative educational experiences by writers like Anzaldúa and Rose and by research on the constructive use of conflict and struggle, such as the research discussed in the first section of this essay.

Such complacency is evident in the works of compositionists like Mary Epes and Ann Murphy. Epes's work suggests that she is aware of recent arguments against the essentialist view of language underlying some composition theories and practices. For example, she admits that error analysis is complex because there is "a crucial area of overlap" between "*encoding*" (defined by Epes as "controlling the visual symbols which represent meaning on the page") and "*composing* (controlling meaning in writing)" (6). She also observes that students are most likely to experience the "conflict between composing and decoding" when the "norms of the written code" are "in conflict" with "the language of one's nurture" (31). Given Epes's recognition of the conflict between encoding and composing, she should have little disagreement with compositionists who argue that learning to use the "codes" of academic discourse would constrain certain types of meanings, such as the formulation of feelings and thoughts towards cultures drastically dissonant from academic culture. Yet, when Epes moves from her theory to pedagogy, she argues that teachers of Basic Writers can and ought to treat "encoding" and "composition" as two separate areas of instruction (31). Her rationale is simple: separating the two could avoid "exacerbating" the students' experience of the "conflict" between these activities (31). The key terms here (for me, at any rate) are "exacerbating" and "conflict." They illustrate Epes's concern to eliminate conflict, disagreement, tension, and complexity from the Basic Writing classroom (cf. Horner).

Ann Murphy's essay "Transference and Resistance" likewise demonstrates the residual power of the earlier view of conflict and struggle as the enemies of Basic Writing instruction. Her essay draws on her knowledge of the Lacanian notion of the decentered and destabilized subject. Yet Murphy argues against the applicability of such a theory to the teaching of Basic Writing on the ground that Basic Writers are not like other students. Basic Writers, Murphy argues, "may need centering rather than decentering, and cognitive skills rather than (or as compellingly as) self-exploration" (180). She depicts Basic Writers as "shattered and destabilized by the social and political system" (180). She claims that "being taken seriously as *adults* with something of value to say can, for many Basic Writing students, be a *traumatic* and *disorienting* experience" (180; emphasis mine). Murphy's argument demonstrates her desire to eliminate any sense of uncertainty or instability in Basic Writing classrooms. Even though Murphy is willing to consider the implications of the Lacanian notion of individual subjectivity for the teaching of other types of students (180), her readiness to separate Basic Writing classrooms from other classrooms demonstrates the residual power of earlier views of conflict and struggle.

Such a residual view is all the more difficult to contest because it is supported by a new generation of minority educators. For example, in "Teacher Background and Student Needs" (1991), Peter Rondinone uses his personal experiences as an open admissions student taking Basic Writing 1 at CCNY during the early 70s and his Russian immigrant family background in the Bronx to argue for the need to help Basic Writers understand that "in deciding to become educated there will be times when [basic writers] will be forced to . . . reject or *betray* their family and friends in order to succeed" ("Teacher" 42). Rondinone's view of how students might best deal with the conflict between home and school does not seem to have changed much since his 1977 essay describing his experience as a senior at City College (see Rondinone, "Open Admissions"). In his 1991 essay, this time writing from the point of view of an experienced teacher, Rondinone follows Bruffee in maintaining that "learning involves shifting social allegiances" ("Teacher" 49). My quarrel with Rondinone is not so much over his having opted for complete deracination (for I honor his right to choose his allegiance even though I disagree with his choice). I am, however, alarmed by his unequivocal belief that his choice is the *a priori* condition of his academic success, which reveals his conviction that conflict can only impede one's learning.

Shelby Steele's recent and popular *The Content of Our Character* suggests similar assumptions about experiences of cultural conflict. Using personal experiences, Steele portrays the dilemma of an African-American college student and professor in terms of being caught in the familiar "trap": bound by "two equally powerful elements" which are "at odds with each other" (95). Steele's solution to the problem of "opposing thrusts" is simple: find a way to "unburden" the student from one of the thrusts (160). Thus, Steele promotes a new, "peacetime" black identity which could "release" black Americans from a racial identity which regards their "middle-class" values, aspirations, and success as suspect (109).

To someone like Steele, the pedagogies of Bruffee, Farrell, and Rondinone would make sense. In such a classroom, the black student who told Steele that "he was not sure he should master standard English because then he 'wouldn't be black no more'" (70) would have the comfort of knowing that he is not alone in wanting to pursue things "all individuals" want or in wishing to be drawn "into the American mainstream" (71). Furthermore, he would find support systems to ease him through the momentary pain, dislocation, and anxiety accompanying his effort to "unburden" himself of one of the "opposing thrusts." The popular success of Steele's book attests to the power of this type of thinking on the contemporary scene. Sections of his book originally appeared in such journals as *Harper's, Commentary,* the *New York Times Magazine,* and *The American Scholar.* Since publication of the book, Steele has been touted as an expert on problems facing African-American students in higher education, and his views have been aired on PBS specials, *Nightline,* and the *MacNeil/Lehrer News Hour,* and in *Time* magazine. The popularity of his book should call our attention to the direct and indirect ways in which the distrust of conflict and struggle continues to be recycled and disseminated both within and outside the academy. At the same time, the weight of the authority of the Wagners and Hellers should caution us to take more seriously the pressures the Rondinones and Steeles can exert on Basic Writing teachers, a majority of us still occupying peripheral positions in a culture repeatedly swept by waves of new conservatism.

But investigating the particular directions taken by Basic Writing pioneers when establishing authority for their expertise and the historical contexts of those directions should also enable us to perceive alternative ways of conversing with the Rondinones and Steeles in the 1990s. Because of the contributions of pioneers like Bruffee, Farrell, and Shaughnessy, we can now mobilize the authority they have gained for the field, for our knowledge as well as our expertise as Basic Writing teachers. While we can continue to benefit from the insights into students' experiences of conflict and struggle offered in the writings of all those I have discussed, we need not let their view of the cause and function of such experiences restrict how we view and use the stories and pedagogies they provide. Rather, we need to read them against the grain, filling in the silences left in these accounts by re-reading their experiences from the perspective of alternative accounts from the borderlands and from the perspective of new language and pedagogical theories. For many of these authors are themselves products of classrooms which promoted uncritical faith in either an essentialist view of language or various forms of discursive utopia that these writers aspired to preserve. Therefore, we should use our knowledge and expertise as compositionists to do what they did not or could not do: re-read their accounts in the context of current debates on the nature of language, individual consciousness, and the politics of basic skills. At the same time, we also need to gather more oppositional and alternative accounts from a new generation of students, those who can speak about the successes and challenges of classrooms which recognize the positive uses of conflict and struggle and which teach the process of repositioning.

The writings of the pioneers and their more established contemporaries indicate that the residual distrust of conflict and struggle in the field of Basic Writing is sustained by a fascination with cures for psychic woes, by two views of education — as acculturation and as accommodation — and by two views of language — essentialist and utopian. We need more research which critiques portrayals of Basic Writers as belonging to an abnormal — traumatized or underdeveloped — mental state and which simultaneously provides accounts of the "creative motion" and "compensation," "joy," or "exhilaration" resulting from Basic Writers' efforts to grapple with the conflict within and among diverse discourses. We need more research analyzing and contesting the assumptions about language underlying teaching methods which offer to "cure" all signs of conflict and struggle, research which explores ways to help students recover the latent conflict and struggle in their lives which the dominant conservative ideology of the 1990s seeks to contain. Most of all, we need to find ways of foregrounding conflict and struggle not only in the generation of meaning or authority, but also in the teaching of conventions of "correctness" in syntax, spelling, and punctuation, traditionally considered the primary focus of Basic Writing instruction.

Author's Note: *Material for sections of this essay comes from my dissertation, directed by David Bartholomae at the University of Pittsburgh. This essay is part of a joint project conducted with Bruce Horner which has been supported by the Drake University Provost Research Fund, the Drake University Center for the Humanities, and the University of Iowa Center for Advanced Studies. I gratefully acknowledge Bruce Horner's contributions to the conception and revisions of this essay.*

Works Cited

Anzaldúa, Gloria. *Borderlands/La Frontera: The New Mestiza.* San Francisco: Aunt Lute, 1987.

Baldwin, James. *Conversations with James Baldwin.* Ed. Fred L. Standley and Louis H. Pratt. Jackson: UP of Mississippi, 1989.

———. *The Price of the Ticket.* New York: St. Martin's, 1985.

Bartholomae, David. "Inventing the University." *When a Writer Can't Write: Studies in Writer's Block and Other Composing Process Problems.* Ed. Mike Rose. New York: Guilford, 1985. 134–65.

———. "Writing on the Margins: The Concept of Literacy in Higher Education." *A Sourcebook for Basic Writing Teachers.* Ed. Theresa Enos. New York: Random, 1987. 66–83.

Bizzell, Patricia. "Beyond Anti-Foundationalism to Rhetorical Authority: Problems Defining 'Cultural Literacy.'" *College English* 52 (Oct. 1990): 661–75.

Brown, Rexford G. "Schooling and Thoughtfulness." *Journal of Basic Writing* 10.1 (Spring 1991): 3–15.

Bruffee, Kenneth A. "On Not Listening in Order to Hear: Collaborative Learning and the Rewards of Classroom Research." *Journal of Basic Writing* 7.1 (Spring 1988): 3–12.

———. "Collaborative Learning: Some Practical Models." *College English* 34 (Feb. 1973): 634–43.

DuBois, W. E. B. *The Autobiography of W. E. B. DuBois: A Soliloquy on Viewing My Life from the Last Decade of Its First Century.* New York: International, 1968.

———. *The Education of Black People: Ten Critiques 1906–1960.* Ed. Herbert Aptheker. Amherst: U of Massachusetts P, 1973.

Epes, Mary. "Tracing Errors to Their Sources: A Study of the Encoding Processes of Adult Basic Writers." *Journal of Basic Writing* 4.1 (Spring 1985): 4–33.

Farrell, Thomas J. "Developing Literacy: Walter J. Ong and Basic Writing." *Journal of Basic Writing* 2.1 (Fall/Winter 1978): 30–51.

———. "Literacy, the Basics, and All That Jazz." *College English* 38 (Jan. 1977): 443–59.

———. "Open Admissions, Orality, and Literacy." *Journal of Youth and Adolescence* 3 (1974): 247–60.

Fiske, Edward B. "City College Quality Still Debated after Eight Years of Open Admission." *New York Times* 19 June 1978: A1.

Flynn, Elizabeth. "Composing as a Woman." *College Composition and Communication* 39 (Dec. 1988): 423–35.

Fox, Tom. "Basic Writing as Cultural Conflict." *Journal of Education* 172.1 (1990): 65–83.

Gould, Christopher, and John Heyda. Literacy Education and the Basic Writer: A Survey of College Composition Courses." *Journal of Basic Writing* 5.2 (Fall 1986): 8–27.

Harris, Joseph. "The Idea of Community in the Study of Writing." *College Composition and Communication* 40 (Feb. 1989): 11–22.

Heller, Louis G. *The Death of the American University: With Special Reference to the Collapse of City College of New York.* New Rochelle, NY: Arlington House, 1973.

Horner, Bruce. "Re-Thinking the 'Sociality' of Error: Teaching Editing as Negotiation." Forthcoming, *Rhetoric Review.*

Howe, Irving. "A Foot in the Door." *New York Times* 27 June 1975: 35.

———. "Living with Kampf and Schlaff: Literary Tradition and Mass Education." *The American Scholar* 43 (1973–74): 107–12.

———. *A Margin of Hope: An Intellectual Autobiography.* New York: Harcourt, 1982.

———. *Selected Writings 1950–1990.* New York: Harcourt, 1990.

———. *World of Our Fathers.* New York: Harcourt, 1976.

Hull, Glynda, and Mike Rose. "'This Wooden Shack Place': The Logic of an Unconventional Reading." *College Composition and Communication* 41 (Oct. 1990): 287–98.

Kriegel, Leonard. "Playing It Black." *Change* Mar./Apr. 1969: 7–11.

———. *Working Through: A Teacher's Journey in the Urban University.* New York: Saturday Review, 1972.

Lu, Min-Zhan. "From Silence to Words: Writing as Struggle." *College English* 49 (Apr. 1987): 433–48.

———. "Redefining the Legacy of Mina Shaughnessy: A Critique of the Politics of Linguistic Innocence." *Journal of Basic Writing* 10.1 (Spring 1991): 26–40.

———. "Writing as Repositioning." *Journal of Education* 172.1 (1990): 18–21.

Lunsford, Andrea A., Helene Moglen, and James Slevin, eds. *The Right to Literacy.* New York: MLA, 1990.

Lyons, Robert. "Mina Shaughnessy." *Traditions of Inquiry.* Ed. John Brereton. New York: Oxford UP, 1985. 171–89.

Mellix, Barbara. "From Outside, In." *Georgia Review* 41 (1987): 258–67.

Murphy, Ann. "Transference and Resistance in the Basic Writing Classroom: Problematics and Praxis." *College Composition and Communication* 40 (May 1989): 175–87.

Quinn, Edward. "We're Holding Our Own." *Change* June 1973: 30–35.

Ritchie, Joy S. "Beginning Writers: Diverse Voices and Individual Identity." *College Composition and Communication* 40 (May 1989): 152–74.

Rondinone, Peter. "Teacher Background and Student Needs." *Journal of Basic Writing* 10.1 (Spring 1991): 41–53.

———. "Open Admissions and the Inward 'I.'" *Change* May 1977: 43–47.

Rose, Mike. *Lives on the Boundary.* New York: Penguin, 1989.

Schilb, John. "Composition and Poststructuralism: A Tale of Two Conferences." *College Composition and Communication* 40 (Dec. 1989): 422–43.

Shaughnessy, Mina. "Diving In: An Introduction to Basic Writing." *College Composition and Communication* 27 (Oct. 1976): 234–39.

———. "The English Professor's Malady." *Journal of Basic Writing* 3.1 (Fall/Winter 1980): 91–97.

———. *Errors and Expectations: A Guide for the Teacher of Basic Writing.* New York: Oxford UP, 1977.

Spellmeyer, Kurt. "Foucault and the Freshman Writer: Considering the Self in Discourse." *College English* 51 (Nov. 1989): 715–29.

Stanley, Linda C. "'Misreading' Students' Journals for Their Views of Self and Society." *Journal of Basic Writing* 8.1 (Spring 1989): 21–31.

Steele, Shelby. *The Content of Our Character: A New Vision of Race in America.* New York: St. Martin's, 1990.

Trilling, Lionel. *The Last Decade: Essays and Reviews, 1965–75.* Ed. Diana Trilling. New York: Harcourt, 1979.

———. *Of This Time, Of That Place, and Other Stories.* Selected by Diana Trilling. New York: Harcourt, 1979.

Trimbur, John. "Beyond Cognition: The Voices in Inner Speech." *Rhetoric Review* 5 (1987): 211–21.

Volpe, Edmond L. "The Confession of a Fallen Man: Ascent to the DA." *College English* 33 (1972): 765–79.

Wagner, Geoffrey. *The End of Education.* New York: Barnes, 1976.

PART SIX

ENGLISH AS A SECOND LANGUAGE

Part VI of *The Bedford Handbook for Writers,* "Editing for ESL Problems," recognizes that increasing numbers of composition students acquired English as a second language, and it focuses on areas of English grammar that typically cause difficulty for nonnative speakers. The purpose of this section of the handbook is to provide students with rules they need to edit their writing and to augment those rules with practical explanations and examples that relate specifically to ESL students.

Instructors encountering ESL students should recognize that language interference in student writing does not necessitate remedial exercises and drills. Instead, instructors should consider ESL problems in a developmental context: Writers make mistakes as they attempt to master conventions in a new language. Further, instructors must understand that ESL writers operate within several competing cultural contexts, and their home cultures may be governed by assumptions radically different from those that they encounter in and out of our classrooms. These differing cultural assumptions affect fundamentally the ways that ESL writers acquire and use English, especially in their writing, which is a social action. Because of the complexities associated with teaching ESL writers, instructors often feel ill equipped to help such students in writing classes. The following selections address questions that arise as a result of that uncertainty:

- What should instructors expect from ESL students? What kinds of culturally conditioned behaviors and expectations do ESL students bring to our classrooms?
- How should instructors construct courses and conduct composition classes for ESL writers?
- How do cultural differences — many of which create fundamental conflicts for students and teachers — affect student writing and student behavior? How can teachers help students negotiate among these apparent conflicts?
- How can instructors promote a classroom environment that encourages learning about and acceptance of the different cultures represented in the student population?

CLASSROOM EXPECTATIONS AND BEHAVIORS
Ilona Leki

[From Understanding ESL Writers: A Guide for Teachers *by Ilona Leki. Portsmouth, NH: Boynton, 1990. 47–57.]*

Ilona Leki is director of English as a Second Language in the University of Tennessee English Department. She is currently working on a revision of

Academic Writing: Techniques and Tasks *(1989), and she coedited (with Joan Carson)* Reading in the Composition Classroom: Second Language Perspectives *(1993).*

In this chapter from Understanding ESL Writers, *Leki offers an overview of the various expectations and behaviors that ESL students bring to the classroom, including their ideas about course work, evaluation, and student-instructor relations. Instructors who are conscious of ESL students' expectations can help make those students' learning experiences more effective and beneficial.*

Most of the time ESL students are not traumatized, just surprised, surprised at the receptions they get here and surprised at some of the customs and behaviors they encounter in U.S. classrooms. International students are often hurt and insulted by American ignorance of, and disinterest in, their home countries. American undergraduates are notorious for such geographical gaffs as placing Canada on a map of Texas; Malaysia may as well be in outer space. One international student was upset to learn that his American classmate had never heard of Thailand. African students are asked if people live in houses in Africa. French students have been asked if they have refrigerators in France.

All this is disheartening coming from college students, but international students have more serious problems to face. Although many faculty members are interested in international students and friendly toward them, in disciplines and perhaps parts of the country where there are many non-natives enrolled as students, these students sometimes encounter hostility from their teachers. Certain professors build a reputation of disliking international students in their classes and of automatically giving them lower grades. How prevalent such a practice is probably cannot be determined, but certainly students believe it happens.

Students have reported other behavior on the part of some professors which is, at the very least, unbelievably insensitive, perhaps racist. One student's content-area teacher took his paper and tore it into pieces, telling the student to learn English before turning in a paper. Another student reports:

> Right at the beginning the professor said that I could not pass the course. He said, "As long as you have a Japanese mind, you can not pass 111." When he said this I thought I could not survive sometimes. I have had a Japanese mind for 30 years how can I change it? I felt so depressed. The teacher said that he had had a Korean student who had taken 111 three times in order to pass. He compared me to the Korean saying that it would take me at least that long. I felt like he thought all Asians were the same — Korean Japanese there's no difference. This felt like racial discrimination to me. (Newstetter et al., 1989)

International students fare as badly in the community. A student from Hong Kong claims that he is regularly overcharged for purchases in his conservative Southeastern community and that residual, confused resentments from the war in Vietnam cause locals to automatically take him for Vietnamese and discriminate against him. (His hilarious and ingenious solution to this problem was to announce that he was not foreign; he was just from California, a location probably as distant and exotic to many of these local residents as any place in Southeast Asia!)

Classroom Expectations

Different national groups and different individuals bring different expectations to the classroom, but many students express surprise at the same aspects of post-secondary classroom culture in the United States. Many of the surprises are pleasant. Some international students come from educational systems in which famous scholars and researchers deliver lectures to several hundred students at once, never getting to know any of them personally, or even speaking to them individually. These students are pleased to find that many of their professors here are approachable, informal, and friendly, that they set up office hours when students are welcome to discuss concerns privately. Some students are also thrilled with the flexibility of the U.S. university system and with the diversity of completely unexpected classes available, like typing or various physical education classes.

On the other hand, ESL students often remark on the apparent lack of respect for teachers here, shown in the casual clothes, sandals, even shorts, that their native classmates wear to class or in the eating and drinking that may go on in some classes. The whole teaching environment is disturbingly casual to some students. Teachers sit on the front desk while lecturing, students interrupt lectures to question or dispute what the teacher has said, teachers sometimes say they do not know the answer to a question. Any of these behaviors may jolt the expectations of non-native students.

Even something as simple as what students and teachers call each other can create confusion. Some international students feel uncomfortable calling teachers by names and prefer to use only titles, addressing their instructors simply as "Doctor" without using a name or using a first name, as in "Professor Ken," or simply using "Teacher." Students from the People's Republic of China tend to address their professors by their last names only: "Good morning, Johnson." By the same token, of course, they may expect to be addressed by their family names only and feel uncomfortable being addressed by their given names, an intimacy reserved for only a few very close family members. Even husbands and wives may refer to each other by their family names. Many of the international names are difficult for linguistically provincial Americans to pronounce, and students often resort to taking on English names while they are here. One Jordanian student writes that his name has been spelled and pronounced in so many different ways that he now responds to anything even vaguely resembling Najib: Jeeb, Nick, Nancy.

Many international university students also have a hard time adjusting to what they see as being treated like high school students. They are amazed to find teachers demanding daily attendance, assigning homework, and policing the class by testing periodically to make sure they have done the homework. These students may come from a system in which students may choose to take advantage of class lectures or not, as long as they pass a comprehensive, end-of-the-year exam. Quite a different attitude toward student responsibilities from our own!

In some countries, students may take pre-departure classes or U.S. culture classes which may cover some of the areas of difference between educational practices at home and abroad and thereby help students prepare for their experiences. But these courses cannot cover every encounter the students may have. One international student, for example, took a multiple choice test here for the first time. Having had no previous experience with this form of testing, the student assumed that multiple choice meant choosing more than one answer per item (Stapleton, 1990). Other students come from educational systems in which competing theories are presented only in order to explain the correct theory. The students are confused when they realize that their professor here assumes none of the theories is entirely correct (Krasnick, 1990). It is important to keep in mind that in addition to learning subject matter in a class, ESL students are also often learning a whole new approach to learning itself.

Classroom Behaviors

It should not come as a surprise to us, then, that these students will not always do what we expect in our classes. International students have stood up when the teacher entered the room; others have insisted on erasing the blackboard after class for the teacher. A student of mine, misconstruing the idea of office hours, complained that he had come by my office, hoping to find me by chance for a conference at 5:00 P.M. Saturday afternoon. That student said he waited for me for an hour!

Some students have a difficult time with the style of class participation they observe. While U.S. teachers may consider class participation an important sign that the students are paying attention, some ESL students will never participate unless specifically called on. They may be especially reluctant to volunteer answers to questions since they may feel that by doing so they are humiliating their classmates who cannot answer the question. A Japanese proverb says something like, "The nail that sticks up gets hammered down." Compare that to our own, "The squeaky wheel gets the oil."

ESL students may also react badly to teacher requests for opinions, especially opinions in conflict with those expressed by the teacher. Such requests may be viewed as evidence of teacher incompetence (Levine, 1983, cited in Scarcella, 1990, 94), and many ESL students are trained specifically *not* to hold opinions differing from those of their teachers. By the same token, ESL students may expect teachers to know the answers to any question they may have; these students may become embarrassed and lose confidence in teachers who honestly state that they do not know an answer but will find out. In one case, an Iranian student whose chemistry teacher had made such a statement dropped the class, explaining that he did not see the point in trying to learn from someone who did not know. In Iran, he explained, a professor would sooner fabricate an answer than admit to not knowing.

Many other types of assumptions come into conflict in culturally mixed classes. In an article on attitudes toward time, Levine (1985) describes a problem familiar to ESL teachers — ESL students' flexible attitude toward deadlines. This professor describes his first day teaching at a university in Brazil. Fearing he will be late for his first class, he asks several people the correct time and gets different answers from everyone he asks, answers differing by twenty minutes! Some of the casual strollers he asks are, he later realizes, students in the very class he was in such a rush to get to on time. Once in class, he notices students coming in fifteen minutes, thirty minutes, even an hour late, and none of them act embarrassed or chagrined or apologetic. And when the class period is over, none of them get up to leave, willing instead to stay on another fifteen, or thirty, minutes or whatever it takes to get their business done. People in many other countries are simply not driven by the clock in the way people in the United States are. As a result, even though ESL students usually know of the U.S. reputation for, they might say, fanatic devotion to punctuality, these students sometimes just cannot bring themselves to conform to class starting times and paper deadline dates. Their priorities are such that they may be unable to refuse to help a friend in need even if their term papers are due tomorrow. In one 8:00 A.M. class of mine, students from Greece, Zaire, and Palestine arrived in class every single day from five to fifteen minutes late; on the other hand, a group of students from the People's Republic of China arrived every single day from five to fifteen minutes early!

Traditional gender roles may also create problems for ESL students. For some of these students, their experience in the United States will be the first time they have been in a mixed-sex classroom. This alone may be intimidating for them. But in addition, in some parts of the world, women are expected not to speak in the presence of males at all, clearly posing a special problem of classroom participation for these students. Even if women students do not have this additional burden placed on them, they, and males from these cultures, may feel awkward working in groups together and, if given the choice, may choose to work only in groups of the same sex.

It is also the case that some of these students, particularly the males, may never have had a female professor and may need some time to adjust themselves to that new experience. ESL professionals also cite instances in which gender prejudices make male ESL students unable to take female authority figures, including teachers, as seriously as they would males. But general respect for authority and for teachers in particular apparently overrides these prejudices for the most part. These problems occur with very few students and far less often in English-speaking countries than in the students' home countries.

Language

Language obviously creates misunderstandings. Even though ESL students may be paying careful attention to what is going on, they may actually understand only a portion of what they hear. New ESL teachers consistently register surprise at their own overestimation of how much their students understand of classroom management talk. Numbers in particular may be difficult, for example, the page numbers of reading assignments. These students may need to have directions repeated even when they claim to have understood. In fact, for students from some cultures where it seems to be taken for granted that all credit for students' learning belongs to the teacher, it may be utterly useless to ask if they understand. For cultural and linguistic reasons, they may always claim to understand even when they don't, either hesitant to bring further attention to themselves by their failure to understand or reluctant to imply that the teacher has not made a point clearly enough.

Sometimes the confusion arises because, for some cultural groups, nodding the head, which indicates agreement or at least understanding to English speakers, may merely indicate that the listener is continuing to listen, while perhaps not understanding the content of what is being said at all (Scarcella, 1990). For some Arabs, blinking the eyes indicates agreement, a gesture unlikely even to be noticed by uninformed native English speakers, and for some Indians, the gesture used is tilting the head to the side in a movement that resembles the English gesture indicating doubt! (This gesture looks like the one which might be accompanied in English by "Oh well" and a shrug.)

Some languages are spoken with a great deal more intonation or emphasis than is usual for English. If students from those language backgrounds have not learned to imitate English oral delivery style well, they may come off sounding more vehement or emotional than they intend. Other students, many Asians, for example, may seem excruciatingly shy because of the longer pauses they customarily take before answering a question put to them. An English speaker may perceive a Vietnamese speaker as not participating in a conversation because the Vietnamese speaker takes so long to reply; the Vietnamese speaker, however, may perceive a series of friendly questions as a barrage implying impatience and not permitting appropriately reflective answers (Robinson, 1985, cited in Scarcella, 1990, 103).

Another aspect of the problems caused by language, even for students who are fairly proficient in English, may occur when a student tries to make a point. The rules for turn-taking vary among languages. A person speaking English is expected to heed verbal and kinetic cues indicating that the listener is now ready to speak, cues like taking a breath or making a sound toward the end of the speaker's sentence. Non-native students may inappropriately interrupt a speaker because turn-taking is handled differently in those students' cultures and they may not yet know the correct signals to send in this culture. In some cultures, interrupting a speaker may not be rude; it may be a sign of listener attentiveness intended to show the listener's involvement in the interaction. But it is also entirely possible that while the speaker is speaking, the non-native student is rehearsing what she or he planned to say and simply has to begin speaking before the planned sentence slips away.

Language-based confusion also arises unexpectedly and in ways impossible to guard against. One example is [an] Asian student . . . who interpreted the comment "It's a shame you didn't have more time to work on this paper" to mean "You should be ashamed of this paper."

The confusion may also be on the teacher's part. Oral English proficiency, for example, including accents, can be extremely misleading. ESL students who have learned English in an environment which precluded much contact with spoken English may speak with accents very difficult to understand but may write quite well. Conversely, particularly with immigrant students, the students' oral English may sound quite native-like but their written English may be a problem. They may be quite proficient at BICS [Basic Interpersonal Communicative Skills] but may have had little experience with CALP [Cognitive Academic Language Proficiency], the language of the academy. In either case, accents cannot be equated one way or the other with proficiency.

Grades and Exams

One very important area in which cultural assumptions may differ and cause friction is evaluation. Some of these students are under tremendous pressure to get good grades either because their financial support depends on maintaining a certain average or because their pride or family honor requires excellent performance. In addition, in many countries around the world, exam results are extremely important, determining much more absolutely than we may be used to here a student's admission to certain types of educational tracks or to certain prestigious schools and ultimately to a desirable job and life style. Even exams taken at age five or six can set children on the road to a comfortable, financially secure future or to a lifetime of factory work. Students from these countries take exams extremely seriously.

Further complicating the exam issue is the fact that it is taken for granted in some countries that friends and relatives have the right to call upon each other for any help they need, and that that call must be answered. Some students feel as much obliged to share exam answers or research papers as they would to share their notes of that day's class or to share their book with a classmate. (See Kuehn, Stanwyck, and Holland, 1990, for a discussion of ESL students' attitudes towards cheating.) Knowledge may be thought of more as communal, less as individual property. The moral obligation to share, to cooperate, to help a friend or relative makes far more pressing demands on some of these students than the obligation our culture may wish to impose of individual work and competition. In other words, what we call cheating is not particularly uncommon or shocking for some of these students. It simply does not carry the onus it does here.

In places where personal relationships have more weight than they do here and adherence to impersonal rules has less weight, bureaucrats and others in authority often have a great deal more flexibility to act than they might here. As a result, arguing, persuading, and bargaining for a better deal is a part of human interaction. That includes, of course, bargaining with teachers for better grades. In situations where students are pleading for higher grades, the justification is nearly always the same: not that the student actually did better, not that the teacher's judgment was wrong, not that the student does not deserve the lower grade, but that the student *needs* a higher grade and that it is in the teacher's power to *help*. When the teacher refuses to help, the student may go away hurt and confused, personally wounded at the teacher's indifference to the student's plight. These are very painful experiences both for the student and for the teacher, but particularly for non-ESL teachers who may not understand that the student (and the teacher as well, obviously) is operating according to another set of culturally determined rules about personal interactions. Non-ESL teachers may well come to resent international students for putting them in such tense, embarrassing situations and making them feel guilty about sticking to their decisions.

In these awful confrontations, it is also not unheard of for students to exhibit more emotion than most U.S. post-secondary teachers are accustomed to dealing with. Men in other cultures, for example, are permitted to cry under a much wider range of circumstances than is permitted here. Unrestrained sobbing is sometimes a student's response to the sadness of failure or defeat.

Body Language and Socio-linguistic Snags

Other conflicting cultural styles may be less dramatic but also disconcerting. Latin American and Arab students may sit or stand too close during conferences; Vietnamese students may feel uncomfortable with a friendly pat on the shoulder; Japanese students may not look at the teacher when addressed. During a discussion of body language, I asked a class of international students whether they noticed that people use eye contact differently in the United States from the way it is used in their home countries. Several students strongly felt that this was the case. When asked to elaborate, a man from El Salvador complained that Americans refused to look him in the eye, as if they were lying, insincere, or hiding something, and a woman from Japan claimed that Americans made her feel uneasy because they seemed to insist on staring at her when they spoke, right in the eye instead of somewhere at the base of the throat, as she was accustomed to doing!

Cultural differences can cause other complications which are not strictly linguistic. One of the experiences Americans abroad often complain about is suffering the injustice of having someone butt in line and be served out of order while those in line continue to wait. But in many other cultures, people assume that those who are waiting in line are in no particular hurry and don't mind not being waited on next. If they did mind, they would be aggressively demanding attention by pushing to the front of the line and stating their desire. Students from these places, then, may feel quite comfortable crowding the teacher after class and demanding attention while other students patiently await their turns.

Other embarrassing moments may occur as a result of socio-linguistic differences among cultures. One of these areas concerns the tacit rules which govern topics of conversation. Teachers may feel intruded upon by questions which are completely normal in the students' cultures: In Asia: Are you married? How old are you? In the Arab world: How much did that cost? Do you have sons? In Eastern Europe: How much money do you make? How much do you weigh? (Wolfson, 1989). The reaction to such questions may be outrage unless we realize that the question of what is appropriate to talk about is a part of the linguistic system of a language that must be learned just as verb tenses must be learned. Just as the questions above may strike us as inappropriate, others take offense at different questions. Muslim students, for example, are offended by questions like "Why don't you drink?" or "Have you ever kissed your boyfriend?" (Wolfson, 1989). Unfortunately, socio-linguistic rules are not visible as rules, are taken for granted, and are assumed to be universal. As a result, while grammatical errors may be ignored, socio-linguistic errors brand the nonnative as rude and offensive.

Notions of modesty about achievements also differ among cultures. Writing teachers may find it difficult, for example, to learn whether a writing assignment went well for given students. When asked how well they did on an assignment, Asian students invariably say they did not do a good job, that they are not good students, while Arab students seem to always reply that their paper is very good, that everything went exceedingly well.

ESL students may actually behave in ways that strike us as unusual, unexpected, or even inappropriate, but difficulties may also arise as we simply misinterpret what appears to be ordinary, recognizable behavior. The Japanese, for example, have an aversion for direct disagreement and instead of saying no to a suggestion may hedge, preferring to indicate vaguely that the decision must be postponed or further studied (Christopher, 1982, cited in Wolfson, 1989, 20). As a result, an English speaker may not recognize that the Japanese speaker has said no and may assume that the Japanese speaker really is still debating the issue. The Japanese apparently do not even like to say the word "no"; when asked whether she liked Yoko Ono, one Japanese student replied, "Yes, I hate her."

Finally, the offices of ESL teachers are often crowded with Chinese paper cuttings, Korean fans, Latin American *mulas,* and pieces of Arabic brass. Non-ESL colleagues of mine with ESL students in their classes have sometimes expressed concern that these gifts look like bribes and have wondered whether or not to accept them from their students. But this type of gift-giving is an accepted part of many cultures, and ESL students often give their teachers small gifts as tokens of respect and gratitude with no baser intentions in mind at all.

Students may misinterpret us as well or feel confused about how to interpret our signals correctly. While they may be happy to learn, for example, that professors have office hours, they may feel unsure about whether or not they are actually invited to take advantage of them. Students may be confused if the decision of whether or not to come by the office during office hours is left up to them and may conclude that an off-hand invitation to come by if they have problems, an invitation which does not *urge* or order the student to come by, is not sincere.

Conclusion

It takes some time for international students to determine exactly what their relationship with a professor is. Many of them come from cultures, such as China, in which teachers are highly respected but also are expected to behave more like mentors, to involve themselves in the students' lives, to know about them as people, and to guide them closely in moral, personal, or educational decisions. These students may then be disappointed to find this is not usually the case here.

Clearly, there is a great deal of room for both misunderstanding and resentment during confrontations involving different cultural styles. For the most part, it is the international students, outnumbered as they are, who will have to make the greater part of the adjustment to accommodate U.S. classroom expectations. But an awareness of some of these students' expectations on the part of their U.S. instructors can certainly make the adjustment easier for all. Anticipating some of the behaviors of culturally mixed groups can help us be more tolerant of them and perhaps at the same time less hesitant about pointing out, if necessary, the inappropriateness of some of these behaviors within the culture of the U.S. college classroom.

References

Krasnick, H. 1990. Preparing Indonesians for graduate study in Canada. *TESL Reporter* 23: 33–36.

Kuehn, P., D. J. Stanwyck, and C. L. Holland. 1990. Attitudes toward "cheating" behaviors in the ESL classroom. *TESOL Quarterly* 24: 313–317.

Levine, R., with E. Wolff. 1985. Social time: The heartbeat of a culture. *Psychology Today* 19 (March): 28–37.

Newstetter, W., T. Shoji, N. Mokoto, and F. Matsubara. 1989. From the inside out. Student perspectives on the academic writing culture. Paper presented at the Conference on Culture, Writing, and Related Issues in Language Teaching, Atlanta, Georgia.

Scarcella, R. 1990. *Teaching language minority children in the multicultural class-room.* Englewood Cliffs, NJ: Prentice-Hall.

Stapleton, S. 1990. From the roller coaster to the round table: Smoothing rough relationships between foreign students and faculty members. *TESL Reporter* 23 (April): 23–25.

Wolfson, N. 1989. *Perspectives: Sociolinguistics and TESOL.* New York: Newbury House.

TAILORING COMPOSITION CLASSES TO ESL STUDENTS' NEEDS

Ann Schlumberger and Diane Clymer

[Teaching English in the Two-Year College 16 (May 1989): 121–128.]

A faculty member at Pima County Community College and the University of Arizona, Tucson, Ann Schlumberger has taught writing from the elementary school to the college level for more than twenty years. With Diane Clymer, Schlumberger wrote "Teacher Education through Teacher Collaboration," a chapter in Richness in Writing: Empowering ESL Students *(1989). The article included here resulted from Schlumberger's and Clymer's ESL teaching experiences and their recognition that fellow teachers regularly have questions about how to teach writing to ESL students.*

Composition teachers encounter ESL students in several different contexts, and Schlumberger and Clymer offer practical advice that applies to any of them. Arguing that learning a language and learning to write are analogous, Schlumberger and Clymer advocate using a process methodology with ESL writers instead of reverting to product-oriented approaches. They explain clearly why and how their four general recommendations for teaching ESL writers will contribute to a more effective pedagogy. Their bibliography will help instructors explore these four recommendations further.

During the past decade, two-year colleges have been providing education to growing numbers of nonnative speakers of English. These English-as-a-second-language students are attracted to two-year campuses for the same reasons as other students: Open enrollment policies provide them with access to postsecondary education, relatively low tuition and fees make education feasible, and the faculty emphasis on teaching rather than research assures students of the personal and academic support necessary to sustain their studies. In addition, many of these students see the two-year college as a low-risk environment in which to improve their English.

Quite often it is the English composition teacher — with little or no background in teaching ESL — who is charged with helping the students realize this goal. Beyond urging novice ESL teachers to subscribe to the *TESOL Quarterly* (the ESL professional journal), this article offers four general recommendations for accommodating composition instruction to the needs of ESL learners. These suggestions are applicable (1) to classes of ESL students sharing the same first language, (2) to classes with students of different first languages, and (3) to classes made up of both ESL and native

English speakers. Also included is a bibliography of suggested readings for teachers who wish to increase their knowledge of ESL pedagogy.

Recommendation 1

Make holistically graded papers a part of the procedure for placing ESL students in composition courses. Placement by objective grammar tests can mask the linguistic facility of ESL students who have grown up in the United States, while misrepresenting the productive skills of foreign ESL students. International students, in particular, can often recognize correct grammatical forms far better than they can use them in their own writing.

While misuse of grammar is often the most salient feature of ESL compositions, holistic scoring permits teachers to assess content, development, organization, and diction as well. When ESL students are literate in their first language, their English writing samples often reflect the rhetorical conventions of their first language. For instance, an argument which is artfully conceived by Korean standards will probably seem confusingly indirect to native English speakers. The repetitious, emphatic language of essays written by Arabic students, while satisfying the phatic purpose of Arabic discourse, will probably be judged redundant hyperbole by an English reader, who wonders when the students will stop repeating themselves and start developing support for their claims.

To minimize misplacement in classes, we further recommend correlating the holistic rating scale with the entrance criteria for courses in the curriculum. When graders are familiar with the sequence of courses, they expedite the placement process by thinking in terms of "This student would benefit from asking _____." In addition, the training session for holistic grading is a useful means of familiarizing new or part-time faculty with the expectations for student performance at different levels of the curriculum. In particular, part-time faculty, who are often hired to teach the same one or two courses each semester, appreciate the experiential overview that participating in a holistic grading session can provide.

At the University of Arizona, ESL students have thirty minutes to write an argumentative placement essay on their choice from three thesis statements. Two teachers independently rate each essay on a scale of 1 to 4; a two-point discrepancy results in the paper's being evaluated by a third reader. Awarding a 1 indicates placement in the preparatory composition course. A 2 indicates the teacher thinks the student can pass the first semester of ESL composition; a 3 indicates that the student will probably do well in that course, and 4 suggests placement in a native-speaker section of freshman composition.

Recommendation 2

Organize courses around thematic units. May Shih describes such "content-based" academic writing courses as "composition courses organized around sets of readings on selected topics" (p. 632). One of the advantages to this format is that recursive encounters with a topic allow both native and nonnative speakers of English to gradually amass a body of material to think and write about. By examining a topic from different perspectives over time, the students' lexical knowledge increases even as their intellectual understanding of the subject deepens: The result is greater fluency. Shih points out that content-based composition instruction enables students to develop the cognitive, evaluative skills needed for work in all academic disciplines.

Teachers of ESL composition students need to remember that developing native-speaker fluency in a foreign language takes time; it is the result of prolonged exposure to the way the language is used in many different contexts. Yet, as Anne Raimes has noted, complete mastery of syntax and expression is not a prerequisite for instruction in English rhetoric ("Composition"). Beginning ESL writing students should not be restricted to grammar drills, sentence combining exercises, and the construction of isolated paragraphs.

Several approaches are possible when designing thematic units. First, since people write best about subjects they know and care about, the choice of unit themes should take into account the students' experiences as well as their writing skills and academic needs. For example, students in a preparatory composition class who have recently arrived in the United States and are just beginning their studies do well reading, discussing, and writing about experiences with language, paralingual communication, and cultural differences — topics which are relevant to their positions as newcomers in a foreign culture. From these personal experiences, they can extract generalizations or inferences that become the focus for expository prose, the type of writing predominant in an academic setting. For instance, a Vietnamese student, reacting in her journal to the informality of American greetings, might develop an essay that classifies and explores the significance of the modes of address used by Vietnamese. Student experiences also yield material for writing personal essays popular in composition classes for native speakers. However, it is important to realize that some ESL students may have traumatic pasts that they do not care to reminisce about.

Another way to ensure that students explore topics that interest them is to enlist their help in selecting thematic units. In some ESL freshman composition classes, students review the table of contents of their anthology of readings and write a proposal to their teacher in which they state the sections of the text they would like the class to cover. Since some international students have been told by their governments what they must study, these students in particular enjoy an opportunity to exercise their freedom of choice. Some semesters an entire class might be in agreement about what they want to read, and they choose to write their papers on the same general topic (such as education or technology). Other semesters, students have divided into interest groups to discuss related readings, to collect copies of library articles to augment their knowledge of a subject, and to garner suggestions for their papers.

At times, however, teachers will want to preserve their control over the choice of theme and materials in order to ensure that students approach one theme from different rhetorical perspectives. For example, in a second-semester freshman composition course, students read essays, poems, short stories, and two short novels — all relating to an overall theme, such as heroism or family and community. Each semester, the teachers of this course agreed on a common theme and the major novels to be studied. Their consensus allowed them to work together in collecting relevant short pieces and developing materials to supplement the literature. The supplementary compilation was copied and sold in the bookstore with the works of fiction. Although many teachers may prefer to work with a thematically arranged reader, using a compilation allows flexibility in the choice of materials, enables teachers to change the thematic focus of their courses frequently, and incidentally, prevents students from plagiarizing the previous semester's papers.

Recommendation 3

Reduce the assigned number of formal, polished essays. As a consequence of the shift in composition instruction from a product to a process orientation, many ESL composition teachers have decreased the number of formal papers they require of students. Instead, students are given more opportunities for revision and for informal, exploratory writing to discover topics. Just as students increase their reading rate and comprehension by extensive reading, so do they gain fluency in writing by extensive writing on a topic. Fluency is more important than correctness of expression in the early stages of the writing process because students are writing to discover ideas, to incorporate new information from a variety of sources, and to explore connections. Eventually, some of this extensive writing evolves into the initial drafts for three or four intensive writing projects, which can culminate in formal, polished essays of 800 to 2500 words.

One advantage of a multidraft approach is that it encourages teachers to vary their responses to student writing according to a paper's stage of development. Vivian Zamel cautions against the dangers of responding to all student writing "as if it were a final draft" (p. 79). When teachers read exploratory writing or early drafts of students' papers, their first concern should be ideas. Extensive correcting of grammar at this point makes it difficult for students to jettison sentences or change passages that do not contribute effectively to ideas that are being developed. ESL composition teachers should de-emphasize mechanics and expression until later stages of revision — a more appropriate time to consider correctness of grammar and niceties of expression.

When marking mechanical errors, we suggest restraint, lest the number of marks overwhelm both ESL students and their teachers. Chastain recommends targeting for correction a maximum of three types of errors per paper. The teacher labels the grammatical structures involved, explains the mistakes, and models correct forms. Thereafter, the student is held accountable for eliminating these errors in papers. Errors are selected for remediation on the basis of their frequency in a paper, their disruption of the text, and their focus in class instruction.

Homburg describes a useful system for classifying mechanical errors according to their serious, irritating, or negligible effects on text comprehensibility. One does not have to be an expert in linguistics to realize that syntax problems severe enough to obscure meaning are more of a concern for teachers than consistent misuse of the definite article or the occasional omission of -s endings on third person verb forms. In fact, composition teachers with experience conducting basic writing classes for native English speakers will recognize some of the same sorts of errors in the work of their ESL students. However, to help teachers understand the ways in which ESL students' native language and background influence their production of English prose, our bibliography includes articles contrasting linguistic and rhetorical features of other languages with those of English. When teachers feel they do not have the resources to interpret the problems a student is having with the language, they may want to consult someone who has specialized training in teaching ESL.

Recommendation 4

Encourage ESL students to develop and use all four language skills in the composition classroom: writing, listening, speaking, and reading. Research supports such a holistic approach to language learning, indicating that instruction and practice in other aspects of language reinforce writing skills.

A standard means of integrating language skills in English classes has been to require students to present oral reports on a topic they have researched and written about. This is a useful practice, but we have found that the spontaneous, informal conversations carried on during small group work are even more beneficial to ESL students' written and oral language development. Long and Porter enumerate the positive effects of group work: It (1) increases opportunities for language practice, (2) improves the quality of student communication, (3) helps individualize instruction, (4) promotes a positive affective environment, and (5) motivates learners (pp. 208–12). From a pedagogical and from a language acquisition perspective, collaborative learning makes sense. Nevertheless, sometimes teachers who have successfully employed peer collaboration in their other classes fear that ESL students' cultural reservations or lack of oral proficiency will cause group work to fail.

We have not found this to be the case. In fact, group activities and peer editing contribute significantly to the invention, drafting, and revision cycles of student writing. We do, though, recommend multilingual groupings, when possible, to ensure the use of English as the medium of discussion. And, as is true for native English speakers, teachers have to explain clearly the rationale for group work since many students will be unfamiliar with this technique. Teachers also need to structure group activities carefully, providing clear directives to the groups and allowing them sufficient time to complete the assigned task. Occasionally misunderstandings develop during peer editing exchanges, but tact, humor, and lessons in the polite subjunctive can help with students who have difficulty expressing or accepting criticism.

Direct instruction in reading also has an important place in the ESL composition curriculum. Indeed, the current literature focuses on the close relationship between reading and writing. We always model for our students how to skim, scan, and annotate a text. In-class previewing of assigned readings is particularly important. The ESL composition teacher — to an even greater extent than the basic writing teacher — cannot assume that students will understand what they read. All students need knowledge of the topic assigned (an issue discussed in the section on thematic units), but ESL students, in particular, may need supplemental background information to help them understand a reading.

One method of previewing a text with students is to have them scan it for words that seem to be important to the text's meaning. These are put on the board, and the teacher uses them to elicit student predictions about what the assigned reading will be about. Idioms, expressions, and difficult vocabulary can thus be explained in a way that highlights the fact that reading, like writing, involves the construction of meaning.

Fraida Dubin stresses the importance of students' knowing "the whole context of a selection so that significant clues to meaning are not overlooked" (p. 157). Echoing the writing teacher's concern for audience, Dubin recommends that ESL students be made aware of the conventions and characteristics of different text types: scholarly prose for experts, popular culture texts for the general public, and nonacademic nonfiction for the educated audience (pp. 155–57).

Students also benefit from direction in how to elaborate on what they read. We have designed an exercise to promote reading/writing connections in ESL freshman composition classes. Whenever students have an assigned reading, they are required to explore, in brief paragraph-length passages, insights or questions that occur to them as they read. The teacher later reads and responds to the content of these informal compositions while modeling active involvement with a text. This exercise ensures that students are prepared for class discussions, and for making connections beyond the literal level of the text. Some of these connections, when explored further, can be the source of ideas which eventually mature into a formal essay.

Conclusion

Composition teachers with a firm grounding in process methodology are in an excellent position to assist ESL students in developing language skills, even though such teachers are not language specialists *per se.* Obviously, a background in linguistics is very valuable to the teacher of ESL composition classes, but current theories of teaching composition complement the current theories in language acquisition.

Stephen D. Krashen, a widely cited theorist on language acquisition, identifies in *The Input Hypothesis: Issues and Implications* (New York: Longman, 1985) two recursive processes in gaining competence in a language: *acquisition* and *learning.* During acquisition, the learner is exposed to "comprehensible input," developing fluency in a language with emphasis on understanding and communicating ideas, not on grammatical correctness. This parallels the early phases of the writing process when the student's focus is comprehending and generating content. Then, during what Krashen calls the learning process ("a conscious process that results in 'knowing about' language"), learners begin to monitor their output, consciously shaping it according to rhetorical, syntactic, and morphological conventions. This process is quite similar to that which student writers engage in as they revise and edit their compositions. What has been discovered about learning a language is applicable to learning to write and vice versa. The analogous nature of these two activities should provide encouragement and reassurance to composition teachers newly assigned to teach ESL classes.

A Bibliography for Tailoring Composition Classes to ESL Students' Needs

Curriculum Design

Farr, Marcia, and Harvey Daniels. "Writing Instruction and Nonmainstream Students." *Language Diversity and Writing Instruction.* Urbana, Ill.: NCTE, 1986. 43–85.

Johnson, Donna M., and Duane H. Roen, ed. *Richness in Writing: Empowering ESL Students.* In press.

Long, Michael H., and Patricia A. Porter. "Group Work, Interlanguage Talk, and Second Language Acquisition." *TESOL Quarterly* 19 (1985): 207–28.

Mackay, Sandra, ed. *Composing in a Second Language.* Rowley, Mass.: Newbury, 1984.

Raimes, Ann. "Composition: Controlled by the Teacher, Free for the Student." *On TESOL '76* (1977): 183–94.

———. "Teaching ESL Writing: Fitting What We Do to What We Know." *The Writing Instructor* 5 (1986): 153–65.

Shih, May. "Content-Based Approaches to Teaching Academic Writing." *TESOL Quarterly* 20 (1986): 617–48.

Spack, Ruth. "Literature, Reading, Writing, and ESL: Bridging the Gaps." *TESOL Quarterly* 19 (1985): 703–25.

Watson-Reekie, Cynthia B. "The Use and Abuse of Models in the ESL Writing Class." *TESOL Quarterly* 16 (1982): 5–14.

RESPONDING TO PAPERS

Brown, H. Douglas. "Interlanguage." *Principles of Language Learning and Teaching.* 2nd ed. Englewood Cliffs: Prentice, 1987. 169–97.

Chastain, Kenneth. "Composition: Toward a Rationale and a System of Accountability." *Toward a Philosophy of Second Language Learning.* Boston: Heinle, 1980. 67–74.

Homburg, Taco Justus. "Holistic Evaluation of ESL Compositions: Can It Be Validated Objectively?" *TESOL Quarterly* 18 (1984): 87–105.

Zamel, Vivian. "Responding to Student Writing." *TESOL Quarterly* 19 (1985): 79–101.

CULTURAL ASPECTS OF WRITING

Connor, Ulla, and Robert B. Kaplan, ed. *Writing across Languages: Analysis of L2 Text.* Reading, Mass.: Addison, 1987.

Derrick-Mescua, Maria, and Jacqueline L. Gmuca. "Concepts of Unity and Sentence Structure in Arabic, Spanish, and Malay." 1985. ERIC ED 260 590.

Hinds, John. "Contrastive Rhetoric: Japanese and English." *Text* 3 (1983): 183–96.

Kaplan, Robert B. "Cultural Thought Patterns in Intercultural Education." *Language Learning* 16 (1966): 1–20.

Lay, Nancy. "Chinese Language Interference in Written English." *Journal of Basic Writing* 1 (1975): 50–61.

Mohan, Bernard A., and Winnie Au-Yeung Lo. "Academic Writing and Chinese Students: Transfer and Developmental Factors." *TESOL Quarterly* 19 (1985): 515–34.

Ostler, Shirley E. "Writing Problems of International Students in the College Composition Classroom." *The Writing Instructor* 5 (1986): 177–89.

Rizzo, Betty, and Santiago Villafane. "Spanish Influence on Written English." *Journal of Basic Writing* 1 (1975): 62–71.

Thompson-Panos, Karyn, and Maria Thomas-Ruzic. "The Least You Should Know about Arabic: Implications for the ESL Writing Instructor." *TESOL Quarterly* 17 (1983): 609–21.

READING

Carrell, Patricia L. "The Effects of Rhetorical Organization on ESL Readers." *TESOL Quarterly* 18 (1984): 441–69.

Carrell, Patricia L., Joanne Devine, and David Eskey, ed. *Interactive Approaches to Second Language Reading.* Cambridge: Cambridge UP, 1988.

Dubin, Fraida, David E. Eskey, and William Grabe, eds. *Teaching Second Language Reading for Academic Purposes.* Reading, Mass.: Addison, 1986. 127–60.

MULTICULTURAL CLASSROOMS, MONOCULTURAL TEACHERS

Terry Dean

[College Composition and Communication 40 (1989): 23–37.]

Terry Dean has taught basic writing for seventeen years and currently is a senior learning-skills counselor at the Learning Skills Center at the University of California, Davis.

Dean addresses the cultural dissonance that results from cultural differences among students in writing classrooms, and he argues that "teachers need to structure learning experiences that both help students write their way into the university and help teachers learn their way into student cultures." Dean surveys a number of teaching strategies designed to help students and teachers negotiate cultural differences, including the use of cultural topics for reading and writing assignments and the use of peer response groups to give students firsthand exposure to other cultures. Dean's article is valuable for its recognition of the reciprocal nature of classroom interactions between students and teachers and for its emphasis on respecting and valuing different cultures.

> Remember gentlemen, John Chrysostom's exquisite story about the day he entered the rhetorician Libanius' school in Antioch. Whenever a new pupil arrived at his school, Libanius would question him about his past, his parents, and his country.
>
> — Renan, *La Réforme intellectuelle et morale*

Sometimes more than others, I sense the cultural thin ice I walk on in my classrooms, and I reach out for more knowledge than I could ever hope to acquire, just to hang on. With increasing cultural diversity in classrooms, teachers need to structure learning experiences that both help students write their way into the university and help teachers learn their way into student cultures. Now this is admittedly a large task, especially if your students (like mine) are Thai, Cambodian, Vietnamese, Korean, Chinese, Hmong, Laotian (midland Lao, lowland Lao), Salvadoran, Afro-American, Mexican, French, Chicano, Nicaraguan, Guatemalan, Native American (Patwin, Yurok, Hoopa, Wintu), Indian (Gujarati, Bengali, Punjabi), Mexican-American, Jamaican, Filipino (Tagalog, Visayan, Ilocano), Guamanian, Samoan, and so on. It may take a while for the underpaid, overworked freshman composition instructor to acquire dense cultural knowledge of these groups. But I have a hunch that how students handle the cultural transitions that occur in the acquisition of academic discourse affects how successfully they acquire that discourse. The very least we can do, it seems to me, is to educate ourselves so that when dealing with our students, in the words of Michael Holzman, "We should stop doing harm if we can help it" (31).

Some would question how much harm is being done. If enough students pass exit exams and the class evaluations are good, then everything is OK. Since we want our students to enter the mainstream, all we need worry about is providing them the tools. Like opponents of bilingual education, some would argue that we need to concern ourselves more with providing student access to academic culture, not spending time on student culture. But retention rates indicate that not all students are making the transition into academic culture equally well. While the causes of dropout are admittedly complex, cultural dissonance seems at the very least to play an important role. If indeed we are going to encounter "loss, violence, and compromise" (142) as David Bartholomae describes the experience of Richard Rodriguez, should we not be directing students to the counseling center? And if the attainment of biculturalism in many cases is painful and difficult, can we be assured, as Patricia Bizzell suggests, that those who do achieve power in the world of academic discourse will use it to argue persuasively for preservation of the language and the culture of the home world view? (299) This was not exactly Richard Rodriguez's response to academic success, but what if, after acquiring the power, our students feel more has been lost than gained? I think as teachers we have an obligation to raise these issues. Entering freshmen are often unaware of the erosion of their culture until they become seniors or even later. Like Richard Rodriguez, many students do not fully realize what they have lost until it is too late to regain it. Let me briefly outline the problem as I see it and offer some possible solutions.

The Problem

A lot is being asked of students. David Bartholomae describes the process: "What our beginning students need to learn is to extend themselves, by successive approximations, into the commonplaces, set phrases, rituals and gestures, habits of mind, tricks of persuasion, obligatory conclusions, and necessary connections that determine 'what might be said' and constitute knowledge within the various branches of our academic community" (146). "Rituals and gestures, tricks of persuasion" mean taking on much more than the surface features of a culture. Carried to an extreme, students would have to learn when it is appropriate to laugh at someone slipping on a banana peel. When we teach composition, we are teaching culture. Depending on students' backgrounds, we are teaching at least academic culture, what is acceptable evidence, what persuasive strategies work best, what is taken to be a demonstration of "truth" in different disciplines. For students whose home culture is distant from mainstream culture, we are also teaching how, as a people, "mainstream" Americans view the world. Consciously or unconsciously, we do this, and the responsibility is frightening.

In many situations, the transitions are not effective. Several anthropological and social science studies show how cultural dissonance can affect learning. Shirley Brice Heath examines the ways in which the natural language environments of working-class Black and white children can interfere with their success in schools designed primarily for children from middle-class mainstream culture. The further a child's culture is from the culture of the school, the less chance for success. Classroom environments that do not value the home culture of the students lead to decreased motivation and poor academic performance (270–72). In a study of Chicano and Black children in Stockton, California, schools, John Ogbu arrives at a similar conclusion. Susan Urmston Philips analyzes the experiences of Warm Springs Native American children in a school system in Oregon where the administrators, teachers, and even some parents thought that little was left of traditional culture. But Philips shows that "children who speak English and who live in a material environment that is overwhelmingly Western in form can still grow up in a world where by far the majority of their enculturation experience comes from their interaction with other

Indians. Thus school is still the main source of their contact with mainstream Anglo culture" (11). Philips describes the shock that Warm Springs Native American children experience upon entering a school system designed for the Anglo middle-class child. Because of differences in the early socialization process of Native American children (especially in face-to-face interaction), they feel alienated in the classroom and withdraw from class activities (128).

Pierre Bourdieu and Jean-Claude Passeron examine how the cultural differences of social origin relate directly to school performance (8–21). Educational rewards are given to those who feel most at home in the system, who, assured of their vocations and abilities, can pursue fashionable and exotic themes that pique the interest of their teachers, with little concern for the vocational imperatives of working-class and farm children. Working-class and farm children must struggle to acquire the academic culture that has been passed on by osmosis to the middle and upper classes. The very fact that working-class and farm children must laboriously acquire what others come by naturally is taken as another sign of inferiority. They work hard because they have no talent. They are remedial. The further the distance from the mainstream culture, the more the antipathy of mainstream culture, the more difficulty students from outside that culture will have in acquiring it through the educational system (which for many is the only way):

> Those who believe that everyone would be given equal access to the highest level of education and the highest culture, once the same economic means were provided for all those who have the requisite "gifts," have stopped halfway in their analysis of the obstacles; they ignore the fact that the abilities measured by the scholastic criteria stem not so much from natural "gifts" (which must remain hypothetical so long as the educational inequalities can be traced to other causes), but from the greater or lesser affinity between class cultural habits and the demands of the educational system or the criteria which define success within it. [Working-class children] must assimilate a whole set of knowledge and techniques which are never completely separable from social values often contrary to those of their class origin. For the children of peasants, manual workers, clerks, or small shopkeepers, the acquisition of culture is acculturation. (Bourdieu and Passeron 22)

Social and cultural conditions in the United States are not the same as in France, but the analyses of Bourdieu, Passeron, Heath, Ogbu, and others suggest interesting lines of inquiry when we look at the performance of students from different cultures and classes in U.S. schools. Performance seems not so much determined by cultural values (proudly cited by successful groups), but by class origins, socio-economic mobility, age at time of immigration, the degree of trauma experienced by immigrants or refugees, and the acceptance of student culture by the mainstream schools. Stephen Steinberg argues in *The Ethnic Myth* that class mobility precedes educational achievement in almost all immigrant groups (131–32). I really do not believe that Black, Native American, and Chicano cultures place less emphasis on the importance of education than Chinese, Jewish, Vietnamese, or Greek cultures do. We do not have over one hundred Black colleges in the United States because Blacks don't care about education. I have never been to a Native American Studies Conference or visited a rancheria or reservation that did not have newsletters, workshops, and fund-raisers in support of education. Bourdieu and Passeron's analysis suggests that educational success depends to a large extent on cultural match, and if an exact match is not possible, there must at least be respect and value of the culture children bring with them. Acculturation (assimilation) is possible for some, but it is not viable for all.

Acculturation itself poses problems. Jacquelyn Mitchell shows how cultural conflict affects the preschool child, the university undergraduate, the graduate student, and the faculty member as well. Success brings with it, for some people, alienation from the values and relationships of the home culture. "In fulfilling our academic roles, we interact increasingly more with the white power structure and significantly less with members of our ethnic community. This is not without risk or consequence; some minority scholars feel in jeopardy of losing their distinctive qualities" (38). The question Mitchell poses is, "How can blacks prepare themselves to move efficiently in mainstream society and still maintain their own culture?" (33) Jacqueline Fleming, in a cross-sectional study of Black students in Black colleges and predominantly white colleges, found Black colleges more effective despite the lack of funding because Black colleges are more "supportive" of students (194). Long before the recent media coverage of racial incidents on college campuses, Fleming noted that "all is not well with Black students in predominantly white colleges" (162). And in California, the dropout rate of "Hispanics" (a term that obscures cultural diversity much as the term "Asian" does) is greater than that of any other group except possibly Native Americans. But despite gloomy statistics, there is hope.

Theoretical Models for Multicultural Classrooms

Several theoretical models exist to help students mediate between cultures. In "Empowering Minority Students: A Framework for Intervention," James Cummins provides one:

> The central tenet of the framework is that students from "dominated" societal groups are "empowered" or "disabled" as a direct result of their interactions with educators in the schools. These interactions are mediated by the implicit or explicit role definitions that educators assume in relation to four institutional characteristics of schools. These characteristics reflect the extent to which (1) minority students' language and culture are incorporated into the school program; (2) minority community participation is encouraged as an integral component of children's education; (3) the pedagogy promotes intrinsic motivation on the part of students to use language actively in order to generate their own knowledge; and (4) professionals involved in assessment become advocates for minority students rather than legitimizing the location of the "problem" in the students. For each of these dimensions of school organization the role definitions of educators can be described in terms of a continuum, with one end promoting the empowerment of students and the other contributing to the disabling of students. (21)

Like Bourdieu, Cummins sees bicultural ambivalence as a negative factor in student performance. Students who have ambivalence about their cultural identity tend to do poorly whereas "widespread school failure does not occur in minority groups that are positively oriented towards both their own and the dominant culture, {that} do not perceive themselves as inferior to the dominant group, and {that} are not alienated from their own cultural values" (22). Cummins argues that vehement resistance to bilingual education comes in part because "the incorporation of minority languages and cultures into the school program confers status and power (jobs, for example) on the minority group" (25). But for Cummins, it is precisely this valuing of culture within the school that leads to academic success because it reverses the role of domination of students by the school.

Shirley Brice Heath's model is similar to Cummins'. The main difference is that she focuses on ethnography as a way for both teachers and students to mediate between home and school cultures. A consideration of home culture is the only way students can succeed in mainstream schools, increase scores on standardized tests, and be motivated to continue school: "Unless the boundaries between classrooms and communities can be broken, and the flow of cultural patterns between them encouraged, the schools will continue to legitimate and reproduce communities of townspeople who control and limit the potential progress of other communities who themselves remain untouched by other values and ways of life" (369). Like Cummins, Heath aims for cultural mediation. As one student stated: "Why should my 'at home' way of talking be 'wrong' and your standard version be 'right'? . . . Show me that by adding a fluency in standard dialect, you are adding something to my language and not taking something away from me. Help retain my identity and self-respect while learning to talk 'your' way" (271). Paulo Freire, on the other hand, wants those from the outside to totally transform mainstream culture, not become part of it: "This, then, is the great humanistic and historical task of the oppressed: to liberate themselves and their oppressors as well" *(Pedagogy* 28). Yet in almost all other respects, Freire's model, like Cummins' and Heath's, is grounded in a thorough knowledge of the home culture by teachers, and actively learned, genuine knowledge by the student. Each of these models has different agendas. Teachers should take from them whatever suits their teaching style, values, and classroom situations. I would simply encourage an inclusion of the study of the wide diversity within student cultures.

Teaching Strategies for Multicultural Classes

Cultural Topics

Culturally oriented topics are particularly useful in raising issues of cultural diversity, of different value systems, different ways of problem solving. Several successful bridge programs have used comparison of different cultural rituals (weddings, funerals, New Year's) as a basis for introducing students to analytic academic discourse. Loretta Petrie from Chaminade University in Hawaii has a six-week summer-school curriculum based on this. Students can use their own experience, interview relatives, and read scholarly articles. Reading these papers to peer response groups gives students additional insights into rituals in their own culture as well as making them aware of similarities and differences with other groups. I have used variations of Ken Macrorie's I-Search paper (Olson 111–22) to allow students to explore part of their cultural heritage that they are not fully aware of. One Vietnamese student, who was three years old when she came to America, did a paper on Vietnam in which she not only interviewed relatives to find out about life there but sought out books on geography and politics; she literally did not know where Vietnam was on the map and was embarrassed when other students would ask her about life there. Several students whose parents were from the Philippines did research that was stimulated by the desire to further understand family customs and to explain to themselves how the way they thought of themselves as "American" had a unique quality to it. One student wrote:

For over eighteen years I have been living in the United States. Since birth I have been and still am a citizen of this country. I consider myself a somewhat typical American who grew up with just about every American thing you can think of; yet, at home I am constantly reminded of my Filipino background. Even at school I was reminded of my Filipino culture. At my previous school, the two other Filipinos in my class and I tried to get our friends to learn a little about our culture.

But classmates were not always open to cultural diversity, and their rejection raised the central question of just how much you have to give up of your culture to succeed in the mainstream society:

> During the Philippine presidential election, there were comments at my school that we Filipinos were against fair democracy and were as corrupt as our ex-President Marcos. Also it was said that Filipinos are excessively violent barbaric savages. This is partly due to our history of fighting among ourselves, mostly one group that speaks one dialect against another group of a different language within the islands. Also maybe we are thought savages because of the food we eat such as "chocolate meat" and "balut," which is sort of a salted egg, some of which may contain a partially developed chicken. So, to be accepted into society you must give up your old culture.

"You must give up your old culture" is misleading. The student had to be careful about sharing home culture with peers, but he isn't giving up his culture; he is gaining a greater understanding of it. His essay ended with:

> I now have a better understanding of why I was doing a lot of those things I didn't understand. For example, whenever we visited some family friends, I had to bow and touch the older person's hand to my forehead. My mother didn't really explain why I had to do this, except it was a sign of respect. Also my mother says my brother should, as a sign of respect, call me "manong" even though he is only two years younger than I. At first I thought all this was strange, but after doing research I found out that this practice goes back a long way, and it is a very important part of my Filipino culture.

Richard Rodriguez's widely anthologized "Aria" (from *Hunger of Memory*) allows students to analyze his assertion that loss of language and culture is essential to attain a "public voice." Although the student above seems to agree in part with Rodriguez, most students find Rodriguez's assertions to be a betrayal of family and culture:

> I understand Rodriguez's assertion that if he learned English, he would lose his family closeness, but I think that he let paranoia overcome his senses. I feel that the lack of conversation could have been avoided if Rodriguez had attempted to speak to his parents instead of not saying anything just because they didn't. I am sure that one has to practice something in order to be good at it and it was helpful when his parents spoke in English to them while carrying on small conversation. To me, this would have brought the family closer because they would be helping each other trying to learn and grow to function in society. Instead of feeling left out at home and in his society, Rodriguez could've been included in both.

I have used this topic or variations on it for a half dozen years or so, and most of my freshmen (roughly 85% of them) believe they do not have to give up cultural and home values to succeed in the university. I find quite different attitudes among these students when they become juniors and seniors. More and more students graduate who feel that they have lost more than they gained. Raising this issue early provides students more choices. In some cases it may mean deciding to play down what seem to be unacceptable parts of one's culture (no balut at the potluck); in other cases it may lead to the assertion of positive values of the home culture such as family cohesiveness and respect for parents and older siblings. Courageous students will bring the balut to the potluck anyway and let mainstream students figure it out. I often suspect that some of the students who drop out of the university do so because they feel too much is being given up and not enough is being received. Dropping out may be a form of protecting cultural identity.

Cultural topics are equally important, if not more so, for students from the mainstream culture. Many mainstream students on predominantly white campuses feel inundated by Third World students. Their sense of cultural shock can be as profound as that of the ESL basic writer. One student began a quarter-long comparison/contrast essay on the immigration experiences of his Italian grandparents with the experiences of Mexicans and Vietnamese in California. As the quarter went on, the paper shifted focus as the student became aware that California was quickly becoming non-white. It scared him. The essay was eventually titled "Shutting the Doors?" and ended with:

> I have had some bad experiences with foreigners. On a lonely night in Davis, three other friends and I decided to go to a Vietnamese dance. When we got there, I couldn't believe how we were treated. Their snobbishness and arrogance filled the air. I was upset. But that was only one incident and possibly I am over reacting. I often reflect on my high school teacher's farewell address. He called for our acceptance of the cultural and religious background of each other. But after long days thinking, I, like many others, am unable to answer. My only hope is that someone has a solution.

The student had grown up in Richmond, California, a culturally diverse East Bay community, and was friendly with students from many cultures (it was his idea to go to the dance). The very recognition on the part of the student of what it feels like to be surrounded by difference at the dance is a beginning step for him to understand what it means to try to be who he is in the midst of another culture. I see this student quite often. He is not racist. Or if he is, he at least has the courage to begin asking questions. The solution for which the student yearned was not immediately forthcoming: his yearning for one is worth writing about.

Language Topics

It is not unusual for ESL errors to persist in the writing or the pronunciation of highly educated people (doctors, lawyers, engineers, professors) because, consciously or unconsciously, those speech patterns are part of the person's identity and culture. The same can be true of basic writers. Language-oriented topics are one way to allow students to explore this kind of writing block. Assignments that require students to analyze their attitudes toward writing, their writing processes, and the role that writing plays in their lives can make these conflicts explicit. For example, one student wrote:

> Moreover, being a Chinese, I find myself in a cultural conflict. I don't want to be a cultural betrayer. In fact, I want to conserve my culture and tradition. I would be enjoyable if I wrote my mother language. For example I like to write letter in Chinese to my friends because I can find warmth in the letter. The lack of interest

in writing and the cultural conflict has somehow blocked my road of learning English.

Overcoming this block may, however, cause problems in the home community. In response to Rodriguez, one student wrote:

> I can relate when Rodriguez say that his family closeness was broken. Even though I speak the language that is understood and is comfortable at home, when I speak proper English around my friends at home, they accuse me of trying to be something I'm not. But what they don't realize is that I have to talk proper in order to make it in the real world.

Jacquelyn Mitchell writes of returning to her community after college:

> My professional attire identified me in this community as a "middle-class," "siddity," "uppity," "insensitive" school teacher who had made her way out of the ghetto, who had returned to "help and save," and who would leave before dark to return to the suburbs. My speech set me up as a prime candidate for suspicion and distrust. Speaking standard English added to the badges that my role had already pinned on me. (31)

In some way problems like this affect us all. In the small town that I grew up in, simply going to college was enough to alienate you from your peers. Although my parents encouraged me to get an education, they and their peers saw college as producing primarily big egos — people who thought they knew everything. No easy choices here. It took my uncle, who made the mistake of becoming a Franciscan priest, forty years to be accepted back into the family by my mother.

Another way to help students with cultural transitions is to make the home language the subject of study along with the different kinds of academic discourse they will be required to learn. Suzy Groden, Eleanor Kutz, and Vivian Zamel from the University of Massachusetts have developed an extensive curriculum in which students become ethnographers and analyze their language patterns at home, at school, and in different social situations, using techniques developed by Shirley Brice Heath. This approach takes time (several quarters of intensive reading and writing), but such a curriculum has great potential for helping students acquire academic discourse while retaining pride and a sense of power in the discourse they bring with them.

Peer Response Groups

Peer response groups encourage active learning and help students link home and university cultures. The Puente Project, in affiliation with the Bay Area Writing Project, combines aggressive counseling, community mentors, and English courses that emphasize active peer response groups. The Puente Project has turned what used to be a 50–60% first-year dropout rate into a 70–80% retention rate in fifteen California community colleges. All of the students are academically high risk (meaning they graduated from high school with a D average), they are Chicanos or Latinos, and all have a past history of avoidance of English classes and very low self-confidence when it comes to writing. Writing response groups give the students a sense of belonging on campus. As students make the transition from home to school, the groups become, in the students' own words, "una familia":

Now after two quarters of Puente, it's totally different. My writing ability has changed to about 110%. I might not be the best speller in the world, but I can think of different subjects faster and crank out papers like never before . . . having Latinos in a class by themselves is like a sun to a rose. This is the only class where I know the names of every student and with their help I decide what to write. (*Puente* 20)

Joan Wauters illustrates how structured non-confrontational editing can make peer response more than a support group. Students work in pairs on student essays with specific training and instructions on what to look for, but the author of the essay is not present. The author can later clarify any point she wishes with the response group, but Wauters finds that the non-confrontational approach allows students to be more frank about a paper's strengths and weaknesses and that it is "especially valuable for instructors who work with students from cultures where direct verbal criticism implies 'loss of face'" (159). Wauters developed these techniques with Native American students, but they apply equally well to other cultures.

Response groups do not have to be homogeneous. Any small group encourages participation by students who may not feel comfortable speaking up in class for whatever reason. They provide a supportive environment for exploring culturally sensitive issues that students might hesitate to bring up in class or discuss with the teacher. The following paragraph was read by a Black student to a group consisting of a Filipino, a Chinese, and two Chicano students:

I am black, tall, big, yet shy and handsome. "I won't hurt you!" Get to know who I am first before you judge me. Don't be scared to speak; I won't bite you. My size intimidates most people I meet. I walk down my dormitory hallway and I can feel the tension between me and the person who's headed in my direction. A quick "Hi!" and my response is "Hello, how are you doing?" in a nice friendly way. It seems that most of the guys and girls are unsure if they should speak to me. I walk through the campus and eyes are fixed on me like an eagle watching its prey. A quick nod sometimes or a half grin. Do I look like the devil? No, I don't. Maybe if I shrink in size and lightened in color they wouldn't be intimidated. Hey, I'm a Wild and Crazy Guy too!

This small group discussion of what it felt like to be an outsider spilled over into the class as a whole, and students that normally would not have participated in class discussion found themselves involved in a debate about dorm life at Davis. I know that peer response groups have limitations, need structure, and can be abused by students and teachers alike. But I have never heard complaints from teachers using peer groups about how difficult it is to get ESL students to participate. In some cases the problem is to shut them up.

Class Newsletters

Class newsletters encourage students to write for an audience different from the teacher, and they generate knowledge about multicultural experiences. I use brief 20-minute in-class writing assignments on differences between the university and home, or how high school is different from the university, or ways in which the university is or is not sensitive to cultural differences on campus. Sometimes I simply have students finish the statement, "The university is like. . . ." These short paragraphs serve as introductions to issues of cultural transition, and when published, generate class discussions and give ideas for students who are ready to pursue the topic in more detail. Newsletters can be done in a variety of formats from ditto masters to desktop publishing. Students who feel comfortable discussing ethnic or cultural tensions establish a forum for those students whose initial response would be one of denial. For example, the story of a Guamanian and a Black student who thought they were not invited to a white fraternity party led to an extended class discussion of whether this kind of experience was typical and whether they had not been invited for ethnic reasons. The next time I had students write, a Chicana student articulated her awakening sense of cultural conflict between the university and her family:

> I was so upset about leaving home and coming to Davis. I was leaving all my friends, my boyfriend, and my family just to come to this dumb school. I was angry because I wanted to be like all my other friends and just have small goals. I was resentful that I had to go away just to accomplish something good for me. I felt left out and angry because it seemed that my family really wanted me to go away and I thought it was because they did not love me. I was not studying like I should because I wanted to punish them. My anger grew when I realized I was a minority at Davis. My whole town is Mexican and I never thought of prejudice until I came to Davis.

Family is central to Chicano/Latino/Mexican-American students. The pull toward home can create ambivalence for students about their school commitments. In this case, the family was aware of this pull, and encouraged the student to give college the priority. The daughter interpreted this as a loss of love. The student's ambivalence about home and school put her on probation for the first two quarters at Davis. She is now a junior, doing well as a pre-med student, and her chances for a career in medicine look good. I don't think just writing about these issues made the difference. The class discussion generated by her article helped her realize that her situation was shared by others who were experiencing the same thing but had not quite articulated it. She was not alone.

Bringing Campus Events into the Classroom

I recently assigned a paper topic for a quarter-long essay that made reading of the campus newspapers mandatory. I was surprised to find that many students did not read the campus newspapers on a daily basis and in many cases were quite unaware of campus issues that directly concerned them, for example, the withdrawal of funding from the Third World Forum (a campus newspaper that deals with Third World issues), compulsory English examinations for international graduate teaching assistants in science and math classes, and increasing incidents of hostility toward Asians (as reflected in bathroom graffiti, "Lower the curve: kill a chink"). Admission policies at UC Berkeley, particularly as reported in the press, have pitted Blacks and Chicanos against Asians, and quite often students find themselves in dorm discussions without having enough specific knowledge to respond. The more articulate students can be about these issues, the greater the chance the students will feel integrated in the university.

Assignments can make mandatory or strongly encourage students to attend campus events where cultural issues will be discussed within the context of campus life — issues such as the self-images of women of color or how Vietnamese students feel they are perceived on campus. A panel entitled "Model Minority Tells the Truth" called for Vietnamese students to become more involved in campus life partly in order to overcome misperceptions of some students:

Vietnamese students feel inferior to Americans because Americans do not understand why we are here. We are refugees, not illegal immigrants. There are a lot of unspoken differences between Vietnamese and Americans because the memory of the Vietnam war is so fresh, and it is difficult for Americans to be comfortable with us because we are the conflict. Vietnamese students also suffer an identity crisis because the Vietnamese community has not established itself yet in America as other Asian groups have.

Anecdotes

Anecdotes about oneself and former class experiences are another way to generate discussion and raise issues of cultural transition and identity. The teacher's own curiosity and experience of cultural diversity will often give students ideas for other topics. Cultural identity does not depend on a Spanish surname alone nor does it reside in skin color. Richard Rodriguez, for example, does not consider himself a Chicano and was insulted when he was so identified at Berkeley during the sixties. I mentioned this in class and described the experiences of several former students whose parents were from different cultures (so-called "rainbow children"). Several weeks later, a student whose mother was Mexican and whose father was Anglo wrote:

> Someone once told me that I'd have to fight everyday to prove to everyone that I wasn't "another stupid Mexican." He was convinced that the whole American population was watching his every move, just waiting for him to slip and make a mistake. Having it emphasized that he is a minority certainly won't help his attitude any. It will just remind him that he is different. All of my life I never considered myself a minority. I didn't speak Spanish, I didn't follow Mexican customs, and I hung around with "American" kids. It is real hard for me to understand why minorities get so much special treatment.

This student found the existence of different student cultural groups on campus to be disturbing:

> When I came to Davis, instead of seeing a melting pot like the one I expected, I saw distinct cultural groups. When I first heard about CHE (Chicanos in Health Education) I was furious. I could not see any need for a special club just for Hispanic students interested in health careers. It seemed that the students in CHE were segregating themselves from the real world. They should actually be interacting with everyone else proving that they weren't different.

After interviewing members of CHE and VSA (Vietnamese Student Association), this student was able to see how some people benefited from these clubs:

> I didn't think I could find some positive aspects about these clubs, bur I found some. Some clubs help immigrants assimilate into the Western culture. They provide the member with a sense of pride about who they are and they strengthen cultural bonds. If students attend classes and become discouraged by lower grades than they expected, they can go to a CHE meeting and see "one of their own" explain how they made it through the bad times and how they came back to beat the odds. I asked Trinh why she joined the VSA. She said she joined to learn more about her culture and to improve her language. But others join to help themselves assimilate into Western culture. I was wondering what was so important about her culture that Trinh couldn't retain unless she went to these meetings. She said, "I can't explain it." But there is an atmosphere there that she can't get anywhere else. And if this gives her a good feeling, then more power to her.

This student still has reservations about cultural differences on campus (primarily because she does not want to see herself as "different"), but the movement from "I was furious about CHE" to "more power to her" is a step toward recognizing her own cultural diversity. Cultural identity is not always simple. I have seen second-generation Vietnamese, Indian, Korean, and Chinese students who saw themselves primarily as "American" (no hyphens), and in some cases as white. One Chinese student, from a Black neighborhood in Oakland, grew up wanting to be Black. It was the cool thing to be.

For some students, examining home culture and the culture of the university can cause anxiety. Teenagers often do not relish the idea of being "different." They have enough difficulty keeping their grades up, forming peer relationships, adjusting to being in a new environment. My sixteen-year-old stepson argues constantly that he is just like his peers. He certainly tries to be. But all you have to do is walk on the school grounds, look around a few minutes, and it is impossible to miss the six-foot-tall, dark-skinned, handsome boy bobbing up and down amongst a sea of white faces: definitely Indian (other Indians can identify him on sight as Telegu). It is becoming increasingly difficult on predominantly white campuses for students to deny differences in culture. What is important to learn is that while differences between home and school can lead to conflict, differences in themselves do not inherently cause conflict. The home culture can be a source of strength which can enable the student to negotiate with the mainstream culture. One of the major factors of success of students coming from cultures least valued by society is the ability of the family to help the student maintain a positive self-image that allows her to withstand rejection and insensitivity of mainstream peers. Occasionally, I have discovered some parents who did not want their children in school at all and did everything in their power to deter the education of their children. But most often, it is not the home culture that causes problems, but a fear on the part of students that elements of that culture will not be accepted in the university environment.

Implications for Teacher Training and Classroom Research

These topics and assignments not only help students mediate between school and home cultures, they provide windows for the teacher into the diversity within each of the cultures that students bring with them. They can serve as a base for ongoing teacher research into the ways in which home and university cultures interact. There simply is no training program for teachers, and can be no definitive research study that will ever account for the realities our students bring with them. Change is constant. Each generation is different. Given the lack of homogeneity in our classes, given the incredible diversity of cultures we are being exposed to, who better to learn from than our students? The culture and language topics I have described here comprise roughly 30–50% of the assignments I give in a ten-week course that meets for two hours twice a week. Some quarters I find myself using more cultural topics than others; it depends on the students. The course is English A, a four-unit course (two units counting toward graduation) with English Department administered, holistically-graded diagnostic, midterm, and final exams. The point is that if one can begin to integrate cultures under these constraints, one should be able to do it anywhere.

The cultural transitions we ask of our students are by no means easy. Cultural transition is ultimately defined by the student, whether she decides to assimilate and leave her culture behind, or attempts to integrate her world view with the academic world view. As composition teachers we are offered a unique opportunity to make these transitions easier for students, and at the same time increase our skills in moving between cultures. Clifford Geertz puts it this way: "The primary question, for any cultural institution anywhere, now that nobody is leaving anybody else alone and isn't ever again going to, is not whether everything is going to come seamlessly together or whether, contrariwise, we are all going to exist sequestered in our separate prejudices. It is whether human beings are going to be able, in Java or Connecticut, through law, anthropology, or anything else, to imagine principled lives they can practicably lead" (234). But we may find, and this has been my experience, that in helping students make cultural transitions, we learn from them how to make transitions ourselves.

Works Cited

Bartholomae, David. "Inventing the University." *When a Writer Can't Write*. Ed. Mike Rose. New York: Guilford, 1985. 134–65.

Bizzell, Patricia. "What Happens When Basic Writers Come to College?" *College Composition and Communication* 37 (October 1986): 294–301.

Bourdieu, Pierre, and Jean-Claude Passeron. *The Inheritors: French Students and Their Relation to Culture*. Chicago: U of Chicago P, 1979.

Cummins, James. "Empowering Minority Students: A Framework for Intervention." *Harvard Educational Review* 56 (February 1986): 18–36.

Fleming, Jacqueline. *Blacks in College; A Comparative Study of Students' Success in Black and in White Institutions*. San Francisco: Jossey-Bass, 1985.

Freire, Paulo. *Pedagogy of the Oppressed*. New York: Continuum, 1982.

———. *The Politics of Education: Culture, Power, and Liberation*. South Hadley, MA: Bergin & Garvey, 1985.

Geertz, Clifford. *Local Knowledge*. New York: Basic, 1983.

Groden, Suzy, Eleanor Kutz, and Vivian Zamel. "Students as Ethnographers: Investigating Language Use as a Way to Learn Language." *The Writing Instructor* 6 (Spring–Summer 1987): 132–40.

Heath, Shirley Brice. *Ways with Words: Language, Life, and Work in Communities and Classrooms*. New York: Cambridge UP, 1983.

Holzman, Michael. "The Social Context of Literacy Education." *College English* 48 (January 1986): 27–33.

Mitchell, Jacquelyn. "Reflections of a Black Social Scientist: Some Struggles, Some Doubts, Some Hopes." *Harvard Educational Review* 52 (February 1982): 27–44.

Ogbu, John. *The Next Generation: An Ethnography of Education in an Urban Neighborhood*. New York: Academic, 1974.

Olson, Carol Booth, ed. *Practical Ideas for Teaching Writing as a Process*. Sacramento: California State Department of Education, 1986.

Petrie, Loretta. "Pulling Together the Multicultural Composition Class." CCCC Convention. New Orleans, March 1986.

Philips, Susan Urmston. *The Invisible Culture: Communication in the Classroom and Community on the Warm Springs Indian Reservation*. New York: Longman, 1983.

The Puente Project: Building Bridges. Berkeley: Bay Area Writing Project, 1985.

Rodriguez, Richard. *Hunger of Memory*. Boston: Bantam, 1982.

Steinberg, Stephen. *The Ethnic Myth: Race, Ethnicity, and Class in America*. New York: Atheneum, 1981.

Wauters, Joan. "Non-Confrontational Critiquing Pairs: An Alternative to Verbal Peer Response Groups." *The Writing Instructor* 7 (Spring/Summer 1988): 156–66.

HOW TO TAME A WILD TONGUE

Gloria Anzaldúa

[From Borderlands/La Frontera: The New Mestiza *by Gloria Anzaldúa. San Francisco: Aunt Lute, 1987. 53–64.]*

Chicana writer Gloria Anzaldúa grew up in southwest Texas, the border-land between the United States and Mexico. In addition to Borderlands/La Frontera, *Anzaldúa coedited* This Bridge Called My Back: Writings by Radi-cal Women of Color *(1983) and edited* Haciendo Caras: Making Face/Mak-ing Soul *(1990).*

ESL problems in the composition class may appear most often as difficul-ties with conventions and grammatical rules, but those problems are mani-festations of larger, more fundamental challenges facing ESL writers, chal-lenges involving their home cultures, and their individual identities. In this chapter from Borderlands/La Frontera, *Anzaldúa tells of the complexities of growing up a Chicana in the "borderland" between the United States and Mexico. In this piece, as in other selections from* Borderlands, *Anzaldúa's prose shifts in language and style in a way that can be confusing. But these shifts have the valuable effect of helping readers understand what it is like to live on linguistic and cultural borderlands. Anzaldúa reminds us of the necessity to respect all cultures.*

"We're going to have to control your tongue," the dentist says, pulling out all the metal from my mouth. Silver bits plop and tinkle into the basin. My mouth is a motherlode.

The dentist is cleaning out my roots. I get a whiff of the stench when I gasp. "I can't cap that tooth yet, you're still draining," he says.

"We're going to have to do something about your tongue," I hear the anger rising in his voice. My tongue keeps pushing out the wads of cotton, pushing back the drills, the long thin needles. "I've never seen anything as strong or as stubborn," he says. And I think, how do you tame a wild tongue, train it to be quiet, how do you bridle and saddle it? How do you make it lie down?

> Who is to say that robbing a people of
> its language is less violent than war?
> — Ray Gwyn Smith[1]

I remember being caught speaking Spanish at recess — that was good for three licks on the knuckles with a sharp ruler. I remember being sent to the corner of the classroom for "talking back" to the Anglo teacher when all I was trying to do was tell her how to pronounce my name. "If you want to be American, speak 'American.' If you don't like it, go back to Mexico where you belong."

"I want you to speak English. *Pa' hallar buen trabajo tienes que saber hablar el inglés bien. Qué vale toda tu educación si todavía hablas inglés con un* 'accent,"' my mother would say, mortified that I spoke English like a Mexican. At Pan American University, I and all Chicano students were required to take two speech classes. Their purpose: to get rid of our accents.

Attacks on one's form of expression with the intent to censor are a violation of the First Amendment. *El Anglo con cara de inocente nos arrancó la lengua.* Wild tongues can't be tamed, they can only be cut out.

Overcoming the Tradition of Silence

> *Ahogadas, escupimos el oscuro.*
> *Peleando con nuestra propia sombra*
> *el silencio nos sepulta.*

En boca cerrada no entran moscas. "Flies don't enter a closed mouth" is a saying I kept hearing when I was a child. *Ser habladora* was to be a gossip and a liar, to talk too much. *Muchachitas bien criadas,* well-bred girls don't answer back. *Es una falta de respeto* to talk back to one's mother or father. I remember one of the sins I'd recite to the priest in the confession box the few times I went to confession: talking back to my mother, *hablar pa' 'tras, repelar. Hociona, repelona, chismosa,* having a big mouth, questioning, carrying tales are all signs of being *mal criada.* In my culture they are all words that are derogatory if applied to women — I've never heard them applied to men.

The first time I heard two women, a Puerto Rican and a Cuban, say the word "*nosotras,*" I was shocked. I had not known the word existed. Chicanas use *nosotros* whether we're male or female. We are robbed of our female being by the masculine plural. Language is a male discourse.

> And our tongues have become
> dry   the wilderness has
> dried out our tongues   and
> we have forgotten speech.
>   — IRENA KLEPFISZ[2]

Even our own people, other Spanish speakers *nos quieren poner candados en la boca.* They would hold us back with their bag of *reglas de academia.*

Oyé como ladra: el lenguaje de la frontera

> *Quien tiene boca se equivoca.*
> — Mexican saying

"*Pocho,* cultural traitor, you're speaking the oppressor's language by speaking English, you're ruining the Spanish language," I have been accused by various Latinos and Latinas. Chicano Spanish is considered by the purist and by most Latinos deficient, a mutilation of Spanish.

But Chicano Spanish is a border tongue which developed naturally. Change, *evolución, enriquecimiento de palabras nuevas por invención o adopción* have created variants of Chicano Spanish, *un nuevo lenguaje. Un lenguaje que corresponde a un modo de vivir.* Chicano Spanish is not incorrect, it is a living language.

For a people who are neither Spanish nor live in a country in which Spanish is the first language; for a people who live in a country in which English is the reigning tongue but who are not Anglo; for a people who cannot entirely identify with either standard (formal, Castilian) Spanish nor standard English, what recourse is left to them but to create their own language? A language which they can connect their identity to, one capable of communicating the realities and values true to themselves — a language with terms that are neither *español ni inglés,* but both. We speak a patois, a forked tongue, a variation of two languages.

Chicano Spanish sprang out of the Chicanos' need to identify ourselves as a distinct people. We needed a language with which we could communicate with ourselves, a secret language. For some of us, language is a homeland closer than the Southwest — for many Chicanos today live in the Midwest and the East. And because we are a complex, heterogeneous people, we speak many languages. Some of the languages we speak are

1. Standard English
2. Working class and slang English
3. Standard Spanish
4. Standard Mexican Spanish
5. North Mexican Spanish dialect
6. Chicano Spanish (Texas, New Mexico, Arizona, and California have regional variations)
7. Tex-Mex
8. *Pachuco* (called *caló*)

My "home" tongues are the languages I speak with my sister and brothers, with my friends. They are the last five listed, with 6 and 7 being closest to my heart. From school, the media, and job situations, I've picked up standard and working class English. From Mamagrande Locha and from reading Spanish and Mexican literature, I've picked up Standard Spanish and Standard Mexican Spanish. From *los recién llegados,* Mexican immigrants, and *braceros,* I learned the North Mexican dialect. With Mexicans I'll try to speak either Standard Mexican Spanish or the North Mexican dialect. From my parents and Chicanos living in the Valley, I picked up Chicano Texas Spanish, and I speak it with my mom, younger brother (who married a Mexican and who rarely mixes Spanish with English), aunts, and older relatives.

With Chicanas from *Nuevo México* or *Arizona* I will speak Chicano Spanish a little, but often they don't understand what I'm saying. With most California Chicanas I speak entirely in English (unless I forget). When I first moved to San Francisco, I'd rattle off something in Spanish, unintentionally embarrassing them. Often it is only with another Chicana *tejano* that I can talk freely.

Words distorted by English are known as anglicisms or *pochismos.* The *pocho* is an anglicized Mexican or American of Mexican origin who speaks Spanish with an accent characteristic of North Americans and who distorts and reconstructs the language according to the influence of English.[3] Tex-Mex, or Spanglish, comes most naturally to me. I may switch back and forth from English to Spanish in the same sentence or in the same word. With my sister and my brother Nune and with Chicano *tejano* contemporaries I speak in Tex-Mex.

From kids and people my own age I picked up *Pachuco*. *Pachuco* (the language of the zoot suiters) is a language of rebellion, both against Standard Spanish and Standard English. It is a secret language. Adults of the culture and outsiders cannot understand it. It is made up of slang words from both English and Spanish. *Ruca* means girl or woman, *vato* means guy or dude, *chale* means no, *simón* means yes, *churro* is sure, talk is *periquiar*, *pigionear* means petting, *que gacho* means how nerdy, *ponte águila* means watch out, death is called *la pelona*. Through lack of practice and not having others who can speak it, I've lost most of the *Pachuco* tongue.

Chicano Spanish

Chicanos, after 250 years of Spanish/Anglo colonization, have developed significant differences in the Spanish we speak. We collapse two adjacent vowels into a single syllable and sometimes shift the stress in certain words such as *maíz/maiz, cohete/cuete*. We leave out certain consonants when they appear between vowels: *lado/lao, mojado/mojao*. Chicanos from South Texas pronounce *f* as *j* as in *jue* (*fue*). Chicanos use "archaisms," words that are no longer in the Spanish language, words that have been evolved out. We say *semos, truje, haiga, ansina*, and *naiden*. We retain the "archaic" *j*, as in *jalar*, that derives from an earlier *h* (the French *halar* or the Germanic *halon* which was lost to standard Spanish in the sixteenth century), but which is still found in several regional dialects such as the one spoken in South Texas. (Due to geography, Chicanos from the Valley of South Texas were cut off linguistically from other Spanish speakers. We tend to use words that the Spaniards brought over from Medieval Spain. The majority of the Spanish colonizers in Mexico and the Southwest came from Extremadura — Hernán Cortés was one of them — and Andalucía. Andalucians pronounce *ll* like a *y*, and their *d*'s tend to be absorbed by adjacent vowels: *tirado* becomes *tirao*. They brought *el lenguaje popular, dialectos y regionalismos*.) [4]

Chicanos and other Spanish speakers also shift *ll* to *y* and *z* to *s*. [5] We leave out initial syllables, saying *tar* for *estar, toy* for *estoy, hora* for *ahora* (*cubanos* and *puertorriqueños* also leave out initial letters of some words). We also leave out the final syllable such as *pa* for *para*. The intervocalic *y*, the *ll* as in *tortilla, ella, botella*, gets replaced by *tortia* or *tortiya, ea, botea*. We add an additional syllable at the beginning of certain words: *atocar* for *tocar, agastar* for *gastar*. Sometimes we'll say *lavaste las vacijas*, other times *lavates* (substituting the *ates* verb endings for the *aste*).

We used anglicisms, words borrowed from English: *bola* from ball, *carpeta* from carpet, *máchina de lavar* (instead of *lavadora*) from washing machine. Tex-Mex argot, created by adding a Spanish sound at the beginning or end of an English word such as *cookiar* for cook, *watchar* for watch, *parkiar* for park, and *rapiar* for rape, is the result of the pressures on Spanish speakers to adapt to English.

We don't use the word *vosotros/as* or its accompanying verb form. We don't say *claro* (to mean yes), *imagínate*, or *me emociona*, unless we picked up Spanish from Latinas, out of a book, or in a classroom. Other Spanish-speaking groups are going through the same, or similar, development in their Spanish.

Linguistic Terrorism

Deslenguadas. Somos los del español deficiente. We are your linguistic nightmare, your linguistic aberration, your linguistic *mestisaje,* the subject of your *burla.* Because we speak with tongues of fire we are culturally crucified. Racially, culturally, and linguistically *somos huérfanos* — we speak an orphan tongue.

Chicanas who grew up speaking Chicano Spanish have internalized the belief that we speak poor Spanish. It is illegitimate, a bastard language. And because we internalize how our language has been used against us by the dominant culture, we use our language differences against each other.

Chicana feminists often skirt around each other with suspicion and hesitation. For the longest time I couldn't figure it out. Then it dawned on me. To be close to another Chicana is like looking into the mirror. We are afraid of what we'll see there. *Pena.* Shame. Low estimation of self. In childhood we are told that our language is wrong. Repeated attacks on our native tongue diminish our sense of self. The attacks continue throughout our lives.

Chicanas feel uncomfortable talking in Spanish to Latinas, afraid of their censure. Their language was not outlawed in their countries. They had a whole lifetime of being immersed in their native tongue; generations, centuries in which Spanish was a first language, taught in school, heard on radio and TV, and read in the newspaper.

If a person, Chicana or Latina, has a low estimation of my native tongue, she also has a low estimation of me. Often with *mexicanas y latinas* we'll speak English as a neutral language. Even among Chicanas we tend to speak English at parties or conferences. Yet, at the same time, we're afraid the other will think we're *agringadas* because we don't speak Chicano Spanish. We oppress each other trying to out-Chicano each other, vying to be the "real" Chicanas, to speak like Chicanos. There is no one Chicano language just as there is no one Chicano experience. A monolingual Chicana whose first language is English or Spanish is just as much a Chicana as one who speaks several variants of Spanish. A Chicana from Michigan or Chicago or Detroit is just as much a Chicana as one from the Southwest. Chicano Spanish is as diverse linguistically as it is regionally.

By the end of this century, Spanish speakers will comprise the biggest minority group in the United States, a country where students in high schools and colleges are encouraged to take French classes because French is considered more "cultured." But for a language to remain alive it must be used.[6] By the end of this century English, and not Spanish, will be the mother tongue of most Chicanos and Latinos.

So, if you want to really hurt me, talk badly about my language. Ethnic identity is twin skin to linguistic identity — I am my language. Until I can take pride in my language, I cannot take pride in myself. Until I can accept as legitimate Chicano Texas Spanish, Tex-Mex, and all the other languages I speak, I cannot accept the legitimacy of myself. Until I am free to write bilingually and to switch codes without having always to translate, while I still have to speak English or Spanish when I would rather speak Spanglish, and as long as I have to accommodate the English speakers rather than having them accommodate me, my tongue will be illegitimate.

I will no longer be made to feel ashamed of existing. I will have my voice: Indian, Spanish, white. I will have my serpent's tongue — my woman's voice, my sexual voice, my poet's voice. I will overcome the tradition of silence.

> My fingers
> move sly against your palm
> Like women everywhere, we speak in code. . . .
> — MELANIE KAYE/KANTROWITZ[7]

"Vistas," corridos, y comida: My Native Tongue

In the 1960s, I read my first Chicano novel. It was *City of Night* by John Rechy, a gay Texan, son of a Scottish father and a Mexican mother. For days I walked around in stunned amazement that a Chicano could write and could get published. When I read *I Am Joaquín*[8] I was surprised to see a bilingual book by a Chicano in print. When I saw poetry written in Tex-Mex for the first time, a feeling of pure joy flashed through me. I felt like we really existed as a people. In 1971, when I started teaching High School English to Chicano students, I tried to supplement the required texts with works by Chicanos, only to be reprimanded and forbidden to do so by the principal. He claimed that I was supposed to teach "American" and English literature. At the risk of being fired, I swore my students to secrecy and slipped in Chicano short stories, poems, a play. In graduate school, while working toward a Ph.D., I had to "argue" with one adviser after the other, semester after semester, before I was allowed to make Chicano literature an area of focus.

Even before I read books by Chicanos or Mexicans, it was the Mexican movies I saw at the drive-in — the Thursday night special of $1.00 a carload — that gave me a sense of belonging. *"Vámonos a las vistas,"* my mother would call out and we'd all — grandmother, brothers, sister, and cousins — squeeze into the car. We'd wolf down cheese and bologna white bread sandwiches while watching Pedro Infante in melodramatic tearjerkers like *Nosotros los pobres*, the first "real" Mexican movie (that was not an imitation of European movies). I remember seeing *Cuando los hijos se van* and surmising that all Mexican movies played up the love a mother has for her children and what ungrateful sons and daughters suffer when they are not devoted to their mothers. I remember the singing-type "westerns" of Jorge Negrete and Miquel Aceves Mejía. When watching Mexican movies, I felt a sense of homecoming as well as alienation. People who were to amount to something didn't go to Mexican movies, or *bailes*, or tune their radios to *bolero, rancherita,* and *corrido* music.

The whole time I was growing up, there was *norteño* music sometimes called North Mexican border music, or Tex-Mex music, or Chicano music, or *cantina* (bar) music. I grew up listening to *conjuntos*, three- or four-piece bands made up of folk musicians playing guitar, *bajo sexto*, drums, and button accordion, which Chicanos had borrowed from the German immigrants who had come to Central Texas and Mexico to farm and build breweries. In the Rio Grande Valley, Steve Jordan and Little Joe Hernández were popular, and Flaco Jiménez was the accordion king. The rhythms of Tex-Mex music are those of the polka, also adapted from the Germans, who in turn had borrowed the polka from the Czechs and Bohemians.

I remember the hot, sultry evenings when *corridos* — songs of love and death on the Texas-Mexican borderlands — reverberated out of cheap amplifiers from the local *cantinas* and wafted in through my bedroom window.

Corridos first became widely used along the South Texas/Mexican border during the early conflict between Chicanos and Anglos. The *corridos* are usually about Mexican heroes who do valiant deeds against the Anglo oppressors. Pancho Villa's song, "*La cucaracha,*" is the most famous one. *Corridos* of John F. Kennedy and his death are still very popular in the Valley. Older Chicanos remember Lydia Mendoza, one of the great border *corrido* singers who was called *la Gloria de Tejas.* Her "*El tango negro,*" sung during the Great Depression, made her a singer of the people. The ever-present *corridos* narrated one hundred years of border history, bringing news of events as well as entertaining. These folk musicians and folk songs are our chief cultural mythmakers, and they made our hard lives seem bearable.

I grew up feeling ambivalent about our music. Country-western and rock-and-roll had more status. In the fifties and sixties, for the slightly educated and *agringado* Chicanos, there existed a sense of shame at being caught listening to our music. Yet I couldn't stop my feet from thumping to the music, could not stop humming the words, nor hide from myself the exhilaration I felt when I heard it.

There are more subtle ways that we internalize identification, especially in the forms of images and emotions. For me food and certain smells are tied to my identity, to my homeland. Woodsmoke curling up to an immense blue sky; woodsmoke perfuming my grandmother's clothes, her skin. The stench of cow manure and the yellow patches on the ground; the crack of a .22 rifle and the reek of cordite. Homemade white cheese sizzling in a pan, melting inside a folded *tortilla.* My sister Hilda's hot, spicy *menudo, chile colorado* making it deep red, pieces of *panza* and hominy floating on top. My brother Carito barbequing *fajitas* in the backyard. Even now and 3,000 miles away, I can see my mother spicing the ground beef, pork, and venison with *chile.* My mouth salivates at the thought of the hot steaming *tamales* I would be eating if I were home.

Si le preguntas a mi mamá, "¿Qué eres?"

> Identity is the essential core of who
> we are as individuals, the conscious
> experience of the self inside.
> — GERSHEN KAUFMAN[9]

Nosotros los Chicanos straddle the borderlands. On one side of us, we are constantly exposed to the Spanish of the Mexicans, on the other side we hear the Anglos' incessant clamoring so that we forget our language. Among ourselves we don't say *nosotros los americanos, o nosotros los españoles, o nosotros los hispanos.* We say *nosotros los mexicanos* (by *mexicanos* we do not mean citizens of Mexico; we do not mean a national identity, but a racial one). We distinguish between *mexicanos del otro lado* and *mexicanos de este lado.* Deep in our hearts we believe that being Mexican has nothing to do with which country one lives in. Being Mexican is a state of soul — not one of mind, not one of citizenship. Neither eagle nor serpent, but both. And like the ocean, neither animal respects borders.

> *Dime con quien andas y te diré quien eres.*
> (Tell me who your friends are and I'll tell you who you are.)
> — Mexican saying

Si le preguntas a mi mamá, "¿Qué eres?" te dirá, "Soy mexicana." My brothers and sister say the same. I sometimes will answer "*soy mexicana*" and at others will say "*soy Chicana*" o "*soy tejana.*" But I identified as "*Raza*" before I ever identified as "*mexicana*" or "Chicana."

As a culture, we call ourselves Spanish when referring to ourselves as a linguistic group and when copping out. It is then that we forget our predominant Indian genes. We are 70–80 percent Indian.[10] We call ourselves Hispanic[11] or Spanish-American or Latin American or Latin when linking ourselves to other Spanish-speaking peoples of the Western hemisphere and when copping out. We call ourselves Mexican-American[12] to signify we are neither Mexican nor American, but more the noun "American" than the adjective "Mexican" (and when copping out).

Chicanos and other people of color suffer economically for not acculturating. This voluntary (yet forced) alienation makes for psychological conflict, a kind of dual identity — we don't identify with the Anglo-American cultural values and we don't totally identify with the Mexican cultural values. We are a synergy of two cultures with various degrees of Mexicanness or Angloness. I have so internalized the borderland conflict that sometimes I feel like one cancels out the other and we are zero, nothing, no one. *A veces no soy nada ni nadie. Pero hasta cuando no lo soy, lo soy.*

When not copping out, when we know we are more than nothing, we call ourselves Mexican, referring to race and ancestry; *mestizo* when affirming both our Indian and Spanish (but we hardly ever own our Black) ancestry; Chicano when referring to a politically aware people born and/or raised in the United States; *Raza* when referring to Chicanos; *tejanos* when we are Chicanos from Texas.

Chicanos did not know we were a people until 1965 when Cesar Chavez and the farmworkers united and I *Am Joaquín* was published and *la Raza Unida* party was formed in Texas. With that recognition, we became a distinct people. Something momentous happened to the Chicano soul — we became aware of our reality and acquired a name and a language (Chicano Spanish) that reflected that reality. Now that we had a name, some of the fragmented pieces began to fall together — who we were, what we were, how we had evolved. We began to get glimpses of what we might eventually become.

Yet the struggle of identities continues, the struggle of borders is our reality still. One day the inner struggle will cease and a true integration take place. In the meantime, *tenémos que hacer la lucha. ¿Quién está protegiendo los ranchos de mi gente? ¿Quién está tratando de cerrar la fisura entre la india y el blanco en nuestra sangre? El Chicano, si, el Chicano que anda como un ladrón en su propia casa.*

Los Chicanos, how patient we seem, how very patient. There is the quiet of the Indian about us.[13] We know how to survive. When other races have given up their tongue we've kept ours. We know what it is to live under the hammer blow of the dominant *norteamericano* culture. But more than we count the blows, we count the days the weeks the years the centuries the aeons until the white laws and commerce and customs will rot in the aeons until the white laws and commerce and customs will rot in the deserts they've created, lie bleached. *Humildes* yet proud, *quietos* yet wild, *nosotros los mexicanos-Chicanos* will walk by the crumbling ashes as we go about our business. Stubborn, persevering, impenetrable as stone, yet possessing a malleability that renders us unbreakable, we, the *mestizas* and *mestizos,* will remain.

Notes

[1] Ray Gwyn Smith, *Moorland Is Cold Country,* unpublished book.

[2] Irena Klepfisz, "*Di rayze aheym*/The Journey Home," in *The Tribe of Dina: A Jewish Women's Anthology,* Melanie Kaye/Kantrowitz and Irena Klepfisz, eds. (Montpelier, VT: Sinister Wisdom Books, 1986), 49.

[3] R. C. Ortega, *Dialectología Del Barrio,* trans. Hortencia S. Alwan (Los Angeles, CA: R. C. Ortega Publisher & Bookseller, 1977), 132.

[4] Eduardo Hernandéz-Chávez, Andrew D. Cohen, and Anthony F. Beltramo, *El Lenguaje de los Chicanos: Regional and Social Characteristics of Language Used by Mexican Americans* (Arlington, VA: Center for Applied Linguistics, 1975), 39.

[5] Hernandéz-Chávez, xvii.

[6] Irena Klepfisz, "Secular Jewish Identity: Yidishkayt in America," in *The Tribe of Dina,* Kaye/Kantrowitz and Klepfisz, eds., 43.

[7] Melanie Kaye/Kantrowitz, "Sign," in *We Speak in Code: Poems and Other Writings* (Pittsburgh, PA: Motheroot Publications, Inc., 1980), 85.

[8] Rodolfo Gonzales, *I Am Joaquín/Yo Soy Joaquín* (New York, NY: Bantam Books, 1972). It was first published in 1967.

[9] Gershen Kaufman, *Shame: The Power of Caring* (Cambridge, MA: Schenkman Books, Inc., 1980), 68.

[10] John R. Chávez, *The Lost Land: The Chicano Images of the Southwest* (Albuquerque, NM: University of New Mexico Press, 1984), 88–90.

[11] "Hispanic" is derived from *Hispanis* (*España,* a name given to the Iberian Peninsula in ancient times when it was a part of the Roman Empire) and is a term designated by the U.S. government to make it easier to handle us on paper.

[12] The Treaty of Guadalupe Hidalgo created the Mexican–American in 1848.

[13] Anglos, in order to alleviate their guilt for dispossessing the Chicano, stressed the Spanish part of us and perpetrated the myth of the Spanish Southwest. We have accepted the fiction that we are Hispanic, that is Spanish, in order to accommodate ourselves to the dominant culture and its abhorrence of Indians. Chávez, 88–91.

PUNCTUATION AND MECHANICS

The parts of *The Bedford Handbook* on punctuation and mechanics, continuing the emphasis of the two preceding parts, present rules in the context of how they affect writers' goals. Students typically encounter these rules only when they have broken them, and too often instructors ask students to learn them through exercises, drills, and rote memorization. The handbook's presentation of the use and application of these rules suggests that students should avoid the counterproductive approach of trying to apply all of the rules every time they write. Instead, students should consider applying particular rules at appropriate stages of the revision process.

Writing teachers regularly face the challenge of convincing students to attend to rules and conventions. No matter what approach teachers use when presenting these rules to writers, the following selections will challenge standard perceptions about teaching the basics and force teachers to consider their answers to the following questions:

- How can teachers challenge students to think about rules (such as punctuation rules) differently?
- Students have covered punctuation and mechanics in one form or another throughout their education. When traditional teaching methods seem to be ineffective or counterproductive, how can teachers question them? What alternatives can they explore? Why?

WHAT GOOD IS PUNCTUATION?
Wallace Chafe

[Center for the Study of Writing Occasional Paper No. 2. Berkeley: Center for the Study of Writing, 1985. ERIC ED 292 120.]

A professor in the Department of Linguistics at University of California–Santa Barbara, Wallace Chafe is coauthor (with Jane Danielewicz) of "Properties of Spoken and Written Language," a chapter in Comprehending Oral and Written Language *(1987). An expanded version of the selection that follows appeared in* Written Communication *in 1988 under the title "Punctuation and the Prosody of Written Language."*

Both articles resulted from Chafe's research on the differences between speaking and writing. He suggests that instructors consider supplementing their presentation of punctuation rules by teaching students to relate punctuation to the "sound of written language." This would encourage students to be more conscious of punctuation as a stylistic option that can contribute to the effectiveness of their writing.

There are few people whose heart will skip a beat at the thought of punctuation. For sheer excitement, punctuation ranks well below spelling, which at least lends itself to interesting games and contests. At best, it seems to be a necessary evil. Since it is present in all normal English writing, anyone who is going to write English needs to learn to use it in an acceptable way, but it is seldom mentioned as an important ingredient of good writing. Interestingly, in the early nineteenth century those in the printing profession believed they knew more about how to punctuate than their authors did. A book called *The Printers' Manual* published in London in 1838 "laments the ignorance of most writers in the art of punctuation and fantasizes about a world in which authors turn in manuscripts with no punctuation at all, leaving that chore to the professional competence of the compositors" (Shillingsburg, 1986, p. 60).

Even if we might now be willing to admit that punctuation is not exactly in a class with setting type, and that authors are best allowed to have some control over it, it continues to suffer from a popular reputation as something that is arbitrary, unmotivated, and governed by rules that make no particular sense. In short, it is in a class with "grammar." Perhaps it is even a part of grammar, but certainly not one of the more interesting parts.

There is a centuries old debate over whether, or to what extent, punctuation is in fact determined by grammar, or whether its primary function is rather to signal the "prosody" — the patterns of pitch and stress and hesitations — that authors have in mind when they write and that readers attribute to a piece of writing. Prosody is an obvious property of *spoken* language, where it takes only a moment of listening to confirm the presence of pitch changes, stresses, and hesitations. But what could it mean to say that these same features are present in written language too? Is not writing something that we see, rather than hear?

Some who have reflected on their own personal experiences in reading and writing have concluded that written language does actually involve a mental image of sound. Just as people can imagine what some familiar piece of music sounds like, readers and writers seem to be able to imagine how writing sounds. Eudora Welty, in her autobiographical book *One Writer's Beginnings,* put it this way: "Ever since I was first read to, then started reading to myself, there has never been a line read that I didn't *hear.* As my eyes followed the sentence, a voice was saying it silently to me. . . . My own words, when I am at work on a story, I hear too as they go, in the same voice that I hear when I read in books. When I write and the sound of it comes back to my ears, then I act to make my changes. I have always trusted this voice." If we can assume that Welty's observations capture something real and important, then the ways writers manage prosody can have an important effect on their writing.

To return to the debate over whether punctuation reflects grammar or whether it has more to do with the prosody of this inner voice, one reason for the inconclusiveness of the debate is the fact that, in the majority of cases, prosody and grammar support each other. Whether the period at the end of a sentence means, "This is the end of a sentence" (signaling something grammatical), or whether it means, "This is where there is a falling pitch and a pause" (signaling something prosodic) may be difficult to decide, since usually both things are true. There are some cases, to be sure, where grammar dictates the presence or absence of punctuation, whereas prosody does the reverse. When one looks at such cases in actual writing, one finds that sometimes grammar has its way, sometimes prosody. There is no clear answer to which predominates, but it is prosody that gives expression to that inner voice.

If we listen a little more carefully to spoken language and its prosody, we find that it is typically produced in brief spurts, each showing a coherent pitch contour and usually followed by a pause. (For more on these spurts and their significance, see Chafe, 1987a.) It is of some interest that these spoken "intonation units" are nicely reflected in the punctuation units of much good writing. (By "punctuation unit" I mean the stretches of language that are separated by punctuation marks.) Notice how Herman Melville used commas, semicolons, and periods to create this effect in *Moby Dick.* I have written the punctuation units on separate lines to emphasize their nature:

1. The prodigious strain upon the mainsail had parted the weather-sheet,
2. and the tremendous boom was now flying from side to side,
3. completely sweeping the entire after part of the deck.
4. The poor fellow whom Queequeg had handled so roughly,
5. was swept overboard;
6. all hands were in a panic;
7. and to attempt snatching at the boom to stay it,
8. seemed madness.
9. It flew from right to left,
10. and back again,
11. almost in one ticking of a watch,
12. and every instant seemed on the point of snapping into splinters.

This example typifies much nineteenth-century writing by including instances of punctuation that are not in accord with grammatically based rules. Most obvious is the fact that the commas and the ends of lines 4 and 7 separate a subject from a predicate, where conventional grammar would not countenance such a separation. But if one thinks of how this passage *sounds* as one reads it to oneself, and presumably as Melville imagined it to himself, the punctuation quite plausibly reflects his prosodic intentions.

Other literature, however, provides us with many examples where punctuation, or the lack of it, seems not to reflect the way the writing sounds. Take, for example, the following long unpunctuated sequence from James Agee's *A Death in the Family,* where a reader may have some difficulty restraining the impulse to insert a few prosodic boundaries:

> He has been dead all night while I was asleep and now it is morning and I am awake but he is still dead and he will stay right on being dead all afternoon and all night and all tomorrow while I am asleep again and wake up again and go to sleep again and he can't come back home again ever any more but I will see him once more before he is taken away.

Doubtless Agee was trying to achieve an effect of breathlessly tumbling, silent ideas. That kind of effect, however, is possible only in writing, and it removes writing from the link with spoken prosody that is so clear in Melville.

The Melville and Agee examples were produced about a hundred years apart, but we can easily find examples of contemporary writing that differ in similar ways. To illustrate with two extremes, there is a marked contrast between the punctuation of the text of a recent automobile advertisement in *Time:*

> Town road.
> The longest straightaway on the course.
> The 16-valve,
> intercooled,
> turbocharged engine,
> capable of doing 130 and more on a test track,
> reaches its mandated maximum of 35 mph and purrs nicely along at that speed.

and the punctuation of a recent scholarly article regarding "paleodemography":

> Persons familiar with the problems inherent in the estimation of demographic parameters for living human groups characterized by small size and a lack of census records should scarcely be surprised to find that paleodemography is controversial.

We can see, then, that writers of different periods as well as of different contemporary styles use punctuation in different ways. Is this because their prosodic intentions are so different, or is it because they differ in the degree to which they make use of punctuation to express their intentions? Both factors undoubtedly play a role, but I will focus here on the second: the assertion that styles of writing are distinguished by the degree to which their punctuation captures the prosody of the inner voice.

Putting things in this way implies that we can have some independent knowledge of the prosody of inner voice, so that we can compare it with a writer's punctuation in order to determine whether that punctuation expresses it well or badly. But how can we know about the inner voice except through punctuation? One way to make it overt might be through reading aloud. In a sense, reading aloud turns written language into spoken language, giving it a prosody that anyone can hear. To see what a systematic investigation along these lines would offer, we listened to tape recordings of a number of people reading aloud various passages of different styles (see Chafe, 1987b, for further details). It was found that they divided the passages into intonation units much like those of normal speech, regardless of how the passages had been punctuated. For example, the Agee passage was divided in the following way by most oral readers:

> He has been dead all night,
> while I was asleep,
> and now it is morning,
> and I am awake,
> but he is still dead,
> and he will stay right on being dead,
> all afternoon,
> and all night,
> and all tomorrow,
> while I am asleep again,
> and wake up again,
> and go to sleep again,
> and he can't come back home again,
> ever any more.
> But I will see him once more,
> before he is taken away.

The average length of these intonation units was just under five words. Five or six words is the typical length for intonation units in ordinary spoken English.

If oral readers create intonation units much like those of speech, regardless of how a passage was punctuated, they show us the degree to which an author punctuated in a spoken-like way. Thus, the automobile advertisement quoted above could be said to be very spoken-like in its punctuation, whereas the Agee passage was very unspoken-like in this respect. Reading aloud can also show associations between specific punctuation marks and specific pitch contours. For example, periods are almost always read aloud as falling pitches (suggesting the end of a declarative sentence), whereas commas are usually read aloud as nonfalling pitches (suggesting that more is to follow).

But it it not necessarily the case that people read something aloud the same way they read it to themselves. Reading aloud is subject to various constraints, both physical and psychological. A speaker has to breathe, for example, and there is a practical limit on how fast one can say something. There seem also to be some mental limitations on the speed with which one can process speech. The inner voice of written language may be freer of these constraints, with the result that more can be included in a written punctuation unit than in a spoken intonation unit. We asked some other readers, instead of reading these passages aloud, to "repunctuate" them, that is, to insert their own punctuation into versions from which the original punctuation had been removed. These repunctuated versions showed us the extent to which the authors had punctuated in ways their readers regarded as appropriate. They also provided clues as to how readers chose between the dictates of grammar and prosody.

The difference between those who read the passages and those who repunctuated them can be illustrated with a brief excerpt from Henry James (taken from *The Turn of the Screw*). James wrote at one point:

We were to keep our heads if we should keep nothing else —

Most of the people who read this little excerpt aloud, in spite of the fact that they were looking at the original punctuation, inserted a prosodic boundary after the word "heads." That is, they read it as if the punctuation had been:

We were to keep our heads, if we should keep nothing else —

In splitting this fragment into two six-word segments, these oral readers were adhering to the five- or six-word limit of spoken intonation units. But the silent readers who repunctuated this passage, even though they did not see the original punctuation, agreed with James: Most of them left the passage whole.

Why did both James and his silent readers prefer a punctuation unit twelve words long, twice the normal length of a spoken intonation unit? They probably were not just being slaves to punctuation rules. In another study writers were found to insert commas before subordinate clauses about 40 percent of the time (Chafe, 1984). Probably it is relevant that very little in this excerpt was "new," in the sense of information being brought up for the first time. Just before this James had written:

. . . we were of a common mind about the duty of resistance to extravagant fancies.

To then write "we were to keep our heads" was to repeat the idea of a "resistance to extravagant fancies," clarifying it and reinforcing it by wording it in a different way. And then to add "if we should keep nothing else" was only to emphasize the resolve by saying that this was the one essential thing to do. The passage in question does little more than strengthen an idea that had already been expressed in the passage before it. In writing, it seems that passages which express little in the way of new information can be all of a piece. Silent readers can absorb them without the need to split them apart. Speakers, locked into the more rigid requirements of spoken language, are more comfortable with a prosody that keeps things shorter. If, among the silent readers, some wish to follow a more leisurely pace, they are free in this example to interpret the conjunction "if " as a prosodic boundary in their own inner prosody. But neither James nor most of his readers saw any need to make this option explicit by inserting a comma.

What does such a study suggest with regard to the teaching of writing? Above all, it suggests how important it is for writers to pay attention to their inner voices. Good writers, whether or not they realize it, *listen to what they write.* They listen while they are writing, and even more importantly they listen while they are reading what they wrote in order to make changes. Paying attention to the sound of written language is absolutely essential to the effective use of punctuation.

It may be a little harder to be a writer these days than it was in the days of Thoreau and Melville. Then, writers were skilled in imagining how something would sound if it were read aloud, and they punctuated accordingly. The trick was to use punctuation marks as if they were stage directions for effective oral presentation. Whether or not these authors specifically intended their works to be read aloud, they punctuated as if that were their intention.

Reading aloud is not so much in fashion any more, nor is punctuation that is based on what reading aloud would sound like. If, as is currently assumed, most reading is going to take place silently and rapidly, more language can be assimilated within single acts of comprehension. A result is the current tendency for longer punctuation units, and for leaving more of a prosodic interpretation up to the reader, allowing the grammar to give prosodic options. This is the style often referred to nowadays as "open" punctuation.

Contemporary writing actually exhibits a broad variety of punctuation styles, so that accomplished writers need to be able to punctuate in ways that are appropriate to whatever kinds of writing they may be doing. An advertising copy writer who punctuated like a professor would soon be out of work, and a professor who punctuated like a nineteenth-century novelist would find journal editors deleting commas right and left.

Students, in addition to being sensitized to their inner voices, will benefit from knowing the range of punctuating options that are available, and from being shown, through examples, what is most appropriate to one style and another. They can learn from practice in writing advertising copy as well as the more academic kinds of exposition, and from experimenting with fiction that mimics the very different punctuation styles of, say, Melville and Agee. At the same time, developing writers need to know that there are certain specific rules for punctuating that violate the prosody of their inner voices, and that simply have to be learned. These arbitrary rules are few in number and well defined, and to learn them need be no burden. The rules themselves may be appropriate to some styles and not to others. For example, the rule against placing a comma between a subject and predicate, violated so often by nineteenth-century writers, was also safely ignored by the person who wrote the following for the outside of a cereal box:

> Two cups of Quaker 100% Natural Cereal mixed with a little of this and a little of that, make the best cookies you've tasted in years.

The bottom line is that punctuation contributes substantially to the effectiveness of a piece of writing, and that its successful use calls for an awareness of something that is, for this and other reasons, essential to good writing: a sensitivity to the sound of written language.

References

Chafe, Wallace. 1984. "How People Use Adverbial Clauses." *Proceedings of the Tenth Annual Meeting of the Berkeley Linguistics Society.*

Chafe, Wallace. 1987a. "Cognitive Constraints on Information Flow." In Russell Tomlin (ed.), *Coherence and Grounding in Discourse.* Amsterdam: John Benjamins.

Chafe, Wallace. 1987b. "Punctuation and the Prosody of Written Language." Technical Report No. 11, Center for the Study of Writing, Berkeley.

Shillingsburg, Peter L. 1986. *Scholarly Editing in the Computer Age: Theory and Practice.* Athens: University of Georgia Press.

Welty, Eudora. 1983. *One Writer's Beginnings.* New York: Warner Books.

From ENCOUNTERING MISSPELLINGS AND SPELLING PERFORMANCE: WHY WRONG ISN'T RIGHT

Alan S. Brown

[Journal of Educational Psychology 80 (1988): 488–94.]

Alan S. Brown is professor of psychology at Southern Methodist University. His research interests include memory dysfunction and multiple-choice tests. His article "A Review of Recent Research on Spelling" appears in the January 1991 Educational Psychology Review. *The following excerpt is the introduction to an article that resulted from Brown's noticing that his own spelling became worse as he experienced students' misspellings.*

The findings that Brown reports from his empirical study of 220 undergraduates support his argument: Using incorrect spellings as teaching aids or as testing methods will not improve spelling performance; students may remember both versions of the spelling. With this in mind, Brown challenges teachers to reconsider their methods for teaching spelling. In addition, he models one form of research that teachers can deploy when questioning traditional methods.

The empirical measurement of spelling ability and its correlates have provided a topic of continuing experimental interest for more than fifty years. At the theoretical level, recent models by Ehri (1980), Morton (1980),

Simon (1976), Simon and Simon (1973), and Smith (1973) have helped to provide the necessary foundation on which to establish a more comprehensive conceptualization of spelling ability. One of the assumptions shared by these models is that there exists a singular memory representation of the orthography of each word, which serves as a template for generated spellings, and which is modified on the basis of the subjects' cumulative experience with correct and incorrect spellings.

This assumption of a unitary representation of each word has not been empirically tested or theoretically challenged. Although Simon and Simon (1973), as well as Ellis (1982), allowed that this singular representation may be incomplete (some letters may be missing), most researchers adhere to the assumption of orthographic singularity. The lack of a direct test of this position may stem from the common wisdom that most people can easily verify that a word is correctly spelled by seeing it (Ellis, 1982; Henderson & Chard, 1980; Nisbet, 1939; Tenney, 1980; Smith, 1973).

An alternative possibility is that different versions of some word's spelling are stored in memory and that the strength of each version is directly related to the frequency with which it has been encountered (Ekstrand, Wallace, & Underwood, 1966). As a version is encountered, its frequency increases automatically (Hasher & Zacks, 1979; Zechmeister, Curt, & Sebastian, 1978). When a word is to be spelled, a version is selected on the basis of a frequency differential: The more frequently one encounters the particular version, the more likely one is to use it, regardless of whether it is correct. The closer two versions are to each other in terms of frequency of experience, the more difficult and/or arbitrary the selection becomes. As Frith (1980) noted, "deviant forms can become acceptable if they are frequent, and normal forms become hard to distinguish from them" (p. 510).

There is some evidence that there exist multiple orthographic memory representations for single words. Nisbet (1939) noted that teachers complained about grading spelling tests from poor spellers because of confusion that occurred after they looked at many incorrect spellings. Their ability to discriminate the correctness of certain words became less efficient as they encountered a number of misspellings. In a similar observation, Frith (1980) pointed out that

> frequent exposure to an incorrect version can make a good speller waver. . . .
> [E]xaminers sometimes report that their spelling ability has been rendered considerably poorer by reading through examination reports. (p. 511)

Nisbet (1939) and Pintner, Rinsland, and Zubin (1929) examined the influence of alternative spelling forms on the subjects' ability to identify correct spellings. Pintner et al. (1929) gave subjects one of two different types of recognition spelling tests, followed by a dictation spelling test on the same words. For some of the subjects, the recognition test was a five-alternative multiple-choice format in which each correct spelling was presented with four misspellings of that same word. For the rest of the subjects, the word was incorrectly spelled and presented with four different correctly spelled words. Pintner et al. were surprised to find that there were a number of words that subjects could not correctly recognize but that they could subsequently spell on the dictation test. Specifically, they found in the two groups that subjects misrecognized 10% and 17% of the words correct in the dictation test.

In a similar type of study, Nisbet's (1939) subjects took an initial dictation test, followed by one of three different recognition tests. For one of these, the "wrongly-spelt" test, subjects were confronted by a misspelled version of a word from the initial test list and were to correct the spelling. Nisbet expressed concern when he discovered that of those words correctly spelled on the first task, 15.1% were wrong on this type of follow-up test. Both Nisbet (1939) and Pintner et al. (1929) suggested that incorrect alternatives may exert a disruptive influence on the recognition decision, especially if the strength level of the alternatives is close to the correct version.

In the remainder of this article, I examine the degree to which exposure to incorrect spellings makes these versions more palatable (apparently correct) to the subject, as indexed by changes that occur from a first to a second spelling test on the same words within a short period of time. Throughout the investigations, the primary focus was on those words correctly spelled (C) on an initial dictation test that are incorrectly spelled (I) on a second test (CI items). In Experiment 1, subjects were given two dictation spelling tests, in succession, on the same words. Between the two tests, half of the subjects generated incorrect spellings for these words, and the other half performed a neutral task. In Experiment 2, the design was modified to include either a final dictation or a recognition test, and subjects either rated misspellings of these words or performed a neutral task between two spelling tests. In Experiment 3 the number of presentations of misspelled versions was varied in the interpolated task.

Notes

This research was supported by Grant RO3 MH38604-01A1 from the National Institute of Mental Health.

I wish to express my gratitude to Jan McDonieal, Sally Smith, Patricia Manos, and Cynthia Griffin for assistance in the data collection and analysis.

Correspondence concerning this article should be addressed to Alan S. Brown, Department of Psychology, Southern Methodist University, Dallas, Texas 75275.

References

Ekstrand, R. R., Wallace, W. P., & Underwood, B. J. (1966). A frequency theory of verbal discrimination learning. *Psychology Review, 73*, 566–578.

Ellis, A. W. (1982). Spelling and writing (and reading and speaking). In A. W. Ellis (ed.). *Normality and pathology in cognitive function* (chap. 4). New York: Academic Press.

Ehri, L. C. (1980). The development of orthographic images. In U. Frith (ed.), *Cognitive processes in spelling* (chap. 14). New York: Academic Press.

Frith, U. (1980). *Cognitive process in spelling.* New York: Academic Press.

Hasher, L. & Zacks, R. T. (1979). Automatic and effortful processes in memory. *Journal of Experimental Psychology; General,* 356–388.

Henderson, L., & Chard, J. (1980). The reader's implicit knowledge of orthographic structure. In U. Frith (ed.) *Cognitive processes in spelling* (chap. 5). New York: Academic Press.

Morton, J. (1980). The logogen model and orthographic structure. In U. Frith (ed.), *Cognitive processes in spelling* (chap. 6). New York: Academic Press.

Nisbet, S. D. (1939). Non-dictated spelling tests (*British Journal of Educational Psychology, 9*, 29–44.

Pintner, R., Rinsland, H. D., & Zubin, J. (1929). The evaluation of self-administering spelling tests. *Journal of Educational Psychology, 20*, 107–11.

Simon, D. P. (1976). Spelling — A task analysis. *Instructional Science, 7,* 301–309.

Simon, D. P., & Simon, H. A. (1973). Alternative uses of phonemic information in spelling. *Review of Educational Research, 43,* 115–37.

Smith, F. (1973). Alphabetic writing — A language compromise? In F. Smith (ed.), *Psycholinguistics and reading* (chap. 10). New York: Holt, Rinehart & Winston.

Tenney, Y. J. (1980). Visual factors in spelling. In U. Frith (ed.). *Cognitive processes in spelling* (chap. 10). New York: Academic Press.

Zechmeister, E. B., Curt, C., & Sebastian, J. A. (1978). Errors in a recognition memory task are a U-shaped function of word frequency. *Bulletin of the Psychonomic Society, 11,* 371–373.

PART NINE

RESEARCH WRITING

The Bedford Handbook recognizes the essential connections between research and much of the writing students will do in school and beyond. Typically, the research paper occupies a central position in freshman writing courses. But as the content and the focus of writing courses have become more interdisciplinary, instructors across the curriculum have recognized the need to incorporate more assignments that require research. The selections that follow focus on several questions worth posing about research writing:

- What do instructors mean by "research" in the context of writing courses? How do we define research (for our students and for ourselves)? How do our different definitions of research affect our writing courses and our teaching?
- If many instructors see the traditional research paper as dysfunctional, what alternative forms of research writing can replace the traditional model?
- How can instructors help students be more critical about the results of their research, and how can students use those results more effectively? How can instructors help students take control of the research instead of letting the research take control of them?
- How can instructors help students understand and avoid plagiarism?

RESEARCH AS A SOCIAL ACT

Patricia Bizzell and Bruce Herzberg

[The Clearing House 60 (1987): 303–6.]

Patricia Bizzell, professor of English at the College of the Holy Cross, is author of an essay collection, Academic Discourse and Critical Consciousness *(1993), and her articles have appeared in* Pre/Text, Rhetoric Review, College English, *and* College Composition and Communication. *Bruce Herzberg is associate professor of English at Bentley College. His articles have appeared in* Professional Communications: The Social Perspective *(1993),* The Politics of Writing Instruction *(1991), and the journal* Rhetoric Review. *Bizzell and Herzberg collaborated on* The Rhetorical Tradition *(1990), winner of the Outstanding Book Award from the Conference on College Composition and Communication, and* The Bedford Bibliography for Teachers of Writing, *now in its third edition.*

Bizzell and Herzberg observe that instructors typically define research in two ways: as discovery or as recovery. Both definitions, they argue, are inadequate and contribute to ineffective assignments and teaching strate-

310

gies. *The authors ask instructors to recognize that research is a "social, collaborative act that draws on and contributes to the work of a community that cares about a given body of knowledge," and they suggest a range of activities to engage students as active participants in knowledge communities.*

"Research" can be defined in several ways. First, it may mean discovery, as in the discovery of new information about the world by a researcher. We often call this work "original" research and think of the researcher as a solitary genius, alone in a study or, more likely, a laboratory. Second, "research" may mean the recovery from secondary sources of the information discovered by others. This is often the way we think of student research: students go to the library to extract information from books for a research paper. These two definitions call for some examination.

The first kind of research — discovery — seems more valuable than the second kind — recovery. Discovery adds to the world's knowledge, while recovery adds only to an individual's knowledge (some might add, "if we're lucky"). No matter how we protest that both kinds of research are valuable, there is a distinctly secondary quality to recovery. After all, recovery is dependent entirely upon discovery, original research, for its materials. Discovery actually creates new knowledge, while recovery merely reports on the results of the work of those solitary geniuses.

Common sense tells us that students, with rare exceptions, do not do original research until graduate school, if then. Students and teachers quite naturally share the feeling that research in school is, thus, mere recovery. Consequently, students and teachers often conclude that students are not likely to produce anything very good when they do this kind of research. Indeed, one cannot be doing anything very good while piling up the required number of facts discovered by others. Research-as-recovery seems to justify writing a paper by copying others' accounts of what they have discovered.

If we try, however, to remedy the defects of the research paper by calling for actual discovery, we run into more problems. Those who hope to do original research must know, before anything else, where gaps exist in current knowledge. And, of course, knowing where the holes are requires knowing where they are not. For most (perhaps all) students, this takes us back to research-as-recovery, that plodding effort to find out some of what others have already figured out.

Even research that evaluates sources of information, relates the accounts of information to one another, frames an argument that ties them together, and either reveals something important about the sources themselves or develops into a new contribution on the same topic requires, like discovery, a grasp of a field of knowledge that students cannot be expected to have.

The problem with both kinds of research, then, hinges on knowledge itself. The popular image of the solitary researcher in the lab or the library does not hint at the problem of knowledge — that these people are workers in knowledge who need knowledge as a prerequisite to their work. According to the popular image, they simply find facts. If that were all, presumably anyone could find them. But we know that is hardly the case.

What successful researchers possess that our students typically do not is knowledge, the shared body of knowledge that helps scholars define research projects and employ methods to pursue them. Invariably, researchers use the work of others in their field to develop such projects and consult others in the field to determine what projects will be of value. In short, all real research takes place and can only take place within a community of scholars. Research is a social act. Research is always collaborative, even if only one name appears on the final report.

This, then, is the third definition of research: a social, collaborative act that draws on and contributes to the work of a community that cares about a given body of knowledge. This definition is also a critique of the popular images that we have been examining. For, by the social definition of research, the solitary researcher is not at all solitary: the sense of what can and should be done is derived from the knowledge community. The researcher must be in constant, close communication with other researchers and will likely share preliminary results with colleagues and use their suggestions in further work. Her or his contributions will be extensions of work already done and will create new gaps that other researchers will try to close. Finally, his/her work of discovery is impossible without continuous recovery of the work of others in the community.

The social definition also allows us to revise the notion of research-as-recovery, for the recoverer in a community of knowledge is not merely rehashing old knowledge or informing himself/herself about a randomly chosen topic — he/she is interpreting and reinterpreting the community's knowledge in light of new needs and perspectives, and in so doing creating and disseminating new knowledge. The activity of interpretation reveals what the community values and where the gaps in knowledge reside. "Study knows that which yet it doth not know," as Shakespeare recognized long ago.

In many fields, the activities of synthesis and interpretation are primary forms of research. Think, for example, of the fields of history, philosophy, art and literary criticism, even sociology, economics, and psychology. But the important point is that no field of knowledge can do without such work. Clearly, the lab-science image of research is inaccurate, unrepresentative, and unhelpful. Research as a social act makes far more sense.

This new definition of research changes what it means for students to do research in school. In what ways do students participate in knowledge communities? One well-known and successful research assignment — the family history — suggests that in this very real community, student researchers find material to be interpreted, contradictions to be resolved, assertions to be supported, and gaps to be filled. They share the information and interpretations with the rest of the community, the family, who do not possess such a synthesis and are grateful to get it. But how do students fit into academic knowledge communities that are so much larger and colder than the family?

First, we must recognize that secondary and middle level students are novices, slowly learning the matter and method of school subjects. But they need not master the knowledge of the experts in order to participate in the sub-community of novices. They will need to know what other students know and do not know about a subject that they are all relatively uninformed about. In other words, they need to have a sense of what constitutes the shared body of knowledge of their community and a sense of the possible ways to increase that knowledge by useful increments. Imagine the classroom as a neighborhood in the larger academic community. Students contributing to the knowledge of the class are engaged in research in much the same way that expert researchers contribute to the larger community. They find out what is known — the first step in research — and identify what is unknown by sharing their knowledge amongst themselves. Then, by filling in the gaps and sharing what they find, they educate the whole community.

There are several practical implications for reimagining research in this way:

1. The whole class must work in the same area of inquiry — not the same topic, but different aspects of the same central issue. A well-defined historical period might do: by investigating work, play, social structure, literature, politics, clothing styles, food, and so on, students would become local experts contributing to a larger picture of the period. We will look at other examples later.

2. Students will need some common knowledge, a shared text or set of materials and, most of all, the opportunity to share with each other what they may already know about the subject. By collaborating on a questionnaire or interviewing each other, students learn valuable ways of doing primary research.

3. They will need to ask questions, critically examine the shared knowledge, and perhaps do some preliminary investigation to determine what the most tantalizing unknowns may be. Here again, some free exchange among class members will be helpful.

4. The exchange of ideas must continue through the process of discovery. Like expert researchers, students need to present papers or colloquia to the research community, distribute drafts and respond to feedback, and contribute to the work of others when they are able. Finally, their work must be disseminated, published in some way, and made available to the group. The early framework of the research community ought not to be reduced to a way to introduce the regular old term paper.

A perfectly good way to choose the general area of research for a class is simply to choose it yourself. Teachers represent the larger community and can be expected to know something about the topic at hand and provide guidance, so if the topic interests the teacher, all the better. Of course, the teacher can lean toward topics that may interest the class. Students may be asked to choose from among several possibilities suggested by the teacher, but it is likely to be needlessly daunting to the students to leave the whole selection process to them. Among the possibilities for class topics: utopia, Shakespeare's England, Franklin's America, the jazz age, the death of the dinosaurs, the year you were born, images of childhood, the idea of school, work and play, wealth and poverty, country and city, quests and heroes, creativity — it's easy to go on and on.

Central texts can be books, photocopied selections, a film, or videotapes. More's *Utopia* might work for some classes, but a utopian science fiction book might be better for others, and the description of the Garden of Eden, a well-known utopia, is only three pages long. Shakespeare plays are easy to come by, as is Franklin's *Autobiography* or selections from it. Not every topic will require such materials, of course. For some topics, the students' interviews or other initial responses might be compiled into the central text.

The shared knowledge of the group might be elicited through alternate writing and discussion sessions, the students answering questions like "what do you know about *x*?" or "what would you like to know about *x*?" Interviews and questionnaires also work, as noted. All of this preliminary reading, writing, and discussion will help to create a sense of community and give students a jump-start on writing for the group, rather than for the teacher. Needless to say, the teacher ought not to grade and need not even read such preliminary work, beyond requiring that it be done.

Identifying a gap in the group's knowledge and choosing a topic for individual research may still be difficult, and it helps to be armed with suggestions if the students run out of ideas or need to be focused. Have a list of questions about utopias, a list of attempted utopian communities, the names of prominent figures in the period under discussion, some key ideas or events or issues to pursue, and so on. Students may not see, in the central text, problems like class differences in opportunities for schooling, or assumptions about the place of women, or attitudes linked to local or historical circumstances. If discussion and preliminary research do not turn them up, the teacher can reasonably help out. We need not pretend that we are inventing a new field of inquiry, but we must beware of the temptation to fall back on assigned topics.

Having students share drafts and give interim reports takes time, but it is usually time well spent. Students can learn to provide useful feedback to other students on drafts of papers — teachers should not read every draft. Students acting as draft-readers can respond to set questions (what did you find most interesting? what do you want to learn more about?) or work as temporary collaborators in attacking problem areas or listen to drafts read aloud and give oral responses. Other kinds of sharing may be worthwhile. Annotated bibliographies might be compiled and posted so that resources can be shared. Groups might lead panel discussions to take the edge off formal presentations. Reading aloud and oral reporting are good ways, too, of setting milestones for writing, and public presentation is important for maintaining the sense of community. Oral reports, by the way, tend to be better as drafts than as final presentations — the feedback is useful then, and anxiety about the performance is muted. Publishing the final results is the last step — copies of the papers might be compiled with a table of contents in a ring binder and put on reserve in the school library, for example.

These activities do not eliminate problems of footnote form and plagiarism, but in the setting of a research community, the issues of footnoting and plagiarism can be seen in a fresh light. Students should be able to articulate for themselves the reasons why members of a community would want to enforce among themselves (and their novices) a common and consistent method of citation. When knowledge exists to be exchanged, footnotes facilitate exchange. So too with plagiarism: members of the community would love to see themselves quoted and footnoted, but not robbed.

An excellent way to teach citation and reinforce community cohesion is to ask students to cite each other. How do you cite another student's paper, especially in draft form? How do you cite an oral report? How do you thank someone for putting you onto an idea? These citation forms may be used rarely, but they are good ways to stir up interest in the need for and uses of footnotes.

If the students are discovering the process of drafting, peer-review, and interim reports for the first time, the problems of discussing work-in-progress may come up in that context. Many students have learned that it is "wrong" to look at someone else's paper and will just be learning about the way professionals share and help each other with their work. A good place to see how collaboration works is to look at the pages of acknowledgments in books. Students will find, in all of their textbooks, long lists of people who are acknowledged for help in the process of writing. Writing their own acknowledgments will allow students to talk about how their ideas were shaped by others, especially by those who cannot reasonably be footnoted.

If the social act of research is successful, students have the opportunity to learn that knowledge is not just found, but created out of existing knowledge. And if people create knowledge, it is reasonable to expect knowledge to change. What people regard as true may be something other than absolute fact. Indeed, it may be only a temporary formulation in the search for better understanding. We can hope that our students will develop ways to evaluate knowledge as a social phenomenon and progress toward a critical consciousness of all claims to knowledge.

BORROWING FROM THE SCIENCES: A MODEL FOR THE FRESHMAN RESEARCH PAPER

Jeff Jeske

[The Writing Instructor *6* (1987): 62–67.]

Jeff Jeske, associate professor of English and director of writing at Guilford College in Greensboro, North Carolina, has published in the International Journal of Women's Studies, Journal of the History of Ideas, *and* The Writing Instructor. *The article included here resulted from Jeske's work at the University of California–Los Angeles, where he developed courses designed to teach graduate students from a variety of disciplines how to write for publication.*

Jeske recognizes that scientific models for writing offer English teachers an alternative to the more traditional approaches for teaching research in freshman writing classes. The format of the generic research paper, he claims, often encourages only the collection and assembly of information about a topic, and students view research as a teacher-sponsored exercise instead of seeing it as a process they can use to answer questions and solve problems. Jeske argues that teachers can use the format of the scientific paper to encourage students to consider actively the aims and methods of the process they use to research. His suggestions are particularly relevant for the increasing number of writing courses with cross-curricular emphasis.

An ongoing classified in the *Los Angeles Weekly* reads: "TERM PAPER ASSISTANCE: 15,728 papers to choose from, all subjects. Read first — then buy. Custom research also available. Research Assistance, ##### Idaho Ave., West L.A., call ###-#### [numbers deleted]." This is one problem facing the instructor who assigns a research paper.

Another is the research paper itself, which has long had a not unde-served reputation as a breakfast of troglodytes, a tedious enterprise best described, like its grizzled great-uncle, the dissertation, as a transferring of bones from one graveyard to another. Signaling its tired, formulaic nature, one wag published a "Brief Guide to the Art of Marking Term Papers" in the *Chronicle of Higher Education* a few years ago. It proposed that besides the all-important counting of pages, all that was required of the grader was to stick a "nice" somewhere in the first quarter of the paper, where the thought might be original, and a "needs elaboration" toward the end, where the writer likely ran out of steam; sprinkled between could be a few "What is your source?'s" attached to random declarative sentences.

Although unhappy mutual tolerance has existed for generations, such is no longer the case. Innocent freshmen are doubtless still willing to shoul-der their cruel burden, but their mentors are not, for "the times they are a' changing." As the gulf widens between old and new composition, all weapons in the teacher's arsenal are being subjected to cold scrutiny. And the research paper is not bearing up well. Clinton Burhans, Jr., for ex-ample, notes damagingly that a preoccupation with the research paper is one of the hallmarks of the "traditional composition course," i.e., one that is on the wrong side of "the knowledge gap."

Worse, Richard Larson asserts that the generic research paper is an "artifice of the composition classroom" ("Richard L. Larson Responds").[1] Because research differs from discipline to discipline, the only way an English instructor can claim to teach research methodology is to teach a field's specific forms — that is, blunder into foreign and thus dangerous jungles of expertise. In other words, the freshman research paper not only has no role in the new freshman English, but it cannot serve the Writing across the Curriculum movement either. In short . . . death!

Professor Larson's proposed abolition of the research paper will not likely occur, however: partly, doubtless, because of the conservatism of the trade, and more importantly, because there are compelling reasons for keeping the old steed saddled. For one thing, the research paper represents an informed immersion in activities which the student *will* use throughout her academic career. In response to Larson, James Doubleday identifies three of these as (1) learning the difference between summary and paraphrase,[2] (2) gaining knowledge of reference sources, and (3) writing a long paper. More abstractly, we know the research paper to be a microcosm of educa-tion itself, inasmuch as it requires first finding information (and teaching oneself how to retrieve it in the process: the islander learning how to handle a pole rather than being doled out a fish) and then evaluating, outside the classroom's *hortus conclusus,* what is relevant and then what is valid, highly sophisticated cognitive activities.

The traditional research paper could use resuscitation, though, for the objections which have been lodged all have partial validity: It definitely needs retooling for its role in the new age of composition.

The following model has actually been around for a long while but at higher strata in the academic atmosphere. I encountered it while working with graduate and professional students and was immediately attracted by the form's clear, crisp presentation of the research paradigm. Explained for professional use by Robert A. Day in his *How to Write and Publish a Scientific Paper,* the model is *de rigueur* in the medical sciences and used with variations by the other hard sciences. I find it in the social sciences as well, and recognize it in the paradigms described in cross-curricular thesis and dissertation manuals. If there is an archetype for the research paper, this is it: the four-part format of Introduction, Materials and Methods, Results, and Discussion.

Besides providing experience with a form which many of my freshmen will later be expected to manipulate fluently, this model is particularly suited to students encountering professional research for the first time, for it can be used to encourage reflection on the research process itself. My interpretation of the model follows. The questions in each section suggest possible focal points for inquiry; I include them in the students' instructions.

I. Introduction
  —What is your key question?
  —Why is the problem significant?
  —Why did you choose it?
  —Was there a narrowing down process?
  —Did you formulate a hypothesis?
  —With what expectations did you begin your research?

The introduction of the standard experimental paper answers the question "What was the problem?" The professional researcher begins not with a topic, but with a specific, limited question; the purpose is to find answers, not to seek out an exercise in debate. Unlike the freshman's characteristic roaming through dark seas congested with towering icebergs of information, the researcher is thus sharply focused in her travel, and not as likely to return to port with an encyclopedia-style pastiche in tow. The energizing focus on question rather than static topic seems to encourage specificity as well as an active, questing spirit. Students in my Los Angeles theme course enthusiastically pursued such questions as Why did Marilyn Monroe commit suicide? Why are there no freeways in Beverly Hills? Why does Santa Monica have the nickname "The People's Republic of Santa Monica"? and Why is there a Venice in Southern California, complete with canals?

With its prompts to explain why the particular question was chosen, the form also encourages students to introduce a personal dimension to the paper and, given that more emphasis is placed on the question than on the answer, to be prepared to modify an initial hypothesis as the inquiry proceeds.

II. Materials and Methods
  —What research strategy did you adopt?
  —What were your primary sources of information, both inside and outside the library?
  —How did you determine what these sources were?
  —Which were the most useful? least useful?
  —Did your focus shift? How did your attitude toward your topic evolve?
  —How did you know when to stop?

The key question here is "How did you study the problem?" In professional research articles, this section is ordinarily the driest of the four, taken up with careful presentation of research design. In our use of the model, it can be the most personal and interesting, combining elements of the traditional literature search with a personal narrative of the student's investigation. I encourage students to be freewheeling and subjective in recounting their research experiences — the frustrations of library research, the blind alleys, the sudden insights, the twists and turns of their hypotheses, the creative extra-library techniques used to find the freshest, most pertinent information.

Teachers employing journals to elicit expressive writing can encourage students to use them here as records of research activity and hence as seed gardens for the Methods section. The goal, as in the Introduction, is for students to develop meta-awareness of themselves as researchers.

III. Results
    —What did you find?
    —Was it what you expected?
    —How did you determine your sources' reliability?
    —How did you resolve contradictory opinions?

Students present the material they found pertinent to their key question and also assess its quality. The assignment requires the students to present dispassionately what they've found and to organize it formally. (Because the key questions ordinarily begin with "Why?," we devote class time to discussing how to organize causal analysis.)

IV. Discussion
    –What is your overall conclusion regarding the key question?
    –What significance do your findings have?
    –What boundaries or weak areas in your research should be pointed
      out to other researchers?
    –Was this a difficult question to investigate?
    –Are you satisfied with the thoroughness of your work?
    –What did you learn about libraries and other sources of information?
    –How would you evaluate your research guide (in our case, Melissa
      Walker's *Writing Research Papers: A Norton Guide*)?
    –How could you make your research strategy more effective?

This section of the paradigm asks "What do your findings mean?" Unlike the professional researcher, though, we interpret "findings" to refer both to the topic and to the research process itself. Regarding the first, students are encouraged to meditate on the larger significance of what they've found; in class, we use a variant of Young, Becker, and Pike's particle-wave-field heuristic to see the topics in different contexts. Some students will have found that there is no answer to their key question; that is all right. Here they can assess the significance of there not being an answer. Or they may have found that their initial hypothesis was incorrect. That is all right, too; a key truth about research is that few hypotheses are not altered or modified in the course of one's investigation.

Just as importantly, we also use the Discussion to overview the research process itself. Students are encouraged to evaluate research strategy and their experience using it. What did they learn about doing research? What would they change? Successfully fusing this type of reflection with interpretation of the Results makes the Discussion section the most challenging to write — as it always is in the real world of research.

One of the model's advantages is its suppleness. In contrast to the traditional research paper, which Professor Larson describes as a "non-form of writing," this four-part model actually has many viable forms, depending on where the individual instructor decides to plot the assignment on such axes as expressive/transactional and topic-oriented/process-oriented. For example, he can emphasize a personal or an empirical tone — or he can encourage the student to follow the lead of the fine writers who synthesize the two.

Other benefits of the model:

- It encourages a free spirit of inquiry. The predetermined format enables the student to experiment with content.
- It provides a focus for discussing the writing of different fields.
- An instructor can bring in professional models to contrast from such sources as the *New England Journal of Medicine,* the *Journal of Social Welfare,* the *Journal of Paleontology* (and there are countless others).
- The four-part structure lends itself well to dividing the project into separate stages spread over time. Each section, with its distinct criteria for successful performance, can become a separate focus — or even a separate paper. The layout is also felicitous for the instructor who wishes to move from a personal to a more analytic mode of writing as the course progresses.

And of course there is one final benefit: This research paper is very difficult to plagiarize. It may finally offer a way to make the research paper vendors fold their tents and caravan into the great barren Beyond, where there will be much weeping and gnashing of teeth over bleached, though well-documented bones.

Notes

[1] See also Larson's "The 'Research Paper' in the Writing Course."

[2] William Irmscher makes the telling point that plagiarism often derives not from dishonesty but from ignorance: Students are often not taught how to read, absorb, quote, and paraphrase the works of others.

References

Burhans, Jr., Clinton S. "The Teaching of Writing and the Knowledge Gap." *College English* 45 (1983): 639–56.

Day, Robert A. *How to Write and Publish a Scientific Paper,* 2nd ed. Philadelphia: ISI Press, 1983, 26–39.

Doubleday, James F. "The 'Research Paper' in the Writing Course: A Comment," *College English,* 46 (1984): 512–13.

Irmscher, William. *Teaching Expository Writing.* New York: Holt, Rinehart, and Winston, 1979, p. 61.

Larson, Richard L. "Richard L. Larson Responds." *College English* 46 (1984): 513–14.

———. "The 'Research Paper' in the Writing Course: A Non-Form of Writing." *College English,* 44 (1982): 811–16.

Young, Richard, Alton L. Becker, and Kenneth L. Pike. *Rhetoric: Discovery and Change.* New York: Harcourt, Brace, and World, 1970, pp. 126–30.

HELPING STUDENTS USE TEXTUAL SOURCES PERSUASIVELY

Margaret Kantz

[College English 52 (1990): 74–91.]

Margaret Kantz, assistant professor of English and director of freshman composition at Central Missouri State University, has written about composing processes in researched student papers. She contributed a chapter to Reading to Write *(1990) by Linda Flower et al. and has published articles in* Poetics.

The following article grew out of Kantz's own experiences as a student writer. In high school she wrote a term paper that received a lower grade than she thought it should and later discovered that the reason for the grade was the paper's lack of rhetorical concept. Since her discovery, Kantz has used her old paper as a teaching device, asking students to try to improve it.

Although the researched essay as a topic has been much written about, it has been little studied. In the introduction to their bibliography, Ford, Rees, and Ward point out that most of the over 200 articles about researched essays published in professional journals in the last half century describe classroom methods. "Few," they say, "are of a theoretical nature or based on research, and almost none cites even one other work on the subject" (2). Given Ford and Perry's finding that 84% of freshman composition programs and 40% of advanced composition programs included instruction in writing research papers, more theoretical work seems needed. We need a theory-based explanation, one grounded in the findings of the published research on the nature and reasons for our students' problems with writing persuasive researched papers. To understand how to teach students to write such papers, we also need a better understanding of the demands of synthesis tasks.

As an example for discussing this complex topic, I have used a typical college sophomore. This student is a composite derived from published research, from my own memories of being a student, and from students whom I have taught at an open admissions community college and at both public and private universities. I have also used a few examples taken from my own students, all of whom share many of Shirley's traits. Shirley, first of all, is intelligent and well-motivated. She is a native speaker of English. She has no extraordinary knowledge deficits or emotional problems. She comes from a home where education is valued, and her parents do reading and writing tasks at home and at their jobs. Shirley has certain skills. When she entered first grade, she knew how to listen to and tell stories, and she soon became proficient at reading stories and at writing narratives. During her academic life, Shirley has learned such studying skills as finding the main idea and remembering facts. In terms of the relevant research, Shirley can read and summarize source texts accurately (cf. Spivey; Winograd). She can select material that is relevant for her purpose in writing (Hayes, Waterman, and Robinson; Langer). She can make connections between the available information and her purpose for writing, including the needs of her readers when the audience is specified (Atlas). She can make original connections among ideas (Brown and Day; Langer). She can create an appropriate, audience-based structure for her paper (Spivey), take notes and use them effectively while composing her paper (Kennedy), and she can present information clearly and smoothly (Spivey), without relying on the phrasing of the original sources (Atlas; Winograd). Shirley is, in my experience, a typical college student with an average academic preparation.

Although Shirley seems to have everything going for her, she experiences difficulty with assignments that require her to write original papers based on textual sources. In particular, Shirley is having difficulty in her sophomore-level writing class. Shirley, who likes English history, decided to write about the Battle of Agincourt (this part of Shirley's story is biographical). She found half a dozen histories that described the circumstances of the battle in a few pages each. Although the topic was unfamiliar, the sources agreed on many of the facts. Shirley collated these facts into her own version, noting but not discussing discrepant details, borrowing what she assumed to be her sources' purpose of retelling the story, and modeling the narrative structure of her paper on that of her sources. Since the only comments Shirley could think of would be to agree or disagree with her sources, who had told her everything she knew about the Battle of Agincourt, she did not comment on the material; instead, she concentrated on telling the story clearly and more completely than her sources had done. She was surprised when her paper received a grade of C– . (Page 1 of Shirley's paper is given as Appendix A.)

Although Shirley is a hypothetical student whose case is based on a real event, her difficulties are typical of undergraduates at both private and public colleges and universities. In a recent class of Intermediate Composition in which the students were instructed to create an argument using at least four textual sources that took differing points of view, one student, who analyzed the coverage of a recent championship football game, ranked her source articles in order from those whose approach she most approved to those she least approved. Another student analyzed various approaches taken by the media to the Kent State shootings in 1970, and was surprised and disappointed to find that all of the sources seemed slanted, either by the perspective of the reporter or by that of the people interviewed. Both students did not understand why their instructor said that their papers lacked a genuine argument.

The task of writing researched papers that express original arguments presents many difficulties. Besides the obvious problems of citation format and coordination of source materials with the emerging written product, writing a synthesis can vary in difficulty according to the number and length of the sources, the abstractness or familiarity of the topic, the uses that the writer must make of the material, the degree and quality of original thought required, and the extent to which the sources will supply the structure and purpose of the new paper. It is usually easier to write a paper that uses all of only one short source on a familiar topic than to write a paper that selects material from many long sources on a topic that one must learn as one reads and writes. It is easier to quote than to paraphrase, and it is easier to build the paraphrases, without comment or with random comments, into a description of what one found than it is to use them as evidence in an original argument. It is easier to use whatever one likes, or everything one finds, than to formally select, evaluate, and interpret material. It is easier to use the structure and purpose of a source as the basis for one's paper than it is to create a structure or an original purpose. A writing-from-sources task can be as simple as collating a body of facts from a few short texts on a familiar topic into a new text that reproduces the structure, tone, and purpose of the originals, but it can also involve applying abstract concepts from one area to an original problem in a different area, a task that involves learning the relationships among materials as a paper is created that may refer to its sources without resembling them.

Moreover, a given task can be interpreted as requiring an easy method, a difficult method, or any of a hundred intermediate methods. In this context, Flower has observed, "The different ways in which students [represent] a 'standard' reading-to-write task to themselves lead to markedly different goals and strategies as well as different organizing plans" ("Role" iii). To write a synthesis, Shirley may or may not need to quote, summarize, or select material from her sources; to evaluate the sources for bias, accuracy, or completeness; to develop original ideas; or to persuade a reader. How well she performs any of these tasks — and whether she thinks to perform these tasks — depends on how she reads the texts and on how she interprets the assignment. Shirley's representation of the task, which in this case was easier than her teacher had in mind, depends on the goals that she sets for herself. The goals that she sets depend on her awareness of the possibilities and her confidence in her writing skills.

Feeling unhappy about her grade, Shirley consulted her friend Alice. Alice, who is an expert, looked at the task in a completely different way and used strategies for thinking about it that were quite different from Shirley's.

"Who were your sources?" asked Alice. "Winston Churchill, right? A French couple and a few others. And they didn't agree about the details, such as the sizes of the armies. Didn't you wonder why?"

"No," said Shirley. "I thought the history books would know the truth. When they disagreed, I figured that they were wrong on those points. I didn't want to have anything in my paper that was wrong."

"But Shirley," said Alice, "you could have thought about why a book entitled *A History of France* might present a different view of the battle than a book subtitled *A History of British Progress. You* could have asked if the English and French writers wanted to make a point about the history of their countries and looked to see if the factual differences suggested anything. You could even have talked about Shakespeare's *Henry V,* which I know you've read — about how he presents the battle, or about how the King Henry in the play differs from the Henrys in your other books. You would have had an angle, a problem. Dr. Boyer would have loved it."

Alice's representation of the task would have required Shirley to formally select and evaluate her material and to use it as proof in an original argument. Alice was suggesting that Shirley invent an original problem and purpose for her paper and create an original structure for her argument. Alice's task is much more sophisticated than Shirley's. Shirley replied, "That would take me a year to do! Besides, Henry was a real person. I don't want to make up things about him."

"Well," said Alice, "You're dealing with facts, so there aren't too many choices. If you want to say something original you either have to talk about the sources or talk about the material. What could you say about the material? Your paper told about all the reasons King Henry wasn't expected to win the battle. Could you have argued that he should have lost because he took too many chances?"

"Gee," said Shirley, "That's awesome. I wish I'd thought of it."

This version of the task would allow Shirley to keep the narrative structure of her paper but would give her an original argument and purpose. To write the argument, Shirley would have only to rephrase the events of the story to take an opposite approach from that of her English sources, emphasizing what she perceived as Henry's mistakes and inserting comments to explain why his decisions were mistakes — an easy argument to write. She could also, if she wished. write a conclusion that criticized the cheerleading tone of her British sources.

As this anecdote makes clear, a given topic can be treated in more or less sophisticated ways — and sophisticated goals, such as inventing an original purpose and evaluating sources, can be achieved in relatively simple versions of a task. Students have many options as to how they can fulfill even a specific task (cf. Jeffery). Even children can decide whether to process a text deeply or not, and purpose in reading affects processing and monitoring of comprehension (Brown). Pichert has shown that reading purpose affects judgments about what is important or unimportant in a narrative text, and other research tells us that attitudes toward the author and content of a text affect comprehension (Asch; Hinze; Shedd; Goldman).

One implication of this story is that the instructor gave a weak assignment and an ineffective critique of the draft (her only comment referred to Shirley's footnoting technique; cf. Appendix A). The available research suggests that if Dr. Boyer had set Shirley a specific rhetorical problem such as having her report on her material to the class and then testing them on it, and if she had commented on the content of Shirley's paper during the drafts, Shirley might well have come up with a paper that did more than repeat its source material (Nelson and Hayes). My teaching experience supports this research finding. If Dr. Boyer had told Shirley from the outset that she was expected to say something original and that she should examine her sources as she read them for discrepant facts, conflicts, or other interesting material, Shirley might have tried to write an original argument (Kantz, "Originality"). And if Dr. Boyer had suggested that Shirley use her notes to comment on her sources and make plans for using the notes, Shirley might have written a better paper than she did (Kantz, "Relationship").

Even *if* given specific directions to create an original argument, Shirley might have had difficulty with the task. Her difficulty could come from any of three causes: 1) Many students like Shirley misunderstand sources because they read them as stories. 2) Many students expect their sources to tell the truth; hence, they equate persuasive writing in this context with making things up. 3) Many students do not understand that facts are a kind of claim and are often used persuasively in so-called objective writing to create an impression. Students need to read source texts as arguments and to think about the rhetorical contexts in which they were written rather than to read them merely as a set of facts to be learned. Writing an original persuasive argument based on sources requires students to apply material to a problem or to use it to answer a question, rather than simply to repeat it or evaluate it. These three problems deserve a separate discussion.

Because historical texts often have a chronological structure, students believe that historians tell stories and that renarrating the battle cast them as a historian. Because her sources emphasized the completeness of the victory/defeat and its decisive importance in the history of warfare, Shirley thought that making these same points in her paper completed her job. Her job as a reader was thus to learn the story, i.e., so that she could pass a test on it (cf. Vipond and Hunt's argument that generic expectations affect reading behavior. Vipond and Hunt would describe Shirley's reading as story-driven rather than point-driven). Students commonly misread texts as narratives. When students refer to a textbook as "the story," they are telling us that they read for plot and character, regardless of whether their texts are organized as narratives. One reason Shirley loves history is that when she reads it she can combine her story-reading strategies with her studying strategies. Students like Shirley may need to learn to apply basic organizing patterns, such as cause-effect and general-to-specific, to their texts. If, however, Dr. Boyer asks Shirley to respond to her sources in a way that is not compatible with Shirley's understanding of what such sources do, Shirley will have trouble doing the assignment. Professors may have to do some preparatory teaching about why certain kinds of tests have certain characteristics and what kinds of problems writers must solve as they design text for a particular audience. They may even have to teach a model for the kind of writing they expect.

The writing version of Shirley's problem, which Flower calls "writer-based prose," occurs when Shirley organizes what should be an expository analysis as a narrative, especially when she writes a narrative about how she did her research. Students frequently use time-based organizing patterns, regardless of the task, even when such patterns conflict with what they are trying to say and even when they know how to use more sophisticated strategies. Apparently such common narrative transitional devices such as "the first point" and "the next point" offer a reassuringly familiar pattern for organizing unfamiliar material. The common strategy of beginning paragraphs with such phrases as "my first source," meaning that it was the first source that the writer found in the library or the first one read, appears to combine a story-of-my-research structure with a knowledge-telling strategy (Bereiter and Scardamalia, *Psychology*). Even when students understand that the assignment asks for more than the fill-in-the-blanks, show-me-you've-read-the-material approach described by Schwegler and Shamoon, they cling to narrative structuring devices. A rank ordering of sources, as with Mary's analysis of the football game coverage with the sources listed in an order of ascending disapproval, represents a step away from storytelling and toward synthesizing because it embodies a persuasive evaluation.

In addition to reading texts as stories, students expect factual texts to tell them "the truth" because they have learned to see texts statically, as descriptions of truths, instead of as arguments. Shirley did not understand that nonfiction texts exist as arguments in rhetorical contexts. "After all," she reasoned, "how can one argue about the date of a battle or the sizes of armies?" Churchill, however, described the battle in much more detail than Shirley's other sources, apparently because he wished to persuade his readers to take pride in England's tradition of military achievement. Guizot and Guizot de Witt, on the other hand, said very little about the battle (beyond describing it as "a monotonous and lamentable repetition of the disasters of Crécy and Poitiers" [397]) because they saw the British invasion as a sneaky way to take advantage of a feud among the various branches of the French royal family. Shirley's story/study skills might not have allowed her to recognize such arguments, especially because Dr. Boyer did not teach her to look for them.

When I have asked students to choose a topic and find three or more sources on it that disagree, I am repeatedly asked, "How can sources disagree in different ways? After all, there's only pro and con." Students expect textbooks and other authoritative sources either to tell them the truth (i.e., facts) or to express an opinion with which they may agree or disagree. Mary's treatment of the football coverage reflects this belief, as does Charlie's surprise when he found that even his most comprehensive sources on the Kent State killings omitted certain facts, such as interviews with National Guardsmen. Students' desire for truth leads them to use a collating approach whenever possible, as Shirley did (cf. Appendix A), because students believe that the truth will include all of the facts and will reconcile all conflicts. (This belief may be another manifestation of the knowledge-telling strategy [Bereiter and Scardamalia, *Psychology*] in which students write down everything they can think of about a topic.) When conflicts cannot be reconciled and the topic does not admit a pro or con stance, students may not know what to say. They may omit the material altogether, include it without comment, as Shirley did, or jumble it together without any plan for building an argument.

The skills that Shirley has practiced for most of her academic career — finding the main idea and learning content — allow her to agree or disagree. She needs a technique for reading texts in ways that give her something more to say, a technique for constructing more complex representations of texts that allow room for more sophisticated writing goals. She also needs strategies for analyzing her reading that allow her to build original arguments.

One way to help students like Shirley is to teach the concept of rhetorical situation. A convenient tool for thinking about this concept is Kinneavy's triangular diagram of the rhetorical situation. Kinneavy, analyzing Aristotle's description of rhetoric, posits that every communicative situation has three parts: a speaker/writer (the Encoder), an audience (the Decoder), and a topic (Reality) (19). Although all discourse involves all three aspects of communication, a given type of discourse may pertain more to a particular point of the triangle than to the others, e.g., a diary entry may exist primarily to express the thoughts of the writer (the Encoder); an advertisement may exist primarily to persuade a reader (the Decoder). Following Kinneavy, I posit particular goals for each corner of the triangle. Thus, the primary goal of a writer doing writer-based discourse such as a diary might be originality and self-expression; primary goals for reader-based discourse such as advertising might be persuasion; primary goals for topic-based discourse such as a researched essay might be accuracy, completeness, and mastery of subject matter. Since all three aspects of the rhetorical situation are present and active in any communicative situation, a primarily referential text such as Churchill's *The Birth of Britain* may have a persuasive purpose and may depend for some of its credibility on readers' familiarity with the author. The term "rhetorical reading," then (cf. Haas and Flower), means teaching students to read a text as a message sent by someone to somebody for a reason. Shirley, Mary, and Charlie are probably practiced users of rhetorical persuasion in non-academic contexts. They may never have learned to apply this thinking in a conscious and deliberate way to academic tasks (cf. Kroll).

The concept of rhetorical situation offers insight into the nature of students' representations of a writing task. The operative goals in Shirley's and Alice's approaches to the term paper look quite different when mapped onto the points on the triangle. if we think of Shirley and Alice as Encoders, the topic as Reality, and Dr. Boyer as the Decoder, we can see that for Shirley, being an Encoder means trying to be credible; her relationship to the topic (Reality) involves a goal of using all of the subject matter; and her relationship to the Decoder involves an implied goal of telling a complete story to a reader whom Shirley thinks of as an examiner — to use the classic phrase from the famous book by Britton et al. — i.e., a reader who wants to know if Shirley can pass an exam on the subject of the Battle of Agincourt. For Alice, however, being an Encoder means having a goal of saying something new; the topic (Reality) is a resource to be used; and the Decoder is someone who must be persuaded that Alice's ideas have merit. Varying task representations do not change the dimensions of the rhetorical situation: the Encoder, Decoder, and Reality are always present. But the way a writer represents the task to herself does affect the ways that she thinks about those dimensions — and whether she thinks about them at all.

In the context of a research assignment, rhetorical skills can be used to read the sources as well as to design the paper. Although teachers have probably always known that expert readers use such strategies, the concept of rhetorical reading is new to the literature. Haas and Flower have shown that expert readers use rhetorical strategies "to account for author's purpose, context, and effect on the audience . . . to recreate or infer the rhetorical situation of the text" (176; cf. also Bazerman). These strategies, used in addition to formulating main points and paraphrasing content, helped the readers to understand a text more completely and more quickly than did readers who concentrated exclusively on content. As Haas and Flower point out, teaching students to read rhetorically is difficult. They suggest that appropriate pedagogy might include "direct instruction . . . modeling, and . . . encouraging students to become contributing and committed members of rhetorical communities" (182). One early step might be to teach students a set of heuristics based on the three aspects of the communicative triangle. Using such questions could help students set goals for their reading.

In this version of Kinneavy's triangle, the Encoder is the writer of the source text, the Decoder is the student reader, and Reality is the subject matter. Readers may consider only one point of the triangle at a time, asking such questions as "Who are you (i.e., the author/Encoder)?" or "What are the important features of this text?" They may consider two aspects of the rhetorical situation in a single question, e.g., "Am I in your intended (primary) audience?"; "What do I think about this topic?"; "What context affected your ideas and presentation?" Other questions would involve all three points of the triangle, e.g., "What are you saying to help me with the problem you assume I have?" or "What textual devices have you used to manipulate my response?" Asking such questions gives students a way of formulating goals relating to purpose as well as content.

If Shirley, for example, had asked a Decoder-to-Encoder question — such as "Am I in your intended audience?" — she might have realized that Churchill and the Guizots were writing for specific audiences. If she had asked a Decoder-to-Reality question — such as "What context affected your ideas and presentation?" — she might not have ignored Churchill's remark, "All these names [Amiens, Boves, Bethencourt] are well known to our generation" (403). As it was, she missed Churchill's signal that he was writing to survivors of the First World War, who had vainly hoped that it would be war to end all wars. If Shirley had used an Encoder-Decoder-Reality question — such as "What are you saying to help me with the problem you assume I have?" — she might have understood that the authors of her sources were writing to different readers for different reasons. This understanding might have given her something to say. When I gave Shirley's source texts to freshmen students. asked them to use the material in an original argument, and taught them this heuristic for rhetorical reading, I received, for example, papers that warned undergraduates about national pride as a source of authorial bias in history texts.

A factual topic such as the Battle of Agincourt presents special problems because of the seemingly intransigent nature of facts. Like many people, Shirley believes that you can either agree or disagree with issues and opinions, but you can only accept the so-called facts. She believes that facts are what you learn from textbooks, opinions are what you have about clothes, and arguments are what you have with your mother when you want to stay out late at night. Shirley is not in a position to disagree with the facts about the battle (e.g., "No, I think the French won"), and a rhetorical analysis may seem at first to offer minimal rewards (e.g., "According to the Arab, Jewish, and Chinese calendars the date was really . . .").

Alice, who thinks rhetorically, understands that both facts and opinions are essentially the same kind of statement: they are claims. Alice understands that the only essential difference between a fact and an opinion is how they are received by an audience. (This discussion is derived from Toulmin's model of an argument as consisting of claims proved with data and backed by ethical claims called warrants. According to Toulmin, any aspect of an argument may be questioned by the audience and must then be supported with further argument.) In a rhetorical argument, a fact is a claim that an audience will accept as being true without requiring proof, although they may ask for an explanation. An opinion is a claim that an audience will not accept as true without proof, and which, after the proof is given, the audience may well decide has only a limited truth, i.e., it's true in this case but not in other cascs. An audience may also decide that even though a fact is unassailable, the interpretation or use of the fact is open to debate.

For example, Shirley's sources gave different numbers for the size of the British army at Agincourt; these numbers, which must have been estimates, were claims masquerading as facts. Shirley did not understand this. She thought that disagreement signified error, whereas it probably signified rhetorical purpose. The probable reason that the Guizots give a relatively large estimate for the English army and do not mention the size of the French army is so that their French readers would find the British victory easier to accept. Likewise, Churchill's relatively small estimate for the size of the English army and his high estimate for the French army magnify the brilliance of the English victory. Before Shirley could create an argument about the Battle of Agincourt, she needed to understand that, even in her history textbooks, the so-called facts are claims that may or may not be supported, claims made by writers who work in a certain political climate for a particular audience. She may, of course, never learn this truth unless Dr. Boyer teaches her rhetorical theory and uses the research paper as a chance for Shirley to practice rhetorical problem-solving.

For most of her academic life, Shirley has done school tasks that require her to find main ideas and important facts; success in these tasks usually hinges on agreeing with the teacher about what the text says. Such study skills form an essential basis for doing reading-to-write tasks. Obviously a student can only use sources to build an argument if she can first read the sources accurately (cf. Brown and Palincsar; Luftig; Short and Ryan). However, synthesizing tasks often require that readers not accept the authors' ideas. Baker and Brown have pointed out that people misread texts when they blindly accept an author's ideas instead of considering a divergent interpretation. Yet if we want students to learn to build original arguments from texts, we must teach them the skills needed to create divergent interpretations. We must teach them to think about facts and opinions as claims that are made by writers to particular readers for particular reasons in particular historical contexts.

Reading sources rhetorically gives students a powerful tool for creating a persuasive analysis. Although no research exists as yet to suggest that teaching students to read rhetorically will improve their writing, I have seen its effect in successive drafts of students' papers. As mentioned earlier, rhetorical reading allowed a student to move from simply summarizing and evaluating her sources on local coverage of the championship football game to constructing a rationale for articles that covered the fans rather than the game. Rhetorical analysis enabled another student to move from summarizing his sources to understanding why each report about the Kent State shootings necessarily expressed a bias of some kind.

As these examples suggest, however, rhetorical reading is not a magical technique for producing sophisticated arguments. Even when students read their sources rhetorically, they tend merely to report the results of this analysis in their essays. Such writing appears to be a college-level version of the knowledge-telling strategy described by Bereiter and Scardamalia *(Psychology)* and may be, as they suggest, the product of years of exposure to pedagogical practices that enshrine the acquisition and expression of information without a context or purpose.

To move students beyond merely reporting the content and rhetorical orientation of their source texts, I have taught them the concept of the rhetorical gap and some simple heuristic questions for thinking about gaps. Gaps were first described by Iser as unsaid material that a reader must supply to/infer from a text. McCormick expanded the concept to include gaps between the text and the reader; such gaps could involve discrepancies of values, social conventions, language, or any other matter that readers must consider. If we apply the concept of gaps to Kinneavy's triangle, we see that in reading, for example, a gap may occur between the Encoder-Decoder corners when the reader is not a member of the author's intended audience. Shirley fell into such a gap. Another gap can occur between the Decoder-Reality corners when a reader disagrees with or does not understand the text. A third gap can occur between the Encoder-Reality points of the triangle if the writer has misrepresented or misunderstood the material. The benefit of teaching this concept is that when a student thinks about a writer's rhetorical stance, she may ask "Why does he think that way?" When a student encounters a gap, she may ask, "What effect does it have on the success of this communication?" The answers to both questions give students original material for their papers.

Shirley, for example, did not know that Churchill began writing *The Birth of Britain* during the 1930s, when Hitler was rearming Germany and when the British government and most of Churchill's readers ardently favored disarmament. Had she understood the rhetorical orientation of the book, which was published eleven years after the end of World War II, she might have argued that Churchill's evocation of past military glories would have been inflammatory in the 1930s but was highly acceptable twenty years later. A gap between the reader and the text (Decoder-Reality) might stimulate a reader to investigate whether or not she is the only person having this problem; a gap between other readers and the sources may motivate an adaptation or explanation of the material to a particular audience. Shirley might have adapted the Guizots' perspective on the French civil war for American readers. A gap between the author and the material (Encoder-Reality) might motivate a refutation.

To discover gaps, students may need to learn heuristics for setting rhetorical writing goals. That is, they may need to learn to think of the paper, not as a rehash of the available material, but as an opportunity to teach someone, to solve someone's problem, or to answer someone's question. The most salient questions for reading source texts may be "Who are you (the original audience of Decoders)?"; "What is your question or problem with this topic?"; and "How have I (the Encoder) used these materials to answer your question or solve your problem?" More simply, these questions may be learned as "Why," "How," and "So what?" When Shirley learns to read sources as telling not the eternal truth but a truth to a particular audience and when she learns to think of texts as existing to solve problems, she will find it easier to think of things to say.

For example, a sophomore at a private university was struggling with an assignment that required her to analyze an issue and express an opinion on it, using two conflicting source texts, an interview, and personal material as sources. Using rhetorical reading strategies, this girl discovered a gap between Alfred Marbaise, a high school principal who advocates mandatory drug testing of all high school students, and students like those he would be testing:

> Marbaise, who was a lieutenant in the U.S. Marines over thirty years ago . . . makes it very obvious that he cannot and will not tolerate any form of drug abuse in his school. For example, in paragraph seven he claims, "When students become involved in illegal activity, whether they realize it or not, they are violating other students . . . then I become very, very concerned . . . and I will not tolerate that."
>
> Because Marbaise has not been in school for nearly forty years himself, he does not take into consideration the reasons why kids actually use drugs. Today the social environment is so drastically different that Marbaise cannot understand a kid's morality, and that is why he writes from such a fatherly but distant point of view.

The second paragraph answers the So what? question, i.e., "Why does it matter that Marbaise seems by his age and background to be fatherly and distant?" Unless the writer/reader thinks to ask this question, she will have difficulty writing a coherent evaluation of Marbaise's argument.

The relative success of some students in finding original things to say about their topics can help us to understand the perennial problem of plagiarism. Some plagiarism derives, I think, from a weak, non-rhetorical task representation. If students believe they are supposed to reproduce source material in their papers, or if they know they are supposed to say something original but have no rhetorical problem to solve and no knowledge of how to find problems that they can discuss in their sources, it becomes difficult for them to avoid plagiarizing. The common student decision to buy a paper when writing the assignment seems a meaningless fill-in-the-blanks activity (cf. Schwegler and Shamoon) becomes easily understandable. Because rhetorical reading leads to discoveries about the text, students who use it may take more interest in their research papers.

Let us now assume that Shirley understands the importance of creating an original argument, knows how to read analytically, and has found things to say about the Battle of Agincourt. Are her troubles over? Will she now create that A paper that she yearns to write? Probably not. Despite her best intentions, Shirley will probably write another narrative/paraphrase of her sources. Why? Because by now, the assignment asks her to do far more than she can handle in a single draft. Shirley's task representation is now so rich, her set of goals so many, that she may be unable to juggle them all simultaneously. Moreover, the rhetorical reading technique requires students to discover content worth writing about and a rhetorical purpose for writing; the uncertainty of managing such a discovery task when a grade is at stake may be too much for Shirley.

Difficult tasks may be difficult in either (or both of) two ways. First, they may require students to do a familiar subtask, such as reading sources, at a higher level of difficulty, e.g., longer sources, more sources, a more difficult topic. Second, they may require students to do new subtasks, such as building notes into an original argument. Such tasks may require task management skills, especially planning, that students have never developed and do not know how to attempt. The insecurity that results from trying a complex new task in a high-stakes situation is increased when students are asked to discover a problem worth writing about because such tasks send students out on a treasure hunt with no guarantee that the treasure exists, that they will recognize it when they find it, or that when they find it they will be able to build it into a coherent argument. The paper on Marbaise quoted above earned a grade of D because the writer could not use her rhetorical insights to build an argument presented in a logical order. Although she asked the logical question about the implications of Marbaise's persona, she did not follow through by evaluating the gaps in his perspective that might affect the probable success of his program.

A skillful student using the summarize-the-main-ideas approach can set her writing goals and even plan (i.e., outline) a paper before she reads the sources. The rhetorical reading strategy, by contrast, requires writers to discover what is worth writing about and to decide how to say it as or after they read their sources. The strategy requires writers to change their content goals and to adjust their writing plans as their understanding of the topic develops. It requires writers, in Flower's term, to "construct" their purposes for writing as well as the content for their paper (for a description of constructive planning, see Flower, Schriver, Carey, Haas, and Hayes). In Flower's words, writers who construct a purpose, as opposed to writers who bring a predetermined purpose to a task, "create a web of purposes . . . set goals, toss up possibilities . . . create a multidimensional network of information . . . a web of purpose . . . a bubbling stew of various mental representations" (531–32). The complex indeterminacy of such a task may pose an intimidating challenge to students who have spent their lives summarizing main ideas and reporting facts.

Shirley may respond to the challenge by concentrating her energies on a familiar subtask, e.g., repeating material about the Battle of Agincourt, at the expense of struggling with an unfamiliar subtask such as creating an original argument. She may even deliberately simplify the task by representing it to herself as calling only for something that she knows how to do, expecting that Dr. Boyer will accept the paper as close enough to the original instructions. My students do this frequently. When students decide to write a report of their reading, they can at least be certain that they will find material to write about.

Because of the limits of attentional memory, not to mention those caused by inexperience, writers can handle only so many task demands at a time. Thus, papers produced by seemingly inadequate task representations may well be essentially rough drafts. What looks like a bad paper may well be a preliminary step, a way of meeting certain task demands in order to create a basis for thinking about new ones. My students consistently report that they need to marshal all of their ideas and text knowledge and get that material down on the page (i.e., tell their knowledge) before they can think about developing an argument (i.e., transform their knowledge). If Shirley's problem is that she has shelved certain task demands in favor of others, Dr. Boyer needs only to point out what Shirley should do to bring the paper into conformity with the assignment and offer Shirley a chance to revise.

The problems of cognitive overload and inexperience in handling complex writing tasks can create a tremendous hurdle for students because so many of them believe that they should be able to write their paper in a single draft. Some students think that if they can't do the paper in one draft that means that something is wrong with them as writers, or with the assignment, or with us for giving the assignment. Often, such students will react to their drafts with anger and despair, throwing away perfectly usable rough drafts and then coming to us and saying that they can't do the assignment.

The student's first draft about drug testing told her knowledge about her sources' opinions on mandatory drug testing. Her second draft contained the rhetorical analysis quoted above, but presented the material in a scrambled order and did not build the analysis into an argument. Only in a third draft was this student able to make her point:

> Not once does Marbaise consider any of the psychological reasons why kids turn away from reality. He fails to realize that drug testing will not answer their questions, ease their frustrations. or respond to their cries for attention, but will merely further alienate himself and other authorities from helping kids deal with their real problems.

This comment represents Terri's answer to the heuristic "So what? Why does the source's position matter?" If we pace our assignments to allow for our students' thoughts to develop, we can do a great deal to build their confidence in their writing (Terri raised her D+ to an A). If we treat the researched essay as a sequence of assignments instead of as a one-shot paper with a single due date, we can teach our students to build on their drafts, to use what they can do easily as a bridge to what we want them to learn to do. In this way, we can improve our students' writing habits. More importantly, however, we can help our students to see themselves as capable writers and as active, able, problem-solvers. Most importantly, we can use the sequence of drafts to demand that our students demonstrate increasingly sophisticated kinds of analytic and rhetorical proficiency.

Rhetorical reading and writing heuristics can help students to represent tasks in rich and interesting ways. They can help students to set up complex goal structures (Bereiter and Scardamalia, "Conversation"). They offer students many ways to think about their reading and writing texts. These tools, in other words, encourage students to work creatively.

And after all, creativity is what research should be about. If Shirley writes a creative paper, she has found a constructive solution that is new to her and which other people can use, a solution to a problem that she and other people share. Creativity is an inherently rhetorical quality. If we think of it as thought leading to solutions to problems and of problems as embodied in questions that people ask about situations, the researched essay offers infinite possibilities. Viewed in this way, a creative idea answers a question that the audience or any single reader wants answered. The question could be, "Why did Henry V win the Battle of Agincourt?" or, "How can student readers protect themselves against nationalistic bias when they study history?" or any of a thousand other questions. If we teach our Shirleys to see themselves as scholars who work to find answers to problem questions, and if we teach them to set reading and writing goals for themselves that will allow them to think constructively, we will be doing the most exciting work that teachers can do, nurturing creativity.

Appendix A: Page 1 of Shirley's paper

The battle of Agincourt ranks as one of England's greatest military triumphs. It was the most brilliant victory of the Middle Ages, bar none. It was fought on October 25, 1414, against the French near the French village of Agincourt.

Henry V had claimed the crown of France and had invaded France with an army estimated at anywhere between 10,000[1] and 45,000 men[2]. During the siege of Marfleur dysentery had taken 1/3 of them[3], his food supplies had been depleted[4], and the fall rains had begun. In addition the French had assembled a huge army and were marching toward him. Henry decided to march to Calais, where his ships were to await him[5]. He intended to cross the River Somme at the ford of Blanchetaque[6], but, falsely informed that the ford was guarded[7], he was forced to follow the flooded Somme up toward its source. The French army was shadowing him on his right. Remembering the slaughters of Crécy and Poictiers, the French constable, Charles d'Albret, hesitated to fight[8], but when Henry forded the Somme just above Amiens[9] and was just

1. Carl Stephinson, *Medieval History*, p. 529.

2. Guizot, Monsieur and Guizot, Madame, <u>The History of France</u>, Volume II, p. 211.

3. Cyril E. Robinson, <u>England: A History of British Progress</u>, p. 145.

4. *Ibid.*

5. Winston Churchill, <u>A History of the English-Speaking Peoples, Volume 1: The Birth of Britain</u>, p. 403.

6. <u>Ibid</u>.

7. <u>Ibid</u>.

8. Robinson, p. 145.

9. Churchill, p. 403.

Works Cited

Asch, Solomon. *Social Psychology*. New York: Prentice, 1952.

Atlas, Marshall. *Expert-Novice Differences in the Writing Process*. Paper presented at the American Educational Research Association, 1979. ERIC ED 107 769.

Baker, Louise, and Ann L. Brown. "Metacognitive Skills and Reading." *Handbook of Reading Research*. Ed. P. David Person, Rebecca Barr, Michael L. Kamil, and Peter Mosenthal. New York: Longman, 1984.

Bazerman, Charles. "Physicists Reading Physics: Schema-Laden Purposes and Purpose-Laden Schema." *Written Communication* 2.1 (1985): 3–24.

Bereiter, Carl, and Marlene Scardamalia. "From Conversation to Composition: The Role of Instruction in a Developmental Process." *Advances in Instructional Psychology*. Ed. R. Glaser. Vol. 2. Hillsdale, NJ: Lawrence Erlbaum Associates, 1982. 1–64.

———. *The Psychology of Written Composition*. Hillsdale, NJ: Lawrence Erlbaum Associates, 1987.

Briscoe, Terri. "To Test or Not to Test." Unpublished essay. Texas Christian University, 1989.

Britton, James, Tony Burgess, Nancy Martin, Alex McLeod, and Harold Rosen. *The Development of Writing Abilities (11–18)*. Houndmills Basingstoke Hampshire: Macmillan Education Ltd., 1975.

Brown, Ann L. "Theories of Memory and the Problem of Development: Activity, Growth, and Knowledge." *Levels of Processing in Memory*. Eds. Laird S. Cermak and Fergus I. M. Craik. Hillsdale, NJ: Laurence Erlbaum Associates, 1979. 225–58.

———, Joseph C. Campione, and L. R. Barclay. *Training Self-Checking Routines for Estimating Test Readiness: Generalizations from List Learning to Prose Recall*. Unpublished manuscript. Univesity of Illinois, 1978.

———, and Jeanne Day. "Macrorules for Summarizing Texts: The Development of Expertise." *Journal of Verbal Learning and Verbal Behavior* 22.1 (1983): 1–14.

———, and Annmarie S. Palincsar. *Reciprocal Teaching of Comprehension Strategies: A Natural History of One Program for Enhancing Learning*. Technical Report #334. Urbana, IL: Center for the Study of Reading, 1985.

Churchill, Winston S. *The Birth of Britain*. New York: Dodd, 1956. Vol. I of *A History of the English-Speaking Peoples*. 4 vols. 1956–58.

Flower, Linda. "The Construction of Purpose in Writing and Reading." *College English* 50 (1988): 528–50.

——. *The Role of Task Representation in Reading to Write.* Berkeley, CA: Center for the Study of Writing, U of California at Berkeley and Carnegie Mellon. Technical Report, 1987.

——. "Writer-Based Prose: A Cognitive Basis for Problems in Writing." *College English* 41 (1979): 1–37.

Flower, Linda, Karen Schriver, Linda Carey, Christina Haas, and John R. Hayes. *Planning in Writing: A Theory of the Cognitive Process.* Berkeley, CA: Center for the Study of Writing, U of California at Berkeley and Carnegie Mellon. Technical Report, 1988.

Ford, James E., and Dennis R. Perry. "Research Paper Instruction in the Undergraduate Writing Program." *College English* 44 (1982): 825–31.

Ford, James E., Sharla Rees, and David L. Ward. *Teaching the Research Paper: Comprehensive Bibliography of Periodical Sources,* 1980. ERIC ED 197 363.

Goldman, Susan R. "Knowledge Systems for Realistic Goals." *Discourse Processes* 5 (1982): 279–303.

Guizot and Guizot de Witt. *The History of France from the Earliest Times to the Year 1848.* Trans. R. Black. Vol. 2. Philadelphia: John Wanamaker (n.d.).

Haas, Christina, and Linda Flower. "Rhetorical Reading Strategies and the Construction of Meaning." *College Composition and Communication* 39 (1988): 167–84.

Hayes, John R., D. A. Waterman, and C. S. Robinson. "Identifying the Relevant Aspects of a Problem Text." *Cognitive Science* 1 (1977): 297–313.

Hinze, Helen K. "The Individual's Word Associations and His Interpretation of Prose Paragraphs." *Journal of General Psychology* 64 (1961): 193–203.

Iser, Wolfgang. *The Act of Reading: A Theory of Aesthetic Response.* Baltimore: The Johns Hopkins UP, 1978.

Jeffery, Christopher. "Teachers' and Students' Perceptions of the Writing Process." *Research in the Teaching of English* 15 (1981): 215–28.

Kantz, Margaret. *Originality and Completeness: What Do We Value in Papers Written from Sources?* Conference on College Composition and Communication. St. Louis, MO, 1988.

——. *The Relationship between Reading and Planning Strategies and Success in Synthesizing: It's What You Do with Them That Counts.* Technical report in preparation. Pittsburgh: Center for the Study of Writing, 1988.

Kennedy, Mary Louise. "The Composing Process of College Students Writing from Sources." *Written Communication* 2.4 (1985): 43–56.

Kinneavy, James L. *A Theory of Discourse.* New York: Norton, 1971.

Kroll, Barry M. "Audience Adaptation in Children's Persuasive Letters." *Written Communication* 1.4 (1984): 407–28.

Langer, Judith. "Where Problems Start: The Effects of Available Information on Responses to School Writing Tasks." *Contexts for Learning to Write: Studies of Secondary School Instruction.* Ed. Arthur Applebee. Norwood, NJ: ABLEX Publishing Corporation, 1984. 135–48.

Luhig, Richard L. "Abstractive Memory, the Central-Incidental Hypothesis, and the Use of Structural Importance in Text: Control Processes or Structural Features?" *Reading Research Quarterly* 14.1 (1983): 28–37.

Marbaise, Alfred. "Treating a Disease." *Current Issues and Enduring Questions.* Eds. Sylvan Barnet and Hugo Bedau. New York: St. Martin's, 1987. 126–27.

McCormick, Kathleen. "Theory in the Reader: Bleich, Holland, and Beyond." *College English* 47.8 (1985): 836–50.

McGarry, Daniel D. *Medieval History and Civilization.* New York: Macmillan, 1976.

Nelson, Jennie, and John R. Hayes. *The Effects of Classroom Contexts on Students' Responses to Writing from Sources: Regurgitating Information or Triggering Insights.* Berkeley, CA: Center for the Study of Writing, U of California at Berkeley and Carnegie Mellon. Technical Report, 1988.

Pichert, James W. "Sensitivity to Importance as a Predictor of Reading Comprehension." *Perspectives on Reading Research and Instruction.* Eds. Michael A. Kamil and Alden J. Moe. Washington, D.C.: National Reading Conference, 1980. 42–46.

Robinson, Cyril E. *England: A History of British Progress from the Early Ages to the Present Day.* New York: Thomas Y. Crowell Company, 1928.

Schwegler, Robert A., and Linda K. Shamoon. "The Aims and Process of the Research Paper." *College English* 44 (1982): 817–24.

Shedd, Patricia T. "The Relationship between Attitude of the Reader towards Women's Changing Role and Response to Literature Which Illuminates Women's Role." Diss. Syracuse U, 1975. ERIC ED 142 956.

Short, Elizabeth Jane, and Ellen Bouchard Ryan. "Metacognitive Differences between Skilled and Less Skilled Readers: Remediating Deficits through Story Grammar and Attribution Training." *Journal of Education Psychology* 76 (1984): 225–35.

Spivey, Nancy Nelson. *Discourse Synthesis: Constructing Texts in Reading and Writing.* Diss. U Texas, 1983. Newark, DE: International Reading Association, 1984.

Toulmin, Steven E. *The Uses of Argument.* Cambridge: Cambridge UP, 1969.

Vipond, Douglas, and Russell Hunt. "Point-Driven Understanding: Pragmatic and Cognitive Dimensions of Literary Reading." *Poetics* 13 (1984): 261–77.

Winograd, Peter. "Strategic Difficulties in Summarizing Texts." *Reading Research Quarterly* 19 (1984): 404–25.

RESPONDING TO PLAGIARISM

Alice Drum

[College Composition and Communication 37 (1986): 241–43.]

Vice president for educational services and adjunct professor of English at Franklin and Marshall College in Lancaster, Pennsylvania, Alice Drum has published numerous articles in professional journals, including World Literature Written in English *and* Magill's Literary Annual. *Currently, she is doing research on Jane Austen.*

Drum wrote the following article as a response to a plagiarism case that was especially troubling to her. After the case was over she surveyed composition texts to see how they presented plagiarism. She concluded that many of the presentations were inadequate and that introductory writing courses needed to do more to prevent plagiarism. With its thorough coverage on pages 477–89, The Bedford Handbook *answers Drum's call for more emphasis on teaching students how to avoid plagiarism.*

Plagiarism is a disease that plagues college instructors everywhere. I believe that our reliance on the classic argument against plagiarism may be one of the reasons for its continued virulence. That argument reads something like this: Plagiarism is both legally and morally wrong because it involves the appropriation of words or ideas that belong to someone else and the misrepresentation of them as one's own. Unfortunately, we tend to place a great deal of emphasis on the first part of the process, the simple act of taking ideas, and very little on the second stage, the more complicated act of passing them off as one's own. In our conferences with students suspected of plagiarism, we carefully point out the legal and ethical implications of what they have done, but we neglect to mention the pedagogical implications of what they have not done — completed an assignment. As the continuing practice of plagiarism testifies, this emphasis on the legalistic rather than the pedagogical consequences of plagiarism has proved an ineffectual way of dealing with the problem. In its place, I would recommend a holistic approach, a recognition that plagiarism involves a student, an instructor, and the structure within which the two interact.

In the first place, we must admit that many students do not know how to avoid plagiarism, that most rhetoric textbooks are of little help in this respect, and that many college composition classes deal inadequately with the problem. The greatest weakness is with the textbooks. A random survey of thirty popular texts reveals that many provide no reference to plagiarism in the index, and that most contain at best a paragraph of explanation and definition. Most textbooks say, in effect, "Do not plagiarize," but they refuse to do much more than remonstrate against the practice. They seldom contain useful writing exercises on the paraphrase, the summary, and the precis, although such exercises would indicate to students that there are varied ways of avoiding plagiarism. Instead, the standard handbook emphasizes the mechanics of documentation — the presentation of footnotes and bibliography in the currently accepted form.

In the classroom, we take our cue from the handbooks and concentrate on rules rather than on the various ways of integrating source materials in a text. Avoiding plagiarism is not simply a matter of following accepted rules, however. If a student changes Harold Bloom's description of Milton, "the severe father of the sublime mode" (*Poetry and Repression*, p. 21), to "a severe father of sublimity," that student has not repeated more than three words in a row, thus adhering to one popular formula on how to avoid plagiarism. On the other hand, the student has not added anything that is original; clearly, the sentence needs a footnote. Occasionally, footnotes are omitted through oversight, but generally the need for documentation is clear to students, once they understand that avoiding plagiarism does not simply involve adhering to a formula but also involves dealing carefully with the style and the content of the original.

In my composition classes, to help students understand this principle, a research paper is due only after I have assigned and returned three or four preliminary assignments and after the students have participated in several research writing workshops. The preliminary assignments may include an abstract, a summary, a brief background paper. The writing workshops include sessions where the students analyze the style and the content of a selected passage and then attempt to put that passage in a different form. They may work on creating an effective paraphrase of a brief article; they may take a single sentence and rewrite it a number of times, making as many stylistic changes as possible without changing the content; they may rewrite a brief passage — an article from *Newsweek* —in the style of a well-known writer. The aim of these exercises is twofold: to help the students understand that writers do give an identity to their words, and to give students confidence in their own ability to create a style of their own in their writing.

These exercises are designed to correct unconscious plagiarism, but we all know that many acts of plagiarism are conscious ones. In regard to these cases, we must examine the myth that plagiarism has everything to do with some anonymous "other" — a critic, an expert — and nothing to do with the teacher of the class, who has, after all, made the assignment which the student has failed to complete. Because written assignments involve at least one, and probably all, of the steps of the cognitive process, they test the student's ability to collect evidence, make inferences, and render judgments. The professor's response in the form of a grade or a written commentary is a means of communicating his or her opinion of the student's intellectual maturity. When students fail to comply honestly with an assignment, the pedagogical process breaks down.

For this reason, the instructor — not deans, chairpersons, nor commissions — should handle initial cases of plagiarism. There are a number of benefits to be derived from this procedure. An important one is that we would not be perpetuating the myth that plagiarism has nothing to do with the instructor and the course. Another benefit is that students are more likely to be concerned about the response of a professor who represents a familiar face than they are about the response of a dean who represents anonymous authority. And professors, only too aware of the difficulties of dealing with bureaucracy, may be more inclined to confer with a student than to involve themselves in the time-consuming procedure of reporting plagiarism to someone else.

Instead, the penalty for plagiarism, at least for initial cases in introductory courses such as composition, should be meted out by the instructor. With initial cases, we can reasonably assume that either the students do not know how to avoid plagiarism or that they have been led to believe that it does not matter. We can assure them that the latter is not true, and we can provide instructions on how to avoid plagiarism in the future. Some persons may argue that the individual professor may not be harsh enough, that stringent punishments are needed to stop the widespread cheating on campuses today. But it can, also, be argued that legalistic punishments have not proved particularly effective, and that they necessitate extensive protections for the student and increasing complications for the professor who attempts to prove plagiarism. I am not arguing for permissiveness in regard to plagiarism, but rather for a recognition that it is at least as much a pedagogical offense as a legalistic one. Certainly, we must insist that we will not tolerate plagiarism, that students will receive significantly lowered grades when they plagiarize. But we should also admit that students may learn more from a second chance to complete an assignment than from an automatic failure in a course. With this alternative procedure, there should be added penalties and added work, but there would, also, be an opportunity for the student to learn how to deal with research material with integrity. And that, after all, is one of the reasons that we assign library papers.

PART TEN

SPECIAL TYPES OF WRITING

Because much of the writing that students will do outside of the composition course asks them to compose arguments to write about literature, many teachers incorporate these kinds of assignments into their course plans. Part Ten of *The Bedford Handbook,* "Special Types of Writing," helps students and teachers with these skills. The discussions of writing arguments, critical thinking, and writing about literature demonstrate specific applications of the composing process presented in Part Two. In these ways the handbook serves as a practical guide and as an important reference source for students in and beyond the freshman writing composition course.

However, even with the thorough coverage and support offered by the handbook, the challenges of teaching these kinds of writing stimulate debates on a variety of issues. The selections that follow offer responses to several central questions that face teachers when they choose to incorporate argumentation and critical thinking of writing about literature into their courses:

- Argumentation and critical thinking are becoming the focus of increasing numbers of composition courses. What is an argument? And what are its various forms?
- Should students learn logic? If so, which form? Why?
- How can teachers interest students in approaching literature from different critical perspectives? Given the sophistication of current critical theory and the complexity of various interpretive approaches to literature, can instructors teach writing about literature without introducing (and suffering) confusion and despair?

WRITING ARGUMENTS

From RECENT RESEARCH IN ARGUMENTATION THEORY

Marie J. Secor

[Technical Writing Teacher 14 (1987): 337–54.]

Marie J. Secor is associate professor of English at Pennsylvania State University. Her interest in argumentation and in style has resulted in numerous publications. With Jeanne Fahnestock, she wrote A Rhetoric of Argument, now in its second edition, and they are working on a new book, A

Rhetoric of Style. *The selection here is the first half of an article in which Secor examines what writing teachers need to know about argumentation.*

The first half of "Recent Research in Argumentation Theory" surveys research conducted in the areas of speech communications and philosophy on the nature and forms of argument. Secor traces the influence of Stephen Toulmin and Chaim Perelman on the study of argumentation. In the remainder of the essay, not included here, she discusses research that attempts to answer the question, "Where is argument?"; and she examines research done in the "informal logic movement." She concludes by reminding her readers that teaching argumentation is much more complex than teaching the rules of logic, and she asks them to consider the findings of recent research in argumentation and critical thinking.

As teachers of writing we are interested in the production, analysis, and evaluation of texts. Even when our pedagogy and research methodology emphasize process, we assume that process aims at the production of written discourse. But recent research in argumentation takes a slightly different approach. It steps back from the methodology of text production in order to address some prior questions: What is an argument? Where is argument to be found? Is it an interaction, a mental process, a series of propositions? What is a good argument? Do principles derived from logic apply to the evaluation of arguments? What does it mean to be reasonable? Is reasonableness the same in all arguments, or does it vary from one field to another? Such questions resemble those asked by researchers in composition and technical writing, and answers to them underlie our most basic assumptions and therefore affect our practice as both teachers and researchers. Awareness of research and scholarship in argumentation can broaden our conception of what argument is, of the forms it may take, and of the motives and purposes that shape scholarly investigation.

This essay surveys two areas of research in argumentation theory: that performed by argumentation scholars in speech communications and that done by informal logicians in philosophy. The two proceed from different histories and assumptions. The informal logicians are a group of philosophers who teach basic courses in logic and critical thinking. Moved by their classroom experience, they have asked how the study of logic can be accommodated to the needs of modern students. Their answer, on the whole, has been that formal, mathematical logic is of limited (or no) applicability, so they have attempted to salvage and describe a kind of informal logic, one that deals with ordinary language and can be used to describe and evaluate the reasoning that people do in everyday life. Their enterprise derives its exigence from the long separation of logic and rhetoric, a gap which they are attempting to repair, and they are just beginning to explore the role of audience and the situational constraints of ordinary language argument. Their work is strengthened by its awareness of structural patterns that can be observed in everyday discourse. It is also somewhat limited by its vision of argument as a structure of propositions that can be described and assessed apart from reference to audiences and fields.

Argumentation scholars in speech, on the other hand, are heavily influenced by the work of two major contemporary theorists, Stephen Toulmin, and Chaim Perelman, both of whom have emphasized the jurisprudential origins and characteristics of argument rather than its connections with formal logic. Even where the work of argumentation theorists does not comment directly on that of Toulmin and Perelman, it shares several of their basic assumptions: that rhetoric is epistemic, the means by which we know whatever it is that can be known to whatever degree of certainty is possible; that rigidly applied standards of deductive validity do little to explain how arguments actually work; that audience and context play crucial roles in determining what counts as good reasoning; that argument can be studied in many different fields, not just in clearly delimited realms of public deliberative, forensic, and epideictic discourse. The work of scholars in argumentation theory draws on that of philosophers and sociologists. It seeks to relate the study of argumentation to theories that emphasize the power of disciplines, audiences, and forums to determine what is knowable, what is arguable, and what are the reasons for accepting any argument.

Toulmin on Argument

Perhaps the single greatest influence on the contemporary study of argumentation is Stephen Toulmin's *The Uses of Argument*, a book that has steadily gained in impact during the past thirty years. For Toulmin the study of argument is concerned not with the manner or technique by which we make inferences; "its primary business," he writes, "is a retrospective justificatory one — with the arguments we can put forward afterwards to make good our claim that the conclusions arrived at are acceptable, because justifiable, conclusions" (1958, p. 6). Perhaps the best known aspect of Toulmin's work is the model of argument he describes in chapter 3, a model that has been adopted and applied by many contemporary scholars of argumentation. For Toulmin, arguments consist of six elements. The first essential component is a *claim*, which can be defined as the conclusion the arguer is attempting to justify. This claim is supported by *data*, which he calls "the facts we appeal to as foundation for the claim" (1958, p. 97). But data and claim alone do not suffice. Arguers may be asked to indicate how the data come to bear on the conclusion. To justify the leap from data to claim, they appeal to a rule or a principle or what Toulmin calls an inference-license that allows data and claim to be connected. This third element is the *warrant*. Warrants may be defined as "general, hypothetical statements, which can act as bridges, and authorise the sort of step to which our particular argument commits us" (1958, p. 98). These three components — data, warrant, and claim — are the primary elements of any argument.

To this simple model Toulmin adds three more elements that may be needed to describe the complete structure of an argument. If the warrant is not obvious or immediately accepted by the audience, it may require *backing* or additional support, statements that indicate the basis for accepting the warrant. The fifth element is called a *modal qualifier*, a word (like "probably" or "presumably" or "usually" or "certainly") that indicates the strength of the connection between the data and the warrant. The qualifier may be needed because not all arguments connect their elements with the force of necessity. The sixth and final element in Toulmin's model of argument is called the *rebuttal*. It consists of a statement that describes the circumstances under which the authority of the warrant might be set aside, the conditions under which the claim would not hold. As this model suggests, Toulmin sees argument as a complex and variable human process, not an abstract or mathematically constrained one; it consists of "the whole activity of making claims, challenging them, backing them up by producing reasons, criticizing those reasons, rebutting those criticisms, and so on" (Toulmin, Rieke, and Janik 1983, p. 13).

In addition to the model of argument, several other concepts and approaches outlined in *The Uses of Argument* have influenced the contemporary study of argumentation. First, Toulmin's rejection of formal logic as a basis for argumentation has made his work especially attractive to rhetoricians. He is quite explicit in rejecting the syllogism as a model for the analysis of arguments. He distinguishes between analytic arguments in which the conclusion is implied in the premises (arguments such as "All men are mortal, Socrates is a man, therefore Socrates is mortal") and what he calls substantial arguments, in which connections between data and claim are not self-evident. He criticizes formal logic for privileging analytic arguments as models to which all others should aspire. For Toulmin the neatness and formality of the analytic syllogism do not constitute arguments for its primacy; in fact, he believes the opposite. He criticizes formal logic for its emphasis on universality, timelessness, and certainty, qualities characteristic of analytic syllogisms but which in his view do not reflect the ways in which we come to know reality or the language we use to describe it.

Another major contribution of Toulmin to the study of argument is his notion of argument fields. Where others have seen all arguments as sharing the same qualities, Toulmin makes distinctions. For him, "Two arguments will be said to belong to the same field when the data and conclusions in each of the two arguments are, respectively, of the same logical type: They will be said to come from different fields when the backing or the conclusions in each of the two arguments are not of the same logical type" (1958, p. 14). Thus arguments in nuclear physics, although they may have the same general structure, will differ essentially from those in sociology, which will differ from those in literary criticism because notions of what constitutes evidence differ from one field to another. The identification of argument fields leads Toulmin to another important question that has inspired further consideration and research: What elements of argument can be said to be field-invariant (the same regardless of field) and what elements are field-dependent (varying as we move from one field to another)? Toulmin answers the question in part by suggesting that the force of the conclusion will be field-invariant but the criteria needed to justify it will vary from one field to another.

In his later book *Human Understanding,* Toulmin continues his investigation of argument as an ongoing human enterprise. Critical of the views expressed by Thomas Kuhn in *The Structure of Scientific Revolutions,* Toulmin argues that conceptual change is evolutionary rather than revolutionary. New ideas, Toulmin believes, are introduced in suitable forums of competition, "within which intellectual novelties can survive for long enough to show their merits or defects; but in which they are criticized and weeded out with enough severity to maintain the coherence of the discipline" (1972, p. 92). Again, in *Human Understanding* Toulmin tries to avoid extremes of absolutism and relativism in assessing the validity of concepts. He shifts the question from one of validity to one of explanatory power. In his view, the most important question to ask of an idea is "would this particular conceptual variant *improve* our explanatory power *more than* its rivals?" (1972, p. 225) The answer depends, of course, on who is doing the explaining. Thus Toulmin appeals to what he calls the "impartial rational standpoint," which is objective to the extent that it does not choose between the views of different cultural and historic environments, but relative to the extent that it remains open to change and the evidence of history.

Toulmin's impact on the study of argument in America was brought about largely through the exposition of his ideas by Wayne Brockriede and Douglas Ehninger (1960). Brockriede and Ehninger summarize Toulmin's model of argument and suggest seven reasons for its superiority in describing and assessing arguments. First, Toulmin's model accounts for warrant-establishing, not just warrant-using arguments; second, it stresses the inferential and relational nature of argument; third, it deals with probable, not just universal claims; fourth, it conceives of argument as dynamic rather than static; fifth, it lays out steps in argument rather than suppressing any; sixth, it reveals rather than obscures deficiencies in arguments; and seventh, it deals with the problem of material validity (that is, the validity of premises rather than just the validity of inference patterns), which has been neglected by formal logic.

Although Brockriede and Ehninger were largely responsible for bringing Toulmin's work to the attention of rhetoricians, Toulmin was not received with universal approbation. Peter Manicas (1966), for example, argues that the Toulmin model really consists of only three elements (data, warrant, and conclusion), not six, and thus is not a new way of seeing arguments at all but only a syllogism laid out on its side. He claims that the challenge of any one of these elements could be overcome simply by constructing a new three-part argument, once again resembling a syllogism, to support the challenging statement. He also accuses Toulmin of relying too heavily on ordinary language and not exploring the full power of formal logic. Along similar lines, Jimmie D. Trent (1968) defends the continuing relevance of logic to the study of argumentation, and Brant R. Burleson (1979) criticizes Toulmin's "impartial standpoint of rationality" for leaning too heavily toward relativism. Other criticisms of Toulmin are voiced by Dale Hample (1977) and J. C. Cooley (1959).

In spite of such qualifications, Toulmin's impact on the study of debate and argumentation has been enormous. Brockriede and Ehninger's popular text, *Decision by Debate* (1963), brought the Toulmin model into wide circulation in debate and argumentation courses, and many other argumentation texts since then have made use of the Toulmin model. Two textbooks of special importance are Richard D. Rieke and Malcolm O. Sillars, *Argumentation and the Decision Making Process* (1975) and the one co-authored by Toulmin with two collaborators, Richard Rieke and Alan Janik, *An Introduction to Reasoning* (1983). The latter, especially, shows how the concept of fields of argument can be fruitfully applied to the pedagogy of discourse production in many disciplines; of particular interest here are the chapters on argumentation in science and in management. Toulmin was brought to the attention of composition researchers by Charles Kneupper (1978); another direct pedagogical application is described in James Stratman (1982). Stratman shows how the Toulmin model can be adapted to the teaching of argumentative sentence-combining exercises and contends that it can help students find new things to say by pointing to areas needing further inquiry and development.

One major product of Toulmin's influence has been the ongoing debate among argumentation scholars over his notion of fields of argument. Although not everyone has agreed with Toulmin, many have taken up the challenge of describing what a field is as a preliminary to distinguishing between field-dependent and -variant qualities of argument. Charles Willard, for instance, emphasizes how understanding the social process of argumentation is an essential preliminary to the study of fields; he urges us to accept "fuzziness and blurred distinctions between fields" and encourages us to think of fields as audiences as well as speakers (1983, p. 21).

Other important work on field theory includes Gronbeck (1981), Fisher (1981), Zarefsky (1981), Rowland (1981), and Miller (1983). The debate in argumentation theory about fields has been protracted, even, to an outsider's view, at times overrefined. Many of the essays can be read as prologomena to a theory of argumentation. Yet such work is valuable and even of special interest to teachers of technical writing. Most of it emphasizes the inherently social nature of argumentative discourse; it suggests that researchers concentrate on studying how groups and institutions are formed and how they determine for themselves what count as good arguments. Such understanding can link the teaching of technical writing directly with a clear rhetorical context.

Perelman on Argument

The other major influence on recent work in argumentation theory has been that of Chaim Perelman, who came to the study of rhetoric from legal philosophy. *The New Rhetoric* of Perelman and Olbrechts-Tyteca (1969) is a rich and complex work that has affected rhetorical theory in many ways; Perelman summarizes and outlines its main ideas in *The Realm of Rhetoric* (1982). First and perhaps most important, for Perelman a theory of rhetoric is a theory of argumentation, and it is not to be identified with formal logic. Like Toulmin, Perelman rejects formal logic as a model for argumentation. Argumentation, in his view, studies the discursive techniques that "induce or increase the mind's adherence to the theses presented for its assent" (1969), p. 4). Unlike mathematical logic, arguments do not demonstrate conclusions that must be accepted; they present discourse that is more or less probable, to which audiences are invited to adhere.

Perelman's theory emphasizes audience, defining it most generally as "the ensemble of those whom the speaker wishes to influence by his argumentation (1969, p. 19). In his view audience is neither a physical assembly nor a demographically describable segment of a population; rather, it is a mental construct of the arguer, an element of the arguer's sense of intention. This audience may vary in size and generality. It can consist of the speaker reflecting on a situation, or it may extend to what Perelman calls the "universal audience," which consists of all of humanity "or at least all those who are competent and reasonable" (1982, p. 14). To convince audiences of whatever magnitude, arguments must proceed from premises that are acceptable to them. Because argument begins in agreement, arguers must be primarily concerned with their audience's acceptance of the premises of their discourse. These points of agreement may be of several kinds. Some deal with reality (which Perelman calls facts, truths, and presumptions), and others concern what is preferable (values, hierarchies of values, and what Perelman calls the *loci* of the preferable). Facts and truths are constituted by audiences' agreement to them; the more people perceive them to be rooted in the structure of reality, the more universal their agreement is likely to be. Facts and truths are thus defined not by external standards but by agreement, which, if withdrawn, would destroy their status. In Perelman's view, facts, truths, and presumptions are accepted by the universal audience, while values, hierarchies, and loci of the preferable are held only by particular audiences, who will vary in the values they hold, in the weight they give to different values, and in their assumptions about what is preferable in any particular circumstance.

Arguing, for Perelman, always consists of procedures by which ideas and values are endowed with what he calls "presence" — that is, emphasized, given prominence in the minds of the audience. Since language is inherently ambiguous, arguments must not only establish the credibility of claims but also endow them in the minds of the audience with the presence they deserve. Finally, Perelman distinguishes a number of means by which concepts are associated or linked with each other in arguments. He uses the term "liaison," which describes a kind of linking or association, to refer to this bonding between ideas (as opposed to the term "entailment" from formal logic). The major techniques of liaison consist of quasi-logical arguments, which draw on patterns resembling but not so rigid as those of formal logic; arguments based on claims about the structure of reality (for example, that causes produce effects); arguments based on examples that imply general laws; arguments that proceed by analogy or metaphor; arguments that dissociate concepts from those that apparently resemble them; and arguments that impose special orders on ideas.

Perelman's approach to argumentation has inspired both controversy and applications. Some of Perelman's commentators have been uneasy with the notion of universal audience. Henry W. Johnstone (1978) has argued that the whole notion of universal audience is unnecessary to Perelman's theory, which would not be seriously affected by its omission. And John Ray claims that the notion is "excessively formal and abstract" (1978, p. 375), to the point that it loses validity when applied to particular situations. Responding to his critics, Perelman defends his own consistent advocacy of philosophical pluralism, pointing out that the word "reasonable" is equivocal, and that "what is reasonable varies in time and in space, what is reasonable for a particular audience may not be so for a universal audience" (1984, p. 193).

A number of essays have attempted to apply and extend Perelman's ideas. Ray Dearin (1982) gives a lucid explication of Perelman's view of quasi-logical argument as an attempt to reconcile the irrelevance of formal logic with the obvious rhetorical power of arguments that use logical structures. Quasi-logical argumentation evokes the prestige of formal logic but resembles a "web" rather than a "chain" of inferentially linked propositions. James Measell explains and elaborates Perelman's comments on analogy and explores some of his theory's implications for the study of argument. He shows how, as an argumentative technique, analogy accommodates to audience by relating the well known from one sphere to the less known from another. He reinforces Perelman's contention that analogies "must be recognized as capable of proof, just as are other argumentative structures" (1985, p. 69). Since to accept an analogy is to accept the importance of the characteristics it highlights, analogies are best kept within limits rather than tested by extension.

Other essays exploring some of the implications of Perelman's ideas include Edward Sciappa's (1985), which applies Perelman's theory of dissociation to the techniques of argumentation used by rhetoricians; J. Robert Cox's (1982), which demonstrates how the concept of *loci* can be applied; Marie Secor's (1984), which identifies some characteristic *loci* of preference in the arguments of literary criticism; and Louise A. Karon's (1976), which investigates the relationship between presence and Perelman's theory of knowledge and defends the concept as an essential ingredient of both adherence and truth.

Perelman's impact on the study of argumentation is just beginning to be felt and will undoubtedly increase as his ideas become familiar to wider audiences. In a pair of essays he wrote at the end of his life, Perelman himself suggests some directions for future research. In "Philosophy and Rhetoric," he reaffirms and articulates his antipositivist approach, insisting that in argumentation there can be "no criteria for objective validity" (1982, p. 292). He urges us to investigate different disciplines, where the value of an argument is to be judged not only by its effectiveness but by "the quality of audience it is able to convince" (1982, p. 293). In "The New Rhetoric and the Rhetoricians: Remembrances and Comments," in addition to answering some of the critics who have written about his work, Perelman compares his own thought with that of Toulmin, which, he claims, ignores the role of audience and neglects reasoning about values, ending with a challenge for rhetoricians to learn from the study of legal and judicial reasoning (1984, p. 195). Thus in his last published essays Perelman seems to be directing future research in argumentation toward the application of his ideas to the study of rhetoric in different disciplines. For this reason, his work holds special significance for teachers of technical writing, who can find in Perelman's work on argument an approach that helps identify the means by which varying kinds of discourse gain the adherence of various audiences.

Values and Good Reasons

Another subject that has engaged theorists of argumentation is what might be called the good reasons issue, that is, the place of values and ethics in argumentation and their role in establishing the force of an argument. Several essays that appeared during the 1960s raised the issue. Ralph T. Eubanks and Virgil Baker (1962) emphasize the centrality of values to rhetoric. Karl Wallace (1963) also discerns values at the basis of rhetorical theory and practice and insists that rhetoric deal with the substance of discourse as well as its structure and style. He borrows from ethics the term "good reasons," which he defines as "statements, consistent with each other, in support of an *ought* proposition or of a value-judgment" (p. 247). By using this term to refer to all the materials of argument and explanation, "we might cease worrying over our failure to find perfect syllogisms in the arguments of everyday life." Wallace sees rhetoric as the art of finding and presenting good reasons, a view that avoids the rigidity of models derived from logic and cuts across what he terms the artificial distinction between ethos, pathos, and logos. Along similar lines, Wayne Booth writes about his pursuit of "good reasons, finding what really warrants assent because any reasonable person ought to be persuaded by what has been said" (1974, p. xiv).

The subject of good reasons, however, concerns more than just the general relationship between rhetoric and ethics and a call for an ethical rhetoric. It also concerns the place of values within argumentation, both as elements of the substance of arguments and as components of the character of the arguer. The question is not only what do we mean by good reasons? We might also ask what does it mean to be reasonable or rational in argument? Walter R. Fisher calls attention to the "indisputable need in contemporary rhetoric for a scheme by which values can be identified and their implications critically considered" (1978, p. 376). Finding Wallace's and Booth's definitions of good reasons useful but too narrowly circular, Fisher conceives of them as: "those elements that provide warrants for accepting or adhering to the advice fostered by any form of communication that can be considered rhetorical" (1978, p. 378). Fisher suggests subjecting the values identified in discourse to the following five questions: questions about fact (What values are embedded in a message?), relevance (Are the values appropriate to the decision called for?), consequence (What are the effects of adhering to such values?), consistency (Does experience confirm these values?); and transcendent issues (Are they an ideal basis for human conduct?). He demonstrates how this logic of good reasons can be fitted to the Toulmin model and notes that some values appear to be field-dependent and others field-invariant.

Fisher explores some further implications of the logic of good reasons in a 1980 essay, where he tries to relate rationality to the logic of good reasons. Distinguishing between rationality and reasonableness, he regards rationality as an ability, an essential attribute of rhetorical competence, and reasonableness more as an attitude, the social aspect of rationality. Ray E. McKerrow pursues the distinction between reason and rationality, defining reasonable discourse as adhering "to the standards of rationality adopted by a communication community" (1982, p. 121) and rationality itself as more of an absolute, associated with mathematics. McKerrow points out, for example, that although it may be *rational* to sterilize rapists, a given society may not consider it reasonable. He calls for a theory of argument that "balances the need for a rational procedure for assessing substantive claims with the equally important need to be cognizant of prevailing values" (1982, p. 121). Another study of values in argumentation is by Joseph W. Wenzel, who claims that argumentation can develop ways of discussing values and that "the study of value-centered argument can clarify the logical and epistemological status of value claims and the reasons supporting them" (1977, p. 152). If we attend to the function of value statements, he claims that we can find a rational basis for every kind of value dispute that people consider significant.

If McKerrow and Wenzel call for the development of a theory of argument that takes account of reasonableness, rationality, and values, Malcolm Sillars and Patricia Ganer (1982) try to explain exactly how prevailing values are deployed in argumentation. Borrowing the social-value system described by Milton Rokeach, they distinguish between beliefs and attitudes (of which we hold many) and values (which are more limited in number). Values back belief warrants and reveal the shared convictions of a community. What argumentation does is not so much ask us to acquire new values or abandon old ones as persuade us to redistribute our values more or less widely, to rescale them, to reemploy them, or to restandardize them. Social values are the real ink between argument and audience; they are the only means of understanding society's presumptions. Sillars and Ganer conclude with a call for more empirical and theoretical research on values to demonstrate exactly how they are used in argumentation.

Henry Johnstone's work on rhetoric and philosophical argumentation also contributes to the good reasons debate. Johnstone's work depicts his increasing conviction that rhetoric is central even to argumentation in philosophy, to which he had first thought it antithetical. In *Validity and*

Rhetoric in Philosophical Argument (1978) he traces his evolving views on the subject. Later, he explores his own conviction that philosophical argument cannot be valid unless it is bilateral; that is, "the arguer must use no device of argument that he could not in principle permit his interlocutor to use" (1982, p. 95). He extends this belief from philosophy to other fields of argument, offering the hypothesis that "no valid communication about anything — shoes or ships or sealing wax — ought to enlist belief by means unavailable to the audience." He notes, "If I can point out your unnoticed assumptions, you can point out mine" (1982, p. 100).

What is the point of this continuing discussion of values and good reasons in argumentation? Certainly it is consistent with the approaches of Toulmin and Perelman, moving away from standards of formal logic as relevant to the description and assessment of arguments. It acknowledges the inevitable presence, indeed the primacy of values in argument. And it directs scholars and researchers to an awareness of how history, social context, and specific disciplinary fields affect our notions of what is reasonable, what is rational, what is valid, and what constitutes good reasons. All of these elements are important to our understanding of arguments, but none of them can be defined as exclusively formal properties. The good reasons discussion represents an attempt to avoid the extremes of an objectivism that would identify and rank values apart from their embodiment in different fields and a relativism that would identify values and good reasons but offer no way to assess them.

References

Booth, Wayne. 1974. *Modern Dogma and the Rhetoric of Assent.* Notre Dame, Ind.: University of Notre Dame Press.

Brockriede, Wayne, and Douglas Ehninger. 1978. *Decision by Debate.* 2d ed. New York: Harper & Row.

———. 1960. Toulmin on argument: An interpretation and application. *Quarterly Journal of Speech 46*: 44–53.

Burleson, Brant R. 1979. On the foundations of rationality: Toulmin, Habermas, and the *a priori* of reason. *Journal of the American Forensic Association* 16: 112–27.

Cooley, J. C. 1959. On Mr. Toulmin's revolution in logic. *Journal of Philosophy 56:* 297–319.

Cox, J. Robert. 1982. The die is cast: Topical and ontological dimensions of the *locus* of the irreparable. *Quarterly Journal of Speech 68:* 227–39.

Dearin, Ray. 1982. Perelman's concept of "quasi-logical argument": A critical elaboration. In *Advances in Argumentation Theory and Research,* pp. 78–94. *See* Cox and Willard.

Eubanks, Ralph T., and Virgil Baker. 1962. Toward an axiology of rhetoric. *Quarterly Journal of Speech 47:* 157–68.

Fisher, Walter R. 1978. Toward a logic of good reasons. *Quarterly Journal of Speech 64:* 376–84.

———. 1980. Rationality and the logic of good reasons. *Philosophy and Rhetoric 13:* 121–30.

———. 1981. Good reasons: Fields and genre. In *Dimensions of Argument,* pp. 114–25. *See* Ziegelmueller and Rhodes.

Gronbeck, Bruce. 1981. Sociocultural notions of argument fields: A primer. In *Dimensions of Argument,* pp. 1–20. *See* Ziegelmueller and Rhodes.

Hample, Dale. 1977. The Toulmin model and the syllogism. *Journal of the American Forensic Association 14:* 1–9.

Johnstone, Henry W. 1978. *Validity and Rhetoric in Philosophical Argument: An Outlook in Transition.* University Park, Pa.: Dialogue Press of Man and World.

———. 1982. Bilaterality in argument and communication. In *Advances in Argumentation Theory and Research,* pp. 95–102. *See* Cox and Willard.

Karon, Louise A. Presence in *The New Rhetoric. Philosophy and Rhetoric 9,* pp. 96–111.

Kneupper, Charles. 1978. Teaching argument: An introduction to the Toulmin model. *College Composition and Communication 29:* 237–41.

Manicas, Peter T. 1966. On Toulmin's contribution to logic and argumentation. *Journal of the American Forensic Association 3:* 83–94.

McKerrow, Ray E. 1982. Rationality and reasonableness in a theory of argument. In *Advances in Argumentation Theory and Research,* pp. 105–22. *See* Cox and Willard.

Measell, James. 1985. Perelman on analogy. *Journal of the American Forensic Association 22:* 65–71.

Miller, Carolyn R. 1983. Fields of argument and special topoi. In *Argument in Transition,* pp. 147–58. *See* Zarefsky, Sillars, and Rhodes.

Perelman, Chaim. 1982. *The Realm of Rhetoric.* Trans. W. Klumack. Notre Dame, Ind.: University of Notre Dame Press.

———. 1982. Philosophy and rhetoric. In *Advances in Argumentation Theory and Research,* pp. 287–97. *See* Cox and Willard.

———. 1984. The new rhetoric and the rhetoricians: Remembrances and comments. *Quarterly Journal of Speech 70:* 188–96.

Perelman, Chaim, and L. Olbrechts-Tyteca. 1969. *The New Rhetoric.* Trans. J. Wilkinson and P. Weaver. Notre Dame, Ind.: University of Notre Dame Press.

Ray, John. 1978. Perelman's universal audience. *Quarterly Journal of Speech 64:* 361–75.

Rieke, Richard D., and Malcolm O. Sillars. 1975. *Argumentation and the Decision Making Process.* New York: John Wiley.

Rowland, Robert. 1981. Argument fields. In *Dimensions of Argument,* pp. 56–79. *See* Ziegelmueller and Rhodes.

Sciappa, Edward. 1985. Dissociation in the arguments of rhetorical theory. *Journal of the American Forensic Association 22:* 72–82.

Secor, Marie. 1984. Perelman's *loci* in literary argument. *Pre/Text* 5:97–110.

Sillars, Malcolm O., and Patricia Ganer. 1982. Value and beliefs: A systematic basis for argumentation. In *Advances in Argumentation Theory and Research,* pp. 184–201. *See* Cox and Willard.

Stratman, James. 1982. Teaching written argument: The significance of Toulmin's layout for sentence combining. *College English 44:* 718–33.

Toulmin, Stephen. 1958. *The Uses of Argument.* Cambridge: Cambridge University Press.

———. 1972. *Human Understanding.* Princeton, N.J.: Princeton University Press.

Toulmin, Stephen, Richard D. Rieke, and Alan Janik. 1983. *An Introduction to Reasoning.* 2d ed. New York: Macmillan.

Trent, Jimmie D. 1968. Toulmin's model of argument: An examination and extension. *Quarterly Journal of Speech 54:* 252–59.

Wallace, Karl. 1963. The substance of rhetoric: Good reasons. *Quarterly Journal of Speech 49:* 239–49.

Wenzel, Joseph W. Toward a rationale for value-centered argument. *Journal of the American Forensic Association 13:* 150–58.

———. 1983. *Argumentation and the Social Grounds of Knowledge.* University: University of Alabama Press.

Zarefsky, David. 1981. "Reasonableness" in public policy argument: Fields as institutions. In *Dimensions of Argument,* 88–100. *See* Ziegelmueller and Rhodes.

TECHNICAL LOGIC, COMP-LOGIC, AND THE TEACHING OF WRITING

Richard Fulkerson

[College Composition and Communication 39 (1988): 436–52.]

(For biographical information, see page 77.)

The article that follows resulted from Fulkerson's frustration with discussions of inductive and deductive reasoning in English textbooks. Fulkerson critiques various unsatisfactory presentations of technical logic by composition texts, and he offers an alternative to the typical textbook suggestions for teaching logic in the writing class. Even if teachers do not adopt his approach, Fulkerson's analysis of the present methods challenges them to reconsider how they present logic to student writers.

Frederick Crews tells a story about teaching logic to composition students at U. C. Berkeley early in his career. He spent "two weeks drawing interlocked circles on the blackboard representing syllogisms and enthymemes" (p. 11). The results, he said, were "stupefyingly irrefutable papers" built on syllogisms such as,

> My major premise is that all freshmen at Berkeley are eager to succeed in life.
> I am a freshman at Berkeley.
> It therefore follows that I am eager to succeed in life. (p. 11)

One illustration of teaching gone awry proves almost nothing, but I find this anecdote revealing. Like Crews, many of us — encouraged by materials that pervade our textbooks — have attempted to introduce some features of what Walter Fisher calls "technical logic" into our classrooms. Rarely, I think, with success.

The rationale for including some technical logic in composition is simple and apparently impeccable. First, much of the writing we teach, even writing we label as exposition, involves argument because it involves the attempt to support some claims (such as theses and topic sentences) with other claims (such as details, examples, and quotation). That attempt is, by definition, argument (see Copi, p. 6). Second, since logic is the intellectual discipline dedicated to analyzing and evaluating argument (Copi, p. 3), then logic should be useful in teaching our students how to improve any writing that involves argument. As Fisher puts it, "argumentation is the theme in the rhetorical tradition that ties rhetoric to logic" (p. 3).

Such borrowings from technical logic also have eminent classical sanction, since it was Aristotle who declared rhetoric to be the counterpart of dialectic and the enthymeme to be a rhetorical syllogism. But it is worth noticing that Aristotle's *Rhetoric*, unlike many current composition texts, includes no discussion of the syllogism.

A glance through current composition textbooks reveals a consequence of that "impeccable" rationale, an apparently accepted paradigm of how logic should be treated in composition, a paradigm I will call comp-logic. It is an attempt to borrow elements of technical logic and make them relevant to rhetorical logic (that term is also Fisher's). Comp-logic includes three parts: "induction," by which composition texts mean generalizing

Special Types of Writing*

from evidence; "deduction," by which composition texts mean reasoning from general principle to specific case; and an array of material fallacies that students are to avoid. Almost always the paradigmatic materials are presented in a separate section or chapter of a larger text.

But the rationale for teaching the comp-logic paradigm is in fact dangerously flawed, and our common textbook presentations are frequently so confused and confusing as to be almost useless either for creating arguments or criticizing them. Furthermore, the goal of assisting students to produce effective argumentative discourse can probably be achieved more successfully by borrowing either from modern informal logic or from the mostly neglected classical stasis theory.

The Terms "Induction" and "Deduction" in Comp-Logic

When English textbooks borrow the technical terms "induction" and "deduction," more limited definitions are given to both terms than they have within technical logic. This would be perfectly reasonable: In rhetoric courses we do not need *all* the logician's baggage. But in addition, the definitions we use invite confusion, partly because they stress an ambiguous motion metaphor, and partly because we present the two terms as complementary and exhaustive (e.g., all arguments are supposed to be one or the other), when, in our usage, they are not.

Here are typical definitions from a 1985 composition textbook: "Reasoning by induction means *moving from* individual pieces of evidence to a conclusion" (Gere, p. 185, emphasis added). The same textbook says that "reasoning by deduction means *moving from* a general statement to a conclusion about the particular case" (Gere, p. 187, emphasis added).

I invite you to go with me now into a freshman class the morning after this material has been assigned. It is, let us say, 9:00 a.m. After checking the roll, collecting daily journals, answering a question or two, the teacher begins:

Teacher:	Now then, what was the main subject of the reading assignment for today?
Class in general:	Induction and deduction.
Teacher:	And what did your text say they were?
First student (reading):	"Inductive reasoning proceeds from a number of particular cases to a generalized conclusion; deductive reasoning proceeds from the application of a general principle to a particular case and then to a particular conclusion" (Adelstein and Pival, p. 356).
Teacher:	O.K. That is *exactly* what it says. Now, in your own words, what does that mean?
Second student:	It means that in induction you go from specific instances to a general conclusion, but in deduction you go from the general to the particular.

Our teacher finds herself at an impasse. She isn't sure of what the students actually understand or even of how to find out. She resists the temptation to resort to a mini-lecture, and finally inspiration strikes. She writes two, almost identical, paragraphs on the board. Both argue for the claim that "Even honors students are sometimes lazy." The first opens with the claim, then gives three examples. The other gives the same three examples, but puts the claim at the end.

Class in general:	Yeah, that's it. The first is deductive reasoning; the second is inductive.
Teacher:	That's what I suspected. You are confusing the *order* of presentation of an argument with the *type* of reasoning. The reasoning in these paragraphs is identical; both show induction.
Second student:	But that's what the book said! "Movement from the general to particulars is deductive; movement from particulars to the general is inductive" (Guinn and Marder, p. 69). That's what the second paragraph does, but the first one is just the opposite. So the first *has* to be deduction.

For the rest of the period, in circles mostly, the conversation continues.

Ironically, the students have just reasoned very well from the textbook definitions. They have applied them to the teacher's sample paragraphs and come out with conclusions, in almost classical syllogistic form.

The fact that the conclusions are wrong, though validly derived, merely indicates the ambiguity of the definitions. Despite the frequent use of motion metaphors like "going from" in English textbooks, the order of presentation is irrelevant to the type of argument. Whether one "goes from" the premises first and follows with the conclusion or "goes from" the conclusion to the premises (or some other combination), the same set of premises and conclusions will always be the same argument.

In technical logic, the difference between an inductive argument and a deductive one involves neither the notion of movement nor the notion of general and specific. In technical logic any argument in which the premises purport to prove the conclusion (*entail* is the technical term) is a deduction. And all other arguments, those in other words in which the premises purport to make the conclusion highly probable, are induction (Copy, p. 169 and 403: see also Hurley, p. 491 and 494; and Kahane, *Logic and Philosophy*, p. 12).

Let me illustrate. Here is an argument that in technical logic is inductive because the premises do not purport to guarantee the conclusion:

Most up-to-date writing teachers stress invention.
She seems from her discussion to be up-to-date.
So she probably emphasizes invention in her classroom.
But in comp-logic this is "deduction" because it "goes from" general to specific.

Comp-logic limits deduction to arguments in the form of the BARBARA syllogism (exemplified by the chestnut upon Socrates' mortality) and structures similar to it like my example above. Comp-logic "deduction" thus leaves out most of what technical logicians mean when they use the term: categorical syllogisms that do not move from general premise to specific conclusion; other sorts of syllogisms (such as hypothetical), plus the entire modern corpus called symbolic logic. Similarly, comp-logic's "induction" excludes much of what logicians mean by induction: arguments from analogy, authority, and sign, for example.

There is nothing inherently wrong in using the terms to mean what we want them to mean. But we should be aware that our definitions differ so dramatically from those used in technical logic that we are not in actuality making much use of whatever that field has to offer. And we should be aware that many types of common arguments do not fit the comp-logic definition of either induction or deduction.

On the other hand, there is something wrong with using the terms in vague and confusing ways as our books do. Furthermore, as Michael Scriven has pointed out, since any inductive argument can be turned into a valid deductive argument by stating the "unstated" premises, "the distinction isn't one you would want to build very much on" (p. 34).

"Induction" in Comp-Logic

Even though many logicians now restrict technical logic to deduction (see Kneale and Kneale), probably the most valuable borrowing in comp-logic is the treatment of what we call "induction." Typically, our texts define it as "the process of drawing a conclusion . . . from particular instances or evidence" (Gefvert, p. 465). It would be more aptly named *argument by generalization*. Because much student writing *does* involve giving examples or details to support a general claim, including discussion of "induction" in this sense seems perfectly sensible.

To show students what makes a good induction, our texts borrow an evaluation system that can be summed up neatly with the acronym STAR. The STAR system requires that there be Sufficient, Typical, Accurate, and Relevant examples in order to support a generalization.

In comp-logic we make the STAR system serve our purposes by applying it contextually instead of logically. That is, instead of asking whether the evidence is extensive enough to justify logically a conclusionary leap, we ask, "Are the examples sufficient to persuade a reader?" and "Will a reader perceive them as typical and accurate?" The concepts of generalizing from examples and of evaluating such inferences by a contextual use of the STAR system are useful in composition. Indeed, they are common sense.

"Deduction" in Comp-Logic

As explained above, comp-logic presents deduction as a syllogism or quasi-syllogism in which a general rule or principle, enunciated in the first or major premise, is applied to a specific case, identified in the second premise. But unlike borrowing the principle of argument by generalization, borrowing the BARBARA syllogism from traditional technical logic is of little use in teaching composition for three reasons.

First, writers rarely build full categorical syllogisms. Instead they use abbreviated forms phrased with noncategorical premises. Consequently, the structure of major, minor, and middle terms, and the distribution rules for validity, and the distinction between soundness and validity rarely fit even writing that does apply general principles to specific cases, such as a *Consumer Reports* product evaluation or a legal brief. So none of this material, which our textbooks frequently import from technical logic, *applies* to most written discourse.

Second, all valid syllogisms, including BARBARA, must have at least one universal premise (e.g., *all humans* have to be mortal).[1] Not surprisingly, our texts do not discuss what sorts of universal, categorical premises students might build arguments on, especially arguments about contingent issues. So students told to write papers based on syllogisms are likely to use as their premises sweeping generalizations, such as "All teachers who give essay tests are unfair" or "All lies are bad." Or even, "All freshmen at Berkeley are eager to succeed."

Third, recall that in both comp-logic and technical logic a deduction is an argument in which the premises purport to entail the conclusion. In other words, in a properly carried out deduction (that is, in a valid one), the truth of the premises guarantees that the conclusion follows. (The most convenient illustration for many of us is a proof in geometry.) Writing, however, almost always deals with contingent issues, issues in which the evidence will never entail the conclusion. (Notice I felt compelled to make even *that* claim a contingent one by saying "almost always.") Given its contingent-ness, writing has little use for the certitudes of deductive reasoning. The moment we acknowledge the contingent nature of our conclusions, we leave the realm of deduction for what Chaim Perelman properly calls, in his book of that title, "the realm of rhetoric." Perelman reminds us, as Aristotle had also done, that most of the argumentation we are concerned about is in the realm of the probable rather than the certain. For that reason, Perelman and Olbrects-Tyteca devote a long section of *The New Rhetoric* to "Quasi-Logical Arguments," arguments which look somewhat like syllogisms but really are not (p. 193–95). Neither technical logic's broad view of deduction, nor comp-logic's more limited view, applies to real-world discourse.

William McCleary conducted a thoughtful empirical study about the effects on student writing of teaching technical deductive logic. A control group of community college freshmen studied composition without studying any logic, and two groups studied traditional syllogistic deduction in slightly different ways. All students were tested on gains in critical thinking, and upon improvements in writing argumentative essays on moral issues.

McCleary concluded, "There is no evidence that studying logic had a positive effect on students' written arguments. In fact, most evidence, though seldom statistically significant, points in the opposite direction" (p. 196). His study found just what the theoretical analysis above would lead one to expect.

I cannot resist adding that since English teachers are not generally trained in syllogistic logic, comp-logic frequently includes bizarre remarks. If students' writing were genuinely affected by what they had studied, they would be in trouble. And if, God forbid, logicians were to read our textbooks, they would have fits, of either laughter or apoplexy.

I have collected a rogues' gallery of the more exotic remarks about the syllogism from our texts. Let me share three of them.

1. Gerald Levin in *Writing and Logic* attempts to distinguish between validity and soundness, a standard and important distinction in technical logic, but one of little relevance to real discourse. He gives the following example:

Mathematics is an exact science.
Astrology is wholly based on mathematics.
Therefore, astrology is an exact science. (p. 93)

He remarks, "As we can see from the last argument, valid syllogistic reasoning has great persuasive force even when it is unsound" (p. 93). That
may be true, but we cannot see it from this syllogism, since the syllogism
is neither valid nor sound. (In technical logic, a syllogism is called *valid* if
it is in proper form; to be *sound* it must be valid and have true premises
as well. But technical logic is not concerned with soundness beyond pointing out that validity does not guarantee it.) Levin's syllogism commits the
four-term fallacy, since its categories are mathematics, exact sciences,
astrology, and "things based on mathematics." Since it is formally fallacious it is invalid. And thus unsound as well.

2. Miller and Judy, after expressing intuitive disdain for formal logic,
nevertheless go on to discuss deductive reasoning and state a rule that
"the same term cannot appear as the direct object of both major and minor
premises" (p. 117). Now since all propositions in a categorical syllogism
must be expressed with copula verbs, there are no direct objects in the
premises. I assume Miller and Judy mean to say that the same term cannot
appear as the *predicate* of both major and minor premises. Which is wrong.
It would make invalid every syllogism of the figure two configuration (see
note 1), when in fact at least four moods of that syllogism are valid (see
Hurley, p. 204–05).

The following syllogism, for example, with "scholars" as the predicate of
both premises is perfectly valid:

All composition teachers are scholars.
No politicians are scholars.
Therefore, no politicians are composition teachers.

3. My nominee for the single most erroneous presentation comes from
Daniel McDonald's *The Language of Argument,* 2nd ed. He claims that
"commonly, 'valid form' means that the general subject or condition of the
major premise must appear in the minor premise as well" (p. 50). That's
confusing, but it might be a mere slip of the pen. However, McDonald uses
it to explain the following syllogism:

All thieves have ears.
All Presbyterians have ears.
All Presbyterians are thieves.

What makes this argument "unreliable syllogistically is that the major term
'thieves' does not appear in the minor premise" (p. 51). Since it is impossible, by definition, for the major term to appear in the minor premise, this
is nonsense. (The analysis is changed somewhat in the third edition of
McDonald's text, made even worse in my view. See p. 71.)

I have found many other examples nearly as erroneous. But I will resist
the temptation to multiply my inductive proof, and simply leap to the
conclusion that our textbooks' presentations about deduction are full of
errors. May God help the naive professor or graduate assistant who falls
innocently into the pit of teaching from such a book and takes it seriously.
It may be necessary for composition teachers to learn about deductive logic
purely to defend themselves from such materials.

Since presentations about "deduction" are likely to be both confused and confusing, since deduction demands absolute entailment of the conclusion and universal premises, and since empirical evidence suggests that student writing is not improved by studying deduction even when presented accurately, our time could be better spent if we deleted the teaching of "deduction" from the comp-logic paradigm. (Now I ask you, does this paragraph involve an inductive argument or a deductive one?)

The Treatment of Material Fallacies in Comp-Logic

The third element of comp-logic involves teaching a list of common nonformal or material fallacies, argument types which though unsound are common enough and deceptive enough to have been given names and studied widely. Such presentations are an honored tradition, going all the way back to Aristotle's *On Sophistical Refutations.* They play a major role in the modern informal logic movement (led by such figures as Ralph Johnson and J. A. Blair, editors of *Informal Logic Quarterly*) as well as in a good number of English textbooks. Some composition authors such as Hartwell prefer a brief list of five or six, realizing that a great deal is left out. Others opt for thoroughness, at the risk of overkill: Barry's *Good Reason for Writing* indexes over thirty fallacies, and Spurgin's *The Power to Persuade* includes twenty-four. (The record number of fallacies discussed may be the more than 112 in David Fischer's *Historians' Fallacies: Toward a Logic of Historical Thought.*)

Teaching some fallacy theory in composition may be a good idea, although I know of no careful study of the question. But at least three problems have to be dealt with.

First, fallacy theory is inherently incomplete. As Horace Joseph put it in 1906, "truth may have its norms, but error is infinite in its aberrations" (p. 569). The fewer fallacies a text presents, the more room for illogic the student is left. But the greater the number of fallacies presented, the greater the chances of confusion. And no matter how many fallacies are included, the list will always remain incomplete. Second, fallacy theory is inherently negative. It tells students some argumentative moves to avoid, but not how to reason well. Teaching fallacies is very much like concentrating on grammar errors as a means of improving sentence structure: It presumes that if all the fallacies/errors are removed, the result is good argument/writing.

Third, and most important, even within the field of logic, material fallacies are not clearly defined and distinguished from each other. C. L. Hamblin noted, in what has become the standard full-length discussion *Fallacies,* that "nobody, these days, is particularly satisfied with this corner of logic. The traditional treatment is too unsystematic for modern tastes. . . . We have no *theory* of fallacy at all in the sense in which we have theories of correct reasoning (p. 11). A decade later, Maurice Finocchiaro, a member of the editorial board of the *Informal Logic Quarterly,* surveyed the ground again. Despite the growth of the informal logic movement, complete with many textbooks concentrating almost exclusively on fallacies, he concluded,

[T]extbook accounts of fallacies are basically misconceived, partly because their concept of fallacy is internally incoherent, partly because the various alleged fallacious practices have not been shown to be fallacies, partly because their classification of fallacies is unsatisfactory, and partly because their examples are artificial.   (p. 18)

When such material becomes part of comp-logic, it rarely improves in the translation.

Some illustrations of the internal incoherence of fallacy theory: Every *post hoc* argument is also a hasty generalization. So is stereotyping. And a *non sequitur*, included in many texts, is any argument in which the conclusion does not follow from the premises — a definition that includes *post hoc*, hasty generalization, and stereotyping.

Since many fallacies parallel good arguments, definitions often seem to fit both a fallacy and its legitimate cousin. We tell students that they must not argue *ad populum*, because an appeal to the crowd's emotions is fallacious. yet we simultaneously tell them that a good argument persuades through *pathos*, certainly an appeal to the emotions.

I tell my technical logic students that they must learn the difference between an irrelevant appeal to pity (such as a student's arguing for a better grade on the ground of having experienced a romantically disastrous semester) and a relevant appeal to pity (such as an argument that we should help save baby seals from being cruelly slaughtered for their pelts). And I tell them they must distinguish between a slippery slope fallacy and its cousin, the legitimate argument from negative consequences. In both cases, they find it difficult to tell the difference.

Many texts that present fallacies conclude with a name-that-fallacy exercise, a task which seems valuable *in a logic class* where there is time to study fallacies at length and where weaknesses in fallacy theory can be discussed. But such exercises are of dubious value in a writing course. Given the vague and overlapping definitions of the fallacies, especially in English texts, it is no wonder that I have frequently had to shepherd even bright graduate teaching assistants through these exercises. Without the teacher's manual to provide the "right" answers, they were often stumped by the questions. (See for example Rottenberg, p. 192–94.)

In a new composition text, Wayne Booth and Marshall Gregory try to turn the definitional difficulty into a virtue. In a section entitled "From 'fallacies' to 'rhetorical resources,'" they analyze twenty-six fallacies and discuss how the same reasoning patterns can be used legitimately. Hasty generalization obviously pairs with generalization, poor analogy with analogy, authority with false authority. Bandwagon they match with tradition or folk wisdom, an ironic pairing since arguments from tradition have also been identified as fallacious (Kahane, *Logic and Contemporary Rhetoric*, p. 56, and Rottenberg, 2nd ed. p. 198). Of the twenty-six fallacies, Booth and Gregory find only two that have no legitimate parallels, card stacking and the appeal to force (p. 408–26). (But see Kielkopf, who argues that there are legitimate appeals to force.) This presentation is honest about the fuzziness of standards for determining an argument to be materially fallacious, but it may leave students even more confused about fallacies than our textbooks typically do.

Comp-Logic and Writing-as-Process

Comp-logic, like technical logic, provides criteria for judging existent argumentative texts. Writing-as-process, on the other hand, describes the complex sequence of recursive and interactive processes which generate and refine texts.

Almost never do the two paradigms meet in composition textbooks. No book that I have examined integrates the two by discussing the processes a student would use to build an argument satisfying the books' criteria. This isn't surprising: Logic and comp-logic are tools for criticizing arguments, not for generating them. Not since Peter Ramus have logicians concerned themselves with how arguments are created.

It is a revealing fact, I think, that most of the full-length argument texts for composition classes are actually argument anthologies with some accompanying apparatus presenting principles of logic. In other words, they stress critical analysis of already written (and usually professional) arguments in the hope that students can imitate what they have read (see Rottenberg, Spurgin, McDonald, Barry). But they do not discuss the procedures the authors went through to build their arguments, and they offer students virtually no advice about generating arguments.

The Toulmin Model of Argument

Recognizing the problems with the common comp-logic paradigm, a few English textbook authors, following the lead of Brockriede and Ehninger in speech, have adopted the six-part Toulmin model of argument first presented in *The Uses of Argument*. Most isolate the model in a single chapter or section, just as the comp-logic paradigm is usually presented (Hairston, Winterowd, Levin, Spurgin, Dodds, Gage, Hartwell). Only one book that I am aware of uses Toulmin as an informing principle with separate chapters on claim, data (or grounds), warrants, and backing — Rottenberg's *Elements of Argument*.

The Toulmin model is attractive in precisely the ways that traditional logic proved troublesome. It does away with any distinction between induction and deduction, rejecting both terms. It concerns both form and substance of an argument, and it raises the question of where one gets "warrants" (the Toulmin counterpart of universal premises). It explicitly deals with the contingent nature of conclusions, as well as with the existence of counterarguments. It continues to stress the STAR evaluation under its heading of "grounds," and it is consistent with any fallacy theory one wants, since all the traditional fallacies can be explained as involving defects in grounds, warrant, or backing.

Yet, there are significant difficulties in using the Toulmin model as it appears in our textbooks. Since Toulmin's model rejects the distinction between induction and deduction, a confusing overlap occurs whenever the model appears side by side with "induction," as in Hairston's *Contemporary Composition*. Within the Toulmin approach, induction is simply any argument with instances as grounds, and a warrant which says "what is true of a sample is very likely true of the group as a whole" (Toulmin, Rieke, and Janik, p. 219).

Presenting Toulmin side by side with traditional deduction, as Levin and Winterowd do, is even more theoretically inconsistent, since Toulmin developed his model as an alternative after a scathing attack on traditional concepts of the syllogism. One of his British colleagues, in fact, continually referred to *A Theory of Argument* as "Toulmin's anti-logic book" (cited by Toulmin, "Logic and the Criticism of Arguments," p. 392).

A second problem arises whenever an author assumes, as some books seem to, that the Toulmin model applies to an entire discourse. The Toulmin model, like traditional deduction and induction, fits only a single argument, that is, any move from rounds to claim. Thus, as Charles Kneupper has argued, it rarely fits full essays, but can be used, with some strain, to explicate any single argumentative move. Kneupper, for example, uses it to explicate the first paragraph of "Civil Disobedience" (p. 239–40).

A third problem is that while the model provides a framework for analyzing an argument, for seeing its various parts and how they interrelate, unlike traditional logic it does not provide a means of evaluation. The fact that an argument has or lacks one or several of the six parts does not make it a good argument or a bad one. Evaluation must come from other sources, and since Toulmin maintains that arguments can be evaluated only within a discourse field according to the canons of that field, evaluating argument in a nondisciplinary writing course becomes problematic.

And finally, Toulmin logic, like traditional logic, is a tool for analyzing existing arguments, rather than a system for creating them. It shares with the more traditional technical logic and comp-logic paradigms difficulties in being integrated into a course attempting to teach a generative process.

Here, however, may be a unique potential of the Toulmin model. Conceivably the six parts could be converted into heuristic questions in a way that comp-logic cannot be. The student would ask the following sequence of questions:

1. "What is my claim?"
2. "What grounds do I have to support it?" (using STAR again).
3. "What statement could warrant any move from the grounds to the claim?"
4. "How can I back up that warrant?"
5. "How much must I qualify my conclusion as contingent?"
6. "What counterarguments that would weaken my conclusion do I need to acknowledge?"

No book currently available turns Toulmin's model into an invention scheme, although Rottenberg makes some gestures in this direction, as does Winterowd, who says the "model provides a guide to *prewriting* the persuasive essay" (p. 248).

John Gage's *The Shape of Reason* fuses parts of Toulmin logic with some traditional syllogistic logic and with classical rhetoric's theory of the enthymeme into the closest thing I have found to an integration of logical concepts and writing as a process. Gage advocates that students learn to phrase each thesis first as a complex enthymeme, consisting of the claim plus the major line of support, and then to add the necessary unstated assumption (or Toulmin warrant) connecting the two. He uses the example of a student who creates the following framework for a paper: "Scientific education should include the issue of moral responsibility so that scientists will learn to consider the harmful effects of their research and weigh them against the potential good, because harmful effects are always possible" (p. 89). In Toulmin's terms we have,

CLAIM: Scientific education should include the issue of moral responsibility.

GROUNDS: Scientists would then learn to consider the harmful effects of their research.

WARRANT: Harmful effects are always possible.

This is obviously not a strong argument. The grounds are not givens already accepted by both arguer and opponents, and the "warrant" does not in fact connect the grounds to the claim. But Gage supplements Toulmin by proposing several standards for evaluating such a frame (p. 87) and shows the student criticizing this initial formulation and creating a more sophisticated one: "Ethics classes for scientists will teach them to weigh the potential harmful effects of their research against the potential good, because raising questions of right and wrong in relation to science will confront them with their compassionate feelings for other people" (p. 103). Notice that not only has the support been changed; the claim is different as well. It has been transformed from a policy assertion to a causal one.

But whether the student can actually make the causal connection plausible, and sustain the implied claim that without such courses scientists will not weigh potential harmful effects of their research, is doubtful. So far the student has only a general framework, a sort of outline; the real ground for this argument, the evidence, has yet to be generated. And neither the Toulmin model, nor comp-logic, nor technical logic tells him how to do that.

In this research, McCleary examined the effects on freshman writing of studying the Toulmin model of argument. Again the students who studied Toulmin logic improved their argumentative writing no more than those who studied no logic at all.

However, because of the complexity of the Toulmin model, and the various ways it might conceivably be presented to a class, including the heuristic possibility above, the McCleary study is less convincing on this matter than on classical deduction.

The verdict on the Toulmin model in composition is still out. And several doctoral dissertations probably are hiding in the jury room.

Stasis Theory: a Nonlogical Approach to Argumentation?

Despite all the above, our students *do* need to learn to write effective arguments. And a precondition of that skill is being able to judge when an argument is effective and when it isn't. If neither comp-logic nor technical logic will help, where are we to look? My answer is that we should look to stasis theory, developed in classical rhetoric but expanded and adapted by several composition theorists in the last fifteen years.

In the rhetorics of Aristotle and Cicero, among others, stasis theory was mainly a system of possible courtroom defenses, but modern adaptations are more inclusive.

Two current composition textbooks are based on stasis theory, *A Rhetoric of Argument* by Fahnestock and Secor and *Real Writing* by Walter Beale. Several others refer to it in passing.

This is not the place for a full-blown discussion of stasis theory. Interested readers should consult the articles by Fahnestock and Secor and by Eckhardt and Stewart in the bibliography. But I do want to outline the essence of stasis theory and to suggest how it achieves the goals of comp-logic yet avoids most of the problems.

Stasis theory classifies arguments in a wholly different way from logic, not by their form (such as categorical or hypothetical syllogism) or by the type of premises used (such as argument from authority or argument from analogy) or even the relationship between premises and conclusions (deductive demonstration or inductive probability), but by the ontological status of the reality claim the conclusion asserts. In stasis theory, an argument of fact differs from an argument of value, and both differ from an argument of policy. In stasis theory, any argument for a policy conclusion is called a policy argument. It is appropriate to use the phrase "stasis of policy" to describe either the conclusion reached or the entire argument.

In no traditional sense is stasis theory a part of technical logic, since it classifies arguments by the substance of the conclusion. But if one considers that the goal of logic is the evaluation of argument strength, then stasis theory can provide at least as strong a methodology as traditional induction or the Toulmin model, through the mechanism of the *stasis-specific prima facie case.*

The notion of a *prima facie* case comes from both law and competitive debate. It means that the case (extended argument) made for a claim is structurally and substantively complete so that if no countercase were presented then the claim would stand. For each type of *stasis* being argued, certain elements must be present before the case can be regarded as complete and in need of evaluating. As an example, in a court of law, a *prima facie* case for the charge of battery must normally include four items:

There must have been a touching by the defendant,
The touching must have been either offensive or harmful,
The touching must have been unconsented,
And it must have been intentional rather than accidental.

If anything is lacking, the prosecution has presented a "bad" argument, and the case will be dismissed without any defense being necessary. Handling all four, however, does not mean that the prosecution will win. It merely means that an argument of sufficient strength has been presented to necessitate some response. The *prima facie* case is thus a minimum but crucial criterion for a satisfactory argument.

In this illustration, the *stasis* can reasonably be called substantiation (Eckhardt and Stewart's term) or interpretation (Beale's term). The defense attorney might counter the case and remain in the same stasis by pointing out that the touching was "privileged" (as when a boxer strikes another boxer, or a parent spanks a child). On the other hand, the defense might choose to shift the stasis to one of value, by admitting that the defendant's acts do indeed fit the definition of battery but were nevertheless proper in terms of some greater good. This was Brutus's defense for murdering Caesar, and it is the standard defense of civil protesters tried on such charges as trespassing on government property. In "Toward a Modern Version of Stasis," Fahnestock and Secor refer to opponents in a federal inquiry chasing "one another up and down the stases" (p. 218).

Books built around stasis theory divide the types of claims a student might need to argue for and then discuss what is required to create a *stasis-specific prima facie* case for each one. The presentations vary, but all are consistent, differing mainly in terminology and the number of major stases presented. In *Real Writing,* Beale presents three: interpretation, value, and policy. Fahnestock and Secor present four in *A Rhetoric of Argument:* "What is it?" "How did it get that way?" "Is it good or bad?" and "What should we do about it?"

Stasis theory does not exclude other potentially useful portions of comp-logic. In every stasis, a rhetor must generalize from evidence, that is, reason "inductively" in the comp-logic sense, and the STAR evaluation system still applies. In fact, the STAR criteria are almost identical to traits of a good argument of the first stasis (interpretation or substantiation). In every stasis a fallacious argument is still fallacious. And every stasis can be fitted into the Toulmin model (see Brockriede and Ehninger), although no composition text that I know of has integrated stasis theory and Toulmin. Furthermore, unlike comp-logic, stasis theory does provide an invention system, because the elements of the *prima facie* case immediately translate into heuristic questions.

Unlike both technical logic and Toulmin logic, stasis theory applies to full discourses rather than single arguments within a discourse. And it can include evaluative principles for each stasis.

In addition, stasis theory provides two extra-argumentative advantages. First, it creates an easily applied discourse taxonomy with increasing levels of complexity as one moves from substantiation to evaluation to policy. Second, it includes concepts of what constitutes effective *arrangement* of an argument in each stasis.

Unfortunately, the textbooks currently built on stasis theory do not integrate stasis theory into a process approach to writing. Each book presents writing as a process in a separate section and then devotes single sections to each stasis. Moreover, these texts are complex and relatively dry and difficult to read. Thus they are not well suited for most freshman classes, although in my experience Beale's *Real Writing* has worked well with honors students.

Conclusion

Based on what our textbooks typically provide, Kaufer and Neuwirth's conclusion seems correct: "Students typically come away from their writing course with a hodgepodge of information about syllogism, Aristotelian topics, fallacy, evidence, and warrants, but they have little idea how to put this information to use when actually composing" (p. 388).

That occurs because our textbook transmutations of technical logic into comp-logic are both ambiguous and ill-conceived to begin with. Even if adapted well, much of what can be borrowed from technical logic is unlikely to be helpful to writers because it describes products not processes and because the absolute nature of deduction ill suits the contingent nature of argumentative discourse. Toulmin logic does suit such contingency, but it has a wealth of unresolved problems of its own.

For contingent arguments, stasis theory can provide heuristic questions leading to sensible procedures for writing each stasis. It also provides criteria for judging arguments of the same stasis, and a progressive taxonomy upon which courses can be built. Thus can a borrowing from classical rhetoric do what our borrowings from technical logic cannot, provide systematic and useful approaches to teaching written argument.

Note

[1] In fact, BARBARA is a mnemonic code to indicate that the syllogism has three Universal Affirmative or type-A propositions.

The vowels *A, E, I,* and *O* were used in medieval times to designate the four types of propositions. The vowels supposedly come from the Latin verbs *affirmo* and *nego*. Thus *A* and *I* designate affirmative propositions, such as "All teachers are hard workers" and "Some teachers are hard workers" respectively. *E* and *O* designate negative propositions of the forms "No teachers are lazy" and "Some teachers are not lazy." The medieval logicians gave personal names to each valid syllogistic form, names in which the three vowels represent the types of propositions in the syllogism. Thus CELARENT refers to a valid syllogism with an *E* major premise, an *A* minor premise, and an *E* conclusion.

But there are four possible syllogisms with that configuration of propositions, depending on the position of the middle term in the two premises. CELARENT is specifically a syllogism in which the middle term appears as the subject of the major premise and the predicate of the minor premise, or what is called Figure 1. If the middle term appears as the predicate of both premises, we have Figure 2. The Figure 2 syllogism with the same types of propositions (EAE) is CESARE. In more modern technical logic these two valid forms are designated simply EAE-1 and EAE-2. EAE-3 and EAE-4 also exist, but both are invalid. Thus they lack medieval names.

The medieval logicians were ingenious; not only did all the valid syllogisms have names whose vowels represented the propositions, but a mnemonic rhyming jingle was used to teach the valid syllogisms for each of the four figures. In Figure 1 these are BARBARA, CELARENT, DARII, and FERIOQUE. Moreover, the consonants in each name represent complex ways by which syllogisms of the second, third, and fourth figures can be transformed into equivalent syllogisms of the first figure (see McCall, p. 157–69).

References (Textbooks are indicated with asterisks.)

*Adelstein, Michael, and Jean G. Pival. *The Writing Commitment.* New York: Harcourt, 1976.

Aristotle. *On Sophistical Refutations.* Trans. E. S. Forster. Cambridge: Harvard University Press, 1955.

*Barry, Vincent. *Good Reason for Writing.* Belmont, Calif.: Wadsworth, 1983.

*Beale, Walter H. *Real Writing.* 2nd ed. Glenview, Ill.: Scott-Foresman, 1986.

*Booth, Wayne, and Marshall Gregory. *The Harper & Row Rhetoric.* New York: Harper & Row, 1987.

Brockriede, Wayne, and Douglas Ehninger. "Toulmin on Argument: An Interpretation and Application." *Quarterly Journal of Speech,* 46 (Feb. 1960): 44–53. Rpt. in *Contemporary Theories of Rhetoric: Selected Readings.* Ed. Richard Johannesen. New York: Harper, 1971, p. 241–55.

Copi, Irving. *Introduction to Logic.* 7th ed. New York: Macmillan, 1986.

Crews, Frederick. "Theory for Whose Sake?" *CCTE Studies* 51 (Sept. 1986): 9–19.

*Dodds, Jack. *The Writer in Performance.* New York: Macmillan, 1986.

*Eckhardt, Caroline, and David Stewart. "Towards a Functional Taxonomy of Composition." *CCC,* 30 (Dec. 30): 338–42. Rpt. in *The Writing Teacher's Sourcebook.* Ed. Gary Tate and Edward P. J. Corbett. New York: Oxford, 1981, pp. 100–06.

———. *The Wiley Reader: Brief Edition.* New York: John Wiley & Sons, 1979.

*Fahnestock, Jeanne, and Marie Secor. *A Rhetoric of Argument.* New York: Random House, 1982.

———. "Teaching Argument: A Theory of Types." *CCC* 34 (Feb. 1983): 20–30.

———. "Toward a Modern Version of Stasis." *Oldspeak/Newspeak Rhetorical Transformations.* Ed. Charles W. Kneupper. Arlington, Va.: Rhetoric Society of America, 1985. 217–26.

Finocchiaro, Maurice A. "Fallacies and the Evaluation of Reasoning." *American Philosophical Quarterly 18* (Jan. 1981): 13–22.

Fischer, David Hackett. *Historians' Fallacies: Toward a Logic of Historical Thought.* New York: Harper & Row, 1970.

Fisher, Walter. "Technical Logic, Rhetorical Logic, and Narrative Rationality." *Argumentation* 1 (1987): 3–21.

*Gage, John. *The Shape of Reason.* New York: Macmillan, 1987.

*Gefvert, Constance. *The Confident Writer: A Norton Handbook.* New York: Norton, 1985.

*Gere, Anne Ruggles. *Writing and Learning.* New York: Macmillan, 1985.

*Guinn, Dorothy M., and Daniel Marder. *A Spectrum of Rhetoric.* Boston: Little, Brown, 1987.

*Hairston, Maxine. *Contemporary Composition.* Short ed. New York: Houghton Mifflin, 1986.

Hamblin, C. L. *Fallacies.* London: Methuen, 1970.

*Hartwell, Patrick. *Open to Language: A New College Rhetoric.* New York: Oxford, 1982.

Hurley, Patrick. *A Concise Introduction to Logic.* 2nd ed. Belmont, Calif.: Wadsworth, 1985.

Johnson, Ralph, and J. A. Blair. *Logical Self-Defense.* 2nd ed. Toronto: McGraw-Hill Ryerson, 1983.

Joseph, Horace William Brindley. *An Introduction to Logic.* 2nd rev. ed. Oxford: Clarendon Press, 1906.

Kahane, Howard. *Logic and Contemporary Rhetoric: The Use of Reason in Everyday Life.* 4th ed. Belmont, Calif.: Wadsworth, 1984.

———. *Logic and Philosophy.* 5th ed. Belmont, Calif: Wadsworth, 1986.

Kaufer, David S., and Christine M. Neuwirth. "Integrating Formal Logic and the New Rhetoric: A Four-Stage Heuristic." *College English* 45 (April 1983): 380–89.

Kielkopf, Charles. "Relevant Appeals to Force, Pity, and Popular Pieties." *Informal Logic Newsletter* 2 (April 1980): 2–5.

Kneale, William, and Martha Kneale. *The Development of Logic.* Oxford: The Clarendon Press, 1962.

Kneupper, Charles W. "Teaching Argument: An Introduction to the Toulmin Model." *CCC* 29 (Oct. 1978): 237–41.

*Levin, Gerald. *Writing and Logic.* New York: Harcourt, 1982.

McCall, Raymond J. *Basic Logic: The Fundamental Principles of Formal Deductive Reasoning.* 2nd ed. New York: Barnes & Noble, 1952.

McCleary, William James. Teaching Deductive Logic: A Test of the Toulmin and Aristotelian Models for Critical Thinking and College Composition." Dissertation, University of Texas at Austin, 1979.

*McDonald, Daniel. *The Language of Argument.* 2nd ed. New York: Harper, 1975.

*———. *The Language of Argument.* 3rd ed. New York: Harper, 1980.

*Miller, James E., and Stephen Judy. *Writing in Reality.* New York: Harper, 1978.

Munson, Ronald. *The Way of Words: An Informal Logic.* Boston: Houghton Mifflin, 1976.

Perelman, Chaim. *The Realm of Rhetoric.* Trans. William Kluback. Notre Dame: University of Notre Dame Press, 1982.

Perelman, Chaim, and L. Olbrects-Tyteca. *The New Rhetoric: A Treatise on Argumentation.* Trans. John Wilkinson and Peircell Weaver. Notre Dame: University of Notre Dame Press, 1969.

*Rottenberg, Annette T. *Elements of Argument,* New York: St. Martin's, 1985.

*———. *Elements of Argument.* 2nd ed. New York: St. Martin's, 1988.

Scriven, Michael. *Reasoning.* New York: McGraw-Hill, 1976.

Sharvy, Robert Lee. "The Treatment of Argument in Speech Text Books." *Central States Speech Journal* 13 (Autumn 1962): 265–69.

*Spurgin, Sally DeWitt. *The Power to Persuade.* Englewood Cliffs, N.J.: Prentice, 1985.

Toulmin. Stephen. "Logic and the Criticism of Arguments." *The Rhetoric of Western Thought.* 3rd ed. Ed. James Golden, Goodwin F. Berquist, and William E. Coleman. Dubuque: Kendall/Hunt, 1983, pp. 391–401.

————. *The Uses of Argument.* Paperback ed. Cambridge, England: Cambridge University Press, 1963.

Toulmin, Stephen, Richard Rieke, and Allan Janik. *An Introduction to Reasoning.* 2nd ed. New York: Macmillan, 1984.

Weddle, Perry. "Inductive, Deductive." *Informal Logic 22* (Nov. 1979): 1–5.

*Winterowd, W. Ross. *The Contemporary Writer.* 2nd ed. New York: Harcourt, 1981.

WRITING ABOUT LITERATURE

A PASSAGE INTO CRITICAL THEORY

Steven Lynn

[College English 52 (1990): 258–71.]

Steven Lynn is associate professor of English and director of the freshman English program at the University of South Carolina, Columbia. He has published several articles on Samuel Johnson, including "Sexual Difference and Johnson's Brain," which appeared in Fresh Reflections on Samuel Johnson *(1987), and an article in the 1990 edition of the annual* The Age of Johnson. *Lynn also authored a book,* Samuel Johnson after Deconstruction, *(1972).*

In the introduction to "A Passage into Critical Theory," Lynn describes the situation that prompted the article: When he attempted to introduce instructors to contemporary literary criticism, they became confused and frustrated. This difficulty is analogous to the problems students have when their instructors try to teach the concept of differing critical perspectives. Lynn's overview demystifies various critical approaches and complements The Bedford Handbook's *discussion on being an active reader by offering teachers expanded options for helping student writers engage literary texts.*

She might have deplored the sentiment, had it come from one of her students, "What we need," she was saying, trying hard not to whine, "is a short cut, a simple guide, a kind of recipe for each of these theories, telling us step by step how to make a particular reading." It was the second week of a three-week institute dedicated to the proposition that all teachers were created equal and that therefore all should share in the excitement and challenge of the ongoing transformation of literary criticism. But these teachers, it was clear, were just on the verge of saying, "Let's just pretend that nothing important has happened since, oh, 1967." I had whipped them into an evangelistic fever at the outset of the institute, ready to receive the spirit of critical theory; and they had read so much and worked so hard. But I nodded. She was right. They were mired in complexity and subtleties. I realized, of course, that no one whose loaf was fully sliced would seriously attempt an overview of recent critical theory in a few pages. But all they needed was to get their bearings, and then the confusion of ideas bouncing around in their heads would probably start falling into some comprehensible order. So I came up with the briefest of guides to some of the recent critical theory, an overview that would succeed when its users began to understand its limitations.

My strategy was to show how a single passage might be treated by a handful of different critical theories — certainly not every theory available, but enough to show how theory shapes practice and to help my students with those most puzzling them. Although multiple readings of the same work are easy to assemble and useful, my effort not only had the virtue of a calculated simplicity and brevity, it also displayed the same reader attempting to act as the extension of various different interpretive codes. The passage I chose, a wonderful excerpt from Brendan Gill's *Here at the New Yorker,* is itself brief, but also rich. In offering these notes I am assuming that my reader, like those teachers, knows enough about recent critical theory to be confused. Obviously, my theorizing will be alarmingly reductive, and the examples won't illustrate what any student at any level can produce, given a sketch of this or that theory. They illustrate only what I can do to provide in a very small space an example of a particular kind of critical behavior. But my teacher/students, as well as my student/students, have found these discussion/examples helpful, and so I'll proceed immediately to Gill's text and then mine, before anyone gets cut on any of these slashes.

Here's Gill's text:

When I started at *The New Yorker,* I felt an unshakable confidence in my talent and intelligence. I revelled in them openly, like a dolphin diving skyward out of the sea. After almost forty years, my assurance is less than it was; the revellings, such as they are, take place in becoming seclusion. This steady progress downward in the amount of one's confidence is a commonplace at the magazine — one might almost call it a tradition. Again and again, some writer who has made a name for himself in the world will begin to write for us and will discover as if for the first time how difficult writing is. The machinery of benign skepticism that surrounds and besets him in the form of editors, copy editors, and checkers, to say nothing of fellow-writers, digs a yawning pit an inch or so beyond his desk. He hears it repeated as gospel that there are not three people in all America who can set down a simple declarative sentence correctly; what are the odds against his being one of this tiny elect?

In some cases, the pressure of all those doubting eyes upon his copy is more than the writer can bear. When the galleys of a piece are placed in front of him, covered with scores, perhaps hundreds, of pencilled hen-tracks of inquiry, suggestion, and correction, he may sense not the glory of creation but the threat of being stung to death by an army of gnats. Upon which he may think of nothing better to do than lower his head onto his blotter and burst into tears. Thanks to the hen-tracks and their consequences, the piece will be much improved, but the author of it will be pitched into a state of graver self-doubt than ever. Poor devil, he will type out his name on a sheet of paper and stare at it long and long, with dumb uncertainty. It looks — oh, Christ — his name looks as if it could stand some working on.

As I was writing the above, Gardner Botsford, the editor who, among other duties, handles copy for "Theatre," came into my office with the galleys of my latest play review in his hand. Wearing an expression of solemnity, he said, "I am obliged to inform you that Miss Gould has found a buried dangling modifier in one of your sentences." Miss Gould is our head copy editor and unquestionably knows as much about English grammar as anyone alive. Gerunds, predicate nominatives, and passive periphrastic conjugations are mother's milk to her, as they are not to me. Nevertheless, I boldly challenged her allegation. My prose was surely correct in every way. Botsford placed the galleys before me and indicated the offending sentence, which ran, "I am told that in her ninth decade this beautiful woman's only complaint in respect to her role is that she doesn't have enough work to do."

I glared blankly at the galleys. Humiliating enough to have buried a dangling modifier unawares; still more humiliating not to be able to disinter it. Botsford came to my rescue. "Miss Gould points out that as the sentence is written, the meaning is that the complaint is in its ninth decade and has, moreover, suddenly and unaccountably assumed the female gender." I said that in my opinion the sentence could only be made worse by being corrected — it was plain that "The only complaint of this beautiful woman in her ninth decade . . ." would hang on the page as heavy as a sash-weight. "Quite so," said Botsford. "There are times when to be right is wrong, and this is one of them. The sentence stands."

New Criticism

I'll start with New Criticism because modern literary study arguably begins with New Criticism, and because it is probably, even today, the most pervasive way of looking at literature. It emerged in the struggle to make literary criticism a respectable profession, which for many scholars meant making it more rigorous, more like the sciences — a goal embodied in Wellek and Warren's landmark *Theory of Literature* in 1949. Wellek's chapter on "The Mode of Existence of a Literary Work of Art" is crucial: "The work of art," Wellek asserts, is "an object of knowledge," "a system of norms of ideal concepts which are intersubjective" (p. 156). What Wellek means by this difficult formulation, at least in part, is that "a literary work of art is in exactly the same position as a system of language" (p. 152). Because the work has the same sort of stable and "objective" status as a language, existing in a "collective ideology," governed by enduring "norms," critical statements are not merely opinions of taste: "It will always be possible to determine which point of view grasps the subject most thoroughly and deeply," as "All relativism is ultimately defeated." This assumption is important, because although New Critics in practice have not always ignored authors, genres, or historical contexts, the purpose of their analysis of particular works, their "close reading," has been finally to reveal how the formal elements of the literary work, often thought of as a poem, create and resolve tension and irony. Great works control profound tensions, and therefore New Criticism's intrinsic analysis, dealing with the work in isolation, is implicitly evaluative.

Common sense might suggest that the function of criticism is to reveal the meaning of a work, but New Criticism attends to *how* a work means, not *what*, for a simple reason: As Cleanth Brooks puts it, the meaning of a work is "a controlled experience which has to be *experienced*, not a logical process" (p. 90). The meaning cannot, in other words, be summed up in a proposition, but the system of norms that constructs a reader's experience can be analyzed. So, the New Critic focuses on "the poem itself" (rather than the author, the reader, the historical context), asking, "What elements are in tension in this work?" and "What unity resolves this tension?"

In Gill's story, the most obvious tension might be seen as that between right and wrong (or editor versus writer, or the world versus *The New*

Yorker, or grammar versus style, or confidence versus doubt, or something else). Whatever the basic tension is determined to be, it must somehow be resolved if the text succeeds, and New Criticism is inevitably teleological: Endings are crucial. Thus a New Critical reading of Gill's passage might well focus on the reconciliation at the end, when Botsford pronounces "right is wrong." The New Critic would then consider, "How does this idea fit into the system of the work's tensions, and how is the tension ordered and resolved?" The following paragraph briefly suggests the sort of discussion that might be produced in response:

> In Gill's story of the dangling modifier, Botsford solves the conflict between Miss Gould's rules and Gill's taste with a paradox that unifies the work: Sometimes "right is wrong." Miss Gould was right to spot the error, but Gill as right to be wrong, to have written the sentence as he did. The irony of this solution is reinforced by various paradoxical images: For example, the dolphin is "diving skyward," an action that in its simultaneously downward ("diving") and upward ("skyward") implications embodies the same logic as a wrong rightness. The "progress downward" of the writer, and even his "becoming seclusion" (appealing to others; unknown to others), convey the same image. In larger terms, the writer's "unshakable confidence" that quickly becomes a "dumb uncertainty" suggests the reversal that informs the story's truth. In such an upside-down world, we would expect to find the imagery of struggle and violence, and such is indicated by the "yawning pit" and the "army of gnats." Such tension is harmonized by Gill's brilliant conclusion: In writing, conducted properly, the demands of correctness and style are unified by the writer's poetic instincts, just as the story itself is resolved by the notion of a correct error.

Structuralism

At first glance, structuralism might appear to be simply the enlargement of New Criticism's project. But instead of focusing on the formal elements that create the experience of a particular work, structuralism aspired to deal, as Terry Eagleton says, "with structures, and more particularly with examining the general laws by which they work" (p. 94). In other words, the structuralist looks at a surface manifestation and theorizes about a deep structure, or s/he interprets surface phenomena in terms of this underlying structure.

In its most ambitious moments, structuralism may aspire to reveal anything from the structure of the human mind itself to the conventions of a literary form. Structuralists have tried, for instance, not only to isolate the conventions of certain kinds of narrative, such as the fantastic and science fiction, but also to determine what features allow us to identify a text as a story. Is Gill's passage a self-contained story, an entity in itself, or it is an excerpt, a fragment, a part of *Here at the New Yorker?* If we consider how we decide whether something is a story, we might well agree that a passage becomes a story when it fits our ideas of what a story is, when it satisfies certain general laws of discourse regarding a story. If we use a very simple and ancient notion of narrative structure, most readers would probably agree that Gill's text does have a beginning, a middle, and an end, moving from harmony, to complication and crisis, and finally to resolution. Readers might also agree it has a hero (the writer, who appears to be Gill), a helper (Botsford), and a villain (Miss Gould), features that Vladimir Propp finds, interestingly enough, in fairy tales. We can identify these elements, which we might argue are essential to a story, because we can relate this story to other ones and to a paradigm of stories. We can imagine (and perhaps even recall) other stories involving a confident neophyte who encounters destructive forces, descends into despair and near helplessness, and then finds an unexpected helper and vindication. Such structuralist analysis moves into the realm of archetypal criticism (as in Northrop Frye's work) when it seeks the universal patterns, the "archetypes" which are the foundation of the system of "literature," rather than isolating the structures and relationships within a particular system of discourse.

To produce a structuralist reading, then, exposing a text's conventions and operations, we must first identify the elements of the text — the genre, the agents, the episodes, the turning points, whatever. Structuralists are naturally attracted to charts and diagrams because these are helpful in reducing the complexity of a text to some understandable pattern, which can be compared to other patterns, or their transmutation, or absence. This concern with conventions rather than discrete works means that structuralism, unlike New Criticism, is not implicitly evaluative. *Gulliver's Travels* and *Gilligan's Island* are equally worthy of analysis, at least structurally: They may, in fact, illuminate one another, since textual conventions appear in the relationship of texts. If all the stories in our culture, regardless of characters or plot, end with a pack of multicolored dogs going off to hunt antelopes, as is indeed apparently the case in one African culture (Grimes, p. vii), then we recognize such an event as a discrete element: the ending element. In the case of Gill's text, one convention of a literary work that we surely recognize as missing is a beginning operation: a title. Does this lack alone disqualify this text as a literary story? If so, could we then add a title (what would it be?) and make the text into a story? If so, who would be the author of this story that didn't exist until we titled it? (We might also consider the status of this story before it was extricated from Gill's book.)

Because students' experience of literature may be limited, it's often helpful to supply comparable texts or to ask students to invent a comparable text, thus making the textual conventions easier to imagine. Here is my very limited attempt to think structurally about this excerpt, offering also another story to highlight the postulated form.

> The structure of Gill's text involves the repetition of an underlying sequence, in which a central figure encounters a contrary force that reverses his fortunes: x + y Æ anti-x. This sequence, which we see in the first two paragraphs, might be represented this way:

> 1. Unrealistic confidence ("unshakable confidence") + critical forces (editors, copy editors, and checkers) Æ unrealistic doubt ("dumb uncertainty").

> The same underlying structure appears in the last two paragraphs, except this time a particular example of the pattern is presented:

> 2. Specific instance: Unrealistic confidence ("boldly challenged her allegation") + critical force (Miss Gould) Æ unrealistic doubt ("Still more humiliating").

> In the final paragraph the pattern is inverted, as confidence becomes doubt, antagonistic forces become helpful, and doubt becomes confidence. This inversion, which is perhaps a common occurrence in the concluding element of a series, heightens by contrast the effect of the hero's success:

> 3. Unrealistic doubt (helpless to "disinter it") + a helpful force (Botsford) Æ realistic confidence (Gill's bold challenge, stoutly maintained, is upheld).

The same underlying pattern can be seen in the following plot:

1. Dreaming of future glory as an artist, a student comes to study at the university and discovers that art professors systematically show students how incompetent they are.
2. The art student turns in a project, and one faculty member explains in public how the project is grossly wrong. The student did not realize that he had departed from the assignment.
3. The chairman of the department then responds to the faculty member's criticism, saying that the assignment was a foolish one, and the student has demonstrated admirable creativity in revising the professor's directions and producing a good project.

Deconstruction

New Criticism, like its sibling philosophy of writing instruction, Current-Traditional Rhetoric, is product-oriented. It is perhaps then not surprising that my New Critical reading of Gill's piece focuses on the centrality of error, one of C-T Rhetoric's fundamental concerns. At first glance, Gill's story may appear to deflate Error's terror, since being wrong turns out to be right. If we press this close reading, however, asking if the text might say something other than what it appears to say, we move into the realm of deconstruction. Composition students in particular might be sensitive to the way Botsford's paradox reverses itself, unravelling Gill's grammatical triumph and plunging "the writer" finally into an even dumber and darker uncertainty. It's bad enough for the writer at *The New Yorker,* not to mention the composer in Freshman English, if the rules of writing are so complex that not even three people in America "can set down a simple declarative sentence correctly," if an experienced and accomplished writer can commit a major blunder without knowing it and without being able to fix it when he does know it. But it's even worse if the rules obtain in one case and not in another, and the rules for determining such exceptions don't seem to exist but are rather invented and applied by whoever happens to be in charge. Basic writing students, mystified by the rules of Standard English, live in just such a nightmare, I suspect.

If we look again at Botsford's vindication, we see it is deceptive, for he does not actually say that sometimes right is wrong and wrong is right. He only says that sometimes "right is wrong." Certainly wrong is also occasionally wrong, and perhaps it is always wrong. But Botsford's apparent reversal of the dismantling of authors at *The New Yorker* is finally ambiguous, since we never know if the writer is ever correct, no matter what he does. "The sentence stands" indeed, but it stands with its error intact, a monument to Gill's inability and the inevitable error of writing — the way language masters us. The passage thus complements the deconstructive commonplace that reading is always misreading.

Although it has been asserted that poststructuralism is not an applicable method (see Tompkins), I am, I think, just applying some basic deconstructive moves to Gill's text, which seems especially receptive, given its overt oppositions and emphasis on language. And despite the reluctance of some theorists to risk the spectacle of defining deconstruction (an action that deconstruction, by definition, renders futile), useful and clear explanations are available. For example, Barbara Johnson says that deconstruction proceeds by "the careful teasing out of warring forces of signification within the text itself" (p. 5). Jonathan Culler says that "to deconstruct a discourse is to show how it undermines the philosophy it asserts, or the hierarchical oppositions on which it relies" (p. 86). This teasing out or undermining might be described as a three-step process: First, a deconstructive reading must note which member of an opposition in a text appears to be privileged or dominant (writers versus editors, error versus correctness, men versus women, etc.); second, the reading shows how this hierarchy can be reversed within the text, how the apparent hierarchy is arbitrary or illusory; finally, a deconstructive reading places both structures in question, making the text ultimately ambiguous. For students to deconstruct a text, they need to locate an opposition, determine which member is privileged, then reverse and undermine that hierarchy. Such activity often makes central what appears to be marginal, thereby exposing "hidden" contradictions. Deconstruction seems to me especially worthwhile because it encourages creativity (my students often enjoy the imaginative playfulness and punning of much poststructuralist criticism) and scrutiny (in order to deconstruct a work, one at least must read it carefully).

Thus, if structuralism shows how the conventions of a text work, then poststructuralism, in a sense, points out how they fail. In our time, the genres fiction and nonfiction have proved especially interesting. Gill's passage would appear to be nonfiction, since Gill really did work at *The New Yorker*, and his book obviously employs the operations of autobiography. But look at Miss Gould's uncannily apt name: She is a Miss Ghoul, having unearthed a "buried" dangling modifier, decomposing Gill's sentence; Botsford, perhaps played by Vincent Price, enters with "an expression of solemnity," carrying this mutilated modifier that the author finds himself unable to "disinter." Miss Gould may not drink human blood, but she does have some strange nutritional ideas: "gerunds, predicate nominatives, and passive paraphrastic conjugations are mother's milk to her." Fortunately, the editor, a gardener, or rather a Gardner, who has the final responsibility for nurturing, pruning, and harvesting the writer's sentences, knows how to deal with buried modifiers. A Botsford, he knows how to get over the unavoidable errors of prose, how to ford the botches of writing (ouch!). Thus, although we initially may place this piece into the nonfiction category, deconstruction calls such placement into question. People in nonfiction usually don't have symbolic numbers — do they? Of course, there was that White House spokesperson named Larry Speakes. And then my allergist in Tuscaloosa, whose name, prophetically enough, was Dr. Shotts. And a hundred other folks I've known with strangely meaningful names. Deconstruction typically leaves us in uncertainty, but with a richer understanding of the categories we have put in motion — thereby unavoidably functioning as a kind of cultural criticism, or at least a prelude to cultural criticism.

Although deconstructive critics may well deal with pervasive, basic issues, they may also choose some marginal element of the text and vigorously explore its oppositions, reversals, and ambiguities. In fact, for some critics, deconstruction is simply a name for "close reading" with a vengeance. The deconstructive critic, for example, might well decide to concentrate on the arguably marginal assertion that because of the editors' merciless correction, "the piece will be much improved." The New Critic, I think, would not be very likely to consider this assertion central, the key to the passage. Yet, proceeding from deconstructive assumptions, bringing the marginal to the center, here is what happened when I turned on this assertion:

Gill's anecdote clearly sets the world's writers against the editors, and the latter control the game. The editors and their henchmen, the checkers and copy editors, get to say what is wrong. They get to dig the "yawning pit" in front of the helpless writer's desk; they determine the "tiny elect" who can write correctly; they make the scores and hundreds of "hen-tracks" on the writer's manuscript, which serve as testimony to the incompetence of writers, the near-impossibility of writing, and the arbitrary power of the editor. To be sure, it is acknowledged that these editorial assaults upon the writer serve their purpose, for "Thanks to the hen-tracks and their consequences, the piece will be much improved." But the cost is clearly terrible. Not only is the writer unable to write his own name with any confidence, he has become a "Poor devil," outside "the elect." In delivering his writing over to the editors, conceding their dominance, the writer inevitably places his own identity, perhaps even his own soul, in jeopardy, as the expostulation "oh Christ!" comes to be an invocation to the only power who can save the writer from the devil and the editor's destructive forces.

In fact, this story of the errors of writing actually reveals that the kingdom of editors is based upon a lie: It simply is not true, despite the beleaguered writer's admission under torture, that "the piece will be much improved" by editorial intervention. Miss Gould's enormous grammatical lore does not improve the piece at all; her effort nearly made it "worse." And Botsford's contribution involves simply leaving the piece as it was written — a strange method of improvement. This instance, in other words, suggests that the writer need not approach dissolution in order to compose his writing. At the same time, Gill can never become again like the gill-less dolphin of the first paragraph, confidently "diving skyward," for the dangling modifier remains, a part of the sea of language the author cannot leave. In the end, both writer and editor are defeated by their inability to control their language, as the status of the writer at *The New Yorker* becomes a paradigm for the alarming status of writing itself: deceptive, mute, and intractable, "The sentence stands," neither improved nor made worse.

Psychological Criticism

In its most commonsensical form, a psychological approach to a text simply involves focusing attention on the motivations and relationships involved in the text's production or consumption. The mental processes of author, character, and/or reader may be involved in such considerations. My students, who have seen their own writing covered by "pencilled hen-tracks of inquiry, suggestion, and correction," are easily interested in what Gill's passage implies about the emotional effects of criticism and why writers react so unconstructively and painfully to correction and advice. Whereas reader-response criticism would build a "reading" from such subjective reaction, psychological criticism would be more interested in analyzing (rather than expressing) the passage's effects. Obviously, terms like "ego," "anxiety," "unconscious," and "obsessive," would be handy in such an analysis, although an introduction to psychological concepts could quickly engulf a course in criticism. And one could easily spend several semesters exploring different psychological schools and the various ways they might influence our reading. My minimal (but still challenging) goal in an introduction to theory is to give my students an extremely basic understanding of some essential Freudian ideas and their application.

Many of my students think they already understand Freud: He's the guy who thought of everything in terms of sex. Freud did of course think that sexuality (in a large sense) pervades our lives, but it is also always in conflict with opposing forces. So that we can function in society, our drive toward pleasure is necessarily contained and suppressed, relegated in part to the unconscious, where it does not slumber peacefully away, but rather asserts itself indirectly, in dreams, jokes, slips of the tongue, creative writing. For instance, dreams of water, Freud tells us, harken back to "the embryo in the amniotic fluid in the mother's uterus"; dreams of diving into water may be expressing a desire to return to the womb (*Lectures,* p. 160). Repression of such desires becomes a problem when the unconscious enlarges its domain, creating hysterical, obsessional, or phobic neuroses that insistently express the desire while still disguising it. If the power of the unconscious begins to take over reality, creating delusion, then we have a psychosis.

This economy of desire is based on Freud's most outrageous (and undeniable) claim: That even infants are sexual beings. Freud's theory of the central sexual phenomenon of early childhood, admittedly based on the development of males, is laid out in a brief and accessible paper, "The Dissolution of the Oedipus Complex." Focusing first on the mother's breasts, the young boy invests his desire in his mother — he "develops an object-cathexis" for her, Freud says. As the boy's "sexual wishes in regard to his mother become more intense," his father is increasingly "perceived as an obstacle to them," thus originating what Freud calls "the simple positive Oedipus complex" (p. 640). The desire to supplant his father and join with his mother cannot be acted out, and it must be repressed, turned away from, put out of sight. This "primal repression" initiates the unconscious, engendering a "place" for repressed desires. If no more than a repression is achieved, however, the Oedipus complex "persists in an unconscious state in the id and will later manifest its pathogenic effect." This "pathogenic effect" can be avoided, Freud says, by "the destruction of the Oedipus complex," which "is brought about by the threat of castration" (p. 664). This threat is embodied in the father and perpetuated by the formation of the super-ego, which "retains the character of the father" (p. 642) and comes to stand for the restraints of "authority, religious teaching, schooling and reading." This constraining law in Lacan's reading of Freud is ultimately the system of language.

Even the most glimmering understanding of Freud, I would argue, can be useful: The idea of the unconscious, for instance, dispenses with the second-most-often-asked question in introductory courses — "Do you think the author really intended to mean any of that?" Further, my students generate thin and uninteresting readings more out of caution and a poverty of options than a plenitude of possibilities, and after an exposure to Freud, what interpretation can be immediately rejected as absurd? Even a basic understanding of "The Dissolution of the Oedipus Concept" opens up Gill's passage in ways my students have found liberating, comic, and revealing. For example, one of the most interesting problems in this passage is the apparent disparity between the emotional content and the actual events. We see a writer bursting into tears, hiding his head on his blotter; a writer who considers himself humiliated, who glares "blankly"; we even see a writer who is unsure of his very name. And what is the cause? A grammatical error? The scene makes so little logical sense that we may well wonder if it makes more psychological sense. The following reading tries to see what might happen when the Oedipal triangle, the unconscious, the super-ego, and the castration complex get Gill's passage on the couch:

> The dolphin diving skyward at the beginning of Gill's passage is an obvious
> Freudian image of birth, and an important clue to the psychic problems being

addressed here. The writer moves from the buoyant amniotic ocean of pure plea-sure and unthreatened ego, the world of "unshakable confidence," into the diffi-cult reality of *The New Yorker,* the world of the anxious, neurotic writer. Gill's longing for an impossible return to the uncomplicated indulgence of an animal state, symbolized by the dolphin, conflicts with his unavoidable status in a pa-rental society of traditions, gospels, grammatical rules, and "editors, copy editors, and checkers." The ambiguity of the image, "diving skyward," reflects this troubled position, suspended between the id's impossible nostalgia and the super-ego's stern correction. Gill's symbol for himself, the dolphin, is an interesting (and no doubt unconscious) play on his name: a "gill" is naturally associated with a fish, which becomes the dolphin; A dolphin, however, does not have a "gill," thus marking again the gulf between the burdened Gill and the free-floating dolphin.

Does Freud's model of psychosexual development also help to explain how this loss of innocence leads to Gill's unexpectedly emotional reaction? Yes, startlingly well in fact, for analysis reveals how Gill's scene reenacts the traumatic dissolu-tion of the Oedipal complex. To see how the Oedipal triangle shapes Gill's pas-sage, how Gill's response bears the emotional charge of reworking his way through this complex, we should first note the writer's special relationship to his editors: He owes his existence, as a writer anyway, to his editors. The union of Miss Gould and Gardner Botsford, in this case, allows "Brendan Gill" to appear. Miss Gould, the copy editor, the symbolic mother, stands for grammatical correctness. At *The New Yorker,* the writer's first desires must be for her "yes." But this identification with Miss Gould, or rather what she represents, is unavoidably frustrated. Like the child who desires union with his mother, the writer is ill-equipped to satisfy Miss Gould: not even one of the "tiny elect," the writer cannot possibly fill in the "yawning pit" of error.

But the writer, like the developing child, must also face the law of the father. Gardner Botsford, the symbolic father, the senior editor, must ultimately direct the writer's attention away from Miss Gould toward the proper object of his attention, outside *The New Yorker* family — the reader. We see that Gill does in fact reveal a turning away from Miss Gould, using in fact the same focus as the child who turns initially from the mother's breasts as an object of desire: Gill finds Miss Gould's "mother's milk," the predicate nominatives and such, distaste-ful. The way Gill chooses to present her name (not "Gloria Gould" but "Miss Gould") marks his recognition of her as a "Miss." As a by-the-book grammarian, she may also be a ghoul, bringing a deadly stiffness to what he handles. Gill's development as a writer thus requires him to reject her.

To see how this rejection is accomplished, again in terms of the Oedipus complex, we must observe how the writer's identification with his writing contrib-utes to his extraordinary anxiety and its symptomatic distortions. Threats to his writing endanger his identity, his ego. Thus we see that although it is the writer's galleys that are covered with "inquiry, suggestion, and correction," Gill shifts these impressions to the writer, and further transforms them from "pencilled hen-tracks" into stings. It is not, as we might suppose, the particular work that may be attacked so much it dies, but instead the writer who may be "stung to death by an army of gnats." In reality, gnats do not, of course, have stingers; they bite, if anything. The dreamlike alteration here again substantiates the threat to his identity that the author has perceived: Being bitten to death by gnats is absurd, but being stung to death is a terrifying prospect.

At this point Freud's assertion that the dissolution of the Oedipus complex is accomplished by the threat of castration is especially helpful. Gardner Botsford, Gill's senior editor, his symbolic father, poses this threat. To see how Botsford plays this role, we must consider what he is threatening to remove. Botsford enters the scene with Gill's play review "in his hand," and we discover eventually that a part of this review has been illegimately "buried," and may subsequently be removed, although Gill himself cannot see how to "disinter it." This threat to Gill's writing is charged by the fear of castration precisely because the writer identifies with his writing. It is no accident that the writer's "dumb uncertainty" becomes a paralyzed silence that threatens to erase the most public sign of his identity, as "his name looks as if it could stand some working on." His name, his signature, organizes the evidence of his potency, his ability (in a sense) to reproduce and promulgate himself. Thus, the writer may well "stare" at his name "long and long," once he realizes he may lose it if he cannot control the prose to which it is attached. Gill realizes that the editorial parents may correct and improve his "piece," but the cost may be terrible, as the piece may be separated from the writer, taken over by the authorities who control the emissions of his pen. Gill's image for what he has lost, the dolphin, thus becomes a rather blatant phallic symbol, reemerging as the pen (the grammatical penis) that the "dumb," unnamed writer loses. In other words, the writer must give up his "piece" to be published, to survive as a writer — but then he is no longer the writer. He cannot get himself into print, so he submits to the authorities of culture, propriety, and correctness, having realized that the self may be cut off from the sign of its identity.

We now may see the fittingness of the error Miss Gould finds: A structure that is "dangling." The writer may see his own fate in the sentence that sticks out, for it suddenly has "assumed the female gender." We would have to agree that the writer who focuses his desire upon grammar and correctness will be impotent, emasculated. The writer, in order to thrive, must get beyond the desire to please the Miss Goulds of the world. We may also see now the fittingness of "Gardner" as the name for the symbolic father: So close to "gardener," Gardner is the one who has the power to prune, to root out, the writer who is stuck on the mother's milk of Miss Gould, grammar. Thus, Gill's story draws on his psychosexual development and an apparently unresolved Oedipus complex to rehearse in powerful terms the advantages of accepting the values of the father and shifting his desire to the reader. Gill evades symbolic castration. "The sentence stands," the father says, saving the writer's pen(is).

Feminist Criticism

I have only recently stopped being amazed at how easily and enthusiastically my students take to feminist criticism. Part of its appeal, I suppose, is its simplicity, at least on the surface: To practice feminist criticism, one need only read as a woman. Such a procedure quickly turns out to have a profound effect on the reader and the text — an effect that hardly can avoid being political. Whatever students' sexual politics might be, feminist criticism unavoidably involves them in significant, timely issues. I do not mean to say that feminist criticism is invariably easy: Reading as a woman, even if one is a woman, may be extremely difficult, requiring the reader to dismantle or discard years of learned behavior. And, of course, I am leaping over the difficult question of what "as a woman" actually means. Since we can't reasonably discuss, as Cheryl Torsney claims, "a single female sexuality" (p. 180), isn't it absurd to assume there is a distinctly feminine way of reading? How can a man even pretend to read "as a woman"?

But these questions need not be answered in order for students to attempt to undo their sexual assumptions, try out new ones, or simply sensitize themselves to the sexual issues present in a work. Feminist criticism thus involves students in reader-response and political criticism. Not all texts, of course, lend themselves easily to feminist criticism, but it is difficult to find one that completely resists a feminist stance. I have found that Gill's passage easily supports a familiar feminist observation, that language itself is phallocentric, as Hélène Cixous and Luce Irigaray have insistently argued. But the passage also repays a more aggressive and perhaps even outrageous (or outraged) approach. Both appear in the following analysis:

> We know not all the writers at *The New Yorker* were men, even some years ago during Brendan Gill's tenure. So, when Gill speaks of "some writer who has made a name for himself in the world," and about the editorial "machinery" that besets "him," Gill is of course referring to writers in the generic sense. One may still assert today, although less confidently than in 1975, that "himself" and "him" in this passage include "herself" and "her." Such a claim, that one sexual marker includes its opposite, is feeble — as if "white" included "black," or "totalitarian" included "democratic." But the motivations for such a claim are revealed even in this brief passage, for Gill's story not only contains this obvious pronominal bias, still accepted by some editors and writers; the story also conveys more subtle messages about sexuality and sexual roles. It is, in fact, a not-so-subtle attack on the image of women.
>
> Miss Gould functions as a familiar stereotype: the finicky spinster, a Miss Thistlebottom, who has devoted her life to English grammar and its enforcement. She is a copy editor, subservient to the male editor and writer, and her lack of imagination and taste testify to the wisdom of this power structure. This division of labor — male/creative, female/menial — is subtly reinforced by reference to the "hen-tracks" (not rooster tracks) that cover the writer's galley, thus further associating petty correction with the feminine, even though surely some copy editors could have been male. These "hen-tracks" are more than an aggravating correction, as they even come to threaten the writer's very identity. The effects of these hen-tracks, feminine marks of correction, allow Gill to assert the disabling consequences of the feminine upon the masculine: The writers become emotional, and even effeminately hysterical, crying on their blotters. Gill receives comfort and approval from the man, Botsford, but Miss Gould lacks the penetrating insight to deal properly with a problem as small as a grammatical error.
>
> Gill's misogyny influences the passage in other ways. The metaphorical threat to the writer is distinctly gynecological, a "yawning pit." Miss Gould's shortcoming is that she fails maternally, providing indigestible "mother's milk." Even the error that Miss Gould locates is subtly connected to the feminine, for the problem with the sentence is that part of it has "assumed the female gender," which may be seen as the underlying problem for Gill: Something has assumed the female gender. That part of the sentence Miss Gould complains of, naturally, is a "complaint" — which, Gill and Botsford determine, should retain its feminine nature. The complaint itself seems strange: In the mode of feminine busybodies like Miss Gould, the nonagenarian laments not having "enough work to do." Miss Gould, similarly overzealous, has herself done more work than is reasonable, and Botsford's pronouncement that "The sentence stands" returns her to her place, negating her feminine fussiness, reasserting masculine mastery of the phallocentric world of writing.

Conclusion

One might want to point out, I suppose, that in offering this rehearsal of critical "approaches," I am assuming that plurality is better than unity, that the relative is better than the absolute (or even a quest for the absolute). And, given what I think we know about language and knowing, it seems silly to me to assume otherwise: As Jane Tompkins says, articulating a current commonplace, we are not "freestanding autonomous entities, but beings that are culturally constituted by interpretive frameworks or interpretive strategies that our culture makes available to us" (p. 734). In other words, the texts we read — when we look at books, at our world, at ourselves — are likewise constituted by these frameworks or strategies. Obviously, if this "reading" of meaning is correct, plurality offers us a richer universe, allowing us to take greater advantage of the strategies our culture makes available — strategies that do not approach a text, but rather make it what we perceive. Our students therefore should learn how to inhabit the theories mentioned here — and a good many others.

To be sure, such plurality is not always comfortable. Furthermore, if we should agree that the more strategies students can deploy (or be deployed by), the more power and insight they can potentially wield, then must we also agree there are no limits? Are all readings welcome, the more the merrier? My initial impulse is to say, "Yes, we can learn from any reading, from any set of interpretive assumptions. Come one, come all." We can see how readings that seem severely inattentive might offer useful insights: Robert Crosman reveals, for example, how one student's reading completely missed the significance of the hair on the pillow at the end of "A Rose for Emily," and yet this reading, comparing Emily to the student's grandmother, profoundly enlarged Crosman's understanding of Faulkner's story. We can even imagine how ludicrous errors might stimulate our thinking: My student who thought *The Hamlet* was by Shakespeare did lead me to ask (mostly in an attempt to ease his embarrassment) about Shakespeare's influence on Faulkner — perhaps *The Hamlet* in some sense is by Shakespeare, or is shaped by *Hamlet.* But we must admit that most readings in violation of shared interpretive strategies will usually be seen as inferior, if not wrong, and that finding insight in such violations often seems an act of kindness, a salvage operation.

I can also imagine theoretical possibilities that would not be welcome in my critical home, should they ever appear: Nazi criticism, racist criticism, electroshock criticism, for example, In other words, if we are not freestanding autonomous entities, we are also not entirely helpless, simply the products of the interpretive operations we inherit, "a mere cultural precipitate," as Morse Peckham puts it (p. xviii). I would like to think we can resist; we can change; we can grow; we can, perhaps, in some sense, even get better. We can, that is, attempt to evaluate ways of making meaning, and their particular applications — and if we are very clever and very lucky, we may even modify interpretive frameworks, or possibly even invent new ones.

But only if we have some awareness that such frameworks exist.

References

Brooks, Cleanth. *The Well-Wrought Urn.* New York: Harcourt Brace, 1947.

Crosman, Robert. "How Readers Make Meaning." *College Literature* 9 (1982): 207–15.

Culler, Jonathan. *On Deconstruction: Theory and Criticism after Structuralism.* Ithaca, N.Y.: Cornell University Press, 1982.

Eagleton, Terry. *Literary Theory: An Introduction.* Minneapolis: University of Minnesota Press, 1982.

Freud, Sigmund. "The Dissolution of the Oedipus Complex." *The Freud Reader.* Ed. Peter Gay. New York: Norton, 1989, pp. 661–66.

———. *Introductory Lectures on Psychoanalysis.* Trans. and ed. James Strachey. New York: Norton, 1966.

Frye, Northrop. *Fables of Identity.* New York: Harcourt, 1951.

Gill, Brendan. *Here at the New Yorker.* New York: Random, 1975.

Grimes, Joseph. *The Thread of Discourse.* Paris: Mouton, 1975.

Johnson, Barbara. *The Critical Difference: Essays in the Contemporary Rhetoric of Reading.* Baltimore: Johns Hopkins University Press, 1980.

Peckham, Morse. *Explanation and Power: The Control of Human Behavior.* New York: Seabury, 1979.

Propp, Vladimir. *The Morphology of the Folktale.* Austin: University of Texas Press, 1968.

Tompkins, Jane. "A Short Course in Post-Structuralism." *College English* 50 (Nov. 1988): 733–47.

Torsney, Cheryl. "The Critical Quilt: Alternative Authority in Feminist Criticism." *Contemporary Literary Theory.* Ed. G. Douglas Atkins and Laura Morrow. Amherst: University of Massachusetts press, 1989, pp. 180–99.

Wellek, Rene, and Austin Warren. *Theory of Literature.* 1942. New York: Harcourt, 1977.

PART ELEVEN

DOCUMENT DESIGN

Many students in composition courses are pursuing business or technical careers, and they need help writing in those fields. Further, as more and more students grow familiar with word processing and desktop publishing software, they have the technology to design documents for a variety of situations, in a variety of fields.

Applying principles of the composing process presented in Part One, Part Eleven of the handbook offers a concise discussion of writing for business and professional purposes, emphasizing that effective communication is direct, clear, and appropriate for the situation. Further, with the new emphasis on document design, the handbook recognizes that effective communication entails more than clear writing; students and teachers must also be conscious of the visual rhetoric of the page. Few teachers of first-year composition have formal training in teaching business or technical writing or in the principles of document design. The selections that follow address several questions that teachers might consider as they attempt to incorporate these issues into their courses.

- What is visual rhetoric? How do the rhetorical features of a document's design relate to the rhetorical features of its text? How can teachers help students integrate writing processes and document design?
- How does teaching business writing compare to teaching other kinds of writing?
- What can teachers of first-year composition courses do to prepare students for the kinds of writing they will have to do in business and professional situations?

THE TROUBLE WITH EMPLOYEES' WRITING
MAY BE FRESHMAN COMPOSITION

Elizabeth Tebeaux

[Teaching English in the Two-Year College (1988): 9–19.]

Elizabeth Tebeaux, professor of English and coordinator of technical writing at Texas A&M University, has written a number of articles on the history of technical writing. Tebeaux authored Design of Business Communications: The Process and the Product *(1990) and, with Tom Pearsall,* Reporting Technical Information *(8th ed., 1994). She has also published articles in* Written Communication, Issues in Writing, Journal of Business and Technical Communication, *and* Technical Communications Quarterly.

Because many students do not take any writing courses after freshman composition, they may find themselves underprepared for jobs that require them to write for a variety of specific purposes. Tebeaux describes her experience as a writing consultant in business and government, observing that many problems employees have in their writing result from writing strategies they learned in first-year composition courses. Tebeaux suggests changes in the design of composition courses — changes that will help students become more effective writers in the "real world." Her argument makes explicit the vital connections between what we ask students to do in writing classrooms and what those same students will do when they write at work.

In the past two decades, programs in rhetoric and composition have expanded in size as well as in range of studies offered. Yet literacy still remains a serious national problem, and business and industry continue to report problems in their employees' ability to write effectively. A number of large corporations are attempting to handle the problem in one of two ways: (1) by developing in-house writing courses that are included as part of company training programs; and (2) by hiring college writing teachers to design and to teach in-house writing courses. After having taught 11 workshops for three large corporations during the past three years and having served as a writing consultant to a large county government for two additional years, I have observed a number of employee writing problems that are traceable to writing strategies learned in freshman composition. While my findings will certainly not be new to technical writing teachers, my purpose here is to share these findings with teachers of freshman composition.

During this five-year period, I have worked with approximately 250 writers in either business organizations or county government. I found that 218 of 250 participants (87 percent) reported that traditional freshman composition was the only writing instruction they had received in college. Of that 250, 91 percent held at least one college degree, and 31 percent had a master's degree. Participants had been out of college 2 to 26 years, although most had been out of college fewer than 10 years. Those who had not earned a four-year degree had completed two years of junior college. Nearly all of these writers (234) reported that they had taken one or two courses in freshman composition. Only 37 reported having taken any kind of course in professional, technical, or business writing, although a course in business letter writing was the most frequent professional writing course mentioned. Forty-four participants reported that spelling, usage, and punctuation errors were marked in some courses in their major field of study. But the most revealing statement was that 87 percent of the employee-participants said that what they knew about how to write they gained in freshman composition.

Designing the Organizational Short Course

Prior to beginning the short courses, I asked employee-participants (all were there because they knew they needed help) to complete a background questionnaire (from which I derived the information given above) and to submit two samples of writing that they knew had been ineffective or that their supervisors had deemed "bad." To each example they submitted, they were asked to answer the following questions:

Figure 1. *Original Sample*

Company Policy on Interduct

The Company's previous position has been not to place interduct direct buried for fiber optic cable. This directive reemphasizes this policy and explains why it is still in effect.

There has recently been a company pursuing sales of interduct for this purpose, stating that their interduct will allow placing of fiber optic cable. Several demonstrations were held that showed the duct being buried and a similar size cable being pulled into the duct with some success.

A recent real life trial of this direct buried interduct was very unsuccessful. It was found that after placing the interduct and allowing the ground to settle for several days, the interduct conformed to the high and low spots in the trench. When these numerous small bends are introduced into the interduct, it becomes impossible to pull more than 400 to 600 feet of fiber optic cable into the interduct before the 600 pound pulling tension is exceeded.

Interduct itself offers little or no advantage as protection to a direct buried fiber optic cable. In fact, it has a negative advantage, in that it will allow the cable to be pulled and fibers shattered or cracked for much greater distances.

As a result of this trial and previous recommendation, there should be no interduct placed for direct buried.

Please direct further questions to H. L. Rogers at 6727. We will appreciate your cooperation in enforcing this matter.

---

1. How did you determine that this piece of writing is "bad" writing?
2. Why did you write it the way you did?
3. What was the purpose of the document? What were the circumstances that led to your writing this document?

Prior to planning each workshop, which consisted of four two-hour settings, I examined these samples and discussed them with the manager who had retained me to design the workshop. Based on the problems discovered in analyzing the samples and talking to each manager, I designed an instructional approach to deal efficiently with the problems. The kinds of problem reports employees submitted were similar to Figure 1. Basically, this memorandum looks just like a freshman essay. The opening paragraph states the purpose. The second and third paragraphs provide support, and the final paragraph concludes by asking for the reader's cooperation.

From the perspective of a reader in an organization who is inundated with routine paperwork like this, the report reveals a number of problems that make it "bad" writing:

- Lack of clearly revealed organization;
- Lack of deductive presentation strategy that gives the reader the main information first;
- Lack of visual presentation techniques for revealing organization and content;

Figure 2. *Revised Sample*

TO: Harlan Stevenson, Manager — Customer Services, BIRMINGHAM

SUBJECT: Company Policy: Interduct shall not be placed for buried lightweight cable.

Contrary to the alleged claims of some overzealous vendors, the above policy remains unchanged.

A field trial was recently conducted where the interduct was buried and cable placement was attempted several days later. The negative observations were as follows:

1. **Cable lengths are reduced between costly splices.**
   The interduct conformed to the high and low spots in the trench. These numerous bends introduced added physical resistance against the cable sheath during cable pulling. Even with application of cable lubricant, the average length pulled was 500 feet before the 600 pound pulling tension was exceeded.

2. **Maintenance liability is increased.**
   Due to shorter cable lengths, the number of splices increases. As the number of splices increases, maintenance liability increases.

3. **Added material costs are counterproductive.**

   Interduct, while adding 16% to the material cost, offers little or no mechanical protection to buried fiber optic cable. In fact, when an occupied interduct was pulled at a 90 degree angle with a backhoe bucket, the fibers were not broken only at the place of contact, as would have been with a direct buried cable. Instead, due to the stress being distributed along the interduct, the fibers shattered and cracked up to 100 feet in each direction.

4. **Increased labor costs are unnecessary.**

   In about the same amount of time required to place interduct, the fiber optic cable could be placed. The added 28% of labor hours expended to pull cable after the interduct is placed cannot be justified.

Please insure that this policy is conveyed to and understood by your construction managers. If you have questions, please call me at 817 334-2178.

> John Doe
> Corporate Engineering Manager

- Lack of analysis of the reader's needs concerning the topic being discussed.

During the workshop, participants were asked to analyze and then revise the two reports they knew to be poorly written. After reviewing the report in figure 1 with the four problem areas in mind, the writer admitted that the main information he wanted to emphasize was not easy to find, much less remember. But after studying visual presentation techniques, the rationale for deductive organization, and the importance of designing any writing with the readers' needs dictating the organization and the visual design, the engineer who wrote Figure 1 submitted the revision in Figure 2.

The most striking aspect of the revision is the effective way in which the writer has visually displayed the information. Through use of visual strategies, the readers have various options for reading the report: they can read the boldface subject line and overview sentence for each reason given and be able to grasp the essential meaning of the report. Or, they can read the subject line, the opening paragraph, the overview sentence for each supporting point, and perhaps as much detail pertaining to each point as they deem necessary. Note, too, that the revision contains more specific reasons for not using interduct than the original version. During analysis of the sample, the writer stated that in designing the message deductively, and in listing each reason for not using interduct, he discovered, in his original, that he had failed to provide all reasons for not using interduct. Thus, the revision is not only visually effective, it is more complete.

Another sample (Figure 3) illustrates the same problems as the previous one; i.e., the report looks like an essay. The report opens with a paragraph stating the thesis. The second and third paragraphs elaborate on that thesis. The final sentence reiterates the thesis statement.

After the discussion on the importance of deductive organization, visual display of information, and the importance of designing writing with readers' needs in mind, the writer stated that she could now see why the MISS Worksheets were not being corrected and/or returned. First, she had not anticipated her readers' needs, particularly that they would not know how to deal with the Profiles and Worksheets. Second, she had not given a date by which she wanted the materials returned to her and additional information that would help readers respond as she wished them to. Third, she had not organized the instructions and presented them on the page so that they could be easily followed. As a result, most profiles had not been returned; she had received numerous calls asking for clarification; several profiles that had been returned were incorrect or had notes attached indicating that the reader was not sure if changes had been done correctly.

In revising her original, the writer places important information first, establishes hierarchies of key information with headings, uses these headings to guide inclusion of information that will make verification easier for readers, and displays all information so that it is visually accessible.

In analyzing the revision by emphasizing the reader's response, other employees observed that the revision was easy to see, easy to follow. In addition, the importance of the message was now apparent.

The essay technique, as applied to short reports and memoranda, the most commonly written documents in business organizations, was apparent in nearly every employee's submission. In fact, the most common answer to Question 2 on the Trouble Analysis Sheet — Why did you write this document the way you did? — yielded some version of the following answers on over 200 samples:

1. this is the way we were taught to write in college;
2. this is the only way I have ever written anything;
3. I don't know any other way to write.

Given the fact the employees in business have too much to read, that they seldom read all of any document, that they "skim" or "search" read most routine writing, participants soon realized why documents, like Figure 3, were not being read or not being read correctly. That is, because of lack

Figure 3. *Original Sample*

MISS

Employee Profiles and Employee Worksheets

The purpose of the following is to explain how the MISS Employee Profiles and Employee Worksheets are to be verified. Your group's worksheets are attached.

The Employee Profiles need to be verified for accuracy before they are filed in the employee's Personal History File. If a change needs to be made that was our error, mark the profile and return it with the Worksheet so that a new profile can be generated. If you are making a change, mark the profile and have it signed and concurred and return both the profile and the Employee Worksheet. After the Employee Profile has been verified, please return the Employee Worksheet to me for my records.

Please note that only information that appeared on the Worksheet was keyed into the MISS data base. Information other than what is on the worksheet is furnished by other data bases. For example, the title is generated by the title code. The title code suffix is generated by the job evaluation number. There have been problems with the title suffix being incorrect. If this is the only correction, please note this on the Employee Profile and worksheet. Please advise me by attaching a note to the employee worksheet when you return it to me. Also, please verify that any other information that may appear to be incorrect is not due to a recent change on payroll records.

If you have problems, please contact me at 6512.

Jane Doe
MISS Administrator

---

of deductive organization to give the reader the "news" immediately and visual presentation technique to reveal organization and content, the memorandum was not "readable"[1] in the sense that the intended audience did not find the document easy to access and process. The revision, Figure 4, however, was deemed a document that would be read because it is visually accessible. You can see organization and content at a glance.

The final assignment required participants to revise some kind of document, usually a policy, which I selected from each organization's policy binder. Like the reports that participants brought to the workshop, many policies too often were not clearly organized and were too visually dense to be read quickly. Figure 5 is one vacation policy statement that participants were asked to revise.

After having revised two of their own reports, participants yielded interesting versions of policies. Figure 6 is one revision of the policy shown in Figure 5. It is concise and clear mainly because it is visually accessible.

Analysis of Samples — Implications for Basic Composition

The opportunity I have had to observe the writing problems and the writing instruction backgrounds of these employees has led me to several initial conclusions which I believe are worth sharing with other composition teachers:

Figure 4. *Revised Sample*

TO: Jane Doe

FROM: MISS Administrator

SUBJECT: Procedures for Reviewing MISS Employee Profiles by

May 22, 1986

If any information is inaccurate on the attached MISS profiles, please return those for correction within the next two weeks.

Each employee should have a MISS profile placed in his/her history file. The profile will replace the SW-1006 in the near future. In addition, all departments within Fabrico's five-state area will be pulling MISS profiles to fill vacancies within their departments.

Procedures for Reviewing MISS Employee Profiles

1. If a change is required because information was keyed incorrectly, mark the profile and return it with the worksheet. A new profile will be sent to you.
2. If you are making a change, mark the profile and have it signed and concurred at the next higher level. Return both the profile and the worksheet. A new profile will be sent to you for review.
3. After the profile has been verified, please return the worksheet to me for my records.

Incorrect Information That May Appear on the MISS Employee Profile

The information that appeared on the worksheet shows the only items that were keyed into MISS. The MISS data base is merged with other data bases to produce the profile.

1. Incorrect title — The title is generated by the title code from the MERT data base. Please check this code on the last PCR and allow one week for the PCR to be worked.
2. Incorrect title code suffix — The title code suffix is generated by the JE number from the Atlanta job evaluation data base. Please note an incorrect title suffix on the worksheet and profile, as I will be working with Atlanta on this problem.
3. Incorrect payroll information — Please allow one week for the last PCR submitted to be worked and merged with new data.

Please call me if you have any questions about how to make changes.

---

(1) If my experience during the past five years is even partially representative of the kinds of problems many employee writers are experiencing, then, more than likely there are many other employees who are attempting to write at work by applying techniques learned in freshman composition to the kinds of writing they are required to do on the job. Yet, traditional freshman composition, as it is usually taught, does not provide adequate preparation for writing at work. While the goal of freshman composition has traditionally been to help students write better in school, too many students and even faculty within English departments and other college departments have assumed that "good writing" is "good writing," and that the student who writes well in school will write well on the job. Too many

Figure 5. *Original Policy*

Joint Practice 27: Vacation Days for Management

General
The purpose of this Joint Practice is to outline the vacation treatment applicable to Management employees.

Eligibility
Vacations with pay shall be granted during the calendar year to each management employee who shall have completed six months' employment since the date employment began. Vacation pay will not be granted if the employee has been dismissed for misconduct. Vacation allowed will be determined according to the following criteria: (a) One week's vacation to any such management employee who has completed six months or more but less than twelve months of service. (b) Two weeks' vacation to any such management employee who has completed twelve months of service but who could not complete seven years of service within the vacation year. Two weeks will be allowed if the employee initially completes six months' service and twelve months' service wtihin the same vacation year. (c) Three weeks' vacation to any management employee who could complete seven or more but less than fifteen years' service within the vacation year and to District level who shall have completed six months' employment within the vacation year. (e) Five weeks' vacation to any management employee who completes twenty-five or more years of service within the vacation year and to Department head level and higher management who shall have completed a period of six months' employment within the vacation year.

The criteria described above are Net Credited Service as determined by the Employees' Benefit Committee. Where eligibility for a vacation week under (a) or (b) above first occurs on or after December 1 of a vacation year, the vacation week may be granted in the next following vacation year if it is completed before April 1 and before the beginning of vacation for the following year. When an authorized holiday falls in a week during which a management employee is absent on vacation, an additional day off (or equivalent time off with pay) may be taken in either the same calendar year or prior to April 1 of the following calendar year. When the additional day of vacation is Christmas Day, it may be granted immediately preceding the vacation or prior to April 1 of the following calendar year.

---

people outside the ranks of technical writing teachers are unaware of the differences between writing in academe and writing in nonacademic settings. English teachers assume, perhaps too optimistically, that what we teach in freshman composition and in writing across the curriculum programs will automatically transfer to nonacademic settings.

(2) Even though technical and business communication programs have grown steadily in the past decade,[2] they are apparently not reaching enough students. In other words, freshman composition is still the main and only "writing instruction" for many students.

(3) Well-meaning faculty in non-English disciplines are not "teaching writing" by assiduously marking errors in spelling, usage, and punctuation

Figure 6.   *Revised Policy*

Joint Practice 27: Vacation Time Allowed Management Employees

The following schedule describes the new vacation schedule approved by the company. This schedule is effective immediately and will remain in effect until a further update is issued.

<u>Vacation Eligibility</u>

1. Vacation with pay shall be granted during the calendar year to each management employee who has completed 6 months' service since the date of employment. Employees who have been dismissed for misconduct will not receive vacation with pay.

<u>Net Credited Service</u>	<u>*Eligible Weeks*</u>
6 mos.–12 mos.	1
12 mos.–7 yrs.	2
7 yrs.–15 yrs. and to District Level with 6 mos. service	3
15 yrs.–25 yrs. and to Division Level with 6 mos. service	4
25 yrs. or more and to Department Head or higher management with 6 mos. service	5

<u>Net Credited Service is determined by the Employee Benefits Committee</u>

2. If eligibility occurs on or after December 1 of a vacation year,
   • vacation may be granted in the next following year if it is taken before April 1.

3. If an authorized holiday falls in a vacation week,
   • an additional day may be taken in either calendar year or before April 1 of the following year.

4. If the additional day of vacation is Christmas day,
   • it may be taken immediately preceding the vacation or before April 1 of the following year.

---

and implying that mechanically correct writing is good writing. The problems I found — the previous samples illustrate these — were not mechanical ones; they stemmed from:

• failing to determine what the audience needed to know so that the writer's purpose (to instruct, persuade, or inform) was achieved;
• failing to organize deductively to reveal the main information first to readers who have more to read than they can and will read carefully;
• failing to use visual design to produce documents that are visually accessible and therefore easy to read;
• failing to understand the importance of creating a visually accessible document and believing that messages that are important to the writer will be important to the reader, and therefore, will be read thoroughly.

The most common problem attributed by any supervisor to the employees attending the workshops was not mechanics; it was lack of clarity and "getting the point across,"[3] both of which, my experience suggests, can be corrected to a great extent by using deductive organization of information and visual design to reveal hierarchies, or levels, of information. Even in original samples that contained a large number of comma splices and nonstandard usage, participants during peer review of each other's work did not think that the main "problem" was mechanics. Employees, in skim- or search-reading routine documents, read holistically. They are looking for answers to the following questions: What is this? Why am I getting this? What am I supposed to do now? The effectiveness of the routine business document is determined by how quickly the reader can answer these questions, not by the mechanical correctness of the content. Correctness becomes an issue if problems in usage, sentence construction, or punctuation hinder the audience's ability to find and process the message.

Reorienting Freshman Composition — Five Recommendations

I am not suggesting that freshman composition be replaced by courses in technical or business writing. Students clearly need the preparation that freshman composition gives them for writing in college. I am suggesting, however, that we need to impress our freshman students and our colleagues in other disciplines with the importance of a course in professional writing to prepare these students for writing in nonacademic contexts. We need to emphasize to students and colleagues that writing at work is not like writing in the classroom and that students need preparation in both areas.

There are, however, some changes that could be implemented in freshman composition programs to make our basic composition courses more relevant to students after they leave school without damaging the basic mission of freshman composition:

(1) Visual design strategies — presenting content in visually effective ways — need to be introduced in composition.[4] Much of the writing in the world of work (brochures, technical reports, articles for publication, advertisements) uses visual rhetoric in making messages persuasive and clear. Why pretend any longer that visual appeal is not an important rhetorical device? Students need to be introduced, even in freshman composition, to basic concepts in producing visually accessible, visually pleasing documents. They need to understand that visual accessibility (one aspect of the difficult area of readability) is as crucial a quality in writing as coherence, unity, and structure. They also need to understand that teachers are the only people who are committed to reading everything students write, that in a work context audiences will read a document only if they believe it will benefit them and if it is easy to access and understand.

(2) The importance of deductive writing in developing "reader-based" prose needs to be emphasized more in freshman composition. In learning to write research papers, students should be taught that placing the conclusions after the introduction is an acceptable organizational method. Students should also be required to use clearly worded informative headings throughout research papers. Doing so enforces the point that developing the outline into headings and subheadings helps the reader follow the presentation and helps the writer organize the discussion, eliminate irrelevant information, and generally "stay on track."

(3) The essay needs to be deemphasized as the main, if not the sole, teaching form in freshman composition. (How many people ever write essays after they graduate from college?) Students may benefit from studying effectively designed sets of instructions, which incorporate visual design.

Students may also benefit from writing instructions and then evaluating them for clarity and visual access during peer review.

(4) Freshman composition should be redefined as Introduction to Writing, to emphasize to our colleagues in other disciplines and to our freshmen that students need more than an introduction to writing to prepare them for the writing they will do after college. We need to explain to students throughout freshman composition how writing in school differs from writing at work, that the standards of "good" writing will ultimately change, that they cannot write on the job the way they have written in the classroom. More freshman composition texts, such as *Four Worlds of Writing,*[5] would be helpful in giving students a perspective on how writing is used beyond the classroom.

(5) To develop competencies that will be valuable outside academic writing, the paradigm in freshman composition needs to be integrated with the paradigm in technical writing. That is, in every writing course, students should have to write for specifically defined audiences; students should have a purpose to achieve with that audience; they should learn to deal with tone, voice, organization, and visual presentation commensurate with that purpose. But ultimately, students need to understand that these common rhetorical elements control all writing, whether it is expressive, referential, literary, or informative.[6]

Conclusion

Much of the published scholarship that fills the pages of rhetoric and composition journals underscores the problem I continue to confront in teaching industrial short courses: little concern is expressed for the usefulness of freshman composition after college, for the differences in which writing in school differs from writing at work, for designing writing curricula to ensure that writing instruction is relevant during students' college years and afterward in nonacademic settings. Basic composition theory, in its emphasis on expressive discourse, continues to foster the traditional goals of writing as learning and writing as thinking, with little attention to ways by which these competencies can be sustained and applied in nonacademic writing environments. The problem, I suspect, stems from the fact that few composition teachers, unless they also teach technical writing, understand, or even care about the relevance of their instruction. However, my consulting experience suggests that we should care and that achieving relevance is not only possible but necessary if our composition instruction is to provide any long-lasting solution to the literacy problem.

Notes

[1] For useful approaches to the design of readable texts, see the following essays in *New Essays in Technical and Scientific Communication: Research, Theory, Practice,* ed. Paul V. Anderson, R. John Brockmann, Carolyn R. Miller (Farmingdale: Baywood, 1983): Lester Faigley and Stephen P. Witte, "Topical Focus in Technical Writing," (pp. 59–68); Jack Selzer, "What Constitutes a 'Readable' Style?" (pp. 71–89); Thomas N. Huckin, "A Cognitive Approach to Readability," (pp. 90–98). Also, Daniel B. Felker, ed. *Document Design: A Review of the Relevant Research* (Washington, DC: American Institutes for Research, 1979): Chapters 1, 2, and 4; Lee Odell and Dixie Goswami, *Writing in Nonacademic Settings* (New York: Guilford, 1985), Chapters 2 and 3.

[2] William E. Rivers, "The Current Status of Business and Technical Writing Courses in English Departments," *ADE Bulletin* 82 (Winter 1985): 50–54.

³ A number of studies suggest the paramount importance of clarity as the most desirable quality in employee writing: Donna Stine and Donald Skarzenski, "Priorities for the Business Communication Classroom: A Survey of Business and Academe," *Journal of Business Communication* 16 (Summer 1979): 15–30; Robert R. Bataille, "Writing in the World of Work: What Our Graduates Report," *CCC* 32 (Oct. 1982): 276–280; Lester Faigley and Thomas P. Miller, "What We Learn from Writing on the Job," *College English* 44 (Oct. 1982): 567–569; Gilbert Storms, "What Business School Graduates Say about the Writing They Do at Work: Implications for the Business Communication Course," *ABCA Bulletin* 46 (Dec. 1983): 13–18; Carol Barnum and Robert Fischer, "Engineering Technologists as Writers: Results of a Survey," *Technical Communication* 31 (Second Quarter, 1984): 9–11.

⁴ The Document Design Center has generated a number of studies on visual design which are available for purchase through DDC. However, only two articles in rhetoric and composition journals have yet dealt with the importance of visual rhetoric as a pedagogical consideration: Robert J. Conners, "*Actio*: A Rhetoric of Manuscripts," *Rhetoric Review* 2.1 (Sept. 1983): 64–73; and Stephen Bernhardt, "Seeing the Text," *CCC* 37 (Feb. 1986): 66–78.

⁵ Janice M. Lauer and others, *The Four Worlds of Writing* (New York: Harper, 1985).

⁶ For a discussion of linking all writing, see Harry P. Kroitor and Elizabeth Tebeaux, "Bringing Literature Teachers and Writing Teachers Closer Together," *ADE Bulletin* 78 (Summer 1984): 28–34.

VISUAL RHETORIC: A READER-ORIENTED APPROACH TO GRAPHICS AND DESIGNS

Charles Kostelnick

[Technical Writing Teacher *16.1 (1989): 77–88.*]

An associate professor of English at Iowa State University, Charles Kostelnick teaches advanced composition and graphic communication in business and technical writing. His articles have appeared in Technical Communications Quarterly, Journal of Business and Technical Communications, College Composition and Communication, *and* Journal of Business Communication.

As sophisticated word processing and desktop publishing software give students more control over the appearance of their writings, students and teachers need to be more conscious of how information is presented visually and how that presentation affects readers. Kostelnick constructs a matrix that teachers can use to explore the "variety of visual elements" in different documents. He also offers detailed guidance for teachers who are unfamiliar with principles of document design.

Most technical writing instructors are better prepared to teach and far more experienced in verbal than visual communication. Rhetoric is practiced with words, not with visible forms. Although a few articles on teaching visual design have appeared recently, textbooks and professional writing pedagogy emphasize primarily the development of language skills, and visual thinking is often treated as a secondary cognitive mode reducible to codified rules and conventions (Barton and Barton 1985). Critics have suggested solutions to the problem: Arnheim (1969, 2–3) argues that visual thinking is central to cognition and should be developed as a general educational goal, while Barton and Barton propose applying concepts of contemporary writing pedagogy — the process approach and rhetorical theory — to instruction in visual design.

To communicate effectively in their disciplines, technical writing students need to learn how to combine visual and verbal strategies in solving rhetorical problems. By "visual rhetoric" (Bonsiepe 1965; see also Buchanan 1985) I mean the ability of the writer to achieve the purpose of a document through visual communication, at any level: for example, through the choice of a typeface (Courier, Helvetica), of graphic cues (bullets, lines, icons), of textual arrangement (lists, flow charts, trees), of data displays (a pie chart, line graph), even of the color, shape, and size of the page. By acknowledging visual rhetoric, we recognize that visual choices make a difference — in readers' attitude toward a document, in how readers process its information, and in which information they value. If the writer designs a document consistent with its purpose, visual rhetoric will enhance the conmmunication; if not, visual cues can misdirect readers, subverting the writer's purpose. Students need to know how to write and design documents consistent with the needs and expectations of their readers.

However, to develop visual rhetoric in a writing course, we need a comprehensive model that (1) enables us to describe the variety of visual elements that comprise each document and (2) provides a framework for evaluating how these elements affect readers. The model should be compatible with the rhetorical nature of language instruction, enabling students to adapt visual design to purpose and audience. The approach to visual rhetoric outlined here has three components: a 12-cell matrix of visual communication, some reader-oriented guidelines for making design choices, and a rationale for integrating design decisions into the writing process.

Four Levels of Visual Design

Technical writing entails visual as well as verbal planning, invention, and problem-solving. To teach these activities, the instructor needs a vocabulary for describing the range of visual choices possible for each writing task. The conventional nomenclature of visual communication (graphics, visuals, layout) is too general and ambiguous to describe the visual modes, levels, and idiosyncrasies of individual documents. These generic terms impede the work of the writing teacher by suggesting that visual tasks are formulaic or performed independently by technicians or typists. Writing itself, however, is an intensely visual activity in which the writer manipulates symbols and marks on a visual field. Through the technology of print, writing becomes "thing-like" (Ong 1982), demanding the visual attention of writer and reader. Since writers create, and readers process, visual as well as linguistic cues, the instructor needs a method for planning and analyzing the design of each document in reader-oriented terms.

Unlike a plan for a building, a set of machine drawings, or an aerial photograph, technical writing is encoded largely through alphanumeric symbols. The "text" provides closure for the message, circumscribing abstract marks or pictorial images contained within, and therefore provides a reference point for the visual schema. Writers make visual choices on four levels: intra-, inter-, extra-, and supra-textual. Each level is encoded

Alphanumerical Symbolic	Spatial	Graphic
1 **Intra** variations in style, size, weight of letters, numbers, symbols	2 local spacing between textual units: picas, CPI, kerning	3 marks: punctuation, underscoring; iconic forms of letters
4 **Inter** levels of headings; letters, numbers signaling textual structure	5 line endings, indentation; matrices, lists, tree configurations	6 bullets, icons; line work, arrows, geometric forms on charts, diagrams
7 **Extra** legends, captions, labels; numerical description of data	8 plotting of data on X-Y axes; viewing angle, size of pictures	9 tone, texture, shading of data displays; details on pictures
10 **Supra** section titles numbers; page headers, tabs; pagination	11 placement of extra-textuals in text; page breaks, section breaks	12 marks, icons, color, line work, logos unifying pages & sections

Figure 1.   *12-Cell Matrix of Visual Communication*

in three visual modes: alphanumeric/symbolic, spatial, and graphic. The combinations of levels and modes are plotted on the 12-Cell Matrix of Visual Communication. (See Figure 1.) Below is a brief description of each of the four levels. Further description of the matrix, especially with regard to business writing, can be found in Kostelnick (1988b, see also 1988a; for a more detailed matrix of graphic communication, see Twyman 1979).

The *Intra-textual* level (cells 1-3) governs the local design of the text. In the alphanumeric/symbolic mode, this includes typeface selection and treatment: boldface, italics, type size (10 versus 12 CPI), and upper and lower case. In the spatial mode, intra-textuality controls the linear distance between characters and semantic units, and in the graphic mode, marks that control the flow of text (punctuation) or that create emphasis (underscoring). Intra-textual choices can affect a textual particle (one word in italics) or the whole text (the selection of a typeface for a 50-page report). Governing a field of invisible points distributed across the page, intra-textuality is essentially a one-dimensional manipulation of the text.

The *Inter-textual* level (cells 4-6) generates the "access structures" (Waller 1979) that enable readers to identify relations among textual units. In the spatial mode, inter-textuality regulates line breaks (and justification) and the vertical arrangement of text. A solid block of text can be divided into paragraphs, paragraphs into lists, and lists into particles (numbers, words, phrases) that form tables, flow charts, and decision trees. In the alphanumeric/symbolic mode, inter-textuality is coded through headings, letters, and numbers, in the graphic mode through bullets, dashes, and line work (e.g., the vertical and horizontal lines on the 12-cell matrix). Through inter-textual treatment in all three modes, a text can be transformed into a hierarchical visual system "surfacing" (Herrstrom 1984, 229) the structure of the document (see also Bernhardt 1986; Twyman 1979).

The *Extra-textual* level (cells 7–9) encompasses images and systems of signs independent from the text. Like speech, textual elements can be perceived aurally. Extra-textual elements, on the other hand, are primarily seen; they may require alphanumeric coding (cell 7), but once their sign systems are understood by the viewer they are comprehended purely by the eye (Bertin 1981, 178–79). Extra-textuals range in level of abstraction from a pie chart or a stylized corporate logo to a realistic drawing or a photograph. Spatially, extra-textual sign systems are constructed on two-dimensional grids, which determine, for example, where the data are plotted (on a line graph) or the viewing angle, size, or depth of an image. Graphic coding controls the resolution of the signs: the tone, color, and fineness of marks on data displays (a dot versus a shaded bar on a graph) or of details on pictures (a stick drawing versus a photograph of workers demonstrating a task).

The *Supra-textual* level (cells 10-12) controls the global organization of a document, securing cohesion among all of its elements, both textual and extra-textual. In the spatial mode, supra-textuality arranges extra-textual elements (charts, graphs, illustrations) within the document and establishes the continuity of the text (breaks in the text between pages, pages separating major sections). In the alphanumeric mode, supra-textual elements include pagination, page headers, and chapter titles, in the graphic mode line work, color, or graphic symbols that define relations between sections, pages, or panels. Extending over several planes, the supra-textual level governs the three-dimensional design of the document. In a proposal, for example, I could use section titles and tabs to divide major units of the text (cell 10); I could design pages that folded out into larger pages (cell 11) to accommodate detailed flow charts; and I could use icons to code pages with similar functions (cell 12). These are just a few of the options I could exercise to create supra-textual cohesion.

Each document combines cells on the matrix to form a unique visual system. The two pages of sample text (see Figure 2), which exclude linguistic coding, illustrate several of the cells on the matrix, each of which is described below:

Intra:

1. Typeface selection (Palatino for text; Helvetica for the section title; Geneva for the flow chart text and for the numbers on the illustration); occasional boldface, upper case, and italic treatment of the typeface; enlarged type size for the section title on the first page.
2. Variations in the spacing between characters at the bottom of the first page.
3. Underlining of headings; various punctuation marks within the text.

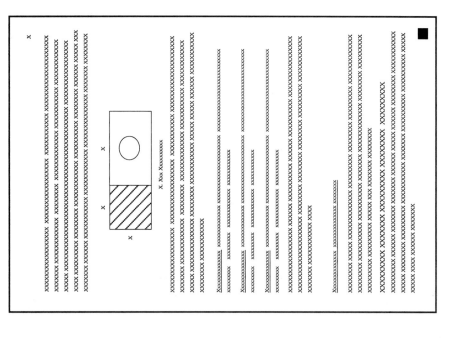

Figure 2. *Sample Text*

Inter:

4. Two levels of headings within the text.
5. Single spacing within paragraphs; double spacing between paragraphs; triple spacing between major headings; indentation of the list with bullets; indentation of text following the subheadings on the second page; spatial arrangement of the flow chart text.
6. Bullets cueing the list; rectilinear line work around the flow chart text; arrows connecting the rectangles.

Extra:

7. Caption for the illustration; numerical tags describing distances on the illustration.
8. Size and spatial orientation of the object in the illustration (front view, cross section of the left part).
9. Shading of the left part of the illustration; minimal graphic coding on the object (a skeletal outline only).

Supra:

10. Section title and number at the top of the first page; pagination on the second page; numbering of the illustration.
11. Break in the text at the bottom of each page.
12. Arrow icon indicating continuity between the first and second pages; square icon on the second page indicating the end of the section.

These elements are the visual raw materials of the document, which any technical writing student could execute with a modicum of desktop publishing equipment. Of course, the sample text contains only a limited number of the available options and in its present state is totally noncontextual. The four levels and three coding modes on the matrix describe a flexible visual vocabulary which the writer/designer can adapt to each communication problem. The rhetorician can use this vocabulary for various purposes — to create emphasis, stimulate reader interest, guide the reader through the text or to the most significant information, enable the reader to compare and contrast data, persuade the reader to take action — in short, for many of the same reader-oriented goals writers achieve with language.

Establishing Reader-Oriented Guidelines for Visual Design

Exercising and integrating the levels and modes on the matrix, however, are complex tasks: how do we provide students with reader-oriented guidelines for making these decisions? The instructor has at least three options: (1) deductively follow conventions outlined in textbooks, (2) inductively extract principles from actual documents and contexts, or (3) consult theories and research encompassing the visual processing of texts.

The first option is a logical place to begin: visual choices, like linguistic ones, are somewhat determined by idiom, protocol, and genre. Readers rely on previous visual experiences to process documents: a message that looks like a sales letter (visual processing always precedes linguistic processing) engenders one set of expectations; a message containing matrices, data displays, and a highly variegated text quite another. Few readers will mistake our sample text for a short story, a refusal letter, a mortgage contract, or a résumé. Generic conventions, however, cannot account for the contextual variables, both visual and rhetorical, of the communication because each document contains a unique combination of cells on the matrix as well as its own audience and purpose. Are we any more able to predict exactly what a "report" is supposed to look like than what it is supposed to *sound* like?

The second teaching method, analyzing rhetorical strategies employed in real-world texts with definable audiences, can supply the necessary contextual dimension, preparing students to make reader-oriented decisions in their own assignments. Tebeaux (1985) and Andrews (1985) have suggested assignments for analyzing visual features of actual documents. These assignments can be used in conjunction with the matrix, which establishes a framework for the systematic visual analysis of virtually any document — an essay, advertisement, brochure, manual, or research report. Examining documents enables students to interact with real texts and to evaluate the rhetorical effects of each visual choice on the matrix. For a beginning exercise, the instructor can distribute a one- or two-page document and have students analyze each visual level or coding mode. For example, on a separate handout students can chart visual elements at each level, and the class can then discuss which elements enhance and which work against the purpose of the document.

Analytical exercises are good "predesigning" techniques that prepare students to make rhetorical choices in their own documents. Additional guidelines about how readers process visual information can be extracted from research in legibility, perception, and psychology as well as from theories of visual information processing. Empirical studies at the intra- and inter-textual levels have clearly demonstrated that readers process some text designs more easily than others (for an overview of these studies, see Benson 1985; Reynolds 1984). For example, Tinker (1963) found that a text set in lower case was more legible than one in upper case, and a relatively small range of type sizes (between 9 and 12 point) produced optimum legibility. Although readers generally preferred type styles that were the most legible, Tinker occasionally found discrepancies between preference and performance, which suggests that visual processing may be mediated by familiarity, contextual variables, or culturally influenced aesthetic norms. Moreover, the "atmosphere value" of typefaces (Spencer 1969, 29) may influence the reader's response to the text, begging the question as to whether or not *any* intra-textual choice can be excluded from rhetorical consideration.

While empirical experiments such as Tinker's establish guidelines based on the perceptual experiences of general readers, more recent studies at the inter-textual level have begun to acknowledge the contextual variables of the communication process. For example, Hartley (1980; 1984; Hartley and Trueman 1985) has conducted studies of the spatial arrangement of text (cell 5) and the use of headings (cell 4), verifying that visual cueing devices aid readers in understanding and retrieving content. Hartley's findings, however, are qualified by context — by the ability and age of readers in the experiment and by the nature and purpose of the text. Wright (1977) has summarized similar experiments (many her own) with tables, flow charts, and decision trees. Like Hartley's experiments, these studies are sensitive to the audience's previous experience with the display device, to the complexity of the tasks being measured, and to the purpose and use of the communication. For instance, readers who are familiar with the key factors in a decision-making process can more quickly draw conclusions from scenarios presented in tables rather than in paragraph form; however, readers who are likely to consider factors not included in the visual display will probably perform better with a branching flow chart than with a table (Wright, pp. 100–102). In all cases, text designers need to analyze carefully the reader's knowledge of the subject and the display technique: inattention to either can defeat the information designer's attempt to make the text transparent. By revealing the benefits and limitations of display techniques for various readers and situations, empirical research in intertextuality has not only generated an array of design guidelines but shown that visual communication, like language use, must always be responsive to contextual variables.

On the extra-textual level, readers "see" rather than "read" information coded in the spatial and graphic modes (Bertin 1981, 179). Whether the sign system is abstract (a bar chart) or realistic (a line drawing), guidelines must respect the perceptual nature of information processing. The numerous empirical studies investigating the perception of data displays (Macdonald-Ross 1977) and pictures (Perkins 1980) have often yielded conflicting or inconclusive results. Macdonald-Ross (1977, 369–75) narrates the controversies surrounding different methods of displaying data (e.g., bars versus circles), concluding that the research findings generally support the practices of experienced information designers. Despite all of the empirical studies on the perception of realistic images, Perkins (1980, 272) maintains that creating pictures is a "profoundly heuristic" activity guided by "tradition and invention rather than law and application."

Instructors are better served by consulting practitioners and theorists, for whom — particularly in regard to data displays — functional economy is the key reader-oriented guideline. In Bertin's semiotic theory of visual information processing, the spatial and graphic coding of quantitative data exploit the eye's ability to process numerous (possibly millions of) pieces of data simultaneously (181). According to Edward Tufte (1983), a well-designed data display presents the maximum information in the smallest area with the minimal graphic coding (51). His graphic standard of "clarity, precision, and efficiency" (51) engenders formulas (the "data-ink" and "data density" ratios) for evaluating the functional performance of charts and graphs. Tufte justifies his guidelines on aesthetic grounds as well: following the dictums of architectural design theorist Robert Venturi, he correlates complexity and structural transparency with "graphical elegance" (177).

At the supra-textual level, the laws of visual gestalt can predict the reader's global perception of the document, providing the designer with guidelines for combining visual forms. For instance, adhering to the law of "equilibrium" assures a balanced arrangement on the page (cell 11), producing visual harmony for the reader; the law of "similarity" helps the reader associate related items (cell 12 graphic cues unifying related pages); and "good figure" enables the reader to differentiate visual elements from their field or background (Bernhardt 1986, 71–72). Computer programs capable of simultaneously displaying several miniature pages of a document can increase the writer's awareness of visual gestalt, affording greater control over supra-textual cohesion. Other disciplines encompassing perception and visual display techniques can also inform supra-textual design. For example, studies derived from hemispheric brain research have found that viewers generally process verbal information more effectively in the right field of vision, visual material in the left, which may provide guidelines for integrating pictures and icons with text (Welford 1984, 14–15; for limitations of combining visual and verbal processing, see Hecht and Juhasz, 1984, 133–36).

Together these sources — including empirical research, graphic communication theory, the psychology of perception, and aesthetics — furnish a wide array of concepts and empirical data (not available in technical writing pedagogy) about how readers process documents visually on all four levels of the matrix. Because context affects perception (Arnheim 1969, 54–72), guidelines extracted from these diverse disciplines must be adapted to the visual and rhetorical variables of each document. The writer must combine the cells on the matrix into a coherent visual system which advances the rhetorical goals of the communication. Discovering an optimal configuration of levels and coding modes can be as complex as discovering an optimal linguistic pattern: rhetoric, visual or verbal, resists prescription. Hence, the designer begins with the same heuristic the writer does: What is the purpose of the communication? Who are the readers? What do the readers expect? How will they use the document? The guidelines outlined above establish valid reader-oriented norms and criteria for defining rhetorical problems and for *finding* solutions rather than prescribing them a priori.

Integrating Visual and Verbal Communication

Despite the variety of visual choices writers make — especially technical writers, who have a good deal of control over in-house documents — visual design is typically regarded as a mechanical skill unrelated to the writing process (Barton and Barton 1985). However, integrating the cells on the matrix into a visual system that complements the rhetorical strategies of the linguistic text demands that the writer solve visual and verbal problems concurrently rather than sequentially. Planning, drafting, and revising require visual as well as verbal thinking: revision is a "re-seeing" guided by the eye as well as the ear, meaning discovered visually as well as linguistically. Visual and verbal thinking are cognitively interdependent, something that design theorists acknowledge in their models of the design process (see Tovey 1984).

Because writing and designing are intertwined in the same process of making meaning, the instructor can use the same principles (and nomenclature) to teach both verbal and visual problem-solving. The matrix contains a vocabulary of visual language subject to the same principles of discourse, arrangement, and style that guide linguistic choices. For example, in an assignment to design a set of instructions — say a manual for a new electronic tool sold to do-it-yourself mechanics — the student needs to consider a range of visual options encompassing several cells on the matrix:

> *Purpose:* to motivate readers to use the document (cell 1: selection of a typeface; 8, 9: illustrations with pertinent detail; 11: size of the document that fits the carrying case); to guide readers to key information about how to solve simple operational problems (5, 6: spatial and graphic cueing devices); to highlight critical warnings that prevent readers from injuring themselves or breaking the tool (1: boldface, upper case; 3: underscoring)
>
> *Discourse Mode:* narrations showing readers how to use and fix the tool (5: steps of a task segmented into a list; 6: bullets highlighting each

major step of the task); forward leaps built visually into the discourse for various readers and situations (5, 6: spatial and graphic cues organizing the text into tree diagrams outlining several contingencies; 12: icons associating similar types of tasks across the whole document).

Arrangement: the steps of each task cued clearly (4: headings, lists coded with numbers; 6: graphic cues signaling a new task); clear divisions between different tasks (5: vertical spacing); illustrations revealing the most useful information (8: selection of appropriate viewing angles; 9: selection of details); cues that enable the reader to either browse through the document or quickly locate answers to questions (10: page headers; 11: illustrations placed strategically in the text).

Style: a low level of technicality (1: familiar symbols; 7: nontechnical labels identifying essential parts of the tool; 9: simple line drawings); a functional but aesthetically pleasing "gestalt" (11: balanced page designs; 12: harmony among page colors).

Tone: an informal, "friendly" document that invites reader use (1: a serif typeface in a medium point size; 3: icons that add interest; 5: ample spacing around textual units; 9: freehand drawings for illustrations); consistent coding throughout the document to avoid shifts in tone.

Readability: an integrated system of visual forms that enables the reader to find and use information with maximum ease (10–12); visual design of all 12 cells adapted to the function of the document and the conditions under which it will be used (in a home workshop or a garage, in an emergency).

Purpose, discourse mode, arrangement, style, tone, readability — these concepts pertain to aspects of the document that readers process visually as well as verbally; hence, the writer of our manual needs to make reader-oriented visual choices *during the drafting of the linguistic text.* Together, from the early planning stages, the visual and linguistic systems should simultaneously drive the rhetoric of the document. By providing a bridge between the two systems, the matrix can be applied to virtually any assignment. As the student shapes the document, recursive stages of "re-seeing," both visually and linguistically, clarify and structure meaning, and develop tone and style consistent with subject, purpose, and audience. Rather than operating as separate or hierarchical functions in the writing course, composing and designing merge into an interdependent, symbiotic process.

Conclusion

Teaching graphics and text design as bona fide, reader-oriented forms of communication enhances the basic rhetorical tenets of the technical writing course. Adapting messages to specific readers requires conscious visual thinking on several levels: the matrix is a tentative first step towards developing a comprehensive system of describing and evaluating these choices. Introducing research and theories in visual communication from various disciplines, along with analyzing actual documents, increases the student's understanding of how readers process texts visually as well as provides guidelines and criteria for visual problem-solving. To play a seminal role in supporting the rhetorical principles of the course, visual thinking must be done during each stage of the writing process. Instead of functioning as merely a specialized skill, visual design will then share with language the same rhetorical responsibilities for patterning the message to the needs of the reader.

References

Andrews, D. C. 1985. Choosing the right visuals. In *Teaching Technical Writing: Graphics*, ed. by Dixie Elise Hickman, Anthology No. 5. Association of Teachers of Technical Writing.

Arnheim, Rudolf. 1969. *Visual Thinking*. Berkeley: Univ. of California Press.

Barton, Ben F., and Marthalee S. Barton. 1985. Toward a rhetoric of visuals for the computer era. *The Technical Writing Teacher* 12:126–45.

Benson, Philippa J. 1985. Writing visually: Design considerations in technical publications. *Technical Communication* 32:35–39.

Bernhardt, Stephen A. 1986. Seeing the text. *College Composition and Communication* 37:66–78.

Bertin, Jacques. 1981. *Graphics and Graphic Information-Processing*. Trans. William J. Berg and Paul Scott. New York: De Gruyter

Bonsiepe, Gui. 1965. Visual/verbal rhetoric. *Ulm* 14–16:23–40.

Buchanan, Richard. 1985. Declaration by design: Rhetoric, argument, and demonstration in design practice. *Design Issues* 2:4–22.

Hartley, James. 1980. Spatial cues in text: Some comments on the paper by Frase and Schwartz. *Visible Language* 14:62–79.

———. 1984. Space and structure in instructional text. In *Information Design: The Design and Evaluation of Signs and Printed Material*, ed. by Ronald Easterby and Harm Zwaga. New York: Wiley.

Hartley, James, and Mark Trueman. 1985. A research strategy for text designers: The role of headings. *Instructional Science* 14:99–155.

Hecht, Peter, and Joseph Juhasz. 1984. Recognition memory: Implications for visual information presentation. In *Information Design: The Design and Evaluation of Signs and Printed Material*. See Hartley 1984.

Herrstrom, David Sten. 1984. Technical writing as mapping description onto diagram: The graphic paradigms of explanation. *Journal of Technical Writing and Communication* 14:223–40.

Kostelnick, Charles. 1988a. Designing for readability: An index for evaluating the visual language of technical documents. In *Proceedings of the 35th ITCC*. Washington, DC: Society for Technical Communication.

———. 1988b A systematic approach to visual language in business communication. *The Journal of Business Communication* 25:29-48.

Macdonald-Ross, Michael. 1977. How numbers are shown: A review of research on the presentation of quantitative data in texts. *AV Communication Review* 25: 359–409.

Ong, Walter J. 1982. *Orality and Literacy: The Technologizing of the Word*. New York: Methuen.

Perkins, D. N. 1980. Pictures and the real thing. In *Processing of Visible Language*, ed. by Paul A Kolers, Merald E. Wrolstad, and Herman Bouma, vol. 2. New York: Plenum.

Spencer, Herbert. 1969. *The Visible Word*. 2d ed. New York: Hastings.

Reynolds, Linda. 1984. The Legibility of Printed Scientific and Technical Information. In *Information Design: The Design and Evaluation of Signs and Printed Material*. See Hartley 1984.

Spencer, Herbert. 1969. *The Visible Word*. 2d ed. New York: Hastings.

Tebeaux, Elizabeth. 1985. Developing a heuristic approach to graphics. In *Teaching Technical Writing: Graphics*. See Andrews 1985.

Tinker, Miles. 1963. *Legibility of Print*. Ames: Iowa State Univ. Press.

Tovey, Michael. 1984. Designing with both halves of the brain. *Design Studies* 5:219–28.

Tufte, Edward. 1983. *The Visual Display of Quantitative Information*. Cheshire, CT: Graphics Press.

Twyman, Michael. 1979. A schema for the study of graphic language. In *Processing of Visible Language,* ed. by Paul A. Kolers, Merold E. Wrolstad, and Herman Bouma, vol. 1. New York: Plenum.

Waller, Robert H. 1979. Typographic access structures for educational texts. In *Processing of Visible Language. See* Twyman 1979.

Welford, A. T. 1984. Theory and application in visual displays. In *Information Design: The Design and Evaluation of Signs and Printed Material. See* Hartley 1984.

Wright, Patricia. 1977. Presenting technical information: A survey of research findings. *Instructional Science* 6:93–134.

From BUSINESS PROSE AND THE NATURE OF THE PLAIN STYLE

Michael Mendelson

[Journal of Business Communication *24 (Spring 1987): 3–18.*]

Associate professor of English and coordinator of the doctoral program in rhetoric and professional communication at Iowa State University, Michael Mendelson has published widely in rhetoric and literary criticism. Currently he is working in the history of rhetoric. The following excerpt concludes "Business Prose and the Nature of the Plain Style," which responds to what Mendelson felt to be a lack of commentary on prose style and business style.

Mendelson opens this article by calling for an alternative to typical presentations of business writing that promote an absence of style. He suggests returning to the plain style of classical rhetoric, especially as it is presented by Demetrius of Alexandria in his third-century B.C. *essay "On Style" in which Demetrius advocates use of various stylistic features while maintaining "lucidity as the principal goal." As Mendelson explains in his overview of Demetrius' presentation, using the plain style encourages a wide range of rhetorical strategies to produce effective prose. Mendelson's conclusion, which follows here, argues that business writers can communicate more effectively if they employ Demetrius' expanded notion of plainness.*

The current standard of prose style promoted by prominent business communications texts is too narrow to accommodate the diversity of situations in business. These texts present a minimal range of stylistic choice and so limit the flexibility and individuality of the writer. An alternative form of the plain style was pioneered by Greek rhetoricians, who insisted on extending the range of options open to writers of even the simplest prose. This expanded version of the plain style is based on the cardinal principles of clarity and conciseness, but it also allows for a repertoire of dictional, syntactic, and figurative choices that make one's prose livelier and more persuasive. This expanded notion of the plain style has already generated considerable interest and promises to radically alter both the writing and teaching of business prose.

An Appropriate Plainness for Business Prose

But what is it that leads to such breadth of style, to a prose that is, as Joseph Williams puts it, "not just clear but vigorous, not just direct but forceful"?[1] The answer is implicit in Demetrius' program for the plain style; for what the writers of our classes and offices need is an expanded range of stylistic choice. I attempted earlier to show that the reigning paradigm of business prose is a uniform standard of stylistic minimalism. By expanding the scope of the plain style, by including options that transcend the "grammatically primitive," the business writer can achieve that vividness, variation, and personality that Demetrius saw as the necessary counterpoint to "pure" plainness.[2]

The distinguished psycholinguist Charles Osgood has defined style as "an individual's deviations from norms for the situations in which he is encoding, these deviations being the statistical properties of those structural features for which there exists some degree of choice in the code."[3] In Standard Business English, the institutional norms of clarity, conciseness, and correctness that govern stylistic range must, of course, be acknowledged; but writers also need to know that an individual style begins to emerge only as they choose from among the myriad of possible transformations in diction, modification, figures, arrangement, even punctuation, transformations that deviate from the strict conventions of standard practice. The goal of these stylistic deviations is not to call attention to one's self or one's prose; rather, a writer alert to style is seeking to stimulate engagement in prominent ideas through recourse to appropriate stylistic ploys.

My argument is that instead of teaching a uniform standard of style to which business writing students are confined, we ought to take a clue from Demetrius and help our students to achieve an adaptable level of diction, to employ a varied texture of syntax, and to utilize apt figures of speech.[4] The only path to such stylistic flexibility is to spend more time in class on style as an integral part of effective business writing.[5] Francis Christensen, in his discussion of generative rhetoric, makes the essential point: "When you know the possibilities, you know the range of choice. Whoever is to call the plays, you will agree, has to know what plays there are to call."[6] The business writer who is introduced only to the skeletal version of the plain style does not have enough plays to meet the challenge of a game with diverse players, situations, and ideas.

Happily, the community of teachers and scholars concerned with business prose style has begun to pay increasing attention to the role of choice and variation in effective business writing. Jack Selzer has been one of the most persistent and articulate champions of flexibility in our stylistic norms. In his essay "Emphasizing Rhetorical Principles in Business Writing," Selzer acknowledges that "Business students do need to know certain forms and conventions peculiar to business writing"; but he also argues that mechanical perfection is not synonymous with stylistic effectiveness. The "rhetorically minded teacher," he adds, will insist that students expand "their stylistic repertoires."[7] And in his spirited indictment of readability formulas as guides to style, Selzer writes that "after all, style is choice," and choice is "perhaps the most important word in any writing course."[8]

My colleagues Helen Rothschild Ewald and Donna Stine, in their essay on "Speech Act Theory and Business Communication Conventions," have indicated that far from being uniform, business style is "context-dependent" and so must seek variations appropriate to specific situations. What is more, they write that speech act theory "allows that communication which is securely governed by . . . rules and regulations — and surely business writing falls into this category — may be particularly enhanced by thoughtful deviance from those rules." Their helpful classification of "areas of intentional deviance" provides a potential tool for calculating the effectiveness of any departure from the stylistic norms of plainness.[9]

In a related development, there has been a good deal of emphasis of late on the role of style in enhancing the "ethos" or personality of working prose. Dorothy Margaret Guinn notes that a writer's ethos emerges not only "through his or her lexical and syntactic choices," but also through deviations from grammatical "hypercorrectness." The sense of the individual writer that is generated through these stylistic departures from convention "becomes a potent means of embedding an identifiable, agreeable personality within one's writing, and drawing readers into agreement with the ideas presented."[10] Merrill Whitburn also argues that any communication can be improved by "the subtle infusion of personality, particularly if the message is intended to be persuasive," and that stylistic deviations can act as enticements for the reader.[11]

All of these concepts (style as choice, as deviation, and as the vehicle for personality) are contemporary expressions of ideas we observed in Demetrius: Choice and deviation are the means by which variation and vividness are achieved, while personality is the result of stylistic individuality. The precedent set both in Demetrius and in this contemporary research argues that business writers need not be held captive by a monolithic ideal of stylistic simplicity. On the contrary, there is powerful evidence that the persuasive effect of the plain style is considerably enriched by the periodic inclusion of "thoughtful deviance," that appropriate plainness is the result not of stylistic conformity but of individual choice.

One of the most intriguing efforts to expand the range of stylistic choice open to business writers has been Craig and Carol Kallendorf's carefully reasoned argument for the use of figures of speech in the practice of business prose.[12] This argument in defense of "a tradition that integrates figures quite thoroughly with the context and purpose of the message" is built on three propositions: first, that the emotional appeal of a well-used figure can create a bond between the writer and the reader; second, that there is a special relation between figures of speech and the logic of certain thought processes; and third, that figures are an effective way to build the "verbal ethos" of a document, an argument we encountered in a more general form above.[13]

The Kallendorfs maintain that taken together these three characteristics of rhetorical figures (their emotion, their logic, and their expression of character) encapsulate the three fundamental appeals of Aristotelian rhetoric; i.e., to persuade by "pathos," "logos," and "ethos." This elegant appeal for a new look at ancient rhetorical devices is grounded in the recognition that all business discourse is persuasive at heart and that figures, as Demetrius suggested, increase the vividness of presentation and so enhance the persuasive power of one's ideas. Also implicit in the Kallendorfs' discussion is the more general notion that an enriched sense of style (by whatever means) is central to the persuasive agenda of business prose. It may be worth noting, however, that almost all the Kallendorfs' examples of rhetorical figures at work in business discourse come either from advertising or from formal speeches, structures in which the latitude for stylistic deviation is greater than it might be in more routine situations. It is important to recognize that the use of rhetorical figures, along with other stylistic options, is in large part contingent upon the persuasive demands of the situation, and that figures may not always be fitting. But this caveat is only a repetition of what we have already heard from Demetrius: that any stylistic choice depends firmly on the nature of the specific situation, or on "kairos." The Kallendorfs are quite right to insist on the addition of figures to the stylistic arsenal appropriate to a large number of business communications situations, and their effort to create a theoretical foundation for an expanded "vision of business writing" is a significant contribution to a new perspective on business style.[14]

At bottom, this entire complex of ideas on choice, deviation, and appropriate figures is a variation on a cardinal principle expressed by Richard Weaver: i.e., all rhetoric is "an art of emphasis," a technique for making some things stand out.[15] The business writer who is fully acquainted with the range of stylistic choices available will be able, when the need arises, to amplify his or her prose and create emphasis in a way that a writer dependent solely on the readability standard of style could not. The value of such an ability is obvious. All effective communication requires procedures designed to bring certain ideas clearly and prominently before the attention of the audience, to lend what we before described as "presence" to one's message.[16] For some time business communication theory has recognized the importance of deliberate training in the analysis of certain extra-linguistic factors, like audience, situation, and purpose.[17] What this study suggests is that the variables of style can also contribute to the presence of our writing, and that more systematic instruction in the purely linguistic features of diction, syntax, and figures of speech could also help enhance the persuasive power of a writer's message.

In 1937, A. Charles Babenroth wrote in *Modern Business English* that "Although personal preferences must necessarily accommodate themselves to house character in many ways, the writer must beware of suppressing his individuality. He should guard individuality jealously as his most prized asset."[18] There is no doubt that the plain style of short words in short sentences is the "house character" of the contemporary business community. What we need to recognize is that the pure plainness of the skeletal style also leads to the phenomenon of the absent author, or what Walker Gibson called "the rhetoric of hollow men."[19] It is through an expanded, more appropriate plainness that business writers can cultivate that "most prized asset" and learn to project themselves as individuals of presence and style.

Notes

[1] Williams, Joseph, "Defining Complexity," *College English,* 40, no. 6, pp. 606–7, February 1979.

[2] The quote is from Broadhead, Glenn J., "Sentence Patterns: Some of What We Need to Know and Teach," in *Sentence Combining: A Rhetorical Perspective,* ed. Donald Daiker et al., Carbondale, Ill.: Southern Illinois University Press, p. 60, 1985.

[3] Osgood, Charles E., "Some Effects of Motivation on Style of Encoding," in *Style in Language,* ed. Thomas Sebeok, New York: John Wiley and Sons, p. 295, 1960.

[4] See Walpole, Jane, "Style as Option," *CCC,* p. 207, May 1980.

[5] The scope of this polemical essay makes it impossible to take up such questions as "What should be taught" and "How should we do it?" For an inventory of practical methods by which style can be taught, see Broadhead, "Some of What We Need to Know and Teach;" Francis Christensen, *The New Rhetoric,* New York: Harper & Row, 1976; Louis T. Milic, "Compositions vs. Stylistics," in *Linguistics, Stylistics, and the*

Teaching of Composition, ed. Donald McQuade, Akron: University of Akron, 1979, pp. 91–102; and Joseph Williams, *Ten Lessons in Clarity and Grace,* Glenview, Ill.: Scott, Foresman, and Company, 1981. A method that dovetails nicely with the plain style's demands for simplicity has recently been outlined by Richard B. Larsen in "Sentence Patterning," *CCC,* pp. 103–4, February 1986. With Larsen's method as a base, the teacher can then go on to those stylistic variations that he or she is most concerned with.

[6] Christensen, p. 166.

[7] Selzer, Jack, "Teaching Rhetorical Principles in Business Writing," in *Teaching Business Writing,* ed. Jeanne W. Halpern, Urbana, Ill.: American Business Communication Association, pp. 6, 14, and 15, resp., 1983.

[8] Selzer, Jack, "Readability is a Four-Letter Word," *The Journal of Business Communication,* 18, no. 4, p. 32, Fall 1981.

[9] Ewald, Helen Rothschild and Donna Stine, "Speech Act Theory and Business Communication Conventions," *The Journal of Business Communication,* 20, no. 2, quotes from pp. 17, 24, and 19, resp., Summer 1983.

[10] Guinn, Dorothy Margaret, "Ethos in Technical Discourse," *The Technical Writing Teacher,* 11, no. 1, pp. 31 and 34, resp., Fall 1983.

[11] Whitburn, Merrill D., "Personality in Scientific and Technical Writing," *The Journal of Technical Writing and Communication,* 6, no. 4, pp. 299–306, 1976.

[12] Kallendorf, Craig and Carol, "The Figures of Speech, 'Ethos,' and Aristotle," *The Journal of Business Communication,* 22, no. 1, pp. 35–50, Winter 1985.

[13] Kallendorf, pp. 30–44.

[14] For quote, see Kallendorf, p. 51. Also of interest is the Kallendorfs' adaptation for the Ciceronian topoi to corporate speeches in "A New Topical System for Corporate Speech Writing," *The Journal of Business Communication,* 21, no. 2, Spring 1984.

[15] Weaver, Richard, *Language Is Sermonic,* ed. Richard L. Johanneson et al., Baton Rouge: Louisiana State University Press, p. 217, 1970.

[16] See Perelman, Chaim, *The Realm of Rhetoric,* trans. William Klublack, Notre Dame: University of Notre Dame Press, pp. xi, xiii, and ch. 4, passim.

[17] See Walpole, pp. 206–7.

[18] Babenroth, A. Charles, *Modern Business English,* rev. ed., New York: Prentice-Hall, p. 134, 1937.

[19] Gibson, Walker, *Tough, Sweet, and Stuffy: An Essay on Modern American Prose Styles,* Bloomington: University of Indiana Press, p. 90, 1966.

PART TWELVE

GRAMMAR BASICS

Though writing teachers no longer consider direct grammar instruction to be central to the teaching of writing, they recognize that students need understandable definitions of grammatical terms and concepts as they revise and edit. Part XII of *The Bedford Handbook* offers a straightforward explanation of the basics of grammar, providing students with an easy-to-use reference source.

The following article explores questions that teachers might confront as they consider how to encourage students to use the handbook's information on grammar:

- What are different definitions of *grammar*? How might these definitions help writing teachers? How can the different kinds of grammar contribute to the teaching of writing?
- How can teachers provide students with the information they need about grammar without hindering their development as writers?

GRAMMAR, GRAMMARS, AND THE TEACHING OF GRAMMAR

Patrick Hartwell

[College English *47 (1985): 105–27.*]

Patrick Hartwell, professor of English at Indiana University of Pennsylvania, is interested in error analysis, basic writing, and literacy. His articles have appeared in College English, Rhetoric Review, *and* Research in the Teaching of English.

In the following article, Hartwell enters the ongoing debate about the role of grammar instruction in writing courses, observing that this is actually a debate about the sequence of instruction in composition classes: should teachers address word- and sentence-level concerns first, or should they use a "top-down" approach, attending first to issues of meaning and purpose? In his attempt to clarify the debate, Hartwell analyzes what we might mean by grammar and describes at least five meanings for the term. His discussion of those meanings can help new and experienced teachers be more specific in their use of grammar instruction and can help them understand more fully what they might or might not want to accomplish when presenting grammar to students.

For me the grammar issue was settled at least twenty years ago with the conclusion offered by Richard Braddock, Richard Lloyd-Jones, and Lowell Schoer in 1963.

> In view of the widespread agreement of research studies based upon many types of students and teachers, the conclusion can be stated in strong and unqualified terms: the teaching of formal grammar has a negligible or, because it usually displaces some instruction and practice in composition, even a harmful effect on improvement in writing.[1]

Indeed, I would agree with Janet Emig that the grammar issue is a prime example of "magical thinking": the assumption that students will learn only what we teach and only because we teach.[2]

But the grammar issue, as we will see, is a complicated one. And, perhaps surprisingly, it remains controversial, with the regular appearance of papers defending the teaching of formal grammar or attacking it.[3] Thus Janice Neuleib, writing on "The Relation of Formal Grammar to Composition" in *College Composition and Communication* (23 [1977], 247–50), is tempted "to sputter on paper" at reading the quotation above (p. 248), and Martha Kolln, writing in the same journal three years later ("Closing the Books on Alchemy," *CCC*, 32 [1981], 139–51), labels people like me "alchemists" for our perverse beliefs. Neuleib reviews five experimental studies, most of them concluding that formal grammar instruction has no effect on the quality of students' writing nor on their ability to avoid error. Yet she renders in effect a Scots verdict of "Not proven" and calls for more research on the issue. Similarly, Kolln reviews six experimental studies that arrive at similar conclusions, only one of them overlapping with the studies cited by Neuleib. She calls for more careful definition of the word *grammar* — her definition being "the internalized system that native speakers of a language share" (p. 140) — and she concludes with a stirring call to place grammar instruction at the center of the composition curriculum: "our goal should be to help students understand the system they know unconsciously as native speakers, to teach them the necessary categories and labels that will enable them to think about and talk about their language" (p. 150). Certainly our textbooks and our pedagogies — though they vary widely in what they see as "necessary categories and labels" — continue to emphasize mastery of formal grammar, and popular discussions of a presumed literacy crisis are almost unanimous in their call for a renewed emphasis on the teaching of formal grammar, seen as basic for success in writing.[4]

An Instructive Example

It is worth noting at the outset that both sides in this dispute — the grammarians and the anti-grammarians — articulate the issue in the same positivistic terms: what does experimental research tell us about the value of teaching formal grammar? But seventy-five years of experimental research has for all practical purposes told us nothing. The two sides are unable to agree on how to interpret such research. Studies are interpreted in terms of one's prior assumptions about the value of teaching grammar: their results seem not to change those assumptions. Thus the basis of the discussion, a basis shared by Kolln and Neuleib and by Braddock and his colleagues—"what does educational research tell us?" — seems designed to perpetuate, not to resolve, the issue. A single example will be instructive. In 1976 and then at greater length in 1979, W. B. Elley, I. H. Barham, H. Lamb, and M. Wyllie reported on a three-year experiment in New Zealand, comparing the relative effectiveness at the high school level of instruction in transformational grammar, instruction in traditional grammar, and no grammar instruction.[5] They concluded that the formal study of grammar, whether transformational or traditional, improved neither writing quality nor control over surface correctness.

> After two years, no differences were detected in writing performance or language competence; after three years small differences appeared in some minor conventions favoring the TG [transformational grammar] group, but these were more than offset by the less positive attitudes they showed towards their English studies. (p. 18)

Anthony Petrosky, in a review of research ("Grammar Instruction: What We Know," *English Journal,* 66, No. 9 [1977], 86–88), agreed with this conclusion, finding the study to be carefully designed, "representative of the best kind of educational research" (p. 86), its validity "unquestionable" (p. 88). Yet Janice Neuleib in her essay found the same conclusions to be "startling" and questioned whether the findings could be generalized beyond the target population, New Zealand high school students. Martha Kolln, when her attention is drawn to the study ("Reply to Ron Shook," *CCC,* 32 [1981], 139–151), thinks the whole experiment "suspicious." And John Mellon has been willing to use the study to defend the teaching of grammar; the study of Elley and his colleagues, he has argued, shows that teaching grammar does no harm.[6]

It would seem unlikely, therefore, that further experimental research, in and of itself, will resolve the grammar issue. Any experimental design can be nitpicked, any experimental population can be criticized, and any experimental conclusion can be questioned or, more often, ignored. In fact, it may well be that the grammar question is not open to resolution by experimental research, that, as Noam Chomsky has argued in *Reflections on Language* (New York: Pantheon, 1975), criticizing the trivialization of human learning by behavioral psychologists, the issue is simply misdefined.

> There will be "good experiments" only in domains that lie outside the organism's cognitive capacity. For example, there will be no "good experiments" in the study of human learning.
> This discipline . . . will, of necessity, avoid those domains in which an organism is specially designed to acquire rich cognitive structures that enter into its life in an intimate fashion. The discipline will be of virtually no intellectual interest, it seems to me, since it is restricting itself in principle to those questions that are guaranteed to tell us little about the nature of organisms. (p. 36)

Asking the Right Questions

As a result, though I will look briefly at the tradition of experimental research, my primary goal in this essay is to articulate the grammar issue in different and, I would hope, more productive terms. Specifically, I want to ask four questions:

1. Why is the grammar issue so important? Why has it been the dominant focus of composition research for the last seventy-five years?
2. What definitions of the word *grammar* are needed to articulate the grammar issue intelligibly?
3. What do findings in cognate disciplines suggest about the value of formal grammar instruction?
4. What is our theory of language, and what does it predict about the value of formal grammar instruction? (This question — "what does our theory of language predict?" — seems a much more powerful question than "what does educational research tell us?")

In exploring these questions I will attempt to be fully explicit about issues, terms, and assumptions. I hope that both proponents and opponents of formal grammar instruction would agree that these are useful as shared points of reference: care in definition, full examination of the evidence, reference to relevant work in cognate disciplines, and explicit analysis of the theoretical bases of the issue.

But even with that gesture of harmony it will be difficult to articulate the issue in a balanced way, one that will be acceptable to both sides. After all, we are dealing with a professional dispute in which one side accuses the other of "magical thinking," and in turn that side responds by charging the other as "alchemists." Thus we might suspect that the grammar issue is itself embedded in larger models of the transmission of literacy, part of quite different assumptions about the teaching of composition.

Those of us who dismiss the teaching of formal grammar have a model of composition instruction that makes the grammar issue "uninteresting" in a scientific sense. Our model predicts a rich and complex interaction of learner and environment in mastering literacy, an interaction that has little to do with sequences of skills instruction as such. Those who defend the teaching of grammar tend to have a model of composition instruction that is rigidly skills-centered and rigidly sequential: the formal teaching of grammar, as the first step in that sequence, is the cornerstone or linchpin. Grammar teaching is thus supremely interesting, naturally a dominant focus for educational research. The controversy over the value of grammar instruction, then, is inseparable from two other issues: the issues of sequence in the teaching of composition and of the role of the composition teacher. Consider, for example, the force of these two issues in Janice Neuleib's conclusion: after calling for yet more experimental research on the value of teaching grammar, she ends with an absolute (and unsupported) claim about sequences and teacher roles in composition.

> We do know, however, that some things must be taught at different levels. Insistence on adherence to usage norms by composition teachers does improve usage. Students can learn to organize their papers if teachers do not accept papers that are disorganized. Perhaps composition teachers can teach those two abilities before they begin the more difficult tasks of developing syntactic sophistication and a winning style. ("The Relation of Formal Grammar to Composition," p. 250)

(One might want to ask, in passing, whether "usage norms" exist in the monolithic fashion the phrase suggests and whether refusing to accept disorganized papers is our best available pedagogy for teaching arrangement.)[7]

But I want to focus on the notion of sequence that makes the grammar issue so important: first grammar, then usage, then some absolute model of organization, all controlled by the teacher at the center of the learning process, with other matters, those of rhetorical weight — , "syntactic sophistication and a winning style" — pushed off to the future. It is not surprising that we call each other names: those of us who question the value of teaching grammar are in fact shaking the whole elaborate edifice of traditional composition instruction.

The Five Meanings of "Grammar"

Given its centrality to a well-established way of teaching composition, I need to go about the business of defining grammar rather carefully, particularly in view of Kolln's criticism of the lack of care in earlier discussions. Therefore I will build upon a seminal discussion of the word *grammar* offered a generation ago, in 1954, by W. Nelson Francis, often excerpted as "The Three Meanings of Grammar."[8] It is worth reprinting at length, if only to re-establish it as a reference point for future discussions.

> The first thing we mean by "grammar" is "the set of formal patterns in which the words of a language are arranged in order to convey larger meanings." It is not necessary that we be able to discuss these patterns self-consciously in order to be able to use them. In fact, all speakers of a language above the age of five or six know how to use its complex forms of organization with considerable skill; in this sense of the word — call it "Grammar 1" — they are thoroughly familiar with its grammar.
>
> The second meaning of "grammar" — call it "Grammar 2" — is "the branch of linguistic science which is concerned with the description, analysis, and formulization of formal language patterns." Just as gravity was in full operation before Newton's apple fell, so grammar in the first sense was in full operation before anyone formulated the first rule that began the history of grammar as a study.
>
> The third sense in which people use the word "grammar" is "linguistic etiquette." This we may call "Grammar 3." The word in this sense is often coupled with a derogatory adjective: we say that the expression "he ain't here" is "bad grammar." . . .
>
> As has already been suggested, much confusion arises from mixing these meanings. One hears a good deal of criticism of teachers of English couched in such terms as "they don't teach grammar any more." Criticism of this sort is based on the wholly unproven assumption that teaching Grammar 2 will improve the student's proficiency in Grammar 1 or improve his manners in Grammar 3. Actually, the form of Grammar 2 which is usually taught is a very inaccurate and misleading analysis of the facts of Grammar 1; and it therefore is of highly questionable value in improving a person's ability to handle the structural patterns of his language. (pp. 300–301)

Francis' Grammar 3 is, of course, not grammar at all, but usage. One would like to assume that Joseph Williams' recent discussion of usage ("The Phenomenology of Error," *CCC*, 32 (1981), 152–168), along with his references, has placed those shibboleths in a proper perspective. But I doubt it, and I suspect that popular discussions of the grammar issue will be as flawed by the intrusion of usage issues as past discussions have been. At any rate I will make only passing reference to Grammar 3 — usage — naively assuming that this issue has been discussed elsewhere and that my readers are familiar with those discussions.

We need also to make further discriminations about Francis' Grammar 2, given that the purpose of his 1954 article was to substitute for one form of Grammar 2, that "inaccurate and misleading" form "which is usually taught," another form, that of American structuralist grammar. Here we can make use of a still earlier discussion, one going back to the days when *PMLA* was willing to publish articles on rhetoric and linguistics, to a 1927 article by Charles Carpenter Fries, "The Rules of the Common School Grammars" (42 [1927], 221–237). Fries there distinguished between the scientific tradition of language study (to which we will now delimit Francis' Grammar 2, scientific grammar) and the separate tradition of "the common school grammars," developed unscientifically, largely based on two inadequate principles — appeals to "logical principles," like "two negatives make a positive," and analogy to Latin grammar; thus, Charlton Laird's characterization, "the grammar of Latin, ingeniously warped to suggest English"

(Language in America [New York: World, 1970], p. 294). There is, of course, a direct link between the "common school grammars" that Fries criticized in 1927 and the grammar-based texts of today, and thus it seems wise, as Karl W. Dykema suggests ("Where Our Grammar Came From," *CE,* 22 (1961), 455–465), to separate Grammar 2, "scientific grammar," from Grammar 4, "school grammar," the latter meaning, quite literally, "the grammars used in the schools."

Further, since Martha Kolln points to the adaptation of Christensen's sentence rhetoric in a recent sentence-combining text as an example of the proper emphasis on "grammar" ("Closing the Books on Alchemy," p. 140), it is worth separating out, as still another meaning of *grammar,* Grammar 5, "stylistic grammar," defined as "grammatical terms used in the interest of teaching prose style." And, since stylistic grammars abound, with widely variant terms and emphases, we might appropriately speak parenthetically of specific forms of Grammar 5 — Grammar 5 (Lanham); Grammar 5 (Strunk and White); Grammar 5 (Williams, *Style);* even Grammar 5 (Christensen, as adapted by Daiker, Kerek, and Morenberg).[9]

The Grammar in Our Heads

With these definitions in mind, let us return to Francis' Grammar 1, admirably defined by Kolln as "the internalized system of rules that speakers of a language share" ("Closing the Books on Alchemy," p. 140), or, to put it more simply, the grammar in our heads. Three features of Grammar 1 need to be stressed: first, its special status as an "internalized system of rules," as tacit and unconscious knowledge; second, the abstract, even counterintuitive, nature of these rules, insofar as we are able to approximate them indirectly as Grammar 2 statements; and third, the way in which the form of one's Grammar 1 seems profoundly affected by the acquisition of literacy. This sort of review is designed to firm up our theory of language, so that we can ask what it predicts about the value of teaching formal grammar.

A simple thought experiment will isolate the special status of Grammar 1 knowledge. I have asked members of a number of different groups — from sixth graders to college freshmen to high-school teachers — to give me the rule for ordering adjectives of nationality, age, and number in English. The response is always the same: "We don't know the rule." Yet when I ask these groups to perform an active language task, they show productive control over the rule they have denied knowing. I ask them to arrange the following words in a natural order:

> French   the   young   girls   four

I have never seen a native speaker of English who did not immediately produce the natural order, "the four young French girls." The rule is that in English the order of adjectives is first, number, second, age, and third, nationality. Native speakers can create analogous phrases using the rule — "the seventy-three aged Scandinavian lechers"; and the drive for meaning is so great that they will create contexts to make sense out of violations of the rule, as in foregrounding for emphasis: "I want to talk to the French four young girls." (I immediately envision a large room, perhaps a banquet hall, filled with tables at which are seated groups of four young girls, each group of a different nationality.) So Grammar 1 is eminently usable knowledge — the way we make our life through language — but it is not accessible knowledge; in a profound sense, we do not know that we have it. Thus neurolinguist Z. N. Pylyshyn speaks of Grammar 1 as "autonomous," separate from common-sense reasoning, and as "cognitively impenetrable," not available for direct examination.[10] In philosophy and linguistics, the distinction is made between formal, conscious, "knowing about" knowledge (like Grammar 2 knowledge) and tacit, unconscious, "knowing how" knowledge (like Grammar 1 knowledge). The importance of this distinction for the teaching of composition — it provides a powerful theoretical justification for mistrusting the ability of Grammar 2 (or Grammar 4) knowledge to affect Grammar 1 performance — was pointed out in this journal by Martin Steinmann, Jr., in 1966 ("Rhetorical Research," *CE*, 27 [1966], 278–285).

Further, the more we learn about Grammar 1 — and most linguists would agree that we know surprisingly little about it — the more abstract and implicit it seems. This abstractness can be illustrated with an experiment, devised by Lise Menn and reported by Morris Halle,[11] about our rule for forming plurals in speech. It is obvious that we do indeed have a "rule" for forming plurals, for we do not memorize the plural of each noun separately. You will demonstrate productive control over that rule by forming the spoken plurals of the nonsense words below:

thole   flitch   plast

Halle offers two ways of formalizing a Grammar 2 equivalent of this Grammar 1 ability. One form of the rule is the following, stated in terms of speech sounds:

a. If the noun ends in /s z š ž č ǰ/, add /ɨz/;
b. otherwise, if the noun ends in /p t k f θ/, add /s/;
c. otherwise, add /z/.

This rule comes close to what we literate adults consider to be an adequate rule for plurals in writing, like the rules, for example, taken from a recent "common school grammar," Eric Gould's *Reading into Writing: A Rhetoric, Reader, and Handbook* (Boston: Houghton Mifflin, 1983):

> *Plurals* can be tricky. If you are unsure of a plural, then check it in the dictionary. The general rules are:
> Add *s* to the singular: *girls, tables*
> Add *es* to nouns ending in *ch, sh, x* or *s; churches, boxes, wishes*
> Add *es* to nouns ending in *y* and preceded by a vowel once you have changed *y* to *i: monies, companies.* (p. 666)

(But note the persistent inadequacy of such Grammar 4 rules: here, as I read it, the rule is inadequate to explain the plurals of *ray* and *tray*, even to explain the collective noun *monies*, not a plural at all, formed from the mass noun *money* and offered as an example.) A second form of the rule would make use of much more abstract entities, sound features:

a. If the noun ends with a sound that is [coronal, strident], add /ɨz/;
b. otherwise, if the noun ends with a sound that is [non-voiced], add /s/;
c. otherwise, add /z/.

(The notion of "sound features" is itself rather abstract, perhaps new to readers not trained in linguistics. But such readers should be able to recognize that the spoken plurals of *lip* and *duck*, the sound [s], differ from the spoken plurals of *sea* and *gnu*, the sound [z], only in that the sounds of the latter are "voiced" — one's vocal cords vibrate — while the sounds of the former are "non-voiced.")

To test the psychologically operative rule, the Grammar 1 rule, native speakers of English were asked to form the plural of the last name of the composer Johann Sebastian *Bach*, a sound [x], unique in American (though not in Scottish) English. If speakers follow the first rule above, using word endings, they would reject a) and b), then apply c), producing the plural as /baxz/, with word-final /z/. (If writers were to follow the rule of the common school grammar, they would produce the written plural *Baches*, apparently, given the form of the rule, on analogy with *churches*.) If speakers follow the second rule, they would have to analyze the sound [x] as [non-labial, non-coronal, dorsal, non-voiced, and non-strident], producing the plural as /baxs/, with word-final /s/. Native speakers of American English overwhelmingly produce the plural as /baxs/. They use knowledge that Halle characterizes as "unlearned and untaught" (p. 140).

Now such a conclusion is counterintuitive — certainly it departs maximally from Grammar 4 rules for forming plurals. It seems that native speakers of English behave as if they have productive control, as Grammar 1 knowledge, of abstract sound features (± coronal, ± strident, and so on) which are available as conscious, Grammar 2 knowledge only to trained linguists — and, indeed, formally available only within the last hundred years or so. ("Behave as if," in that last sentence, is a necessary hedge, to underscore the difficulty of "knowing about" Grammar 1.)

Moreover, as the example of plural rules suggests, the form of the Grammar 1 in the heads of literate adults seems profoundly affected by the acquisition of literacy. Obviously, literate adults have access to different morphological codes: the abstract print -s underlying the predictable /s/ and /z/ plurals, the abstract print -ed underlying the spoken past tense markers /t/, as in "walked," /əd/, as in "surrounded," /d/, as in "scored," and the symbol /Ø/ for no surface realization, as in the relaxed standard pronunciation of "I walked to the store." Literate adults also have access to distinctions preserved only in the code of print (for example, the distinction between "a good sailer" and "a good sailor" that Mark Aranoff points out in "An English Spelling Convention," *Linguistic Inquiry*, 9 [1978], 299–303). More significantly, Irene Moscowitz speculates that the ability of third graders to form abstract nouns on analogy with pairs like *divine: :divinity* and *serene: :serenity*, where the spoken vowel changes but the spelling preserves meaning, is a factor of knowing how to read. Carol Chomsky finds a three-stage developmental sequence in the grammatical performance of seven-year-olds, related to measures of kind and variety of reading; and Rita S. Brause finds a nine-stage developmental sequence in the ability to understand semantic ambiguity, extending from fourth graders to graduate students.[12] John Mills and Gordon Hemsley find that level of education, and presumably level of literacy, influence judgments of grammaticality, concluding that literacy changes the deep structure of one's internal grammar; Jean Whyte finds that oral language functions develop differently in readers and non-readers; José Morais, Jesús Alegria, and Paul Bertelson find that illiterate adults are unable to add or delete sounds at the beginning of nonsense words, suggesting that awareness of speech as a series of phones is provided by learning to read an alphabetic code. Two experiments — one conducted by Charles A. Ferguson, the other by Mary E. Hamilton and David Barton — find that adults' ability to recognize segmentation in speech is related to degree of literacy, not to amount of schooling or general ability.[13]

It is worth noting that none of these investigators would suggest that the developmental sequences they have uncovered be isolated and taught as discrete skills. They are natural concomitants of literacy, and they seem best characterized not as isolated rules but as developing schemata, broad strategies for approaching written language.

Grammar 2

We can, of course, attempt to approximate the rules or schemata of Grammar 1 by writing fully explicit descriptions that model the competence of a native speaker. Such rules, like the rules for pluralizing nouns or ordering adjectives discussed above, are the goal of the science of linguistics, that is, Grammar 2. There are a number of scientific grammars — an older structuralist model and several versions within a generative-transformational paradigm, not to mention isolated schools like tagmemic grammar, Montague grammar, and the like. In fact, we cannot think of Grammar 2 as a stable entity, for its form changes with each new issue of each linguistics journal, as new "rules of grammar" are proposed and debated. Thus Grammar 2, though of great theoretical interest to the composition teacher, is of little practical use in the classroom, as Constance Weaver has pointed out *(Grammar for Teachers* [Urbana, Ill.: NCTE, 1979], pp. 3–6). Indeed Grammar 2 is a scientific model of Grammar 1, not a description of it, so that questions of psychological reality, while important, are less important than other, more theoretical factors, such as the elegance of formulation or the global power of rules. We might, for example, wish to replace the rule for ordering adjectives of age, number, and nationality cited above with a more general rule — what linguists call a "fuzzy" rule — that adjectives in English are ordered by their abstract quality of "nouniness": adjectives that are very much like nouns, like *French* or *Scandinavian,* come physically closer to nouns than do adjectives that are less "nouny," like *four* or *aged.* But our motivation for accepting the broader rule would be its global power, not its psychological reality.[14]

I try to consider a hostile reader, one committed to the teaching of grammar, and I try to think of ways to hammer in the central point of this distinction, that the rules of Grammar 2 are simply unconnected to productive control over Grammar 1. I can argue from authority: Noam Chomsky has touched on this point whenever he has concerned himself with the implications of linguistics for language teaching, and years ago transformationalist Mark Lester stated unequivocally, "there simply appears to be no correlation between a writer's study of language and his ability to write."[15] I can cite analogies offered by others: Francis Christensen's analogy in an essay originally published in 1962 that formal grammar study would be "to invite a centipede to attend to the sequence of his legs in motion,"[16] or James Britton's analogy, offered informally after a conference presentation, that grammar study would be like forcing starving people to master the use of a knife and fork before allowing them to eat. I can offer analogies of my own, contemplating the wisdom of asking a pool player to master the physics of momentum before taking up a cue or of making a prospective driver get a degree in automotive engineering before engaging the clutch. I consider a hypothetical argument, that if Grammar 2 knowledge affected Grammar 1 performance, then linguists would be our best writers. (I can certify that they are, on the whole, not.) Such a position, after all, is only in accord with other domains of science: the formula for catching a fly ball in baseball ("Playing It by Ear," *Scientific American,* 248,

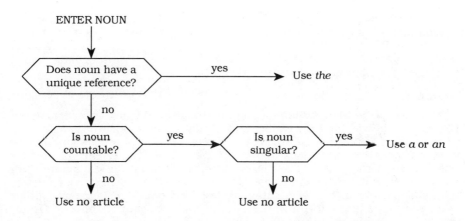

ENTER NOUN

No. 4 [1983], 76) is of such complexity that it is beyond my understand-ing — and, I would suspect, that of many workaday centerfielders. But perhaps I can best hammer in this claim — that Grammar 2 knowledge has no effect on Grammar 1 performance — by offering a demonstration.

The diagram above is an attempt by Thomas N. Huckin and Leslie A. Olsen (*English for Science and Technology* [New York: McGraw-Hill, 1983]) to offer, for students of English as a second language, a fully explicit formulation of what is, for native speakers, a trivial rule of the language — the choice of definite article, indefinite article, or no definite article. There are obvious limits to such a formulation, for article choice in English is less a matter of rule than of idiom ("I went to college" versus "I went to a university" versus British "I went to university"), real-world knowledge (using indefinite "I went into a house" instantiates definite "I looked at the ceil-ing," and indefinite "I visited a university" instantiates definite "I talked with the professors"), and stylistic choice (the last sentence above might alternatively end with "the choice of the definite article, the indefinite ar-ticle, or no article"). Huckin and Olsen invite non-native speakers to use the rule consciously to justify article choice in technical prose, such as the passage below from P. F. Brandwein (*Matter: An Earth Science* [New York: Harcourt Brace Jovanovich, 1975]). I invite you to spend a couple of min-utes doing the same thing, with the understanding that this exercise is a test case: you are using a very explicit rule to justify a fairly straightfor-ward issue of grammatical choice.

Imagine a cannon on top of _____ highest mountain on earth. It is firing _____ cannonballs horizontally. _____ first cannonball fired follows its path. As cannonball moves, _____ gravity pulls it down, and it soon hits ground. Now _____ velocity with which each succeeding cannonball is _____ fired is increased. Thus, _____ cannonball goes farther each time. Cannonball 2 goes farther than _____ cannonball 1 although each is being pulled by _____ gravity toward the earth all _____ time. _____ last cannonball is fired with such tremendous velocity that it goes completely around _____ earth. It returns to _____ mountaintop and continues around the earth again and again. _____ cannonball's inertia causes it to continue in motion indefi-nitely in _____ orbit around earth. In such a situation, we could consider cannonball to be _____ artificial satellite, just like _____ weather satellites launched by _____ U.S. Weather Service. (p. 209)

Most native speakers of English who have attempted this exercise report a great deal of frustration, a curious sense of working against, rather than with, the rule. The rule, however valuable it may be for non-native speakers, is, for the most part, simply unusable for native speakers of the language.

Cognate Areas of Research

We can corroborate this demonstration by turning to research in two cognate areas, studies of the induction of rules of artificial languages and studies of the role of formal rules in second language acquisition. Psychologists have studied the ability of subjects to learn artificial languages, usually constructed of nonsense syllables or letter strings. Such languages can be described by phrase structure rules:

$S \Rightarrow VX$

$X \Rightarrow MX$

More clearly, they can be presented as flow diagrams, as below:

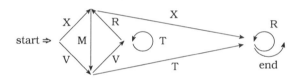

This diagram produces "sentences" like the following:

VVTRXRR.	XMVTTRX.	XXRR.
XMVRMT.	VVTTRMT.	XMTRRR.

The following "sentences" would be "ungrammatical" in this language:

*VMXTT.	*RTXVVT.	*TRVXXVVM.

Arthur S. Reber, in a classic 1967 experiment, demonstrated that mere exposure to grammatical sentences produced tacit learning: subjects who copied several grammatical sentences performed far above chance in judging the grammaticality of other letter strings. Further experiments have shown that providing subjects with formal rules — giving them the flow diagram above, for example — remarkably degrades performance: subjects given the "rules of the language" do much less well in acquiring the rules than do subjects not given the rules. Indeed, even telling subjects that they are to induce the rules of an artificial language degrades performance. Such laboratory experiments are admittedly contrived, but they confirm predictions that our theory of language would make about the value of formal rules in language learning.[17]

The thrust of recent research in second language learning similarly works to constrain the value of formal grammar rules. The most explicit statement of the value of formal rules is that of Stephen D. Krashen's monitor model.[18] Krashen divides second language mastery into *acquisition* — tacit, informal mastery, akin to first language acquisition — and formal learning—conscious application of Grammar 2 rules, which he calls "monitor-ing" output. In another essay Krashen uses his model to predict a highly individual use of the monitor and a highly constrained role for formal rules:

> Some adults (and very few children) are able to use conscious rules to increase the grammatical accuracy of their output, and even for these people, very strict conditions need to be met before the conscious grammar can be applied.[19]

In *Principles and Practice in Second Language Acquisition* (New York: Pergamon, 1982) Krashen outlines these conditions by means of a series of concentric circles, beginning with a large circle denoting the rules of English and a smaller circle denoting the subset of those rules described by formal linguists (adding that most linguists would protest that the size of this circle is much too large):

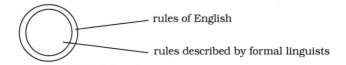

Krashen then adds smaller circles, as shown below—a subset of the rules described by formal linguists that would be known to applied linguists, a subset of those rules that would be available to the best teachers, and then a subset of those rules that teachers might choose to present to second language learners:

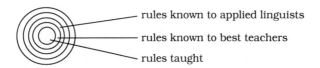

Of course, as Krashen notes, not all the rules taught will be learned, and not all those learned will be available, as what he calls "mental baggage" (p. 94), for conscious use.

An experiment by Ellen Bialystock, asking English speakers learning French to judge the grammaticality of taped sentences, complicates this issue, for reaction time data suggest that learners first make an intuitive judgment of grammaticality, using implicit or Grammar 1 knowledge, and only then search for formal explanations, using explicit or Grammar 2 knowledge.[20] This distinction would suggest that Grammar 2 knowledge is of use to second language learners only after the principle has already been mastered as tacit Grammar 1 knowledge. In the terms of Krashen's model, learning never becomes acquisition (*Principles*, p. 86).

An ingenious experiment by Herbert W. Seliger complicates the issue yet further ("On the Nature and Function of Language Rules in Language Learning," *TESOL Quarterly*, 13 [1979], 359–369). Seliger asked native and non-native speakers of English to orally identify pictures of objects (e.g., "an apple," "a pear," "a book," "an umbrella"), noting whether they used the correct form of the indefinite articles *a* and *an*. He then asked each speaker to state the rule for choosing between *a* and *an*. He found no correlation between the ability to state the rule and the ability to apply it correctly, either with native or non-native speakers. Indeed, three of four adult non-native speakers in his sample produced a correct form of the rule, but they did not apply it in speaking. A strong conclusion from this experiment would be that formal rules of grammar seem to have no value whatsoever. Seliger, however, suggests a more paradoxical interpretation. Rules are of no use, he agrees, but some people think they are, and for these people, assuming that they have internalized the rules, even inadequate rules are of heuristic value, for they allow them to access the internal rules they actually use.

The Incantations of the "Common School Grammars"

Such a paradox may explain the fascination we have as teachers with "rules of grammar" of the Grammar 4 variety, the "rules" of the "common school grammars." Again and again such rules are inadequate to the facts of written language; you will recall that we have known this since Francis' 1927 study. R. Scott Baldwin and James M. Coady, studying how readers respond to punctuation signals ("Psycholinguistic Approaches to a Theory of Punctuation," *Journal of Reading Behavior,* 10 [1978], 363–83), conclude that conventional rules of punctuation are "a complete sham" (p. 375). My own favorite is the Grammar 4 rule for showing possession, always expressed in terms of adding -'s or -s' to nouns, while our internal grammar, if you think about it, adds possession to noun phrases, albeit under severe stylistic constraints: "the horses of the Queen of England" are "the Queen of England's horses" and "the feathers of the duck over there" are "the duck over there's feathers." Suzette Haden Elgin refers to the "rules" of Grammar 4 as "incantations" *(Never Mind the Trees,* p. 9: see note 3).

It may simply be that as hyperliterate adults we are conscious of "using rules" when we are in fact doing something else, something far more complex, accessing tacit heuristics honed by print literacy itself. We can clarify this notion by reaching for an acronym coined by technical writers to explain the readability of complex prose — COIK: "clear only if known." The rules of Grammar 4 — no, we can at this point be more honest — the incantations of Grammar 4 are COIK. If you know how to signal possession in the code of print, then the advice to add -'s to nouns makes perfect sense, just as the collective noun *monies* is a fine example of changing -y to -i and adding -es to form the plural. But if you have not grasped, tacitly, the abstract representation of possession in print, such incantations can only be opaque.

Worse yet, the advice given in "the common school grammars" is unconnected with anything remotely resembling literate adult behavior. Consider, as an example, the rule for not writing a sentence fragment as the rule is described in the best-selling college grammar text, John C. Hodges and Mary S. Whitten's *Harbrace College Handbook,* 9th ed. (New York: Harcourt Brace Jovanovich, 1982). In order to get to the advice, "as a rule, do not write a sentence fragment" (p. 25), the student must master the following learning tasks:

Recognizing verbs.

Recognizing subjects and verbs.

Recognizing all parts of speech. *(Harbrace* lists eight.)

Recognizing phrases and subordinate clauses. *(Harbrace* lists six types of phrases, and it offers incomplete lists of eight relative pronouns and eighteen subordinating conjunctions.)

Recognizing main clauses and types of sentences.

These learning tasks completed, the student is given the rule above, offered a page of exceptions, and then given the following advice (or is it an incantation?):

> Before handing in a composition, . . . proofread each word group written as a sentence. Test each one for completeness. First, be sure that it has at least one subject and one predicate. Next, be sure that the word group is not a dependent clause beginning with a subordinating conjunction or a relative clause. (p 27)

The school grammar approach defines a sentence fragment as a conceptual error — as not having conscious knowledge of the school grammar definition of *sentence*. It demands heavy emphasis on rote memory, and it asks students to behave in ways patently removed from the behaviors of mature writers. (I have never in my life tested a sentence for completeness, and I am a better writer — and probably a better person — as a consequence.) It may be, of course, that some developing writers, at some points in their development, may benefit from such advice — or, more to the point, may think that they benefit — but, as Thomas Friedman points out in "Teaching Error, Nurturing Confusion" (*CE*, 45 [1983], 390–399), our theory of language tells us that such advice is, at the best, COIK. As the Maine joke has it, about a tourist asking directions from a farmer, "you can't get there from here."

Redefining Error

In the specific case of sentence fragments, Mina P. Shaughnessy *(Errors and Expectations* [New York: Oxford University Press, 1977]) argues that such errors are not conceptual failures at all, but performance errors— mistakes in punctuation. Muriel Harris' error counts support this view ("Mending the Fragmented Free Modifier," *CCC*, 32 [1981], 175–182). Case studies show example after example of errors that occur *because* of instruction — one thinks, for example, of David Bartholomae's student explaining that he added an -*s to children* "because it's a plural" ("The Study of Error," *CCC*, 31 [1980], 262). Surveys, such as that by Muriel Harris ("Contradictory Perceptions of the Rules of Writing," *CCC*, 30 [1979], 218–220), and our own observations suggest that students consistently misunderstand such Grammar 4 explanations (COIK, you will recall). For example, from Patrick Hartwell and Robert H. Bentley and from Mike Rose, we have two separate anecdotal accounts of students, cited for punctuating a *because*-clause as a sentence, who have decided to avoid using *because.* More generally, Collette A. Daiute's analysis of errors made by college students shows that errors tend to appear at clause boundaries, suggesting short-term memory load and not conceptual deficiency as a cause of error.[21]

Thus, if we think seriously about error and its relationship to the worship of formal grammar study, we need to attempt some massive dislocation of our traditional thinking, to shuck off our hyperliterate perception of the value of formal rules, and to regain the confidence in the tacit power of unconscious knowledge that our theory of language gives us. Most students, reading their writing aloud, will correct in essence all errors of spelling, grammar, and, by intonation, punctuation, but usually without noticing that what they read departs from what they wrote.[22] And Richard H. Haswell ("Minimal Marking," *CE*, 45 [1983], 600–604) notes that his students correct 61.1% of their errors when they are identified with a simple mark in the margin rather than by error type. Such findings suggest that we need to redefine error, to see it not as a cognitive or linguistic problem, a problem of not knowing a "rule of grammar" (whatever that may mean), but rather, following the insight of Robert J. Bracewell ("Writing as a Cognitive Activity," *Visible Language*, 14 [1980], 400–422), as a problem of metacognition and metalinguistic awareness, a matter of accessing knowledges that, to be of any use, learners must have already internalized by means of exposure to the code. (Usage issues—Grammar 3—probably represent a different order of problem. Both Joseph Emonds and Jeffrey Jochnowitz establish that the usage issues we worry most about are linguistically unnatural, departures from the grammar in our heads.)[23]

The notion of metalinguistic awareness seems crucial. The sentence below, created by Douglas R. Hofstadter ("Metamagical Themas," *Scientific American*, 235, No. 1 [1981], 22-32), is offered to clarify that notion; you are invited to examine it for a moment or two before continuing.

Their is four errors in this sentance. Can you find them?

Three errors announce themselves plainly enough, the misspellings of *there* and *sentence* and the use of *is* instead of *are*. (And, just to illustrate the perils of hyperliteracy, let it be noted that, through three years of drafts, I referred to the choice of is and *are* as a matter of "subject-verb agreement.") The fourth error resists detection, until one assesses the truth value of the sentence itself — the fourth error is that there are not four errors, only three. Such a sentence (Hofstadter calls it a "self-referencing sentence") asks you to look at it in two ways, simultaneously as statement and as linguistic artifact — in other words, to exercise metalinguistic awareness.

A broad range of cross-cultural studies suggest that metalinguistic awareness is a defining feature of print literacy. Thus Sylvia Scribner and Michael Cole, working with the triliterate Vai of Liberia (variously literate in English, through schooling; in Arabic, for religious purposes; and in an indigenous Vai script, used for personal affairs), find that metalinguistic awareness, broadly conceived, is the only cognitive skill underlying each of the three literacies. The one statistically significant skill shared by literate Vai was the recognition of word boundaries. Moreover, literate Vai tended to answer "yes" when asked (in Vai). "Can you call the sun the moon and the moon the sun?" while illiterate Vai tended to have grave doubts about such metalinguistic play. And in the United States Henry and Lila R. Gleitman report quite different responses by clerical workers and PhD candidates asked to interpret nonsense compounds like "house-bird glass": clerical workers focused on meaning and plausibility (for example, "a house-bird made of glass"), while PhD candidates focused on syntax (for example, "a very small drinking cup for canaries" or "a glass that protects house-birds").[24] More general research findings suggest a clear relationship between measures of metalinguistic awareness and measures of literacy level.[25] William Labov, speculating on literacy acquisition in inner-city ghettoes, contrasts "stimulus-bound" and "language-bound" individuals, suggesting that the latter seem to master literacy more easily.[26] The analysis here suggests that the causal relationship works the other way, that it is the mastery of written language that increases one's awareness of language as language.

This analysis has two implications. First, it makes the question of socially nonstandard dialects, always implicit in discussions of teaching formal grammar, into a non-issue.[27] Native speakers of English, regardless of dialect, show tacit mastery of the conventions of Standard English, and that mastery seems to transfer into abstract orthographic knowledge through interaction with print.[28] Developing writers show the same patterning of errors, regardless of dialect.[29] Studies of reading and of writing suggest that surface features of spoken dialect are simply irrelevant to mastering print literacy.[30] Print is a complex cultural code — or better yet, a system of code — and my bet is that, regardless of instruction, one masters those codes from the top down, from pragmatic questions of voice, tone, audience, register, and rhetorical strategy, not from the bottom up, from grammar to usage to fixed forms of organization.

Second, this analysis forces us to posit multiple literacies, used for multiple purposes, rather than a single static literacy, engraved in "rules of grammar." These multiple literacies are evident in cross-cultural studies.[31] They are equally evident when we inquire into the uses of literacy in American communities.[32] Further, given that students, at all levels, show widely variant interactions with print literacy, there would seem to be little to do with grammar — with Grammar 2 or with Grammar 4 — that we could isolate as a basis for formal instruction.[33]

Grammar 5: Stylistic Grammar

Similarly, when we turn to Grammar 5, "grammatical terms used in the interest of teaching prose style," so central to Martha Kolln's argument for teaching formal grammar, we find that the grammar issue is simply beside the point. There are two fully-articulated positions about "stylistic grammar," which I will label "romantic" and "classic," following Richard Lloyd-Jones and Richard E. Young.[34] The romantic position is that stylistic grammars, though perhaps useful for teachers, have little place in the teaching of composition, for students must struggle with and through language toward meaning. This position rests on a theory of language ultimately philosophical rather than linguistic (witness, for example, the contempt for linguists in Ann Berthoff's *The Making of Meaning: Metaphors, Models, and Maxims for Writing Teachers* [Montclair, N.J.: Boynton/Cook, 1981]); it is articulated as a theory of style by Donald A. Murray and, on somewhat different grounds (that stylistic grammars encourage overuse of the monitor), by Ian Pringle. The classic position, on the other hand, is that we can find ways to offer developing writers helpful suggestions about prose style, suggestions such as Francis Christensen's emphasis on the cumulative sentence, developed by observing the practice of skilled writers, and Joseph Williams' advice about predication, developed by psycholinguistic studies of comprehension.[35] James A. Berlin's recent survey of composition theory (*CE*, 45 [1982], 765–777) probably understates the gulf between these two positions and the radically different conceptions of language that underlie them, but it does establish that they share an overriding assumption in common: that one learns to control the language of print by manipulating language in meaningful contexts, not by learning about language in isolation, as by the study of formal grammar. Thus even classic theorists, who choose to present a vocabulary of style to students, do so only as a vehicle for encouraging productive control of communicative structures.

We might put the matter in the following terms. Writers need to develop skills at two levels. One, broadly rhetorical, involves communication in meaningful contexts (the strategies, registers, and procedures of discourse across a range of modes, audiences, contexts, and purposes). The other, broadly metalinguistic rather than linguistic, involves active manipulation of language with conscious attention to surface form. This second level may be developed tacitly, as a natural adjunct to developing rhetorical competencies — I take this to be the position of romantic theorists. It may be developed formally, by manipulating language for stylistic effect, and such manipulation may involve, for pedagogical continuity, a vocabulary of style. But it is primarily developed by any kind of language activity that enhances the awareness of language as language.[36] David T. Hakes, summarizing the research on metalinguistic awareness, notes how far we are from understanding this process:

> the optimal conditions for becoming metalinguistically competent involve growing up in a literate environment with adult models who are themselves metalinguistically competent and who foster the growth of that competence in a variety of ways as yet little understood. ("The Development of Metalinguistic Abilities," p. 205: see note 25)

Such a model places language, at all levels, at the center of the curriculum, but not as "necessary categories and labels" (Kolln, "Closing the Books on Alchemy," p. 150), but as literal stuff, verbal clay, to be molded and probed, shaped and reshaped, and, above all, enjoyed.

The Tradition of Experimental Research

Thus, when we turn back to experimental research on the value of formal grammar instruction, we do so with firm predictions given us by our theory of language. Our theory would predict that formal grammar instruction, whether instruction in scientific grammar or instruction in "the common school grammar," would have little to do with control over surface correctness nor with quality of writing. It would predict that any form of active involvement with language would be preferable to instruction in rules or definitions (or incantations). In essence, this is what the research tells us. In 1893, the Committee of Ten *(Report of the Committee of Ten on Secondary School Studies* [Washington, D.C.: U.S. Government Printing Office, 1893]) put grammar at the center of the English curriculum, and its report established the rigidly sequential mode of instruction common for the last century. But the committee explicitly noted that grammar instruction did not aid correctness, arguing instead that it improved the ability to think logically (an argument developed from the role of the "grammarian" in the classical rhetorical tradition, essentially a teacher of literature — see, for example, the etymology of *grammar* in the *Oxford English Dictionary).*

But Franklin S. Hoyt, in a 1906 experiment, found no relationship between the study of grammar and the ability to think logically; his research led him to conclude what I am constrained to argue more than seventy-five years later, that there is no "relationship between a knowledge of technical grammar and the ability to use English and to interpret language" ("The Place of Grammar in the Elementary Curriculum," *Teachers College Record,* 7 [1906], 483-484). Later studies, through the 1920s, focused on the relationship of knowledge of grammar and ability to recognize error; experiments reported by James Boraas in 1917 and by William Asker in 1923 are typical of those that reported no correlation. In the 1930s, with the development of the functional grammar movement, it was common to compare the study of formal grammar with one form or another of active manipulation of language; experiments by I. O. Ash in 1935 and Ellen Frogner in 1939 are typical of studies showing the superiority of active involvement with language.[37] In a 1959 article, "Grammar in Language Teaching" *(Elementary English,* 36 [1959], 412-421), John J. DeBoer noted the consistency of these findings.

> The impressive fact is . . . that in all these studies, carried out in places and at times far removed from each other, often by highly experienced and disinterested investigators, the results have been consistently negative so far as the value of grammar in the improvement of language expression is concerned. (p. 417)

In 1960 Ingrid M. Strom, reviewing more than fifty experimental studies, came to a similarly strong and unqualified conclusion:

> direct methods of instruction, focusing on writing activities and the structuring of ideas, are more efficient in teaching sentence structure, usage, punctuation, and other related factors than are such methods as nomenclature drill, diagramming, and rote memorization of grammatical rules.[38]

In 1963 two research reviews appeared, one by Braddock, Lloyd-Jones, and Schorer, cited at the beginning of this paper, and one by Henry C. Meckel, whose conclusions, though more guarded, are in essential agreement.[39] In 1969 J. Stephen Sherwin devoted one-fourth of his *Four Problems in Teaching English: A Critique of Research* (Scranton, Penn.: International Textbook, 1969) to the grammar issue, concluding that "instruction in formal grammar is an ineffective way to help students achieve proficiency in writing" (p. 135). Some early experiments in sentence combining, such as those by Donald R. Bateman and Frank J. Zidonnis and by John C. Mellon, showed improvement in measures of syntactic complexity with instruction in transformational grammar keyed to sentence combining practice. But a later study by Frank O'Hare achieved the same gains with no grammar instruction, suggesting to Sandra L. Stotsky and to Richard Van de Veghe that active manipulation of language, not the grammar unit, explained the earlier results.[40] More recent summaries of research — by Elizabeth I. Haynes, Hillary Taylor Holbrook, and Marcia Farr Whiteman — support similar conclusions. Indirect evidence for this position is provided by surveys reported by Betty Bamberg in 1978 and 1981, showing that time spent in grammar instruction in high school is the least important factor, of eight factors examined, in separating regular from remedial writers at the college level.[41]

More generally, Patrick Scott and Bruce Castner, in "Reference Sources for Composition Research: A Practical Survey" *(CE,* 45 [1983], 756–768), note that much current research is not informed by an awareness of the past. Put simply, we are constrained to reinvent the wheel. My concern here has been with a far more serious problem: that too often the wheel we reinvent is square.

It is, after all, a question of power. Janet Emig, developing a consensus from composition research, and Aaron S. Carton and Lawrence V. Castiglione, developing the implications of language theory for education, come to the same conclusion: that the thrust of current research and theory is to take power from the teacher and to give that power to the learner.[42] At no point in the English curriculum is the question of power more blatantly posed than in the issue of formal grammar instruction. It is time that we, as teachers, formulate theories of language and literacy and let those theories guide our teaching, and it is time that we, as researchers, move on to more interesting areas of inquiry.

Notes

¹ *Research in Written Composition* (Urbana, Ill.: National Council of Teachers of English, 1963), pp. 37–38.

² "Non-magical Thinking: Presenting Writing Developmentally in Schools," in *Writing Process, Development and Communication*, Vol. II of *Writing: The Nature, Development and Teaching of Written Communication*, ed. Charles H. Frederiksen and Joseph F. Dominic (Hillsdale, N.J.: Lawrence Erlbaum, 1980), pp. 21–30.

³ For arguments in favor of formal grammar teaching, see Patrick F. Basset, "Grammar — Can We Afford Not to Teach It?" *NASSP Bulletin*, 64, No. 10 (1980), 55–63; Mary Epes et al., "The COMP-LAB Project: Assessing the Effectiveness of a Laboratory-Centered Basic Writing Course on the College Level" (Jamaica, N.Y.: York College, CUNY, 1979) ERIC 194 908; June B. Evans, "The Analogous Ounce: The Analgesic for Relief," *English Journal*, 70, No. 2 (1981), 38–39; Sydney Greenbaum, "What Is Grammar and Why Teach It?" (a paper presented at the meeting of the National Council of Teachers of English, Boston, Nov. 1982) ERIC 222 917; Marjorie Smelstor, *A Guide to the Role of Grammar in Teaching Writing* (Madison: University of Wisconsin School of Education, 1978) ERIC 176 323; and A. M. Tibbetts, *Working Papers: A Teacher's Observations on Composition* (Glenview, Ill.: Scott, Foresman, 1982).

For attacks on formal grammar teaching, see Harvey A. Daniels, *Famous Last Words: The American Language Crisis Reconsidered* (Carbondale: Southern Illinois University Press, 1983); Suzette Haden Elgin, *Never Mind the Trees: What the English Teacher Really Needs to Know about Linguistics* (Berkeley: University of California College of Education, Bay Area Writing Project Occasional Paper No. 2, 1980) ERIC 198 536; Mike Rose, "Remedial Writing Courses: A Critique and a Proposal," *College English*, 45 (1983), 109–128; and Ron Shook, Response to Martha Kolln, *College Composition and Communication*, 34 (1983),491–495.

⁴ See, for example, Clifton Fadiman and James Howard, *Empty Pages: A Search for Writing Competence in School and Society* (Belmont, Cal.: Fearon Pitman, 1979); Edwin Newman. *A Civil Tongue (Indianapolis,* Ind.: Bobbs-Merrill, 1976); and *Strictly Speaking* (New York: Warner Books, 1974); John Simons, *Paradigms Lost* (New York: Clarkson N. Potter, 1980); A. M. Tibbets and Charlene Tibbets, *What's Happening to American English?* (New York: Scribner's, 1978); and "Why Johnny Can't Write, *Newsweek*, 8 Dec. 1975, pp. 58–63.

⁵ "The Role of Grammar in a Secondary School English Curriculum." *Research in the Teaching of English*, 10 (1976), 5–21; *The Role of Grammar in a Secondary School Curriculum* (Wellington: New Zealand Council of Teachers of English, 1979).

⁶ "A Taxonomy of Compositional Competencies," in *Perspectives on Literacy*, ed. Richard Beach and P. David Pearson (Minneapolis: University of Minnesota College of Education, 1979), pp. 247–272.

⁷ On usage norms, see Edward Finegan, *Attitudes toward English Usage: The History of a War of Words* (New York: Teachers College Press, 1980), and Jim Quinn, *American Tongue in Cheek: A Populist Guide to Language* (New York: Pantheon, 1980); on arrangement, see Patrick Hartwell, "Teaching Arrangement: A Pedagogy," *CE*, 40 (1979), 548–554.

⁸ "Revolution in Grammar," *Quarterly Journal of Speech*, 40 (1954), 299–312.

⁹ Richard A. Lanham, *Revising Prose* (New York: Scribner's, 1979); William Strunk and E. B. White, *The Elements of Style*, 3rd ed. (New York: Macmillan, 1979); Joseph

Williams, *Style: Ten Lessons in Clarity and Grace* (Glenview, Ill.: Scott, Foresman, 1981); Christensen, "A Generative Rhetoric of the Sentence," *CCC*, 14 (1963), 155–161; Donald A. Daiker, Andrew Kerek, and Max Morenberg, *The Writer's Options: Combining to Composing*, 2nd ed. (New York: Harper & Row, 1982).

[10] "A Psychological Approach," in *Psychobiology of Language*, ed. M. Studdert-Kennedy (Cambridge, Mass.: MIT Press, 1983), pp. 16–19. See also Noam Chomsky, "Language and Unconscious Knowledge," in *Psychoanalysis and Language: Psychiatry and the Humanities*, Vol. III, ed. Joseph H. Smith (New Haven, Conn.: Yale University Press, 1978), pp. 3–44.

[11] Morris Halle, "Knowledge Unlearned and Untaught: What Speakers Know about the Sounds of Their Language," in *Linguistic Theory and Psychological Reality*, ed. Halle, Joan Bresnan, and George A. Miller (Cambridge, Mass.: MIT Press, 1978), pp. 135–140.

[12] Moscowitz, "On the Status of Vowel Shift in English," in *Cognitive Development and the Acquisition of Language*, ed. T. E. Moore (New York: Academic Press, 1973), pp. 223–260; Chomsky, "Stages in Language Development and Reading Exposure," *Harvard Educational Review*, 42 (1972), 1–33; and Brause, "Developmental Aspects of the Ability to Understand Semantic Ambiguity, with Implications for Teachers," *RTE*, 11 (1977), 39–48.

[13] Mills and Hemsley, "The Effect of Levels of Education on Judgments of Grammatical Acceptability," *Language and Speech*, 19 (1976), 324–342; Whyte, "Levels of Language Competence and Reading Ability: An Exploratory Investigation," *Journal of Research in Reading*, 5 (1982), 123–132; Morais et al., "Does Awareness of Speech as a Series of Phones Arise Spontaneously?" *Cognition*, 7 (1979), 323–331; Ferguson, *Cognitive Effects of Literacy: Linguistic Awareness in Adult Non-readers* (Washington, D.C.: National Institute of Education Final Report, 1981) ERIC 222 857; Hamilton and Barton, "A Word Is a Word: Metalinguistic Skills in Adults of Varying Literacy Levels" (Stanford, Cal.: Stanford University Department of Linguistics, 1980) ERIC 222 859.

[14] On the question of the psychological reality of Grammar 2 descriptions, see Maria Black and Shulamith Chiat, "Psycholinguistics without 'Psychological Reality,'" *Linguistics*, 19 (1981), 37-61; Joan Bresnan, ed., *The Mental Representation of Grammatical Relations* (Cambridge, Mass.: MIT Press, 1982); and Michael H. Long, "Inside the 'Black Box': Methodological Issues in Classroom Research on Language Learning," *Language Learning*, 30 (1980), 1–42.

[15] Chomsky, "The Current Scene in Linguistics," *College English*, 27 (1966), 587–595; and "Linguistic Theory," in *Language Teaching: Broader Contexts*, ed. Robert C. Meade, Jr. (New York: Modern Language Association, 1966), pp. 43–49; Mark Lester, "The Value of Transformational Grammar in Teaching Composition," *CCC*, 16 (1967), 228.

[16] Christensen, "Between Two Worlds," in *Notes toward a New Rhetoric: Nine Essays for Teachers*, rev. ed., ed. Bonniejean Christensen (New York: Harper & Row, 1978), pp. 1–22.

[17] Reber, "Implicit Learning of Artificial Grammars," *Journal of Verbal Learning and Verbal Behavior*, 6 (1967), 855–863; "Implicit Learning of Synthetic Languages: The Role of Instructional Set," *Journal of Experimental Psychology: Human Learning and Memory*, 2 (1976), 889–94, and Reber, Saul M. Kassin, Selma Lewis, and Gary Cantor, "On the Relationship Between Implicit and Explicit Modes in the Learning of a Complex Rule Structure," *Journal of Experimental Psychology: Human Learning and Memory*, 6 (1980), 492–502.

[18] "Individual Variation in the Use of the Monitor," in *Principles of Second Language Learning*, ed. W. Richie (New York: Academic Press, 1978), pp. 175-185.

[19] "Applications of Psycholinguistic Research to the Classroom," in *Practical Applications of Research in Foreign Language Teaching*, ed. D. J. James (Lincolnwood, Ill.: National Textbook, 1983), p. 61.

[20] "Some Evidence for the Integrity and Interaction of Two Knowledge Sources," in *New Dimensions in Second Language Acquisition Research*, ed. Roger W. Andersen (Rowley, Mass.: Newbury House, 1981), pp. 62–74.

[21] Hartwell and Bentley, *Some Suggestions for Using Open to Language: A New College Rhetoric*. (New York: Oxford University Press, 1982), p. 73; Rose, *Writer's Block: The Cognitive Dimension* (Carbondale: Southern Illinois University Press, 1983), p. 99; Daiute, "Psycholinguistic Foundations of the Writing Process," *RTE*, 15 (1981), 5–22.

[22] See Bartholomae, "The Study of Error"; Patrick Hartwell, "The Writing Center and the Paradoxes of Written-Down Speech," in *Writing Centers: Theory and Administration*, ed. Gary Olson (Urbana, Ill.: NCTE, 1984), pp. 48–61; and Sondra Perl, "A Look at Basic Writers in the Process of Composing," in *Basic Writing: A Collection of Essays for Teachers, Researchers, and Administrators* (Urbana, Ill.: NCTE, 1980), pp. 13–32.

[23] Emonds, *Adjacency in Grammar: The Theory of Language-Particular Rules* (New York: Academic, 1983); and Jochnowitz, "Everybody Likes Pizza, Doesn't He or She?" *American Speech*, 57 (1982), 198–203.

[24] Scribner and Cole, *Psychology of Literacy* (Cambridge, Mass.: Harvard University Press 1981); Gleitman and Gleitman, "Language Use and Language Judgment," in *Individual Differences in Language Ability and Language Behavior*, ed. Charles J. Fillmore, Daniel Kemper, and William S.-Y. Wang (New York: Academic Press, 1979), pp. 103–126.

[25] There are several recent reviews of this developing body of research in psychology and child development: Irene Athey, "Language Development Factors Related to Reading Development," *Journal of Educational Research*, 76 (1983), 197–203; James Flood and Paula Menyuk "Metalinguistic Development and Reading/Writing Achievement," *Claremont Reading Conference Yearbook*, 46 (1982), 122–132; and the following four essays: David T. Hakes, "The Development of Metalinguistic Abilities: What Develops?," pp. 162–210; Stan A. Kuczaj, II, and Brooke Harbaugh "What Children Think about the Speaking Capabilities of Other Persons and Things," pp. 211–227, Karen Saywitz and Louise Cherry Wilkinson, "Age-Related Differences in Metalinguistic Awareness," pp. 229–250; and Harriet Salatas Waters and Virginia S. Tinsley, "The Development of Verbal Self-Regulation: Relationships between Language, Cognition, and Behavior." pp. 251–277; all in *Language, Thought, and Culture*, Vol. II of *Language Development*, ed. Stan Kuczaj, Jr. (Hillsdale, N.J.: Lawrence Erlbaum. 1982). See also Joanne R. Nurss. "Research in Review: Linguistic Awareness and Learning to Read," *Young Children*. 35, No. 3 (1980), 57–66.

[26] "Competing Value Systems in Inner City Schools," in *Children In and Out of School. Ethnography and Education*, ed. Perry Gilmore and Allan A. Glatthorn (Washington, D.C.: Center for Applied Linguistics, 1982), pp. 148–171; and "Locating the Frontier between Social and Psychological Factors in Linguistic Structure," in *Individual Differences in Language Ability and Language Behavior*, ed. Fillmore, Kemper, and Wang, pp. 327–340.

[27] See, for example, Thomas Farrell, "IQ and Standard English," *CCC*, 34 (1983), 470–484, and the responses by Karen L. Greenberg and Patrick Hartwell, *CCC*, in press.

[28] Jane W. Torrey, "Teaching Standard English to Speakers of Other Dialects," in *Applications of Linguistics: Selected Papers of the Second International Conference of Applied Linguistics*, ed. C. E. Perren and J. L. M. Trim (Cambridge, Mass.: Cambridge University Press, 1971), pp. 423–428; James W. Beers and Edmund H. Henderson, "A Study of the Developing Orthographic Concepts among First Graders," *RTE*, 11 (1977), 133–148.

[29] See the error counts of Samuel A. Kirschner and C. Howard Poteet, "Non-Standard English Usage in the Writing of Black, White, and Hispanic Remedial English Students in an Urban Community College," *RTE,* 7 (1973), 351–355; and Marilyn Sternglass, "Close Similarities in Dialect Features of Black and White College Students in Remedial Composition Classes," *TESOL Quarterly,* 8 (1974), 271–283.

[30] For reading, see the massive study by Kenneth S. Goodman and Yetta M. Goodman, *Reading of American Children Whose Language Is a Stable Rural Dialect of English or a Language Other than English* (Washington, D.C.: National Institute of Education Final Report, 1978) ERIC 175 754; and the overview by Rudine Sims, "Dialect and Reading: Toward Redefining the Issues," in *Reader Meets Author/Bridging the Gap: A Psycholinguistic and Sociolinguistic Approach,* ed. Judith A. Langer and M. Tricia Smith-Burke (Newark, Del.: International Reading Association 1982), pp. 222–232. For writing, see Patrick Hartwell, "Dialect Interference in Writing: A Critical View," *RTE,* 14 (1980), 101–118; and the anthology edited by Barry M. Kroll and Roberta J. Vann, *Exploring Speaking-Writing Relationships: Connections and Contrasts* (Urbana, Ill.: NCTE, 1981).

[31] See, for example, Eric A. Havelock, *The Literary Revolution in Greece and its Cultural Consequences* (Princeton, N.J.: Princeton University Press, 1982); Lesley Milroy on literacy in Dublin, *Language and Social Networks* (Oxford: Basil Blackwell, 1980); Ron Scollon and Suzanne B. K. Scollon on literacy in central Alaska, *Interethnic Communication: An Athabascan Case* (Austin Tex.: Southwest Educational Development Laboratory Working Papers in Sociolinguistics, No. 59, 1979) ERIC 175 276; and Scribner and Cole on literacy in Liberia, *Psychology of Literacy* (see note 24).

[32] See, for example, the anthology edited by Deborah Tannen, *Spoken and Written Language: Exploring Orality and Literacy* (Norwood, N.J.: Ablex, 1982); and Shirley Brice Heath's continuing work: "Protean Shapes in Literacy Events: Ever-Shifting Oral and Literate Traditions," in *Spoken and Written Language,* pp. 91–117; *Ways with Words: Language, Life and Work in Communities and Classrooms* (New York: Cambridge University Press, 1983); and "What No Bedtime Story Means," *Language in Society,* 11 (1982), 49–76.

[33] For studies at the elementary level, see Dell H. Hymes et al., eds., *Ethnographic Monitoring of Children's Acquisition of Reading/Language Arts Skills In and Out of the Classroom* (Washington, D.C.: National Institute of Education Final Report, 1981) ERIC 208 096. For studies at the secondary level, see James L. Collins and Michael M. Williamson, "Spoken Language and Semantic Abbreviation in Writing," *RTE,* 15 (1981), 23–36. And for studies at the college level, see Patrick Hartwell and Gene LoPresti, "Sentence Combining as Kid-Watching," in *Sentence Combining: Toward a Rhetorical Perspective,* ed. Donald A. Daiker, Andrew Kerek, and Max Morenberg (Carbondale: Southern Illinois University Press, in press).

[34] Lloyd-Jones, "Romantic Revels — I Am Not You," *CCC,* 23 (1972), 251–271; and Young, "Concepts of Art and the Teaching of Writing," in *The Rhetorical Tradition and Modern Writing,* ed. James J. Murphy (New York: Modern Language Association, 1982), pp. 130–141.

[35] For the romantic position, see Ann E. Berthoff, "Tolstoy, Vygotsky, and the Making of Meaning," *CCC,* 29 (1978), 249–255; Kenneth Dowst, "The Epistemic Approach," in *Eight Approaches to Teaching Composition,* ed. Timothy Donovan and Ben G. McClellan (Urbana, Ill.: NCTE, 1980), pp. 65–85; Peter Elbow, "The Challenge for Sentence Combining"; and Donald Murray, "Following Language toward Meaning," both in *Sentence Combining: Toward a Rhetorical Perspective* (in press; see note 33). and Ian Pringle, "Why Teach Style? A Review-Essay," *CCC,* 34 (1983), 91–98.

For the classic position, see Christensen's "A Generative Rhetoric of the Sentence" and Joseph Williams' "Defining Complexity," *CE*, 41 (1979), 595–609; and his *Style. Ten Lessons in Clarity and Grace* (see note 9).

[36] Courtney B. Cazden and David K. Dickinson, "Language and Education: Standardization versus Cultural Pluralism," in *Language in the USA*, ed. Charles A. Ferguson and Shirley Brice Heath (New York: Cambridge University Press, 1981), pp.446–468; and Carol Chomsky, "Developing Facility with Language Structure," in *Discovering Language with Children*, ed. Gay Su Pinnell (Urbana, Ill.: NCTE,1980), pp.56–59.

[37] Boraas, "Formal English Grammar and the Practical Mastery of English." Diss. University of Illinois, 1917; Asker, "Does Knowledge of Grammar Function?" *School and Society*, 17 (27 January 1923), 109–111; Ash, "An Experimental Evaluation of the Stylistic Approach in Teaching Composition in the Junior High School," *Journal of Experimental Education*, 4 (1935), 54–62; and Frogner, "A Study of the Relative Efficacy of a Grammatical and a Thought Approach to the Improvement of Sentence Structure in Grades Nine and Eleven," *School Review*, 47 (1939), 663–675.

[38] "Research on Grammar and Usage and Its Implications for Teaching Writing," *Bulletin of the School of Education*, Indiana University, 36 (1960), pp. 13–14.

[39] Meckel, "Research on Teaching Composition and Literature," in *Handbook of Research on Teaching*, ed. N. L. Gage (Chicago: Rand McNally, 1963), pp. 966–1006.

[40] Bateman and Zidonis, *The Effect of a Study of Transformational Grammar on the Writing of Ninth and Tenth Graders* (Urbana, Ill.: NCTE, 1966); Mellon, *Transformational Sentence Combining: A Method for Enhancing the Development of Fluency in English Composition* (Urbana, Ill.: NCTE, 1969); O'Hare, *Sentence-Combining: Improving Student Writing without Formal Grammar Instruction* (Urbana, Ill.: NCTE, 1971); Stotsky, "Sentence-Combining as a Curricular Activity: Its Effect on Written Language Development," *RTE*, 9 (1975), 30–72; and Van de Veghe, "Research in Written Composition: Fifteen Years of Investigation," ERIC 157 095.

[41] Haynes, "Using Research in Preparing to Teach Writing," *English Journal*, 69, No. 1 (1978), 82–88; Holbrook, "ERIC/RCS Report: Whither (Wither) Grammar," *Language Arts*, 60 (1983), 259–263; Whiteman, "What We Can Learn from Writing Research," *Theory into Practice*, 19 (1980), 150–156; Bamberg, "Composition in the Secondary English Curriculum: Some Current Trends and Directions for the Eighties," *RTE*, 15 (1981), 257–266; and "Composition Instruction Does Make a Difference: A Comparison of the High School Preparation of College Freshmen in Regular and Remedial English Classes," *RTE*, 12 (1978), 47–59.

[42] Emig, "Inquiry Paradigms and Writing," *CCC*, 33 (1982), 64–75; Carton and Castiglione, "Educational Linguistics: Defining the Domain," in *Psycholinguistic Research: Implications and Applications*, ed. Doris Aaronson and Robert W. Rieber (Hillsdale, N.J.: Lawrence Erlbaum, 1979), pp. 497–520.

APPENDIX

WRITING ACROSS THE CURRICULUM

As educators have come to recognize that writing and learning are fundamentally related, they have become more interested in the concept of "writing across the curriculum" (commonly referred to as WAC). Though WAC has been around for more than a century in one form or another, the concept gained national attention only in the late 1970s. Increasingly, administrators are asking writing teachers to "do" writing across the curriculum in their introductory writing courses, a request that is often difficult to enact. WAC has a wide range of manifestations. At one end of the continuum are "writing to learn" approaches, in which writing is used in a variety of subjects — chemistry, history, sociology, and so on — to increase students' engagement and enhance their learning. At the other end of the continuum are "learning to write" approaches, in which students learn to write as members of specific disciplines. Recognizing this diversity of approaches and the continuing interest in WAC, the following articles address questions that teachers and administrators face as they attempt to incorporate WAC principles in their writing courses or as they consider developing their own WAC programs:

- What is WAC and where did it come from? How can teachers learn more about it?
- How does WAC affect students, teachers, and the academy?
- How can teachers incorporate WAC in writing courses?
- Where is the WAC movement headed?

WRITING ACROSS THE CURRICULUM:
A BIBLIOGRAPHIC ESSAY
Patricia Bizzell and Bruce Herzberg

[From The Territory of Language: Linguistics, Stylistics, and the Teaching of Composition. *Ed. Donald A. McQuade. Carbondale: Southern Illinois UP, 1986. 340–52.]*

[For biographical information, see page 310.]

In this extensive bibliographical survey, Bizzell and Herzberg define writing across the curriculum, discuss its several manifestations, and offer an overview of WAC's origins and theoretical premises. They also examine problems associated with WAC initiatives and explore the future of the movement. They conclude their essay with a bibliography, current through 1985.

["Further Resources in Writing across the Curriculum," following this selection, extends bibliographical information through 1992.]

"Writing across the curriculum" has come to mean three things to writing teachers in America. It denotes, first, a theory of the function of writing in learning; second, a pedagogy to encourage particular uses of writing in learning; and third, a program that applies the pedagogy in a particular school. American interest in the theoretical, pedagogical, and institutional aspects of writing across the curriculum has been growing rapidly in recent years, in part as a response to perceived declines in students' writing ability. Harvey Wiener, president of the Council of Writing Program Administrators, estimates that there are now about four hundred college-level writing-across-the-curriculum programs. Most American scholarship in the field is also recent, appearing after 1975.

The concept of writing across the curriculum was introduced in the 1960s by James Britton and his colleagues at the University of London Institute of Education. They studied language in secondary-level classrooms and found that most speaking, reading, and writing is used to convey information (Barnes et al.). In the London group's seminal work, *The Development of Writing Abilities* (11–18), Britton and his colleagues found that the overwhelming majority of student writing is "transactional," that is, writing used to convey information to a relatively distant and impersonal audience, usually the teacher in the role of examiner. Britton and his colleagues contrasted transactional writing with two other kinds, "poetic" and "expressive." Poetic writing allows the student to step back from the role of active participant in the world, to contemplate and speculate, and to share his or her thoughts with an intimate audience, for example, the teacher in the role of trusted adult. Expressive writing also allows students to explore ideas informally, but in expository modes such as the class journal rather than in fiction or poetry. (For summaries of the London group's work, see Applebee, "Writing"; Rosen; Shafer.)

The London group's studies in developmental psychology and the philosophy of language suggest that adolescents, like younger children, need to use language in personal, exploratory ways, with the support of a friendly audience, in order to learn (Britton). In other words, they need more opportunities for poetic and expressive writing. This need is particularly great for students whose social origins put them at a comparatively greater remove from school conventions of language use. Students need to be able to make connections in their own vernacular between school knowledge and their own interests and values before they can be expected to master transactional writing.

Out of this understanding of the function of the language in learning grew the London group's Writing across the Curriculum Project, headed by Nancy Martin. The Writing across the Curriculum Project published a series of pamphlets demonstrating, with many examples of expressive and poetic writing and talking, the academic benefits of allowing students to use language in the full range of ways. The pamphlets *(Information; Why Write?; Talking; Science; Options)* also suggest assignments for expressive and poetic writing in a variety of disciplines (see also Martin et al.).

A Language for Life, the report of the Bullock Commission, on which Britton served, advocates similar changes in language instruction across the curriculum (See Brunetti.) This commission was appointed by then Secretary of State for Education and Science Margaret Thatcher to respond to Britain's version of the "back-to-basics" furor. Britton wrote the Bullock

Report's chapters on early language development and collaborated on chapters dealing with writing instruction and language across the curriculum.

Britton and his colleagues were influenced by James Moffett's curriculum for *Teaching the Universe of Discourse* on the elementary and secondary levels, a curriculum recently detailed, with suggestions for college use, in Moffett's *Active Voice*. Moffett sorts language along a continuum from private, oral, concrete uses to public, written, abstract uses. Students will more easily master the full range of uses if they are encouraged to begin with those closest to their own speech. These beginning forms of language use are what Britton would call expressive — such as dialogues and letters — and poetic — such as plays and fictional autobiographies. Like Britton, Moffett does not aim to replace all transactional writing with expressive and poetic writing, but rather to help students feel comfortable with the full range of ways to use language to explore and communicate ideas.

Janet Emig was one of the first American theorists to make use of Britton's work. In *The Composing Processes of Twelfth Graders,* she revises Britton's classification of language uses. Her "reflexive" resembles his expressive, and her "extensive" resembles his transactional. Like Britton, she finds that when secondary-level students are given more opportunities to write reflexively, they engage in a more thoughtful writing process, write better and feel better about what they write, and learn more. Emig's argument for the importance of reflexive or expressive writing, however, differs from Britton's. In her seminal essay, "Writing as a Mode of Learning," Emig looks more to cognitive than to developmental psychology for evidence of the importance of all ways to use writing in learning. Whereas the London group emphasizes the continuity between speech and writing, Emig emphasizes the unique cognitive advantages conferred by writing. Writing requires imagining the audience and reinforces learning by involving hand, eye, and brain. The written text facilitates reflecting on and reformulating ideas. Writing thus becomes a central means to constitute and propagate knowledge.

Emig agrees with Britton that students must be given more opportunities to write reflexively (expressively) in all disciplines. Several studies have confirmed her finding that American students on the secondary and college levels do not have such opportunities now, because the great majority of the writing they do is transactional (Donlan; Tighe and Koziol; Eblen). The most comprehensive of these studies is Arthur N. Applebee's *Writing in the Secondary Schools: English and the Content Areas.* American interest in writing across the curriculum has been strengthened by the conjunction of findings that most student writing is transactional, and of widespread feelings that student writing ability is declining. Suspecting a causal relationship, many composition administrators have argued for a program to inform college faculty in all disciplines of the need for expressive and poetic writing, as well as the usual transactional assignments.

In addition to encouraging cross-disciplinary uses of expressive and poetic writing, some work on writing across the curriculum explores uses of language peculiar to the academy. The aim of this work is to reform freshman composition pedagogy as well as writing instruction in courses outside the English department. Elaine Maimon has argued that this new freshman composition pedagogy should teach academic discourse *(Instructor's Manual).* She explains that each academic discipline has its own way of making sense of experience, which is embodied in the discourse conventions of the discipline. Moreover, some discourse conventions are shared by all academic disciplines — that is, there is an academic discourse as well as disciplinary discourses. A D. Van Nostrand argues that studying academic discourse teaches students how to find — or create — significant relationships between facts, rather than simply to report facts. The freshman composition course, where students learn what ways of relating facts are significant in the academy, is the place where they are initiated into academic discourse (Bizzell).

Writing program administrators have been eagerly exchanging ideas on how to implement the various aims of writing across the curriculum. A national network of writing-across-the-curriculum programs has been formed; several newsletters circulate. College-level writing-across-the-curriculum programs typically take one of two forms, Laurence Peters has found. One common kind of program is centered in an interdisciplinary freshman composition course. The other is centered in upper-level writing-intensive courses in various disciplines.

The most complete account of an interdisciplinary freshman composition course can be found in *Writing in the Arts and Sciences,* a textbook by Elaine Maimon and several of her colleagues from other departments at Beaver College. The book begins with the section "Writing to Learn," which discusses cross-disciplinary uses of expressive writing, heuristics, and informal academic writing, such as class notes and library work. The second major section, "Learning to Write," comprises chapters on discipline-specific discourse such as the humanities research paper, the social science case study, and the natural science laboratory report. A few other textbooks for writing across the curriculum have appeared, and more are likely to come out in the near future (Behrens; Bizzell and Herzberg). Another model for the interdisciplinary course has been developed by David Hamilton: students practice "serious parodies" of disciplinary discourse in order to grasp the underlying conceptual activities specific to each discipline (See also Rose, "Remedial Writing ").

Writing-across-the-curriculum programs based in upper-level writing-intensive courses frequently stress the importance of expressive writing in all disciplines. Toby Fulwiler has shown how journals can be used both to explore academic content and to relate knowledge to one's own values ("Journals"). With Art Young, he has also edited a collection of essays on the teaching of poetic, expressive, and transactional writing in the Michigan Technological University writing-across-the-curriculum program. On the other hand, in collections such as those edited by C. William Griffin *(Teaching Writing)* and by Christopher Thaiss, the assumption is not necessarily that expressive writing needs to be increased. Rather, teachers in all disciplines should use writing for learning in ways particularly useful in their disciplines. (See also Odell.)

Faculty development has become an important aspect of writing across the curriculum. Professors who have not been trained to teach writing, whether they teach literature or other academic disciplines, often have too narrow a notion of "good" writing as grammatically correct writing. If they do not see themselves as writers, experiencing the complexities of the composing process, they often do not appreciate students' need for guidance through this process. They may be reluctant to take on the extra work of teaching writing, or fear that it will take time away from essential course content. They may be wary of the writing program administrator's expanded influence in college affairs.

This need for faculty development has prompted much work on how to start a writing-across-the-curriculum program and conduct writing workshops for faculty from all disciplines. Elaine Maimon has given practical advice on coping with intracampus politics ("Cinderella"; "Writing"). Some workshops, such as those conducted by Anne Herrington and Ann Raimes, seek to sensitize faculty to the ways they are teaching academic discourse and to make their assignment design and essay evaluation more effective through discussion of examples from their own courses (see also Rose, "Faculty Talk"; Walvoord). Another kind of workshop aims to develop faculty's view of themselves as writers by asking them to write expressively and to critique each other's work. Toby Fulwiler has been an influential proponent of such workshops ("Showing"). (See also Bergman, "Inclusive Literacy"; Freisinger.)

This American work on pedagogical and institutional concerns has relied for its theoretical underpinnings on the scholarship by Britton — by far the most frequently cited authority — Emig, and Moffett. Their work has helped us to understand the function of writing in the intellectual development of the individual student. But Britton, Emig, and Moffett have done most of their work on the elementary and secondary level. We are only now beginning to realize that new American theoretical work in writing across the curriculum is needed, work which addresses concerns particular to American, college-level writing instruction. This new theoretical work is beginning to take shape around the question of whether all students should be required to learn academic discourse. Mina Shaughnessy has diagnosed basic writers' fundamental problem as ignorance of academic discourse conventions.

In exploring this question, theorists are reexamining the importance of expressive writing in writing-across-the-curriculum programs. Expressive writing plays a part in most programs. It can be regarded as one important stage in a writing process which will issue eventually in finished pieces of academic writing. But C. H. Knoblauch and Lil Brannon have argued that keeping up a student-teacher dialogue through expressive writing should be the main goal of writing across the curriculum, because it is through such dialogue that inquiry methods are learned. They see the teaching of academic discourse as drill in "formal shells," leading to nothing more than "grammar across the curriculum." They fear that students whose home languages are at a relatively greater remove from academic discourse will be unduly penalized by a policy which requires all students to master academic discourse. These students will spend so much time on superficial aspects of academic discourse, such as Standard English usage, that they will have little time left for substantive learning.

Other theorists argue that learning and discourse conventions cannot be separated in the academy. Students must be able eventually to use academic discourse if they are to master the full complexities of academic thinking. The notion of dialogue or conversation as a mode of learning here is redefined to mean not a face-to-face encounter, but a sustained communal enterprise. Charles Bazerman has explained that learning how to enter this ongoing conversation means learning how the academic community talks and writes about what it does. As Elaine Maimon has argued, this is a matter of "Talking to Strangers" for students unfamiliar with the academic discourse community. But if students are not required to learn this discourse, they risk not participating fully in college intellectual life. To help them, we need more study of how this community develops and transmits its discourse conventions, a study in which scholars trained in literary criticism may be particularly well suited to engage (Maimon, "Maps and Genres").

Such study would help to return rhetoric to its eminent place in the curriculum. James Raymond has argued that rhetoric is the least reductive, most interdisciplinary methodology in the liberal arts. Taking a similar position, James Kinneavy has observed that increased attention to rhetoric helps faculty in all disciplines to communicate better with each other about the intellectual problems upon which they are working. They are thus better prepared to train their students not only to develop complex arguments within the disciplines but also to explain their areas of expertise cogently to a general audience. Kinneavy hopes that the spread of writing-across-the-curriculum programs will eventually revivify informed public discourse in our democracy, since citizens will be better able to sift evidence and evaluate debates on complex issues.

The study of "rhetoric across the curriculum," to coin a phrase, is becoming the study of how the academic community constitutes and legitimates its knowledge through its discourse. We are learning, as Kenneth Bruffee has shown, that knowledge is a "social entity," always collaboratively produced. From such study, too, we learn how other communities similarly constitute themselves in language. Because this is becoming the focus of rhetoric, literary critics have recently been studying it together with composition specialists. In one such fruitful exchange (Horner), eminent scholars agree that the establishment of English departments was justified by a false distinction between literary discourse and discourse that conveys information. This distinction leads to a separation between reading instruction, which focuses upon interpreting literary texts, and writing instruction, which focuses upon producing expository texts. Because this separation not only devalues composition studies but also impoverishes literary theory, it is now ending. A new kind of English department is emerging, united under a rhetorical paradigm, and well suited to study all kinds of discourse, not just fiction and poetry, and to foster rhetoric across the curriculum.

Bibliography

Applebee, Arthur N. "Writing across the Curriculum: The London Projects." *English Journal* 66 (1977): 81–85.

———. *Writing in the Secondary School: English and the Content Areas.* Urbana NCTE, 1981. Eighty-two percent of teachers surveyed agree that writing instruction is the responsibility of all faculty. But only 3 percent of lesson time is spent on writing of paragraph length or more. Very little attention is given to the writing process. Virtually all writing is informational (transactional), for an audience of teacher-as-examiner.

Barnes, Douglas, James Britton, and Harold Rosen *Language, the Learner, and the School.* Harmondsworth: Penguin, 1969.

Bazerman, Charles "A Relationship between Reading and Writing: The Conversation Model." *College English* 41 (1980): 656–61.

Behrens, Laurence "Meditations, Reminiscences, Polemics: Composition Readers and the Service Course." *College English* 41 (1980): 561–70. Surveying composition readers, Behrens finds that almost all selections are meditations, reminiscences, or polemics. Most of the writing that students do in other courses, however, seeks to convey information, and students are better at conveying information than they are at writing meditations, reminiscences, and polemics. A new kind of reader is needed to "serve" students by teaching the kinds of writing they do in other courses.

Bergman, Charles A. "An Inclusive Literacy: U.S. Schools Are Teaching and Writing in All the Subject Disciplines." *AAHE Bulletin* (Dec 1982): 3–5. Bergman argues for writing across the curriculum as a way of demystifying the conventions of academic discourse, and describes the "conversation experience" of faculty at his university after a workshop with Kenneth Bruffee in which they learned to see themselves as writers.

———. "Writing across the Curriculum: An Annotated Bibliography." *AAHE Bulletin* (1983–84): 33–38. Bergman selects forty-one entries, citing some important theoretical works and a number of articles that describe writing-across-the-curriculum programs at specific schools.

Bizzell, Patricia. "College Composition: Initiation into the Academic Discourse Community." *Curriculum Inquiry* 12 (1982): 191–207. Bizzell argues that students' unequal distance from school discourse is a function of social class, that access to academic discourse is a prerequisite for social power, and that linguistically disenfranchised students can be helped by a writing-across-the-curriculum approach that seeks to demystify the conventions of academic discourse.

Bizzell, Patricia, and Bruce Herzberg. "Writing-across-the-Curriculum Textbooks: A Bibliographic Essay." *Rhetoric Review* 3 (Jan. 1985): 202–17.

Britton, James. *Language and Learning*. Harmondsworth: Penguin, 1970. Britton develops the theory that we construct our understanding of the world through language, an individual task shaped by social interaction.

Britton, James, et al. *The Development of Writing Abilities* (11–18). London: Macmillan Education, 1975; Urbana: NCTE, 1977.

Bruffee, Kenneth. "The Structure of Knowledge and the Future of Liberal Education." *Liberal Education* 67 (1981): 177–86. We have assumed that knowledge is determined by external reality and should be attained by individual effort in a hierarchical educational system. But the work of Einstein, Heisenberg, and Godel suggests that knowledge is created and promulgated through social activity. Hence education should be restructured for collaborative work, as in peer-tutoring workshops and writing-across-the-curriculum programs.

Brunetti, Gerald J. "The Bullock Report: Some Implications for American Teachers and Parents." *English Journal* 67 (1978): 58–64.

Bullock Commission. *A Language for Life*. London: HMSO, 1975.

Donlan, Dan. "Teaching Writing in the Content Areas: Eleven Hypotheses from a Teacher Survey." *Research in the Teaching of English* 8 (1974): 250–62.

Dunn, Robert F. "A Response to Two Views." *AAHE Bulletin* (Dec. 1982): 7–8.

Eblen, Charlene. "Writing-across-the-Curriculum: A Survey of a University Faculty's Views and Classroom Practices." *Research in the Teaching of English* 17 (1983): 343–48.

Emig, Janet. *The Composing Processes of Twelfth Graders*. Urbana: NCTE, 1971.

———. "Writing as a Mode of Learning." *College Composition and Communication* 28 (1977): 122–28. Rpt. in *The Writing Teacher's Sourcebook*. Ed. Gary Tate and E. P. J. Corbett. New York: Oxford UP, 1981. 69–78.

Freisinger, Randall R. "Cross-Disciplinary Writing Workshops: Theory and Practice." *College English* 42 (1980): 154+. Following Britton, Freisinger strongly defends the use of expressive writing in all disciplines, in spite of faculty resistance to this notion. He uses Piaget to argue that the absence of expressive writing retards cognitive development in college-age students.

Fulwiler, Toby. "Journals across the Disciplines." *English Journal* 69 (1980): 14–19. Fulwiler cites Britton and Emig on the need for expressive writing across the curriculum, and argues that journals have served this end well. He describes both the "academic journal," which focuses on course content, and the "personal journal," which focuses on ethical responses to course content.

———. "Showing, Not Telling, at a Writing Workshop." *College English* 43 (1981): 55–63. A good account of Fulwiler's methods in faculty workshops. He details five strategies and recommends conducting the workshop like a retreat.

Fulwiler, Toby, and Art Young, ed. *Language Connections: Writing and Reading across the Curriculum.* Urbana: NCTE, 1982. Twelve essays from the Michigan Tech writing-across-the-curriculum program, written by professors of literature, rhetoric, and reading. Essays address the interdisciplinary teaching of poetic, expressive, and transactional writing. The book includes three essays on reading, two on peer critiquing, and a selected bibliography.

Griffin, C. Williams, ed. *Teaching Writing in All Disciplines.* San Francisco: Jossey-Bass, 1982. Ten essays on writing-across-the-curriculum theory and practice, including John C. Bean, Dean Drenk, and F. D. Lee, "Microtheme Strategies for Developing Cognitive Skills"; Toby Fulwiler, "Writing: An Act of Cognition"; Elaine Maimon, "Writing across the Curriculum: Past, Present, and Future"; Chris Thaiss, "The Virginia Consortium of Faculty Writing Programs: A Variety of Practices"; Barbara Fassler Walvoord and Hoke L. Smith, "Coaching the Process of Writing."

Hamilton, David. "Interdisciplinary Writing." *College English* 41 (1980): 780+. Hamilton describes the Iowa Institute on Writing for writing program administrators, which developed an interdisciplinary freshman composition course using "serious parodies" of discourse modes of various disciplines, with the aim of teaching transferable processes of conceptualization. The article also analyzes the limitations of other interdisciplinary writing courses, such as those that ask students to write about their areas of expertise for a lay audience.

Herrington, Anne J. "Writing to Learn: Writing across the Disciplines." *College English* 43 (1981): 379–87. Following a defense of writing across the curriculum that draws on the work of Emig and Lee Odell, Herrington describes her workshops to help faculty design writing-intensive courses in their own disciplines. She describes good assignments in economics, sociology, and psychology.

Horner, Winifred, ed. *Composition and Literature: Bridging the Gap.* Chicago: U of Chicago P, 1983. Twelve essays by eminent literary critics and composition specialists, including Wayne Booth, E. P. J. Corbett, E. D. Hirsch, Jr., Richard Lanham, Elaine Maimon, and J. Hillis Miller.

Kinneavy, James L. "Writing across the Curriculum" *ADE Bulletin* 76 (1983): 14–21 Rpt. in *Profession 83.* Ed. Richard Brod and Phyllis Franklin. New York: MLA, 1983: 13–20.

Knoblauch, C. H., and Lil Brannon. "Writing as Learning through the Curriculum." *College English* 45 (1983): 465–74.

Maimon, Elaine. "Cinderella to Hercules: Demythologizing Writing across the Curriculum." *Journal of Basic Writing* 2 (1980): 3–11. Maimon describes and debunks several "myths" that obstruct writing-across-the-curriculum programs, such as the Myth of the Simple Rules, which leads misguided college deans to think that writing across the curriculum is simply a matter of enforcing a few grammar guidelines; the Myth of Cinderella, which casts writing teachers in a menial role; the Myth of Hercules, which envisions an effective program being launched by the writing program administrator alone; and more. This issue of *JBW* includes seven other essays on writing across the curriculum.

———."Maps and Genres" *Composition and Literature: Bridging the Gap.* Ed. Winifred Horner. Chicago: U of Chicago P, 1983: 110–25.

————."Talking to Strangers." *College Composition and Communication* 30 (1979): 364–69.

————."Writing in All the Arts and Sciences: Getting Started and Gaining Momentum." *Writing Program Administration* 4 (1981): 9–13. Maimon discusses administrative problems of launching writing-across-the-curriculum programs; how to deal with resistance within the English department; general curriculum guidelines. This issue of *WPA* also includes Toby Fulwiler, "Writing across the Curriculum at Michigan Tech," an account of his successful faculty seminars there; and a response to both Fulwiler and Maimon by Ann Raimes.

————. *Instructor's Manual: Writing in the Arts and Sciences.* Cambridge Winthrop, 1981. Maimon, Elaine P., and Gerald L. Belcher, Gail W. Hearn, Barbara F. Nodine, and Finbarr W. O'Connor. *Writing in the Arts and Sciences.* Cambridge: Winthrop, 1981.

Martin, Nancy, et al. *Writing and Learning across the Curriculum* 11–16. London: Ward Lock, 1976.

Moffett, James. *Active Voice: A Writing Program across the Curriculum.* Upper Montclair: Boynton/ Cook, 1981.

————. *Teaching the Universe of Discourse.* Boston: Houghton, 1969

Odell, Lee "The Process of Writing and the Process of Learning." *College Composition and Communication* 31 (1980): 42–50. In faculty writing workshops, Odell discovered that writing in different disciplines requires a wide variety of conceptual activities; the inability to perform them is the chief cause of bad student writing. Workshops should not, therefore, seek to persuade faculty to teach any one heuristic method. Elements from a few powerful heuristics, however, can be combined to provide an invention method useful across the disciplines.

Peters, Laurence. "Writing across the Curriculum: Across the U.S." Writing to *Learn: Essays and Reflections by College Teachers across the Curriculum.* Ed. Christopher Thaiss. Fairfax: George Mason U Faculty Writing Program, 1982. 4–19.

Raimes, Ann. "Writing and Learning across the Curriculum: The Experience of a Faculty Seminar." *College English* 41 (1980): 797–801. To attend a seminar led by Raimes and Charles Persky, faculty in several disciplines received released time during the semester so that they could work on writing assignments and use student writing from current courses as the principal "text." Discussions focused on assignment design and essay evaluation.

Raymond, James C. "Rhetoric: The Methodology of the Humanities." *College English* 44 (1982): 778–83.

Rose, Mike. "Remedial Writing Courses: A Critique and a Proposal." *College English* 45 (1983): 109–28. Rose argues against the focus on personal writing common to many remedial composition programs, and for an interdisciplinary course that introduces developmental students immediately to college-level reading, writing, and thinking tasks.

————. "When Faculty Talk about Writing." *College English* 41 (1979) 272–79. A cross-disciplinary group of faculty, teaching assistants, and student counselors met to discuss their perceptions of student writing problems and agreed on some action — give professional recognition for composition teaching and research; teach academic discourse in freshman composition; and move university-wide standards for evaluating writing beyond a narrow focus on grammar.

Rosen, Lois. "An Interview with James Britton, Tony Burgess, and Harold Rosen. Closeup: The Teaching of Writing in Great Britain." *English Journal* 67 (1978): 50–58.

Shafer, Robert E. "A British Proposal for Improving Literacy." *Educational Forum* 46 (1981): 81–96 Shafer summarizes work of Britton and his colleagues, giving particular attention to theory. He discusses Britton's spectator/participant distinction; the work of Barnes and Rosen on the chasm between academic discourse and the students' own language; the influence of Sapir, Kelly, and Vygotsky; and the relation between speaking and writing.

Shaughnessy, Mina. "Some Needed Research on Writing." *College Composition and Communication* 28 (1977): 317–21. Shaughnessy argues that basic writers are those "unskilled in the rituals and ways of winning arguments in academe." To help them, we need a taxonomy of academic discourse conventions.

Thaiss, Christopher, ed. *Writing to Learn: Essays and Reflections by College Teachers across the Curriculum.* Fairfax: George Mason U Faculty Writing Program, 1982. Sixteen essays by professors of accounting, education, English, finance, mathematics, nursing, physical education, and psychology. They argue for the value of writing across the curriculum while describing classroom ideas that have worked well.

Tighe, M. A, and S. M. Koziol, Jr. "Practices in the Teaching of Writing by Teachers of English, Social Studies, and Science." *English Education* 4 (1982): 76–85.

Van Nostrand, A. D. "Writing and the Generation of Knowledge." *Social Education* 43 (1979): 178–80. This article heads a special section, "Writing to Learn in Social Studies," edited by Barry K. Beyer and Anita Brostoff, and aimed at secondary-level teachers.

Walvoord, Barbara E. Fassler. *Helping Students Write Well: A Guide for Teachers in All Disciplines.* New York: MLA, 1982. A good book for faculty who have not yet thought about how they teach writing. Walvoord concentrates on ways to respond effectively to student writing above the developmental level. Many specific examples of assignments and student papers.

Writing across the Curriculum Project. *From Information to Understanding: What Children Do with New Ideas.* London: Ward Lock, 1973; Upper Montclair: Boynton/Cook, 1983.

———. *Why Write?* London: Ward Lock, 1973; Upper Montclair Boynton/Cook, 1983. Children should be encouraged to write about knowledge important to them, rather than forced to learn particular essay forms.

———. *From Talking to Writing.* London: Ward Lock, 1973; Upper Montclair: Boynton/Cook, 1983. This pamphlet argues for expressive talk, but also argues that some kinds of thinking can only be accomplished in writing, because writing facilitates reflection and reformulation. Writing assignments should call on these unique powers rather than simply asking for a report on what has been learned.

———. *Writing in Science: Papers from a Seminar with Science Teachers.* London: Ward Lock, 1973.

———. *Keeping Options Open: Writing in the Humanities.* London: Ward Lock, 1973; Upper Montclair: Boynton/Cook, 1983.

FURTHER RESOURCES IN WRITING ACROSS THE CURRICULUM

Glenn B. Blalock

The following references were selected to complement Bizzell and Herzberg's bibliography and to suggest how research and study in writing across the curriculum has expanded and developed in recent years. These citations are grouped under five general headings: Bibliographies; Theoretical Premises; Overviews, Definitions, Different Approaches; Practical Applications, Writing in the Disciplines, Reports on Research; and Establishing and Maintaining a WAC Program.

Bibliographies

ERIC. Available on CD-ROM, the ERIC system collects an extensive array of materials on writing across the curriculum (and writing in the content areas).

Longman Bibliography of Composition and Rhetoric. New York: Longman, 1984–86. Continued yearly from 1987 by the *College Composition and Communication Bibliography of Composition and Rhetoric.* Though the volumes through 1990 do not include a category labeled "writing across the curriculum," entries relating to WAC appear primarily under the subheading "communication in other courses." Entries are annotated.

Griffin, C. W. "Bibliography." *Programs That Work: Models and Methods for Writing across the Curriculum.* Ed. Toby Fulwiler and Art Young. Portsmouth: Boynton/Cook, 1990. 295–319. Griffin provides an extensive annotated bibliography.

Theoretical Premises

Although none of the following articles specifically addresses writing across the curriculum, each discusses the theoretical premises that inform social views of writing, views that have become more central to WAC theories since Bizzell and Herzberg composed their essay.

Bartholomae, David. "Inventing the University." *When a Writer Can't Write: Studies in Writer's Block and Other Composing Problems.* Ed. Mike Rose. New York: Guilford, 1985. 143–65. [See page 14 of *Background Readings* for an excerpt from this work.]

Bizzell, Patricia. "Cognition, Convention, and Certainty: What We Need to Know about Writing." *Pre/Text* 3 (1982): 213–43.

Bizzell argues for a different emphasis in composition instruction, one that resists then prevailing cognitivist views of writing.

Bizzell, Patricia. "What Happens When Basic Writers Come to College?" *College Composition and Communication* 37 (1986): 294–301.

Bizzell argues that the difficulties of basic writers stem from "the initial distance between their worldviews and the academic worldview, and perhaps also from the resistance to changing their own worldviews that is caused by this very distance."

Bruffee, Kenneth A. "Collaborative Learning and the 'Conversation of Mankind.'" *College English* 46 (1984): 635–52.

Bruffee traces the history of the collaborative learning movement and says that students should come to understand that intellectual pursuit is a social activity.

———. "Social Construction, Language, and the Authority of Knowledge: A Bibliographical Essay." *College English* 48 (1986): 773–89.

In addition to providing a bibliographical survey, Bruffee explains the fundamental premises of social construction and explores how those premises have informed recent educational initiatives, including writing across the curriculum.

Cooper, Marilyn. "The Ecology of Writing." *College English* 48 (1986): 364–75.

Cooper argues that we should see writing as "one of the activities by which we locate ourselves in the enmeshed systems that make up the social world."

Elbow, Peter. "Reflections on Academic Discourse: How It Relates to Freshmen and Colleagues." *College English* 53 (1991): 135–55.

Elbow challenges the notion of a distinct and homogeneous academic discourse and contends that "we need nonacademic discourse . . . for the sake of helping students produce good academic discourse — academic language that reflects sound understanding of what they are studying in disciplinary courses."

Harris, Joseph. "The Idea of Community in the Study of Writing." *College Composition and Communication* 40 (1989): 11–22.

Instead of seeing communities in terms of insiders and outsiders, Harris argues for an understanding of community as a more dynamic entity, one not necessarily organic or unified.

Reither, James A. "Writing and Knowing: Toward Redefining the Writing Process." *College English* 47 (1985): 620–28.

Reither challenges the view of the writing process as linear and as simply goal-oriented or problem solving.

Reither, James A., and Douglas Vipond. "Writing as Collaboration." *College English* 51 (1989): 855–67.

The authors propose that, instead of using the term "social" to describe writing and knowing, instructors describe these activities as "collaborative."

Overviews, Definitions, Different Approaches

The following articles provide overviews of the WAC movement, present definitions of WAC and its various manifestations, and discuss various approaches to WAC.

Barr, Mary A., and Mary K. Healy. "School and University Articulation: Different Contexts for Writing across the Curriculum." *Strengthening Programs for Writing across the Curriculum.* Ed. Susan McLeod. San Francisco: Jossey-Bass, 1988. 43–53.

Explores how WAC programs have developed differently in secondary schools and in colleges and universities.

Bergman, Charles A. "Writing across the Curriculum: Students as Scholars, Scholars as Students." *Journal of Advanced Composition* 5 (1984): 79–86.

Bergman argues that faculty members do not necessarily recognize explicit conventions of academic writing any more readily than do students. He calls for more attention to teaching the various forms of academic writing.

Colomb, Gregory G. "Where Should Students Start Writing in the Disciplines?" Paper presented at the 39th Annual Meeting of the Conference on College Composition and Communication, St. Louis, Mar. 1989. ERIC ED 297 341.

Colomb holds that by thinking of students as outsiders trying to join disciplinary communities, we can see that they need to learn the epistemological and formal conventions of those communities in order to participate in them. Colomb argues that writing instruction should take place in the disciplines.

Comprone, Joseph J. "Writing across the Disciplines: Where Do We Go from Here?" Paper presented at the 42nd Annual Meeting of the Conference on College Composition and Communication, Boston, 21-23, Mar. 1991. ERIC ED 331 053.

Comprone explores the connections between literacy theory and WAC practice.

Fulwiler, Toby, and Art Young. *Writing across the Disciplines: Research into Practice.* Upper Montclair: Boynton, 1986.

This collection includes essays that explain WAC, show how to establish a WAC program, present specific techniques for including writing in a variety of courses, and discuss problems and possibilities of WAC.

Goodkin, Vera, and Robert P. Parker. *The Consequences of Writing: Enhancing Learning in the Disciplines.* Upper Montclair: Boynton/Cook, 1987.

This book explores the principles and practices of writing to learn in the content areas. In addition to examining writing and the construction of knowledge and exploring the connections between language and thinking, the book offers examples of using writing in five different content area courses.

Graham, Joan. "What Works: The Problems and Rewards of Cross-Curriculum Writing Programs." *Current Issues in Higher Education* (1983–84): 16–26.

Graham explores alternative WAC approaches, discusses faculty responsibilities, and describes training workshops to help prepare faculty for WAC courses.

Hedley, Jane, and Jo Ellen Parker. "Writing across the Curriculum: The Vantage of the Liberal Arts." *ADE Bulletin* 98 (Spring 1991): 22–28.

The authors challenge the premises of WAC, arguing that a common academic discourse does exist and that it is grounded in the liberal arts.

Jones, Robert, and Joseph J. Comprone. "Where Do We Go Next in Writing across the Curriculum?" *College Composition and Communication* 44 (1993): 59–68.

The authors identify several problems with current WAC programs, offer solutions, establish four goals for WAC efforts, and illustrate their proposals with examples of how their suggestions have worked at their university.

Kuriloff, Peshe C. "Writing across the Curriculum and the Future of Freshman English: A Dialogue between Literature and Composition." *ADE Bulletin* 98 (Spring 1991): 34–39.

In an imaginary dialogue between the two "residents" of English departments — literature proponents and composition proponents — Kuriloff makes the point that both should support a broader approach to writing instruction.

Mahala, Daniel. "Writing Utopias: Writing across the Curriculum and the Promise of Reform." *College English* 53 (1991): 773-89.

Pointing out that current WAC initiatives are in part based on British programs that were intended as institutional critiques, Mahala argues that U.S. manifestations of WAC have retreated from that critical stance and questions the current goals of WAC programs.

McLeod, Susan H. "Writing across the Curriculum: The Second Stage and Beyond." *College Composition and Communication* 40 (1989): 337–43.

McLeod offers an overview of the WAC movement, discussing why programs have survived and changed over the years. She also speculates about the future of WAC initiatives.

McLeod, Susan, ed. *Strengthening Programs for Writing across the Curriculum.* San Francisco: Jossey-Bass, 1988.

This collection of essays discusses establishing and maintaining new WAC programs, evaluating existing programs, conducting research, and preparing for future challenges facing WAC.

McLeod, Susan. "Defining Writing across the Curriculum." *Writing Program Administration* 11 (Fall 1987): 19–24.

McLeod defines WAC according to its philosophical bases — cognitive or rhetorical. She also describes the several different institutional manifestations of WAC.

Ronald, Kate. "On the Outside Looking In: Students' Analyses of Professional Discourse Communities." *Rhetoric Review* 7.1 (1988): 130–49.

Ronald describes her students' attempts to study professional discourse by using rhetorical analysis. She questions whether analyzing discourse conventions can help students become novice participants in a community, and she explores how analyses of this sort contribute to WAC efforts generally.

Russell, David R. *Writing in the Academic Disciplines, 1870–1990: A Curricular History.* Carbondale: Southern Illinois UP, 1991.

Russell explores a wide range of academic writing over the years, examining the effects of specialization on writing instruction. He concludes with a history of the WAC movement, placing the movement within the extensive historical context he has uncovered.

Walker, Anne. "Writing-across-the-curriculum: The second decade." *English Quarterly* 21 (1988): 93–103.

Walker presents the rationale for and the theoretical basis of WAC, offers evidence that WAC programs are effective, discusses opposition to WAC efforts, and examines research that attempts to demonstrate the efficacy of WAC.

Ward, Jay A. "WAC Reconsidered: Issues for the 90s." Paper presented at the 42nd Annual Meeting of the Conference on College Composition and Communication, Boston, 21–23, Mar. 1991. ERIC ED 333 456.

Most content area instructors (and many composition instructors) do not share a view of writing that is compatible with contemporary composition theory. If WAC programs are to be successful, Ward argues, composition instructors must attempt to approach writing in ways that include the diverse discourse communities of the academy.

Williamson, Michael W. "Basic Writers Writing across the Disciplines I: An Historical and Theoretical Introduction." *Research and Teaching in Developmental Education* 4 (Fall 1987): 57–70.

Williamson offers a historical survey of WAC programs and explores the theoretical premises of two manifestations of WAC: writing to learn and learning to write in a discipline.

———. "Basic Writers Writing across the Curriculum II: The Structure of Programs, Implications for Basic Writers, and Strategies for Teaching." *Research and Teaching in Developmental Education* 4 (Spring 1988): 72–88.

Williamson describes different manifestations of WAC, explores WAC programs for basic writers, and discusses some practical strategies for implementing WAC in basic writing courses.

Practical Applications, Writing in the Disciplines, Reports on Research

The following articles discuss specific applications of WAC, both in general writing courses and in various content area courses. Many of these articles also report on various kinds of research done in support of WAC efforts.

Anderson, Worth, et al. "Cross-Curricular Underlife: A Collaborative Report on Ways with Academic Words." *College Composition and Communication* 41 (1990): 11–36.

This article reports on and examines the experiences of five students who completed a standard first-year writing course taught by Susan Miller at the University of Utah. The students' reports suggest that their introductory writing course was not necessarily an effective introduction to the kinds of writing they had to do in other academic courses.

Bridgeman, Brent, and Sybil B. Carlson. "Survey of Academic Writing Tasks." *Written Communication* 1.2 (1984): 247–80.

The authors surveyed 190 departments in thirty-four universities to determine what kinds of writing were required and what kinds of topics were preferred.

Connolly, Paul, and Teresa Vilardi, eds. *Writing to Learn Mathematics and Science.* New York: Teachers College Press, 1989.

This book includes twenty-three chapters focusing on pedagogical issues of using ordinary language to teach math and science. Topics include writing as problem solving, classroom applications, and learning in context.

Diaz, Diana M. "Language across the Curriculum and ESL Students: Composition, Research and 'Sheltered Courses.'" Paper presented at the Annual Meeting of the National Conference of Teachers of English, Baltimore, Nov. 1989. ERIC ED 326 057.

Diaz argues that incorporating the principles of WAC into ESL courses would make those courses more effective at helping ESL students become language "acquirers" and participants in several different academic discourse communities.

Faigley, Lester, and Kristine Hansen. "Learning to Write in the Social Sciences." *College Composition and Communication* 36 (1985): 140–49.

Faigley and Hansen examine the problems that composition teachers and students have with content area assignments. The authors include results from observations of and interviews with participants in social science classes.

Gopen, George D., and David A. Smith. "What's an Assignment Like You Doing in a Course like This?: Writing to Learn Mathematics." *College Mathematics Journal* 21.1 (1990): 2–19.

The authors describe an experimental mathematics course that incorporated regular writing assignments. They discuss common problems that students encountered and discuss several procedures used to help students.

Gratz, Ronald K. "Improving Lab Report Quality by Model Analysis, Peer Review, and Revision." *Journal of College Science Teaching* 19.5 (1990): 292–95.

Gratz describes his methods for teaching lab report writing to undergraduates and discusses results of using these methods.

Gray, Donald J. "Writing across the College Curriculum." *Phi Delta Kappan* (June 1988): 729–33.

Exploring how teachers might integrate WAC principles in their courses, Gray discusses several different kinds of writing assignments and examines why some are more effective than others. Gray offers an excellent overview of the goals of programs that argue for more writing in the disciplines.

Hirsch, Linda. "Are Principles of Writing across the Curriculum Applicable to ESL Students in Content Courses? Research Findings." Paper presented at the Annual Meeting of the National Conference of Teachers of English, Baltimore, Nov. 1989. ERIC ED319 264.

Hirsch describes two studies that suggest that WAC initiatives help ESL students in content area courses.

Joliffe, David A., ed. *Advances in Writing Research, Volume Two: Writing in Academic Disciplines.* Norwood, NJ: Ablex, 1988.

This book includes research articles about writing processes and written texts in different disciplines.

Mallonee, Barbara C., and John R. Breihan. "Responding to Students' Drafts: Interdisciplinary Consensus." *College Composition and Communication* 36 (1985): 213–31.

In successful WAC programs, the authors argue, teachers from across the disciplines agree on how to respond to student writing. They identify four areas in which teachers should try to reach consensus and include examples of response checklists that they have used.

McCarthy, Lucille Parkinson. "A Stranger in Strange Lands: A College Student Writing across the Curriculum." *Research in the Teaching of English* 21 (1987): 233–65.

For two years, McCarthy studied one college student's attempts to write effectively in different disciplines. She found that the degree of the student's success was affected as much by the social, classroom contexts for writing as by the requirements of assignments.

Moss, Andrew, and Carol Holder. *Improving Student Writing: A Guidebook for Faculty in All Disciplines.* Pomona: California State UP, 1988.

This guide offers practical ideas for constructing effective assignments, helping students through the writing process, and evaluating writing.

Moynihan, Mary Minard. "Writing in Sociology Classes: Informal Assignments." *Teaching Sociology* 17 (1989): 346–50.

Moynihan describes three writing-to-learn assignments: a diary entry, a marriage contract, and a letter to a friend.

Powell, Alfred. "A Chemist's View of Writing, Reading, and Thinking across the Curriculum." *College Composition and Communication* 36 (1985): 414–18.

Arguing that WAC initiatives will work in the natural sciences, Powell describes two different kinds of assignments he uses.

Price, J. J. "Learning Mathematics through Writing: Some Guidelines." *College Mathematics Journal* 20.5 (1989): 393–401.

Price describes written homework used in a math course and gives examples of homework problems.

Shamoon, Linda K., and Robert A. Schwegler. "Sociologists Reading Student Texts: Expectations and Perceptions." *The Writing Instructor* 7 (1988): 71–81.

The authors examine the ways sociologists perceive and evaluate student writing and, based on their findings, suggest that writing teachers think of how academic readers respond to student texts as one way to characterize disciplinary discourse communities.

Sills, Caryl K. "Paired Composition Courses: `Everything Relates.'" *College Teaching* 39.2 (Spring 1991): 61–64.

Sills describes a link between a first-year composition course and an introductory sociology course.

Tchudi, Stephen N. *Teaching Writing in the Content Areas: College Level.* West Haven: NEA Professional Library, 1986.

This book includes chapters on formal and informal writing assignments as well as projects in various content areas.

Thall, Edwin, and Gary Bays. "Utilizing Ungraded Writing in the Chemistry Classroom." *Journal of Chemical Education* 66.8 (1989): 662–63.

The authors describe assignments they use to improve communication skills in a first-year course for chemistry majors.

Walvoord, Barbara, and Lucille McCarthy. *Thinking and Writing in College: A Naturalistic Study of Students in Four Disciplines.* Urbana: NCTE, 1990.

This book describes a seven-year study in which writing specialists worked with professors in business, history, psychology, and biology. The study documents the effectiveness of using writing to help students become members of disciplinary communities.

Wilkinson, A. M. "A Freshman Writing Course in Parallel with a Science Course." *College Composition and Communication* 36 (1985): 160–65.

Wilkinson describes a writing course with assignments linked to a biology course.

Establishing and Maintaining a WAC Program

The following articles discuss the problems that confront WAC programs, and many suggest practical solutions.

Cornell, Cynthia, and David J. Klooster. "Writing across the Curriculum: Transforming the Academy?" *Writing Program Administration* 14 (Fall–Winter 1990): 7–16.

Recognizing that WAC challenges institutional structures and practices, the authors discuss several reasons why WAC programs struggle to survive.

Fulwiler, Toby, and Art Young, eds. *Programs That Work: Models and Methods for Writing across the Curriculum.* Portsmouth, NH: Boynton/Cook, 1990.

This book includes essays on numerous successful WAC programs and includes an extensive annotated bibliography assembled by C. W. Griffin.

Sipple, Jo Ann M. "A Planning Process for Building Writing across the Curriculum Programs to Last." *Journal of Higher Education* 60 (1989): 444–57.

Sipple discusses management and political issues associated with WAC programs.

Smith, Louise Z. "Opinion: Why English Departments Should 'House' Writing Across the Curriculum." And Blair, Catherine Pastore. "Opinion: Only One of the Voices: Dialogic Writing across the Curriculum." *College English* 50 (1988): 390–95; 383–89.

Smith and Blair offer opposing views on who should control WAC efforts, discussing in the process the fundamental premises of WAC.

Stout, Barbara R., and Joyce N. Magnotto. "Writing across the Curriculum at Community Colleges." *Strengthening Programs for Writing across the Curriculum.* Ed. Susan McLeod. San Francisco: Jossey-Bass, 1988. 21–30.

The authors survey the wide range of WAC programs in community colleges and discuss how institutions have adapted WAC to meet the needs of their students and faculty.

Strenski, Ellen. "Writing across the Curriculum at Research Universities." *Strengthening Programs for Writing across the Curriculum.* Ed. Susan McLeod. San Francisco: Jossey-Bass, 1988. 31–42.

Strenski describes several apparent roadblocks to successful WAC programs at research universities, arguing that in spite of potential barriers, WAC can be successful in these institutions.

White, Edward M. "Shallow Roots or Taproots for Writing across the Curriculum?" *ADE Bulletin* 98 (Spring 1991): 29–33.

Using his own university as an example, White discusses problems with establishing ongoing WAC programs and offers several suggestions for ensuring their survival.

THE QUIET AND INSISTENT REVOLUTION: WRITING ACROSS THE CURRICULUM

Toby Fulwiler

[From The Politics of Writing Instruction: Postsecondary. Ed. Richard Bullock and John Trimbur. Portsmouth, NH: Boynton/Heinemann, 1991. 179–87.]

Toby Fulwiler, director of writing at the University of Vermont, edited The Journal Book (1987) and coedited Programs That Work: Models and Methods for Writing Across the Curriculum (1990) and A Community of Voices (1992). His articles have appeared in the Journal of Education, among other publications. The following selection grew out of Fulwiler's observations of the politics of teaching writing.

Contending that writing across the curriculum in the fullest sense is an educational reform movement, Fulwiler discusses three necessary changes caused by WAC programs: "1) a faculty's relationship to students, 2) its relationship with one another, and 3) its relationship to the whole institution in which it operates." Fulwiler encourages teachers and administrators to understand the full potential of WAC programs.

Movements become political to the extent that they ask institutions to make choices about goals, governance, methods, and the allocation of resources. What will have to change and why? Who will gain, who lose? How much will it cost? What will be the long-term effect? And how will we know it works? The movement identified as Writing Across the Curriculum (WAC) has become political, maybe even quietly revolutionary, as it asks educational institutions these questions.

In most cases, writing-across-the-curriculum programs did not start with political intentions. In the mid-1970s, at small schools and large, public as well as private, they were instituted to improve the general writing and learning abilities of college students. To do this, most programs focused on the primary movers and shakers of the academic curriculum, the college professors themselves, asking them to include more writing in all classes in all disciplines. The majority of academic courses, it was reasoned, already included a substantial set of required readings; few, however, included an equally substantial set of writing assignments.

However, asking historians, chemists, and engineers to help students improve their writing and learning ability has proved to he no simple matter. To effect real change in abilities as basic as writing and learning, these programs have asked, tacitly in most cases, that instructors alter as well their perceptions of other dimensions of the academic community: for example, 1) the role of language in learning, 2) their relationship to students in the classroom, 3) their interactions with colleagues in other disciplines, and 4) the nature of the academic institution itself. Intentionally or not, Writing Across the Curriculum has become an educational reform movement that asks hard, politically charged questions of the whole academic curriculum. This essay examines the nature of these political questions.

Premises

At first glance, the premises that underlie writing-across-the-curriculum programs seem more practical and pedagogical than political. That is, they sound like good, solid, reasonable, ideologically neutral ideas with some chance of helping teachers teach better and students learn better, while allowing educational institutions to conduct business as usual. John Dewey, for example, would surely approve of them all. But so would Paulo Freire. I might formulate these premises as follows:

1. Learners construct knowledge for themselves. Learning is not something that happens *to* learners, but something they make happen to and for themselves with the help of others. So, the more students write to themselves and talk with one another about what they are trying to learn, the more they own and take responsibility for their own education. And the less, by implication, they depend on the teacher to tell them what to think and know.

2. Learners learn best when they pose and solve meaningful problems for themselves. The best model for active, engaged learning probably comes

from the students' world (home, street, and workplace), where real, every-day problems need to be solved, but where nobody has an instructor's manual or answer key. In other words, students will become more motivated, knowledgeable, skillful, and thoughtful when colleges and universities invite them "inside" to work on the real issues of the day. And, of course, to pose and solve such problems, students will necessarily use various modes of language.

3. Language is an instrument for learning. Learners read, write, talk, and listen to comprehend, understand, create, imagine, ask and answer questions, pose and solve problems, and in general to figure things out. They do all this with language all the time, in addition to using it to demonstrate to instructors that they *have* comprehended, understood, created, imagined and asked — which, of course, they do on tests and in term papers. As such, language — verbal, numerical, visual, musical — is the very center of the academic curriculum.

4. Language is an avenue to personal growth, social success, political power. People who speak and write persuasively in one or more languages are more likely to thrive in our culture than those who don't. In some instances skill with spoken and written language means mastering the King's English; in other instances, it means being adept in a particular dialect community; in all instances, those who use language well are more likely to understand themselves and to influence and perhaps even govern others within their language communities. Educational communities that understand and support this premise provide curricula that are rich in language experiences for learners; those that understand and do not support this premise do not provide such experiences; some do not seem to understand this premise at all.

5. The faculty are the primary determiners of the way language is perceived and used within academic institutions. Their beliefs, knowledge, skills, methods, and attitudes shape, to a large extent, how colleges operate and what they stand for. And what colleges stand for and teach shapes, in many instances, what students learn and stand for.

You will most likely notice that none of these premises is focused exclusively on writing. Instead, each treats language as a whole, complex, intertwined, mutually dependent symbolic network, not easily divisible into discrete entities, skills, achievements, or outcomes. However, the term "*writing* across the curriculum" caught on first because, of all the language modes, writing seemed to be the most easily misunderstood and abused in school curricula. A better term than "writing" would be "language and learning," but we'll dance with what brung us.

You will also notice that none of these particular premises focuses on the specialized writing of particular "discourse communities." Some WAC programs teach students the kind of reasoning and conventions required of specialists within particular disciplines, where history majors learn to write like historians, political-science majors like political scientists, and so on. In my view, those programs address an important but more specialized need than those that stress the language and learning connection as it functions *across* disciplinary boundaries — that is, which treats the academic community itself as a more generalized discourse community.

In articulating these premises to reasonable people who care about student learning, they sound pretty much like God, mother, and apple pie.

However, if and when they are used as the basis for reformulating or restructuring academic programs, they begin to threaten business as usual. Why?

For one thing, WAC has given new meaning to the concept of faculty development. The interdisciplinary writing workshop was invented to transmit WAC ideas convincingly to college faculty. Such multiday workshops have been the most common method for introducing writing-across-the-curriculum ideas to college instructors (Knoblauch and Brannon; Fulwiler, "Showing," "How Well"). At such workshops, instructors from a variety of disciplines explore the role of writing throughout the curriculum by sharing ideas and talking with one another, and by reading short articles by the likes of Peter Elbow, James Britton, Janet Emig, and Donald Murray. In addition — and more important — they do a substantial amount of writing themselves and examine what happens at various stages along the way — discovering, composing, revising, editing, sharing, and responding. In other words, most writing-across-the-curriculum programs begin with experiential learning for teachers to convince them to try more experiential learning with their students.

In addition, WAC programs address real deficiencies in college curricula with workable solutions. It seems clear that writing-across-the-curriculum programs develop at institutions of various sizes and missions because of perceived needs within their institutions (Huber and Young). They are most likely to be found at two- and four-year colleges with heavy teaching loads and large classes. They are less likely to be found — though no less needed — at huge research universities with large classes and equally high expectations for research and publication pressure. In many of these cases instructors have deliberately decreased the writing they require of students because writing assignments — as they conceive of them — take too much faculty reading and grading time. In some cases they want to do something about it; in other cases they do not.

At other institutions, with lighter teaching loads, smaller classes, and less research pressure, the need for more writing may take a different and even more insidious form: professors in the quantitative disciplines often find qualitative written expressions difficult to evaluate; professors in the humanities commonly believe it their duty to critique and correct everything their students write; professors in the sciences sometimes see little value in the verbal written exploration and speculation of undergraduates. A writing-across-the-curriculum program challenges all of these notions.

Finally, WAC programs cost somebody something. In economic terms, all instructional choices are political in one way or another: one decision reinforces the status quo, another challenges it, still another tries to ignore it. Consider, for example, that college instructors have only a limited amount of time and energy with which to teach each class. When they assign more writing, and when they use class time to talk about that writing, they take time and energy away from something else — lectures, discussions, quizzes — that they did before. When one teacher chooses to do this, it makes an individual difference in the quality of classroom education; when many teachers within the same curriculum make similar choices, it makes a political difference. The more students educate themselves through the active use of their own language, the more ownership they exert over what they learn, and the more they trust (own) their own perceptions. Students so educated are more likely to speak with their own authority within the academic community. When students learn (are allowed to learn? encouraged to learn?) that knowledge is not something received whole and memorized — or put in the bank (Freire) — but rather a construct that they themselves participate in making, the nature of so-called higher education changes (Bruffee). Let me conclude by looking at three necessary changes caused by strong WAC programs: 1) a faculty's relationship to students, 2) its relationship with one another, and 3) its relationship to the whole institution in which it operates.

Faculty-Student Relationships

Writing-across-the-curriculum classrooms change from places in which professors talk and students copy to places in which teachers and students together participate as partners in dialogue, as co-learners in asking questions, pursuing truth, constructing knowledge. The writing makes a difference, giving learners the time to focus, find, collect, organize, and rehearse ideas, allowing them stronger, more equal voices in their own learning. In other words, instructors who adopt the ideas promoted at writing-across-the-curriculum workshops change more than just their writing assignments: They change the nature of the classroom learning from individual, passive, and competitive to communal, active, and collaborative. Following are some of the practices that draw the students inside:

Expressive Writing.   Instructors who provide time in class for students to explore their own ideas and beliefs through informal (expressive) writing help students find their own voices, some of which will be antagonistic to the instructor's own agenda. In free and open classrooms, this is as it should be. Journal writing and freewriting — writing that the instructor will not grade or necessarily even read — are commonly explored topics at WAC workshops and become common practices at schools with WAC programs.

Open-Ended Assignments.   When students are invited to ask and answer their own questions (or pose and solve their own problems), they gain a powerful voice in determining their own curriculum even within the disciplinary constraints that particular courses of instruction impose. Instructors who invite students to design the writing assignments, select research topics, and invent forms, for reporting the results necessarily increase students' involvement, investment, and ownership in their learning.

Collaborative Learning Groups.   When students work together to pose and solve problems they best replicate the kind of learning that goes on in the world outside the academy — at home, on the streets, or within institutions. Real learning means that people put their heads together to both pose and solve problems. Instructors who give over class time for student-student meetings alter student-teacher relationships in important ways. Student ideas command center stage along with instructor ideas, and both are seen as legitimate and vital parts of the academic community. When students talk to one another in small groups, they take power and responsibility for their ideas and often work together as a group to support, refine, and defend those ideas — which strengthens, at the same time, their confidence and individual voices.

Real-World Writing.   Students are more easily engaged in writing tasks that seem real and useful; a regular workout with real-world tasks (case studies, hypothetical situations, letters to real editors, etc.) increases student motivation and strengthens their voices. That is, teachers who make assignments that deal with real-world problems *and* who provide real-world circumstances under which the work takes place continue to give students more power in determining and deciphering their curriculum. For example, instructors who provide opportunities for students to write rough drafts, to confer with teacher and classmates about the ideas in those drafts, and to write further in light of those comments invest school writing with an uncommon kind of authenticity. The audiences now include the students' peers as well as the teacher in a collaborative role. The resultant process by which the writing gets done is real, and students know that and are, again, allowed inside rather than kept outside.

Response to Student Writing. Responses recognized as honest yet friendly are most likely listened to by young writers. Instructors who respond to student writing with questions, approval, empathy, and suggestions — rather than commands, corrections, hostility, and grades — demonstrate to students that not all writing — nor by extension all student ideas — needs to be submitted for instructor approval, revision, or correction. The lesson here? That students must take responsibility for and make choices about their own ideas, writing, and learning. The reading of — rather than the evaluating of — writing demonstrates the collaborative and subjective nature of the making of meaning and knowledge.

Faculty Writing with Students. This practice is commonly modeled by leaders at writing workshops and demonstrates to students that instructors are co-learners in their own classes; learning is never finished, not all wrapped up before the class starts. Students witness the process of their teachers still wrestling with and generating ideas related to the course of study, giving them more purpose in the pursuit of their own ideas. When students watch their teachers write with them, they feel like participants in a community of learners, which is quite different from being the subjects (objects?) of instruction. In addition, instructors who share their writing — warts and all — with their students subject themselves to some of the same risks of self-disclosure and potential ridicule that students must regularly take; it is a leveling process, giving instructors — as well as students — only as much authority as their current written ideas warrant.

Faculty-Faculty Relationships

Writing workshops, by their very nature, introduce faculty to one another in settings that neutralize traditional university hierarchies and cut across both disciplinary and college lines. It is common for participants to express, sometime during the first day of a workshop, that this is the first or the best experience they've ever had in sharing ideas with colleagues across the curriculum. In the process, workshop participants often find social and intellectual connections with one another that suggest further work and mutual exploration after the workshop is over. In other words, one of the outcomes of writing workshops is the generation of a true community of scholars, often at odds with normal university categories, compartments, and channels, a community of scholars generating new possibilities for collaborating rather than competing with one another in the generation of knowledge.

Expanding the Canon. One of the central conventions of writing workshops is the serious consideration they give to student writing. Formal student papers are collaboratively examined to find out *what is right* as well as what is deficient. Informal writing, such as that found in student journals, is looked at for evidence of cognitive activity rather than stylistic or grammatical correctness. When workshop leaders treat seriously the texts that previously many instructors have only criticized or rejected, they begin to make room for new voices in the traditional textual canon — which includes the sciences and social sciences as well as the humanities and fine arts (Hairston).

Collaborative Publication. When faculty meet one another at workshops, it is not uncommon for them to embark on mutually beneficial publication projects (Maimon; Fulwiler and Young). For one thing, most workshops model the positive benefits of collaborating on a piece of writing — either by co-writing, sharing, or writers' receiving peer responses. For another, people who share ideas often find that they have more ideas in common than not and find something about which to write. Finally, and commonly, participants are encouraged to see their own writing in a more positive light than they may be accustomed to — resulting in the courage to try to publish more. This latter is especially important for college faculty who have not published much in their academic careers. Co-writing, in fact, is one of the best, easiest, and most common ways for neophytes to break into academic print — and workshops commonly provide faculty with the means and courage to do so. Being able to publish their work in some avenue of the academic community is akin to finding and owning their own voices in that community, making them more likely to become stronger political players in the academic power game.

Interdisciplinary Scholarship. When faculty talk, write, and research together, they are more likely to dismantle the needlessly sharp disciplinary barriers that separate one view of knowledge from another. Writing workshops attended by faculty from a variety of disciplines make it more likely that interdisciplinary research and publication will result in the university community. In addition, the act of writing itself is an integrating mechanism, asking authors to make their ideas clear to audiences beyond themselves — an idea also promoted at writing workshops. In a number of college settings, the writing workshops have provided the impetus and ideas for cross-departmental, cross-college, and cross-disciplinary scholarship (McCarthy and Walvoord).

Pedagogical Research. Faculty who take seriously the idea that writing promotes better learning often want to find out whether or not the learning really is better in their own classes (Thaiss). Consequently, a number of research studies have now emerged as a result of teachers asking — and trying to answer — questions about their teaching (Young and Fulwiler). In many blue-ribbon institutions, such research has been traditionally and strictly the province of professors in the schools of education. Writing across the curriculum is changing that, making such classroom-based pedagogical research a legitimate activity for professors in any discipline. Knowledge so generated is bound to have a positive effect on the nature of teaching, learning, and community at the institutions where it takes place.

Faculty-Institution Relationships

Institutions that encourage and nourish WAC programs may find themselves changed in ways for which they did not bargain. If faculty and students locate more egalitarian and open ways of approaching learning, the institution itself may follow.

Balance. The degree to which teachers ask for more student writing across the curriculum may be the degree to which they bring in fewer research dollars or spend fewer hours pursuing their own specialized research. I believe that research and scholarship are essential functions of the modern college or university at least where course loads make room for such professional activities. But writing-across-the-curriculum programs argue, first and foremost, for balance. They argue that teachers should, indeed, spend more time on their teaching — at least more thoughtful time, sharing teacher voices and values with students and using writing to help accomplish that.

A Language-Centered Curriculum. The net result of admitting more writing into the whole curriculum is a tilt toward a multidimensional, more decentralized, less authoritarian curriculum. An institution encouraging its faculty to pay attention to qualitative measures of student learning — which writing necessarily is — will pay less attention to more simplistic objective measures of learning. It is also more likely to pay similar attention to subjective expression and exploration in other areas of institutional measurement and achievement, perhaps even more time in creative teacher-student projects and less in strictly esoteric, isolationist research activities.

An Empathetic Curriculum. The degree to which teachers admit more student writing in their course of study is the degree with which they begin to empathize with younger learners, champion their voices, and question the necessity of absolute and often arbitrary standards of performance and behavior. An empathetic curriculum is a student-centered curriculum and, as a result, a more politically egalitarian one.

Altered Reward Structures. In many colleges and universities, teachers who pay more attention to assigning and responding to student writing spend more time on their teaching — especially in generating more dialogue between themselves and their students — than instructors who communicate with their students primarily through objective tests. However, the current reward structure at many institutions does not favor increased attention to teaching, a condition leading to further debates about the goals of higher education and the allotment of resources. More faculty attention to student writing and learning in the curriculum may challenge the publish-or-perish principle of tenure and promotion as well as the impersonal modes of student evaluation that currently dominate so many of our institutions of higher learning.

Writing-across-the-curriculum programs ask all participants in the learning community to use language thoughtfully, to shape and extend their ideas and voices. They do so quietly but insistently, believing that the degree to which students find and trust their voices is the degree to which they — minority and middle class alike — influence and help direct our society. Higher education is passive and stuffy by habit, not intention. I don't buy conspiracy theories ("It's dangerous to teach them to think!"), but I do believe in the inertia of institutions, the deadliest enemy of change, reform, and revolution. Writing Across the Curriculum creates change because it addresses simultaneously the inertia of student, faculty, and institution alike. It starts from within, with ideas from without, and addresses the real teacher in all of us — which is why we entered education in the first place.

Works Cited

Berthoff, Ann E. *Forming the Thinking Writing: The Composing Imagination.* Rochelle Park, NJ,: Hayden, 1981.

Britton, James, Tony Burgess, Nancy Martin, Alex McLeod, and Harold Rosen. *The Development of Writing Abilities* 11–18. London: Macmillan, 1975.

Britton, James. *Prospect and Retrospect* Ed. G. M. Pradl. Portsmouth, NH: Boynton/Cook, 1982.

Bruffee, Kenneth. "Collaborative Learning and the 'Conversation of Mankind,'" *College English* 46:7 (November 1984): 635–652.

Elbow, Peter. Writing without Teachers. New York: Oxford University Press, 1973.

Emig, Janet. "*Writing as a Mode of Learning,*" *CCC* 28:2 (May 1977): 122–28.

Freire, Paulo. *Pedagogy of the Oppressed.* New York: Herder and Herder, 1970.

Fulwiler, Toby. "How Well Does Writing across the Curriculum Work?" *College English* 46 (February 1984): 113–125.

———. "Showing, Not Telling, at a Writing Workshop." *College English* 43 (January 1981): 55–63.

Fulwiler, Toby, and Art Young, eds. *Language Connections.* Urbana, IL: NCTE, 1982.

Gere, Anne Ruggles, ed. *Roots in the Sawdust: Writing to Learn across the Disciplines.* Urbana, IL: NCTE, 1985.

Hairston, Maxine. "The Winds of Change: Thomas Kuhn and the Revolution in the Teaching of Writing," *CCC* 33 (February 1982): 76–88.

Huber, Bettina, and Art Young. "Report on the 1983–84 Survey of the English Sample," *ADE Bulletin* 84 (Fall 1986): 45–46.

Knoblauch, C. H., and Lil Brannon. "Writing as Learning through the Curriculum," *College English* 45 (September 1983): 465–474.

Maimon, Elaine, Gerald Belcher, Gail Hern, Barbara Nodine and Finbar O'Connor. *Writing in the Arts and Sciences.* Cambridge MA: Winthrop, 1981.

McCarthy, Lucille Parkinson, and Barbara E. Walvoord. "Models for Collaborative Research in Writing across the Curriculum." *Strengthening Programs for Writing across the Curriculum.* Ed. S. McLeod. San Francisco: Jossey-Bass, 1989.

Murray, Donald. "The Maker's Eye: Revising Your Own Manuscripts." In *Learning by Teaching*, Portsmouth, NH: Boynton/Cook, 1982, 68–72.

Thaiss, Christopher, ed. *Writing to Learn: Essays and Reflections by College Teachers across the Curriculum.* The George Mason Faculty Writing Program, Fairfax, VA: George Mason University, 1982.

Young, Art, and Toby Fulwiler. *Writing across the Disciplines: Research into Practice.* Portsmouth, NH. Boynton/Cook, 1986.

CONTENT-BASED APPROACHES TO TEACHING ACADEMIC WRITING

May Shih

[TESOL Quarterly 20 (1986): 617–48.]

May Shih is an associate professor of English at San Francisco State University. She has taught ESL and TESL courses at Washington State University, the University of Wisconsin–Madison, the University of Oregon, and the University of Washington.

Though Shih discusses ESL composition instruction in this excerpt, her proposals also apply to composition classrooms with native speakers. She describes three typical approaches to teaching writing in composition programs — "pattern-centered," "functional," and "process-centered" — and compares these approaches with the content-based instruction that she does. Shih explains the benefits of content-based instruction, noting how it helps students develop the skills they will need to handle various academic writing assignments. She concludes with a description of five ways that teachers and administrators can structure content-based academic writing instruction.

In recent years, composition programs for native and nonnative students have experimented with a range of content-based approaches to teaching academic writing — in which writing is linked to concurrent study of specific subject matter in one or more academic disciplines. This may mean that students write about material they are currently studying in an academic course or that the language or composition course itself simulates the academic process (e.g., minilectures, readings, and discussion on a topic lead into writing assignments). Students write in a variety of forms (e.g., short-essay tests, summaries, critiques, research reports) to demonstrate understanding of the subject matter and to extend their knowledge to new areas. Writing is integrated with reading, listening, and discussion about the core content and about collaborative and independent research growing from the core material.

This article presents a rationale for content-based approaches to teaching academic writing skills and describes five instructional approaches for ESL programs. . . .

Studies . . . indicate that many types of writing tasks are assigned in university courses; types of tasks emphasized vary from one academic level to another (especially lower division undergraduate versus graduate), from one academic field to another, and even within disciplines. Writing is often required as a mode of demonstrating knowledge (e.g., in essay exams, summaries) and is also used by instructors as a mode of prompting independent thinking, researching, and learning (e.g., in critiques, research papers). Especially in the academic fields chosen most often by nonnative students, tasks require mostly transactional or informative writing; writing from personal experience only is rare.

Writing instruction for students at the beginning of their undergraduate education needs to prepare them to handle a variety of tasks across disciplines. As students begin to specialize, they must learn to gather and interpret data according to methods and standards accepted in their fields, to bring an increasing body of knowledge to bear on their interpretations, and to write in specialized formats. . . .

Approaches to Teaching Writing in ESL Programs

Intermediate- and advanced-level ESL academic writing courses generally have one of four orientations, depending on which element of composing is taken as the basis for course organization: rhetorical patterns (form), function, process, or content.

Pattern-centered approaches ask students to analyze and practice a variety of rhetorical or organizational patterns commonly found in academic discourse: process analysis, partition and classification, comparison/contrast, cause-and-effect analysis, pro-and-con argument, and so on. Kaplan (1966,1967) and others point out that rhetorical patterns vary among cultures and suggest that nonnative students need to learn certain principles for developing and organizing ideas in American academic discourse, such as supporting generalizations by presenting evidence in inductive and deductive patterns of arrangement.

Model essays are generally used to help build this awareness. (Eschholz, 1980, & Watson, 1982, recommend using models after students have started writing — as examples of how writers solve organizational problems — rather than as ideals to be imitated.) Writing assignments require students to employ the specific patterns under study. Traditionally, the source of the content for these essays has been students' prior personal experience (how to make something, to practice process analysis; one city versus another city, to practice comparison/contrast). The assumption has been that once student writers assimilate the rhetorical framework, they will be able to use the same patterns appropriately in future writing for university courses.

Functional approaches recognize that in real writing, purpose, content, and audience determine rhetorical patterns. Starting from given patterns and asking students to find topics and produce essays to fit them is thus a reversal of the normal writing process. Instead of having students write a comparison/contrast essay, a functional approach would ask students to start with a specified purpose and audience, for example, "Persuade one of your friends who is planning to move that City X is a better place to live than City Y." A rhetorical problem motivates writing. Students should not be asked "to fit their ideas into preexisting organizational molds (implying that there is a limited number of correct ways to organize)"; rather, they should see that "organization grows out of meaning and ideas" (Taylor, 1981, p. 8).

Typically, in a functionally oriented writing program, writers assume a variety of roles; academic writing is only one context and usually not the sole focus. Contexts for writing tasks are carefully defined; purpose and audience are always specified. If the writer is placed in unfamiliar roles in which background knowledge about the topic may be lacking, data may be supplied in the form of facts, notes, tables or figures, quotations, documents, and so on. Specific-purpose tasks posed in McKay (1983) and McKay & Rosenthal (1980) and case problems such as those in Hays (1976), Field & Weiss (1979), and Woodson (1982) are good examples of functionally based composition assignments.

Process-centered approaches help student writers to understand their own composing process and to build their repertoires of strategies for prewriting (gathering, exploring, and organizing raw material), drafting (structuring ideas into a piece of linear discourse), and rewriting (revising, editing, and proofreading). Tasks may be defined around rhetorical patterns or rhetorical problems (purpose), but the central focus of instruction is the *process* leading to the final written product. Students are given sufficient time to write and rewrite, to discover what they want to say, and to consider intervening feedback from instructor and peers as they attempt to bring expression closer and closer to intention in successive drafts (Flower, 1985; Murray, 1980, 1985; Taylor, 1981; Zamel, 1982, 1983). Hartfiel, Hughey, Wormuth, & Jacobs (1985) and Flower (1985) are good examples of process-centered composition textbooks for ESL and for native English writers respectively.

A process approach which is student centered takes student writing (rather than textbook models) as the central course material and requires no strict, predetermined syllabus; rather, problems are treated as they emerge. "By studying what it is our students do in their writing, we can learn from them what they still need to be taught" (Zamel, 1983, p. 182). Revision becomes central, and the instructor intervenes throughout the composing process, rather than reacting only to the final product. Individual conferences and/or class workshops dealing with problems arising from writing in progress are regular features of process-centered instruction.

At least in early stages, the focus is on personal writing — students explore their personal "data banks" (Hartfiel et al., 1985, pp. 18–33 Hughey, Wormuth, Hartfiel, & Jacobs, 1983, p. 11).

> Most students begin to write in personal papers about subjects that are important to them. Once they have successfully gone through the writing process, taking a subject that is not clear to them and developing and clarifying it so that it is clear to others, they are able to write about increasingly objective subjects, and they can see how to apply the process to a variety of writing tasks, academic and professional as well as personal. (Murray, 1985, p. 240)

Later in the course, students may move to academically oriented topics. They may continue to write primarily from personal experience and beliefs, or they may move to writing from sources, practicing new prewriting, drafting, and rewriting strategies as they tackle academic tasks like the library research paper.

Content-based approaches differ from traditional approaches to teaching academic writing in at least four major ways:

1. Writing from personal experience and observation of immediate surroundings is de-emphasized; instead, the emphasis is on writing from sources (readings, lectures, discussions, etc.), on synthesis and interpretation of information currently being studied in depth. Writing is linked to ongoing study of specific subject matter in one or more academic disciplines and is viewed as a means to stimulate students to think and learn (Beach & Bridwell, 1984; Emig, 1977; Fulwiler, 1982; Newell, 1984).
2. The focus is on *what is* said more than on *how* it is said (Krashen, 1982, p. 168) in preparing students for writing and in responding to writing. The instructor who guides and responds to writing must know the subject matter well enough to explain it, field questions, and respond to content and reasoning in papers. Treatment of matters of form (organization, grammar, mechanics) and style do not dictate the composition course syllabus, but rather follow from writers' needs.
3. Skills are integrated as in university course work: Students listen, discuss, and read about a topic before writing about it — as contrasted to the traditional belief that in a writing course, students should only write.
4. Extended study of a topic (some class treatment of core material and some independent and/or collaborative study/research) precedes writing, so that there is "active control of ideas" and "extensive processing of new information" (Anthony, 1985, p. 4) before students begin to write. A longer incubation period is permitted, with more

input from external sources, than in traditional composition classes, in which students rely solely or primarily on self-generated ideas and write on a new topic for each composition. Writing assignments can build on one another with "situational sequencing" (Schuster, 1984).

Intuition and experience suggest that when students write to a topic about which they have a great deal of well-integrated knowledge, their writing is more likely to be well organized and fluent; conversely, when students know little about a topic, their writing is more likely to fail. When students have few ideas about a topic, or when they are unwilling to risk stating the ideas they do have, their writing may rely on glib generalizations, unsupported by argument or enriching illustrations. (Langer, 1984, pp. 28–29)

Rationale for Content-Based Approaches to Teaching Academic Writing: Skills Developed

The formal writing tasks assigned in university courses . . . require students to exercise complex thinking, researching, and language skills. Traditional composition courses have often fallen short in helping ESL students to develop the skills needed to handle real academic writing tasks. Content-based academic writing instruction may be a more effective means of prompting students to develop the requisite skills because it deals with writing in a manner similar (or identical) to how writing is assigned, prepared for, and reacted to in real academic courses.

Prewriting

The formal academic writing tasks identified in the survey literature require students to restate or recast information presented in course lectures, readings, and discussions or to report on original thinking and research (primary or secondary) connected to the course content. Important prewriting skills needed to handle such tasks include the following:

1. Recalling, sorting, synthesizing, organizing, interpreting, and applying information presented in course lectures, readings, and class discussions (for essay exams, controlled out-of-class essays). The material must be mentally reordered as necessitated by the question, so that the essay will not be merely a "memory dump" (Flower, 1985, p. 66) — that is, a writer-based, rote recital of information in the order stored — but a coherent essay directly answering the question posed (Jacobs, 1984).
2. Calling upon personal experience and knowledge; selecting, interpreting, and connecting relevant ideas; reflecting; imagining (for personal essays, creative writing).
3. Relating concepts presented in course reading (and lectures, discussions) to personal experience (for response essays in the social sciences, journals).
4. Conducting primary (firsthand) research (for data-based reports) .
   a. Defining the research question and working hypotheses.
   b. Collecting appropriate and sufficient data, with appropriate methods and instruments. Designing data-collection procedures and objectively recording data through systematic observations (for observational studies, field trip reports, case studies, etc.); experiments (for lab reports, other experimental reports); surveys and questionnaires (for research reports in social science, business, and other fields); tests (for research reports in social science, education, and other fields); and letters of inquiry.

c. Analyzing and interpreting data correctly — using appropriate statistical tests and appropriate lines of reasoning; drawing, from events, appropriate inferences at various levels of abstraction (Applebee, Auten, & Lehr, 1981; Britton, Burgess Martin, McLeod, & Rosen, 1975; Moffett, 1968): record of ongoing events, record of observed events, analysis and interpretation, theory and speculation.

5. Reading a text (poem, story, novel, play, historical document, etc.) carefully and critically (for critical analyses, reviews/critiques); identifying an interpretive problem and the appropriate techniques of analysis; isolating and analyzing points important for the chosen interpretive problem, for example, theme, plot, characters, language, style (Bazerman, 1985, pp. 354–358; Maimon, Belcher, Hearn, Nodine, & O'Connor, 1981, pp. 155–163).

6. Obtaining and organizing information from secondary sources (for research proposals, library research papers).
   a. Choosing a suitable and compelling research topic and restricting it; making hypotheses about the central question/ problem to be investigated.
   b. Locating appropriate reference sources (library skills).
   c. Evaluating sources (to judge relevance and usefulness); selecting sources that work well together.
   d. Skimming, scanning, and close reading; taking notes—to record information, aid understanding, and prompt own thinking; distinguishing more important and less important information; differentiating own ideas from those of sources; using direct quotation, paraphrase, and summary; recording page references.
   e. Synthesizing information from secondary sources with writer's own thoughts and firsthand data.

7. Recasting data and ideas collected from primary and/or secondary investigation, using schemata common in academic writing: listing, definition, process analysis, classification, comparison/contrast, analysis, and so on (D'Angelo, 1975, 1980; Kiniry & Strenski, 1985; Rose, 1979a, 1983). D'Angelo assumes a loose connection between thought processes and the organizational patterns which express ideas. Rose (1979a, p. 64) suggests that these are not only categories of rhetoric (ways to present information) but also of epistemology (ways to gain, explore, and order information); they are "thinking strategies as well as discourse strategies" (1983, p. 123).

Writing assignments in many traditional composition courses may fall short in preparing students for real academic writing because they require a different set of prewriting strategies than do writing tasks in university subject-matter courses. Pattern-centered approaches have traditionally given more attention to the form of the final written product than to the prewriting (and rewriting) process. Moreover, requiring student writers to find a topic to fit a pattern reverses the normal prewriting process (finding a pattern suitable to topic and purpose).

Functional approaches, by placing student writers in a variety of roles for which they may sometimes lack background knowledge, often shortcut the prewriting process by providing a great deal of guidance. For example, case assignments often provide students with the precise rhetorical problem and specific content for writing, rather than requiring them to go through the process of defining a problem and gathering information for themselves. Such writing is not self-initiated in the sense that most academic writing is (in which students must define their own rhetorical problems and gather relevant materials themselves).

Process-centered approaches often focus solely or primarily on personal writing and develop too narrow a repertoire of prewriting strategies; some strategies which are productive for personal and creative writing may be counterproductive if inappropriately applied to academic writing tasks.

> Some current invention strategies like brainstorming and freewriting encourage the student to generate material without constraint. . . . But . . . the more prescribed the task is, the less effective such freewheeling strategies might be: the student generates a mass of ideas that can lead to more disorder than order, more confusing divergence than clarifying focus. (Rose, 1984, p. 91)

In teaching writing apart from reading and in asking students to write primarily from personal experience, immediate observation, and preselected content, traditional composition courses may help student writers develop strategies for tapping their internal knowledge and attitudes (Skill 2 listed above), but often to the neglect of strategies for collecting, synthesizing, and interpreting new information from external sources (Skills 1, 3–7) — skills basic to the academic learning process.

It has been noted that few academic assignments ask students "to narrate or describe personal experiences, to observe immediate objects like the architecture of campus buildings, to express a general opinion on something not studied closely, to reflect on self" (Rose, 1983, p. 111), that "in most college courses, students are less often asked to do independent thinking than they are required to work with assigned sources — textbooks, lecture notes, and outside readings" (Spatt, 1983, p. v). There is evidence that academic discourse is different, more cognitively demanding, and requiring different skills from personal writing.

> Formal, disciplined writing on academic and impersonal themes teaches skills different from those taught in narrative writing about personal experiences . . . the more difficult type of writing, which the school must teach, is that which requires more abstract thinking and more hierarchic structure, and that which is less immediate to the writer's concrete, everyday experience. (Freedman & Calfee,1984, pp. 472–473)

Student motivation may be higher when personal writing is de-emphasized and a link to university content courses is made evident, as the relevance of composition instruction to academic studies can more easily be seen (Irmscher, 1979, p. 75; Rose, 1983, p. 113).

In content-based composition instruction, writing tasks require students to restate and recast information and ideas from readings, lectures, and discussions on a topic and possibly also to report on results of independent or group research on related topics. Thus, students develop strategies for collecting, synthesizing, and interpreting new information from external sources (Skills 1, 4, 5, 6) as well as for connecting such new information to previous knowledge and beliefs (Skills 3, 5, 7). As in real academic writing, writing serves to help students consolidate and extend their understanding of the topics under study.

Writing the First Draft

In writing the first draft of a paper, writers take material previously gathered and organized and structure it into a linear piece of discourse; it is "the process of putting ideas into visible language" (Flower & Hayes, 1981, p. 373). While producing the draft, writers continue to discover what they want to say and alter and refine initial plans. Especially when producing formal analytical discourse, it is rare that ideas and organization of the piece are fully formulated in a writer's mind before drafting begins (Flower & Hayes, 1981; Murray, 1980, 1985; Taylor, 1981; Zamel 1982). Since it is difficult to attend to considerations on many levels (essay, paragraph, sentence, word/phrase) all at once, writers typically write multiple drafts — that is, a first draft with revisions — for important papers. Writing the *first* draft of an academic paper requires at least the following skills:

1. Applying an efficient and productive writing process; being able to begin and continue writing; being able to alter initial plans as new ideas are discovered.
2. Monitoring one's own process and progress while drafting without being excessively diverted by premature editing, which is counterproductive (Rose, 1984, pp. 5, 72–73).
3. Having lexical/semantic knowledge and fluency — conveying intended meaning in words.
4. Having morphological and syntactic knowledge and fluency — communicating in words and sentences that are well formed, sentences that properly express coordinate and subordinate relationships among ideas.
5. Knowing discourse frames, conventions, and techniques, being able to adapt familiar discourse patterns or invent new patterns appropriate to the task.
   a. Providing an appropriate overall design, using a standard format if necessary, for example, problem/purpose statement; review of research; methods, materials, and apparatus results; discussion; conclusion.
   b. Providing a clear statement of thesis or purpose at the beginning and adhering to this unifying idea/focus throughout the paper: "decenteredness: the ability to maintain all parts of a piece of writing under the control of a unified purpose" (Mellon, 1978, p. 264).
   c. Giving credit to secondary sources, in text and final reference list, in an appropriate format.
6. Knowing mechanical conventions: orthography, spelling, capitalization, punctuation, manuscript form.

In content-based approaches to developing academic writing skills, writing tasks require student writers to produce first drafts under the same or similar conditions as those faced in tackling assignments for subject-matter courses. Students must develop an efficient and productive writing process (Skills 1, 2) and apply knowledge of conventions of English discourse, lexicon/semantics, morphology, syntax, and mechanics (Skills 3, 4, 5, 6) to produce a draft in a format well suited to the specific assignment and under strict time constraints in the case of essay tests. Writers need to be able to adapt and combine familiar discourse patterns (e.g., comparison/contrast, cause/effect analysis).

Traditional pattern-centered approaches have often required students to produce essays in strict organizational molds — for example, a series of five-paragraph essays, each according to a given method of organization (process analysis, comparison/ contrast). Certainly, student writers need to become thoroughly familiar with the basic schemata, or "superframes," for processing and communicating information in academic writing — for example, listing, definition, seriation, classification, summary, comparison/ contrast, analysis, and academic argument (Kiniry & Strenski, 1985, pp. 192–195). However, more important, they need to be able to apply such schemata to content studied in course-related readings and lectures and to analyze the wording of course writing assignments and determine appropriate organizational formats. Longer papers require an ability to combine different schemata in primary and secondary organizational plans.

Revising

Revising refers to reviewing and reworking a text. Two kinds of revision have been distinguished in research on composing processes. In "internal revision" (Murray, 1978, p. 91), or "revising to fit intentions" (Nold, 1982, p. 19), writers reread their drafts, discover what they said, match this message with what they intended to say, and rework (expand, delete, rearrange, alter) the content and structure of the written piece to make it congruent with their intentions. In "external revision" (Murray, 1978, p. 91), or "revising to fit conventions" (Nold, 1982, p. 18), writers edit and proofread their text to detect and correct any violations of conventions of grammar, diction, style, and mechanics. In revising, a writer transforms writer-based prose (common in first drafts) into reader-based prose (Flower, 1979). Skills exercised during revising include the following:

1. Evaluating and revising content — testing what the paper says and the reader's probable response against what the writer intends to say and how the writer intends the reader to react; adding, deleting, reordering, and altering material to make all parts of the discussion relevant, substantive, and informed.
2. Evaluating and revising organization — making any changes needed to create a reader-based (rather than a writer-based) organization.
3. Editing grammar — applying awareness of one's own grammatical weaknesses and knowledge of English grammatical forms and rules to identify and correct grammatical errors.
4. Editing vocabulary and style — using knowledge of lexical and stylistic conventions and reference works (dictionary, thesaurus, handbook) to identify and correct problems and improve style.
5. Editing mechanics — applying knowledge of mechanical rules of English and using reference works to identify and correct errors in spelling, capitalization, punctuation, word division, abbreviations, manuscript form.
6. Checking documentation of sources.

When university faculty read student papers, they respond primarily to content: Does the paper discuss a topic accurately, thoroughly, logically, and creatively, with responsible acknowledgment of sources? Student writers receive feedback on how well their writing demonstrates understanding of the subject matter and original thinking.

In content-based approaches to teaching academic writing, student writers receive this type of feedback to use in subsequent revision (helping to develop Skills 1, 2). In contrast, in traditional composition classes, instructor feedback has often been largely aimed at matters of form and style rather than of substance and organization (e.g., Sommers, 1982; Zamel, 1985). If students write about topics in their own academic specializations, composition instructors often lack background knowledge to respond meaningfully to the content, reasoning, and organization of the paper.

When writing complex academic essays, student writers need to be able to edit their own papers for grammatical, lexical, stylistic, mechanical, and documentation errors (Skills 3, 4, 5, 6). The ability to produce highly accurate prose in controlled compositions and personal writing does not necessarily transfer across discourse types.

> We have evidence to suggest that while a writer might eventually produce grammatically correct prose for one kind of assignment, that correctness might not hold when she faces other kinds of tasks. Brooke Nielson, for example, found that when her sample of traditional writers shifted registers from the informal (writing to peers) to the formal (writing to an academic audience), their proficiency fell apart. . . . So we might guide a student to the point where she writes with few errors about her dorm, but when she is asked, say, to compare and contrast two opinions on dormitory housing, not to mention two economic theories, the organizational demands of comparing and contrasting and the more syntactically complicated sentences often attending more complex exposition or argument put such a strain on her cognitive resources and linguistic repertoire that error might well reemerge. . . . We cannot assume a simple transfer of skills across broadly different discourse demands. (Rose, 1983, pp. 113–114)

Five Instructional Approaches

Content-based academic writing instruction can be structured in a number of ways. For ESL students who are beyond an elementary proficiency level in English, at least five approaches can be distinguished:

1. Topic-centered "modules" or "minicourses" (attention to all four language skills) — in practice, most commonly used with students in the upper levels of preacademic (intensive) ESL programs
2. Content-based academic writing courses, that is, composition courses organized around sets of readings on selected topics (reading and writing skills emphasized) — appropriate for newly matriculated undergraduate ESL students, to prepare them to handle writing tasks across disciplines
3. Content-centered English-for-special-purposes (ESP) courses, that is, field-specific, "sheltered" subject-matter courses (multiskill) — workable with students at any level beyond elementary proficiency, since complexity of material is adjusted to suit student level; at any stage of university study, since course is designed around students' backgrounds, needs, and interests; whenever students share an interest in a particular subject
4. Composition or multiskill English-for-academic-purposes (EAP) courses/tutorials as adjuncts to designated university content courses—feasible for students in the upper level(s) of an intensive ESL program and for matriculated ESL students
5. Individualized help with course-related writing at times of need (through faculty in writing-across-the-curriculum programs, tutors, and writing center staff)—for matriculated ESL students

Krashen (1985, pp. 69-74) has proposed a four-stage plan as a general schema for acquisition-based second language teaching programs. In Stage 1, General Language Teaching, second language input comprehensible to beginners is provided in a low-anxiety situation and in an organized way. In Stage 2, Sheltered Language Teaching, sheltered subject-matter courses (in which native speakers of the language of instruction are excluded, helping to ensure that instructor input is adjusted to student level) serve to ease students into learning academic subject matter in the second language. In Stage 3, Partial Mainstream, students further develop second language competence through exposure to unmodified input on selected topics ("narrow input") which they have the best chance of understanding and strong motivation to study. ESL students who only take courses in their majors may never leave the early part of this stage (p. 76). In Stage 4, Full Mainstream, second language competence is expanded to a greater number of subject areas.

If Krashen's four-stage plan is used as a framework, Approaches 1 and 3 (cited above) for teaching academic writing fit into Stage 2 (sheltered classes, modified input), Approach 2 (and possibly Approach 3) fits into Stage 3 (partial mainstream, narrow but unmodified input), and Approaches 4 and 5 fit into Stages 3 and 4 (partial/full mainstream).

The five approaches are described below; examples are given from programs for native and nonnative students.

Topic-Centered Modules or Minicourses

In one content-based approach to teaching writing (as well as other language skills), instructional units, or modules (Baker Baldwin, Fein, Gaskill, & Walsleben, 1984), or minithematic units (Dubin, 1985) simulate actual university courses through intensive reading, live or videotaped lectures, films, discussions, writing tasks, quizzes, tests, and other activities. The units may be independent modules or minicourses — as in the UCLA Extension American Language Center's 3-week modules on topics such as "The Brain," "Marketing and Advertising," "Rich and Poor Nations," and "The Roles of Men and Women" (Baker et al., 1984), or the University of Wisconsin-Madison Summer Language Institute's 3-week minicourses on topics such as "The United Nations," "NASA Space Programs," "American Music," or "Current Events."

Alternatively, thematically related units may be tied together in an extended, content-based course (same length as a real academic course). Examples of such extended courses are the American culture courses offered by many intensive ESL programs (readings, lectures, films, discussions, oral skills activities, and writing about a series of cultural topics) and the ecology course offered in *Critical Thinking, Critical Choices* (Aebersold, Kowitz, Schwarte, & Smith, 1985), which draws information from natural sciences, politics, economics, anthropology, and engineering.

Thematic units may be part of an orientation to American universities or part of an academic skills course (Eskey, Kraft, & Alvin, 1984; Eskey, Kraft, Shaw, & Alvin, 1981), as in the University of Southern California American Language Institute's EAP courses (Dubin, 1985, pp. 11-15). In the Institute's EAP-Regular course ("Acculturation to Academic Life"), students first work through a diagnostic miniunit using the theme of "Levels of Language," then a thematic unit on "American Education" to orient themselves to university organization, requirements, services, and academic skills, and finally other thematic units on topics such as "Nature vs. Nurture," "Issues in American Media," "Crime and Punishment," and "Corporate Responsibility." In the EAP Science and Technology course, the last segment of the course consists of three 3-week science units based on material from the fields of astronomy, geology, and biology.

In these minicourses, the focus is on comprehending and learning new content. The classroom is a place where second language acquisition takes place, as well as learning. Writing practice is integrated with practice of other language skills (reading, listening, speaking) as in actual academic situations, and in similar proportion, so writing may *not* be stressed (writing and speaking being secondary to reading and listening, as noted by A. M. Johns, 1981).

Reading and discussion of core material could be followed by individualized reading, research, and writing tasks. For example, Cortese (1985) describes an experimental course (University of Turin) on the topic of American Indians; in the latter part of the course, students selected a book on the topic to read independently, made an oral report to class, wrote the report, and participated in a debate.

Possible difficulties in implementing the minicourse or thematic-modules approach include instructor hesitation about teaching in certain content areas and the need for staff time and expertise to select, adapt, and/or develop readings, minilectures, and study materials appropriate to student level. Topics with the greatest potential to hold student interest may not also be areas in which ESL instructors are knowledgeable. Thus, this approach requires that instructors be open to acquiring new knowledge along with their students and willing to exert effort on curriculum development. As the approach has, in practice, been aimed at upper level, preacademic ESL students interested in diverse academic disciplines, the materials selected should not assume any specialized background knowledge on a topic; thus, language instructors should easily be able to understand the materials and lead discussions on them.

Content-Based Academic Writing Courses (Reading and Writing Intensive)

Content-based academic writing courses prepare students who are at the beginning of undergraduate study to handle writing tasks across disciplines. Typically, a course may be organized around sets of readings on selected topics — narrow input, in Krashen's sense (1985, p. 73). In recent years, a number of texts of this nature have been published — generally aimed at academic writing courses for native English writers.

For example, *Writing and Reading across the Curriculum* (Behrens & Rosen, 1985) uses sets of readings on topics such as artificial intelligence, obedience to authority, fairy tales, death and dying, nuclear war, morality and the movies, and the business of college sports. *Making Connections across the Curriculum* (Chittenden & Kiniry, 1986) clusters readings around such topics as power, the origins of the nuclear arms race, the urban experience, the working world, the nature of learning, the treatment of cancer, and the impact of animals. *The Course of Ideas* (Gunner & Frankel, 1986) offers readings in Western civilization from Greek antiquity to the 20th century. Integrated sets of readings are also offered in Zimbardo and Stevens (1985), Bean and Ramage (1986), and Anselmo, Bernstein, and Schoen (1986).

Students are guided to practice reading skills, study skills, and forms of writing common to many academic writing assignments, such as summary, personal response, synthesis, and critique/evaluation (Behrens & Rosen, 1985; Spatt, 1983), and basic expository schemata such as listing, definition, seriation, classification, and comparison/contrast (Kiniry & Strenski, 1985, pp. 192–195). This type of content-based course also serves to introduce students to the nature of inquiry, techniques and standards for gathering and evaluating evidence, and writing formats characteristic of different academic fields (Bazerman, 1985; Bizzell, 1982; Faigley & Hansen, 1985; Maimon et al., 1981).

Later in the course, individual writing tasks may be given, using material from students' academic courses, ideally with the help of cooperating teachers. Clark (1984), who describes formalized procedures for enlisting such help, asks students to write a 10-page paper investigating both sides of a controversial issue in a chosen discipline. Examples of such issues are, "Is the formation of memory a chemical or electrical process?" (psychology) and "Should the British have used large aircraft formations against the Germans in World War II?" (history) (p. 186). Cooperating professors in students' concurrent academic courses are asked to assist by (a) helping the student to focus on a controversial issue that can be handled in 10 pages and (b) critiquing a draft of the student's paper, "commenting on accuracy in reporting the data and clarity of the summary and resolution of the arguments" (p. 189). This arrangement helps solve the problem of a composition instructor lacking the knowledge about a student's topic to comment substantively. In addition, "students have the opportunity . . . to engage in the process of collaborative learning characteristic of the work of professional scholars and writers" (p. 188).

A content-based academic writing course is attractive because it can be incorporated into an existing composition program without necessitating the cooperation of instructors in other academic disciplines (although limited cooperation may be desirable, e.g., to facilitate the individualized research papers just described).

For ESL composition programs, this approach requires instructors to be resourceful in assembling sets of readings which will be comprehensible, suitable, and interesting for members of a particular class. Published ESL texts with sets of closely related readings are scarce, as noted earlier, most currently available anthologies are aimed at native English writers. ESL instructors can selectively use native-speaker texts but should recognize that the topics in such texts may not appeal to a certain class or that selections can be discouragingly difficult for a particular group.

Instructors should be prepared to conduct an initial needs assessment to guide materials selection, and they should be knowledgeable about places to turn for course readings. Possible sources for readings on a topic include textbook anthologies in specific fields, periodicals, and reference tools. Examples of the latter are *The Reference Shelf* series (H. W. Wilson Company), which reprints from the year's periodicals articles and speeches on current topics (e.g., arms control, the world food crisis, crime and society, ethnic America, the issue of gun control), and the *Opposing Viewpoints* series (Greenhaven Press), which reprints articles on issues with opposing viewpoints (e.g., male/female roles, the arms race, American values).

Instructors must also be willing to spend time constructing reading, discussion, and study questions (serving as prewriting materials, to prompt students to think through a topic), essay tests, and good academic writing assignments:

> Good assignments can help students remember information and master general concepts through writing about them; they can help students master through writing the skills and the ways of thinking of a particular discipline; they can engage students, through writing, in the process of discovering connections between themselves and their subject, of understanding the world they live in; and they can evoke, instead of bloodless responses or mere regurgitation of information, independent, even creative, thought. (Brostoff, 1979, p.184)

For assistance, instructors can turn to the writing-across-the-curriculum literature, much of which seeks to clarify how writing tasks can be formulated and sequenced so as to engage students and stimulate thinking on a topic, how students can be prepared for writing, and how to respond to the content of student writing. (See, for example, Bean, 1981–1982; Bean, Drenk, & Lee, 1982; Beyer, 1979; Brostoff, 1979; Fulwiler & Jones, 1982; Giroux, 1979; and articles in Fulwiler & Young, 1982; Gere, 1985; and Griffin, 1982.)

Content-Centered ESP Courses

Content-based composition instruction may also be tied to the content of a specific academic discipline. Any or all language skills may be emphasized in ESP courses. In "sheltered" subject-matter courses, native speakers of the language of instruction are excluded. This helps to ensure that instructors will speak to students in comprehensible language and that texts and other materials will be explained as needed (Krashen, 1985, p. 17). Thus, sheltered ESP courses can be offered to students at any level beyond elementary, whenever a group of students at a given level share an interest in a particular subject and instructors have, or are willing to acquire, content knowledge.

Examples of such courses are the sheltered psychology classes offered to English and French immersion students at the University of Ottawa (Edwards, Wesche, Krashen, Clement, & Kruidenier, 1984; Krashen, 1985; Wesche, 1985), a course in English for business and economics offered at Oregon State University's English Language Institute (McDougal & Dowling, 1980), and ESP courses offered at Western Illinois University's WESL Institute—courses in English for business/economics (Proulx, 1984), English for agriculture and biology (Smith, 1984), and English for computer science (McKee, 1984).

Team teaching by a subject teacher and a language teacher may be desirable when a single teacher does not possess both the subject knowledge and the language teaching expertise. For example, the English for Overseas Students Unit at the University of Birmingham has implemented team teaching to meet student needs in lecture comprehension and the writing of examination questions in such fields as transportation and plant biology (Dudley-Evans, 1984; T. F. Johns & Dudley-Evans, 1980). The subject teacher and language teacher divide the work of recording lectures and preparing comprehension checks (including exam questions), and during class time, both help students with problems that arise.

A similar team-teaching arrangement is reported at the English Language Unit at Ngee Ann Polytechnic in Singapore (Dudley-Evans, 1984). An

English-for-occupational-purposes writing course was designed to prepare students for writing tasks they might have to carry out in future jobs in building maintenance and management (e.g., writing of specifications, memos, accident reports, progress reports, and meeting reports). The subject teacher finds authentic or realistic situations that are the basis for report assignments. As students work on these assignments, both teachers act as consultants. Models written by the subject teacher or based on the best student work are later presented and discussed.

As in the minicourse or thematic-modules approach, a major potential difficulty in implementing content-centered ESP courses is the subject-matter knowledge required of the language instructor. In practice, this problem has been handled in various ways: (a) asking subject-area instructors to teach the course (as in Edwards et al., 1984; Wesche, 1985) — and perhaps provide guidance on strategies to use with the nonnative students; (b) employing language instructors who happen also to have the necessary expertise in the chosen subject (e.g., assigning an ESL instructor who is knowledgeable about microcomputers to teach a course on microcomputer programming/applications); (c) using team teaching (as in Dudley-Evans, 1984; T. F. Johns & Dudley-Evans, 1980); or (d) choosing materials aimed at a general audience (i.e., that assume minimal previous specialized knowledge). In the latter case, the instructor learns alongside the students (as in Proulx, 1984; Smith, 1984) and uses additional supports such as guest speakers, films, and field trips.

Composition or Multiskill EAP Courses/Tutorials as Adjuncts to Designated University Courses

A fourth approach for connecting composition instruction to the study of academic subject matter is to link composition or multiskill EAP courses (or tutorials) to selected university content courses. Students enroll in both courses; writing assignments center on the material of the content course. In this "interdependent method" (Press, 1979), responsibility for guiding student thinking and writing is shared between academic content instructors and composition/EAP instructors.

The university content course is typically an introductory course, often a survey course. Composition-section adjuncts to such courses have become popular in programs for native students. For example, Wilkinson (1985) describes a freshman composition course at Cornell University which is taught in parallel with an elementary biology course. Griffin (1985, pp. 401–402) gives additional examples.

The content course could be an interdisciplinary course. For example, composition courses have been linked to the Freshman Interdisciplinary Studies Program at Temple University (Scheffler 1980). Freshmen (all levels — remedial to honors) join four to six faculty members in a year-long interdisciplinary study of a broad topic such as "The Environment," "The Human Condition," "Law and Disorder," and "Creativity."

The content course could also be an upper division or graduate course. Examples are a composition adjunct course to a University of Michigan History Department colloquium on the Indochina conflict (Reiff, 1980) and a joint composition and metallurgical engineering class given at Ohio State University (Andrews, 1976). In such upper division writing adjunct courses, students can be taught to write according to conventions within a particular discipline.

Tutorial adjuncts are another possible arrangement; then students would not be limited to selecting among only a few designated university courses. For example, individualized writing adjunct courses have been offered at all levels (freshman through graduate) California State University campuses (Sutton, 1978).

While the adjunct model has spread to many university composition programs for native students, it has been slower in getting established in ESL programs. ESL adjunct courses tend to be multiskill EAP courses, rather than focusing on composition, as in the courses described for native students. At UCLA and the University of Southern California, ESL courses have been linked with introductory courses in the liberal arts and sciences (Snow & Brinton, 1985). At Macalester College, ESL students may elect a "bridge course" in which an ESL academic study skills course immediately follows a subject course such as geography (Peterson, 1985; Peterson & Guyer, 1986). "Pre" and "post" ESL classes "sandwiched" around content courses have been used at the English Language Institute at Oregon State University (Longenecker, 1982; Polensek, 1980).

The potential contributions and possible limitations of the adjunct-course approach for ESL programs in general, and for preparing ESL students to handle university writing tasks in particular, remain to be evaluated. What is needed, minimally, is cooperation from subject-area instructors and ESL faculty willingness to step into subject-area classrooms and keep up with class events. For ESL instructors seeking to set up adjunct courses, the experiences of composition adjunct programs already in place for native students are a rich source of information.

Individualized Help with Course-Related Writing at Times of Need

A final content-based approach for helping students develop academic writing skills is to provide assistance with course-related writing at times of need. Such assistance might be given by subject area faculty, tutors, and/or writing center staff.

Many writing-across-the-curriculum programs now in existence place some responsibility for writing instruction with instructors in all academic disciplines. A basic premise is that "writing skills must be practiced and reinforced throughout the curriculum; otherwise they will atrophy, no matter how well they were taught in the beginning" (Griffin, 1985, p. 402). In addition, faculty have discovered that writing helps students to analyze and synthesize course material — that writing is learning and that faculty need to be actively involved in stimulating students' thinking and writing.

Through channels such as collaboration with writing center staff and faculty workshops and seminars on writing, subject-area instructors learn more about writing — what it is; how it can be done; how it can promote learning; and how it can be effectively assigned, guided, and evaluated. Published discussions of such programs and faculty development seminars include Connelly & Irving (1976), Maimon (1979), Rose (1979b), Raimes (1980), Fulwiler (1981), Herrington (1981), Thaiss (1982), Abraham (1983), and Young & Fulwiler (1986). Guidance for instructors in all disciplines is provided by Anderson, Eisenberg, Holland, Wiener, and Rivera-Kron (1983), Moss & Holder (1982), Walvoord (1982), and Griffin (1982).

ESL staff should establish ongoing communication with content instructors when the latter guide student writing in courses enrolling ESL students. Different forms of contact can be explored, for example, contact through writing center tutors, ESL program-sponsored faculty development seminars, or participation in established faculty seminars.

Finally, ESL students might receive guidance for course-related writing through ESL tutors and campus writing centers. TESL/ TEFL programs can help to train tutors who have not worked extensively with ESL students.

A potential problem with relying on tutors and writing center staff may be lack of sufficient trained personnel. Effective procedures must be established for student referral, writing diagnosis, tutor recruitment and matching, and staff development. Another limitation can be a tutor's lack of knowledge about the topics on which students write; in such cases, feedback can be given on a paper's form, but not on substance. Ideally, students who are writing papers in specific fields would be matched with peer tutors majoring in these fields.

Conclusion

Instructors who choose to use a content-based approach to teach academic writing skills recognize that in the academic community, writing is a tool for assessing and promoting student understanding and independent thinking on specific subject matter; they seek to give developing student writers the same experience of "writing to learn."

For all academically oriented ESL students who are beyond an elementary proficiency level in English, there are ways to structure academic content-based instruction. ESL instructors can draw ideas from a variety of established native and nonnative programs.

To determine the most suitable approach for a particular group of students, a number of factors must be considered: student status (where students are at in their studies — their knowledge base), academic interests shared by class members, English proficiency level, need/desire for intensive work on all skills versus emphasis on reading and writing, types of cooperative arrangements with subject-area instructors which are feasible, and subject-matter knowledge and interests of language instructors.

At present, content-based ESL curricula are still relatively new at the university level. On a practical level, there is a need for faculty to develop, evaluate, refine, and share materials and pedagogical strategies for each of the five frameworks discussed in this article. On an empirical level, there is a need for research of all types — needs assessment studies to guide syllabus design and materials selection, curriculum evaluation studies, and controlled evaluation studies on the effects of receiving specific types of content-based instruction. Student and teacher reactions need to be documented systematically. Empirical data are needed to support the belief held by many that content-based instruction can help ESL students to become more confident and competent when they tackle academic writing.

References

Abraham, G. W. (1983). Writing: An institutionwide approach. In W. K. Sparrow & N. A. Pickett (Eds.), *Technical and business communication in two-year programs* (pp. 69–75). Urbana, IL: National Council of Teachers of English.

Aebersold, J. A., Kowitz, J., Schwarte, B., & Smith, E. L. (1985). *Critical thinking, critical choices: Book 1. Reading and writing; Book 2. Listening and speaking.* Englewood Cliffs, NJ: Prentice-Hall.

Anderson, J. R., Eisenberg, N., Holland, J., Wiener, H. S., & Rivera-Kron, C. (1983). *Integrated skills reinforcement: Reading, writing, speaking. and listening across the curriculum.* New York: Longman.

Andrews, D. C. (1976). An interdisciplinary course in technical communication. Technical Communication, 23, 12–15.

Anselmo, T., Bernstein, L., & Schoen, C. (1986). *Thinking and writing in college.* Boston: Little, Brown.

Anthony, T. P. (1985). Writing in EAP: Climate and process *ESP Newsletter,* 95, 1–6.

Applebee, A. N., Auten, A., & Lehr, F. (1981). *Writing in the secondary school: English and the content areas.* Urbana, IL: National Council of Teachers of English.

Baker, L., Baldwin, R., Fein, D., Gaskill, W., & Walsleben, M. (1984, March). *Content-based curriculum design in advanced levels of an intensive ESL program.* Workshop presented at the 18th Annual TESOL Convention, Houston.

Bazerman, C. (1985). *The informed writer: Using sources in the disciplines* (2nd ed.). Boston: Houghton Mifflin.

Beach, R., & Bridwell, L. (1984). Learning through writing: A rationale for writing across the curriculum. In A. D. Pellegini & T. D. Yawkey (Eds.), *The development of oral and written language in social contexts (pp.* 183–198). Norwood, NJ: Ablex.

Bean, J. C. (1981–1982). Involving non-English faculty in the teaching of writing and thinking skills. *International Journal of Instructional Media,* 9, 51–69.

Bean, J. C., Drenk, D., & Lee, F. D. (1982). Microtheme strategies for developing cognitive skills. In C. W. Griffin (Ed.), *Teaching writing in all disciplines* (pp. 27–38). San Francisco: Jossey-Bass.

Bean, J. C., & Ramage, J. D. (1986). *Form and surprise in composition: Writing and thinking across the curriculum.* New York: Macmillan.

Behrens, L. (1978). Writing, reading and the rest of the faculty: A survey. *English Journal,* 67(6), 54–60.

Behrens, L., & Rosen, L. J. (1985). *Writing and reading across the curriculum* (2nd ed.). Boston: Little, Brown.

Beyer, B. K. (1979). Pre-writing and re-writing to learn. *Social Education,* 43, 187–189, 197.

Bizzell, P. (1982). College composition: Initiation into the academic discourse community. *Curriculum Inquiry,* 12, 191–207.

Boyan, D. R., & Julian, A. C. (Eds.). (1984). *Open doors 1982–83: Report on international educational exchange.* New York: Institute of International Education.

Bridgeman, B., & Carlson, S. (1983). *A survey of academic writing tasks required of graduate and undergraduate foreign students* (TOEFL Research Rep. No. 15). Princeton, NJ: Educational Testing Service.

Bridgeman, B., & Carlson, S. (1984). Survey of academic writing tasks. *Written Communication,* 1, 247–280.

Britton, J., Burgess, T., Martin, N., McLeod, A., & Rosen, H. (1975). *The development of writing abilities (11–18).* London: Macmillan Education.

Brostoff, A. (1979). Good assignments lead to good writing. *Social Education,* 43, 184–186.

Chittenden, P., & Kiniry, M. (Eds.). (1986). *Making connections across the curriculum. Readings for analysis.* Boston: Bedford Books of St. Martin's Press.

Clark, W. (1984). Reaching across the curriculum with the documented research paper. *The Writing Instructor,* 3, 185–91.

Connelly, P. J., & Irving, D. C. (1976). Composition in the liberal arts: A shared responsibility. *College English,* 37, 668–670.

Cortese, G. (1985). From receptive to productive in post-intermediate EFL classes: A pedagogical "experiment." *TESOL Quarterly, 19,* 7–25.

D'Angelo, F. (1975). A *conceptual theory of rhetoric.* Cambridge, MA: Winthrop.

D'Angelo, F. (1980). *Process and thought in composition* (2nd ed.). Cambridge, MA: Winthrop.

Dubin, F. (Ed.). (1985, August). American Language Institute. *Curriculum Clearing House Newsletter,* pp. 3–25.

Dudley-Evans, T. (1984). The team-teaching of writing skills. In R. Williams, J. Swales, & J. Kirkman (Eds.), *Common ground: Shared interests in ESP and communication studies* (British Council ELT Document 117) (pp. 127–133). Oxford: The British Council/Pergamon Press.

Eblen, C. (1983). Writing across the curriculum: A survey of a university faculty's views and classroom practices. *Research in the Teaching of English, 17,* 343–348.

Edwards, H., Wesche, M., Krashen, S., Clement, R., & Kruidenier, B. (1984). Second language acquisition through subject-matter learning: A study of sheltered psychology classes at the University of Ottawa. *Canadian Modern Language Review, 41,* 268–282.

Emig, J. (1977). Writing as a mode of learning. *College Composition and Communication, 28,* 122–128.

Eschholz, P. A. (1980). The prose models approach: Using products in the process. In T. R. Donovan & B. W. McClelland (Eds.), *Eight approaches to teaching composition* (pp. 21–35). Urbana, IL: National Council of Teachers of English.

Eskey, D. E., Kraft, C., & Alvin, M. (1984, March). *Structuring a content-based ESL syllabus.* Workshop presented at the 18th Annual TESOL Convention, Houston.

Eskey, D., Kraft, C., Shaw, P., & Alvin, M. (1981, March). *Teaching English for academic purposes: Rationale, syllabus, and pedagogy.* Intensive study session at the 15th Annual TESOL Convention, Detroit.

Faigley, L., & Hansen, K. (1985). Learning to write in the social sciences. *College Composition and Communication, 36,* 140–149.

Field, J. P., & Weiss, R. H. (1979). *Cases for composition.* Boston: Little, Brown.

Flower, L. (1979). Writer-based prose: A cognitive basis for problems in writing. *College English, 41,* 19–37.

Flower, L. (1985). *Problem-solving strategies for writing* (2nd ed.). New York: Harcourt Brace Jovanovich.

Flower, L., & Hayes, J. R. (1981). A cognitive process theory of writing. *College Composition and Communication, 32,* 365–387.

Freedman, S. W., & Calfee, R. C. (1984). Understanding and comprehending. *Written Communication, 1,* 459–490.

Fulwiler, T. (1981). Sharing, not telling, at a faculty workshop. *College English, 43,* 55–63.

Fulwiler, T. (1982). Writing: An act of cognition. In C. W. Griffin (Ed.), *Teaching writing in all disciplines* (pp. 15–26). San Francisco: Jossey-Bass.

Fulwiler, T., & Jones, R. (1982). Assigning and evaluating transactional writing. In T. Fulwiler & A. Young (Eds.), *Language connections: Writing and reading across the curriculum* (pp. 45–55). Urbana, IL: National Council of Teachers of English.

Fulwiler, T., & Young, A. (Eds.). (1982). *Language connections: Writing and reading across the curriculum.* Urbana, IL: National Council of Teachers of English.

Gere, A. R. (Ed.). (1985). *Roots in the sawdust: Writing to learn across the disciplines.* Urbana, IL: National Council of Teachers of English.

Giroux, H. A. (1979). Teaching content and thinking through writing. *Social Education, 43,* 190–193.

Griffin, C. W. (Ed.). (1982). *Teaching writing in all disciplines.* San Francisco: Jossey-Bass.

Griffin, C.W. (1985). Programs for writing across the curriculum: A report. *College Composition and Communication, 36,* 398–403.

Gunner, J., & Frankel, E. (1986). *The course of ideas: College reading and writing.* New York: Harper & Row.

Hartfiel, V. F., Hughey, J. B., Wormuth, D. R., & Jacobs, H. L. (1985). *Learning ESL composition.* Rowley, MA: Newbury House.

Hays, R. (1976). Case problems improve tech writing courses and seminars. *Journal of Technical Writing and Communication, 6,* 293–298.

Herrington, A. J. (1981). Writing to learn: Writing across the disciplines. *College English, 43,* 379–387.

Herrington, A. J. (1985). Writing in academic settings: A study of the contexts for writing in two college chemical engineering courses. *Research in the Teaching of English, 19,* 331–359.

Hughey, J. B., Wormuth, D. R., Hartfiel, V. F., & Jacobs, H. L. (1983). *Teaching ESL composition: Principles and techniques.* Rowley, MA: Newbury House.

Irmscher, W. F. (1979). *Teaching expository writing.* New York: Holt, Rinehart and Winston.

Jacobs, S. (1984). Composing the in-class essay: A case study of Rudy. *College English, 46,* 34–42.

Johns, A. M. (1981). Necessary English: A faculty survey. *TESOL Quarterly, 15,* 51–57.

Johns, T. F. & Dudley-Evans, A. (1980). An experiment in team teaching of overseas postgraduate students of transportation and plant biology. In *Team teaching in ESP* (British Council ELT Document 106) (pp. 6–23). London: The British Council.

Kaplan, R. B. (1966). Cultural thought patterns in intercultural education. *Language Learning, 16,* 1–20.

Kaplan, R. B. (1967). Contrastive rhetoric and the teaching of composition. *TESOL, Quarterly, 1*(4), 10–16.

Kiniry, M., & Strenski, E. (1985). Sequencing expository writing: A recursive approach. *College Composition and Communication, 36,* 191–202.

Krashen, S. D. (1982). *Principles and practice in second language acquisition.* Oxford: Pergamon.

Krashen, S. D. (1985). *The input hypothesis: Issues and implications.* New York: Longman.

Kroll, B. (1979). A survey of the writing needs of foreign and American college freshmen. *ELT Journal, 33,* 219–226.

Langer, J. A. (1984). The effects of available information on responses to school writing tasks. *Research in the Teaching of English, 18,* 27–44.

Longenecker, W. E. (1982). Incorporating English for specific purposes programs into an on-going intensive program. In R. P. Barrett (Ed.), *The administration of intensive English language programs* (pp. 57–67). Washington, DC: National Association for Foreign Student Affairs.

Maimon, E. (1979). Writing in the total curriculum at Beaver College. *CEA Forum, 10,* 7–10.

Maimon, E. P., Belcher, G. L., Hearn, G. W., Nodine, B. F., & O'Connor, F. B. (1981). *Writing in the arts and sciences.* Boston: Little, Brown.

McDougal, M., & Dowling, B. T. (1980). English for business and economics: A new elective at OSU. *ESP Newsletter, 35,* 3–4.

McKay, S. (1983). *Fundamentals of writing for a specific purpose.* Englewood Cliffs, NJ: Prentice-Hall.

McKay, S., & Rosenthal, L. (1980). *Writing for a specific purpose.* Englewood Cliffs, NJ: Prentice-Hall.

McKee, M. B. (1984, November). English for computer science. *TTT Review: Teachers, Texts, and Technology in EFL/ESL Training,* pp. 19–20.

Mellon, J. C. (1978). A taxonomy of compositional competencies. In R. Beach & P. D. Pearson (Eds.), *Perspectives on literacy: Proceedings of the 1977 Perspectives on Literacy Conference* (pp. 247–272). Minneapolis: University of Minnesota, College of Education.

Moffett, J. (1968). *Teaching the universe of discourse.* Boston: Houghton Mifflin.

Moss, A., & Holder, C. (1982). *Improving student writing: A guidebook for faculty in all disciplines. Pomona:* California State Polytechnic University.

Murray, D. M. (1978). Internal revision: A process of discovery. In C. R. Cooper & L. Odell (Eds.), *Research on composing* (pp. 85–103). Urbana, IL: National Council of Teachers of English.

Murray, D. M. (1980). Writing as process: How writing finds its own meaning. In T. R. Donovan & B. W. McClelland (Eds.), *Eight approaches to teaching composition* (pp. 3–20). Urbana, IL: National Council of Teachers of English.

Murray, D. M. (1985). *A writer teaches writing* (2nd ed.). Boston: Houghton Mifflin.

Newell, G. E. (1984). Learning from writing in two content areas: A case study/ protocol analysis. *Research in the Teaching of English, 18,* 265–287.

Nold, E. (1982). Revising: Intentions and conventions. In R. A. Sudol (Ed.), *Revising: New essays for teachers of writing* (pp. 13–23). Urbana, IL: National Council of Teachers of English.

Ostler, S. (1980). A survey of academic needs for advanced ESL. *TESOL Quarterly, 14,* 489–502.

Peterson, P. W. (1985). The bridge course: Listening comprehension in authentic settings. *TESOL Newsletter, 19*(6), 21.

Peterson, P. W., & Guyer, E. C. (1986, March). *Academic study skills: A bridge course in human geography.* Paper presented at the 20th Annual TESOL Convention, Anaheim, CA.

Polensek, H. (1980). < Sandwiches >. *ESP Newsletter, 35,* 5–6.

Press, H. B. (1979). Basic motivation for basic skills: The interdependent approach to interdisciplinary writing. *College English, 41,* 310–313.

Proulx, G. (1984, November). English for business/economics. *TTT Review: Teachers, Texts, and Technology in EFL/ESL Training,* p. 17.

Raimes, A. (1980). Writing and learning across the curriculum: The experience of a faculty seminar. *College English, 41,* 797–801.

Reiff, J. D. (1980). The in-course writing workshop in a program of writing across the curriculum. *Journal of Basic Writing, 2*(4), 53–61.

Rose, M. (1979a). Teaching university discourse: A theoretical framework and a curriculum. In *Working Papers, 2* (pp. 61–82). Los Angeles: University of California Office of Undergraduate Affairs, Writing Research Project.

Rose, M. (1979b). When faculty talk about writing. *College English, 41,* 272–279.

Rose, M. (1983). Remedial writing courses: A critique and a proposal. *College English, 45,* 109–128.

Rose, M. (1984). *Writer's block: The cognitive dimension.* Carbondale: Southern Illinois University Press.

Scheffler, J. A. (1980). Composition with content: An interdisciplinary approach. *College Composition and Communication, 31,* 51–57.

Schuster, C. I. (1984). Situational sequencing. *The Writing Instructor, 3,* 177-184.

Smith, S. (1984, November). English for agriculture and biology, Or how to plan a content-centered course from scratch. *TTT Review: Teachers Texts, and Technology in EFL/ESL Training,* pp. 17–18.

Snow. M. A., & Brinton, D. (1985, April). *Linking ESL courses with content courses: The adjunct model.* Paper presented at the 19th Annual TESOL, Convention, New York.

Sommers, N. (1982). Responding to student writing. *College Composition and Communication, 33,* 148–156.

Spatt, B. (1983). *Writing from sources.* New York: St. Martin's Press.

Sutton, M. (1978). The writing adjunct program at the Small College of California State College, Dominiguez Hills. In J. P. Neel (Ed.), *Options for the teaching of English Freshman composition* (pp. 104–109). New York: Modern Language Association.

Taylor, B. P. (1981). Content and written form: A two-way street. *TESOL Quarterly, 15,* 5–13.

Thaiss, C. (1982). The Virginia Consortium of Faculty Writing Programs: A variety of practices. In C. W. Griffin (Ed.), *Teaching writing in all disciplines* (pp. 45–52). San Francisco: Jossey-Bass.

Walvoord, B. E. F. (1982). *Helping students write well: A guide for teachers in all disciplines.* New York: Modern Language Association.

Watson B. (1982). The use and abuse of models in the ESL writing class *TESOL Quarterly, 16,* 5–14.

Wesche, M. B. (1985). Immersion and the universities. *Canadian Modern Language Review, 41,* 931–940.

West, G. K., & Byrd, P. (1982). Technical writing required of graduate engineering students. *Journal of Technical Writing and Communication, 12,* 1–6.

Wilkinson, A. M. (1985). A freshman writing course in parallel with a science course. *College Composition and Communication, 36,* 160–165.

Woodson, L. (1982). *From cases to composition.* Glenview, IL: Scott Foresman.

Young, A., & Fulwiler, T. (Eds.). (1986). *Writing across the disciplines: Research into practice.* Upper Montclair, NJ: Boynton/Cook.

Zamel, V. (1982). Writing: The process of discovering meaning. *TESOL Quarterly, 16,* 195–209.

Zamel, V. (1983). The composing processes of advanced ESL students: Six case studies. *TESOL Quarterly, 17,* 165–187.

Zamel, V. (1985). Responding to student writing. *TESOL Quarterly, 19,* 79–101.

Zimbardo, R., & Stevens, M. (1985). *Across the curriculum: Thinking, reading, and writing.* New York: Longman.

THE FUTURE OF WRITING ACROSS THE CURRICULUM

Christopher Thaiss

[From Strengthening Programs for Writing across the Curriculum. *Ed. Susan McLeod. San Francisco: Jossey-Bass, 1988. 91–102.]*

Christopher Thaiss is director of writing across the curriculum and director of composition at George Mason University. He is the author of Write to the Limit *(1991) and* The Sense of Value *(1993). He also contributed to* Writing across the Curriculum: A Guide to Developing Programs, *(1992).*

Thaiss examines the trends and continuing problems that writing across the curriculum planners face and considers how the success of the WAC movement might be sustained. He argues that, instead of seeing content and method in opposition, educators should view "writing-to-learn" methods as a key to learning content. Thaiss also discusses the relation between WAC and general education reform and the ever-present problem of apparently conflict-

ing disciplinary standards for "good writing." Thaiss's overview can help teachers and administrators recognize the possibilities for change in current WAC programs.

It's impossible for me to talk about the future without first estimating where writing across the curriculum is now. Many ideas fit under the WAC umbrella. At more and more schools, WAC means the writing-intensive or writing-emphasis courses taught within a major. This can imply careful instruction in the phases of the writing process — discovery, revision, and editing — or it can merely mean increasing the required word count in a course. At many schools, including some of those with writing-emphasis courses, WAC means teachers in diverse fields using writing-to-learn techniques, such as journals, reading response logs, systematic note making, impromptu exercises, role playing, field studies, I-Search papers, collaborative research, informal and formal debates, process analyses, formative assessments, and so on.

Writing across the curriculum also means research. Curiosity drives the vanguard. Although many of us got into this movement (it is, for all our modest disclaimers, messianic) because someone in our institution consulted us based on our experience as teachers of writing, we stick with it because we quickly see the limits of our knowledge and find, humbly and gratefully, that we can learn a lot about our profession from the people "out there," teachers in other fields. . . . Collaborative research projects . . . raise to the level of art the spontaneous collaborations that ideally go on in every cross-curricular workshop — indeed, in any earnest exchange of ideas and questions among teachers.

The cross-curricular urge is not, in my view, an offshoot of the teaching of writing but is its foundation. We can't know what and how to teach unless we mess around in the beautiful muck of people's texts and their purposes, backgrounds, fears, fantasies, and delusions in regard to writing. And to do this we must go outside the boundaries of our departments and beyond the fringe parking of our campuses.

I talk as if this is simple truth, but I realize how revolutionary — and evolutionary — it is. People who enjoy studying writing across the curriculum in its myriad guises, or writing in the workplace, or the composing processes of young children are people who marvel at the diversity and unpredictability of culture. These are not the same people who think of "writing across the curriculum" as a mandate to impose a single standard of syntactical correctness or a short list of required readings across the curriculum. Those, I would argue, are antithetical meanings of the concept and reasons why the term occasions resistance and confusion. Most of the WAC people one meets have swum around in cultural stews throughout their careers. We tend to be the ESL people, the writing center people, the pop culturists, the Third World historians, the Geertzian anthropologists, the quantum physicists, the epidemiologists, the systems engineers — entrepreneurs of every stripe.

We have seen that using language can empower people, enable them to survive in body and flourish in spirit. We have seen how the force to limit communication—whether that force takes the form of monopoly in mass media or the radical narrowing of standards of "acceptable language"—can intimidate, passify (not pacify), and disenfranchise people. Yes, writing across the curriculum advocates want people to write about whatever they study, because they see writing as power, whether that power be political or spiritual or therapeutic or intellectual.

WAC has succeeded because workshop participants have felt this power themselves in the workshops and then in their classrooms. They have reached the same insights as those achieved by such writing-process researchers as Emig (1977) and Shaughnessy (1977), who convinced our profession more than a decade ago that writing is learning and growth, that the act of writing defines writing, and that no text is more than a step in anyone's development. WAC would never have spread had its advocates had nothing more to offer fellow teachers than correction symbols, syntax rules, and pious lectures about the need for "good" writing. When workshop participants praise their experience, they always focus on how writing serves intellectual and social purposes: "I feel that I understand my students better," "Writing gives them an outlet for their confusion, their frustrations," "They reach insights I never hoped for before." Not surprisingly, as Shaughnessy predicted in *Errors and Expectations,* teachers also see gains in the quality of student texts: "They write a lot better than previous classes."

As we confront trends and issues in planning new and continuing WAC programs, we need to keep in mind the bases of our success: our desire to learn from our colleagues and our sense of the power of writing. It is on these strengths that we can build the future of the movement.

The Future of WAC: Two Troubling Trends

Ironically, as I look to the future of WAC, our very success troubles me. Just as "the writing process," through the perseverance of many teachers and researchers, has become so successful that now almost everyone in our field slaps the name onto whatever they do, so the term "writing across the curriculum" stands in danger of the same thing. Two trends need to be watched closely: the textbook-title syndrome and the top-down decree.

The Textbook-Title Syndrome

When I review manuscripts with "across the curriculum" or "in the content areas" or "across the disciplines" in the title, I've learned to ask a simple question: What makes the book different from the books published before the "across the curriculum" furor began? A disappointingly large number have merely substituted sample essays about physics, sociology, and computers for such previous staples as E. B. White's trip to the lake, Annie Dillard's sojourn at the creek, or John Updike's idyll of the grocery store. Though they provide different grist for the composition mill, such "content area" essays still exist as static texts, imposing for their polish and learnedness while the processes of their writers remain opaque. Such textbooks assume, as their predecessors did, that the composition course stands isolated from the rest of the curriculum. If it did not, then students in the composition course would write about what they are reading, hearing, discussing — and writing — in the other courses they actually take. They wouldn't need a book full of assorted essays.

Indeed, I feel that such texts can actually hinder writing across the curriculum more than they promote it. The student who must write about Loren Eiseley or Stephen Jay Gould in the composition class will not have the chance to get her or his peers' or the writing teacher's feedback on the draft of the research paper she is writing in cell biology. Even those text-books that present samples closer to the actual college curriculum (for example, sample lab reports, field studies, or business case analyses written by students) essentially privilege static texts that have very little to do with the actual classes our students are taking now. If faculty at an institution really talk with their colleagues on the next floor or in the next building and if they take steps to find out what their students are really studying and writing in their other classes, then there is no need for any teacher or publisher to have to fabricate reading matter, topics, purposes, or audiences for their students. If our message is that "writing is important in every field, "then what better way to show this than by taking seriously in the writing class the writing that the students really must do?

If you suspect that your students are not writing in their other classes (many teachers use a student questionnaire to find this out), then that "cross-curricular" textbook won't convince students that they should be. Yet even if students are not writing on assignment in those classes, they are still reading, hearing lectures, perhaps doing hands-on work, and taking notes (so they *are* writing). You can turn your writing class into a writing across the curriculum class by teaching your students such writing-to-learn strategies as double-entry note making, reading response logs, and I-Search papers, using the readings and lectures from their other classes as topics. Meanwhile, you can be politicking for more WAC faculty development workshops on your campus.

The Top-Down Decree

The other problem with success is that administrators try to decree it by decreeing WAC programs, rather than by assisting the growth of grassroots efforts. One assumption on which this sourcebook is based is that some faculty development, primarily voluntary, should precede legislated or decreed changes in curriculum. The activities described in Chapter Two presuppose a cross-disciplinary core of faculty who have already understood some writing-process and writing-to-learn theory. This core need not be large. Every faculty has at least a few, maybe many, teachers who quickly pick up the spirit of the workshop, probably because of their own experience as writers or because, like many teachers I've met, they are already using writing-to-learn or process techniques in their classes. Without these people—and without some faculty development structure to spread their ideas—faculty are liable to think that "WAC" merely means: (1) "adding the English teacher's job" to theirs or (2) "adding writing" to their courses.

At our meetings of the National Network of Writing Across the Curriculum Programs and in my conversations with program directors, I keep hearing the same lament about mandated WAC curricula, particularly of the writing-intensive or writing-emphasis variety. Several large public universities, plus many smaller schools, have decreed such programs, in some cases without prior faculty development, sometimes even without faculty debate and consent. Often faculty resist, and those in charge either can't meet their quota of writing-intensive sections or are forced to accept as writing intensive some sections taught by faculty who don't know how to handle student writing but who understandably want the usual reward of reduced class size or release time. Let me suggest, first of all, that the granting of such rewards reinforces the misconception that writing is additive, not instrumental. Experienced WAC folks know that sensibly using writing as a mode of learning in classes does not mean that we reach fewer students or expend more time in teaching; it just means that teaching and learning occur more efficiently.

Another common complaint concerns students: They'll tolerate the one or two writing courses they need to graduate, but woe to the teacher who requires writing in any other course! As long as writing is presented as the production of more words, rather than as an essential tool of thought, then we can only expect that students will resent it as an imposition.

Suggestions for Resisting These Trends

If mandatory WAC, either through decreed writing-intensive courses in the majors, through committee selection of a so-called writing across the curriculum anthology, or through some other expedient, is considered by a college or department before a cross-campus enthusiastic core of faculty has been developed, we should resist it, even though it might appear to represent an administrative commitment to writing. We need to keep pointing out to administrators that every WAC program that has endured and flourished was built on a firm basis of faculty development before sweeping changes in requirements were made.

As for compensation, rather than doling out release time and reduced student loads to faculty who teach writing-intensive courses, spend the release time or some other suitable reward on faculty development workshops and on continuing coordination of the faculty development program. The same amount of money or time that is spent to support the same small percentage of writing-intensive courses could be spent each year instead to train new faculty in writing-process and writing-to-learn techniques, with a far greater payoff. In doing so, the number of trained faculty will increase continually, hence the number of potential WAC sections will increase as well. Under this plan, there is no limit to the spread of WAC in the institution; moreover, students will not regard writing requirements as extraordinary, because no classes will be identified exclusively as "writing-intensive."

As for text selection, keep in mind that no externally published text can give your faculty working knowledge of their colleagues' courses, assignments, and ways of dealing with student writing. Questioning fellow faculty from other departments or assigning your students to conduct interviews with their other teachers will give you better data about writing across the curriculum than any anthology. Anyone experienced in cross-disciplinary workshops has learned that what is asked of students in writing and how the teacher handles it can vary drastically from one course or one teacher to another within the same subject.

For a writing across the curriculum course itself, choose texts that help you teach students ways to identify each of their "discourse communities" during the current semester, rather than assigning them any anthology's homogenized ideas about "writing in science" or "writing in the humanities." If your current text teaches writing-to-learn techniques and if it helps students understand the writing process so that they write discovery drafts, get good feedback, and revise, don't change it. Understanding the process of writing and how to use writing to learn will allow students to handle any form, format, or criterion a teacher may throw at them, regardless of the discipline.

Other Issues in the Future of WAC

Cultural Literacy or "Method" versus "Content"

This is not an issue of the future, really, since WAC people have always had to answer the skepticism of faculty who see the time devoted to writing-to-learn activities as time taken away from the teaching of content. We have always had to confront the unexamined notion that people learn any body of information (whether the names of Greek philosophers or the lyrics of a rock song) merely by being given a text and being told to read it, or by having someone stand before a class and tell it to them. What is new is the slick term "cultural literacy" and the facile coupling of this boost for a certain list of names, events, and abstract terms with an attack on schools' alleged overemphasis on methods of learning.

Those who have studied writing and learning across the curriculum — to use Nancy Martin's (Martin, D'Arcy, Newton, and Parker, 1976) still-incisive phrase — know, of course, that real attention to how we learn has always taken a backseat to schools' and colleges' concern about the books required and the content of lectures. College faculty discover that students can't match dates with events and that they look puzzled when classic authors are mentioned. Faculty therefore assume that students were never told about the events and were never required to read Shakespeare or Hawthorne. Even a brief look at high school curricula, however, would tell college teachers that all the stuff was in the books and on the syllabus but that it somehow didn't become part of students' knowledge (or, if it did, the college teacher just hasn't used enough writing-to-learn exercises to access it!). After more than twenty years of research in what James Britton (1970) called "language and learning," we know that it is method that makes the difference. Content and method are not opposed; one is the means to the other. To place them in opposition is to assert, ironically, that the content is not worth achieving.

There is no better way to achieve cultural literacy (or cross-cultural literacy or intercultural literacy) than through writing to learn. A WAC workshop could even be called "The Pragmatics of Cultural Literacy," if that is your interest. And if you want to cite classical precedents for your methodology, they are everywhere. Is there a better example of a language-intensive class than that of Socrates? All those teachers who just lectured their students have been forgotten; Socrates, the expert and patient discussion leader, has continued to teach through the ages. And how does he continue to teach? Through the student, Plato, who kept the most complete learning log. If it weren't for Plato's writing in order to understand the intense debates led by his mentor, would we even have a Greek philosophical "content" to talk about? Without the "thinkwriting" of a Newton or Darwin or . . . well, you can see what I mean.

General Education Reform

Though colleges and universities continually tinker with required courses, enthusiam for general education reform has been fueled by Secretary of Education Bennett in Washington, by privately funded studies and association reports, and, most recently, by the cultural literacy debate. Much WAC activity has come about as part of institutions' desire to upgrade students' writing, and this improvement has been seen as a task of the general education curriculum. Rarely (there are exceptions) does a school undertake a writing across the disciplines effort unless it already has what it considers to be a strong freshman composition course or unless it creates one. Happily, almost all faculties now see written communication as a vital component of any core. A primary goal of WAC in the future should be to make writing to learn as widely accepted.

I would urge any WAC planner, if he or she is not already part of the institution's general education or core curriculum committee, to politick for membership. Such membership offers a wonderful opportunity to raise faculty consciousness about the essential link between writing and learning. And, if you are already a member of the committee, you are in the right position to suggest WAC alternatives to a ghettoized English composition course: (1) You can design a composition course that teaches writing-to-learn skills as well as drafting, peer feedback, and research techniques; (2) you can suggest pairing or clustering the writing course with other courses so that some assignments apply to more than one class; (3) you can suggest writing-to-learn techniques that suit each course in the core and that give students practice in a variety of skills; (4) you can argue the necessity of regular faculty development for general education teachers, and you can write the proposal for the funding of these workshops; and (5) you can counter every iteration of the content-or-method myth.

Cooperation between Colleges and Secondary Schools

At last year's Virginia Conference on Language and Learning, a high school history teacher asked if college history teachers were doing things with writing to learn that she and her colleagues were trying in their classes. Though the answer was an emphatic yes, I realized that all disciplines face the same lack of across-levels communication among practitioners that we in English have always faced. Before WAC, college teachers of writing were concerned about what went on in the high school English classes their students had taken; high school teachers wanted to know the same about college English classes and customarily invited the local college composition director in for a chat. Now, as WAC succeeds in diffusing responsibility and spawning variety, it will be harder to isolate a spokesperson about an institution's writing program. Who can speak authoritatively about writing in the university after WAC workshops have been going on for several years? Who can represent "the writing program" at a WAC-inspired public high school?

If we accept both the intimate connection of writing and learning and the teacher's freedom to adapt WAC theory and strategies in new ways, then we can't ask a high school or a college for a definitive outline of required writing skills. I think we need to be forthright about this in our communication with secondary schools and make a virtue of necessity. Rather than pretend that there is consensus where there are only individuals experimenting and adapting, talk up the dynamic nature of the enterprise. Rather than pretend that you are the expert on your campus, list the names and numbers of your WAC nucleus. If you have gone the extra mile and have developed an in-house WAC newsletter (the National Network of Writing Across the Curriculum Programs has about fifty of these among its 500 member institutions), be sure to show copies to those who inquire about your program; the articles by teachers give substance to your anecdotes.

It will become important to use whatever liaison between your college and the schools that you have (for example, a National Writing Project site or another in-service or recertification program) as a launchpad for networking across the curriculum. Like Bernadette Glaze, the high school history chair who serves as assistant director of the Northern Virginia Writing Project and who has organized annual language and learning conferences in Virginia, take as your goal to find out what's going on in your area in both colleges and schools. Use the easiest means — newsletter, conferences, informal meetings between the WAC rep from a college department and the WAC rep from its high school counterpart — to get people talking. Knowing that college professors are using writing-process and writing-to-learn techniques can boost the high school's WAC effort, and vice versa. Ignore conventional prejudice that says that high school teachers can't change the teaching methods of college faculty. I've seen it happen many times on my own campus, and every other National Writing Project site tells similar stories.

WAC, LAC, and ?AC

From the inception of WAC, logic has exerted pressure on the narrowness of the concept. The British Schools Council research teams in the 1960s saw that the marvelous teaching they witnessed cultivated all modes of language. Robert Parker (Martin, D'Arcy, Newton, and Parker, 1976), the American coauthor of *Writing and Learning Across the Curriculum, 11–16* (still one of the best books in the field), has always insisted that the movement be called "language across the curriculum." Anyone who has been involved in WAC knows that the writing part works only if reading, talking, and listening work with it. That WAC has remained a viable term probably shows that we have not yet succeeded in freeing the concept from its association with the English composition course and from our preoccupation with the production of student texts.

Logic and experience demand that we go outside conventional associations and share our findings with those who have achieved expertise in other language areas, such as reading specialists and oral communication specialists. A few years ago, a book project (Thaiss and Suhor, 1984) allowed me to work closely with several speech specialists. We were surprised to learn from one another how many techniques we shared, yet how bound we were in our assumptions about the preeminence of the language area each represented. As language teachers, we saw how much we had to teach each other about our specific fields. I've had a similar experience the past two years in working with reading specialist Tom Estes (Estes and Vaughn, 1986) in a faculty development program for Blue Ridge Community College (Virginia).

Logic also demands that we listen to those colleagues who (sometimes facetiously) remark, "If we have writing across the curriculum, why not math and science across the curriculum?" Indeed, and why not music and economics and physical exercise? In a way, of course, such remarks beg the question: "Do you mean to imply that we don't already have these subjects across the curriculum?" Just as the WAC planner should never assume that writing process and writing to learn are *not* going on in unexpected places, so no other discipline specialist should assume that students are not learning important lessons about his or her field in a nonspecialist's classroom. One of the underemphasized spinoffs of the WAC workshop is that each of us learns a lot about other subjects — as long as all the participants get opportunities to demonstrate their teaching. And, as we learn from one another, we gradually reshape our teaching to accommodate the new and varied knowledge. I am no longer the same teacher of Shakespeare or of freshman composition that I was before I began to design general education courses with sociologists and global historians and natural scientists. They are not the same teachers they were before they heard about journals and practiced in-class writing. It's no wonder that the folks who meet at the WAC workshop show up again on the general education reform committee.

I think that WAC planners should expect, even hope, to see their programs merge into more broadly conceived interdisciplinary ventures. One way to measure the success of your WAC workshops is to see, over the years, how many other cross-curricular initiatives sprout up, from research projects to team-taught courses to general education reforms to grant proposals to degree programs to administrative offices. We have to be patient. We also have to abjure possessiveness. The longer we hold onto the WAC workshop as "our program" and the longer we stay chained to one format, the longer WAC will remain unassimilated.

Reports I hear through the network assure me that being willing to loosen the reins will not lead to our being thrown off. Indeed, as more and more people begin to own stock in branches of the endeavor, the calls for our experience become more frequent. Granted, those branches may not look like something we would have designed, but we have to live with the realization that inviting people into any workshop means that they will go off and do unique, sometimes disquieting things with the information. These variations are built into the model. Sometimes we will feel that we must intercede, as I, for example, sometimes do when a colleague's writing across the curriculum course appears to ignore process and just increase the required word count. Probably fortunately, we won't have time to intercede nearly as often as we would like. In talking with students, I have been surprised to learn how much they say they've benefited from writing assignments and teacher methods that I thought were misguided.

WAC and "Good Writing": Who's in Charge?

. . . Ellen Strenski [raised] the issue of style by describing a conflict between an English teacher and a teacher in another department, both of whom evaluated a student's paper. The other professor wanted technical language; the English professor wanted language for the layperson. To my mind, this shouldn't be an issue; it is an example of the success of WAC. The student felt the challenge of writing on the same topic for different audiences; how fortunate to have this experience before going into the business world! To demand that either teacher change criteria would falsify the experience and rob the student of a chance to learn.

While I say that conflicts in style should not be an issue, I realize that, as WAC proliferates and control of writing becomes diffused among departments (for example, through writing-intensive courses), students may encounter an even more bewildering variety of criteria than they would find in a non-WAC English sequence, where students always complain about inconsistency from teacher to teacher. If students do encounter a teacher who won't permit the first person, another who thrives on personal experience essays, a third who wants footnotes for every line, and a fourth who wants only original observations, lucky for them. That's the real world of writing, where tastes and formats differ wildly. If they get a sense of this from their WAC experience, hurray!

On the other hand, diffusion of responsibility and control may mean that the student of computer design or sociology or literary criticism might write only in a major-sponsored writing-intensive course, hence missing the fortunate frustration of writing for a teacher who doesn't know any of the jargon — one thing that can always be said for us composition teachers is that our students always have to write down to us! It is of no small concern to many teachers of writing in schools with writing-intensive programs that students will not get the important practice of translating specialized knowledge for a lay reader. This is potentially serious, since a frequent complaint about college graduates is that they can't communicate except with fellow specialists.

We can look at this situation positively. After all, it's better for students to do substantial writing in at least one or two courses than to do none at all, even if the vocabulary is esoteric and the writer does not have to defend the assumptions of the discipline to the reader. If the writing environment in the specific writing-intensive class is salutary, then students can use the experience to overcome writing anxiety and learn through the composing process. Thus, if the alternative is nothing, then "writing intensive only" is certainly preferable.

However, this potential hazard should inspire us to richer possibilities: First, we can argue for ongoing faculty development money, in lieu of release time for writing-intensive sections, in order to train new groups of teachers each year in a variety of writing-to-learn and writing-process techniques, hence varying the experiences for students. This method truly spreads writing across the curriculum. Second, we can opt for an upper-level required writing course, taught by faculty who are not specialists in the students' majors (the University of Maryland and George Mason University do this through the English department), in addition to the writing that students do in major courses. And, third, at the very least, this problem allows us to argue more convincingly for faculty development, including release time for one or more WAC specialists who can support the writing-intensive teachers by showing them how to vary audience for their students (for example, through the case method, through writing for outside readers, and through peer response groups).

Our Best Hopes: People and Writing

Though it's tempting to see our enterprise in terms of program models, teaching techniques, and course syllabi, the future of WAC, just like its present, depends on the imaginations and goodwill of people. The greatest thing we've got going for us is that people in every locale, every sort of school, and every subject area have become enthusiastic about the writing-learning connection. We may indeed have achieved a critical mass: I keep encountering teachers who've been using writing in their teaching for years — "I just started doing it one day and it worked" — and who only now are discovering that what they've been doing has been named — "I never called it anything, but I guess it was a learning log" — and that there are lots of other teachers who are equally excited about their success.

We have to remember to trust what we claim. We say that writing promotes thought, both critical and creative; we say that people who write about what they hear, read, and say come to fuller understanding. If we believe in these claims, then we can feel confident that WAC will continue to grow as long as people write and are encouraged to do so. Whatever else we have faculty do in our workshops, we must at least have them write. If we believe what we claim about writing, then the benefits of the writing will be so evident to our colleagues that they will need no push to share them with their students. Conversely, if participants do not feel these rewards, then no amount of pressure will spread writing across the curriculum, and the movement will vanish. This does not appear to be happening.

Further, I think we can also trust in the continued widening and intensifying of networks. People want to talk about these writing, learning, and teaching techniques; they want to write about them; they want to learn from others. Not a day goes by when I do not hear from two or three or six or more people, on my own campus and from all over the country, about what's going on in WAC. Nothing speaks so eloquently about the future of the movement as this frequent note: "I just wanted to let you know that I've asked for information from other people in the network. Everyone has been so willing to help."

References

Britton, J. *Language and Learning.* Harmondsworth, England: Pelican, 1970.

Emig, J. "Writing as a Mode of Learning." *College Composition and Communication,* 1977, *28,* 122–128.

Estes, T., and Vaughn, J. *Reading and Reasoning beyond the Primary Grades.* Boston: Allyn & Bacon, 1986.

Martin, N., D'Arcy, P., Newton, B., and Parker, R. *Writing and Learning Across the Curriculum, 11–16.* Upper Montclair, N.J.: Boynton/Cook, 1976.

Shaughnessy, M. *Errors and Expectations.* New York: Oxford, 1977.

Thaiss, C., and Suhor, C. (eds.). *Speaking and Writing, K–12: Classroom Strategies and the New Research.* Urbana, Ill.: National Council of Teachers of English, 1984.

BIBLIOGRAPHY FOR FURTHER READING

This bibliography points out further books and articles related to the variety of topics discussed in *Background Readings*. For convenience, it follows the organization of *Background Readings*.

Part One: Composing and Revising

The Writing Situation

Bizzell, Patricia. "Cognition, Convention, and Certainty: What We Need to Know about Writing." *Academic Discourse and Critical Consciousness*. Pittsburgh: U of Pittsburgh P, 1992. 75–104. (First published in *Pre/Text* 3 (1982): 213–43.)

Booth, Wayne C. "The Rhetorical Stance." *College Composition and Communication* 14 (1963): 139–45.

Cooper, Marilyn. "The Ecology of Writing." *College English* 48 (1986): 364–75.

Ede, Lisa, and Andrea Lunsford. "Audience Addressed/Audience Invoked: The Role of Audience in Composition Theory and Pedagogy." *College Composition and Communication* 35 (1984): 155–71.

Elbow, Peter. "Closing My Eyes as I Speak: An Argument for Ignoring Audience." *College English* 49 (1987): 50–69.

Fulkerson, Richard. "Composition Theory in the Eighties: Axiological Consensus and Paradigmatic Diversity." *College Composition and Communication* 41 (1990): 409–29.

Harris, Joseph. "Rethinking the Pedagogy of Problem–Solving." *Journal of Teaching Writing* 7 (1988): 157–65.

Kinneavy, James L. *A Theory of Discourse.* New York: Norton, 1971. 17–40, 48–68.

Kroll, Barry. "Writing for Readers: Three Perspectives on Audience." *College Composition and Communication* 35 (1984): 172–85.

Lindemann, Erika. *A Rhetoric for Writing Teachers.* 2nd ed. New York: Oxford UP, 1987. 11–20.

Reither, James A. "Writing and Knowing: Toward Redefining the Writing Process." *College English* 47 (1985): 620–28.

Roth, Robert G. "The Evolving Audience: Alternatives to Audience Accommodation." *College Composition and Communication* 38 (1987): 47–55.

Williams, James D. *Preparing to Teach Writing.* Belmont: Wadsworth, 1989. 3–14, 27–49.

The Writing Process

Berlin, James A. "Contemporary Composition: The Major Pedagogical Theories." *College English* 44 (1982): 765–77.

Berlin, James A. *Rhetoric and Reality.* Urbana: NCTE, 1987.

Emig, Janet. *The Composing Processes of Twelfth Graders.* NCTE Research Rept. No. 13. Urbana: NCTE, 1971.

Flower, Linda, and John R. Hayes. "A Cognitive Process Theory of Writing." *College Composition and Communication* 32 (1981): 365–87.

Flower, Linda, and John R. Hayes. "The Cognition of Discovery: Defining a Rhetorical Problem." *College Composition and Communication* 31 (1980): 21–32.

Hairston, Maxine. "Different Products, Different Processes: A Theory about Writing." *College Composition and Communication* 37 (1986): 442–52.

Hillocks, George, Jr. *Research on Written Composition*. Urbana: ERIC, 1986. 1–62.

Perl, Sondra. "Understanding Composing." *College Composition and Communication* 31 (1980): 363–69.

Selzer, Jack. "Exploring Options in Composing." *College Composition and Communication* 35 (1984): 276–84.

Planning and Drafting

Corbett, Edward P. J. *Classical Rhetoric for the Modern Student*. New York: Oxford UP, 1965: 94–174.

Elbow, Peter. *Writing with Power: Techniques for Mastering the Writing Process*. New York: Oxford UP, 1981.

Hesse, Douglas D. "Insiders and Outsiders: A Writing Course Heuristic." *The Writing Instructor* 7 (1988): 84–94.

Hilbert, Betsy S. "It Was a Dark and Nasty Night It Was a Dark and You Would Not Believe How Dark It Was a Hard Beginning." *College Composition and Communication* 43 (1992): 75–80.

Hillocks, George, Jr. *Research on Written Composition*. Urbana: ERIC, 1986. 169–86.

LeFevre, Karen Burke. *Invention as a Social Act*. Carbondale: Southern Illinois UP, 1987.

Lindemann, Erika. *A Rhetoric for Writing Teachers*. 2nd ed. New York: Oxford UP, 1987. 74–92.

Nelson, Victoria. *Writer's Block and How to Use It*. Cincinnati: Writer's Digest Books, 1985.

Podis, JoAnne M., and Leonard A. Podis. "Identifying and Teaching Rhetorical Plans for Arrangement." *College Composition and Communication* 41 (1990): 430–42.

Reynolds, Mark. "Make Free Writing More Productive." *College Composition and Communication* 39 (1988): 81–82.

Wyche–Smith, Susan. "Teaching Invention to Basic Writers." *A Sourcebook for Basic Writing Teachers*. Ed. Theresa Enos. New York: Random, 1987. 470–79.

Young, Richard. "Recent Developments in Rhetorical Invention." *Teaching Composition: 12 Bibliographic Essays*. Ed. Gary Tate. Forth Worth: Texas Christian UP, 1987. 1–38.

Revising

Berthoff, Ann E. "Recognition, Representation, and Revision." *A Sourcebook for Basic Writing Teachers*. Ed. Theresa Enos. New York: Random House, 1987. 545–55.

Coles, Nicholas. "Empowering Revision." *Facts, Artifacts, and Counterfacts: Theory and Method for a Reading and Writing Course*. Ed. David Bartholomae and Anthony Petrosky. Upper Montclair, NJ: Boynton/Cook, 1986. 167–98,

Faigley, Lester, and Stephen Witte. "Analyzing Revision." *College Composition and Communication* 32 (1981): 400–14.

Flower, Linda, et al. "Detection, Diagnosis, and the Strategies of Revision." *College Composition and Communication* 37 (1986): 16–55.

Hillocks, George, Jr. *Research on Written Composition*. Urbana: ERIC, 1986. 39–49.

Lanham, Richard. *Revising Prose*. New York: Scribner's, 1979.

Lindemann, Erika. *A Rhetoric for Writing Teachers*. 2nd ed. New York: Oxford UP, 1987. 171–88.

Raymond, Richard C. "Teaching Students to Revise: Theories and Practice." *Teaching English in the Two–Year College* 16 (1989): 49–58.

Schwartz, Mimi. "Revision Profiles: Patterns and Implications." *College English* 45 (1983): 549–58.

Wall, Susan V. "The Languages of the Text: What Even Good Students Need to Know about Re–Writing." *Journal of Advanced Composition* 7 (1987) 31–40.

Word Processing

Curtis, Marcia S. "Windows on Composing: Teaching Revision on Word Processors." *College Composition and Communication* 39 (1988): 337–44.

Hawisher, Gail E., and Cynthia L. Selfe. "The Rhetoric of Technology and the Electronic Writing Class." *College Composition and Communication* 42 (1991): 55–65.

Tuman, Myron C., ed. *Literacy Online: The Promise (and Peril) of Reading and Writing with Computers.* Pittsburgh: U of Pittsburgh P, 1992.

Tuman, Myron C. *Word Perfect: Literacy in the Computer Age.* Pittsburgh: U of Pittsburgh P, 1992.

Responding to Student Writing

Grimm, Nancy. "Improving Students' Responses to Their Peers' Essays." *College Composition and Communication* 37 (1986): 91–94.

Harris, Muriel. *Teaching One–to–One.* Urbana: NCTE, 1986.

Lees, Elaine O. "Evaluating Student Writing." *College Composition and Communication* 30 (1979): 370–74.

Lindemann, Erika. *A Rhetoric for Writing Teachers.* New York: Oxford UP, 1987. 207–23.

Murray, Donald M. "Teaching the Other Self: The Writer's First Reader." *College Composition and Communication* 33 (1982): 140–47.

Robertson, Michael. "Is Anybody Listening?" *College Composition and Communication* 37 (1986): 87–91.

Assessing Student Writing

Belanoff, Pat, and Marcia Dickson, eds. *Portfolios: Process and Product.* Portsmouth, NH: Boynton/Cook, 1991.

Cooper, Charles R., and Lee Odell, eds. *Evaluating Writing: Describing, Measuring, Judging.* Urbana: NCTE, 1977.

Lloyd-Jones, Richard. "Tests of Writing Ability." *Teaching Composition: 12 Bibliographic Essays.* Ed. Gary Tate. Fort Worth: Texas Christian UP, 1987. 155–76.

White, Edward M. *Teaching and Assessing Writing: Recent Advances in Understanding, Evaluation, and Improving Student Performance.* Jossey-Bass Higher Education Series. San Francisco: Jossey-Bass, 1985.

Part Two: Paragraphs

Braddock, Richard. "The Frequency and Placement of Topic Sentences in Expository Prose." *Research in Teaching Writing* 8 (1974): 287–304.

Christensen, Francis. "A Generative Rhetoric of the Paragraph." *Notes toward a New Rhetoric: Six Essays for Teachers.* New York: Harper, 1967. 52–81.

D'Angelo, Frank. "The Topic Sentence Revisited." *College Composition and Communication* 37 (1986): 431–41.

Laib, Nevin. "Conciseness and Amplification." *College Composition and Communication* 41 (1990): 443–59.

Lindemann, Erika. *A Rhetoric for Writing Teachers.* 2nd ed. New York: Oxford UP, 1987. 141–57.

Meyer, Emily, and Louise Z. Smith. *The Practical Tutor.* New York: Oxford UP, 1987. 91–112.

Shaughnessy, Mina P. *Errors and Expectations: A Guide for the Teacher of Basic Writing.* New York: Oxford UP, 1977. 226–74.

Smith, Rochelle. "Paragraphing for Coherence: Writing as Implied Dialogue." *College English* 46 (1984): 8–21.

Stern, Arthur A. "What Is a Paragraph?" *College Composition and Communication* 27 (1976): 253–57.

Parts Three and Four: Effective Sentences and Word Choice

Effective Sentences

Carkeet, David. "Understanding Syntactic Errors in Remedial Writing." *College English* 38 (1977): 682+.

Christensen, Francis. "A Generative Rhetoric of the Sentence." *Notes toward a New Rhetoric: Six Essays for Teachers.* New York: Harper, 1967. 1–22.

Corbett, Edward P. J. "Approaches to the Study of Style." *Teaching Composition: 12 Bibliographical Essays.* Ed Gary Tate. Fort Worth: Texas Christian UP, 1987. 83–130.

Crowhurst, Marion. "Sentence Combining: Maintaining Realistic Expectations." *College Composition and Communication* 34 (1983): 62–72.

Daiker, Don, Andrew Kerek, and Max Morenberg. *Sentence Combining: A Rhetorical Perspective.* Carbondale: Southern Illinois UP, 1985.

Faigley, Lester. "Names in Search of a Concept: Maturity, Fluency, Complexity, and Growth in Written Syntax." *College Composition and Communication* 31 (1980): 291–300.

Freeman, Donald C. "Linguistics and Error Analysis: On Agency." *The Territory of Language.* Ed. Donald McQuade. Carbondale: Southern Illinois UP, 1986. 165–73.

Laib, Nevin. "Conciseness and Amplification." *College Composition and Communication* 41 (1990): 443–59.

Lanham, Richard. *Analyzing Prose.* New York: Scribner's, 1983.

——. *Style: An Anti-Textbook.* New Haven: Yale UP, 1977.

Lindemann, Erika. "Teaching about Sentences." *A Rhetoric for Writing Teachers.* 2nd ed. New York: Oxford UP, 1987. 131–40.

Meyer, Emily, and Louise Z. Smith. *The Practical Tutor.* New York: Oxford UP, 1987. 159–76.

Noguchi, Rei R. *Grammar and the Teaching of Writing: Limits and Possibilities.* Urbana: NCTE, 1991. 38–58.

Phelps, Terry D. "A Life Sentence for Student Writing: The Cumulative Sentence." *Journal of Teaching Writing* 6 (1987): 319–24.

Pixton, William H. "The Dangling Gerund: A Working Definition." *College Composition and Communication* 24 (1973): 193–99.

Shaughnessy, Mina P. *Errors and Expectations: A Guide for the Teacher of Basic Writing.* New York: Oxford UP, 1977. 44–89.

Strong, William. "Creative Approaches to Sentence Combining." Urbana: ERIC, 1986. ERIC ED 274 985.

Walpole, Jane R. "The Vigorous Pursuit of Grace and Style." *Writing Instructor* 1 (1982): 163–69.

Williams, Joseph. *Style: Ten Lessons in Clarity and Grace.* 3rd ed. Glenview: Scott, 1989.

Word Choice

Coe, Richard M. "Public Doublespeak — Let's Stop It." *English Quarterly* 19 (1986): 236–38.

Corbett, Edward P. J. *Classical Rhetoric for the Modern Student.* New York: Oxford UP, 1965. 438–47.

Devet, Bonnie. "Bringing Back More Figures of Speech into Composition." *Journal of Teaching Writing* 6 (1987): 293–304.

Frank, Francine Wattman, and Paula A. Treichler, et al. *Language, Gender, and Professional Writing: Theoretical Approaches and Guidelines for Nonsexist Usage.* New York: MLA, 1989.

Lanham, Richard. *Revising Prose.* New York: Scribner's, 1983.

Lutz, William, ed. *Beyond Nineteen Eighty–Four: Doublespeak in a Post–Orwellian Age.* Urbana: NCTE, 1989.

Lutz, William. *Quarterly Review of Doublespeak.* Urbana: NCTE.

Ohmann, Richard. "Use Definite, Specific, Concrete Language." *College English* 41 (1979): 390–97.

Vardell, Sylvia M. "'I'm No Lady Astronaut': Nonsexist Language for Tomorrow." Urbana: ERIC, 1985. ERIC ED 266 472.

Part Five: Grammatical Sentences

Bamberg, Betty. "Periods Are Basic: A Strategy for Eliminating Comma Faults and Run-on Sentences." *Teaching the Basics — Really!* Ed. Ouida Clapp. Urbana: NCTE, 1977. 97–99.

Byrony, Shannon. "Pronouns: Male, Female, and Undesignated." *ETC.: A Review of General Semantics* 45 (1988): 334–36.

Epes, Mary. "Tracing Errors to the Sources: A Study of the Encoding Processes of Adult Basic Writers." *Journal of Basic Writing* 41 (1985): 4–33.

Harris, Muriel. "Mending the Fragmented Free Modifier." *College Composition and Communication* 32 (1981): 175–82.

Hull, Glynda. "Constructing Taxonomies for Error." *A Sourcebook for Basic Writing Teachers.* Ed. Theresa Enos. New York: Random, 1987. 231–44.

Kagan, Dona M. "Run-on and Fragment Sentences: An Error Analysis." *Research in the Teaching of English* 14 (1980): 127–38.

Kline, Charles R., Jr., and W. Dean Memering. "Formal Fragments: The English Minor Sentence." *Research in the Teaching of English* 11 (1977): 97–110.

Kolln, Martha. "Everyone's Right to Their Own Language." *College Composition and Communication* 37 (1986): 100–02.

Kroll, Barry, and John Schafer. "Error Analysis and the Teaching of Composition." *College Composition and Communication* 29 (1978): 242–48.

Mathews, Alison, and Martin S. Chodorow. "Pronoun Resolution in Two–Clause Sentences: Effects of Ambiguity, Antecedent Location, and Depth of Imbedding." *Journal of Memory and Language* 27 (1988): 245–60.

Moskovit, Leonard. "When Is Broad Reference Clear?" *College Composition and Communication* 34 (1983): 454–69.

Noguchi, Rei R. *Grammar and the Teaching of Writing: Limits and Possibilities.* Urbana: NCTE, 1991.

Shaughnessy, Mina P. *Errors and Expectations: A Guide for the Teacher of Basic Writing.* New York: Oxford UP, 1977.

Sklar, Elizabeth S. "The Tribunal of Use: Agreement in Indefinite Constructions." *College Composition and Communication* 39 (1988): 410–22.

Williams, Joseph M. "The Phenomenology of Error." *College Composition and Communication* 32 (1981): 152–68.

Wolfram, Walt, and Ralph W. Fasold. *The Study of Social Dialects in American English.* Englewood Cliffs: Prentice, 1974.

Part Six: English as a Second Language

Chappel, Virginia A., and Judith Rodby. "Verb Tense and ESL Composition: A Discourse Level Approach." Urbana: ERIC, 1982. ERIC ED 219 964.

Leki, Ilona. "Coaching from the Margins: Issues in Written Response." *Second Language Writing: Research Insights for the Classroom.* Ed. Barbara Kroll. Cambridge: Cambridge UP, 1990. 57–68.

MacGowan–Gilhooly, Adele. "Fluency First: Reversing the Traditional ESL Sequence." *Journal of Basic Writing* 10.1 (1991): 73–87.

Master, Peter. "Teaching the English Articles as a Binary System." *TESOL Quarterly* 24 (1990): 461–78.

Nelson, Gayle L., and John M. Murphy. "Peer Response Groups: Do L2 Writers Use Peer Comments in Revising Their Drafts?" *TESOL Quarterly* 27 (1993): 135–41.

Rinnert, Carol, and Mark Hansen. "Teaching the English Article System." Urbana: ERIC, 1986. ERIC ED 284 436.

Ur, Penny. *Grammar Practice Activities: A Practical Guide for Teachers.* Cambridge: Cambridge UP, 1988.

Williams, James D. "English as a Second Language and Nonstandard English." *Preparing to Teach Writing.* Belmont, CA: Wadsworth, 1989. 131–76.

Zamel, Vivian. "Recent Research on Writing Pedagogy." *TESOL Quarterly* 21 (1987): 697–715.

Parts Seven and Eight: Punctuation and Mechanics

Cruttenden, Alan. "Intonation and the Comma." *Visible Language* 25.1 (1991): 54–73.

Hashimoto, Irvin. "Pain and Suffering: Apostrophes and Academic Life." *Journal of Basic Writing* 7 (1988): 91–98.

Martin, Charles L., and Dorothy E. Ranson. "Spelling Skills of Business Students: An Empirical Investigation." *Journal of Business Communication* 27.4 (1990): 377–400.

Meyer, Charles F. *A Linguistic Study of American Punctuation.* New York: Peter Lang, 1987.

Meyer, Charles F. "Functional Grammar and Its Application in the Composition Classroom." *Journal of Teaching Writing* 8 (1989): 147–67.

Meyer, Charles F. "Teaching Punctuation to Advanced Writers." *Journal of Advanced Composition* 6 (1985–1986): 117–29.

Meyer, Emily, and Louise Z. Smith. *The Practical Tutor.* New York: Oxford UP, 1987. 177–201, 286–96.

Shaughnessy, Mina. *Errors and Expectations: A Guide for the Teacher of Basic Writing.* New York: Oxford UP, 1977. 14–33, 36–38, 160–86.

"Vygotsky and the Bad Speller's Nightmare." *English Journal* 80.8 (1991): 65–70.

Williams, Joseph. "Punctating Beginnings" and "Punctuating Middles." *Style: Ten Lessons in Clarity and Grace.* 3rd ed. Glenview: Scott, 1989. 169–87.

Part Nine: Research Writing

Coon, Anne C. "Using Ethical Questions to Develop Autonomy in Student Researchers." *College Composition and Communication* 40 (1989): 85–89.

Daemmrich, Ingrid. "A Bridge to Academic Discourse: Social Science Research Strategies in the Freshman Composition Course." *College Composition and Communication* 40 (1989): 343–48.

Dellinger, Dixie G. "Alternatives to Clip and Stitch: Real Research and Writing in the Classroom." *English Journal* 78 (1989): 31–38.

Fulkerson, Richard. "Oh, What a Cite! A Teaching Tip to Help Students Document Researched Papers Accurately." *Writing Instructor* 7 (1988): 167–72.

Holland, Robert M., Jr. "Discovering Forms of Academic Discourse." *Audits of Meaning: A Festschrift in Honor of Anne E. Berthoff.* Ed. Louise Z. Smith. Portsmouth, NH: Boynton/Cook, 1988. 71–79.

Johnson, Jean. *The Bedford Guide to the Research Process.* 2nd ed. Boston: Bedford, 1992.

Kennedy, Mary Lynch. "The Composing Process of College Students Writing from Sources." *Written Communication* 2 (1985): 434–56.

Kleine, Michael. "What Is It We Do When We Write Papers like This One — And How Can We Get Students to Join Us?" *Writing Instructor* 6 (1987): 151–61.

Kroll, Barry M. "How College Freshmen View Plagiarism." *Written Communication* 5 (1988): 203–21.

Larson, Richard L. "The 'Research Paper' in the Writing Course: A Non–Form of Writing." *College English* 44 (1982): 811–16.

Lazere, Donald. "Teaching the Political Conflicts: A Rhetorical Schema." *College Composition and Communication* 43 (1992): 194–213.

Lutzker, Marilyn. *Research Projects for College Students: What to Write across the Curriculum.* Westport: Greenwood, 1988.

Marino, Sarah R., and Elin K. Jacob. "Questions and Answers: The Dialogue between Composition Teachers and Reference Librarians." *The Reference Librarian* 37 (1992): 129–42.

Page, Miriam Dempsey. "'Thick Description' and a Rhetoric of Inquiry: Freshmen and the Major Fields." *Writing Instructor* 6 (1987): 141–50.

St. Onge, Keith R. *The Melancholy Anatomy of Plagiarism.* Lanham, MD: UP of America, 1988.

Schmersahl, Carmen B. "Teaching Library Research: Process, Not Product." *Journal of Teaching Writing* 6 (1987): 231–38.

Schwegler, Robert A., and Linda K. Shamoon. "The Aims and Processes of the Research Paper." *College English* 44 (1982): 817–24.

Strickland, James. "The Research Sequence: What to Do before the Term Paper." *College Composition and Communication* 37 (1986): 233–36.

Tyryzna, Thomas N. "Research outside the Library: Learning a Field." *College Composition and Communication* 37 (1986): 217–23.

Williams, Nancy. "Research as a Process: A Transactional Approach." *Journal of Teaching Writing* 7 (1988): 193–204.

Part Ten: Special Types of Writing

Writing Arguments

Bator, Paul. "Aristotelian and Rogerian Rhetoric." *College Composition and Communication* 31 (1980): 427–32.

Dyrud, Marilyn A. *Teaching Logic.* Urbana: ERIC, 1984. ED 284 311.

Fahnestock, Jeanne, and Marie Secor. "Teaching Argument: A Theory of Types." *College Composition and Communication* 34 (1983): 20–30.

Frisch, Adam. "The Proposal to a Small Group: Learning to 'See Otherwise.'" Urbana: ERIC, 1989. ED 303 796.

Kaufer, David S., and Neuwirth, Christine M. "Integrating Formal Logic and the New Rhetoric: A Four-Stage Heuristic." *College English* 45 (1983): 380–89.

Lamb, Catherine E. "Beyond Argument in Feminist Composition." *College Composition and Communication* 42 (1991): 11–24.

McCleary, William J. "A Case Approach for Teaching Academic Writing." *College Composition and Communication* 36 (1985): 203–12.

Rapkin, Angela A. "The Uses of Logic in the College Freshman English Classroom." *Activities to Promote Critical Thinking: Classroom Practices in Teaching English.* Urbana: NCTE, 1986. 130–35.

Writing about Literature

Biddle, Arthur W., and Toby Fulwiler, eds. *Reading, Writing, and the Study of Literature.* New York: Random, 1989.

Chamberlain, Lori. "Bombs and Other Exciting Devices, or the Problem of Teaching Irony." *College English* 51 (1989): 29–40.

Commeyras, Michelle. "Using Literature to Teach Critical Thinking." *Journal of Reading* 32 (1989): 703–07.

Dragga, Sam. "Collaborative Interpretation." *Activities to Promote Critical Thinking: Classroom Practices in Teaching English.* Urbana: NCTE, 1986. 84–87. ERIC ED 273 985.

Gould, Christopher. "Literature in the Basic Writing Course: A Bibliographic Survey." *College English* 49 (1987): 558–74.

Holman, C. Hugh, and William Harmon. *A Handbook to Literature.* 5th ed. New York: Macmillan, 1986.

Lentriccia, Frank, and Thomas McLaughlin, eds. *Critical Terms for Literary Study.* Chicago: U of Chicago P, 1990.

Meyer, Emily, and Louise Z. Smith. "Reading and Writing about Literature." *The Practical Tutor.* New York: Oxford UP, 1987. 256–85.

Moran, Charles, and Elizabeth F. Penfield. *Conversations: Contemporary Critical Theory and the Teaching of Literature.* Urbana: NCTE, 1990.

Oster, Judith. "Seeing with Different Eyes: Another View of Literature in the ESL Class." *TESOL Quarterly* 23 (1989): 85–102.

Reilly, Jill M., et al. "The Effects of Prewriting on Literary Interpretation." Urbana: ERIC, 1986. ED 276 058.

Roskelly, Hephzibah. "Writing to Read: The Stage of Interpretation." Urbana: ERIC, 1988. ED 297 268.

Swope, John W., and Edgar H. Thompson. "Three R's for Critical Thinking about Literature: Reading, 'Riting, and Responding." *Activities to Promote Critical Thinking: Classroom Practices in Teaching English.* Urbana: NCTE, 1986. 75–79. ERIC ED 273 985.

Wentworth, Michael. "Writing in the Literature Class." *Journal of Teaching Writing* 6 (1987): 155–62.

Part Eleven: Document Design

Anderson, W. Steve. "The Rhetoric of the Résumé." Urbana: ERIC, 1984. ED 249 537.

Bernhardt, Stephen A. "Seeing the Text." *College Composition and Communication* 37 (1986): 66–78.

Hall, Dean G., and Bonnie A. Nelson. "Initiating Students into Professionalism: Teaching the Letter of Inquiry." *Technical Writing Teacher* 14 (Winter 1987): 86–89.

Kostelnick, Charles. "The Rhetoric of Text Design in Professional Communication." *Technical Writing Teacher* 17.3 (1990): 189–202.

Lanham, Richard A. *Revising Business Prose.* New York: Scribner's, 1981.

Mansfield, Margaret A. "Real World Writing and the English Curriculum." *College Composition and Communication* 44 (1993): 69–83.

Matalene, Carolyn B., ed. *Worlds of Writing: Teaching and Learning in Discourse Communities of Work.* New York: Random, 1989.

Norman, Rose. "Resumex: A Computer Exercise for Teaching Résumé-Writing." *Technical Writing Teacher* 15 (Spring 1988): 162–66.

Odell, Lee, and Dixie Goswami, eds. *Writing in Nonacademic Settings.* New York: Guilford, 1986.

Pickett, Nell Ann. "Achieving Readability through Layout." *Teaching English in the Two-Year College* 10 (1984): 154–56.

Redish, Janice C., Robbin M. Battison, and Edward S. Gold. "Making Information Accessible to Readers." *Writing in Nonacademic Settings.* New York: Guilford, 1985. 129–54.

Shenk, Robert. "Ghost-Writing in Professional Communications." *Journal of Technical Writing and Communication* 18 (1988): 377–87.

Sterkel, Karen S. "The Relationship between Gender and Writing Style in Business Communication." *Journal of Business Communication* 25 (Fall 1988): 17–38.

Part Twelve: Grammar Basics

Baron, Dennis. *Grammar and Good Taste: Reforming the American Language.* New Haven: Yale UP, 1982.

Connors, Robert J. "Grammar in American College Composition: An Historical Overview." *The Territory of Language: Linguistics, Stylistics, and the Teaching of Composition.* Ed. Donald A. McQuade. Carbondale: Southern Illinois UP, 1986. 3–22.

Crowley, Sharon. "Linguistics and Composition Instruction: 1950–1980." *Written Communication* 6 (1989): 480–505.

D'Eloia, Sarah. "The Uses — and Limits — of Grammar." *A Sourcebook for Basic Writing Teachers.* Ed. Theresa Enos. New York: Random, 1987. 373–416.

Harris, Muriel, and Katherine E. Rowan. "Explaining Grammatical Concepts." *Journal of Basic Writing* 8.2 (1989): 21–41.

Lindemann, Erika. *A Rhetoric for Writing Teachers.* 2nd ed. New York: Oxford UP, 1987. 93–116.

Noguchi, Rei R. *Grammar and the Teaching of Writing: Limits and Possibilities.* Urbana: NCTE, 1991.

Quirk, Randolph, and Sidney Greenbaum. *A Concise Grammar of Contemporary English.* New York: Harcourt, 1975.

Sedgwick, Ellery. "Alternatives to Teaching Formal, Analytical Grammar." *Journal of Developmental Education* 12 (Jan. 1989): 8+.

National Council of Teachers of English. Reprinted with permission.

Ronald A. Sudol, "The Accumulative Rhetoric of Word Processing," *College English,* December 1991. Copyright © 1991 by the National Council of Teachers of English. Reprinted with permission.

Elizabeth Tebeaux, "The Trouble with Employees' Writing May Be Freshman Composition," *Teaching English in the Two-Year College,* February 1988. Copyright © 1988 by the National Council of Teachers of English. Reprinted with permission.

Christopher Thaiss, "The Future of Writing Across the Curriculum." From *Strengthening Programs for Writing Across the Curriculum,* edited by Susan H. McLeod. Copyright © 1988 by Jossey-Bass, Inc. Reprinted by permission.

James D. Williams, excerpts from *Preparing to Teach Writing* by James D. Williams (pages 124–130, 256–261). Copyright © 1989 by Wadsworth Publishing Co. Reprinted by permission of the publisher.

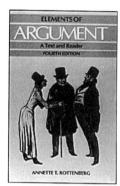